"I bowed my head surveying Merton's erudition, captured here in his careful reading of Saint Bernard, aligned with skills that deployed his scholarship as a spur to his students' contemplation. The energy he expended on preparing classes, while maintaining daily life as monk and writer, is extraordinary. No less impressive is the wildly capacious skill-set exhibited by Patrick O'Connell as he introduces and annotates Merton's 'notes.' His expert summoning of the entire Merton corpus to bear on whatever Merton text he annotates astounds me. O'Connell wins first honors as the most agile transmitter of Merton's legacy. My admiring his accomplishment here and elsewhere defies adequate expression."

— Jonathan Montaldo
Co-editor of *We Are Already One: Thomas Merton's Message of Hope*

"Anticipating by a number of years the Second Vatican Council's call for religious orders to return to the wisdom of their founders, Merton's in-depth teaching notes, skillfully annotated by Patrick F. O'Connell, show us Merton's intimate knowledge of the works of St. Bernard, St. Aelred, and others, along with his giftedness as a teacher and an interpreter of this rich tradition."

— Paul M. Pearson
Director, Thomas Merton Center

MONASTIC WISDOM SERIES

Marsha Dutton, Executive Editor

Advisory Board

Michael Casey, ocso
Lawrence S. Cunningham
Patrick Hart, ocso
Robert Heller

Terrence Kardong, osb
Kathleen Norris
Miriam Pollard, ocso
Bonnie Thurston

---

INITIATION INTO THE MONASTIC TRADITION SERIES

BY

THOMAS MERTON

*Cassian and the Fathers:*
*Initiation into the Monastic Tradition* (MW 1)

*Pre-Benedictine Monasticism:*
*Initiation into the Monastic Tradition 2* (MW 9)

*An Introduction to Christian Mysticism:*
*Initiation into the Monastic Tradition 3* (MW 13)

*The Rule of St. Benedict:*
*Initiation into the Monastic Tradition 4* (MW 19)

*Monastic Observances:*
*Initiation into the Monastic Tradition 5* (MW 25)

*The Life of the Vows:*
*Initiation into the Monastic Tradition 6* (MW 30)

*Charter, Customs, and Constitutions of the Cistercians:*
*Initiation into the Monastic Tradition 7* (MW 41)

MONASTIC WISDOM SERIES: NUMBER FORTY-TWO

# The Cistercian Fathers and Their Monastic Theology
*Initiation into the Monastic Tradition 8*

by
## Thomas Merton

Edited with an Introduction by
Patrick F. O'Connell

Preface by
James Finley

## α
Cistercian Publications
www.cistercianpublications.org

LITURGICAL PRESS
Collegeville, Minnesota
www.litpress.org

A Cistercian Publications title published by Liturgical Press

Cistercian Publications
Editorial Offices
161 Grosvenor Street
Athens, Ohio 45701
www.cistercianpublications.org

© 2016 by Merton Legacy Trust. All rights reserved. No part of this book may be reproduced in any form, by print, microfilm, microfiche, mechanical recording, photocopying, translation, or by any other means, known or yet unknown, for any purpose except brief quotations in reviews, without the previous written permission of Liturgical Press, Saint John's Abbey, P.O. Box 7500, Collegeville, Minnesota 56321-7500. Printed in the United States of America.

**Library of Congress Cataloging-in-Publication Data**

Names: Merton, Thomas, 1915–1968.
Title: The Cistercian Fathers and their monastic theology : initiation into the monastic tradition 8 / by Thomas Merton ; edited with an introduction by Patrick F. O'Connell ; preface by James Finley.
Description: Collegeville, Minnesota : Cistercian Publications, 2016. | Series: Monastic wisdom series ; no. 42 | Includes bibliographical references and index.
Identifiers: LCCN 2015035165 | ISBN 9780879070427 | ISBN 9780879074814 (ebook)
Subjects: LCSH: Cistercians—Theology—History. | Monasticism and religious orders—History.
Classification: LCC BX3402.3 .M47 2016 | DDC 271/.12—dc23
LC record available at http://lccn.loc.gov//2015035165

# CONTENTS

Preface    vii

Introduction    xi

THE CISTERCIAN FATHERS AND THEIR MONASTIC THEOLOGY    1

APPENDICES I–VII    307

Appendix A: Textual Notes    397

Appendix B: Table of Correspondences    448

Appendix C: For Further Reading    451

Index    459

# PREFACE

We are fortunate to have access to these notes that Thomas Merton made for the conferences he presented to the novices at the Abbey of Gethsemani. For me, personally, reading these notes awakens fond memories of being a novice at the monastery, listening to Thomas Merton speak from the notes that you are about to read in this book.

Thomas Merton gave conferences to the novices during the week in the small novitiate library. Then, on Sunday afternoons, before vespers, he would give a conference in the community chapter room. All the novices were expected to attend these Sunday afternoon conferences, and any professed members of the community were welcome to attend as well. Merton spoke seated at a small table with these notes open in front of him. He read from these notes when he was quoting from St. Bernard or whatever source he was reflecting on at the time. He would occasionally glance at his notes as he spoke to be sure he was keeping on track with the basic content he intended to cover. But, for the most part, he spoke from memory, passing on to us basic information about and insights into Saint Bernard and other classical sources of contemplative wisdom. Merton shared all this in a clear, sometimes funny manner that made it easy to relax and enjoy the richness of the spiritual wisdom that was being passed on to us as he taught.

The playful humor that was present when Merton spoke tends not to be evident in these notes. But what is present here are passages that resonate with that trustworthy guidance and insight that I treasured most in listening to Merton deliver his conferences and in being with him in spiritual direction. I am referring to Merton's gift as a spiritual teacher to say things that were so beautiful and clarifying that I felt compelled to write them down so that I could reflect upon them later. I realized that what made these seminal sayings beautiful is that my soul recognized they were true. Resting in that truth provided inner clarity and reassurance that helped me to get my bearings in my own search for God. I would listen to Merton speak, waiting for those moments in which these soulful illuminations would pour out of him. In those moments I would feel grateful to God that this man existed, and for my good fortune in being in his presence, hearing him saying these life-giving things that guided and reassured me in my search for God. In reading these notes I found myself pausing to savor passages that resonate with that same depth and clarity that was Merton's gift to share.

When I left the monastery I was pleased to discover that I still had access to Merton's guidance in his writings that shed a steady light on solitude, silence, compassion, contemplative prayer, concern for the world, and other transformative themes of contemplative living. But there is something that tends not to be overtly present in Merton's spiritual writings that is very present in these notes—namely, the extent to which Merton carefully studied and prayed with the classical texts of the monastic fathers and the mystics as sources of the wisdom that he passed on to us in his writings. When we try to read the sermons of Saint Bernard and other writings of the Christian mystical traditions on our own, we might become discouraged in realizing how hard it is for us to access by ourselves the depth and beauty these texts contain. It is precisely at this point that we can begin to appreciate these notes.

What makes these notes unique and helpful is that they allow us to look over Merton's shoulder, as it were, as we see how Merton mentors us in the art of reading and entering into the interior richness of the classical texts of contemplative Christianity. Better yet, Merton invites us to accompany him in his explorations. But we can join Merton in this way only to the extent that we read these notes in the same careful, prayerful manner in which Merton wrote them. And it is here that we can learn from Merton how to enter into a particularly challenging and rewarding kind of contemplative spiritual reading.

What are we to look for in ourselves that allows us to discern that we are entering the ancient stream of contemplative wisdom that Merton is inviting us to encounter? It's hard to say due to the intimate manner in which the transition into this deeper place occurs. But we can look for certain aspects that tend to occur as we learn to read, study, and pray in this way. There is first the tendency to realize that we are entering deep water, and so we would do well to begin by asking God for guidance and to continue to ask for God's guidance every step of the way. We can also look for signs that we are beginning to discover that the very slowness that is required to understand what we are reading embodies the patience that grants entrance into the deep things of God. We can look for signs that we are beginning to realize that being perplexed is not an obstacle to understanding. Rather, perplexity, deeply accepted, embodies the experiential humility and unknowing in which the unseen light of God shines gently in our minds and hearts.

As we continue to read these notes in this patient, humble manner, we can begin to notice graced shifts in our awareness of God's presence in our life. We can begin to realize that our dependence on Merton in helping us to understand Bernard's sermons is falling into the background as we begin to see for ourselves and take to heart Bernard's profound teachings about the mysterious process in which we are transformed in God's love. We might find ourselves encouraged to further hone our mystic reading skills by seeking out other well-written introductions by other authors that help us to access the inner richness of the classical texts of contemplative Christianity.

As transitions such as these unfold within us, we are able to realize that Merton is such a good teacher because he was such a good student, and we are able to realize that in these notes Merton is being a good teacher in helping us to be good students of the spiritual wisdom and trustworthy guidance that lies waiting to be discovered in the careful, prayerful reading of the classical texts of contemplative Christianity. Merton is teaching us in these notes how to be grateful and amazed that the ancient wisdom that shimmers and shines in the eloquent and beautiful things that mystics say is now flowing in our sincere desire to learn from God how to find our way to God.

James Finley

# INTRODUCTION

Thomas Merton first encountered St. Bernard of Clairvaux (1090–1153), the principal subject of the novitiate conferences found in the present volume, even before his conversion to Roman Catholicism. In his autobiography,[1] he recounts his purchase in February 1937 of Étienne Gilson's *The Spirit of Mediaeval Philosophy*,[2] his initial "feeling of disgust" when he discovered "it was a Catholic book," replete with *Nihil Obstat* and *Imprimatur* giving it ecclesiastical sanction, and his realization soon afterward that it provided an intellectually convincing explanation for the nature and existence of God. Chapter 14 of Gilson's book, "Love and Its Object," includes a substantial appendix entitled "Note on the Coherence of Cistercian Mysticism"[3] that defends Bernard's teaching on "the problem of love," a discussion that Merton will call in the first version of these novitiate conferences "[o]ne of the best short introductions to St. Bernard."[4] As Merton relates a few pages later in *The Seven Storey Mountain*, this topic interested him enough "that one day I had gone and looked up St. Bernard's *De Diligendo Deo* in the catalogue of the University Library. It was one of the books Gilson had frequently mentioned:

---

1. Thomas Merton, *The Seven Storey Mountain* (New York: Harcourt, Brace, 1948), 171–72.
2. Étienne Gilson, *The Spirit of Mediaeval Philosophy*, trans. A. H. C. Downes (New York: Charles Scribner's Sons, 1936) (Merton consistently presents the title as *Medieval* rather than *Mediaeval*).
3. *Spirit of Mediaeval Philosophy*, 289–303.
4. See Appendix A, page 399, below.

but when I found that there was no good copy of it, except in Latin, I did not take it out."[5]

There the matter apparently remained until Merton made his life-changing Holy Week retreat at the Abbey of Gethsemani in April 1941, having been baptized at Corpus Christi Church two and a half years earlier, on November 16, 1938.[6] In the autobiography he mentions in passing that while at the monastery he "read St. Bernard's *De Diligendo Deo*,"[7] and his journal from April 8 through April 12 (Tuesday through Saturday of Holy Week) is filled with passages quoted from this treatise (in the original Latin version!),[8] accompanied as he nears the end of his reading by extended commentary on St. Bernard's insights on love:

> Inseparable from the notion of charity is that of freedom. The *servus* and *mercenarius* are bound and restricted, one by fear, the other by self-love. Only charity is perfectly free. Love is loved for itself: that means, it is not drawn by any necessary attraction towards the satisfaction of anything less than itself, or conflicting with itself. Only in charity is love perfectly spontaneous, and free from determination or necessity. . . . All imperfect love, short of charity, ends in something not itself; perfect charity is its own end, therefore is free, because it is not determined by anything outside itself. Love that loves itself is God, and only God is absolutely free. . . . But we are constituted in His image . . . we are free to love Love for itself, and to find ourselves again in that truly perfect freedom of Love's own self-sufficing and eternal action. . . . Pride, self-love, are the love of death, because these turn away from God, in whom is all Being: therefore they necessarily turn to non-being, or death.[9]

---

5. *Seven Storey Mountain*, 184.
6. *Seven Storey Mountain*, 221–25.
7. *Seven Storey Mountain*, 331.
8. Thomas Merton, *Run to the Mountain: The Story of a Vocation. Journals*, vol. 1, *1939–1941*, ed. Patrick Hart (San Francisco: HarperCollins, 1995), 337–38, 342–43, 344–45, 349–54 (the transcriptions and accompanying translations are not always completely accurate).
9. *Run to the Mountain*, 352–53.

Introduction xiii

In such reflections on "find[ing] ourselves again" in authentic freedom by imaging God's own love, which "is not a quality, or accident of God, it is His substance,"[10] can be heard early articulations of Merton's own characteristic exploration of the meaning of authentic human identity.

Having returned to the monastery to stay on December 10, 1941, Merton deepened his acquaintance with Bernard. He notes in *The Seven Storey Mountain*[11] that the "one small box" that "was to represent all the privacy I had left" included two books, "a volume of St. John of the Cross and Gilson's *Mystical Theology of St. Bernard*."[12] In a letter to his friend Robert Lax dated November 21, 1942, Merton mentions the Cistercian custom of listening to readings during meals and the wide variation in quality of the books read: "Sometimes very good, like St. Bernard's sermons on the Canticle of Canticles—sometimes very bad like a few I forget"[13]—Merton, however, will later comment about these readings that "There was a time when I was tempted not to like St. Bernard at all (when the *Sermons in Cantica* were read in the refectory, during my novitiate, I was irritated by the breasts of the Spouse)."[14](!) Merton's familiarity with Bernard was increased when he was given the task in autumn 1947 of cataloguing the manuscripts and early printed editions of Cistercian authors that had been collected by the previous abbot, Dom Edmond Obrecht,[15]

---

10. *Run to the Mountain*, 353.
11. *Seven Storey Mountain*, 384.
12. Étienne Gilson, *The Mystical Theology of Saint Bernard*, trans. A. H. C. Downes (New York: Sheed & Ward, 1940).
13. Thomas Merton, *The Road to Joy: Letters to New and Old Friends*, ed. Robert E. Daggy (New York: Farrar, Straus & Giroux, 1989), 166; Thomas Merton and Robert Lax, *When Prophecy Still Had a Voice: The Letters of Thomas Merton & Robert Lax*, ed. Arthur W. Biddle (Lexington: University Press of Kentucky, 2001), 91.
14. Thomas Merton, *Entering the Silence: Becoming a Monk and Writer. Journals*, vol. 2, *1941–1952*, ed. Jonathan Montaldo (San Francisco: HarperCollins, 1996), 403 [1/27/1950].
15. See *Entering the Silence*, 106–19 [9/12–18/1947].

a job that would first bring him into contact with Dom Jean Leclercq,[16] the great modern editor of Bernard,[17] who would become a lifelong friend.[18] Eventually the abbot assigned to Merton for his exclusive use a set of volumes of St. Bernard's works[19] that he would annotate profusely,[20] and he began to study and write on Bernard extensively. His first substantial prose work, issued anonymously in 1948, was an annotated translation from the original French of *The Spirit of Simplicity*, an official report on simplicity in Cistercian life, approved by the General Chapter of the Order in 1925,[21] to which he added "St. Bernard on Interior Simplicity," a translation and discussion of selected excerpts from Bernard's *Sermons on the Song of Songs* and his treatise *On the Love of God* on the topic

16. See Jean Leclercq, OSB, "Thomas Merton and St. Bernard of Clairvaux," *The Merton Annual* 3 (1990): 37–38, and Thomas Merton and Jean Leclercq, *Survival or Prophecy? The Letters of Thomas Merton and Jean Leclercq*, ed. Brother Patrick Hart (New York: Farrar, Straus & Giroux, 2002), 3–6.

17. *Sancti Bernardi Opera, ad Fidem Codicum Recensuerunt*, ed. Jean Leclercq, C. H. Talbot, and H. M. Rochais, 8 vols., in 9 (Rome: Editiones Cistercienses, 1957–1977).

18. It was Dom Leclercq who was responsible for the invitation to Merton to participate in the meeting of Asian monastics in Thailand at which Merton died. See *Survival or Prophecy*, 162–63 (12/30/1967 letter of Leclercq to Merton).

19. J. P. Migne, ed., *Patrologiae Cursus Completus, Series Latina* [PL], 221 vols. (Paris: Garnier, 1844–1865), vols. 182–85.

20. See Chrysogonus Waddell, OCSO, "Merton of Gethsemani and Bernard of Clairvaux," *The Merton Annual* 5 (1992): 129; see also Jean Leclercq, OSB, introduction to *Thomas Merton on St. Bernard*, Cistercian Studies Series [CS], vol. 9 (Kalamazoo, MI: Cistercian Publications, 1980), 19.

21. According to Waddell ("Merton of Gethsemani and Bernard of Clairvaux," 109), the report, also anonymous, was written by Dom Jean-Baptiste Chautard, the Abbot of Sept-Fons, whose famous book *The Soul of the Apostolate* had been translated anonymously by Merton and issued two years earlier in the same series as *The Spirit of Simplicity* (Trappist, KY: Abbey of Gethsemani, 1946); a new edition with a revised preface (Garden City, NY: Doubleday Image, 1961) would identify Merton as the translator.

of simplicity.[22] While Merton calls himself the "translator and editor" of the volume in his introductory note, his extensive discussion of Bernard in part 2 qualifies him to be given the title of author as well, as is indicated by the reprinting of this material as the second part of the posthumously published *Thomas Merton on St. Bernard*.[23] Along with a brief foreword in which he summarizes the meaning of simplicity in the Cistercian tradition as *"getting rid of everything that did not help the monk to arrive at union with God by the shortest possible way,"*[24] that is, through charity, and explains that the discussion of interior simplicity based on the teaching of Bernard has been included as a complement to the official report, which concentrates principally on the externals of simplicity (in clothing, buildings, liturgy, etc.), and a briefer conclusion calling for a deeper acquaintance on the part of Cistercians with the sources of their tradition, ideally through reading of the texts themselves, Merton's major contribution to the volume is a series of four sets of texts translated from Bernard with substantial commentary. After providing an overview of Bernard's theology of image and likeness, which identifies natural simplicity as one of the main aspects of the divine image in the human

---

22. *The Spirit of Simplicity Characteristic of the Cistercian Order: An Official Report, demanded and approved by the General Chapter; Together with Texts from St. Bernard of Clairvaux on Interior Simplicity; Translation and Commentary by a Cistercian Monk of Our Lady of Gethsemani* (Trappist, KY: Abbey of Our Lady of Gethsemani, 1948). For discussions, see Paul R. Dekar, "*The Spirit of Simplicity*: Merton on Simplification of Life," *The Merton Annual* 19 (2006): 267–82; Patrick F. O'Connell, "*Spirit of Simplicity, The*," in William H. Shannon, Christine M. Bochen, and Patrick F. O'Connell, *The Thomas Merton Encyclopedia* (Maryknoll, NY: Orbis Books, 2002), 446–48; M. Basil Pennington, "Father Louis' First Book: *The Spirit of Simplicity*," in *Thomas Merton My Brother: His Journey to Freedom, Compassion, and Final Integration* (Hyde Park, NY: New City Press, 1996), 65–78; Waddell, "Merton of Gethsemani and Bernard of Clairvaux," 109–17.

23. *Thomas Merton on St. Bernard*, 105–57; this version does not include Merton's foreword or conclusion to the volume.

24. *Spirit of Simplicity*, iii.

person, the section on "Man's Original Simplicity"[25] stresses Bernard's emphasis on the centrality of self-knowledge, of discovering one's "real self, in the image of God" as well as on the necessity "to get rid of . . . the overlying layer of duplicity that is *not* ourselves"[26]—the roots of Merton's own understanding of the true and false self can be recognized here. The following two sections focus respectively on "Intellectual Simplicity,"[27] in which knowledge is seen as oriented toward love, which alone makes possible that union with God that is the highest knowledge, and on "The Simplification of the Will,"[28] divided into two subsections, the first emphasizing obedience as the key for overcoming self-will, the second focusing on the danger, both for one's own salvation and for the peace of the community, of relying on one's own judgment. Finally, the last set of texts, headed "Perfect Simplicity—Unity of Spirit with God,"[29] considers the full restoration of one's likeness to God as a union not of substance but of wills, in which the soul, transcending multiplicity to become one spirit with God, can be said *"to become God"*[30] in so far as it loses itself in God: this is the perfection of simplicity.

The previous year, in a journal entry for May 14, 1947, Merton had written: "I read some St. Bernard on the Mystical Marriage. The tenth chapter of *De Diligendo Deo* and the last sermons *In Cantica* bring St. Bernard and St. John of the Cross into line together. When they reach their goal, they are together in their way of looking at things: we are made for the mystical marriage, it fulfills our nature."[31] This is the origin of Merton's first article on Bernard, "Transforming Union in St. Bernard of Clairvaux and St. John of the Cross," published in five parts in

---

25. *Spirit of Simplicity*, 81–91; *Thomas Merton on St. Bernard*, 111–20.
26. *Spirit of Simplicity*, 90; *Thomas Merton on St. Bernard*, 118–19.
27. *Spirit of Simplicity*, 92–110; *Thomas Merton on St. Bernard*, 121–36.
28. *Spirit of Simplicity*, 111–30; *Thomas Merton on St. Bernard*, 137–52.
29. *Spirit of Simplicity*, 131–35; *Thomas Merton on St. Bernard*, 153–57.
30. *Spirit of Simplicity*, 131; *Thomas Merton on St. Bernard*, 157.
31. *Entering the Silence*, 73.

Introduction                                     xvii

the official Cistercian journal in 1948–1950[32] and later reprinted in *Thomas Merton on Saint Bernard*.[33] Merton begins by indicating that the purpose of the essay is to show that while their terminology differs, for Bernard and John "the same goal lies at the end of both their journeys."[34] It is on some level Merton's effort to reconcile his predilection for the great Carmelite mystic with his own Cistercian calling, about which he felt some degree of ambivalence almost from the beginning.[35] The first section focuses on the two saints' respective views of human nature, which initially seem incompatible, but only because "St Bernard is talking about nature in its essential definition, in itself" while "St John is talking about nature as it finds itself, *per accidens*, in its present, actual, fallen condition."[36] In part 2, Merton compares Bernard's description of the process of stripping away the false garments of sin that obscure the "naked" natural dignity of the human person to John's doctrine of emptiness and annihilation in the experience of the dark night and concludes that despite the difference in imagery the experience described is the same. The third section notes that whereas John makes a distinction between two phases of the unitive life, the deep yet transient experiences of the divine presence in the spiritual betrothal and the incomparably greater state of transforming union he calls the spiritual

32. M. Louis Merton, "Transforming Union in St. Bernard of Clairvaux and St. John of the Cross," *Collectanea Ordinis Cisterciensium Reformatorum* 9, no. 2 (1948): 107–17; 9, no. 3 (1948): 210–23; 10, no. 1 (1949): 41–52; 10, no. 3 (1949): 353–61; 11, no. 1 (1950): 25–38.

33. *Thomas Merton on St. Bernard*, 159–226; for a somewhat more extended discussion see Patrick F. O'Connell, "*Thomas Merton on St. Bernard*," *Merton Encyclopedia*, 480–81.

34. *Thomas Merton on St. Bernard*, 161.

35. See the journal entry for August 14, 1947: "And so tomorrow we stars of the active life will celebrate Mary's contemplation. So much activity in the spirituality of St. Bernard! Pure contemplation only for the weak. I don't know, maybe that is common teaching. But I still prefer St. John of the Cross" (*Entering the Silence*, 98).

36. *Thomas Merton on St. Bernard*, 169.

marriage, Bernard's descriptions in his early works of the visits of the Bridegroom seem to refer only to John's "betrothal," whereas in Bernard's view "the perfect union with God described by St. John of the Cross as mystical marriage was only to be attained in the next life."[37] But in the following section, Merton suggests that in the final sermons on the Song of Songs Bernard is speaking of "a perfect union of wills, a perfect union of love with God, perfect likeness to God . . . and therefore mystical marriage even on earth,"[38] a description that Merton considers to be based on personal experience.[39] The concluding section deals with what Merton considers to be the biggest difficulty of all in reconciling the teaching of the two saints: is the pure love Bernard describes a permanent state, a union that has permanently and irrevocably transformed the soul? Merton maintains that Bernard himself "no longer has any hesitation in calling this union of love a permanent and habitual state,"[40] though he makes the necessary distinction between "the union of the *faculties*" of the soul, which cannot be continual, and the "uninterrupted union" of the "substance of the soul," which is marked by *"an uninterrupted joy."*[41]

As one would of course expect, Bernard has a prominent role in Merton's 1949 history of the Cistercian Order, *The Waters of Siloe*,[42] though the focus is on his teaching rather than on biographical data. In the opening chapter, the Cistercian emphasis on simplicity once again is evident, highlighted by Bernard's critique in his *Apologia* of a decadent monasticism marked by pomp and display[43] and by the inspiration his writings provided

---

37. *Thomas Merton on St. Bernard*, 200.
38. *Thomas Merton on St. Bernard*, 206.
39. *Thomas Merton on St. Bernard*, 211.
40. *Thomas Merton on St. Bernard*, 215.
41. *Thomas Merton on St. Bernard*, 217.
42. Thomas Merton, *The Waters of Siloe* (New York: Harcourt, Brace, 1949).
43. *The Waters of Siloe*, 13.

for the austere beauty of Cistercian architecture.[44] Merton pays particular attention to Bernard's treatise on *The Degrees of Humility* with its emphasis on authentic self-knowledge and on the *spiritus lenitatis*, the compassionate gentleness that grows out of a sense of one's own weakness and "is a perfect preparation for mystical prayer"[45] because it fosters docility to the working of the Holy Spirit. He also points out that the spiritual serenity fostered by the Cistercian life is evident in the pellucid style of Bernard and the Cistercian "school" generally and in their acute psychological ruminations on the nature of the soul as "capable of love,"[46] a capacity that is actualized by a participation in the mystery of the passion, particularly in union with the Mother of God: "Compassion for the crucified Savior was as important a means to dispose the soul for mystical prayer as compassion for one's neighbor."[47] In the shorter second section of the book, an examination of the central characteristics of Cistercian life, Bernard's appreciation of nature as a setting for contemplation is distinguished from Wordsworthian nature mysticism but also presented as a corrective to the distorted view that as an ascetical practice the Cistercians deliberately chose unhealthy locations for their abbeys.[48] Bernard's emphasis on love for the person of Christ as the foundation of his mystical teaching is shown to be an attractive and effective means to engage "men of all kinds"[49] who were joining the early Cistercians, an experiential rather than theoretical foundation for contemplative union that began with an appreciation of the accessible human Jesus but prepared the way for "the infused and experimental knowledge of Christ in His divinity."[50] Bernard's teaching on the "common will" as

44. *The Waters of Siloe*, 15.
45. *The Waters of Siloe*, 24.
46. *The Waters of Siloe*, 28.
47. *The Waters of Siloe*, 29.
48. *The Waters of Siloe*, 267–73.
49. *The Waters of Siloe*, 291.
50. *The Waters of Siloe*, 295.

constitutive for authentic community life[51] is complemented by an investigation of the place of solitude in Bernard's teaching, a rejection of both outer and inner isolation joined to an affirmation of the necessity for "a solitude which empties our hearts and isolates us from the desires and ambitions and conflicts and troubles and lusts common to all the children of this world."[52] The paradoxical life of solitude in community is finally seen to be directed to the discovery of the "real self," a daunting task "because, in St. Bernard's language, our true personality has been concealed under the 'disguise' of a false self, the *ego* whom we tend to worship in place of God."[53] It is the recovery of this perspective and the realization of this transformation, Merton suggests, that is the task of a renewed Cistercian spirituality, "a return to the integrity of the Cistercian life in its letter and spirit."[54]

The biographical material largely absent from *The Waters of Siloe* turns up quite unexpectedly in a two-page sketch of Bernard's life included in *The Ascent to Truth*,[55] Merton's 1951 volume on the teachings of St. John of the Cross, added at the last minute to brief overviews of other mystical theologians because, according to Merton, "many in the Order would be offended if he were left out"[56]—even though he is virtually absent from the text itself. Bernard is identified not only as "one of the greatest and most characteristic figures of the Middle Ages" but also as the "last of the Church Fathers" because of "his loyalty to the spirit of Patristic theology" at a time when the first stirrings of a movement that would lead to the scholastic theology of the next century had begun. He notes the paradox of Bernard's with-

51. *The Waters of Siloe*, 336–38.
52. *The Waters of Siloe*, 345.
53. *The Waters of Siloe*, 349.
54. *The Waters of Siloe*, 350.
55. Thomas Merton, *The Ascent to Truth* (New York: Harcourt, Brace, 1951), 321–22.
56. Letter to Robert Giroux dated July 22, 1951 (*The Letters of Robert Giroux and Thomas Merton*, ed. Patrick Samway [Notre Dame, IN: University of Notre Dame Press, 2015], 104).

drawal from the world and sacrifice of his own noble status that eventually leads to the establishment of Cistercian monasteries throughout Europe, thereby "turning the Order into a world movement," and to his own paramount role in the ecclesiastical and even political life of the first half of the twelfth century, as well as the complexity of his personality, "one of ardent lyricism combined with seriousness and strength," the "mellifluous Doctor" whose letters of instruction and admonition were often marked by "a certain note of violence." In the context of *The Ascent to Truth*, Merton focuses on Bernard's "crucially important part in the theological developments of his age," particularly his role in "the detection of singularly dangerous errors" in Abelard and others, which is said to have "prepared the way for the sane intellectualism of the scholastics" such as Aquinas by exposing the faulty use of the scholastic method in contemporary theology, while at the same time he "saved true Christian mysticism" by opposing attempts to undermine divine "transcendence by narrowing it down to the limitations of a philosopher's concept"— neat formulations with little nuance that a more mature Merton would qualify in the conferences found in the present volume.

In January 1950, Merton signed a contract with his principal publisher, Harcourt, Brace, for four books, one of which was to be on Bernard.[57] At the time he wrote in his journal (in the same entry that mentions his unease as a novice with the breasts of the Bride):

> The more I read St. Bernard and the Cistercian Fathers, the more I like them. . . . I think that now, after eight years and more, I am really beginning to discover the depth of St. Bernard. This is because I have realized that the foundation of his whole doctrine . . . is that God is Truth and Christ is Truth Incarnate and that salvation and sanctity for us means being true to ourselves and true to Christ and true

---

57. See the journal entry for January 18, 1950 (*Entering the Silence*, 399); the other books were to be on Aelred of Rievaulx, Bernard's younger Cistercian contemporary, the work that eventually became *The Ascent to Truth*, and a book on the liturgy that was never written.

to God. It is only when this emphasis on truth is forgotten that St. Bernard begins to seem sentimental.[58]

But by mid-1952, he was having second thoughts about this project, as he indicated in his journal: "It seemed to me an impertinence and waste of time to write a book about St. Bernard, as I am supposed to do. . . . What need is there for me to do all over again what has been done by Gilson and Leclercq and by our own Father Pacificus from Tilburg in Rome, these recent days!" Somewhat overwhelmed by his new responsibilities as master of students at Gethsemani, he asks, "Where will I get the time to write anything?" and exclaims, "If obedience thinks it desirable for me to write about St. Bernard, obedience must also make it possible for me to do so!"[59] There is also the fact of a certain lack of enthusiasm for Bernard, despite the obvious influence of his Cistercian predecessor on his own developing spiritual theology. A few months earlier he had written to the Carthusian Jean-Baptiste Porion:

> It does not seem to me to be a reserved or even a mortal sin to live in a Cistercian monastery with more actual sympathy for St. John of the Cross than St. Bernard of Clairvaux. Though I by no means refuse to read St. Bernard. I just cannot assert that he nourishes me as much as others do. . . . For when I read St. Bernard, I am more drawn to study than to contemplation. He does not draw me to rest in silence and darkness: he evokes spontaneous admiration for a rather brilliant theological manner of meditating on the

---

58. *Entering the Silence*, 403 [1/27/1950].
59. Thomas Merton, *A Search for Solitude: Pursuing the Monk's True Life. Journals*, vol. 3, *1952–1960*, ed. Lawrence S. Cunningham (San Francisco: HarperCollins, 1996), 12 [8/28/1952]. The references are to Gilson's *The Mystical Theology of Saint Bernard*, Jean Leclercq's *Saint Bernard Mystique* (Paris: Desclée de Brouwer, 1948), and Pacificus Delfgaauw's 1952 doctoral dissertation, *Saint Bernard, Maître de l'Amour de Dieu: Étude de Théologie Monastique*, later published as *Saint Bernard, Maître de l'Amour Divin* (Paris: FAC-Éditions, 1994).

Scriptures which is, for me, something short of prayer. . . . I am happy with St. John of the Cross among the rocks.[60]

The solution to his conundrum would develop as a result of the nine-hundredth anniversary of the death of St. Bernard on August 20, 1153, which prompted no less than five separate publications on Bernard by Merton, including a book-length study. The shortest, but probably the most widely diffused, was originally written as a foreword for a collection of Bernard's selected letters, translated by Merton's friend Bruno Scott James,[61] which Merton would later include in slightly revised form as part of the "Mentors and Doctrines" section of *A Thomas Merton Reader*.[62] After a brief quotation from Newman about the saint as one who not only transmits but lives out the message of the Gospel, Merton identifies the "scandal"[63] of Bernard's extraordinary career, as monk and abbot of a new order seeking obscurity who became the most visible public figure of the age, with the folly and mystery of the cross. But he implies that the "scandal" has also a less scriptural dimension. The paradox of Bernard's

---

60. Thomas Merton, *The School of Charity: Letters on Religious Renewal and Spiritual Direction*, ed. Patrick Hart (New York: Farrar, Straus & Giroux, 1990), 33 [2/9/1952].

61. *St. Bernard of Clairvaux Seen through His Selected Letters*, trans. Bruno Scott James (Chicago: Henry Regnery, 1953), v–viii. About half of this foreword was included in the August 1953 issue of Merton's friend Edward Rice's new magazine *Jubilee*, along with a new introductory paragraph calling attention to the anniversary and providing highlights of Bernard's public life, and followed by excerpts from nine of the letters, each with a marginal explanatory note by Merton (*Jubilee* 1, no. 4 [August 1953]: 32–37). The same piece, with the references to the letters removed, was reused a decade later as a foreword to Henry Daniel-Rops, *Bernard of Clairvaux*, trans. Elisabeth Abbott (New York: Hawthorn Books, 1964), 5–7. The bibliographies are not completely clear on the relationship of these various versions.

62. Thomas Merton, *A Thomas Merton Reader*, ed. Thomas P. McDonnell (New York: Harcourt, Brace, 1962), 315–18 (immediately following an essay on St. John of the Cross); this piece on Bernard was omitted from the revised edition of the *Reader* (Garden City, NY: Doubleday Image, 1974).

63. *Merton Reader*, 315; *Selected Letters*, v.

activity being rooted in his contemplation is linked with his own awareness of the dangers of an activism that could easily exhibit the foibles of one's own personality and character, as is often evident in the letters. Here Merton confronts the humanity of his subject, "the faults of frailty and passion which even a saint could commit in the heart of ruthless and energetic action"[64] of which, he maintains, Bernard himself was quite conscious. Without judging how much of Bernard's anger, where the translator finds him "at his best"[65]—his "bold and grandiose impatience"[66] even with royal correspondents—is truly righteous indignation, Merton emphasizes that the other side of Bernard is just as prominent in the letters: "the gentle and long-suffering monk who . . . had in his heart something of Christ's unending patience with the weak sinner and compassion for the publican."[67] Calling attention to examples of amusing comments and aphoristic remarks in the letters, to one particular letter[68] on "pure love" that "takes us at once to the heart of St. Bernard's theology,"[69] as well as to the translator's rare ability to capture Bernard's "vigor and life and rhythm" in English,[70] Merton emphasizes that his Cistercian predecessor is an "imposing personality" who "is too important to be overlooked," and that while the "whole Bernard is not to be found in the *Letters* alone . . . the whole Bernard can never be known without them."[71] He concludes that acquaintance with Bernard should prompt not only respect but admiration and love, and finally imitation, and even that "perhaps our own century needs nothing so much as the combined anger and gentleness of

---

64. *Merton Reader*, 316; *Selected Letters*, vi.
65. *Merton Reader*, 316; *Selected Letters*, vii.
66. *Merton Reader*, 316; *Selected Letters*, vi.
67. *Merton Reader*, 317; *Selected Letters*, vii.
68. This is the famous letter to the Carthusians, appended to his treatise *On the Love of God*, that Merton will discuss in detail in the conferences found in this volume (see pages 96–107).
69. *Merton Reader*, 317; *Selected Letters*, vii.
70. *Merton Reader*, 317; *Selected Letters*, viii.
71. *Merton Reader*, 317; *Selected Letters*, viii, which reads: ". . . an imposingly important personality."

Introduction                                                    xxv

another Bernard"[72]—a suggestion in which the first word should not be overlooked! Two of the articles from this year appeared first in French translation. The anniversary would of course be celebrated much more widely in Bernard's native land than in America, and various publications were eager to have a contribution by the best-known contemporary Cistercian. An extensive collection of scholarly articles on Bernard was prefaced by Merton's "Saint Bernard, Moine et Apôtre,"[73] which Jean Leclercq suggests was included because "the editor thought that it would reach a wider reading public"[74] with a prominent contribution by Merton (a decision, he notes, that was not universally endorsed). As in the *Letters* preface, Merton begins with a general consideration of the nature of sanctity, presenting a saint as a sign or "sacrament" of God,[75] an embodiment of the continuing presence of Christ in the Church and in the world through the indwelling power of the Holy Spirit. Recognizing the controversial aspects of Bernard's career as preacher of an unsuccessful crusade, vociferous opponent of theological innovation, and, initially, overenthusiastic ascetic, Merton emphasizes that Bernard's vocation as witness to Christ, rather than as reformer of the Church or proponent of

---

72. *Merton Reader*, 318; *Selected Letters*, viii.

73. Commission d'Histoire de l'Ordre de Cîteaux, *Bernard de Clairvaux* (Paris: Éditions Alsatia, 1953), vii–xv; in his *Thomas Merton: A Bibliography* (New York: Farrar, Straus & Cudahy, 1956), Frank Dell'Isola erroneously refers to this volume as "a biography" of Bernard (35), a mistake repeated in the headnote to Merton's preface to *Marthe, Marie et Lazare* (Thomas Merton, *"Honorable Reader": Reflections on My Work*, ed. Robert E. Daggy [New York: Crossroad, 1989], 15). The original version appeared in England in two installments in *The Tablet* 201, no. 5896 (May 23, 1953): 438–39; 201, no. 5897 (May 30, 1953): 466–67; and in America in *Cross and Crown* 5, no. 3 (September 1953): 251–63; it was eventually included in Thomas Merton, *Disputed Questions* (New York: Farrar, Straus and Cudahy, 1960), 274–90.

74. Leclercq, "Merton and St. Bernard," 38; perhaps in response, Chrysogonus Waddell emphasizes that this inclusion was "by no means a publicity ploy" ("Merton of Gethsemani and Bernard of Clairvaux," 122).

75. *Disputed Questions*, 274.

devotion to the "humanity of Christ" or to the Virgin Mary, must be recognized as the unifying element of his remarkably multifaceted life. His "apostolate" is to be found not so much in his various activities on behalf of the Church as in his "radiation of Christ, by the grace of the Holy Spirit,"[76] by his dying and rising with Christ, "plunging to the depths of his human nothingness" and "com[ing] back to us resplendent with the divine mercy."[77] If this experience prompted in Bernard "a holy impatience,"[78] this is in essence because he "thirsts for God Himself" and speaks above all to other "souls athirst for God,"[79] especially the monks under his charge. Bernard himself sees the monastic vocation as at once apostolic in leaving all things to follow Christ, angelic in its paradisal chastity, and prophetic in its eschatological expectation, three dimensions of a contemplative life that "makes possible the fullness of the Christian vocation to divine union in so far as that union can be achieved on earth."[80] It is this experience, inspired by the gift of the Spirit, that leads Bernard to recognize "clearer than anyone else in his time"[81] the true meaning of the incarnation as the definitive outpouring of divine love for humanity, reenacted through the mediation of the Mother of God in the lives of individuals and in the Church, "in His mystical as well as his physical body . . . in our hearts as well as in His own flesh."[82] This recognition, Merton concludes, is evident not simply in what Bernard said but in who he was—and is: "Bernard remains a sign of God because like all the saints he has been filled with the revelation of the living God"[83] and leads his listeners through the wound in Christ's side "into the heart which is the sanctuary of God."[84] While Merton proved himself quite capable

76. *Disputed Questions*, 279.
77. *Disputed Questions*, 281.
78. *Disputed Questions*, 283.
79. *Disputed Questions*, 284.
80. *Disputed Questions*, 286.
81. *Disputed Questions*, 287.
82. *Disputed Questions*, 288.
83. *Disputed Questions*, 289.
84. *Disputed Questions*, 290.

of more technical studies of the Cistercian saint, here he has provided the inspirational prelude to the scholarly theological articles by others that was evidently expected of him by the compilers of this anniversary volume.

The second French article,[85] a translation of a conference entitled "The Sacrament of Advent in the Spirituality of St. Bernard" that Merton had given to his students the year before,[86] was not published in English until it was included in Merton's 1965 collection of liturgical essays, *Seasons of Celebration*.[87] Drawing extensively on Bernard's series of Advent sermons, Merton focuses on his use of the term *"sacramentum,"* the Latin equivalent of the Pauline *"mysterion"* that in Ephesians refers to the divine plan for creation that finds its fulfillment in the once and future coming of Christ but is "already present and realized in a hidden manner" in those who have responded to Christ's proclamation of the Kingdom of God "in the midst of us."[88] Paradoxically, Advent is seen by Bernard as a paschal season, the beginning of Christ's passage through the world and back to the Father, "gathering the elect to Himself by the effects of His death and resurrection"[89] so that the incarnation may find its fulfillment in the ingathering of "the *Whole Christ*" in union with the risen and glorified Lord at the Father's right hand, a reality foreshadowed by "the highest contemplation . . . a participation of the Mystery of Christ, the Mystery of the Cross."[90] This experience becomes possible through the self-emptying of

---

85. Thomas Merton, "Le Sacrement de l'Avent dans la Spiritualité de Saint Bernard," *Dieu Vivant* 23 (1953): 21–43.

86. Thomas Merton, "Monastic Orientation," Series 3 (Advent 1951–August 1952)," Part 1, 1–14; found in volume 16 of "Collected Essays," the twenty-four-volume bound set of published and unpublished materials assembled at the Abbey of Gethsemani and available both there and at the Thomas Merton Center, Bellarmine University, Louisville, KY.

87. Thomas Merton, *Seasons of Celebration* (New York: Farrar, Straus & Giroux, 1965), 61–87.

88. *Seasons of Celebration*, 64.

89. *Seasons of Celebration*, 66.

90. *Seasons of Celebration*, 67.

compunction, "a breaking out of the prison of 'selfhood,' . . . a liberation from a miserable preoccupation with our own failings,"[91] so that the "interior life" becomes Christ's own presence dwelling within as the true source of life, as one's deepest identity. This is the essence of Bernard's teaching on the three Advents, the first coming on Christmas, the final coming at the parousia, and the *"medius Adventus,"* which "is in a certain sense the most important for us," the "present Advent that is taking place at every moment of our own earthly life as wayfarers."[92] Christ's coming now, in this time and place, above all in Scripture, the nourishing *"viaticum"* that is not merely to be studied and remembered but eaten, "absorb[ed] into the depths of our being,"[93] both puts us in touch with the foundational events of faith and with their final realization and is an invitation and challenge to ongoing conversion. All this is both modeled by and made available through Mary, herself the *"regia . . . via per quam Salvator advenit,"* the "royal way"[94] of Christ's coming and therefore the most apt place to encounter and receive the saving Word.

There is actually a third "pseudo-article" that also appeared in French during this year, a piece entitled "Saint Bernard et l'Amérique"[95] that was actually a cobbled-together substitute for an essay on this topic that, according to Fr. Chrysogonus Waddell, Merton was for some reason not allowed to write.[96] It consists of

---

91. *Seasons of Celebration*, 70–71.
92. *Seasons of Celebration*, 76.
93. *Seasons of Celebration*, 80–81.
94. *Seasons of Celebration*, 88.
95. Thomas Merton, "Saint Bernard et l'Amérique," *Temoignages* 38–39 (July 1953): 88–98.
96. Waddell, "Merton of Gethsemani and Bernard of Clairvaux," 122; in an unpublished letter of October 26, 1952 to Gethsemani Abbot James Fox (archives of the Thomas Merton Center [TMC], Bellarmine University, Louisville, KY), *Temoignages* editor Claude Jean Nesmy, osb, responds to an October 5 letter from Dom James: "there is nothing we can do but agree that it would be quite impossible for Father Louis to contribute to our April issue on St. Bernard by anything yet unpublished. But, as we are quite anxious to give this issue on Saint Bernard every possible and adequate illustration,

Introduction                                    xxix

passages from the French translation of *The Waters of Siloe* preceded by excerpts from Merton's apologetic letter to the editor, explaining that Bernard is little known and appreciated by Cistercians in America, including his own students, only one of whom, a convert, truly understands and loves the saint; the pragmatism of most of the rest finds it difficult to resonate with Bernard's allegorical approach to Scripture. It is noteworthy mainly for the fact that Merton would subsequently pen a kind of retraction in a letter dated September 2, 1953, to Fr. Charles Dumont, the editor of the Order's journal *Collectanea*, to whom he writes: "Pray for me, Father, and my scholastics. They are such wonderful monks. They gave some very good conferences on St. Bernard, conferences that belied the hasty note of mine that was published in *Témoignages*. They *do* love and understand his spirit."[97]

Actually a fourth article for that year was in fact appearing serially in *Collectanea* itself (in English) at the time of his writing this letter to Dumont. "Action and Contemplation in St. Bernard"[98]

---

we wonder if it would not be possible for us to select a few passages out of some of the well-known books . . . with the due agreement of Fr Louis himself and the French editors. . . . Well, to crown our insatiate wishes, we would indeed—if it is ever possible—ask Fr Louis to let us have only a few lines, let us say a paragraph, of introduction to the passages." In an unpublished letter to Merton himself dated March 14, 1953, Dom Nesmy specifies the final arrangements: "J'ai décidé de profiter de votre autorisation pour publier ce que vous me disiez des réactions de vos clercs devant Saint Bernard. . . . Avec tout cela et les extraits que je pourrais prendre au besoin dans Aux Sources du Silence . . . je pense que l'on pourrait arriver à faire quelque chose de pas trop mal" ("I have decided to take advantage of your permission to publish what you have told me of the responses of your students to Saint Bernard. . . . With all that and the extracts I have been able to take as needed from *The Sources of Silence* [*The Waters of Siloe*] . . . I think we could put together something that is not too bad") [TMC archives].

97. *School of Charity*, 67; Waddell mentions some of these conferences and their presenters (including himself) in "Merton of Gethsemani and Bernard of Clairvaux," 123.

98. M. Louis Merton, "Action and Contemplation in St. Bernard," *Collectanea Ordinis Cisterciensium Reformatorum* 15, no. 1 (January 1953): 26–31; 15, no. 2 (July 1953): 203–16; 16, no. 2 (April 1954): 105–21; this version of

was another long, more technical essay comparable to that on Bernard and John of the Cross published in the same periodical some four years earlier. The complete version of the essay consists of five parts.[99] The first, "Action and Contemplation in the Mystery of Christ," surveys the topic from the New Testament up to the time of Bernard. While the focus in John's Gospel is on love of God manifesting itself in the two forms of contemplative abiding in God and active witness to others, both exemplified by Jesus, St. Paul stresses that members of the Body of Christ have different functions, some more active, some more contemplative. The early monastic literature teaches the superiority of the contemplative life to the active, respectively represented by the figures of Mary and Martha, though both are seen as necessary and indeed complementary. Thus Bernard is seen as building on a long tradition of evangelical and monastic teaching in his exploration of the paradoxical relation of action and contemplation in the Christian life. The three central sections of the essay look at "Action in the Monastic Life," "The Contemplative Life," and "The Apostolate," respectively. Merton notes that Bernard typically considers not two types of monastic life but three, including Lazarus with his two sisters as models: he represents the penitents, Mary the contemplatives, and Martha the active administrators or preachers. For most monks, the life of penance in itself or a life of penance that leads to contemplation is the road to sanctification, but for some, the further dimension of care for others becomes the completion of their vocation. Bernard teaches that the way of contemplation is to be preferred as more conducive to peace and rest in God, but that "the 'mixed' life, composed of action and contemplation together, is in a certain sense more necessary to the Church than contemplation alone, and therefore it has a higher dignity than the life of pure and unmixed contem-

---

the essay consists of the second, third, and fourth of the five parts included in the expanded version published in *Thomas Merton on St. Bernard*, 23–104.

99. For a somewhat more extensive presentation of this material, see O'Connell, "Thomas Merton on St. Bernard," *Merton Encyclopedia*, 479–80.

plation,"[100] but to be fruitful, "the apostolic vocation . . . is not *substituted* for contemplation" but "*added* to contemplation, and becomes an integral part in the interior, contemplative life of the soul perfectly united to the Word."[101] As in "The Sacrament of Advent," in the final section Merton looks at Bernard's teaching on Mary, presented here as the perfect model of both contemplation and action, receiving the Word into her soul and body in intimate union and offering him to the world in an act of supreme love, prompting Merton to exhort his readers to turn to her and "to seek, by prayer and ardent desire, for a charity that will bring us to that spiritual maturity in Christ which will, to some extent, unify both action and contemplation in our own souls."[102]

Merton had plans to include "Action and Contemplation"—"made more readable"[103]—as part of his projected book-length study, and wrote a new preface for it, but nothing came of the idea except a French translation of an expanded version of the article entitled *Marthe, Marie et Lazare*[104] with the preface included.[105] These introductory pages orient the reader by emphasizing the importance of seeing Bernard's teaching as a whole as focused on the mystery of Christ and on contemplation as the experience of participation in this mystery. By taking certain of Bernard's statements out of context, his understanding of the relation between action and contemplation can easily be distorted in one direction or the other or judged to be inconsistent. Likewise an anachronistic introduction of later considerations of the definition, functions, and relative importance of active and contemplative religious orders can only confuse the issue, since such

---

100. *Thomas Merton on St. Bernard*, 60.
101. *Thomas Merton on St. Bernard*, 71.
102. *Thomas Merton on St. Bernard*, 87.
103. Letter dated April 30, 1953 to Robert Giroux (*Letters of Robert Giroux and Thomas Merton*, 151).
104. Thomas Merton, *Marthe, Marie et Lazare*, trans. Marie Tadié (Paris: Desclée de Brouwer, 1956).
105. It is available in English only in "*Honorable Reader*", 17–22.

distinctions did not exist in Bernard's day. Hence the importance, Merton declares, of the study that is to follow, which will point out the complementarity of the vocations of Lazarus, Martha, and Mary in the monastic context and remind the reader that contemplation is ultimately a gratuitous divine gift rather than simply the choice of an individual, but that according to Bernard, "we can always orient our desires and our efforts in one or the other of these two directions," and if possible "the chief object of our aspirations" should be "the vocation of Mary." This, Merton indicates, "is the most important point of our study."[106]

Merton's final contribution to the Bernardine anniversary did at last result in a book-length work. On June 30, 1953, Merton wrote to Sr. Thérèse Lentfoehr, "Have you seen the new Encyclical on St. Bernard? At first, when I heard about it in a newspaper clipping, it sounded tame. I never saw anything so strong on the mystical life."[107] Soon Merton had the idea of making the encyclical, entitled *Doctor Mellifluus*,[108] widely available to an English-speaking audience, and on July 23, his editor Robert Giroux wrote, "If you're not going to get to the big biography in the next year or so, this might afford a means of doing a small book on St. Bernard."[109] Merton responded on August 12[110] that he was interested in pursuing the idea, still as "a good appetizer for the future book on St. Bernard,"[111] but at this point he was thinking

---

106. *"Honorable Reader"*, 21.
107. *Road to Joy*, 214.
108. The encyclical is dated May 24, 1953; according to Waddell, it was composed principally by Dom Sighard Kleiner, the abbot general of the "other branch" of the Cistercians, the Common Observance ("Merton of Gethsemani and Bernard of Clairvaux," 124).
109. *Letters of Robert Giroux and Thomas Merton*, 157.
110. *Letters of Robert Giroux and Thomas Merton*, 158–59.
111. He had written in a previous letter of July 26, "I feel a great distaste for writing an official biography of St. Bernard, and think I won't. When the time comes for that book . . . well, it will have to be something other than a biography. Perhaps three long essays on important aspects of his thought" (*Letters of Robert Giroux and Thomas Merton*, 158).

Introduction                                                    xxxiii

of a very short volume, "around thirty pages or less"—simply
an English translation of the five thousand-word encyclical[112]
with a brief introduction. But less than two weeks later, he wrote
to Giroux that his "picture of it has changed. I think it ought to
include three sections: first, a sketch of St. Bernard's life and
character, second an outline of his chief works, and third the
notes on the Encyclical," as a way to "make this book more accessible to the general reader."[113] He received a positive response
from his editor on September 23: "It ought, in short, to be a little
book on Saint Bernard, with this encyclical as a taking-off
point,"[114] and on October 9, he sent a substantially complete draft
of his own contributions,[115] corresponding to the tripartite structure he had indicated in his August 22 letter, which ended up

---

112. Despite what is sometimes written (see M. Basil Pennington,
"Thomas Merton and His Own Cistercian Tradition," in *Thomas Merton My
Brother*, 83; William H. Shannon, *"Last of the Fathers, The," Merton Encyclopedia*, 244), the translation is not by Merton: it is substantially the official
Vatican translation (see Merton's letters to Giroux of August 24 and October
3, 1963 [*Letters of Robert Giroux and Thomas Merton*, 160, 163]), though Giroux
made a few revisions to the text, "so we'll be sure not to call it the 'Vatican
translation' anywhere" (letter to Merton, November 4, 1953 [*Giroux-Merton
Letters*, 165]), and Merton himself subsequently reworked some of the language "and tried to put it into proper English . . . to make the text idiomatic
at least in the most important passages" (letter to Giroux, January 14, 1954
[*Letters of Robert Giroux and Thomas Merton*, 170]). Giroux later wrote with
evident amusement to Merton that "a new magazine called *The Pope Speaks*,
which is devoted to Papal documents, asked us if they could use *your* translation of the text of Dr. Mellifluus. I hastily assured them it was *not* your
translation, but you may nevertheless hear from them" (letter of May 28,
1954 [*Letters of Robert Giroux and Thomas Merton*, 178]).
    113. Letter of August 24, 1953 (*Letters of Robert Giroux and Thomas Merton*,
160).
    114. *Letters of Robert Giroux and Thomas Merton*, 162.
    115. *Letters of Robert Giroux and Thomas Merton*; on January 14, 1954,
Merton sent to Giroux "two significant and rather long additions . . . one
on the book De Consideratione, which I had not treated at all, the other on
St. Bernard's Mariology" (*Letters of Robert Giroux and Thomas Merton*, 170).

being almost three times as long as the text of the encyclical itself. Though it was not published until the beginning of June of the following year, *The Last of the Fathers*[116] is of course the work most closely tied to the 1953 anniversary.

As with his writing on St. Bernard generally, Merton is concerned here with seeing and presenting him whole. In his preface[117] he notes that "like other complex and many-sided characters, he suffered a rapid and disconcerting fragmentation at the hands of his own fame" and points to the celebration of the eighth centenary generally and the publication of *Doctor Mellifluus* in particular as an opportunity to "bring these fragments together,"[118] an enterprise to which he hopes this publication will contribute. He also glosses the term *"mellifluus"*—"flowing-with-honey"—pointing out both its apparent incompatibility with Bernard's sometimes inflated reputation for anger and its potential to misrepresent his richness of style and doctrine as "insipid sentimentality."[119] The opening section, "The Man and the Saint,"[120] situates Bernard in the context of his time and place, surveying the highlights of his life and work chronologically, with somewhat more emphasis on the monastic dimension than the more public activities, but without neglecting the problematic aspects, above all the preaching of the Second Crusade. Merton stresses particularly the importance of resisting the temptation to oversimplify Bernard by "dividing him against himself," failing to realize that for Bernard the inner and outer life, the life of

---

116. Thomas Merton, *The Last of the Fathers: Saint Bernard of Clairvaux and the Encyclical Letter*, Doctor Mellifluus (New York: Harcourt, Brace, 1954); for brief overviews see M. Basil Pennington, "Like Father Like Son: Bernard of Clairvaux and Thomas Merton," *Thomas Merton My Brother*, 96–97; Shannon, "Last of the Fathers, The," *Merton Encyclopedia*, 244–45; Waddell, "Merton of Gethsemani and Bernard of Clairvaux," 123–25.
117. *Last of the Fathers*, 9–15.
118. *Last of the Fathers*, 9.
119. *Last of the Fathers*, 11.
120. *Last of the Fathers*, 23–44.

the soul and the life of the Church, are, or at least should be, a single unified whole: "the invisible and interior peace of the members among themselves and with their God is not separable . . . from an exterior and visible order which reflects the purposes of God in the world, and which guarantees the effect of His salvific action upon souls."[121] The second section, "St. Bernard's Writings,"[122] begins by identifying Bernard not just as a pious "spiritual writer" but as a theologian with a "definite and coherent doctrine."[123] He then provides pithy summaries of virtually all Bernard's main works, first the treatises, then the sermons, above all the series of eighty-six on the Canticle of Canticles, "his greatest and most important single work."[124] Bernard's preaching revolves around "two great themes: the mystery of Christ in Himself and in those who are conformed to Him in the Holy Spirit. In other words: Christ and the Church."[125] Again Merton's focus is on the "inner unity" of Bernard's life and work: "In all that he writes, in all that he says, in all that he does, Bernard has only one end in view: the integration of nations, dioceses, monasteries, and individuals into the life and order of the Church."[126] Finally, in part 3, "Notes on the Encyclical *Doctor Mellifluus*,"[127] which is only slightly shorter than the text of the encyclical itself,[128] Merton highlights the document's focus on wisdom, "the repose of the soul in an embrace of love that attains to God beyond all understanding," transcending the approach of theology

---

121. *Last of the Fathers*, 40–41.
122. *Last of the Fathers*, 47–67; Waddell, himself one of the most distinguished contemporary scholars of early Cistercianism, says that in this section Merton "in astonishingly few words, goes to the heart of each of Bernard's major writings and communicates their substance" ("Merton of Gethsemani and Bernard of Clairvaux," 124).
123. *Last of the Fathers*, 48.
124. *Last of the Fathers*, 61.
125. *Last of the Fathers*, 63–64.
126. *Last of the Fathers*, 66–67.
127. *Last of the Fathers*, 71–90.
128. *Last of the Fathers*, 93–116.

as "faith in search of understanding"[129] and rejecting a "false 'curiosity'" that divorces knowledge from love.[130] "It is hard to imagine," Merton declares of the pope, "how his treatment of the theme [of mystical wisdom] could have been more direct, more forceful, or more succinct."[131] He likewise praises the encyclical's extensive use of Bernard's Sermon 83 on the Canticle to epitomize the saint's teaching on the mutual love of God and the human person that is the essence of Bernard's doctrine and experience of contemplative union, a love that overflows into "fruitful action and . . . apostolic charity."[132] Once again Merton brings his commentary to a close with a discussion of Bernard's teaching on Mary, since the encyclical itself climaxes with a lengthy quotation of the famous passage on the meaning of the name Mary as "Star of the Sea,"[133] which Merton himself will consider in detail in his novitiate conferences (see 61–65), and he suggests that Bernard's teaching as presented by the pope might well "foreshadow a dogmatic definition of Our Lady's universal mediation."[134] In any case, Merton evaluates the encyclical as a document not only of "fulsome and unqualified praise" for its subject but above all as "a call to sanctity, to divine union, uttered in our own troubled time by the Vicar of Jesus Christ with all the impassioned ardor of the great Saint Bernard himself."[135]

129. *Last of the Fathers*, 72.
130. *Last of the Fathers*, 75.
131. *Last of the Fathers*, 77.
132. *Last of the Fathers*, 84.
133. *Last of the Fathers*, 113–14.
134. *Last of the Fathers*, 89; Merton will later become more restrained in his Mariology, writing in his journal for January 30, 1965, "I do not agree with the medieval idea of *Mediatrix apud mediatorem* . . . (without prejudice to her motherhood which is a much better statement and truth)" (Thomas Merton, *Dancing in the Water of Life: Seeking Peace in the Hermitage. Journals*, vol. 5, *1963–1965*, ed. Robert E. Daggy [San Francisco: HarperCollins, 1997], 197); for an overview of Merton's writing on Mary, see Patrick F. O'Connell, "Mary," *Thomas Merton Encyclopedia*, 285–87.
135. *Last of the Fathers*, 90.

While *The Last of the Fathers* marks the culmination of Merton's literary commemoration of the anniversary of St. Bernard's death, Bernard makes a significant contribution to two subsequent books published over the next few years. *The Silent Life*[136] includes a chapter on the Cistercians[137] that focuses principally on the spirituality, or as Merton himself says, the "theological notions,"[138] of Cistercian life, and thus draws largely on Bernard. Merton begins by modifying the common perception that the founders of Cîteaux were determined to observe the Benedictine *Rule* "to the letter,"[139] but does emphasize the "sense of Law"[140] that provided the structure for what was in fact the first religious "order" in the modern sense of the word but was also directed to the realization of a life of selfless love. In St. Bernard, it is God's own law of infinite charity and freedom that becomes central, the "Law of divine Liberty, hidden and active in the Person of Christ."[141] The "Ordo" or "observance" that characterizes Cistercian life in Bernard's teaching and in subsequent practice is not a matter simply of external conformity to rules but the realization of *"the more excellent way*, which is charity,"[142] learned in the "school of Christ"[143] which is the monastery. For Bernard, humility, generosity, discretion, and compunction in living out the *Rule* guard against a rigid conception

---

136. Thomas Merton, *The Silent Life* (New York: Farrar, Straus & Cudahy, 1957); for an overview, see Christine M. Bochen, "*Silent Life, The*," *Merton Encyclopedia*, 436–39.

137. The second section of the book, on the cenobitic life, which includes this chapter, was actually added to the original version of *The Silent Life* when the censor objected that Merton gave too much emphasis in his text to eremitic forms of monasticism: see the unpublished letter from Cistercian Abbot General Gabriel Sortais to Merton dated February 3, 1957 (TMC archives) and Merton's reply of February 7, 1957 (*School of Charity*, 99–101).

138. *Silent Life*, 117.
139. *Silent Life*, 95.
140. *Silent Life*, 101.
141. *Silent Life*, 104.
142. *Silent Life*, 106.
143. *Silent Life*, 105.

of observance that might give rise to a self-righteous pride in keeping all its precepts punctiliously; they lead to "interior peace, which is nothing but the realization of our true selves, as we actually are, in Christ,"[144] which is both the foundation of peace with others in community and the indispensable precondition for the deepest experience of peace, contemplative oneness with God. Whether called to individual mystical union in this life or not, all Cistercians, in the view of St. Bernard, share in the identity of the Spouse, the "mystical Bride" that is the Church loved by Christ and called to love him in return; this "is the whole reason for the call to the Cistercian cloister"[145] and the basis for the "devotion to the Incarnate Word and to the Blessed Virgin Mary"[146] that are hallmarks of traditional Cistercian spirituality. Only in this context do the monk's "fasts, labors, poverty and solitude"[147] make sense: "For the peace of the monastic life does not rest on ascetic or mystical achievements, but on faith in the mercy of God, selfless compassion for our brethren, and pure love for the Father, in union with the charity of Christ."[148]

*The New Man*,[149] largely written before *The Silent Life* but published four years later,[150] is perhaps Merton's most systematic presentation of his anthropology and his soteriology, his contemporary restatement of the traditional patristic teaching on the human person as made in the image and likeness of God; alienated from that identity, from the true self, in the Fall, a quest for

144. *Silent Life*, 112.
145. *Silent Life*, 116.
146. *Silent Life*, 116.
147. *Silent Life*, 117.
148. *Silent Life*, 117.
149. Thomas Merton, *The New Man* (New York: Farrar, Straus & Cudahy, 1961); for an overview, see William H. Shannon, "*New Man, The*," *Merton Encyclopedia*, 322–23.
150. See Merton's journal entry for November 23, 1959, in which he speaks of completing the process of "editing and correcting" this book, "written in five weeks in 1954 (during the fall vacation)" (*Search for Solitude*, 348); in a May 21, 1960, letter to Dom Gabriel Sortais, Merton dates the book's composition to 1955 (*School of Charity*, 132).

an illusory autonomy; and restored to authentic selfhood, to union in love with the Creator, through participation in the paschal mystery, the passage from death to life with and in Christ, the Second Adam, effected and symbolized above all in the sacrament of baptism and in the liturgy of the Easter Vigil, the baptismal setting par excellence. Much of this material, of course, has parallels in St. Bernard, rooted as he is in the patristic tradition, as is evident from Merton's writing as early as *The Spirit of Simplicity*. This connection is made explicit in the chapter titled "Spirit in Bondage," in which Merton says he will "sketch out some of the broad outlines" of the Fall, the combination of "pride, compulsive drives, anxiety and all the rest of the elements that evolve from the original act by which Adam wrecked the human spirit," by "following the thought of St. Bernard."[151] As Bernard says in his treatise on *The Steps of Humility and Pride*, it is the desire for knowledge as a possession—what he terms *curiositas*—that prompts Adam to want to "add to the knowledge of good, which he already had, the knowledge of evil."[152] It is the desire for autonomy, for self-assertion, for existence apart from the gift of life received from God and totally dependent on God, and therefore it is an alienation from reality, the choice of illusion over truth, of death over life. "St. Bernard puts this *sapor mortis*, this taste for death, at the very heart of original sin. It is the exact opposite of the wisdom, the *sapida scientia* or existential ('tasting') knowledge of the divine Good. . . . They cannot exist together. Consequently, having acquired the one, Adam necessarily lost the other."[153] By placing himself at the center of his existence, Adam has created a false relationship with the rest of creation, seeking permanent satisfaction from what is by nature impermanent, as Bernard points out in his Sermon 82 on the Canticle:[154] "St. Bernard sees the fall not as a descent from the supernatural to the natural, but as a collapse into ambivalence in which the

---

151. *New Man*, 104.
152. *New Man*, 106.
153. *New Man*, 108.
154. *New Man*, 111.

historical 'nature' in which man was actually created for supernatural union with God is turned upside down and inside out, and yet still *retains its innate capacity and 'need' for divine union.*"¹⁵⁵ It is of course this radical lack of fulfillment, this fruitless, aimless wandering in "regions of unreality"¹⁵⁶ (Bernard's *"regio dissimilitudinis"*—the "land of unlikeness"), a life of contradiction that is inevitably a life of frustration, which paradoxically makes sinful humanity receptive to the message of the Gospel: in Christ the Word of God, "the eternal and uncreated Image of the Father,"¹⁵⁷ can be found the pattern of true human identity, as Bernard points out in Sermon 80 on the Canticle,¹⁵⁸ the still-present image of God that can be uncovered when likeness to the Word is restored by dying to one's self-centered, self-created, illusory identity and being reborn through and with the risen Christ, finding one's true self in Christ, as Christ—in the familiar words of St. Paul that Merton will later cite: "I live, now not I, but Christ liveth in me"¹⁵⁹ (Gal 2:20). As Bernard, the "last of the fathers," expressed this patristic doctrine in the idiom of his own time, so Merton, drawing here and throughout his work on this entire tradition up to and including Bernard, endeavors to do the same for a contemporary audience.

While *The New Man* marks Bernard's last explicit contribution of any significance to Merton's published work, he had also repeatedly been a key focus of attention and discussion throughout Merton's years of teaching novices and newly professed monks that would culminate in the conferences found in the present volume. Even before being appointed the abbey's first master of students in May 1951, Merton had taught a course to novices and newly professed monks entitled "An Introduction to Cistercian Theology,"¹⁶⁰ based principally on Bernard, that

---

155. *New Man*, 112.
156. *New Man*, 112.
157. *New Man*, 132.
158. *New Man*, 132.
159. *New Man*, 141.
160. Included in "Collected Essays," vol. 19.

Introduction xli

began by considering the contrast between vain *curiositas* and a genuine desire for knowledge, went on to explore "The Region of Unlikeness," pervaded by self-will, and the process of conversion through humility and self-knowledge, concluding with the Cistercian presentation of monastic life as a school of charity, drawing particularly on Bernard's sermons for Pentecost and for the Dedication of a Church, as well as his teaching on the degrees of love in the *De Diligendo Deo*.[161] His third series of "Monastic Orientation" notes, conferences given between Advent 1951 and August 1952, begins with the original version of "The 'Sacrament of Advent' in the Spirituality of St. Bernard"[162] and includes sections on Bernard's Lenten Sermons,[163] on the Ordering of Charity in his Sermons 49 and 50 on the Song of Songs,[164] and on his treatise *On Precept and Dispensation*.[165] Series 4, conferences from September 1952 through November 1953, includes discussion of modesty in St. Bernard, part of a broader treatment of the topic;[166] consideration of self-will and the common will as taught by Bernard in his sermons, and on contemplative quiet as found in the treatises *The Steps of Humility and Pride* and *On Loving God*, as well as in the Sermons on the Canticles, particularly Sermon 52;[167] a brief "Introduction to St. Bernard" (which would be incorporated into the revised version of the *Cistercian Fathers* conferences—see 13–31) looks at him as father and Doctor of the Church, as monk and spiritual master, and in the early days of

---

161. See Waddell, "Merton of Gethsemani and Bernard of Clairvaux," 119–20, for the table of contents of the course, which subsequently was given to the scholastics as well.

162. "Monastic Orientation," Series 3, 1–14 ("Collected Essays," vol. 16).

163. "Monastic Orientation," 3, 38–52; this and the following section will be included in the Appendices of *The Cistercian Fathers and Their Monastic Theology*: see pages 320–38, 338–55.

164. "Monastic Orientation," 3, 53–71.

165. "Monastic Orientation," 3, 91–115.

166. "Monastic Orientation," Series 4, 29–35 ("Collected Essays," vol. 17).

167. "Monastic Orientation," 4, 54–86.

his conversion and novitiate at Cîteaux;[168] and a couple of conferences for May discuss Bernard's Fourth Sermon for the Assumption.[169] Series 5, from Advent 1953 through the rest of the liturgical year until November 1954, includes conferences on "Aspects of Saint Bernard's Mariology"[170] as part of the commemoration of the Marian Year proclaimed by Pope Pius XII, as well as a brief discussion of "St. Bernard on Compunction, Fear, Graces of Prayer."[171] The final series, running from December 1954 until October 1955, when Merton became master of novices, incorporates brief notices of St. Bernard on Monastic Peace,[172] on poverty,[173] and on the monastic vocation.[174]

There are frequent references to Bernard throughout Merton's novitiate conferences as well;[175] he draws on Bernard particularly

168. "Monastic Orientation," 4, 88–99.
169. "Monastic Orientation," 4, 133–37.
170. "Monastic Orientation," Series 5, 17–33 ("Collected Essays," vol. 17).
171. "Monastic Orientation," 5, 96–99.
172. "Monastic Orientation," Series 6, 17–21 ("Collected Essays," vol. 17).
173. "Monastic Orientation," 6, 70.
174. "Monastic Orientation," 6, 83.
175. See the indices to the previous volumes published in this series: Thomas Merton, *Cassian and the Fathers: Initiation into the Monastic Tradition*, ed. Patrick F. O'Connell, Monastic Wisdom [MW], vol. 1 (Kalamazoo, MI: Cistercian Publications, 2005); Thomas Merton, *Pre-Benedictine Monasticism: Initiation into the Monastic Tradition 2*, ed. Patrick F. O'Connell, MW 9 (Kalamazoo, MI: Cistercian Publications, 2006); Thomas Merton, *An Introduction to Christian Mysticism: Initiation into the Monastic Tradition 3*, ed. Patrick F. O'Connell, MW 13 (Kalamazoo, MI: Cistercian Publications, 2008); Thomas Merton, *The Rule of Saint Benedict: Initiation into the Monastic Tradition 4*, ed. Patrick F. O'Connell, MW 19 (Collegeville, MN: Cistercian Publications, 2009); Thomas Merton, *Monastic Observances: Initiation into the Monastic Tradition 5*, ed. Patrick F. O'Connell, MW 25 (Collegeville, MN: Cistercian Publications, 2010); Thomas Merton, *The Life of the Vows: Initiation into the Monastic Tradition 6*, ed. Patrick F. O'Connell, MW 30 (Collegeville, MN: Cistercian Publications, 2012); Thomas Merton, *Charter, Customs, and Constitutions of the Cistercians: Initiation into the Monastic Tradition 7*, ed. Patrick F. O'Connell, MW 41 (Collegeville, MN: Cistercian Publications, 2015).

in "Liturgical Feasts and Seasons,"[176] part 2, his series of conferences on the sanctoral cycle of the Church year. The pair of conferences entitled "Saint Bernard's Sermons for the Feast of Saint Andrew"[177] (November 30) focus on the love of the cross and on obedience as exemplified for Bernard by the apostle; "Saints Peter and Paul"[178] (June 29) draws on Bernard's sermon on these saints as models not of speculative knowledge but of the science of life—how to live in Christ; "Office of the Feast of Saint Bernard"[179] (August 20) and "Feast of Saint Bernard (second conference),"[180] which follows, reflect on the liturgical readings for Vespers and Nocturns of the feast, respectively, while "Sermon outline—Feast of St. Bernard (1958)"[181] presents Bernard as the one who helps the monk find the springs of living water mentioned in the book of Ecclesiasticus (Sirach) through his life, his character and his doctrine. In "Feast of the Immaculate Heart of Mary"[182] (August 21) Bernard's sermon *De Aquaeductu* presents Mary in the role of Mediatrix, while "Feast of the Holy Name of Mary"[183] (September 12) considers Bernard's famous second sermon on the *"Missus Est"* with its lyrical invocation of Mary as "Star of the Sea." "St. Bernard on the Guardian Angels"[184] draws on Bernard's twelfth sermon on Psalm 90, read in the second nocturn of the feast of the Guardian Angels, with its reflections on the angels as present companions in struggle and future companions in glory. Finally "St. Bernard's First Dedication Sermon"[185] considers

176. Included in "Collected Essays," vol. 24.
177. "Liturgical Feasts and Seasons," 2.4–7.
178. "Liturgical Feasts and Seasons," 2.36.
179. "Liturgical Feasts and Seasons," 2.52.
180. "Liturgical Feasts and Seasons," 2.53–54.
181. "Liturgical Feasts and Seasons," 2.55–56.
182. "Liturgical Feasts and Seasons," 2.57.
183. "Liturgical Feasts and Seasons," 2.62.
184. "Liturgical Feasts and Seasons," 2.71–72.
185. "Liturgical Feasts and Seasons," 2.90–91; another one-page handwritten conference on Bernard's first Dedication sermon is found in Merton's original typescript of his liturgical conferences but is not included in the multigraphed version.

the church building as simply the outward sign of the living Church of the monastic community dedicated to divine service.

As St. Bernard of Clairvaux was the most important, but by no means the only important, author among the early Cistercian Fathers, so he is the major but not the exclusive focus of Merton's reading and writing about the theology and spiritual teaching of the twelfth-century Cistercians.[186] The other three "Cistercian evangelists," William of St. Thierry, Aelred of Rievaulx, and Guerric of Igny, as well as their contemporary Isaac of Stella and slightly later successor Adam of Perseigne, also attract Merton's attention and interest. In a list of projected works Merton submitted to the Cistercian General Chapter in 1946, he includes a book on "The Cistercian Way of Contemplation," drawing on the teaching of all the major Cistercian Fathers;[187] an anthology of Cistercian Marian texts with commentary, especially but not exclusively from Adam of Perseigne and Amadeus of Lausanne; a biography of Aelred; a study of the doctrine of Guerric; translations and analysis of William's writings on the love of God; and much else on early Cistercianism. Almost none of this was actually composed as Merton's writing went in other directions after the appearance of his autobiography (also mentioned at the end of the list), but these planned works provide an indication of his deep enthusiasm for the early Cistercian writers that was an important element of his own monastic formation and would continue to play a significant role in his developing spiritual teaching and in his formation of those who came under his charge in the years to come.

Surprisingly, William (ca. 1085–1148) is the only one of these figures to appear in the extensive collection of Cistercian biographical sketches from the Golden Age, titled *In the Valley of*

---

186. For a survey of the topic see M. Basil Pennington, "Thomas Merton and His Own Cistercian Tradition," *Thomas Merton My Brother*, 79–91.

187. See Chrysogonus Waddell, ocso, "Merton and the Tiger Lily," *The Merton Annual* 2 (1989): 59–84, which includes extensive discussion of this document and a translation from the French of the text itself as an appendix (80–84).

*Wormwood*,[188] that Merton composed in the mid-1940s but that was published only in 2013.[189] In his essay, Merton points out the centuries of relative neglect and the recent rediscovery of William, his role as St. Bernard's first biographer, and his stature as a great theologian and mystic with a particular emphasis on the nature of love, the role of the Holy Spirit, and the Augustinian identification of the divine image with the three powers of the soul. Other than this biographical sketch, Merton has no other article devoted exclusively to William, but he sometimes appears in tandem with Bernard, as when Merton quotes from his treatise *On the Nature and Dignity of Love* in *The Waters of Siloe*,[190] and his classification of the three levels of spiritual life—*carnales, animales,* and *spirituales*—in his famous *Golden Epistle* appears more than once in other sets of conferences.[191]

Aelred (which Merton usually spells Ailred) (1110–1167) was one of Merton's early discoveries in the novitiate, as he recalls "with nostalgia" in a journal entry dated August 31, 1947: "the old days when I got so much consolation out of the Cistercian Fathers . . . the bright fall days four years ago when I opened Migne and found St. Ailred."[192] The book on Aelred was the one

---

188. Thomas Merton, *In the Valley of Wormwood: Cistercian Blessed and Saints of the Golden Age*, edited with an introduction by Patrick Hart, OCSO, foreword by Brian Patrick McGuire, CS 233 (Collegeville, MN: Cistercian Publications, 2013), 327–37.

189. Presumably Merton considered it both difficult and unnecessary to condense so well-known a life as Bernard's into the brief scope of a mini-biography (though his parents, two brothers, and sister are represented), but Waddell speculates that Merton may have removed the Bernardine material at some point to use for other purposes ("Merton of Gethsemani and Bernard of Clairvaux," 109); perhaps the same reason may explain the absence of Aelred and Guerric, while the absence of an established cult for Isaac and Adam would account for their omission.

190. *Waters of Siloe*, 279–80, 343, 347–48.

191. See *Cassian and the Fathers*, 229–30; *Pre-Benedictine Monasticism*, 284; *Introduction to Christian Mysticism*, 73–74; *Life of the Vows*, 19.

192. *Entering the Silence*, 104; he adds, "But God has taken all the joy out of what was then a brave new world"—being at the time in the midst of one of his episodic vocation crises, longing to become a Carthusian.

project on his list for the General Chapter that continued to attract him, mentioned first in a letter to Robert Giroux dated September 9, 1949, as a combined "biography, study of his doctrine and selected texts from his writings."[193] This is one of the four works that in 1950 Merton contracted to write, and as late as June 5, 1954, he is still writing to Giroux, "I also want to finish that St. Ailred job," but the book never appeared. In five segments between 1985 and 1989, the biographical material was published in *Cistercian Studies* as "St. Aelred of Rievaulx and the Cistercians,"[194] which situates Aelred in the Cistercian movement as a whole and in the development of English Cistercianism, provides a detailed portrait of Aelred's character and of most of the major events of his life, and touches on some but by no means all of his works.[195] Merton includes a section entitled "Saint Ailred—Cister-

---

193. *Letters of Robert Giroux and Thomas Merton*, 49. The book is mentioned repeatedly in Merton's correspondence with Giroux through the rest of 1949, and on January 11, 1950, Giroux writes of it, "I hope we may expect the St. Aelred manuscript soon. . . . It ought to be in proof before Easter" (*Letters of Robert Giroux and Thomas Merton*, 58). Merton responds that he would like to wait for the publication of Aelred's *De Anima*, expected soon, as "it will naturally affect many of my statements about other parts of his work" (January 16, 1950 letter [*Giroux-Merton Letters*, 61]), Giroux reassures him that "there is no rush about it" (February 13, 1950, letter [*Giroux-Merton Letters*, 62]), and no more is heard of the project for more than four years.

194. Thomas Merton, "St. Aelred of Rievaulx and the Cistercians," ed. Patrick Hart, *Cistercian Studies* 20, no. 3 (1985): 212–23; 21, no. 1 (1986): 30–42; 22, no. 1 (1987): 55–75; 23, no. 1 (1988): 45–62; 24, no. 1 (1989): 50–68. Though an initial editorial note identifies the manuscript as "written in the mid-fifties," it is evident from Merton's correspondence with Giroux that it was largely composed in the late 1940s.

195. Though he had claimed in his letter dated September 9, 1949, that "I have finished the biographical part" (*Letters of Robert Giroux and Thomas Merton*, 49), in fact the concluding pages of the essay as published (*Cistercian Studies* 24, no. 1 [1989]: 67–68 [Part 5]) veer off into a discussion of the antagonism between Thomas Becket and Gilbert Foliot, the bishop of London, to whom Aelred had dedicated a set of sermons, without returning to Aelred himself; there is no discussion of his final days and death, so unless there

*cian Life in His Time*" for his feast (February 3) in "Liturgical Feasts and Seasons,"[196] drawing on the *Life of Aelred* written by his disciple Walter Daniel and on the encomium his fellow Cistercian abbot and author Gilbert of Hoyland included in his Sermons on the Canticle at the time of Aelred's death. His final look at Aelred,[197] an introduction to the English translation of Amédée Hallier's study of the monk[198] completed on September 2, 1968, just days before leaving for Asia,[199] provides an explicitly postconciliar perspective, emphasizing the "humanism full of psychological insight with plenty of relevance for our own day"[200] of monastic theology generally and Aelred in particular, with his emphasis on a theology of community and of friendship, on the divine image as a creative openness to love and the defacing of

---

was more material that had disappeared, "the biographical part" still had some remaining work. Merton also writes, "We shall consider Aelred's *Rule for his sister on a later page*" (*Cistercian Studies* 24, no. 1 [1989]: 61 [Part 5]), which does not happen, and earlier had referred in a footnote to meditations from the same text as being "among the excerpts printed below" (*Cistercian Studies* 22, no. 1 [1987]: 65 [Part 3]), a reference to the translated selections intended as part of the volume as a whole.

196. "Liturgical Feasts and Seasons," 2.15–16.

197. Merton gives a conference on Aelred and the idea of the memory of God on May 7, 1964, while the Cistercian Fathers conferences are in progress, but it is not connected to them (Gethsemani tape 114.1).

198. Amédée Hallier, ocso, *The Monastic Theology of Aelred of Rievaulx*, trans. Columban Heaney, CS 8 (Spencer, MA: Cistercian Publications, 1969), vii–xiii.

199. See Thomas Merton, *The Other Side of the Mountain: The End of the Journey. Journals*, vol. 7, *1967–1968*, ed. Patrick Hart (San Francisco: HarperCollins, 1998), 163 [9/3/1968]; the possibility of Merton's providing a preface had first been raised by Hallier a decade earlier when he was preparing to publish, in French, what had originally been his doctoral dissertation (see Roger Lipsey, *Make Peace Before the Sun Goes Down: The Long Encounter of Thomas Merton and His Abbot, James Fox* [Boston: Shambhala, 2015], 116–17), but evidently nothing was composed by Merton until the English translation was being readied for publication.

200. *Monastic Theology*, vii.

that image as a kind of Sartrian "bad faith,"[201] and on monastic life as an education in "authentic freedom by loving and creative consent"[202] to the Word and the Cross of Christ.

In an April 1959 letter to a fellow novice master stressing the importance of introducing their charges to the Cistercian Fathers, Merton writes: "Guerric is one of the easiest to break into in Latin. And perhaps the most representative."[203] Later that same year, the Abbey of Gethsemani published a translation of the five Christmas sermons of the fourth Cistercian "evangelist," Guerric of Igny (d. 1157), a monk of Clairvaux whom St. Bernard had appointed abbot of the daughter house of Igny in the Marne valley. The volume begins with a lengthy introductory essay by Merton,[204] highlighting four key themes of the sermons: Christ's birth as God's supreme gift for us and to us; the necessity of accepting that gift personally and communally in a spirit of joy for the gift to be efficacious; the role of "motherhood" of the infant Christ that belongs to the Church, to the monastic community, and to each individual member of both; and the importance of receiving Christ the Incarnate Word in the same humility and silence revealed by the Infant in the crib.[205] Following his own

201. *Monastic Theology*, x.
202. *Monastic Theology*, xi.
203. *School of Charity*, 119 (April 15, 1959, letter to Mark Weidner, ocso).
204. *The Christmas Sermons of Bl. Guerric of Igny*, trans. Sr. Rose of Lima, essay by Thomas Merton (Trappist, KY: Abbey of Gethsemani, 1959), 1–25.
205. Merton presents the anti-Jewish allegory found in these sermons, contrasting Church and Synagogue, without evaluative comment, but he will later write, at the conclusion of a longer analysis of the growth of medieval anti-Semitism: "In the theology of the time, the transition from Old to New Testament was more and more the esoteric privilege of those who, understanding the 'mystical sense' of the Old Testament types, were able to see the Charity and the Spirit of Christ in the 'carnal figures' of the Old Testament. But since the mystical understanding implied, in fact, not only a very special culture, but also a highly developed spirituality, it was not the affair of many. The fact that in monasteries there were many monks who could not transcend in this way the Old Testament symbolism and ritual of the monasteries constituted something of a problem. Blessed Guerric of Igny, the Cistercian, in his Christmas sermons (which like all his sermons are very

Introduction                                        xlix

advice in his letter, Merton also gives a pair of conferences to the novices on Guerric's three Easter sermons in April 1964,[206] and another pair on his Advent sermons in late 1965.[207] In his commentary on the Easter sermons, later transcribed and published,[208] Merton points out that Guerric uses the Genesis story of his brothers' encounter with Joseph and Jacob's reaction—the revival of his spirit—as a foreshadowing of the resurrection and the gift of the Spirit to the disciples on Easter night, an experience made available to his—and Merton's—listeners as well.

Merton's admiration for Isaac of Stella (d. ca. 1169) is evident in his journal entry dated December 5, 1960, in which he remarks on the "Magnificent light in the lapidary sentences" of the English-born Cistercian abbot's Easter sermon: "Fire struck from stone: but how marvelous!"[209] Thus he was quite receptive to his friend A. M. Allchin's request in October 1963 that he provide an introduction to a selection of Isaac's sermons by the English Anglican nun Penelope Lawson.[210] The translation did not actually arrive until almost two years later, shortly after Merton had

---

Pauline) upbraids these severe and rather pessimistic monks and calls them 'the Jews.' Thus again there was a renewal of a very bad conscience among those who were thought and supposed to be the best of Christians. If many of these were still 'no better than Jews,' what about the Jews themselves, down at the bottom of the social scale?" (Thomas Merton, *Conjectures of a Guilty Bystander* [Garden City, NY: Doubleday, 1966], 120).

206. April 6 and 7, 1963 (Gethsemani tapes 51.2 and 48.4); the first was issued commercially as "Life and Celebration" (Tape 12A), *The Merton Tapes*, Series 1 (Chappaqua, NY: Electronic Paperbacks, 1972).

207. November 30 and December 7, 1964 (Gethsemani tapes 134.1 and 134.4); the first was published as "Consent to God 1" (tape 1A), *The Merton Tapes*, Series 3 (Chappaqua, NY: Electronic Paperbacks, 1983).

208. Thomas Merton, "Guerric of Igny's Easter Sermons," *Cistercian Studies* 7 (1972): 85–95.

209. Thomas Merton, *Turning Toward the World: The Pivotal Years. Journals*, vol. 4, *1960–1963*, ed. Victor A. Kramer (San Francisco: HarperCollins, 1996), 72.

210. Thomas Merton, *The Hidden Ground of Love: Letters on Religious Experience and Social Concerns*, ed. William H. Shannon (New York: Farrar, Straus & Giroux, 1985), 25 [10/21/1963].

moved permanently to his hermitage,[211] where he carefully read the English versions against the original Latin,[212] finding in the "coherence" and "solidity" of Isaac's language a steadying influence[213] and in his teaching "an unquestioningly deep and austere intuition, and very modern. But deeply mystical," and having "Profound implications for my own prayer and solitude."[214] In a Sunday afternoon conference in November, he compared Isaac's teaching on prayer to that of the hesychasts of the Eastern Church.[215] He had written his introduction by the following July,[216] but when no publisher was found for the volume, the introduction appeared by itself in *Cistercian Studies*.[217] Merton notes Isaac's more speculative theological perspective, less influenced by St. Bernard than other early Cistercian Fathers; the difference between the medieval worldview articulated by Isaac, in which the all-encompassing presence of Christ is found everywhere in Scripture and in creation, and that of modernity; and the particular setting of Isaac's monastery of Stella on the island of Ré in the Atlantic off the west coast of France,[218] which gave to his sermons a particular element of solitude and exile, an emphasis on austerity, simplicity, and honesty and on the necessity for trust in the Word in the midst of trial.

211. See the journal entry for September 21, 1965 (*Dancing in the Water of Life*, 298).
212. See Merton's October 17, 1965, letter to Sr. Penelope Lawson (*Hidden Ground of Love*, 478–79).
213. *Dancing in the Water of Life*, 338 [late 1965].
214. *Dancing in the Water of Life*, 309 [10/29/1965].
215. November 17, 1965 (Gethsemani tape 156.2); issued as "Prayer: The Response of a Creature" (AA2261.2) (Kansas City, MO: Credence Cassettes, 1988).
216. See Merton's July 27, 1966, letter to Sr. Penelope Lawson (*Hidden Ground of Love*, 480).
217. Louis Merton, ocso, "Isaac of Stella: An Introduction to Selections from his Sermons," *Cistercian Studies* 2 (1967): 243–51.
218. Merton had included a passage from Isaac's Sermon 14 on the solitude of this island abbey in the Cistercian chapter of *The Silent Life* (98–99).

The last major early Cistercian writer who attracted Merton's attention was Adam of Perseigne (ca. 1145–ca. 1221), the son of a serf who became a Cistercian abbot in Normandy and the counselor and spiritual director of Richard the Lionheart, among many others. Merton had planned to translate Adam's Marian writings as early as his 1946 General Chapter proposal, and while this never happened, he did give conferences to the scholastics in May 1952 on Adam's *Mariale*,[219] focused on finding Mary as the surest way of finding her Son[220] and as the model of the hidden life of silence and humility.[221] Merton evidently found Adam's reflections on monastic formation in his letters particularly helpful in carrying out his own duties as master of novices, writing successive versions of an article on the topic[222] that eventually was included as the introduction to a volume of Adam's letters.[223] Here he focuses on the newness of life—monastic formation as inner transformation—that should characterize the vow of conversion of manners, a rebirth that is a share in the divine infancy

219. "Monastic Orientation," 3, 72–80.

220. As early as May 1, 1949, Merton had written in his journal of "marvelous things in Adam of Perseigne about Mary being 'the way,'" commenting, "She is that. Through her we come quickly to—everything" (*Entering the Silence*, 307).

221. This is followed by further texts on silence from Adam's letters (81–88), some of which will be included in the appendices to the *Cistercian Fathers* conferences (see 356–59).

222. In an August 19, 1956, letter to Fr. Charles Dumont, Merton writes that he is "pleased and grateful to have you as my translator, in the article on Adam" (*School of Charity*, 96); it appeared in French as M. Louis Merton, "La Formation Monastique selon Adam de Perseigne," trans. Charles Dumont, *Collectanea Ordinis Cisterciensium Reformatorum* 19 (January 1957): 1–17. Thomas Merton, "Christian Freedom and Monastic Formation" (*American Benedictine Review* 13 [September 1962]: 289–313) is an expanded English version.

223. Thomas Merton, "The Feast of Freedom: Monastic Formation according to Adam of Perseigne," in *The Letters of Adam of Perseigne*, vol. 1, trans. Grace Perigo, Cistercian Fathers [CF] vol. 21 (Kalamazoo, MI: Cistercian Publications, 1976), 3–48.

of Jesus in humility and self-emptying, again seen as realized through the mediation of Mary, and leading to the stillness of the contemplative sabbath experienced as the liberation effected by the seven gifts of the Holy Spirit, imaged by Adam as the "feast of freedom" mentioned in the title of the essay. It is Adam, finally, whom Merton cites in his presentation on "Marxism and Monastic Perspectives," on the final day of his life, as exemplifying the early Cistercians' understanding of the period of formation as "a kind of monastic therapy"[224] in which the novitiate is seen as "a period of cure, of convalescence," making possible "the education of the 'new man'" in selfless love that is "the whole purpose of the monastic life."[225]

Thus his studies of the major Cistercian writers of the twelfth century had quite thoroughly prepared Merton to expand his novitiate conferences beyond the focus on "The Life, Works and Doctrine of St. Bernard," as they were originally titled, to encompass the broader consideration of the movement indicated by the new title *The Cistercian Fathers and Their Monastic Theology*, though in the event the expansion goes in different, non-Cistercian directions, and, except for the added discussion, written earlier, of William's biography of Bernard, other Cistercian Fathers make only very minor appearances in a few of the appendices to the revised version of these conferences.

*******

Merton began his series of conferences on "The Life, Works and Doctrine of Saint Bernard" during the summer of 1956, some eight or nine months after he had been appointed Gethsemani's master of novices in October 1955. They were part of a sequence

---

224. The phrase is of course familiar from the title of Merton's 1968 essay "Final Integration: Toward a 'Monastic Therapy,'" in Thomas Merton, *Contemplation in a World of Action* (Garden City, NY: Doubleday, 1971), 205–17.

225. Thomas Merton, *The Asian Journal*, ed. Naomi Burton Stone, Brother Patrick Hart and James Laughlin (New York: New Directions, 1973), 333.

on "HISTORY OF THE ORDER—(to follow Carta Caritatis and Consuetudines)" as he had typed at the top of the opening page of his lecture notes and presumably followed immediately on the completion of his conferences on these early Cistercian documents.[226] According to a handwritten schedule for classes to be given between Friday, August 31, and Friday, September 14, 1956, inserted into the typescript,[227] the weekly St. Bernard conferences took place on Fridays, and by the end of August, Merton was already well into his discussion of Bernard's *De Diligendo Deo*, which had been preceded by a biographical overview of Bernard's life. Since Merton was on his trip to St. John's University in Minnesota for a conference on psychiatry and religious life between July 22 and August 4, 1956,[228] it is tempting to think that the new set of conferences might have begun after his return, on Friday, August 10, but this almost certainly leaves too little time for his introductory section. On the verso sides of his typescript pages, Merton often jotted brief notes of announcements to be made at the beginning of class, and opposite his text on "*Passage from the second to {the} third degree of love*" (122), at the top of the last of his six pages of material on the *De Diligendo*, is a rather detailed note on Brother Albert,[229] who according to a journal entry of August 20, 1956, was anointed on that day,[230] so presumably Merton must have reached this point in his discussion on August 24, the probable date for his comments on the old monk, making it extremely unlikely that he had been able to present all the

---

226. See *Charter, Customs, and Constitutions* for the texts of these conferences and discussion of their presentation.

227. This page immediately follows the six pages of notes on the *De Diligendo Deo* and precedes the first page of notes on the *Apologia*.

228. See *Search for Solitude*, 49–63; this was of course the occasion of Merton's famous, or notorious, encounter with psychiatrist Gregory Zilboorg: for an account of the meeting see Michael Mott, *The Seven Mountains of Thomas Merton* (Boston: Houghton Mifflin, 1984), 290–99.

229. "*De Diligendo Deo*," 5v.

230. *Search for Solitude*, 69.

preceding material in the two available half-hour Friday conference periods earlier in August. Hence sometime in early July, or even in June, would seem to be a likely starting point for these conferences.[231]

Few other notes provide any indication of the progression of the conferences. After completing his discussion of the treatise *De Praecepto et Dispensatione*, Merton turns to Bernard's third sermon for paschal time, with its discussion of the common and the proper will (234–37), and on the verso of the first of his two pages of notes on this sermon is a fairly detailed note on "Ash Wed + 3 following days" that suggests Merton was discussing this material at the beginning of Lent, 1957. Mention of "paschal mystery" on the verso of the page where Merton begins his discussion on "*St. Bernard and the Scriptures*" (257) might well be connected with Easter 1957, but of course need not be a reference to the liturgical calendar at all. A note on work assignments, opposite material on Sermons 9–12 on the Song of Songs (269), includes a list of five novices designated as "Waterboys," suggesting that their job is to take water to monks at work in the fields, which would indicate that it is now probably harvest season (many monks must have been at work for five waterboys to be needed). This is the last note that provides any clues as to the dating of the conferences. There are still fifteen pages of Merton's typescript remaining, which would suggest that the conferences probably continued well into the fall of 1957, but all that can be

---

231. One piece of apparently contrary evidence is an undated fragment of a letter to Dom Jean Leclercq, osb, in which Merton writes, "I have spent the year teaching a course on Cassian, on the Cistercian Consuetudines, and now on St. Bernard—I am just beginning" (*Survival or Prophecy?*, 75–76). The letter is assigned by the editor to "Fall 1956"—presumably on the basis of Merton's reference to "the year" of his novitiate teaching, which would be completed in October 1956; but from the evidence already cited it is clear that either the reference to "the year" or to "just beginning"—or perhaps both—could not have been literally accurate and therefore cannot be used to determine in any precise way when the conferences began.

said with a fair degree of certainty is that they began in the summer of 1956 and went on for more than a year.

There are two versions of the text of "Life, Works and Doctrine of Saint Bernard." The first is Merton's own typescript, which he would have had in front of him while teaching the novices. The text of the conference material consists of sixty-four typed pages, with Merton's own handwritten additions and alterations. The first seven pages are numbered—except for pages 1 and 3, which are the beginning of the work as a whole and of the section providing a capsule summary of Bernard's life—with the running head "[St] Bernard." They are followed by six pages on the *De Diligendo Deo* with their own pagination and running head ("de diligendo") and the non-text handwritten page listing the schedule for conferences from August 31 through September 14. Then follow pages numbered 7 through 29, with the running head "St Bern[ard]"; the handwritten number 7, added after the canceled typewritten 6 on the first of these pages, should of course be 8, so the pagination from this point on is one page less than the actual count. Inserted between pages 26 and 27, four handwritten pages, the first entitled "St Bernard on Pure Love" and the following three entitled "The First Epistle of St. John,"[232] interrupt the material on the treatise *De Praecepto et Dispensione*, which concludes on page 27. Pages 28–29, on Bernard's Sermon 3 on the Resurrection, are followed by three pages numbered 29a-c, entitled "A Note on Contemplation and Mystical Theology," then by pages 30–54, all (except 29c) with the same running head. After the typescript proper are six handwritten pages: two on an article in French by Jean Mouroux from the 1953

---

232. In a journal entry for December 29, 1957, Merton writes: "Preparing notes on first epistle of St. John for the novices' conference" (*Search for Solitude*, 150). These pages were probably kept with the St. Bernard typescript because of the importance of this epistle for Bernard's theology, as Gilson had emphasized (*Mystical Theology of Saint Bernard*, 22–25).

collection *Saint Bernard Théologien*,[233] two on "the Mystical Doctrine of St. Bernard," and two on "St Ailred's Marian Sermons." The second version of the text is a seventy-four page multigraph[234] reproduced from "spirit master" (purple) stencils for distribution to the novices at the conclusion of the course. It was copied directly from Merton's typescript, as is evident from occasional notes made on the typescript by the novice(s) assigned to retype the material, marking the beginning of a new page on the stencils,[235] presumably as a reminder where the next round of typing should resume. This text therefore has no independent authority, except that the fact that it omits the handwritten pages in the middle and at the end of the typescript is a strong indication that they were not intended by Merton to be included as an integral part of this set of conferences. Consequently, they are included in the textual notes of this edition but not in the text proper. In the main an accurate transcription, this version includes occasional misreadings of Merton's handwritten additions, omissions of some underlinings, a few cases of material

233. Jean Mouroux, "Sur les Critères d'Expérience Spirituelle d'après les Sermons sur le Cantiques des Cantique," *Saint Bernard Théologien*, Actes du Congrès de Dijon, 15–19 Septembre 1953, *Analecta Sacri Ordinis Cisterciensis* 9, nos. 3–4 (1953): 253–67.

234. It is numbered 1–41, 41a–d, 42–49, 53–73, with the running head "St[.] Bernard"; pages 41a–d comprise "A NOTE ON CONTEMPLATION AND MYSTICAL THEOLOGY" corresponding to pages 29a–c of Merton's original typescript, indicating that they had evidently been added to the original text after the typist had reached this point in his copying; a note on the bottom of page 49 reads: "There are no pages 50–52"—presumably added when it was noted that these page numbers had inadvertently been skipped over.

235. On page 13 of the typescript (page 155 of this edition) the typist has interlined the number "24" between "offerings" and "rather"—corresponding to the division between pages 23 and 24 on the stencil; on page 29 of the typescript the note "start p. 41" above the beginning of the quotation "*Non intendentes* . . ." (page 236 of this edition) corresponds to the beginning of page 41 on the stencil; on page 48 of the typescript the typist's note "p 66" with an arrow pointing to the words "*Ipse prior dilexit nos*" corresponds to the beginning of that page on the stencil (page 292 of this edition).

missing due to eyeskip, and other generally minor inaccuracies. There are also a few instances where Merton evidently added handwritten material to his typescript after the typist had passed that point in the text, so that these additions are not included on the stencils.

This first version of the St. Bernard conferences consists of eight sections. It begins with a "Preamble"[236] summarizing the 1953 encyclical *Doctor Mellifluus*, followed by a detailed chronology of St. Bernard's life.[237] The references and quotations in the preamble are taken from Merton's own volume *The Last of the Fathers*,[238] and the sequence of topics considered—Bernard's significance as highlighted in the encyclical, his doctrine and style, the emphasis on union with God through love and humility, mediated through the Mother of Jesus—parallels that found in the commentary he had provided there on *Doctor Mellifluus* but expressed much more succinctly and with little repetition in language. For example, Merton compresses his earlier emphasis on the importance of wisdom for Bernard by providing a brief definition—"the combination of knowledge and love"—and twice calling his approach "'sapiential' rather than scholastic . . . sapiential rather than speculative" (2),[239] using a term that does not appear in his commentary or in the encyclical itself but that will become quite familiar in Merton's subsequent writings.[240] He concludes this brief introductory overview, the "authoritative

---

236. Pages 1–10 in this edition.
237. Pages 12, 32–48 in this edition.
238. The fact that these conferences begin with an overview of *Doctor Mellifluus* apparently accounts for the erroneous statement in the introductory note to Merton's preface to *Marthe, Marie et Lazare* that "*One of two longer studies, originally called 'The Life, Works and Doctrine of St. Bernard' . . . appeared in 1954 as* The Last of the Fathers" (*"Honorable Reader,"* 15).
239. For the sake of consistency all quotations will be taken from the edited text found in the present volume, with any significant substantive variants from the "Life, Works and Doctrine" version included in a footnote.
240. See Patrick F. O'Connell, "Wisdom," *Thomas Merton Encyclopedia*, 533–35, for an overview of Merton's teaching on wisdom and the terminology he employs.

outline" provided by this papal document, with "[p]ractical conclusions" directed specifically to his audience of novices, emphasizing what taking Bernard as guide and model actually entails in terms of both study and practice (10). This consideration of the concrete implications of what is being discussed for the formation process, for the novices' monastic—and indeed Christian and human—lives, will be a recurring focus throughout these conferences, as it was in all Merton's novitiate courses.

This introductory section is completed by a biographical outline. After concisely situating Bernard in the context of the religious, political, and cultural developments of the High Middle Ages and of the territory of Burgundy where he grew up and would live out his monastic life, Merton provides a year-by-year chronology of Bernard's adult life from his "conversion" in 1111, the year before he joined the Cistercians, through his death in 1153; only four years, all from his early monastic life, are not listed as marked by some significant event. The five periods into which Merton divides Bernard's career give some sense of overall shape and order to the plethora of activities, travels, interactions, and writings that mark his complicated and busy involvement in the major issues, developments, and controversies of his era: the first encompassing his early monastic years up through 1125 as novice and young monk at Cîteaux and as founding abbot of Clairvaux; the second (1126–1130), when "not much {is} going on, except writing" (!) (33), that concludes with his emergence onto the public stage as a champion of Pope Innocent II in the papal schism; the third (1131–1138), marked by his efforts on behalf of Innocent until the schism comes to an end in 1138, but also noteworthy for the beginning of his series of sermons on the Song of Songs and the death of his brother Gerard, also in 1138; the fourth (1139–1148), which finds Bernard involved in many political and ecclesiastical matters, including the preaching of the Second Crusade at the behest of the former Clairvaux monk Bernardo Pignatelli, now Pope Eugene III; the fifth and final period (1149–1153), begun with the failure of the crusade and ending with Bernard's illness and death on August 20, 1153, but also including the composition for his disciple Eugene of *De Consideratione*, his last great treatise.

Each of the sections that follow focuses on a particular literary work, beginning with the treatise *On the Love of God* (*De Diligendo Deo*),[241] which Merton in the "Life, Works and Doctrine" text calls an appropriate starting point both because it is an early work and because it introduces the theme of love that is central to Bernard's theology. He then goes on to consider the controverted question of whether Bernard's doctrine of love, viewing love as a continuum developing as it does from the "*amor carnalis*" of self-preservation to the heights of the pure love of God, was consistent. Merton endorses Étienne Gilson's position that the human person, made in the divine image, is thus made for love, and that even in a fallen state, "defiled, debased, vitiated by sin" (78), this image remains, and that growth in love is the process of the restoration of divine likeness through the power of the Holy Spirit until "the divine Law of Charity is fulfilled in our own lives; we are perfectly ourselves, and yet we are outside ourselves and lost in God. We have found ourselves at last in Him" (79). Characteristic Mertonian language is evident here, commenting on a book (*The Spirit of Mediaeval Philosophy*) that, as noted above, Merton had first encountered at the very outset of the intellectual and spiritual journey that would lead him to baptism and into the monastery. The rest of this section is a summary and commentary on the treatise, beginning with the first eight chapters that explain why God is to be loved: both objectively because He is God and therefore deserving of all love, and subjectively because He has first loved us, undeserving as we are, both in the total and totally free self-gift of the Son's incarnation and redemption, and in the gift of life and of all that sustains life, and of those qualities of dignity, knowledge—especially self-knowledge—and virtue that give life true meaning.

---

241. Pages 78–80, 107–25 in this edition; see also Appendix A, pages 398–99, for the unrevised version of the introductory material of this section.

This is followed by Merton's résumé of chapters 8–11 in which Bernard sets out the four degrees of love: first comes love of oneself for one's own sake—the fleshly love of self-preservation that *"is well-ordered* if it limits itself to natural necessity" (119) and that logically entails the social love, the love of neighbor as oneself, that sees others as having the same needs and therefore the same rights as oneself. This is followed by love of God for our own sake, an awareness of human contingency and dependence that leads through trial to the "experience of our own nothingness and *gratitude for the love of God"* (122), the source of all good. Gratitude for God's gift of His love then leads to a deepened realization of God as lovable, to be loved for His own sake, a love that is progressively purified of self-interest: *"amor castus, justus* and *'gratus' "* (123)—pure, just, freely given. Finally the highest degree of love is to love even ourselves for God's sake, that is, to love completely as God loves, to love all, including ourselves, in and through God, even in some sense as God, being " 'one spirit' with Him"—an experience fully realized only in the next life, possible in this life "only in passing," but intimated by the self-surrender of a mystical death to self, when "Our love is God's love, and our knowledge is His knowledge. Hence our limitations are drowned and overwhelmed in the inrush of His divine Spirit, and we no longer know ourselves, but only His love" (125).

After this elevated exploration of the power of love to bring the human person into a participation in the very life of the trinitarian God, the following discussion of Bernard's *Apologia*[242] is a decided, perhaps even disconcerting, change of focus and change of pace. The treatise is an important document in early Cistercian history, which certainly justifies its inclusion in a set of conferences devoted to that subject (as the general rubric of the sequence has it), but it also shows a different side of Bernard: his skill not only as a polemicist but also as a literary stylist and talented satirist, employing quite down-to-earth resources on

---

242. Pages 126, 132–34, 139–56 in this edition.

behalf of a high spiritual ideal. The *Apologia* was actually composed a year or two before the *De Diligendo Deo*, at the behest of Bernard's friend William of St. Thierry, at the time still a Black Benedictine abbot but later to become a Cistercian at the Abbey of Signy, who was concerned about the growing antagonism between the new Cistercians and the Cluniac Benedictines. Merton first provides some background about Bernard's own prior relations with Cluny, including his criticisms of what he considered its lax practices in his Letter 1 to his cousin Robert, whom he accused the Cluniacs of seducing away from Clairvaux, and his generally positive relations with Peter the Venerable, the abbot of Cluny, who was working to effect reforms there after the brief but calamitous reign of his immediate predecessor, Pontius. Merton warns that the *Apologia* must be read as a whole, with equal attention given to Bernard's opening critique of those Cistercians who have attacked Cluny in a spirit of pharisaic pride and his own subsequent denunciation of what he sees as excesses and deviations in the Cluniac system (the Cistercians violating the spirit of the Benedictine *Rule* as much as—if not more than—the Cluniacs do its letter). He defends Bernard's severe criticisms as evidently just, if at times heightened for rhetorical effect, and as a "necessary and salutary" restatement of the essential elements of Benedictine monasticism, motivated not by "mere partisan feeling" (142) but by "an intense and passionate love for the *reality of the monastic ideal* . . . something to *be lived and put into practice*" (143). The opening chapters of the treatise (1–7) as Merton now summarizes them show Bernard undermining Cistercian claims to moral superiority, contradicted by the very pride that motivates them, professing his own love and admiration for Cluny and its gifts to the Church, defending the principle of unity in diversity among the different forms of monastic life, and defending dispensations from the *Rule* as provided for in the *Rule* itself. "But one must distinguish between rightful dispensations in case of need and *wholesale mitigation reaching the point of abuse*" (148), as Bernard proceeds to do in the remainder of the treatise, with its scathing critique of monastic authorities relaxing regulations from a false sense of "charity" and of the resulting violation of both letter and spirit of Benedictine life in matters of food and drink, dress, and particularly the lavish adornment of monastic churches, which he sees both as a distraction from prayer and as a kind of religious "consumerism" that attracts donations from the rich and deprives the poor of alms that would otherwise be theirs. All this is expressed in masterful prose from which Merton quotes particularly vivid examples. Merton sums up Bernard's conclusions in the principle "Let each one hold to the good which he possesses and not judge the other" (156), which he himself may seem to have violated, but only if his motives are not taken into account; his main point is that Cluny does not have to adopt Cistercian customs, nor should individual Cluniacs become Cistercians, in order to live a faithful Christian and monastic life—but rather all monks should be faithful to the spirit that animates their own observance at its best. As Merton had pointed out to the novices earlier in this discussion:

> We must remember not to apply these standards of St. Bernard too literally today. The situation is no longer quite the same; at best there might be a remote analogy. But it is for us to remember, as individual monks, that it is necessary to keep a high ideal of mortification and of charity at the same time. We must deny ourselves if we are followers of Christ. There must be, in the world, men of penance and prayer, and our renunciation must be a fact, and not just a word. The *Apologia* reminds us of this. We must never forget it. (143)

The section that follows looks at Bernard's famous sermon *On Conversion*,[243] delivered to students at Paris in 1140 at a time when intellectual life in the capital that would lead to the founding of the university and the development of scholasticism was beginning to flourish, albeit in some forms that could be controversial and even dangerous, as with Peter Abelard. Merton rejects the characterization of Bernard as anti-intellectual, pointing out

---

243. Pages 160, 166, 196–214 in this edition.

his friendship with and support of many of the great scholars of the period; what he is opposed to, as the sermon makes clear, is a "sterile intellectualism, a life that is lived entirely in the mind, and has little effect in changing one's morals" (197). Commitment to the truth is not a matter of the mind alone for Bernard but of the whole person and is above all a commitment to the Truth incarnate in the person of Christ. Thus Bernard's point in his address to the students, many of whom "lived disedifying lives, while talking about the Truth," was that authentic communion with the Truth required "a *metanoia*, a conversion, a change of heart—a change that takes place deep in one's being and re-orientates the whole course of one's life" (198). Merton presents the sermon as composed of two complementary parts, the first nine chapters describing the meaning and process of conversion and the last nine considering the progress in virtue and the stages of the ascent to God and "the perfect restoration by charity of the divine likeness in the soul" (198). Bernard begins by analyzing both the call of the divine Word to inner transformation and the strategies of avoidance that result only in a pseudo-conversion, a change of outward practice without a change of heart, graphically expressed in Bernard's allegory of the divided faculties of the soul engaged in a struggle comparable to that of a sick woman resisting her own healing. Merton traces Bernard's depiction of the stages of conversion and spiritual growth, from the mind to the will to the memory, experienced through the progressive appropriation of the beatitudes, becoming poor and meek, "mourning for the fact that there is no consolation save in hope" (205), hungering and thirsting "for the life of virtue and its rewards" (208), finding purity of heart through the divine mercy that cleanses even the memory of one's own failures, and so becoming merciful toward others and a peacemaker who returns good for evil. Failure to walk this path, Bernard concludes, is particularly disastrous in the clergy, who are charged with directing others to God but who are all too often simply careerists motivated by "*worldly ambition*" and the desire "for political and human prestige and for wealth" (213). This of course is a final direct challenge to his audience of theological students to examine their motives for choosing to become clerics—is it service or status? In his summation, Merton points out Bernard's concern for authenticity, for his listeners "be[ing] what they are supposed to be . . . not a mere sham"; his analysis of "the psychological reality of the spiritual life," rooted in experience, beyond the level of abstract concepts; his emphasis on clerics and monks seeking "the highest perfection of love" both for their own sake and for the sake of the fruitfulness of the entire Church; and the effectiveness of Bernard's rhetorical strategy, first describing "the beauties of the Christian vocation to sanctity" in compelling and attractive detail, and only then exposing and condemning the abuses rampant in clerical life of the period. "They are," Merton concludes, "truly the words of a saint" (214).

The next text Merton discusses, *De Praecepto et Dispensatione*,[244] is probably the most exclusively "monastic" of Bernard's treatises, concerned as it is with answering the question posed to Bernard by some Black Benedictines about whether monks were obliged under pain of sin to keep the *Rule* of St. Benedict. In this initial version of the material,[245] Merton contextualizes Bernard's response by first considering the historical background and the contemporary canonical regulations concerning this question. In his detailed and rather complex discussion, he points out that the degree of obligation depends on the intention of the original compiler of a particular rule, and that different religious orders (Franciscans, Carmelites, Dominicans) vary in their level of obligation, though the presence of contempt, scandal, or habitual inconstancy (and of course a violation of the moral law in general) would constitute a sinful act in any order. There is also the fact that a violation of the virtue of obedience can be

---

244. Pages 214–24 in this edition, but see also Appendix A, pages 405–11, for the extensive introductory material cut from the final version of the text.

245. This section corresponds fairly closely in structure and content, though not in wording, to Merton's discussion of the *De Praecepto* in "Monastic Orientation," 3, 91–115.

sinful even when it is not a question of a direct violation of the vow. Against this background, Merton turns to the specific question of whether the Benedictine *Rule* obliges under the pain of sin, and if so in what circumstances. He refers to the semiofficial *Spiritual Directory* of the Order,[246] which accepts the principle that since the *Rule* does not specify the author's intent in the matter, its obligations are not to be considered binding under pain of serious sin, but that Cistercian tradition seems to favor the idea that breaking the *Rule* does involve commission of venial sin, a position that Merton finds to be less than perfectly clear or convincing. He then turns to St. Thomas's discussion of the topic,[247] which points out that to make every violation of the rule of a religious order a matter of serious sin would make religious life a morally perilous state, which would be contrary to the whole point of such a vocation. According to Thomas, distinctions must be made between obligations that bear on the very essence of religious life—the vows of poverty, chastity, and obedience—and observances designed to assist one to seek perfection, which are not binding and become a matter of sin only to the extent that their neglect stems from some sinful motive. Merton then turns to Bernard and his response to the question whether the prescriptions of the *Rule* are to be regarded as obligatory precepts or as counsels for spiritual growth. Bernard's starting point is clear: "To vow to live under the *Rule* of St. Benedict is to oblige oneself to live according to the *Rule*" (215). But he goes on to distinguish between those precepts found in the *Rule* that are part of the fundamental moral law that even God cannot change, obligations that God alone can abrogate, and observances that are subject to

---

246. [Vital Lehodey, ocso], *A Spiritual Directory for Religious*, trans. from the Original French Text "*Directoire Spirituel à l'Usage des Cisterciens de la Stricte Observance*" by a Priest of New Melleray Abbey, Peosta, Iowa (Trappist, KY: Abbey of Our Lady of Gethsemani, 1946), 206–9.

247. *Sancti Thomae Aquinatis Doctoris Angelici Ordinis Praedicatorum Opera Omnia, secundum Impressionem Petri Fiaccadori Parmae 1852–1873 Photolithographice Reimpressa*, 25 vols. (New York: Misurgia, 1948), 3:638–39 (*Secunda Secundae*, q. 186, a. 9).

human (i.e., superiors') dispensation, with the promotion of charity being the determining criterion for enforcing or altering particular usages. He also differentiates between *"peccata,"* faults of weakness that are not serious and involve sin only if one neglects to perform the penance assigned for them, and *"crimina,"* deliberate violations that may be seriously sinful if they involve malice or scandal. He concludes: "St. Bernard certainly seems to believe that in infractions of our most notable observances, like silence, fasting and so forth, there can be real sin, perhaps serious sin, if there is formal disobedience to the *Rule*, and that other kinds of transgression out of weakness and inadvertence are not really to be regarded as sins, but as faults of frailty which we have come to the monastery to correct," and adds: "There is no possibility of foisting on St. Bernard an opinion that the *Rule* can be observed or not according to the discretion of the individual!" (216).

Merton then considers Bernard's specific instruction in the treatise concerning obedience and stability. With regard to the former, Bernard distinguishes between perfect obedience—not simply formal adherence to the letter of the law or command but the loving and generous submission of the will to God, encountered in the person of the superior, in imitation of and union with Christ—and imperfect obedience, motivated by fear of adverse consequences or by a legalistic attitude, or demanding, at least implicitly, rational justification for commands that one finds onerous or unclear. Bernard points out that "No ONE VOWS TO BE ACTUALLY PERFECT IN OBEDIENCE" (220), an obvious impossibility for even the most dedicated religious, but rather to form one's life according to the pattern found in the *Rule* and to accept willingly and carry out humbly the penitential remedies imposed for infractions of the *Rule*. As for stability, Bernard lays down the fundamental principle that one is never permitted to substitute a lesser for a greater good, therefore to abandon one form of religious life for a less strict one (unless one's salvation is somehow at stake). One is not even permitted to leave a less strict monastery for a stricter one without a superior's permission, unless the former is somehow "irregular"—not conforming to the *Rule* (*regula*). As for the particular question of Benedictines becoming

Cistercians, which Bernard would consider a stricter and therefore a higher form of religious life, Bernard is opposed in principle because of the danger of scandal and the risk of failure, though if observance in a given monastery is so lax that the *Rule* is not being lived, Bernard would consider a transfer legitimate, and Merton points out that in practice, he not infrequently accepted Benedictines at Clairvaux.

Complementing the rather technical discussion of monastic observance and obligation in *De Praecepto et Dispensatione* is Merton's relatively brief consideration of Bernard's teaching on self-will and the common will in a more homiletic fashion in his Third Sermon for Paschaltide,[248] a key text for Merton as early as *The Spirit of Simplicity*[249] and the only one of Bernard's liturgical sermons that he comments on in this set of conferences. The spiritual disease of self-will (*voluntas propria*), focused on the satisfaction of one's own desires, reinforcing and reinforced by attachment to one's own judgment (*proprium consilium*), is identified by Bernard in the sermon with the leprosy of Naaman in the Fourth [or Second] Book of Kings.[250] It can only be healed by a conversion that brings a commitment to the common will,[251] to "charity, [which] shares a universal good, a real good, with God and with others. Its good is not diminished by being shared. It is therefore united to others in love. It is, in fact, LOVE. The common will and the common good are the same: they are love. Wherever there is real love, that reaches out to God and to other

---

248. Pages 234–37 in this edition.

249. See *The Spirit of Simplicity*, 111–27: virtually the entire discussion on "The Simplification of the Will" (see above, page xvi) is based on this sermon.

250. 4 Kings 5:1-14 in the Vulgate numbering used by Bernard and Merton; 2 Kings in the Hebrew and contemporary translations.

251. For a highly critical discussion of Merton's understanding—and practice—of the common will, see Michael Casey, ocso, "Merton's Teaching on the 'Common Will' and What the Journals Tell Us," *The Merton Annual* 12 (1999): 62–84; Casey seems unaware of the extent to which Merton is following Gilson in his emphasis on this concept (see *Mystical Theology of Saint Bernard*, 55, 74–75, 95, 101–2, 135, 233, n. 94).

men and excludes none, then *we cannot have self-will*" (236). Humans suffer from the frustration of their own wishes and the rejection of their own judgment, but this suffering is ultimately the result of self-contradiction, of the denial of one's own deepest nature and orientation, the union of wills with God that is true human fulfillment: "As soon as we accept what is contrary, and embrace it as the will of God, our will is 'common' and the basic suffering of opposition to Him is removed" (236). As Naaman was healed of his leprosy in the waters of the Jordan, so Bernard teaches that "the remedy for all the 'leprosy' of our soul is in the mysteries of Christ, particularly in the Passion and Resurrection" (235). In his humble obedience to Mary and Joseph, "Jesus, though He was Wisdom Itself, . . . judged it better to embrace the common view rather than to maintain His own." In his total self-surrender to the Father's will, as Merton sums up Bernard's message, "The obedience of Jesus Crucified is the most perfect example of the 'common will'—what was pleasing to the Father, to Jesus Himself, and salutary for us" (237).

The remaining material, which constitutes about 45 percent of the text (thirty-three of the seventy-four multigraph pages), is directly or indirectly focused on Bernard's greatest work, the Sermons on the Canticle of Canticles: an introductory "Note on Contemplation and Mystical Theology," inserted into the text after the typist had reached this point, as the pagination of both the original typescript (29a-c) and the stencil copy (41a-d) make clear; an overview of Bernard's own mystical teaching, of the composition of the series of sermons, and of Bernard's approach to the Scriptures; and a detailed commentary on the first twenty-three of the sermons, grouped in six segments.

The "Note,"[252] a brief historical survey of the meaning of the term "mystical theology," extending from the New Testament to the present-day Church and monastic life, is intended to provide a context for a proper understanding and appreciation of Bernard's own teaching. Merton begins by pointing out that there is no

---

252. Pages 237–44 in this edition.

distinct concept of "contemplation" or "mystical theology" in the New Testament or the Apostolic Fathers, but that the invitation to enter into "the mystery of Christ" (237) that is found throughout the scriptural and immediate postscriptural Christian writings is a call to participate in the experience of God that these terms come to describe. It is in the Greek fathers that this terminology begins to be used to describe "the hidden knowledge of God by experience," with the distinction between "*theologia*" and "*theoria*" corresponding to the difference between the contemplation of God in Himself and the experience of God in creation, redemption, and scriptural revelation (238). The Latin fathers made no distinction between dogmatic and mystical theology, seeing all theology as the discovery of wisdom in "an experiential realization of the mysteries of faith" (238)—knowing God rather than just knowing about God. Merton then jumps to the late Middle Ages and the Renaissance, when mystical theology becomes more narrowly a study of the life of prayer and spiritual growth, differentiated from the more objective and intellectual realm of dogma. This split becomes even wider in the eighteenth century, when mysticism becomes identified with rare and extraordinary supernatural phenomena of virtually no relevance to the ordinary life of faith. But in the twentieth century, the earlier understanding of contemplation as "the 'normal' development of the life of grace" has been recovered (239); though Merton finds much of the recent scholarly conversation about mysticism "sterile and misleading" (239), he does see valuable contributions being made by the various contemporary approaches—the phenomenological, the speculative, the patristic (historical), and even some of the popularizations that endeavor "to bring mysticism to the level of the ordinary religious and the faithful" (241).

Merton's personal evaluation of this renewal of interest in the mystical life is that it is frequently vague and superficial on the level of popular knowledge, but that the impression of strangeness and irrelevance has largely dissipated, and the fact that many of the faithful do experience preliminary stages of contemplative prayer and can have legitimate aspirations for a deeper contemplative life is more widely recognized and accepted in the Church. On the other hand, the tendency to characterize even "the most insignificant of consolations" as coming from "mystical grace" (242) tends to trivialize authentic contemplative experience and to deemphasize the need for "a true *metanoia*, a complete inner change" (242) in order to experience the presence of God in a deep, immediate way. He also notes that despite the change in focus and understanding, much contemporary mysticism is still comprised of *"extraordinary and charismatic* gifts" that may or may not involve the "graces of contemplation properly so called" (242). Turning to monastic life, Merton suggests that the prayer life of many monks is contemplative in a broad sense, but that growth toward union with God does not ordinarily *"conform to the clear outlines laid down in the books"* (243) and that even genuine spiritual experiences may not lead to lasting holiness, particularly when they result in a tendency toward introspection and self-absorption that can often turn morbid. Merton reminds his novices that the ordinary "virtues of the monastic life itself" make the most powerful contribution to the development of a truly contemplative life, and that "not taking ourselves too seriously" (244) and focusing on Jesus rather than oneself is the best guard against an illusory spiritual elevation that cannot be sustained.

Having provided this background, Merton can more confidently discuss what he calls "THE MYSTICAL DOCTRINE OF ST. BERNARD'S SERMONS ON THE CANTICLE OF CANTICLES" (244), beginning with a general presentation of the sermons[253] as the product of "the last, most mature and most productive period of his life," in which he elaborates "the essence of his teaching" (245) in "a great work of art" (246) that is *"not only a theoretical exposition of spiritual doctrine, but a living expression of the spiritual experience that was common in the Cistercian monasteries of the twelfth century"* (245), especially his own spiritual experience. Writing in the patristic tradition, Bernard presents a holistic, integrated

---

253. Pages 244–62 in this edition.

vision of the Christian life in which the spiritual development of the individual is recognized as a participation in and appropriation of the central mysteries of faith, deeply rooted in Scripture and in the life of the Church as a whole. The goal is not extraordinary visions or revelations but "a prolongation of the Incarnation, an effect intended by God when the Word became incarnate" (248), the perfection and fulfillment of unitive love through faithful conformity to the person and teaching of Christ. After dating the successive stages of Bernard's composition of the sermons, from their beginnings in the mid-1130s until the very end of his life—interrupted for periods of varying length because of other private and public obligations—Merton then considers the very different approach to the Scriptures taken in the patristic tradition that Bernard brings to its culmination, an approach that rejects a narrow focus on the literal sense that fails to hear the Word of God calling the listener to conversion and transformation. For Bernard and his tradition, "true contemplative reading of the Scriptures is an infused and divinely given understanding of the way the texts all point to Jesus Christ as to the center of all revelation, how they show us more or less how we must live to be united to Him and to have Him living in us, and how we are all tending to our last end, the Kingdom of God, the glorification of Christ in His Church, the Heavenly Jerusalem" (258). It draws on the stories and images of the Bible to provide a language for communicating the deep personal spiritual experience that had been directed and nurtured by immersion in the Word in the first place: "St. Bernard's commentary on the Canticle is then an elaboration of what he himself has found, by experience, in the sacred text, after having entered into it guided by the Church and by the tradition of her Fathers and Doctors" (259), as Bernard himself describes the process in Sermons 73 and 74 on the Canticle.[254]

---

254. As with Guerric's Christmas Sermon, Bernard's equation here and elsewhere of sterile literalism with the Jew and spiritual insight with the Christian is of course profoundly disturbing to a contemporary reader, as is Merton's failure to critique such a reading. Merton generally presents such material simply as a literary trope without considering its real-world

Then follows Merton's detailed commentary on the first twenty-three of the sermons; stopping at this point is not simply an arbitrary decision on his part or evidence of a flagging of interest or energy, but apparently a deliberate choice to focus on this initial group of sermons, probably given between 1135 and 1137, after which Bernard is called away from the monastery by the pope for about a year. While these are not the culmination of Bernard's mystical teaching (found in Sermons 82–85, written at the end of his life), they do provide a coherent and comprehensive introduction to the major ideas and themes of the entire series. By discussing a continuous sequence of sermons, taken from the beginning of the work, rather than selecting individual examples from throughout the series, Merton is able to give the novices a better sense of the "rhythm" that Bernard develops, the ways he is able to remain faithful to the verse-by-verse progression of the scriptural text (only the first three verses of which are discussed in this entire segment, which constitutes more than

---

consequences—as perhaps Bernard himself did, since he mounted a strong defense of the Jews when preparations for the Second Crusade set off waves of anti-Jewish persecution. It should be noted that it was in this general period that Merton wrote in his journal: "One has either got to be a Jew or stop reading the bible. For the bible really cannot make sense to anyone who is not spiritually a 'Semite.' The spiritual sense of the Old Testament is not and cannot be first an emptying out of its Israelitic content. The New Testament is the fulfillment of the Old, not its destruction. The fulfillment of the promises made to Abraham, the promises Abraham believed in. . . . Hence, the terrible mystery of the persecution of Israel in our time. *Salus ex Judaeis.* Christ crucified again in His people 'according to the flesh.' Israel remains the Servant of Yahweh even though Jesus has fulfilled the type in Isaias. Israel is still His people even though Israel has denied Him" (*Search for Solitude*, 127 [11/24/1957]). See also the revised version of the beginning of this passage, which reads: ". . . The New Testament is the fulfillment of that spiritual content, the fulfillment of the promise made to Abraham, the promise that Abraham believed in. It is never therefore a denial of Judaism, but its affirmation. Those who consider it a denial have not understood it" (*Conjectures of a Guilty Bystander*, 5–6).

a quarter of the entire set!), while at the same time developing and communicating his teaching on the key dimensions and successive phases of the contemplative life in an integration of allegorical exegesis, the resources of tradition and personal experience. To consider these sermons in their proper order, Merton implies, is to discover the subtle artistry with which Bernard has designed a flexible, adaptable structure that owes part of its power and attraction to the apparently spontaneous, informal, even somewhat meandering yet never disorganized unfolding of his instruction, delivered in an accessible voice that invites rapport between speaker and audience yet maintains an authority based not only on abbatial office but also on a wisdom formed and tested by the discipline of the Gospel.

In the first grouping of eight sermons,[255] all commenting on the opening verse of the Canticle, "Let him kiss me with the kiss of his mouth," "the whole doctrine of the Sermons *in Cantica*"— the desire for mystical union and the nature of that union—"is pretty well sketched out," Merton claims, "in broad outlines" (263). As Merton summarizes, Bernard first characterizes the Canticle of Canticles as the love song of the union of Christ and the Church, longed for by the patriarchs and prophets of Israel and made possible by the perfect union of divinity and humanity in the incarnation. The kiss of the mouth is the culmination of the process of deepening spiritual intimacy preceded by the kiss of the feet and of the hands—images that prompt a kind of excursus by Bernard on God as immaterial spirit and thus the need to understand properly the use of material, corporeal imagery for God in the Scriptures. The kiss of the mouth symbolizes "a union of wills and spirits in which the soul is perfectly united with God to the point of spiritual identification (not metaphysical!) by *pure love*" (265), an image of personal union that is not an alternative to the ecclesial interpretation already given but a recognition that it is precisely as a member of the Church that

---

255. Pages 263–68 in this edition.

one shares the identity of the Bride of Christ. Finally, the kiss of the mouth is identified with the gift of the Holy Spirit: "To be 'kissed' by God is simply to receive the Holy Spirit, and to be united to the Father in the Son," a union of both knowledge and love, more precisely "the knowledge of God by love" (267), which is a participation in the Son's own exchange of love with the Father that is the Holy Spirit: "we share the love of Jesus for the Father; or Jesus, by His Spirit, loves the Father in us" (268).

The second grouping, Sermons 9–12,[256] begins what Merton calls "a series of instructions on what we should call the *illuminative life*" (269) that will continue through Sermon 22. The focus here is on "the anointing of the soul" by the Holy Spirit, symbolized by the ointments of contrition, devotion, and *pietas* (fraternal compassion), "that prepares the way for pure love" (269). These three ointments are all dimensions of the essential gift of the *"experience of the divine mercy"* that is "the very heart of the illuminative way" and that calls forth the equally essential "response to the mercy of God by gratitude and confidence in our own hearts, and by compassion for our brothers" (270). It is the spiritual father, the abbot, who is the principal channel in the monastery through which this triple anointing is received, through which divine mercy is mediated. It is he who draws his spiritual sons to humility and compunction, encourages growth in gratitude and trust that is given voice in the praise of God, and models the merciful identification with the sorrows and struggles of others and the willingness to share their burdens, a very practical self-forgetfulness that for Bernard "is the secret of progress in the mystical life" (274).

The third segment, Sermons 13–18,[257] focuses on Jesus as the source and goal of all spiritual good, centering in the celebrated Sermon 15 on the Name of Jesus as "oil poured out" (Cant 1:2). This is preceded, Merton points out, by two sermons on the phari-

---

256. Pages 269–74 in this edition.
257. Pages 274–87 in this edition.

saical spirit that fails to acknowledge the absolute necessity for the divine mercy made flesh in the person of Christ, "the *absolute gratuity* of the salvation offered to man by God" (276), and that is therefore marked by ingratitude toward God and contempt toward others who do not measure up to their own standards of "virtue." It is not the Pharisee but the Spouse, who has responded to the free gift of salvation with confidence rooted in love, who is the true model for the *"adolescentulae,"* the young maidens who are inspired by the example of the Bride to follow in her footsteps: "In the good lives of the saints His Name is as 'oil poured out' upon all the faithful" (277). Thus Bernard turns to the healing oil of the holy name of Jesus, which expresses the saving power of God: "The *reality* that is in the divine Person of the Incarnate Word is communicated to us as though by a sacrament in the Name of Jesus. Meditation and love of the Holy Name is as it were a prolonged spiritual communion. . . . By the constant invocation of the Holy Name, *all our senses and actions* become directed to Jesus and centered on Him" (278–80). It is Christ the new Eliseus (Elisha) who restores life by breathing the divine life of grace into the soul and makes it possible to distinguish the presence of the Holy Spirit from merely natural or even diabolic influences. "Without this knowledge," according to Bernard, *"we do not desire Him when He is absent; we do not glorify Him when He is present."* Merton comments: "This simple phrase speaks volumes" (281). The action of the Holy Spirit is considered further in the concluding sermon of this group, in which is found Bernard's famous distinction between canals and reservoirs, an admonition not to try to communicate what one has not truly experienced and not to "retain for ourselves the charisms that have been given us for others" (282)—again an emphasis on the necessity for discernment and self-knowledge, a realistic appraisal of one's own spiritual development, "this time in function of a love that builds up to an apostolic and charismatic mission" (284). Only those who are empty of vanity and self-regard are able to share the gifts and fruits of contemplation, for they alone are "filled with reality, with God Himself . . . . This fullness is the complete work of the Holy Spirit, the *infusio* of sanctifying grace upon which must follow the other work, the *effusio* of charismatic graces, also His work in us for souls" (287).

In the following pair of sermons,[258] Bernard turns back to those still in the earlier stages of spiritual progress, "the beginners that follow the Bride as her escort and seek the Spouse after her example" (287), represented in the monastic context by those who have recently joined the community. In Sermon 19 he cautions against mistaking an enthusiastic but superficial spiritual fervor for mature and responsible commitment to a Christ-centered life and emphasizes the importance of obedience, discretion, and fidelity to the direction of the spiritual father in overcoming the tendency even in spiritual matters to confuse self-will with the will of God and self-satisfaction with genuine fulfillment. Sermon 20, among the most important and best known of the series, as Merton notes, presents the solution to the central "problem of the spiritual life" that the preceding sermon has raised: how "to get rid of self-love and self-will and to cultivate true love of God" (291). The answer is simple: to respond with love to the love of Jesus, marked by its deeply human compassion, its elevated wisdom, its unwavering strength that endured and overcame death itself. "The way to 'perfection' is not the love of an abstraction but the love of a person" (291), a love, Bernard goes on to say, that begins with "*amor carnalis*," human affection for the human Jesus that engages the emotions in order to purify and elevate them to become that love of the "whole heart" (294) spoken of in the great commandment. Thus the incarnate Christ meets and engages beginners in the spiritual life where they are, at their own level, but then draws them beyond a love based mainly in feeling to "a love not merely of the flesh of Christ, but of the TRUTH and LIGHT of Christ" (296)—"*amor rationalis*": loving with the whole mind as well as the whole heart. Finally there is "*amor fortis . . . constancy* and the ability to stand firm and resist

---

258. Pages 287–97 in this edition.

evil in all its forms, not by our own power but by the power of God" (297)—loving God with one's whole strength. With these three dimensions of love, the disciple's love responds and corresponds to the sweetness, wisdom, and strength of Christ's love, those qualities that "complete one another to produce a *perfect spiritual love*" (293).

The next two sermons,[259] "of relatively lesser importance" (297) according to Merton, consider the Spouse's request to the Bridegroom "to draw me after Thee" (Cant. 1:3) as indicating that even one well advanced on the way to union is limited by "the incapacity of a created being to respond perfectly, of its own accord, to the Love of God" (297–98) and is subject to the vicissitudes, the spiritual highs and lows, consolations and desolations, inevitable in any human journey to God, and taking different forms depending not just on the diverse subjective experiences of people with widely varying personalities but objectively on "the diversity of gifts, and of vocations" that result in differing ways of responding to "the same mystical ointments" (299). Nevertheless, underlying these fluctuations in individual experience and variations in the way Christ's loving call is experienced between one individual and another, what is common and constant is the fact that "Christ must be wisdom, justice, sanctification and redemption" for all, and all "must seek all virtue, strength, wisdom and prudence in Him" (299).

The final sermon to be discussed,[260] and thus the concluding focus of the entire set of conferences, constitutes its own group. Merton writes that Sermon 23, on the "cellars" or storerooms of the Spouse, "sums up the first group of sermons and is the culminating point of St. Bernard's early maturity," filled with teaching "about the interior life and about contemplation, drawn from St. Bernard's own experience" (299). In the context of scriptural interpretation, the cellars can be equated with the moral sense,

---

259. Pages 297–99 in this edition.
260. Pages 299–306 in this edition.

the personal application of the message to one's own life appropriate to "progressives," those in the illuminative way, beyond the literal sense symbolized by the gardens where the attendants wait but preceding the mystical or spiritual sense identified with the bedchamber where the Bride experiences full union with her divine Spouse. Bernard then suggests that the cellars themselves are threefold, filled with the resources of asceticism that make possible "the restoration of human nature in Christ and its divinization" (301), evidence of Bernard's traditional patristic understanding of human nature as fundamentally good. First comes the discipline of submission to the *Rule* and to those more advanced in the spiritual life, in order to reorder and reorient "the natural power to love" and do away with "the *selfish* and *self-centered* love which actually is not natural, according to his view" (302). Thus is made possible a "life according to nature," life in community lived not just under another but with another, a life marked by "gentleness, charity, kindness, meekness, non-violence and pure affection—*humanitas*" (303). The third cellar is the wine-cellar, the cellar of grace that is assigned to the superior, whose responsibility for those under his apostolic care requires "a special charity which goes 'out of itself' and 'is lost to itself' . . . . and fervent zeal, without which one cannot rightly take charge of other souls" (303), aptly represented by the wine with which he is refreshed and strengthened to carry out his duties. Finally Bernard looks ahead to the *cubiculum*, the bedchamber, the secret place of rest where the Bridegroom awaits. It is not to be identified with the study associated with intellectual contemplation, "a place of *lights*, but *not of rest*" (304). It is not the *"locus terribilis"* where one sees the evils of those who should be models of righteousness, "the pride, avarice, sacrilege, simony and callous indifference of prelates to truth and justice" (304) and is moved by dread "lest the roots of the same evil be hidden in himself" (305), a "dark night" experience that Bernard paradoxically identifies with that fear of the Lord that is the beginning of wisdom, because it brings an existential awareness of the holiness of God "through the experience of the mystery of evil" (305).

Introduction                                                                   lxxix

In the bedchamber of "true contemplation . . . God Himself is experienced, passively, in rest and in deepest secrecy" (306), an experience of the divine mercy that transcends strict justice, that is certain and stable and permanent, an experience of peace and rest beyond "all curiosity, all striving of the mind, all strain, all agitation of the interior and exterior senses" (306), a foretaste of that everlasting rest in the embrace of God promised to those who love Him; but in this life, Bernard concludes his sermon (perhaps in the rueful awareness that in having to deal once more with the papal schism he is about to be drawn again into a confrontation with the pettiness and machinations of the human quest for power in a fallen world), "unfortunately one does not remain there for long" (306). On this realistic note, this return from the mountaintop, Merton's commentary on the Canticles sermons and thus his conferences on "The Life, Works and Doctrine of St. Bernard" come to their end.

This set of conferences is of course not fully comprehensive. Not only does it omit any extended discussion of the remaining Sermons on the Canticle; it considers none of the other sermons in Bernard's vast corpus except for the Third Sermon in Paschal Time; a number of Bernard's treatises, notably *The Steps of Humility and Pride*, *On Grace and Free Choice*, and *On Consideration*, are referred to only in passing, and little attention is given to Bernard's letters. Nevertheless, Merton has provided his novices with a detailed exposure to Bernard the man, the monk, and the writer and certainly has made them aware of his central position in Cistercian history and spirituality. The St. Bernard conferences both continue and contrast with those on the *Carta Caritatis* and the *Consuetudines* that preceded them: Merton brings his audience to the next major phase of early Cistercian history, turning from documents that focus primarily on observances and organizational structure to a figure and a body of work that do not ignore the institutional dimension, as is evident in *De Praecepto et Dispensatione* and elsewhere, but that make it emphatically clear that the central purpose of Cistercian monastic life, from its origins in medieval France to the present day in rural Kentucky, is to live out the call of the Gospel to radical conversion and to a life of selfless love, made possible by conformation to the crucified and risen Christ and leading ultimately to participation in the very life of the Trinity.

\* \* \* \* \* \* \*

While the precise time frame for the initial presentation of the St. Bernard conferences remains somewhat nebulous, exact dating can be established for the final presentation of this material, the revised version now entitled *The Cistercian Fathers and Their Monastic Theology*, because Merton's classes had begun to be recorded in April 1962. These conferences began on January 5, 1963, and continued through August 8, 1964, a total of fifty-four classes spread out over the course of nineteen months. The new year of 1963 had brought two significant changes to the formation process at Gethsemani[261]—the merging of the novitiates of the choir monks and the brothers[262] and the beginning of a new monastic formation program in which recently professed monks in simple vows, rather than moving on immediately to classes preparing them for priestly ordination, continued their studies in monastic theology and spirituality, including most of Merton's conferences.[263] It thus seemed particularly appropriate to Merton, evidently, to include a revamped version of his St. Bernard conferences among the inaugural classes for this considerably larger and more varied group.

Only a single version of the text of *The Cistercian Fathers and Their Monastic Theology* is extant—the 176-page mimeographed

---

261. For an overview of these changes see *Pre-Benedictine Monasticism*, xi–xvi.

262. See *Turning toward the World*, 285 [1/4/1963].

263. See *School of Charity*, 155 (11/13/1962 letter to Ronald Roloff, osb); *Hidden Ground of Love*, 581 (1/11/1963 letter to E. I. Watkin); *School of Charity*, 163 (4/4/1963 letter to Archbishop Paul Philippe, op); *School of Charity*, 185 (11/25/63 letter to Mother M. L. Schroen).

reproduction[264] that was distributed to the novices and also made available to formation directors at other monasteries. Merton's own teaching typescript apparently has not survived, but it is apparent from an examination of the text of the mimeograph that it was based on the ditto reproduction of "The Life, Works and Doctrine of St. Bernard" rather than on Merton's own original typescript, since the various misreadings and other errors present in the ditto are found in the mimeograph as well. But the new text includes not only hundreds of brief additions and alterations to the first version of these conferences but also the incorporation of numerous large blocks of completely new material. The increase in length is indicated by the relative number of pages in old and new texts: while the final forty-five pages of the mimeograph contain seven appendices that have no equivalent in the "Life, Works and Doctrine" text, the seventy-three pages of the ditto have grown to 130 pages in the mimeo, more than 40 percent longer.[265] It is evident both from the new title and from the fact that the material is now labeled "PART ONE: SAINT BERNARD" (1) that Merton intended at the outset of these conferences to expand his coverage to discuss other significant writers of the early Cistercian tradition, but in fact all the additional material in the body of the text is incorporated into the existing St. Bernard material (and most of the appendices are also about Bernard). In fact, even after nineteen months of conferences, Merton will bring this course to a close not only without any discussion of William, Aelred, or other Cistercian fathers, but also without presenting all the material he had prepared on Bernard himself.

264. The title page and first page of text are unnumbered; consecutive numbering begins with "3" on the second page of text, running through "175" with "170" repeated erroneously on two pages—thus constituting 175 pages of text.

265. The comparison is not exact because part of the ditto is typed in pica and part in elite, whereas all of the mimeo is in elite, so that the new text is in fact somewhat more than 44 percent longer than the old, the percentage indicated by the relative number of pages in each.

Merton's additions begin on the very first page, as he adds a few sentences of explanatory material on the encyclical before beginning his numbered outline of its major points, and he also expands the single introductory sentence on Bernard's background to compare and contrast the eleventh and twelfth centuries with regard to the three-fold reaction of the new religious orders, the protomendicant evangelicals and the rise of a new humanism (10–11). But the first major insertion of new material is "An Introduction to St. Bernard of Clairvaux as a Person" (13–31), which is actually taken almost entirely[266] from conferences Merton gave as master of students at some point between September 1952 and November 1953,[267] a most unusual procedure for his novitiate conferences.

The contents of this added material raise the question of whether there may have been an intermediate version of the text, perhaps corresponding to a second presentation of the "Life, Works and Doctrine" conferences, at some time after the completion of the initial course in the latter part of 1957. More specifically, had Merton at least begun to revise his text before October 1958, when Pope Pius XII died? He makes a comparison here between the perspective of William of St. Thierry's hagiographic biography of Bernard and an article on Pius in a popular magazine, which he mentions in the original version of this text had been read in the refectory on the day he was presenting his conference back in the early 1950s.[268] It seems unlikely—though not impossible—that Merton would have retained this reference to a pope who had died more than four years earlier if he were

---

266. The section on *"Nature and Character of St. Bernard"* (18–19), drawing largely on the work of Jean Leclercq and Louis Bouyer, is inserted, and the transitional final sentence (31) has been added.

267. Thomas Merton, "An Introduction to St. Bernard of Clairvaux," "Monastic Orientation," 4, 88–99; it is likely from its position in the volume that this material was presented sometime in 1953, the Bernardine anniversary year.

268. "Introduction to St. Bernard," 88.

incorporating this material for the first time in 1963, and in fact when he discusses this material in his recorded conferences,[269] he substitutes an article on President Lyndon Johnson as a point of comparison with William's biography. A somewhat similar question arises in relation to the criteria for selecting the material included in his seven appendices, five of which are also borrowed from "Monastic Orientation": why were these particular conferences chosen from among a considerably wider group of Bernardine and other early Cistercian materials found in these conference collections from the early 1950s? A plausible explanation would be that Merton actually re-presented them to the novices, but this did not happen in connection with the *Cistercian Fathers* conferences, nor at any time after April 1962 when recording of the conferences began. Might he have done so in connection with a second presentation of the "Life, Works and Doctrine" course, sometime in the late 1950s? There is no documentary evidence indicating such a repetition, but it is at least possible and could explain the otherwise enigmatic appearance of these recycled materials in the final version of these conferences.

Whatever the case, the inclusion of a discussion of William's *Vita Prima*, or more precisely of the opening chapters of the *Vita* on Bernard's early life and education, his conversion, vocation, and novitiate at Cîteaux, provides a detailed prelude to the biographical outline of Bernard's monastic career, which had allotted only a single sentence to the earlier period of Bernard's life. Merton points out both that William is using the "conventional tropes of hagiography," which may seem "odd, artificial, absurd" to a contemporary audience, and that he is "unusual as medieval writers go in his objectivity" (13), writing from personal experience of the saint during his own lifetime. Merton counsels his audience: "remember he is a *panegyrist*—so beware—but take his fundamental view. Bernard {was} formed by special grace as a

---

269. Conference of June 20, 1964 (#118.3), available commercially as the first of four recorded conferences included in *Thomas Merton and St. Bernard of Clairvaux* (Rockville, MD: NowYouKnowMedia, 2014).

saint, a man of God, a sign of God for his times" (14). William provides helpful details about Bernard's upbringing and education but is primarily focused on the working of grace in one already much gifted by nature. As was already noted, Merton inserts new material from Leclercq and Bouyer that balances William's elevated portrait, pointing out that there was in Bernard "a definite aggressivity" along with a basic shyness, and that there is no reason to believe "that *all* St. Bernard's power-drives and initiatives were purely supernatural" (18). The complexity and even contradictions of his personality were not only an integral aspect of his extraordinary influence on his contemporaries but also a source of "dangers and problems" (19) that he had to wrestle with in his own life.[270] Merton is particularly interested in William's description of Bernard's conversion, which despite his virtuous behavior throughout his early life is presented as a definite change in direction, "a CONVERSION FROM VANITY TO TRUTH, FROM ILLUSION TO REALITY, operated by the fear of the Lord, in response to the personal call of Truth from within the depths of his own soul, promising him *rest* in certitude in exchange for *labor* and *anxiety* caused by the pursuit of illusion" (23), language that resonates with Merton's own characteristic understanding of the emergence of the true self. The momentous decision to enter Cîteaux is thus seen by William as marked by a *"flight from illusion,* flight from all that *savors of worldliness,* of

---

270. Merton's own ambivalence about Bernard at the very time he is presenting these conferences is evident in his journal entry for August 20, 1963, the saint's feast day: "Feast of the enigmatic Saint Bernard—whom we 'know' so well that we do not know him at all. That is, in the Order we are satisfied with a very rudimentary image of him (not yet a decent ikon!) or, at best, with an aspect of him. I am unable to resist the brilliance of his writing, especially the early treatises—I do not mean his rhetoric, which I can very easily resist. I prefer the dialectic of Anselm. The personality of Bernard is, to me, difficult and unappealing. Yet I admit I have never really known him and agree with Knowles that it is very difficult to know B." (*Dancing in the Water of Life,* 10–11).

*self-display*, pride, ambition, power, {along with a} positive desire to give himself to Christ and to rest secure" (26), and already in his time as a novice, the combination of his natural gifts, special graces, and generosity of response set Bernard apart as a special instrument of God's work. Merton sums up by pointing out that while Bernard's gifts and graces are unique to himself, his "zeal for the service of God" (30), carried out in prayer, work, and community life, can and should be imitated, and while his ascetic practices, which permanently damaged his health, were taken to an extreme, as even William recognized, Merton suggests that his commitment to self-discipline, his mortification of the senses, can be an inspiration, if not precisely an example, for contemporary Cistercians (perhaps a perspective more characteristic of 1953 than of 1963).

The first completely new block of material added to the conferences is Merton's detailed discussion of Bernard's set of four Marian sermons on the *Missus Est* (the opening words of the Annunciation story in Luke 1:26-38),[271] which is inserted before the commentary on the *De Diligendo Deo* in a section now headed "THE EARLIER WORKS OF SAINT BERNARD" (48). It is preceded by some prefatory comments (48–50) indicating Merton's belief that an objective, mainly academic approach to Bernard is ineffective in a monastic setting; much more beneficial for his audience is a more existential engagement with "a few characteristic works" of Bernard that allows them "to share in his experience and his worship, which were those of his time" (48). This requires a shift in perspective that will be able not only to recognize Bernard's eminence as both saint and writer but also "to see him as an example of the religious sensibility of the twelfth century with its deep *sense of the sacred*, {its} sense of the *reality of mystery*, {the} capacity to *reach sacred reality through symbol*, in which the invisible and visible are brought together" (48–49), a capacity largely lost in the modern era but one that is necessary in order

---

271. Pages 50–68 of this edition.

to appreciate Bernard and one that a sympathetic and personally engaged study of Bernard and his era can help to recover as a crucially important dimension of mature religious commitment.

Among the earliest of Bernard's works, the *Missus Est* homilies are thus a good starting point "to enter into the *mind* of Bernard as a saint and genius, and as a writer" (48).[272] They exemplify "the *symbolic* mentality of the Middle Ages," an aesthetic rather than scientific approach to reality that requires personal commitment to be understood: "A symbol *signifies*—it does not *explain*. It points to an invisible and sacred reality which we attain not by comprehension but by love and sacred awe, {by an} initiation to a higher world, and {by} the gift of ourselves" (54). For St. Bernard, "through such forms and figures as we have, principally in the Scriptures, we must learn to penetrate to this supreme reality in mystery" (58). Thus the significance of the (largely fanciful) etymologies of the various names in the Annunciation story—they are a means to draw the reader into a participation in the drama of the incarnation being described. This is true above all of the name of Mary, glossed as "Star of the Sea" by Bernard and his tradition and the focus of the most lyrical and most celebrated passage in these homilies, the repeated injunction in the second homily to call on Mary as guiding light for the journey (61–66). It is in this context that Merton considers the often exaggerated reputation of Bernard as a Marian theologian, pointing out that his approach is actually quite traditional; his contribution is less in the area of doctrine (where he opposed the "novelty" of the Immaculate Conception) than of a "powerful and personal development of Marian DEVOTION. . . . He still sees the mystery of Mary as inseparable from the mystery of the Incarnation and as an important aspect of that mystery. He does not separate the Mother from the Son" (66).

---

272. Merton in fact discusses only the first sermon at length, with attention to the key "*Stella Maris*" section of Sermon 2 and almost no consideration of the specific material of the two final sermons.

The *Missus Est* discussion is the only newly added section that is completely independent of the first version of the text. The other major blocks of additional material are all related to works already included in "Life, Works and Doctrine," but they radically reconfigure the original treatment, usually in quite interesting and revealing ways. Turning now to the *De Diligendo Deo*, Merton first rewrites and expands his introductory overview on the Cistercian theology of love,[273] drawing not only on the doctoral dissertation of the Cistercian Pacifique Delfgaauw but also on the earlier work of Gilson to refute the claim that Bernard's doctrine on the degrees of love is inconsistent. Merton endorses Delfgaauw's contention that Bernard's "theology is *synthetic* but not *systematic*" and is marked by a "profound internal coherence" (71) exhibiting the "real *completeness*, unity and wholeness which underlies all Cistercian thought in {the} twelfth century" (73). While this discussion basically makes the same points already found in the earlier version of the text, though in much greater detail, the other new material added to the *De Diligendo* section, entitled "BERNARD AND GUIGO,"[274] is completely new, and is about one and one-half times as long as the original discussion of the text of the treatise itself. In the original "Life, Works and Doctrine" text, Merton had not mentioned the letter to the Carthusians that Bernard had appended to the *De Diligendo* to comprise the final section of the work. In the revised text he calls this "*Epistola* 11 to Guigo" Bernard's "first short 'treatise' on love" (81) (indicating only in passing that it was incorporated into the *De Diligendo* text [see 72]), and he eventually outlines the teaching of the letter in twelve numbered points, emphasizing the importance of friendship in the development of Cistercian teaching on love; he highlights Bernard's use of the traditional trope of the three motivations for love—the fear of slaves, the hope of reward of mercenaries, and the selfless love of sons, which responds in

---

273. Pages 70–77 in this edition.
274. Pages 81–107 in this edition.

kind to the law of God's own being that is inscribed in the very order of creation itself: "*Charity, selfless love, is built into the very nature of things by God the Creator, for creation resembles the Creator*" (103), and it ultimately "FULFILLS BOTH THE LAWS OF FEAR AND OF DESIRE. It makes fear chaste; it makes desire ordinate" (107). But before considering the letter itself Merton looks at the gift that had prompted it, a copy of the *Meditations* of the Carthusian prior Guigo, called by its editor "the most original work of the period" (81), which had captured Merton's interest and aroused his enthusiasm to such an extent that he gives this work significantly more attention than Bernard's response. He quotes dozens of the aphoristic reflections of Guigo on truth, on self-love and attachments, on true and false charity, which directly influenced St. Bernard, on the power of good to overcome evil. Merton comments on this last saying: "*Guigo's doctrine is not only speculative on this point—it is a true Christian exposition of* AHIMSA (*non-violent love of truth*)" (86); earlier he had compared Guigo's idea of worldly (i.e., illusory) peace as rooted in ignorance to the Buddhist notion of *avidya* (82). Clearly Merton recognized in Guigo's laconic observations a medieval Christian expression of some of the insights he found most stimulating in his encounters with the wisdom of other religious traditions. Though largely a tissue of quotations, most still in the original Latin, the section on Guigo manifests a degree of fascination, the excitement of new, or renewed, discovery,[275] that is less evident in his subsequent discussion of Bernard's reply.

---

275. Merton's initial encounter with the *Meditations* was considerably less enthused: in a September 7, 1947 journal entry, he wrote, "I don't think as much of Guigo I's *Meditations* as I once thought I might. Very lapidary, but not on an interesting enough level. Why was he apparently writing for seculars? Or was he? I'd better read them some more before I can say" (*Entering the Silence*, 105). He evidently did not pursue the study of Guigo to any great extent at this time, writing to Jean Leclercq on October 9, 1950, that "we would like to get Wilmart's *Pensées du B. Guigue*, if this is Guigo the Carthusian. I have never yet gone into him. His lapidary style fascinates

In the additional material inserted into the *Apologia* discussion, Peter the Venerable, abbot of Cluny, plays a role comparable to, if rather less prominent than that of Guigo in the preceding section. There are actually three discrete blocks of new text.[276] The first and shortest provides an expanded analysis of Bernard's first letter, to his cousin Robert, "the 'first shot' in the battle between the White and Black monks" (126), in which he excoriates the Cluniacs for inducing his young relative to abandon the Cistercians for the less strenuous life of the Black Benedictine monastery. Then Merton follows up on his original paragraph about the importance of setting the *Apologia* in the context of Bernard's relationship with Peter by providing a detailed summary

---

me. He is better than Pascal. Yet I love Pascal" (*Survival or Prophecy?*, 24). He later writes to his Carthusian friend J.-B. Porion that his own current writing is mainly in the form of maxims, adding, "sometimes they seem to be a little like Guigo. I think he is very fine. I like his lapidary quality"; he goes on to say that he sometimes uses Guigo's maxims in spiritual direction (*School of Charity*, 33–34 [2/9/1952 letter]). Merton's rekindling of interest in Guigo at the time of the Cistercian Fathers lectures is evidently connected with "this beautiful letter of Guigo [misread as "Guido"] on solitude" that he translated on February 5, 1963 (*Turning toward the World*, 296), which was published in a limited edition by the Benedictine nuns of Stanbrook Abbey (*The Solitary Life: A Letter of Guigo*, trans. Thomas Merton [Worcester, UK: Stanbrook Abbey Press, 1963]). In his introduction, dated "Lent 1963," the very time when he was giving his conferences on Guigo, Merton calls him "one of those extraordinary figures in literature and in spirituality who, unknown and perhaps in some sense inaccessible to the many, have been accorded the most unqualified admiration by the discerning few" (1), and in reference to the *Meditations* he adds, "Some of the most fundamental ideas in Bernard's own doctrine of love were inspired by his Carthusian friend" (2). He concludes: "There is an inimitable naked power in the austere style of Guigo the Carthusian from which every suggestion of ornament, indeed every useless word is ruthlessly excluded. The extraordinary compression of this thought and language convey something of the fervor, the passionate seriousness of this saint and genius, a pure exemplar of the Carthusian spirit and certainly the greatest Carthusian writer" (4).

276. Pages 126–33, 134–39, 157–60 in this edition.

of the latter's early epistle to Bernard defending Cluniac usages with its "appeals to charity as against 'formalism' and 'rigidity'" (135). Merton comments: "*His principles are perfectly sound*, and St. Bernard not only agreed with them but adopted them. *His practice was dubious* and he himself made a serious reform at Cluny" (139). This is followed by a much briefer summary of a later, more conciliatory letter that still emphasizes the principle of charity but is considerably less defensive, "no longer criticizing the Cistercians but saying each should follow his own (order's) way to God. What matters is purity of intention in either case" (139). Then, following his analysis of the text of the *Apologia*, Merton adds a section on the reforms that Peter undertook at Cluny at least in part in consequence of Bernard's critique. He looks first at a late "encyclical letter" Peter wrote to the priors of all the Cluniac houses, criticizing a general atmosphere of complacency and indicating "that Peter had largely come around to St. Bernard's point of view" (158), and then examines in considerable detail the revision of the Cluniac *Statuta* four years earlier, in 1146, which "undoubtedly gives us the spirit and letter of the reforms carried on by Peter" (158): considering regulations on the office, fasting and abstinence, clothing, silence, formation, and manual labor, Peter appeals to the principle that distinguishes between essential elements of monastic life that cannot be changed—charity, humility, chastity—and those "aids to the practice of virtue" (159) that can and should be changed when, due to altered circumstances, they no longer fulfill that function; the revised regulations both lighten some of the burdensome requirements associated with liturgical life and "useless or merely external formalities" at Cluny (160) and tighten up much of the laxness in ascetical practice that had gradually become accepted there. Thus Bernard's treatise is now framed by consideration of the Cluniac perspective as it evolved under the leadership of Peter the Venerable, who became a close friend of Bernard.

Whereas Guigo was an inspiration and Peter a dialogue partner for Bernard, the figure who dominates the inserted material in the *De Conversione* section, the lengthiest of all, is Bernard's great adversary Peter Abelard, who virtually takes over this part of the text as Merton devotes twice as much space to discussing Abelard as he gives to the sermon analysis retained from the original text. He first adds a new overview of the intellectual ferment centered in Paris in the first half of the twelfth century,[277] slightly abridges and revises a paragraph on the Parisian schools that originally led directly into the discussion of Bernard's own attitude toward the intellectual life and the background to his sermon, and then launches into *"The Case of Peter Abelard,"*[278] the most important contemporary intellectual figure on the Parisian or even the European scene, with the rationale that "We cannot understand St. Bernard completely without knowing Abelard. At the same time, we cannot know Abelard if we merely look at him through the eyes of the Cistercians" (167). Merton's own fascination with Abelard soon becomes evident.[279]

Merton first rejects the reductive myths about Abelard as either the first rationalist and "apostle of free thought" or the proud, faithless rebel, seeing him as a flawed but brilliant innovator and situating him particularly in a monastic context, as one who "strove earnestly to find his place as a monk and finally . . . did die a holy death as a monk at Cluny, after admitting his errors" (167). Relying particularly on Gilson's *Héloise and Abélard*, he provides the basic facts of Abelard's life, his affair with Heloise, their marriage and the subsequent withdrawal into religious life,

---

277. Pages 160–65 in this edition.
278. Pages 167–96 in this edition.
279. See *Conjectures of a Guilty Bystander*, 245: "Meanwhile I have developed a great sympathy for Abelard, and a profound admiration for the human greatness of Héloise, which Gilson brings out so well in his book about them. Abelard in the end suffered far more than St. Bernard ever did (if one can estimate such things: and what would be the point of running up a score?). Abelard's weaknesses were great, his character had enormous flaws, he was vain and impulsive, he never learned to control himself as Bernard did (and Bouyer has rightly shown that Bernard's character had its flaws too). Bernard had vanity but overcame it, or controlled it. Abelard could never control his. It ruined him."

more turbulent for Abelard than for Heloise as abbess of the Paraclete, and his pious death, related to Heloise by Peter the Venerable in a "beautiful letter" (171) in which the abbot of Cluny consoles her by assuring her that "Christ reserves Abelard to be reunited to her after the resurrection" (172). Merton then turns to Abelard's wrestling with important theological and philosophical problems, not only the shortcomings and ambiguities of his thought but also its intellectual power and systematic approach that anticipates the great Summas of the next century, and quotes approvingly a long passage by David Knowles that finds him, despite his shortcomings, "one of the half-dozen most influential names in the history of medieval thought" (176). He then looks at the controversy between Abelard and both William of St. Thierry and Bernard, actually giving more attention to William's profound unease with Abelard's overly rationalistic lack of sensitivity to the dimension of divine mystery than to Bernard's more apodictic position that "Abelard is in the power of the devil, 'the very power which he denies!' " (181). Then come the circumstances of Abelard's condemnation at Sens and his retirement to Cluny, with a more detailed report of Peter's letter to Heloise, praising both herself and Abelard, who according to Peter was for Cluny "a treasure more precious than any gold or precious stone" (185) and who died in the odor of sanctity. (The implicit contrast in tone and content with Bernard is striking.) Finally, Merton turns to a topic that is least relevant to the ostensible focus of the section, Bernard's conversion sermon, but is obviously of considerable interest to him: Abelard's monastic doctrine as set forth in his Letter 8 to Heloise. Not only his quite traditional teaching on the vows (with special attention to "Abelard's concept of obedience since he has an established reputation as a rebel" [192]) and on the importance of silence and solitude for an authentic monastic life (a position firmly rooted in the desert tradition and highly critical of contemporary accommodations) but also the structure of the community, the physical arrangements ("almost Cistercian in simplicity," Merton comments [195]), and the roles of the various officers—all the way down to the portress and the vestiarian—are considered in detail by Merton, who is clearly attracted and even moved by a side of Abelard that is virtually unknown to his champions and critics alike.[280]

The final major insertion[281] in the text proper comes at the end of the *De Praecepto et Dispensatione* section, which Merton had radically abridged by cutting out all the long preliminary discussion on the history of the question of the obligation to obey a religious rule under pain of sin—the only significant omission of material from the "Life, Works and Doctrine" text—presumably because it was so technical and could easily be dispensed with without affecting the discussion of Bernard's own treatment of the topic (though a few salient details, like the date of the treatise—1128—get lost in the process of cutting). Perhaps in compensation, Merton follows the "points on stability" that conclude the discussion of *De Praecepto* with "a few samples of ordinary letters about the routine business of deciding vocations, recommendations and advice concerning vocations, and especially regarding transfer to another monastery" (225). He looks at more than a dozen letters *in toto*, some very briefly and others in more detail, the first three recommending acceptance or re-acceptance of particular persons, but almost all the rest dealing with cases in which religious of other observances (mainly Benedictines) had been allowed to become Cistercians. Merton emphasizes the differences in tone and strategy found in the different letters, from that of a "politician" (226) in Letter 34, to "effusive affection" (227) in Letter 35 (addressed to the subject of the controversy brought up in the previous letter), to "gracious and

---

280. In a journal entry dated January 18, 1964, Merton writes: "I wonder if anyone reads the monastic letters, etc. of Abelard. They are full of fine traditional material, in the manner of Jerome, clear, precise, and among the best monastic writings of the twelfth century. I am reading them now for the course on Bernard, in connection with *De Conversione*. Ought to do an article on them but I don't have time" (*Dancing in the Water of Life*, 63–64).

281. Pages 224–33 in this edition.

clever" (227) in equating Clairvaux with the Jerusalem to which an English cleric had set out on pilgrimage in Letter 67, to conciliatory in Letters 68 and 69, to rather pugnacious, even "in some sense cynical" (229) in Letters 70 and 71 (to an obscure but supercilious abbot for whom Bernard obviously has little respect), to defensive in response to a letter from the abbot of Prémontré in Letter 328. This pendant to the *De Praecepto* material not only provides concrete examples illustrating the extent to which Bernard's practice does or does not accord with the theory put forth in the treatise but also gives some sense of the ordinary give-and-take of unremarkable situations and relationships that would have occupied much of Bernard's attention on a day-to-day basis, quite different from composing mystical masterpieces or intervening in major political and ecclesial crises.

This is the last of the new material added to the revised text of the conferences. The material has become, from one perspective, less unified and coherent. But it is also richer and more comprehensive with its evidence of Merton's broadened sympathies and interests. The new "fathers" whose "monastic theology" is explored are not Cistercians but the Carthusian Guigo and the Cluniac Peter the Venerable and even, or perhaps especially, the complex rebel turned monastic founder and legislator Peter Abelard, with whom the Merton of 1964 obviously felt a sympathy and rapport far different from the conventional condemnation expressed in the biographical sketch of Bernard found in *The Ascent to Truth*. Thus in its final form, *The Cistercian Fathers and Their Monastic Theology* is a more intriguing and more revealing volume than it would have been if it had continued to focus exclusively on Bernard and, perhaps, than it would have been if it had added sections on other early Cistercians rather than the less-expected figures who now interact in varied ways with the "Last of the Fathers."

The other Cistercian fathers, however, are not completely excluded. For whatever obscure reason, Merton has appended seven appendices to the revised text, all but the first and third drawn from his scholasticate conferences of the early 1950s; four of these are still completely focused on Bernard, the other three, considerably shorter, incorporating material from four other early Cistercian writers. Appendix 1[282] considers Sermons 37 and 38 *De Diversis*, a carefully balanced pair of which the first emphasizes the fulfillment already present in the monastic community which seeks God only because they have already found Him in being found by Him; the second makes clear that this finding and being found is not realized simply in sensible consolation but in the patience and poverty of those who put their trust not in their own frail powers but in God alone, experienced "in loving acceptance and trust and {a} spirit of penance and compunction" (310). Appendix 4[283] is a long examination of Bernard's Lenten spirituality as found in his sermons for the season. As he had in his conference/article on Advent, Merton finds Bernard approaching Lent as a "sacrament," the continuing presence of Christ in the world, in this case "the mystery of Christ still suffering in the world in His Mystical Body" (321). He points out that for Bernard it is not simply exterior penitential practices but interior conversion that is the heart of the Lenten journey, a deepening of humility that incorporates joy as well as sorrow, "two different aspects of one thing: that charity which unites us to God the Father, in Christ, by the bond of the Holy Spirit" (332); it is compunction that integrates these two dimensions by fostering genuine interior detachment and undermines any tendency toward formalism and false piety, an insight that Merton finds Bernard and John of the Cross to have in common: for Bernard, the "freedom of the perfectly detached soul . . . the same thing

---

282. Pages 307–11 in this edition (not found in "Monastic Orientation").

283. "Monastic Orientation," 3, 38a–51 (pages 320–38 in this edition). Page 44 of this material, headed "joy and sorrow" and preceding the text with the identical heading (page 328 in this edition), was not included in the *Cistercian Fathers* typescript; it consists of an X-shaped diagram showing the different consequences of charity and concupiscence, leading to God and to hell respectively, followed by a listing of characteristics of the contrasting pairs of evil joy and evil sorrow, true joy and true sorrow.

that we find in St. John of the Cross . . . is the true fruit and grace of Lent, the *'mysterium'* which makes God known to His friends" (337–38). The following Appendix, titled "ORDINAVIT IN ME CARITATEM,"[284] is intended by Merton to build on "the idea of the total conversion of our whole being to God by love" (338) found in the Lenten sermons. The theme of the "ordering of charity" is found in Sermons 49 and 50 on the Canticle of Canticles, another contrasting pair, of which the first "is a regular, thoughtful ascetic conference on the interior life, an objective series of reflections on the function of *discretion* in keeping our movements of fervor in order" (339) that suddenly raises the question of the proper ordering of charity in Bernard's own life and responsibilities as a superior, a topic that is raised but not resolved in this sermon, but which in the following sermon Bernard "treats . . . (to his own satisfaction) on an entirely new level—profound speculation, deep psychology, in which he is completely involved as a person: he not only thinks the problem out, he *lives* it out for his monks. . . . Here St. Bernard is most original and most himself—{and} also most profound" (339–40). The first not only emphasizes the central importance of discretion in bringing order to the life of virtue but also considers the significance of communal order in the Church and in the monastery, the integration and synthesis of complementary roles in the Body of Christ, including that of the superior, who experiences the tension between the call to personal union with God and his responsibility to the community. This issue is resolved in Sermon 50 with Bernard's recognition that "there are *two* charities to be ordered, and they must be balanced together" (353)—effective charity regulated by concrete needs of particular people in particular circumstances, and affective charity that "sees values as they are in themselves—eternally in God—hence it places God first, contemplation first" (353). These horizontal and vertical

---

284. "Monastic Orientation," 3, 53–63 (pages 338–55 in this edition); this material was originally followed by a five-page appendix (64–68) focusing on discretion in Gregory the Great and Thomas Aquinas as well as Bernard that was not included in the *Cistercian Fathers* typescript.

dimensions intersect and are integrated "in so far as by discretion we learn to direct our love to God as He is concretely found in the requirements of the present situation, especially in the service of our neighbor, even though at the sacrifice of contemplation" (354). The seventh and final Appendix,[285] on the rest or repose of contemplation ("*Quies Contemplationis*"), is the longest and does serve as an appropriate culmination of the entire text, though some of its sources are also discussed in the main body of the conferences. The first of its three parts focuses on the ascent to contemplative rest outlined in the three degrees of truth that Bernard describes in the *De Gradibus Humilitatis*, an important early treatise not discussed elsewhere in the text. In the first degree, reason, blinded by ignorance and enslaved by the illusions and anxieties of a life given over to pursuit of material satisfaction, is liberated by the humility of self-knowledge. In the second, the reason is led from recognition of the justice of its own condemnation to the experience of divine mercy that instills a spirit of merciful compassion toward the failings of others: "It is Jesus Whom I love in the weakness and imperfection of my brother" (364). As ascent to the first degree of truth is prompted by the Word and to the second by the Holy Spirit, so ascent to the third degree, contemplative union with the divine Spouse, is associated with the action of the Father. It is a "sleep" (372) that is also on a deeper level an awakening to the ineffable reality of God, "a new world *more real than the everyday reality of life*" (373), sometimes seen in and through this reality and sometimes transcending and leaving ordinary reality behind, a "*raptus*" that "takes us *entirely out of ourselves*" (374). The second section traces the same path to contemplation according to the four degrees of love set forth in the *De Diligendo Deo*, already discussed by Merton in the commentary on that treatise, but focusing here particularly on the fourth and final degree, loving ourselves for God's sake, fulfilling the purpose of creation and redemption, "find[ing] ourselves in

---

285. "Monastic Orientation," 4, 67–86 (pages 359–95 in this edition).

God and see[ing] ourselves from within God, loving ourselves with His love of us, which is also His love of Himself" (377). Such a perfectly pure, totally self-forgetful love is possible only for brief periods in the world of space and time, limitations and responsibilities, but will be the permanent state of the resurrected life. The final section looks at Bernard's teaching on the *"quies contemplationis"* in the Sermons on the Canticle, first Sermon 23, with its "cellars" (380–83) and "bedchambers" (383–89), paralleling in somewhat more detail the analysis of the sermon that concludes the conferences proper, then Sermon 52, in which the divine Bridegroom, having embraced His Spouse with the left hand of fear of judgment and the right hand of "assured hope of heaven" (390), now "protects and guards the 'sleeping' soul so that it may not be disturbed or awakened by anything from without or from within itself" (392). This is the true repose of contemplation, "a watchful and life-giving sleep which is a beginning of eternal life and puts an end to our 'death' here below" (392), at peace in the divine presence beyond restless desires and temptations and distractions, beyond "all images and representations and words and reasonings and human concepts and manners of thinking" (394). This is a fitting if apparently somewhat fortuitous "last word" on Bernard's contemplative teaching.

The remaining three appendices do finally bring out four other early Cistercian authors for brief "cameo" appearances. Appendix 2[286] considers the topic of "SELF-WILL AND DISOBEDIENCE" as found in Isaac of Stella's Third Sermon on the Assumption. It consists largely of Merton's translations of excerpts from the sermon, in which Isaac is criticizing those (monks in particular) who have formally renounced their own will and yet in practice are constantly trying to arrange things so that they are able to have their own way. This attitude marks their relationships not only with other people—self-will as the "source of all conflict and social division" (312)—but also with God Himself, a futile attempt to make reality bend to one's own wishes. "Obe-

---

286. "Monastic Orientation," 6, 96 (pages 311–13 in this edition).

dience to God," Merton interprets Isaac as saying, "is simply adaptation to reality—the consent to conform to what is. If we insist on acting as if reality were other than it is, and try to force it to be so, then we are compelled against our will and judgement to submit to reality unwillingly" (312). Only by submitting to the will of God, as Mary above all demonstrates, does one discover "a life of joy and gratitude, liberty and peace" (312–13).

The following Appendix, on spiritual rest,[287] considers two early Cistercian commentaries on the verse "In all things I sought rest" (Sir. 24:11): Guerric of Igny's Sermon 3 on the Assumption and the treatise *"De Requie Caelesti"* of Baldwin of Ford (later the archbishop of Canterbury). Guerric relates the pause in harvesting work due to the mid-August celebration of the Marian feast to the deeper rest in Christ, which he likens to being at the still center of the turning wheel of this world. Mary is the pattern for this stillness, finding rest in the bosom of the Father as the divine Wisdom found rest in her flesh: "Unless Wisdom can find rest in our hearts, we will never find rest in heaven" (316), and Wisdom, Christ the Word, is at rest when He is recognized and cared for in the poor, when work is done not in restless anxiety but in quiet liberty of spirit. Wisdom is at rest in the "generosity and self-forgetfulness that enables us to find rest in all things, because we are ready for everything . . . . upset by nothing," and "do all things willingly, in order to rest in Christ" (317). Like Guerric, Baldwin sees the words of Wisdom seeking rest as Christ's quest for rest in us and for ourselves in Him: "so that God might rest in man, being perfectly pleased with man (image–likeness) and man might rest in God, loving all God's will and separated in no way from God" (317). To "rest" from sin, finding a place of repose in the "tabernacle" of the Church, in the "unity of the common life," is to become a place of rest for God, made possible because God first "rested in the 'Tabernacle of the Humanity of Christ'" (318). Even distractions and temptations and human weaknesses, one's own and those of others, can assist in the search for "true

---

287. Pages 313–20 in this edition (not found in "Monastic Orientation").

rest" when they are recognized as evidence that it is "a gift of God," a peace "that we cannot attain . . . merely by our own powers" (319) but only through the redemptive work of Christ. "Make in me Thy Tabernacle," Baldwin prays, "and rest in me that I might rest in Thee. For Thou dost rest in us by making us rest" (319).

The shortest (and oddest) of the appendices consists almost entirely of excerpts on silence, in the original Latin, from Adam of Perseigne's Letter 29.[288] This material was originally appended to a conference from May 1952 on exterior and interior silence in Adam,[289] drawing both on this letter and on Letter 2, which in turn followed on a broader consideration of Adam's *Mariale*,[290] where his doctrine on silence is developed at length. For some reason, perhaps to serve as a prelude to the long final appendix on the "*quies contemplationis*," Merton decided to include only the quotations, with none of the preceding explanatory material, in this sixth Appendix. Silence is presented by Adam first as the appropriate response of attentiveness in listening to the Word, then as true receptivity to the Spirit, who comes upon the disciples as tongues of flame, with seven gifts that are experienced as seven silences as they still the uproar of vices, "above all the Gift of *Fortitude*," which "produced the silence most favorable to the generation of the Word" (358). The brief final excerpts focus on the silence of spiritual childhood that is necessary in order to receive the saving Word and the role of discernment in fruitful silence—the ability to know when, why, and how a true word may and should arise out of silence.

This supplementary material, an apparently random selection of Cistercian teachings with no obvious criteria for inclusion, complements but also at times overlaps the contents of the main body of the conferences to which they are attached. As has already been suggested, their appearance here may be the result of their being re-presented orally (or in the case of the two appendices

288. "Monastic Orientation," 3, 87–88 (pages 356–59 in this edition).
289. "Monastic Orientation," 3, 81–86.
290. "Monastic Orientation," 3, 72–80.

not found in "Monastic Orientation," perhaps presented for the first time) for an audience of novices, but this did not happen during the nineteen months beginning in January 1963 when the *Cistercian Fathers and Their Monastic Theology* conferences were being given, nor in the eight months immediately preceding, nor at any time after the conferences ended in November 1964. In fact, the recordings of this course reveal that Merton did not include a significant portion of the revised text of the St. Bernard conferences themselves in his series of classes.

\* \* \* \* \* \* \*

In his opening conference for this course, on January 5, 1963, Merton uncharacteristically seems somewhat ill at ease, almost apologetic about subjecting his audience to the work of St. Bernard, whose "flowery" style is not in tune with a contemporary sensibility, at best an acquired taste—like Tibetan food with the Dalai Lama! This apparent discomfort might be attributed to the fact that his class size had just increased substantially with the addition of the brother novices and newly professed monks, but in his journal entry for that day he indicates that his audience had actually expanded considerably beyond even these contingents:

> Large group of brothers at my class on St. Bernard today—more than I thought—not only all the simple professed but perhaps also solemn professed (I am not sure!). Somebody is probably making them come, and some surely looked as if they had no reason of their own to be there. This is embarrassing, and also quite foolish. I have suddenly, and for no real reason, become part of a magic and desperate answer someone has dreamed up for the Brothers. I have to take the assignment as it comes, from God, and treat them with sincerity and concern for their *real* needs. They do not need a "course on St. Bernard"!! I would much prefer simply to have small and quiet classes with my novices—after all, that is supposed to be my job![291]

291. *Turning toward the World*, 286.

It is not surprising, therefore, that Merton was more than a little disconcerted as he looked out on the group assembled before him on that first day. He had in fact already decided, and announced to his audience, that a conventional "course" on St. Bernard would be a "waste of time" for present-day monks, and that what is needed is to put Bernard's teaching into a contemporary context, to figure out what he was trying to do and to do something analogous for today.[292] Thus rather than spending any time on historical and biographical background as found in the opening section of the printed text, he will jump immediately into a discussion of Bernard's Marian sermons, which he proceeds to do, in the process becoming more relaxed and leaving behind the somewhat constrained tone with which he had begun.

This "engaged" reading of texts, to try to understand both what they would have meant for Bernard and his monks and what they might mean for Merton and his monks and novices, will be the approach Merton will continue to take throughout this set of conferences, often developing more explicitly the concrete applications already present in the written text. As was his customary method in his classes, he is selective about the particular details from the written text that he includes in his actual presentation; his intention here, as in all his conferences, is to highlight the connections of the topic at hand to the formation of his audience.

The first few minutes of the conferences, as was his usual practice, were often given over to details about the monastery or to news items Merton thought it important for his listeners to be

---

292. Merton is simply repeating here what he has written in the revised text: "The best thing to do with St. Bernard is to read him together and explain what he is trying to do. A mere 'course on' St. Bernard is practically useless in our monasteries. It is of no avail to know the list of the books he wrote or even the main themes he treated, nor even to know the outlines of his theological thought. These matters are helpful only when they serve to clarify a reading of St. Bernard that helps us to share in his experience and his worship, which were those of his time" (48).

aware of. For example, on February 2, 1963, and again on May 18, he reports on the whereabouts of former novices who have recently gone elsewhere; he mentions putting up screens and fighting a brush fire on March 30; the anticipated arrival of a yogi (and the upcoming celebration of "Derby Day") is announced on May 4, the imminent visits of Benedictine Aelred Graham, an Argentinian poet (Miguel Grinberg), and a Czech theologian (Jan Lochman), all on March 7, 1964, and later the visits of Archbishop Thomas Roberts and Rabbi Zalman Schachter (May 23); the rearrangement of novitiate Scripture classes (no longer taught by Merton himself) is announced on June 15. He mentions trouble in Haiti on May 11, 1963; the election of Pope Paul VI ("a great man" in need of prayers) on June 22; the stained glass windows being made at Gethsemani's daughter house in South Carolina for bombed Negro churches on July 20; the Vatican Council's approval of a vernacular liturgy on October 12; the coup in Vietnam on November 9, and of course the assassination of President Kennedy, which takes up most of the conference period on November 23, the day after the shooting; he gives news of one of his correspondents (Evora Arca de Sardinia) having to separate from her husband (a Bay of Pigs prisoner) on February 15, 1964; on May 2 he predicts, correctly, a long hot summer for the civil rights movement; on July 18 he mentions the nomination of Barry Goldwater for president, and on August 8 the Tonkin Gulf incident. The effect of these juxtapositions of current events, local and global, with the spirituality and theology of a twelfth-century Cistercian abbot is to remind his audience, at least implicitly, that such teachings are not to be considered in a vacuum but incarnationally, in the context of the minor and major events of their own and other people's actual daily lives.

In the three conferences (January 5 to February 9) he devotes to the *Missus Est* homilies, he tries to teach the students how to remember and interiorize the content of the material—first by paying attention, then by pinpointing the subject (as though preparing to report for a newspaper), then most importantly by adopting the appropriate perspective on the material—in the case of Bernard, realizing that he is not using an Aristotelian logical approach but trying to develop a sense of the sacred to help his readers or listeners to experience the reality of mystery themselves through the mediation of symbols that point beyond the literal level. He contrasts Bernard's movement from words to the Word to experiencing the sweetness of God's love with Aquinas's movement from beings to Being to experiencing the light of Truth—adding that he actually prefers the second, the focus on Being as the ultimate goal. As usual, he uses humor to enliven his presentations, here provoking laughter by his droll retelling of the legend that after his death, Bernard was seen in a vision with a stain on his white cowl because of his failure to accept the Immaculate Conception.

No fewer than twenty conferences (February 9 to August 26) are taken up with the *De Diligendo Deo*—though almost half of these first provide a general overview of Bernard's understanding of love and then focus mainly on Guigo and Bernard's letter to the Carthusians. Merton distinguishes more explicitly than in the written text the three terms Bernard uses: *amor*, which is equivalent to the Greek *eros*—passionate desire; *dilectio*, the calm, harmonious love of friendship (*philia*); and *caritas*, the fruition and fulfillment of divine union (*agape*). He relates Bernard's theology of image and likeness to the purpose of the new monastic formation program—to connect with sources that can "slake the thirst" for meaning, for God, that brought each of them to the monastery, and goes all the way back to Gilson's *The Spirit of Mediaeval Philosophy* to ground the fundamental insight that the more the image is faithful to the original, the more it is true to itself: "therefore only by loving do we find our true self," and to love truly is possible only through the Holy Spirit—it is "the divine action in us" that enables us "to discover our true identity." He emphasizes not only Guigo's importance for Bernard but also the importance of his insights for today's monks: that the first step toward truth is to accept the truth of our own falsity, or that pure subjectivity paradoxically turns the beloved into an object, because it has no real relationality, or that happiness consists in letting go of a limited goal, not latching on to some "thing" instead of the infinite, or that God is immediately present to the soul but is not experienced immediately. In discussing Bernard's letter and its three types of love, he notes that neither fear nor desire leads to authentic freedom, which is found only in doing the will of God without any concern for something else, and warns against an attitude in which "my idea becomes more important than the truth." He notes in passing that they are making slow progress: what should take fifteen minutes takes five weeks because he gets going on a particular point rather than following the chain of reasoning—but this observation doesn't motivate him to move more rapidly, recognizing as he does that making the material come alive is more important than keeping to some strict timetable. Looking at charity as the "law" by which God Himself lives, he points out that living by another law, the law of one's own will, is a burden that is ultimately insupportable; this insight has a "fabulous implication": "punishment" is actually allowing one to have one's own way! He later notes that they're not "getting anyplace" with St. Bernard, but adds that "you don't have to get anyplace in the monastery," since "we're already there"—there's no need to see results but just to abide in God's love. He emphasizes that Bernard's teaching on the degrees of love in the *De Diligendo* emphasizes that human beings were made for love, that even in loving naturally one is giving glory to God, because living "according to nature"—human nature as God intended it—is good, and that it is only disordered love, misdirected love, that fails to honor God. In discussing Bernard's four degrees of love, he not only points out the traditional use of this number but also notes that seven is a famous number, referring to St. Teresa's seven mansions in *The Interior Castle* and making a humorous allusion to *The Seven Storey Mountain* and the seven levels of Mount Purgatory. He finishes up his discussion of the *De Diligendo* by praising Bernard as a great creative writer who appealed to the whole person, to the imagination and the emotions as well as the mind, but notes that a different approach is needed today, depending less on rhetoric, which can tend to antagonize as much as to convince, than on person-to-person contact.

After a month's gap due to time spent in the hospital for his back problems, Merton returns to Bernard at the end of September with seven conferences on the *Apologia*, taking the course up to the beginning of Advent (September 28 to November 23).[293] As in the written text, he prefaces his discussion of the treatise with a look at Bernard's first letter, to his cousin Robert, where the interior struggle between the severe Bernard and the gentle Bernard is on display. He goes on to emphasize the importance of discretion, noting in an aside that imprudence, lack of discretion, wrecked Bernard's own health as a young monk. Providing an initial overview of the controversy between Cîteaux and Cluny, Merton points out that Peter the Venerable's principle of "charity first" will be taken up by Bernard and that Bernard's practical applications will be adopted by Cluny, so that there is a mutual learning process that ensues. The whole affair demonstrates that tradition and renewal must go together—a matter that is relevant to the reform of the liturgy at the present time. While you can't wait for everybody to agree with change, for then it will never happen, there must be continuity in essentials. The need for charity is central, but there is also a need for flexibility and even variety in accidentals—"don't argue about the color of the habit!" As Bernard admonishes his own fellow Cistercians, lack of charity undermines monastic life even more than lack of austerity: "there's an easier way to hell than this!" he warns—pride in one's own deprivations.

Returning to Bernard at the beginning of 1964, after a month's break, Merton gives a conference, not taken from his Cistercian fathers text, on Bernard's Epiphany sermons (January 4, 1964), then turns to the sermon on conversion that will occupy him, directly or indirectly, for the next seventeen classes (January

---

293. In a journal entry for September 28, 1963, Merton writes: "Today started conferences on Cîteaux and Cluny and was happy that everyone really seemed so glad to have me back. And probably they were so because they could see I was glad to be back with them" (*Dancing in the Water of Life*, 20).

11 to June 13). He first sets the stage by looking at the intellectual ferment and social upheaval of the twelfth century, then turns to Abelard as the embodiment of both the potential and the problems of this new era—Bernard sees only the latter. As in the written text, in these conferences Merton actually spends more time on Abelard—as a figure of controversy in his personal and his public life and as theological innovator and as monastic founder—than on Bernard here, with only the four concluding conferences (May 16 to June 13) actually focused on the *De Conversione* itself. But when he does get to the sermon, he notes that "important truth always changes your life," whereas Abelard's conception of "truth" was largely abstract and without personal application. Bernard challenged the "clerics" (seminarians) in his audience to take the quest for truth personally—to recognize the need for conversion, that it is good to feel bad, to have a sense of moral culpability, a rational (not neurotic) guilt. He emphasizes the need to face reality, to see the truth: the reason is converted when it stands back and evaluates actions according to faith; this, in turn, leads the will to begin to desire and to love the good, to reach the point where it becomes easier to live a good life than a bad life, enslaved to illusion and passion. The final step is to purify the memory, the third of the soul's powers, which can "torpedo the whole thing," Merton says, if one is unable to let go of the after-effects of sin, a fixation on one's past; this entails not "spiritual amnesia" but "seeing myself in a new light—as a forgiven sinner," and so as one able to forgive myself and to forgive another like myself as well. This is the culmination of Bernard's message in the *De Conversione*.

In the last of the conferences on this sermon, Merton actually says that Bernard "gets boring" because what he's talking about ultimately can't be expressed in words, so that the language becomes a barrier. It's apparent at this point that Merton is getting ready to wind up the class, and to do so, he circles back almost to the beginning of his written text, spending three classes (June 20 to July 18) looking at William of St. Thierry's biographical account of Bernard's own conversion and early monastic life as a follow-up to his call to conversion in the sermon, emphasizing once again as he had at the outset that there is a need to avoid the danger of a stereotyped image of Bernard and to "translate" his story into today's context. For contemporary monks, as for Bernard, the fundamental problem, Merton maintains, is idolatry, making a means into an end, and so living in contradiction to reality. While today's monastics cannot replicate Bernard's unique gifts of nature and grace, they can find and use their own gifts with the same generosity that Bernard showed. Merton then concludes the course with a single class (August 8) that looks at a few of the "vocation letters" Bernard had appended to the *De Praecepto et Dispensatione* section, calling the letters a good source of insight on Bernard as a person and a monastic leader, though difficult to read in succession from beginning to end.

There are no conferences on *De Praecepto* itself, which is mentioned only in passing in the context of the *Apologia*, no discussion of the Third Resurrection Sermon and its doctrine of self-will and the common will, and an astonishing omission—no conferences at all on what Merton himself calls Bernard's greatest and most important work, the Sermons on the Canticle. By this point, he is evidently burned out on Bernard, or at least perceives that his audience has had enough or more than enough and needs to move on to something else (which turns out to be a decided change of pace, a series on art and poetry that continues until Merton retires as novice master and enters the hermitage a full year later), and so the Canticles section is left unmentioned—though it is available in the printed mimeograph—along with those seven appendices—to anyone who might have been interested in extending his acquaintance with Bernard beyond the confines of the live presentations.

\* \* \* \* \* \* \*

The final version of the *Cistercian Fathers and Their Monastic Theology* conferences is available only in the mimeograph reproduction, which therefore serves as the copy text for all the blocks of material added in the main body of this second recension, as well as for the additions and alterations made to the original

"Life, Works and Doctrine of Saint Bernard" text. Because the basis for the revised text was, however, not Merton's own typescript of "Life, Works and Doctrine" but the "ditto" reproduction that introduced various misreading and other errors, the critical text of these conferences found in the present volume has restored all the correct readings of the original material found in the typescript but not in the two subsequent versions.[294] The text of the material in "AN INTRODUCTION TO ST. BERNARD OF CLAIRVAUX AS A PERSON" and in the five appendices drawn from the "Monastic Orientation" volumes incorporates numerous readings from the original versions that in the judgment of the editor were inadvertently altered or omitted in the process of being retyped for inclusion in *Cistercian Fathers and Their Monastic Theology*. Appendix A records first the additions and alterations made by Merton for the revised *Cistercian Fathers and Their Monastic Theology* text, including transcriptions of material (chiefly the first part of the *De Praeceptione et Dispensatio* section) omitted in the revised text or inserted in the typescript but not included as part of the text in the ditto and consequently not found in the mimeograph as well; secondly, all readings accepted from the original typescript are recorded; a list is provided of all additions and alterations found in the typescript itself, including those made in the process of typing as well as those that are handwritten, to make available at least for this first version of the text a record of Merton's changes made in the process of composition; finally two lists of variant readings between material first appearing in the volumes of "Monastic Orientation," the first consisting of readings adopted from the earlier texts and the second of substantive variants not adopted in this volume, are provided.

---

294. *The Cistercian Fathers and Their Monastic Theology* is the only set of conferences given by Merton as novice master that has previously appeared in print. The mimeograph text was published in a lightly edited form by Chrysogonus Waddell, ocso, in his journal *Liturgy O.C.S.O.* 26, no. 3 (1992): 9–51; 27, no. 1 (1993): 15–53; 27, nos. 2–3 (1993): 37–62; 28, no. 1 (1994): 9–46; 28, no. 2 (1994): 27–52; 28, no. 3 (1994): 29–74; 29, no. 1 (1995): 33–57; 29, no. 2 (1995): 33–50; 29, no. 3 (1995): 9–36.

All substantive additions made to the text, in order to turn elliptical or fragmentary statements into complete sentences, are included in braces, as are the few emendations incorporated directly into the text, so that the reader can always determine exactly what Merton himself wrote. No effort is made to reproduce Merton's rather inconsistent punctuation, paragraphing, abbreviations, and typographical features; a standardized format for these features is established that in the judgment of the editor best represents a synthesis of Merton's own practice and contemporary usage: e.g., all Latin passages are italicized unless specific parts of a longer passage are underlined by Merton, in which case the underlined section of the passage is in Roman type; all other passages underlined by Merton are italicized; words in uppercase in the text are printed in small caps; periods and commas are uniformly included within quotation marks; patterns of abbreviation and capitalization, very inconsistent in the copy text, are regularized. All references to primary and secondary sources are cited in the notes. Untranslated Latin passages in the original text are left in Latin but translated in the notes; if Merton has himself used or cited a particular translation, that source is used in the notes; otherwise, the translations are by the editor.[295] Scripture passages are quoted from the Douay-Rheims version customarily used by Merton.

Appendix B provides a table correlating the written text and the taped lectures, including indications of those conference recordings that have been made available commercially, in order to facilitate comparison of Merton's written version of the material as published in this edition with the conferences as actually delivered to the novices and young monks in his class. Appendix C lists Merton's other works in which St. Bernard and the other

---

295. I have found the translations provided by Waddell in his published texts, both those taken from existing English versions and those made by Waddell himself, very helpful, but except for those translations referred to by Merton himself I have preferred to translate as literally as possible to facilitate an understanding of the passages Merton has quoted in the original Latin.

Cistercian Fathers are discussed, followed by a selected list of important recent translations and studies of these figures, which will provide helpful updating on material discussed by Merton.

* * * * * * *

In conclusion I would like to express my gratitude to all those who have made this volume possible:

- to the Trustees of the Merton Legacy Trust, Peggy Fox, Anne McCormick, and Mary Somerville, for permission to publish *The Cistercian Fathers and Their Monastic Theology* conferences;

- to the late Robert E. Daggy, former director of the Thomas Merton Center, Bellarmine College (now University), Louisville, Kentucky, for first alerting me to the project of editing Merton's monastic conferences, and for his encouragement in this and other efforts in Merton studies;

- to Brother Patrick Hart, ocso, the founding editor of the Monastic Wisdom series, for his friendship and guidance in the publication of this series of volumes of Thomas Merton's monastic conferences;

- to James Finley, whose writing and speaking on the work of his former novice master have contributed significantly to making Merton's work known and appreciated, for his insightful preface to this volume;

- to Paul M. Pearson, director and archivist of the Merton Center, and Mark C. Meade, assistant archivist, for their gracious hospitality and valued assistance during my research visits to the Center;

- to publisher Hans Christoffersen, managing editor Lauren Murphy, copy editor Patrick McGowan, and production manager Colleen Stiller at Liturgical Press, for guiding this and previous volumes of Merton's conferences through the publication process with grace and efficiency;

- to the Gannon University Research Committee, which provided a grant that allowed me to pursue research on this project at the Merton Center and at various libraries;
- to Mary Beth Earll of the interlibrary loan department of the Nash Library, Gannon University, for once again providing invaluable assistance by locating and procuring various obscure volumes;
- to library staff of the Hesburgh Library of the University of Notre Dame, the Latimer Family Library of St. Vincent College, and the Institute of Cistercian Studies Collection at the Waldo Library of Western Michigan University, especially Neil Chase, for assistance in locating important materials in their collections;
- again and always to my wife Suzanne and our children for their continual love, support, and encouragement in this and other projects.

# The Cistercian Fathers and Their Monastic Theology

*Novitiate–Abbey of Gethsemani–1963*

## Part One: Saint Bernard

A most important part of Cistercian formation {is} getting acquainted with our Father St. Bernard, who did more than any other to shape the spirituality of the Order—to be a Cistercian is in fact to have the spirit of Bernard, and since he has left so many writings in which that spirit is found, we must learn to read him at no matter what cost. It is very rewarding.

I. Preamble—The Encyclical *Doctor Mellifluus* (May 24, 1953–Pentecost):[1] to begin with, we can consider the Encyclical of Pius XII on the eighth centenary of the death of St. Bernard. It will show us something of St. Bernard's position as a doctor of the Church. We here briefly outline the points made by Pope Pius XII, who emphasizes the mystical and ascetical teaching of St. Bernard, and in particular his doctrine of *charity*, which is the root of his teaching on contemplation. Cistercian theology is primarily a theology of *love*.

1. The importance of St. Bernard: Bernard, the Last of the Fathers, stood out above all others in his age ({the} twelfth century {was} the Age of Bernard) by gifts of nature and grace—by

---

1. Thomas Merton, *The Last of the Fathers: Saint Bernard of Clairvaux and the Encyclical Letter*, Doctor Mellifluus (New York: Harcourt, Brace, 1954), 91–116.

sanctity and wisdom. His doctrine is "sapiential" rather than scholastic, {focusing on} contemplative rather than speculative knowledge of God and the things of God. This is important—it shows the very special (patristic) character of Cistercian doctrine.

2. {The} Purpose of the Encyclical: Pope Pius XII wishes to add to the chorus of praise that has been constant since Bernard's death, and thus to celebrate his eighth centenary. He wishes to meditate on his merits and expound them to all, first of all to Cistercians, then to all who find their delights principally in what is true, holy, etc., {in order} that all may be inspired to follow his example (especially monks).

3. His doctrine *in general*: Bernard's doctrine is drawn entirely from Scripture and {the} Fathers, especially Scripture. {It is} sapiential rather than speculative, but Bernard does not despise philosophy in the right sense of the word—only vain philosophy that does not lead to God (read p. 95[2]). {With regard to} the *order* of knowledge, it should be ordered to love for God. What is wisdom? the combination of knowledge and love (read p. 96[3]).

---

2. "His doctrine was drawn almost exclusively from the pages of Sacred Scripture and from the Holy Fathers, which he had at hand day and night in his profound meditations; and not from the subtle reasonings of dialecticians and philosophers, which on more than one occasion he appeared to hold in low esteem. But it should be remarked that he does not reject human philosophy which is genuine philosophy, namely, that which leads to God, to correct living, and to Christian wisdom. Rather does he repudiate that philosophy which, by recourse to empty verbiage and sophistry, aspires with presumptuous boldness to ascend to divine heights and to delve into all the secrets of God, with the result that, as often happened in those days, it violated the integrity of faith and fell miserably into heresy" (*Last of the Fathers*, 94–95).

3. "In the following words, he describes most appropriately the doctrine, or rather the wisdom, which he follows and ardently loves: 'It is the spirit of wisdom and understanding which, like a bee bearing both wax and honey, is able both to kindle the light of knowledge and to pour in the savor of grace. Hence, let neither one think he has received the "kiss" [i.e., of mystical grace], neither he who understands the truth but does not love it,

St. Bernard's aim, in studying God, {is} unity, union, in contemplation (read p. 97[4]). Studying under the guidance of charity leads to union (97–98[5]).

---

nor he who loves the truth but does not understand it.' 'What would be the good of learning without love? It would puff us up. And love without learning? It would go astray.' 'Merely to shine is futile; merely to burn is not enough; to burn and to shine is perfect.' Then he explains the source of true and genuine doctrine, and how it must be united with charity: 'God is Wisdom, and wants to be loved not only affectionately, but also wisely. . . . Otherwise, if you neglect knowledge, the spirit of error will most easily lay snares for your zeal; nor has the cunning enemy a more efficacious means of removing love from the heart, than if he can make a man walk carelessly and imprudently in the path of love'" (*Last of the Fathers*, 96–97, quoting from *In Cantica*, 8.6; *In Cantica*, 69.2; *In Nativitate S. Joannis Baptistae*, 3; *In Cantica*, 19.7 [J. P. Migne, ed., *Patrologiae Cursus Completus, Series Latina* [PL], 221 vols. (Paris: Garnier, 1844–1865), vol. 183, cols. 813AB, 1113A, 399B, 866D]).

4. "From these words it is clear that in his study and his contemplation under the influence of love rather than through the subtlety of human reasoning, Bernard's sole aim was to direct toward the Supreme Truth all the rays of truth which he had assembled from many different sources; drawing from them light for the mind, the fire of charity for the soul, and correct norms for the guidance of conduct. This is indeed true wisdom, which transcends all things human, and brings everything back to its source, that is, to God, in order to convert men to Him. The Mellifluous Doctor makes his way with deliberate care through the uncertain and precarious circuits of reasoning, not trusting in the keenness of his own mind nor depending upon the labored and artful syllogisms which many of the dialecticians of his time frequently abused, but, like an eagle, attempting to fix his eyes on the sun, he pushes on with swift flight to the summit of truth."

5. "The charity which activated him makes light of obstacles and, so to speak, gives wings to the mind. For him, learning is not the final goal, but rather a path leading to God; it is not the cold object of empty speculation, an intellectual diversion, fascinating the mind with its play of light and glory, but it is moved, impelled, and governed by love. Wherefore, borne up by this wisdom and by means of meditation, contemplation, and love, Bernard ascends the peak of the mystical life and is united with God Himself, tasting at times almost infinite happiness even in this mortal life."

4. His style truly fulfills the function of good rhetoric, to make the soul love and seek what is proposed to the mind in his doctrine.

5. His *Mystical Theology*: the Pope examines this part of St. Bernard's doctrine "for the edification of all." In some sense, every soul is called to perfect union. In what sense? We shall see (read quote: p. 98–99[6]). Mystical Marriage is conformity to God by perfect charity (p. 99[7]). It is a union of perfect *love* (read

6. "It is a pleasure, Venerable Brethren, for the edification of all, to quote some fine passages, from his works, on this mystical teaching: 'We have taught that every soul, even though weighed down with sins, ensnared in vice, caught in the allurements of the passions, held captive in exile, and imprisoned in the body . . . even, I say, though it be thus damned and in despair, can find within itself not only reasons for yearning after the hope of pardon and the hope of mercy, but also for making bold to aspire to marriage with the Word, not hesitating to establish a covenant of union with God, and not being ashamed to be yoked in one sweet bond of love along with the King of the Angels. What will the soul not dare with Him whose marvelous image it sees within itself, and whose striking likeness it recognizes in itself'" (quoting from *In Cantica*, 83.1 [*PL* 183, col. 1181CD]).

7. "'By this conformity of charity . . . the soul is wedded to the Word, when, namely, loving even as she is loved, she exhibits herself in her will conformed to Him to Whom she is already conformed in her nature. Therefore, if she loves Him perfectly she has become His Bride. What can be more sweet than such a conformity? What can be more desirable than this charity, whereby thou art enabled of thyself to draw nigh with confidence to the Word, to cleave to Him steadfastly, to interrogate Him familiarly, and to consult Him in all thy doubts, as audacious in thy desires as thou art capacious in thy understanding? This is in truth the alliance of holy and spiritual marriage. But it is too little to call it an alliance: it is rather an embrace. Surely we have then a spiritual embrace when the same likes and the same dislikes make one spirit out of two. Nor is there any occasion to fear lest the inequality of the persons should cause some defect in the harmony of wills, since love knows nothing of reverence. Love means an exercise of affection, not an exhibition of honor. . . . Love is all-sufficient for itself. Whithersoever love comes, it subjugates and renders captive to itself all the other affections. Consequently, the soul that loves, simply loves and knows nothing else except to love'" (*Last of the Fathers*, 99–100, quoting from *In Cantica*, 83.3 [*PL* 183, col. 1182CD]).

pp. 100–101–102[8]). The Holy Father reproves those "who neglect and relegate to a secondary place" this doctrine, in favor of {the} worries and business of everyday life. We must not become so immersed in temporal things as to forget our vocation to union with God! (read p. 101[9]). *Not all* can or will attain to mystical marriage, but all *can and must* "lift their hearts from the earthly things around them to those of heaven and most earnestly love the Supreme Giver of all good things" (read p. 102[10]); "Wherefore,

---

8. "After pointing out that God wants to be loved by men rather than feared and honored, he adds this wise and penetrating observation: 'Love is sufficient of itself; it pleases of itself, and for its own sake. It counts as merit to itself and is its own reward. Besides itself love requires no motive and seeks no fruit. Its fruit is its enjoyment of itself. I love because I love, and I love for the sake of loving. A great thing is love, if yet it returns to its Principle, if it is restored to its Origin, if it finds its way back again to its Fountainhead, so that it may be thus enabled to continue flowing with an unfailing stream. Amongst all the emotions, sentiments, and feelings of the soul, love stands distinguished in this respect, that in this one case alone has the creature the power to correspond and to make a return to the Creator in kind, though not in equality.' Since in his prayer and his contemplation he had frequently experienced this divine love, whereby we can be intimately united with God, there broke forth from his soul these inspired words: 'Happy is the Soul to whom it has been given to experience an embrace of such surpassing delight! This spiritual embrace is nothing else than a chaste and holy love, a love sweet and pleasant, a love perfectly serene and perfectly pure, a love that is mutual, intimate, and strong, a love that joins two, not in one flesh, but in one spirit, that makes two to be no longer two but one undivided spirit, according to the testimony of St. Paul, where he says, "He who cleaves to the Lord is one spirit with Him"'" (*Last of the Fathers*, 100–101, quoting from *In Cantica*, 83.6 [*PL* 183, col. 1184C]; the scriptural reference is to 1 Cor. 6:17).

9. "In our day the sublime teaching of the Doctor of Clairvaux on the mystical life, which exceeds and can satisfy all human desires, seems sometimes to be neglected and relegated to a secondary place, or even forgotten by many who, completely taken up with worries and business of daily life, seek and desire only what is useful and profitable for this mortal life, almost never lift their eyes and minds to heaven, and almost never aspire after heavenly things and values that cannot perish."

10. *Last of the Fathers*, 101–2.

since love for God is gradually growing cold today in the hearts of many, or is even not infrequently utterly extinct, we feel that these writings of the Mellifluous Doctor should be attentively meditated; from [them] a new and heavenly force can pour forth, both into individual and into social life" etc. (read p. 102[11]). In a powerful paragraph (p. 102[12]), the Holy Father shows how the doctrine of love taught by St. Bernard is indeed the pure doctrine of the Gospel and is badly needed to counteract the evils of our time: "The divine love which burned so mightily in the Doctor of Clairvaux must be re-enkindled in the hearts of all men . . . if the Catholic religion is to carry out its mission successfully." These words, addressed to all, apply especially to us (read

11. "Wherefore, since love for God is gradually growing cold today in the hearts of many, or is even not infrequently utterly extinct, we feel that these writings of the Mellifluous Doctor should be attentively meditated; because from their content, which for that matter comes from the Gospels, a new and heavenly force can pour forth, both into individual and into social life, in order to guide morality, make it conform with Christian precepts, and thus be able to provide timely remedies for the many great evils now troubling and attacking society. For when men do not have the proper love for their Creator, from Whom comes everything they have; when they do not love one another, then, as often happens, they are separated from one another by hatred and deceit and turn upon one another in bitter conflict. But God is the most loving Father of us all, and we are all brethren in Christ, we whom He redeemed by shedding His Precious Blood. Hence, as often as we fail to return God's love or reverently to recognize His divine fatherhood, the bonds of brotherly love are sundered in disaster and—as alas so often happens—discord, contention and enmity burst out with tragic effects, going so far as to undermine and destroy the very foundations of human society."

12. "Hence, that divine love which burned so mightily in the Doctor of Clairvaux must be re-kindled in the hearts of all men, if we desire the restoration of Christian morality, if the Catholic religion is to carry out its mission successfully, and if, through the calming of dissension and the restoration of order in justice and equity, serene peace is to shine forth for a worn and anguished humanity."

p. 103[13]). It is clearly God's will that we cultivate in our hearts the spirit of charity of St. Bernard. This is most urgently important. It is for this that we have been called to the cloister. If we fail to develop something of his spirit we will fail in our vocation. Hence the Holy Father goes on to a special exhortation addressed to monks first of all and then to the clergy. We must be "MOST ARDENTLY INFLAMED WITH THAT LOVE WHICH OUGHT ALWAYS TO UNITE US MOST PERFECTLY WITH GOD." Why? (1) it is most urgently needed in our time; (2) where this love is fervent, all the other virtues flourish; where it is tepid, they all languish. {The} reason {is} because love keeps us in contact with God our supreme end; it gives life and purpose to the virtues, for their life must come from Him; it keeps us in contact with the source of all life—God.

6. *His doctrine on Charity*: it is most important for us to know *what love is*, and not just {to} struggle blindly for "more love" with no idea {of} what we are doing. This is an aspect of his mystical theology—the same thing from another point of view. {Here lies the} excellence of his doctrine: "Of this charity no one, perhaps, has spoken more excellently, more profoundly, or more ardently than Bernard."[14] Its foundation stone {is the} *purity of love*: loving God for His own sake "because He is God";[15] *generosity*:

---

13. "May those who have embraced the Order of the Mellifluous Doctor, and all the members of the clergy, whose special task it is to exhort and urge others to the fervor of divine love, be most ardently inflamed with that love which ought always to unite us most perfectly with God. In our own day, more than at any other time—as we have said—men need this divine love; family life needs it; the whole of human society needs it. Where it burns and urges souls on to God, Who is the supreme goal of all mortals, all other virtues wax strong; when, on the contrary, it is absent or has died out, then tranquillity, peace, joy, and all other genuine good things gradually disappear or are completely destroyed, since they flow from Him who 'is love'" (cf. 1 John 4:8).

14. *Last of the Fathers*, 103, which reads: "Of this divine charity . . . ."

15. "'The reason for loving God . . . is God'" (*Last of the Fathers*, 103, quoting from *De Diligendo Deo*, 50 [*PL* 182, col. 974A]).

loving Him without limit; *efficacy*: it turns all labor to joy. It transforms us into the perfect likeness of God. It brings perfect peace (*Tranquillus Deus tranquillat omnia*[16]). The real meaning of contemplative "rest" {is} not quietistic apathy, "not the death of the mind but its life" (p. 104[17]). It is a perfect return of love to God, {which} flows from perfect forgetfulness of self. It awakens apostolic zeal (see quote: p. 105[18])—{the prime} example {being} the apostolic zeal of Bernard himself. It means, then, ardent fraternal charity, love for the Church of God, especially love of suffering for the Church, defense of the faith and unity of the Church, {and} support of the papal authority, {a} recognition of infallibility.[19]

7. *Humility*: speaking of St. Bernard's own humility, rather than of his doctrine of this virtue, the Holy Father shows how Bernard's strength lay in his humility and all the other virtues which went to make up his sanctity uniting him to God (see p. 110[20]). The source of Bernard's humility {was} contemplation and prayer.

---

16. "The tranquillity of God tranquillizes all about Him" (*Last of the Fathers*, 104, quoting from *In Ps. 90*, 18.4 [*PL* 183, col. 252C]).

17. Text reads: ". . . but its true life."

18. "This perfect tranquillity of mind, in which we enjoy the loving God by returning His love, and by which we turn and direct ourselves and all we have to Him, does not reduce us to laziness, sloth and inertia, but awakens an assiduous, efficient and active zeal that spurs us on to procure our own salvation and, with the help of God, that of others also."

19. See *Last of the Fathers*, 109: "In clear and simple fashion he acknowledges the infallible magisterium of the Roman Pontiff in questions of faith and morals."

20. "Although he was held in great favor and esteem by popes, princes and peoples, he was not puffed up, he did not grasp at the vain, fleeting glory of men, but ever shone with that Christian humility which 'acquires other virtues . . . having acquired them, keeps them . . . keeping them, perfects them'; so that 'without it the others do not even seem to be virtues.' Wherefore 'proferred honor did not tempt his soul, nor did he set his foot on the downward path of worldly glory; tiara and ring had no more appeal

8. *Love for Jesus and Mary*: the mystery of the Incarnation {was} the center of Bernard's spirituality. The fervor of his love for Jesus the Man-God {is} illustrated {in the} Encyclical (p. 111[21]). His devotion to Mary centers in his confidence in her *mediation*.

---

for him than rake or hoe.' And while he undertook such great and frequent labors for the glory of God and the benefit of the Christian name, he was wont to call himself 'the useless servant of the servants of God,' 'a vile worm,' 'a tree without fruit,' 'a sinner, ashes. . . .' This Christian humility, as well as the other virtues, he nourished by assiduous contemplation of heavenly things, and by fervent prayer to God, by which he called down grace from on high on the labors undertaken by himself and his followers" (*Last of the Fathers*, 110–11, quoting from *De Moribus et Officiis Episcoporum*, 5.17; *Vita Prima*, 2.25; *Epistola* 37; *Epistola* 215; *Vita Prima*, 5.12; *In Cantica*, 71.5 [*PL* 182, col. 821A; *PL* 185, col. 283B; *PL* 182, cols. 143B, 379B; *PL* 185, col. 358D; *PL* 183, col. 1123D]).

21. "So ardent was the love he bore in a special manner to Jesus Christ Our Divine Savior that under its influence and inspiration he penned the fine and profound pages which still arouse the admiration and enkindle the devotion of all readers. 'What can so enrich the soul that reflects upon it [the holy name of Jesus]? What can . . . fortify the virtues, engender good and honorable dispositions, foster holy affections? Dry is every kind of spiritual food, which this oil does not moisten. Insipid, whatever this salt does not season. If thou writest, thy composition has no charms for me, unless I read there the name of Jesus. If thou disputest or conversest, I find no pleasure in thy words, unless I hear there the name of Jesus. Jesus is honey in the mouth, melody in the ear, a cry of joy in the heart. Yet not only is that name light and food. It is also medicine. Is any amongst you sad? Let the name of Jesus enter his heart; let it leap thence to his lips; and lo! the light that radiates from that name shall scatter every cloud and restore tranquillity. Has someone sinned, and is he, moreover, abandoning hope, rushing in desperation toward the snare of death? Let him but invoke this life-giving name, and straightway he shall experience a renewal of courage. . . . Whoever, when trembling with terror in the presence of danger, has not immediately felt his spirits revive and his fears departing as soon as he called upon this name of power? . . . There is nothing so efficacious as the name of Jesus for restraining the violence of anger, repressing the swellings of pride, healing the smarting wound of envy. . . .'" (*Last of the Fathers*, 112, quoting from *In Cantica*, 15.6 [*PL* 183, cols. 846D–847B]).

In this he is a model for us: we should love Mary as he did. The Holy Father closes by praying to Our Lady for the world, in the spirit of St. Bernard and in union with him (p. 115[22]).

Practical conclusions: (1) As monks, we have a God-given model and guide in our Father St. Bernard. (2) We have a special obligation to take advantage of this grace and to have devotion to him. (3) But "devotion" must take a practical turn. It must mean (a) reading and studying his works; (b) nourishing a fervor like his, based entirely on the Love of God; (c) cultivating like him a spirit of contemplation and desire for divine union, as the source and cause of all other virtues—an efficacious way to sanctity; (d) fostering a love that desires union and at the same time overflows in zeal for souls and for the Church of God; (e) by the chief means used by St. Bernard—cultivating humility, loving Jesus and trusting Mary. Here we have an authoritative outline of what our Cistercian spirituality should be based on. These elements are of course common to us and to all other orders; but if they do not receive a central position with us and a very marked emphasis, then we are not Cistercians.

### The Career of St. Bernard in Outline:

BACKGROUND—*The Age*: the twelfth century is an age of *transition* and *awakening*. In the eleventh century {came the} high point of feudal society, {of} papal power (Gregory VII) {and} religious reform. Cîteaux {was} a fruit of the religious and monastic revival of the feudal period. Intellectually, the eleventh

---

22. "Therefore as the Doctor of Clairvaux sought and obtained from the Virgin Mother Mary help for the troubles of his times, let us all through the same great devotion and prayer so strive to move our divine Mother that she may obtain from God timely relief from these grave evils which have either already come upon us or may yet befall, and that she who is benign and most powerful will by the help of God grant that the sincere, solid and fruitful peace of the Church may at last dawn on all nations and peoples."

century is *static* and *conservative*. It looks back to Charlemagne. Its attitude is discernible in the heavy, the solid, the monumental mysticism of Romanesque architecture. It believes that the peace of feudal Christendom is the Kingdom of God, and seeks only to preserve this condition, offering praise to God, unaware of the coming changes and developments that will undermine this structure. In the twelfth century there are various reactions against this heavy conservatism of the eleventh century, a century of power and tradition:

a) {The} reaction of poverty, solitude, labor, flight from the world of power into *mystical* love, *ecstasy* (the Cistercians, {the} Victorines)—but this is essentially *conservative* and static;

b) {The} reaction of evangelism—evangelical poverty and preaching (canons, preachers like Robert of Arbrissel)—{a} prelude to the mendicant movement and the new age of {the} thirteenth century;

c) {The} reaction of humanism and dialectics—{a} prelude to scholasticism: (1) the humanists of Chartres discover *nature* and the *cosmos* (as a religious epiphany but also as {an} object of scientific thought); (2) the dialecticians (Abelard) discover the autonomy of *reason*; (3) {the} beginning of anti-clericalism, {a} revolt against {the} power of {the} Church, new heresies, seeds of secularism, {a} prelude to {the} commercial age.

It is very important to note that in the twelfth century the *vernacular* becomes important in literature and in preaching. {An} awakening of the common man begins. {There is} growth of a new economy—the merchants and craftsmen of the towns. Physically speaking, life is *primitive* compared to ours—castles, walled towns, difficulty of communications, {a} dangerous life, lack of comforts we are used to (but this lack is not felt). {There is an} essential *simplicity* of the times: {a} unity of culture; as it stands, everybody has the same beliefs, the same outlook. Yet the individual is less lost in the crowd than today where we talk so much of individuality. In the Middle Ages there is *much less standardization*. In the overall agreement on essentials, there is also much more room for accidental differences and individual development within the unified framework of the whole. Note, for instance, hermits, pilgrims, monks, wanderers, crusaders, craftsmen, jongleurs, wandering clerics, poets, etc.; {there is} plenty of latitude for variegated types, all accepted as natural. {There is a} *vitality* of the culture and of the individual—{a} vitality in every field—earthiness and spirituality. {It is} unfortunate {that there is} vitality in the realm of sin as well as in the realm of sanctity (n.b. religion penetrates everything). The Middle Ages can then appear as an age of extremes, but is it really? Fundamentally there is a certain *psychological balance* in the Middle Ages, which we have lost today. Whatever may have been the shortcomings of medieval society, man could develop tremendously in it, once he found favorable conditions. Hence, though there is much *violence*, and the age must not be idealized, the Middle Ages is on the whole a *healthy* period, and with all its lacks, this is a great advantage. Our age, on the other hand, is spiritually and psychologically unhealthy, and our lack of health comes precisely from the things which we imagine give us an advantage over the Middle Ages—our "progress"—but this is material rather than spiritual. The Middle Age is balanced because the material and spiritual levels of man's life are more or less in harmony, whatever their shortcomings. One feels that though the problems of the age were great, the men of those times loved and flourished in the midst of their problems. With us, they are separated by an abyss.

*The Immediate Background of St. Bernard*—at the time of his birth, Burgundy {was a} rich, independent duchy, powerful and cultured; {it was a} wine-growing country; Dijon {had many} crafts {and} trades. Cluny {was} now being built; Molesme is thriving. {There is} monastic reform everywhere: {the} Grande Chartreuse {was} founded six years before St. Bernard's birth. Other new movements {include the} growth of cloister schools, giving place to cathedral schools from which will spring universities. {In} literature, *The Song of Roland* {is written around this time}. Political life {is marked by} St. Gregory VII vs. Emperor Henry IV (until 1088); then Urban II succeeds him; and when Bernard is six years old, the First Crusade leaves for the Orient.

## An Introduction to St. Bernard of Clairvaux as a Person

We are following William of St. Thierry in the *Vita Prima Bernardi*.[23] A few peculiarities of this kind of writing must be remembered: we are dealing with conventional tropes of hagiography. To us these tropes seem odd, artificial, absurd. But let us remember that we have our own conventional tropes and clichés, creating an "image" to which we respond favorably. Contrast with a magazine article on Pope Pius XII.[24] {The} *modern writer* seeks to bring the "hero" down to everybody's level—to enable us to realize that the Pope is "just like other folks" (he loves his pet goldfinch[25]). At the same time, the "heroic" side of the Pope is presented with an American touch. We admire versatility, the "freedom" with which a man can nonchalantly turn his hand to anything and *succeed easily*. His many languages {are noted—he is} ready with a greeting in Gaelic;[26] {you} "can't catch him napping"; "he can do anything"[27]—talk about statistics, business, astronomy, etc.[28] Our reverence for the "all-round threat" {is evident}. Note {the} apology {for} "his *almost* ascetic look."[29] *William of St. Thierry* {is} unusual as medieval writers go in his objectivity—a friend of St. Bernard, writing in his lifetime. (William died five years before St. Bernard.) His picture is human, not by virtue of standard "homey" traits, but by its authenticity. But he stresses the *superhuman and charismatic* in St. Bernard, brings out factors that make the saint *extraordinary, not like us*,

---

23. *PL* 185, cols. 225–68 (Bk. 1).

24. Anne Fromer, "The Many Lives of Pope Pius XII," *Coronet* 33 (November 1952): 71–86.

25. See Fromer, "Many Lives," 74.

26. See Fromer, "Many Lives," 77.

27. "[He] is . . . so universal in his interests and so many-sided in his abilities as to make even his closest associates marvel" (Fromer, "Many Lives," 73).

28. See Fromer, "Many Lives," 77, which doesn't actually mention astronomy specifically, but science in general and the resources provided by the Pontifical Academy of Sciences.

29. "He is almost ascetic in appearance" (Fromer, "Many Lives," 73).

*a man of God*. {In} following William, remember he is a *panegyrist*—so beware—but take his fundamental view. Bernard {was} formed by special grace as a saint, a man of God, a sign of God for his times.

I. *The Early Formation of St. Bernard*

a) *Childhood*: {the} birth of St. Bernard {took place} sometime between April and August 1090, in a lower room of the tower in the Castle of Fontaines, near Dijon. His parents {were} *Tescelin*, a knight in the service of {the} Duke of Burgundy, {noted for his} piety, justice, love of {the} poor; {he was} brave, humble (hated praise), used force of arms only in the right way—for his lord or for {a} just cause; {and} Aleth (Alette), {who} wanted to enter {a} convent but {was} given in marriage at fifteen; {she was a} perfect Christian wife, living for the family, {filled with} love of {the} poor and of the sick—{a} "*mulier fortis*,"[30] "*apostolicam regulam tenens*"[31] (living according to the rules in the Epistles of St. Paul[32]). "*Filios enutriens in omni disciplina. Septem liberos genuit non tam viro suo quam Deo.*"[33] William of St. Thierry insists on the fact that she willed to give them all to God (in fact, all died in religion) and Alette would not let anyone else nurse them but herself, as if to give the goodness that was in her to them. She brought them up for the desert rather than the court—{with} coarse simple food, etc. Later,[34] St. Bernard sums up {the} work of conversion proposed to Humbeline by telling her to live as their mother had lived.

b) *His education at Châtillon*: Châtillon-sur-Saône {was a} fortified town in {the} diocese of Langres, where Tescelin had a house. He was one of the defenders of the town. At five, St. Bernard starts studying with the canons of the church of Vorles. {He}

30. "strong woman" (Prov. 31:10, which reads "*mulierem fortem*").
31. "holding to the apostolic rule" (*Vita Prima*, 1.1.1 [col. 227B]).
32. See Eph. 5:21-33; Col. 3:18.
33. "Raising her sons in all discipline. She bore seven children not so much to her husband as to God" (*Vita Prima*, 1.1.1 [col. 227B], which reads: ". . . *Septem quippe liberos* . . .").
34. See *Vita Prima*, 1.6.30 (col. 245A).

learned reading, writing, singing; {his} textbook {was} the *Psalter*. At seven {came} his vision or dream of the birth of Jesus, on Christmas Eve (*"dormit ad ostium"* says the hymn;[35] rather, he was still sleeping at home). This had a profound effect on his future life and teaching, which centered so much on the Incarnation and the love of Jesus and Mary. Bernard as a child {showed} precocious intelligence {and} great virtue. {He was} shy to a fault, afraid of speaking in public {and} of meeting strangers. ({See the} antiphons of {the} votive office {for} *prime*: *"Beatus Bernardus ab infantia spiritum sortitus est bonum, per quem erat puer docilis et amabilis valde."*[36] {See} William of St. Thierry, *Vita Prima* [PL 185, col. 228]: "*Erat* simplicissimus in saecularibus, amans habitare secum . . . mire cogitativus, *parentibus obediens et subditus*; omnibus benignus et gratus, domi simplex et quietus, foris rarus . . . Deo devotus, ut puram sibi pueritiam *conservaret; litterarum studio deditus*, PER QUAS IN SCRIPTURIS DEUM DISCERET ET COGNOSCERET."[37]) The happy natural gifts of Bernard were developed quietly and harmoniously by grace. {He was} a wise child who grew in wisdom under the secret guidance of Wisdom. If there was anything of this in our past life in our childhood, and if we have lost it, the monastery should enable us to *recover* it. But the modern world does its best to ruin these qualities in children—the harshness, the worldliness, competitive spirit, *thoughtlessness* {that is} encouraged in children. {He engaged in the} study of the liberal

---

35. "he sleeps at the entrance" (from the hymn *"Bernardus Inclytis"* [*Breviarium Cisterciense Reformatum*, 4 vols. (Westmalle, Belgium: Typis Cisterciensibus, 1951), *Pars Aestivalis*, 585]).

36. "The blessed Bernard was allotted a good spirit from infancy, through which he was a docile and very lovable boy" (*Breviarium Cisterciense, Aestivalis*, 585).

37. "He was very simple in worldly matters, loving to dwell by himself. . . . He was marvelously thoughtful, obedient and submissive to his parents; kind and gracious to all; simple and quiet at home; rarely outside . . . devoted to God, so as to keep for himself his pure childhood; given to the study of books, through which he might learn about and come to know God in the Scriptures" (*Vita Prima*, 1.1.3, which reads: "*Erat namque in . . . litterarum etiam studio . . .*").

arts (see Cassiodorus, *De Septem Artibus Liberalibus*[38]): {the} trivium {involved} cultivation and discipline of the mind {through} grammar, rhetoric, logic; {the} quadrivium {consisted in} elementary "sciences": arithmetic, geometry, astronomy, music. Grammar {included instruction in} how to speak and write correctly, including metrics; {the} writing of Latin composition and Latin verses. {Bernard was} never much of a poet {but became} a conscious and effective prose stylist. This developed at Châtillon, {where he} studied Cicero, Virgil, Seneca, Horace, Ovid, Terence, Persius; perhaps {he was} already studying the Latin Fathers and *Origen* (a favorite). The character of these great writers must be understood to gain an appreciation of St. Bernard. The genius of classical Latin {was} mixed with echoes of the Christian orient and Platonism, and all immersed in the BIBLE and in a rich interior experience of the mysteries of faith and the liturgy. ({The} theory that Bernard knew Greek {was} held by W. Williams.[39] Bernard more probably learned all he knew of {the} Greek Fathers from William of St. Thierry.) {Did he have a} knowledge of law— Roman and canon? {There are} possible influences, {seen in} many traces of legal expressions in his works. {As for} philosophy and theology, Manrique[40] thinks St. Bernard's theology was all di-

---

38. Cassiodorus, *De Artibus ac Disciplinis Liberalium Litterarum* (*PL* 70, cols. 1140C–1220A).

39. Williams actually writes, "he had apparently but very slight knowledge of Greek" (Watkin W. Williams, *Studies in St. Bernard of Clairvaux* [London: SPCK, 1927], 51), providing in his notes two instances where Bernard apparently shows familiarity with some Greek terms. In *Saint Bernard of Clairvaux* (Manchester, UK: Manchester University Press, 1935), Williams notes two quotations in the *De Conversione* that follow the Septuagint and comments, "It would be interesting to know how these translations from the Greek come to be explained" (15); he also remarks in his appendix, "his translation of two passages from the LXX is certainly stimulating" (365–66).

40. Angel Manrique, *Cisterciensium seu Verius Ecclesiasticorum Annalium a Condito Cistercio*, 4 vols. (Leyden: G. Boissat & Laurent Anisson, 1642–1659; repr. Farnborough: Gregg International, 1970), 1:45; *"Theologiam infusam a Deo fuisse fortitum"* (1105: c. 2, n. 6).

rectly infused! We know nothing of his formation, but his authority as a theologian shows clearly that he received one.

*Trials of St. Bernard as a Young Man:*

a) {The} death of his mother {took place} in 1103 or 1104, after a saintly life of prayer and penance, in her declining years. {She was a} shining example, {a} powerful influence on Bernard. Her death made a great impression on {the} fourteen-year-old boy.

b) The attraction of the world. His relatives orient him towards {the} secular clergy {and an} ecclesiastical career. *His gifts of nature* {were a} potential temptation, {along with} his good looks, his manners ("*suavissimis ornatus moribus*"[41]), his brilliant mind, his facility and elegance of speech. William of St. Thierry says many roads opened out before him—all of them enticing prospects. Should he take one of these roads for the sake of his own pleasure and ambition? {There were also} dangerous friendships ("*amicitiae procellosae*"[42]). {William relates} how he began to be attracted to worldly pleasure {but} resisted the first step of curiosity. According to William,[43] Bernard was never seriously tempted to lust, only to *curiosity*—to look at women with the wrong kind of interest. His resistance to the first impulse was so complete and generous that the business never went any further. In the other "temptations" he felt no movement of desire. (Note {the} relation between *Vita Prima*, iii, 6 [col. 230], and the twelve degrees of Pride: {the} first degree.[44]) {After} various temptations {involving} women, {he} resolves to leave the world.

---

41. "adorned with very polished manners" (*Vita Prima*, 1.3.6 [col. 230B]).
42. "stormy friendships" (*Vita Prima*, 1.3.6 [col. 230B]).
43. See *Vita Prima*, 1.3.6 (col. 230C): "*aliquando curiosius aspiciendo*" ("sometimes by gazing more curiously").
44. See *De Gradibus Humilitatis et Superbiae*, 10.28: "*De primo superbiae gradu, qui est curiositas*" ("On the First Step of Pride, Which Is Curiosity") (*PL* 182, col. 957B).

*Nature and Character of St. Bernard*: Dom Leclercq (*SBM* = *Saint Bernard Mystique*) stresses the fact that St. Bernard was *not* naturally aggressive, but was timid, characterized by *"verecundia."*[45] This may be exaggerated. There was probably a conflict between his shyness and a definite aggressivity. It is not *de fide*[46] that *all* St. Bernard's power-drives and initiatives were purely supernatural. Bouyer remarks that when in 1130 St. Bernard returned to Clairvaux for an interval of silence, it was more of a lion to his den, "sated for a moment but still growling rather than a lamb delighted to rejoin the fold which he had left against his will."[47] {As for} Blessed Aleth, her sanctity was perhaps *unusual* in feudal society. Her influence in the life of Bernard and of her other sons were preponderant. He was a sickly child. His childhood vision of the Nativity before Christmas vigils {was} important for his later development. These factors added to St. Bernard make him an exceptional figure, and his spirituality is more "Bernardine" than simply "Cistercian"—a special modality of the "Cistercian." *Bouyer* says: "Such a monastic career was at the antipodes of what the reformers of Cîteaux had intended."[48] The paradox of his career was not unnoticed. His contemporaries accused him of inconsistency, of not staying in his proper place in the Church, etc. "What does a monk have to do with courts and councils?"[49] a certain cardinal asked him. The only answer is that God willed this exceptional vocation which was not easily

---

45. "shyness" (Jean Leclercq, OSB, *Saint Bernard Mystique* [Paris: Desclée de Brouwer, 1948], 16).

46. i.e., to be held as a matter of faith.

47. "le lion qui regagne sa tanière, un moment repu mais toujours grondant, que l'agneau trop heureux de retrouver le bercail auquel on l'aurait arraché malgré lui" (Louis Bouyer, *La Spiritualité de Cîteaux* [Paris: Le Portulan, 1955], 35).

48. "Mais une telle carrière monastique apparaît d'abord aux antipodes de ce que les réformateurs cisterciens avaient voulu" (Bouyer, *Spiritualité*, 33).

49. "Qu'est-ce qu'un moine a de commun avec la cour et avec les conciles?" (Bouyer, *Spiritualité*, 34); the cardinal was Haimeric, to whom Bernard addressed his treatise *De Diligendo Deo* (see PL 182, col. 973A).

accountable in human terms. Bernard was a creature of contradictions, and out of these contradictions, with God's grace, came his extraordinary power in his time. But it was not without dangers and problems.

### THE VOCATION OF SAINT BERNARD (*Vita Prima*, n. 8 [231])

{With regard to} the motives of his vocation, it is strictly a *conversio*, operated by the *fear of the Lord*. {As for} what *it is not*—at least here we follow William of St. Thierry, St. Bernard's good friend, giving what was not only probably the mind of St. Bernard, but the common attitude of the time and also the mind of St. Benedict: St. Bernard's vocation is *not*, in his mind, the consecration by a generous soul of himself to God in order to do more perfectly in the monastery what he is already doing in the world. {It} is *not* a step higher taken by a soul already high in sanctity seeking "the highest" vocation, in which he can relish the consolations of contemplative prayer; {it} is *not* the offering of an active and gifted man who places his talents at the disposal of a struggling new foundation; {it} is *not* precisely the enthusiastic embracing of penance by a penitential soul looking for a chance to embrace a hard rule and a place in which many penances are practiced. However, penance is one of the moving forces in the vocation of St. Bernard, but {this} must be seen in the right perspective.

What went on in his mind? Read *De Conversione*, cc. 1–3,[50] where St. Bernard teaches how the voice of God and the word of

---

50. "CHAPTER I *None may be converted unto the Lord, save only he who is prevented by the Divine will inwardly revealed to him in conscience.* You have assembled, as we believe, to hear the word of the Lord. We can think of no other reason for this your so eager concourse. We certainly approve of this desire, and rejoice with you in your praiseworthy zeal. For blessed are they who hear the word of God, provided that they keep it (*Luke* xi, 28). Blessed are they who remember his commandments, provided that they fulfil them (*Ps.* cii, 18). Forsooth he has the words of eternal life, and the hour will

God act in the soul to produce the transformation ("*metanoia*")

come—would that it were now present—in which the dead shall hear his voice, and they who have heard shall live (*John* v, 25), inasmuch as life is in his will (*Ps.* xxix, 6). Finally, hear what he says himself: *Is it my will that a sinner should die, saith the Lord God, and not that he should be converted from his ways and live?* (*Ezech.* xviii, 23). From which words we clearly recognize that our true life is found only through conversion; nor is there any other entrance into life, as the Lord says again: *Unless you be converted and become as little children, you shall not enter into the kingdom of heaven* (*Matt.* xviii, 3). Fittingly indeed is it only little children who enter in, for it is a little Child who leads them (*Isa.* xi, 6), he who to this very end was born and given to us. I am seeking then a voice which the dead may hear, and hearing it may live (*John* v, 25). For perhaps it is necessary for the gospel to be preached to the dead (1 *Pet.* iv, 6). And here comes to mind a word, brief but full of meaning, which the mouth of the Lord spoke, as the prophet testifies: *Thou hast said*, referring undoubtedly to the Lord his God, *Be converted, O ye sons of men* (*Ps.* lxxxix, 3). Deservedly indeed should conversion be required of the sons of men; it is necessary, seeing that they are sinners. Upon the heavenly spirits is enjoined what better befits the righteous, namely, praise; as the same prophet sings: *Praise thy God, O Sion* (*Ps.* cxlvii, 12). Moreover the phrase used, *Thou hast said*, should not, as I think, be lightly accounted of or understood in an ordinary sense. For who would dare to compare what we are told God has said with human words? The word of God is living and effective (*Heb.* iv, 12), and his voice a voice of great deeds and of power (*Ps.* xxviii, 4). In short, *he spoke and they were made* (*Ps.* cxlviii, 5); he said: *Be light made. And light was made* (*Gen.* i, 3). He said: *Be converted*, and the sons of men have been converted. Quite evidently, then, conversion of souls is the work of the Divine, not of the human voice. Simon, son of John (*John* xxi, 15), called and appointed by the Lord to be a fisher of men, even he will toil all night in vain and take nothing, until casting the net at the Lord's word he encloses a great multitude of fishes. To-day may we too cast the net at his word, and learn the truth of what is written: *He will give to his voice the voice of power* (*Ps.* lxvii, 34). If we speak falsehood, plainly it will be of our own that we speak (*John* viii, 44). Then too, perchance, if we seek our own and not the things which are Jesus Christ's (*Phil.* ii, 21), it will be judged to be our own voice, not the Lord's. For the rest, even if we speak the righteousness of God and seek the glory of God, it will yet be necessary to look for the effect from him alone and to ask him to lend to his voice a voice of power. We admonish you therefore that the ears of your hearts be aroused to this interior voice, in

which he calls *conversio*. The word of God is a *life-giving* and

---

order that you may be zealous to hear God speaking within rather than man without. For it is a voice of great deeds and of power (*Ps.* xxviii, 4), shaking the desert (*Ps.* xxviii, 8), revealing secrets, dispelling the torpor of souls. CHAPTER II *None may escape the appeal of the Divine voice, which, whether a man will or no, brings the soul face to face with itself.* Truly it needs not that we labour to hear this voice; rather were it a labour so to close thine ears as not to hear it. Indeed it offers itself; it imposes itself; never does it cease to knock at the door of each one of us. In a word: *Forty years*, the Scripture tells us, *was I very near to this generation and said: These men always err in heart* (*Ps.* xciv, 10). Still is he very near to us; still does he speak, and perchance there is none to listen. Still he says: *These men err in heart*. Still wisdom cries aloud in the streets (*Prov.* i, 20): *Return, ye transgressors, to the heart* (*Isa.* xlvi, 8). Now this is what the Lord said to begin with, and this word addressed to all these who are being converted in heart seems to have come first, a word which not merely calls them back, but leads them back and sets them before their own faces. For it is not only a voice of power, but it is also a ray of light, equally declaring to men their sins and revealing the hidden things of darkness (1 *Cor.* iv, 5). For there is no difference between this voice and light, seeing that one and the same Person is the Son of God, the Word of the Father and the splendour of his glory (*Heb.* i, 3); so too the substance of the soul would seem to be, in its own kind, spiritual and simple; unaffected by any distinction between the senses, but the whole soul—if indeed it is to be spoken of as a whole—alike seeing and hearing. What then is the purpose of that ray of light, of that word, if not that the soul may know itself? Indeed the book of conscience is laid open, a wretched past is recalled, a sad story is unfolded. The reason is enlightened and the record of the memory is, as it were, submitted to its scrutiny. But both reason and memory are not so much possessions of the soul, as they are the soul itself; thus it is the soul which, at once both inspector and inspected, is set before its own face and compelled by the violent apparitors of thoughts which arise against it (*Rom.* ii, 15) to be judged in the first instance at its own bar. *My soul is troubled within myself*, says the prophet of the Lord (*Ps.* xli, 7), and thou, dost thou wonder that thou canst not without conviction of sin, without distress, without confusion be set before thine own face? CHAPTER III *The soul, instructed by the Divine voice, may discover and judge its own evil state.* It is not from me that thou must expect to learn what in thy memory reason discovers and blames. Apply thy hearing within, use the eyes of thy heart, and by thine own testing thou wilt learn its state. For no one knows what is in man,

active expression of His will which stirs us up, separates us from what is not willed by God, moves our minds and our wills powerfully towards the fulfillment of His will, eventually uniting us to

---

except the spirit of man which is in him (1 *Cor.* ii, 11). If there be hidden within thee pride, or envy, or avarice, or ambition, or any such pest, scarcely will it be able to escape this scrutiny. If fornication, or rapine, or cruelty, or any kind of deceit, indeed, whatever fault you will, be there, it may not be hidden from the judge within who is himself the accused; nor in his presence will it be denied. For, however quickly passed all the prurience of sinful flesh, however soon ended all voluptuous charm, it impressed the thoughts of its bitterness upon the memory; it left its foul traces. Forsooth into that depository, as into some cesspit, all the abomination, all the filth has run. It is a great volume, in which everything has been written; written, mark you, with the pen of truth. And now the belly bears this bitter stuff, however the poor palate seemed to enjoy for a brief moment a certain sorry sweetness. My belly, my belly! In my misery I bewail it. The belly of my memory in which is congested so much putrid stuff, why should I not bewail it? My brothers, which of us, were he suddenly to discover that this outside garment which he wears was smeared all over with filthy spittle and defiled by some fetid dirt, would not vehemently abhor it, would not quickly put it off, would not fling it from him with disgust? So then a man, who finds in such a state, not his garment, but his very inner self beneath his garment, must so much the more lament, so much the more be distressed in mind, as what he shrinks from enduring is nearer to his person. For the infected soul will not be able, as a man flings away his tunic, so to fling away itself. Who of us is so patient and so brave, were he perchance, as we read of Moses's sister Mary, to see his own flesh glittering with the deadly candour of leprosy, as to be able to stand by unmoved and give thanks to his Creator? But what is that flesh of yours, if not the corruptible tunic with which we are clothed? Or how should this bodily leprosy be accounted of by all the elect, if not as the rod of a Father's correction and as the cleansing of their hearts? Then is it that there is strong tribulation, then most just cause for grief, when a man, roused from the sleep of wretched pleasure, begins to discover the inward leprosy which he himself has sought for himself with such effort and such toil. Be it that no man hates his own flesh (*Eph.* v, 29), still less will the soul be able to hate itself" (*Of Conversion: A Sermon to the Clergy by Saint Bernard of Clairvaux*, trans. Watkin Williams [London: Burns, Oates & Washbourne, 1938], 1–7; *PL* 182, cols. 833B–837B).

Him in love. (For {the} word of God in this context, understand *actual grace*—inspiration of the Holy Spirit—usually coupled with {the} influence of some Scripture passage.) Remember (cf. St. Anthony,[51] St. Francis,[52] etc.): conversions of the saints {are} usually powerfully influenced by some Scripture passage. William of St. Thierry cites a passage which he thinks sums up St. Bernard's vocation to the monastery. (In all probability {it} sums up William's own vocation to Cîteaux): "*Venite ad me omnes qui laboratis et onerati estis et ego reficiam vos. Tollite jugum meum super vos ET INVENIETIS REQUIEM ANIMABUS VESTRIS*" (Matt. 11:28-29).[53] The essence of St. Bernard's vocation is a CONVERSION FROM VANITY TO TRUTH, FROM ILLUSION TO REALITY, operated by the fear of the Lord, in response to the personal call of Truth from within the depths of his own soul, promising him *rest* in certitude in exchange for *labor* and *anxiety* caused by the pursuit of illusion. The price of this rest is complete self-denial, the total gift of self to God, by obedience ("*tollite jugum meum super vos*"). The reason why St. Bernard chooses Cîteaux is that he thinks Cîteaux has the *Real Thing*—it is a monastery where there are no illusions and compromises; the monastic life is lived in its simplicity and truth, as it should be lived, and there is nothing fake about it. At Cîteaux, therefore, he can rest in the certitude that he is really doing the right thing, and really giving himself to God.

51. St. Anthony was inspired to renounce the world and become a hermit by Matt. 19:21. See Thomas Merton, *Cassian and the Fathers: Initiation into the Monastic Tradition*, ed. Patrick F. O'Connell, Monastic Wisdom [MW], vol. 1 (Kalamazoo, MI: Cistercian Publications, 2005), 32.

52. St. Francis "understood as addressed to himself the Gospel text: *If you wish to come after me, deny yourself and take up your cross and follow me* (Mt. 16:24)" (St. Bonaventure, *Major Life of St. Francis*, c. 1.5, in Bonaventure, *The Soul's Journey into God; The Tree of Life; The Life of St. Francis*, trans. Ewert Cousins, Classics of Western Spirituality [New York: Paulist Press, 1978], 189).

53. "Come to me, all you that labour, and are burdened, and I will refresh you. Take up my yoke upon you, . . . and you shall find rest to your souls" (*Vita Prima*, 1.3.8 [col. 231BC]).

Let us now discuss these statements in detail:

1. *Conversion from vanity to truth*: (a) {We must recognize} the *danger* of vanity. It is not safe to remain in the world where the soul is surrounded by illusion, in appeals to the passions which blind the conscience: *"non esse tutum diu cohabitare serpenti"*[54] (231). (b) In what precisely did "vanity" consist? It *is not* a question of St. Bernard fleeing from women. It is clear that he had completely overcome the flesh (cf. n. 6—it seems that the phrase *"a calore carnalis concupiscentiae totus refriguit"*[55] may be taken as a *permanent* change, to judge by the opening lines of n. 7 [230D][56]). {It} *is* centered in the concupiscence of the eyes, partly, but especially in the *pride of life*. He sees the devil offering him *"magna res* [possessions], *spes majores* [ambitions, positions, honors], SED FALLACES OMNES"[57]—HONORS, ETC., ARE A BAIT OF ILLUSION. What precisely was this temptation? His family was pushing him towards a Church career in which he would be able to *exercise his talents*, and taste the pleasure and success that followed from this, and in which he would be *admired* for learning, ability and *sanctity*. Although this in itself was not wrong, he saw in it the occasion for sin, for a turning away from God, a contempt of God. *"Appetitus vanitatis* contemptus est veritatis."[58] Read *Letter*

---

54. "It is not safe to live together with the serpent for any length of time" (*Vita Prima*, 1.3.8 [col. 231B]).

55. "he was completely cooled from the heat of carnal concupiscence" (*Vita Prima*, 1.3.6 [col. 230C]).

56. "*Circa idem tempus instinctu daemonis in lectum dormientis injecta est puella nuda. Quam ille sentiens, cum omni pace et silentio partem ei lectuli quam occupaverat, cessit, et in latus alterum se convertit, atque dormivit*" ("Around that same time a naked girl, by the inspiration of the demon, threw herself into the bed of the sleeping Bernard. Becoming aware of her, he moved in complete peace and silence from the part of the bed she had occupied, turned away to the other side, and slept").

57. "great possessions, greater hopes, but all illusory" (*Vita Prima*, 1.3.8 [col. 231B]).

58. *Epistola* 18 (*PL* 182, col. 121A, which reads: ". . . *contemptus veritatis*") ("To desire vanity is the same thing as to ignore the truth" [*The Letters*

2, to Fulk, a youth with the same problem.[59] Ambition is "*contemptus caritatis*" (8).[60] But St. Bernard is personally concerned because it seems that this same Fulk's uncle, who is now trying to turn him away from religious life, tried to do the same to Bernard. ("*In me certe fervorem novitium extinguere voluit; sed Deo gratias non valuit*" [81B][61]). Read n. 4—the animated "dialogue" between the wicked uncle and Christ.[62] Relatives who strive to

---

*of St. Bernard of Clairvaux*, trans. Bruno Scott James (Chicago: Henry Regnery Company, 1953), 52] [#19]).

59. *PL* 182, cols. 79C–87C (*Letters*, 10–18); according to James's headnote, "*Little seems to be known about Fulk beyond what can be gathered from this letter. Evidently he was a young man who, after he had been professed as a Canon Regular of St. Augustine, was persuaded by his rich uncle to return to the world. As he later became Archdeacon of Langres we may assume that he did not follow the advice of St. Bernard and return to his Order*" (10).

60. "*Contemptus oblita sui*" (col. 80A) ("She [i.e., Charity] will forget how you repudiated her" [*Letters*, 11]); the enumeration here is evidently a reference to the pagination of the Mabillon edition that is reprinted, with these numbers, in *PL* 182.

61. "He certainly tried to damp my novice's ardour but, thanks to God, he was not able" (*Letters*, 11).

62. "But what shall I say of the malice of this uncle of yours who draws his nephews from the army of Christ that he may drag them with him to hell? Is this the way he rewards those he loves? Whom Christ calls to share with him his heavenly kingdom, this uncle invites to burn forever with him in hell. I should not wonder if Christ were not already angry with him and saying to him, 'How often have I not been ready to gather thy nephews together, and thou didst refuse it. Behold your house is left desolate to you.' Christ says, 'Let the little children be, do not keep them back from me, the kingdom of heaven belongs to such as these.' But your uncle says, 'Leave my nephews to me that they may burn with me.' 'They are mine,' says Christ, 'and must serve me.' 'They shall perish with me,' says your uncle. 'I redeemed them, they are mine,' says Christ. 'But I fed them,' says your uncle. 'The bread you fed them with was mine not yours, but my blood not yours redeemed them,' says Christ. Thus their uncle after the flesh fights with their heavenly father for his nephews in order to disinherit them of heavenly joys and burden them with earthly gifts" (*Letters*, 12 [*PL* 182, cols. 81C–82A]).

make others remain in the world and live according to the world are greatly to be condemned. Note how St. Bernard's experience affects his whole view of the monastic vocation.

2. *The Voice of Truth*: the action of vanity is *exterior*, working on our senses, the passions, sometimes through human instruments. But the action of truth is *from within*. The voice of truth is *sweetly persistent*. It promises rest, and *asks a complete gift of self*. "*Veritatem vero ipsam et interius jugiter audiebat clamantem ac dicentem, Venite ad me, omnes qui laboratis*" etc. (231B).[63]

3. *The Choice of Cîteaux*: it was clear that the choice of a monastery would be dictated by St. Bernard's principal motives—*flight from illusion*, flight from all that *savors of worldliness*, of *self-display*, pride, ambition, power, {along with a} positive desire to give himself to Christ and to rest secure. He begins to ask himself: "UBI CERTIUS AC PURIUS INVENIRET REQUIEM ANIMAE SUAE SUB JUGO CHRISTI."[64] But this "*certius*" and "*purius*" are fulfilled most of all at Cîteaux. Two other factors, which might have deterred another, accidentally CONFIRM his choice of Cîteaux: (1) the place is poor and severely criticized; (2) the place is extraordinarily austere. Note {that} St. Bernard does not choose Cîteaux precisely because of the poverty and bad reputation of the place, its instability, its hard life; but these factors also attract him and confirm his attraction to the *essential* point he seeks in a complete conversion to God by a *purely* and *authentically* monastic life. They are integral to such a vocation. They might have frightened him, says William, but they did not do so, because he was really seeking God. He set aside all hesitation.

4. *Motives in going to Cîteaux*: William then describes the state of mind of Bernard in going to Cîteaux: (1) he seeks above all a

---

63. *Vita Prima*, 1.3.8 (col. 231B, which reads: ". . . *ipsam interius* . . .") ("But within he heard Truth itself constantly calling and saying, 'Come to me, all you who labor,'" etc.).

64. *Vita Prima*, 1.3.8 (col. 231C) ("Where he might more surely and more purely find rest for his soul under the yoke of Christ").

hidden life—"*omnino delitescere*";[65] (2) peace in this hidden life with God: "*abscondi in abscondito faciei Dei omni conturbatione hominum*";[66] (3) above all to flee illusion: "MAXIME AD EFFUGIUM VANITATIS,"[67] {which was especially} dangerous either (a) because of his nobility; or (b) because of his gifts; or (c) because of his fame for sanctity (231D).

### NOVITIATE OF SAINT BERNARD—*St. Bernard's Monastic Formation*

1. William of St. Thierry stresses the fact that the entrance of St. Bernard at Cîteaux with his thirty companions was the sign of the Lord's blessing. It began the expansion of the Order. The novitiate of St. Bernard, who was a mystic from the beginning, is marked by *special graces* and *extraordinary austerity* which belonged to his extraordinary vocation.

2. "*Vitam angelicam in terris vixit.*"[68] This is not the normal way to live. William of St. Thierry stresses that it is a special gift of God, and that those who have not received the gift are unable even to understand what it is all about. Nevertheless, the extraordinary austerity and the special graces of prayer in St. Bernard's novitiate were given to him as a father and master of souls. He was to lead others by the same way of *austerity* and *contemplation*, although they would not be able to go as far as he, either in mortification or in the contemplation of the divine truth. It is above all stressed that St. Bernard did not arrive at contemplation

---

65. *Vita Prima*, 1.3.8 (col. 231C, which reads: "*omnino ibi* [there] *delitescere*") ("to hide away completely").
66. *Vita Prima*, 1.3.8 (col. 231CD, which reads: ". . . *Dei ab omni* . . .") ("to be hidden away from every disturbance of men in the secret of the face of God" [Ps. 30[31]:21]).
67. *Vita Prima*, 1.3.8 (col. 231D, which reads; "*maximaeque* . . .") ("especially for escape from vanity").
68. *Vita Prima*, 1.4.19 (col. 237D, which reads: ". . . *angelicam gerens in* . . .") ("He lived an angelic life on earth").

by means of a technique of mortification. Rather it was the other way round. His extraordinary mortification was made possible, in large measure, by the profound absorption of his soul in God. William of St. Thierry also repeatedly asserts that St. Bernard's experience of God was richly consoling: *"benedictiones dulcedinis"*;[69] {he} tasted the goodness and sweetness of God constantly for long periods, as one who was to communicate that sweetness to others. *"Totus absorptus in spiritum, spe tota in Deum directa, intentione seu meditatione spirituali tota occupata memoria, videns non videbat, audiens non audiebat; nihil sapiebat gustanti, vix aliquid sensu aliquo corporis sentiebat"* (n. 20 [238]).[70] *"Curiositatis sensu mortificato, nil hujusmodi sentiebat; vel si forte aliquando eum contingebat videre, memoria alibi occupata non advertebat"* (238).[71]

3. *How did St. Bernard arrive at this state?* (a) by a special preparation in the order of nature; (b) by special gifts of grace; (c) by extraordinary generosity and application.

a) *Gifts of Nature*: *"Ad contemplanda spiritualia quaeque seu divina, cum gratia spirituali, naturali quadam {virtute} pollebat ingenii."*[72] {He} quotes *Wisdom* 8:19-20: "I was a talented child and a noble nature had fallen to my lot; gentle birth above the

---

69. *Vita Prima*, 1.4.19 (col. 237D–238A) ("the blessings of sweetness").

70. *Vita Prima*, 1.4.20 (col. 238CD, which reads: *"totusque . . ."*) ("Totally taken up into the spirit, with all his hope directed toward God, with his memory totally occupied by spiritual attentiveness or meditation, seeing, he did not see, hearing, he did not hear; he enjoyed the flavor of nothing he tasted; he scarcely felt anything with any sense of his body").

71. *Vita Prima*, 1.4.20 (col. 238D, which reads: *"Curiositatis enim sensu . . . memoria, ut dictum est* [as it is said], *alibi . . ."*) ("With his sense of curiosity mortified, he felt nothing of this sort; or if by chance it sometimes happened that he did see, he did not pay attention to it, his memory being otherwise occupied").

72. *Vita Prima*, 1.4.21 (col. 239A, which reads: *"Ad contemplanda quippe spiritualia . . ."*; *"virtute"* omitted in copy text) ("In order to contemplate every spiritual or divine thing, along with spiritual grace he was strong with a certain natural strength of character").

common had endowed me with a body free from blemish"[73] (partly Knox[74]). What was this perfect nature? It was *not inclined to curiosity or sensuality*. It was spontaneously obedient to the spirit, and *inclined to the things of God*. His flesh had never known sin, and followed the spirit as a most apt instrument for the service of God. St. Bernard hardly ever felt any of the struggle of flesh against spirit: "*cum caro . . . vix aliquid concupisceret adversus spiritum*" (239).[75] {He} was able to do without food and sleep to an extraordinary degree (because of the effects of {the} graces of prayer, largely).

b) *Special gifts of grace* {included} absorption in the sweetness of God (as we have seen above). {He also had a} special grace to be without distractions at manual labor—even involuntary ones: "*Ipse* privilegio majoris gratiae *in virtute spiritus simul et totus quodammodo exterius laborabat, et totus interius Deo vacabat*" ({240}).[76] Even though his nature was perfectly adapted to the graces of contemplation, by excessive penance he ruined his health. "The spirit listed so strongly against the flesh, exceeding the powers and the strength of flesh and blood, that the poor beast of burden fell under the load and has never since been able

---

73. *Vita Prima*, 1.4.21 (col. 239A) ("*Puer eram ingeniosus, et sortitus sum animam bonam; et cum magis essem bonus, veni ad corpus incoinquinatum*").

74. See *The Old Testament*, trans. from the Vulgate by Ronald Knox, 2 vols. (New York: Sheed & Ward, 1950), 2:983: "I was, indeed, a boy of good parts, and nobility of nature had fallen to my lot; gentle birth above the common had endowed me with a body free from blemish."

75. "*cum caro in eo ex dono praevenientis gratiae, et adjutorio subsequentis naturae, et usu bono spiritualis disciplinae, vix jam aliquid . . .*" (*Vita Prima*, 1.4.21 [col. 239B]) ("when the flesh in him, through the gift of prevenient grace, and the aid of nature that followed, and the good use of spiritual discipline, now scarcely desired anything contrary to the spirit").

76. *Vita Prima*, 1.4.23 (col. 240C; copy text reads: "239") ("By a privilege of a greater grace, in the power of the Spirit, in some way exteriorly he himself was totally at work, and at the same time interiorly was totally open to God").

to get on its feet" (239).[77] But miraculous aids helped him to continue, in spite of ruined health, to perform superhuman feats of endurance. "*Vigilat ultra possibilitatem humanam.*"[78] {He has} no appetite for food {and} eats only to keep {his} body from failing: "*Etenim comesturus, priusquam comedat, sola cibi memoria satiatus est*" ({this is} hyperbole) (239).[79] {His} ruined stomach no longer permits him to digest food.

c) *Generosity and application*: this is the important part for us. We cannot have his gifts merely for the asking: God gives such things to whom He pleases, and usually only to those who have some special vocation. But we must all imitate St. Bernard's zeal for the service of God: (1) on entering the monastery he gave himself entirely to the *hidden life*: "*Intentione ibi* moriendi a cordibus et memoria hominum *et spe delitescendi et latendi tanquam vas perditum*" (238);[80] (2) what was his first concern? purity of heart and perseverance: "*custodiam sui cordis et propositi constantiam*" (238);[81] (3) {this} went beyond mortification of desires—{it} mortified the senses themselves, so that they lost their usefulness (this is not to be imitated, and he never urged anyone to imitate him in this, but we must imitate his mortification of the desires, and be austere with the flesh on principle); (4) *zeal for the common life*: "*Inter novitios novitius, monachus inter monachos*"[82]—{he} felt that

---

77. "*spiritus supra vires, supra virtutem carnis ac sanguinis, tanta adversus carnem concupiscebat, ut infirmum animal cadens sub onere, usque in hanc diem non adjiciat ut resurgat*" (*Vita Prima*, 1.4.21 [col. 239B]).

78. *Vita Prima*, 1.4.21 (col. 239B) ("He keeps watch beyond human possibility").

79. *Vita Prima*, 1.4.22 (col. 239D) ("In fact, when about to eat, but before eating, he was satisfied by the mere recollection of food").

80. *Vita Prima*, 1.4.19 (col. 238A) ("With the intention of dying away from the hearts and memory of men, and the hope of hiding away and escaping notice like a lost vessel").

81. *Vita Prima*, 1.4.19 (col. 238A) ("the custody of his heart and the constancy of his offering").

82. *Vita Prima*, 1.4.22 (col. 240A) ("a novice among the novices, a monk among the monks").

he was indeed a novice, less perfect than the others, and *much in need of monastic discipline*; {having a} sense of the need of monastic discipline is a great grace, because it implies humility and poverty of spirit, as opposed to the pride of those who think they excel in discipline and embrace it not because they "need" it {but} as if the monastery needs them; (5) *zeal for manual labor*: {he was} hungry for work to do {but} could not keep up with the others, {so} took on humble jobs {and} prayed for strength to be a good harvester, and his prayer was answered; (6) *zeal for prayer and solitude*: "*Ad orandum si se solitudo offeret, ea utebatur: sin autem, ubicunque, seu apud se, seu in turba esset, solitudinem cordis sibi ipse efficiens, ubique solus erat*" (241);[83] (7) *lectio divina*: {he} gave himself with zeal to the study of Scripture and the Fathers, reading the Bible "*simpliciter et seriatim*"[84]—{he} derived most profit from meditation of Scripture while working in the woods, so that he said his best masters had been the oaks and beeches of the forest, and that all the lights of later days went back to these hours in the fields and in the woods (240).[85] So much for St. Bernard as a person. We cannot go into the details of his life and activity here. An *outline* must suffice, then we will pass on to his works.

---

83. *Vita Prima*, 1.4.24 (col. 241A, which reads: ". . . *ipse sibi* . . .") ("If solitude offered itself, he used it for praying; but if not, wherever he was, whether by himself or in a crowd, making for himself a solitude of the heart, he was everywhere alone").

84. *Vita Prima*, 1.4.24 (col. 241A) ("simply and sequentially").

85. "*Nam usque hodie quidquid in Scripturis valet, quidquid in eis spiritualiter sentit, maxime in silvis et in agris meditando et orando se confitetur accepisse; et in hoc nullos aliquando se magistros habuisse, nisi quercus et fagos, joco illo suo gratioso inter amicos dicere solet*" (*Vita Prima*, 1.4.23 [col. 240CD]) ("For up to the present day he acknowledges that whatever he finds valuable in the scriptures, whatever he experiences spiritually in them, he received by meditating and praying in the woods and in the fields; and he is accustomed to say among his friends as a pleasant jest of his that in this respect he had no teachers at all except the oaks and beeches").

## Life of St. Bernard

{During his} *childhood*, {he} studies with the canons of St. Vorles; Aleth dies {in} 1103 or 1104 (St. Bernard {was} then thirteen or fourteen).

{The} *First Period*. {In} 1111 the "conversion" of St. Bernard {takes place} (see {earlier}[86] in more detail). {In} 1112, St. Bernard enters Cîteaux with thirty companions. {In} 1113 {he} makes profession, {and in} 1115 {is} sent as superior to {the} new foundation of Clairvaux. {In} 1116, Bernard, after {the} abbatial blessing by William of Champeaux ({a} philosopher), becomes ill under {the} care of {a} quack doctor, {and} brings in {the} first big catch of souls, at Châlons. {During} 1117–1118 Bernard, still sick, meets William of St. Thierry, abbot of {the} Order {of} St. Benedict. {In} 1118 Clairvaux makes {its} first foundation—Trois Fontaines. {In} 1119 {Bernard writes} Letter 1[87] to Robert, his cousin, who "apostatizes" to Cluny, {which} reflects his outlook at this period; Tescelin comes to Clairvaux, {and there is an} economic crisis at Clairvaux. {In} 1123 {his} first miracles {are performed}; 1124–1125 {sees} the affair of Arnold of Morimond (read *Letters*, 4;[88] top {of} page 5[89]), the end of the economic crisis of Clairvaux, due to the

---

86. Copy text reads "later" (inadvertently retained from the earlier version).

87. *PL* 182, cols. 67D–79C (*Letters*, 1–10).

88. "*Arnold was the first Abbot of Morimond, an abbey founded from Cîteaux in the year 1115. . . . This letter belongs to the year 1124 and was occasioned by a sad moral disaster to the Order. Arnold, tiring of the difficulties of his charge (apparently his lay-brothers were lazy, his monks disobedient, and his neighbours hostile), suddenly, and without consulting anyone, left his charge and with a handful of monks set out for the Holy Land 'where,' says Bernard in another letter concerning the same subject, 'it is well known that soldiers to fight and not monks to sing are what is wanted.' But he died suddenly in Belgium the next year without having either accomplished his purpose or corrected his error*" (*Letters*, 19–20 [headnote to Letter 4, to Arnold of Morimond]).

89. "So as not to keep your anxiety in any longer suspense we must tell you that one of our brother abbots, styled of Morimond, has ill-advisedly enough left the monastery over which he ruled and, impelled by a spirit of

intervention of Theobald of Champagne and Geoffrey de la Roche ({the} prior); Bernard {now} writes the *Apologia*;[90] he has begun other treatises. {In} 1125 Bernard {is} again sick. This brings us to the end of the first period of St. Bernard's career: {it is} entirely monastic, with great trials and personal struggles, and difficulties with his abbey. The foundations are *few*, three so far. His writing activity has hardly begun. He is not yet prominent in public life.

{The} *Second Period*. {In} 1126 not much {is} going on, except writing; {Bernard is} busy with *De Diligendo Deo*[91] {and} *De Gradibus Humilitatis*;[92] these are the fruit of St. Bernard's first period; he is sick in bed again this year. {In} 1127 {he composes} *De Gratia et Libero Arbitrio*,[93] again characteristic of his early thought; Bernard resists {making a} foundation in Spain—{he} has been trying to check expansion, but now gives in and founds Igny, {the} fourth {Clairvaux} foundation; foundations now follow rapidly; again St. Bernard is sick in bed and nearly dies. {In} 1128, St. Bernard writes {a} spiritual directory for the Knights Templar,[94] acts as secretary at {the} Council of Troyes ({where} approbation of {the} Templars {is given}), {and makes} intervention in secular affairs, pleading for victims of injustice, etc., {as well as} advising

---

frivolity, has determined to set out for Jerusalem. But first, they say, he will try whether he can, in any way, wring a licence from you for his blunder. If you were to countenance him at all in this matter (which God forbid), consider, we implore you, how great an occasion of harm it would be to our Order. With such an example before him any abbot would believe himself at liberty to throw over the burden of his office as soon as it became irksome, and especially would this be the case with us where the burden seems great and the honour small" (*Letters*, 23 [to Pope Calixtus]; *Epistola* 359 [*PL* 182, cols. 560C–561A]).

90. *PL* 182, cols. 895D–918A.
91. *PL* 182, cols. 974A–1000B.
92. *PL* 182, cols. 941A–972C.
93. *PL* 182, cols. 1001A–1030A.
94. *De Laude Novae Militiae ad Milites Templi Liber* (*PL* 182, cols. 921A–940B).

and correcting bishops (read Letters 67,[95] 101,[96] 224;[97] {see also the}

> 95. To Alexander, Bishop of Lincoln (*Letters*, 90–92; *PL* 182, cols. 169A–170C [#64]), mainly concerning his canon, Philip, who has joined the community at Clairvaux (see below, pages 227–28); in the final section, Bernard writes: "And now I turn to yourself. I feel impelled and even inspired by the Charity of God to exhort you not to regard the passing glory of the world as if it would never pass away; and so lose the glory that endures for ever; not to love your possessions more than your self or only for your own sake, and so lose both your possessions and your self; not to allow the flattery of present prosperity to hide from you the inevitable end, so that when it comes it will bring endless adversity; not to allow the pleasures of this world to beget for you and conceal from you the endless woe which they beget by concealing, so that when you think death is far off, it may come upon you unawares, and while you are counting on a long life, life itself may suddenly leave you ill prepared, according to what has been written: 'It is just when men are saying, All quiet, all safe, that doom will fall upon them suddenly, like the pangs that come to a woman in travail, and there will be no escape from it'" (91–92; col. 170BC).
>
> 96. To a Certain Chancellor (*Letters*, 149): "To the noble and honourable S., Chancellor, health in the Lord, from Bernard, Abbot of Clairvaux. God has given you many good things in this life, but it is much to be feared that, unless you derive from your worldly and temporal goods some profit for your soul, you will lose the eternal joys of heaven for the sake of the passing and deceitful pleasures of time. In all simplicity, I would therefore suggest that some . . . of our brothers wish to divide and build an abbey. If you wish to keep them by building for them a place on your property, as you can easily do, I beg you to notify me by the bearer of this letter. Surely your great sickness, of which I have heard, is a warning from God that you should succour your soul endangered among the false pleasures of the world, by this or some other good work" [the ellipsis in the text denotes missing material].
>
> 97. To Henry, Archbishop of Sens (*Letters*, 303–4; *PL* 182, cols. 344C–345B [#182]): "I confess that I have often intended to write to you for your own sake on behalf of other people, and then have decided not to do so on account of your hateful hardness: but charity shall prevail. I want to keep your friends for you, but you will not condescend to it. I wish to reconcile your enemies to you, but you will not suffer it. You will not have peace, you are set on rushing to your own shame, confusion, and deposition. You are multiplying your accusers and driving away your supporters. In everything your own sweet will is law, you think only of power and not at all of the

letter *De Moribus Episcoporum*[98]). {In} 1129 {he} refuses to make {a} foundation in {the} Holy Land, but is more and more out of his monastery; {he becomes involved in the} conflict over the Archbishop of Paris. {In} 1130, Letters 21[99] and 51.3[100] explain his position and {he} defends himself against criticism for intervening in public affairs; {there is a} double papal election, {and} Bernard at {the} Council of Étampes swings France to {the} cause of Innocent II; {he} also has {a} conference with {the} King of England and swings him to Innocent. From now on St. Bernard is in the center of everything. This ends the second period, one of transition, in which Bernard finds his place as the leading light of his age, as a writer, as a figure in Church councils and affairs of state.

{The} *Third Period* (SCHISM). {In} 1131 (March), {Bernard made a} voyage through north France and Flanders; {his} first skirmish with Abelard {took place} (after {a} visit to {the} Convent of {the} Paraclete); {there was a} visit of {the} Pope and cardinals to Clairvaux (see {the} *Vita Prima*[101]). {In} 1132 {the} foundation of Rievaulx {was made} (read {the} Letter to Henry {I}[102] of

---

fear of God. All your enemies are laughing about you, all your friends complaining. How could you have unfrocked that man when he had not been, I do not say convicted in court, but even summoned. Everyone will be shocked by this, everyone will be whispering about it, everyone will jeer at it, everyone will be indignant. Do you really think that the whole world is as void of all sense of justice as you seem to be, so that you can deprive a man of his archdeaconry in this way without causing remark? Or perhaps it pleases you more to give it and then take it away, than to retain his gratitude for the gift of it? Do not, I pray, do not do this thing, which will shock everyone and please no one. Perhaps I have written more boldly and more bitingly than you could wish, but if you will correct your ways you will see it has been for your good."

98. *PL* 182, cols. 809A–834A, also written to Archbishop Henry of Sens.
99. *Letters*, 55 (*PL* 182, col. 123AB [#20]).
100. *Letters*, 80–81 (*PL* 182, cols. 156B–157B [#48]); both this letter and the preceding are addressed to Cardinal Haimeric, the papal chancellor.
101. *Vita Prima*, 2.1.6-7 (*PL* 185, cols. 272A–273A).
102. Copy text reads "II".

England: #95[103]), {as well as the} foundation of Moruela in Spain, along with many others; {Bernard was} still travelling and working for Innocent II. {In} 1133 {he makes a} voyage to Italy, arbitrates between Pisa and Genoa, enters hostile Rome ({cf.} Letter 141[104]) {and} returns to Tours in {the} summer to negotiate {a} local schism. 1135 {finds} Bernard in Brittany, {then in} Poitou ({the} conversion of William of Angoulême {takes place}), {the} Rhineland, Bamberg, Lombardy ({for the} Council of Pisa—May), Milan (June), Pavia (August), Cremona; {he} returns to France in November (read Letter 137;[105] read letters 145,[106] 146,[107] 164,[108] 165[109]);

103. "To Henry, the illustrious King of England, that in his earthly kingdom he may faithfully serve and humbly obey the King of heaven, from Bernard, styled Abbot of Clairvaux. In your land there is an outpost of my Lord and your Lord, an outpost which he has preferred to die for than to lose. I have proposed to occupy it and I am sending men from my army who will, if it is not displeasing to you, claim it, recover it, and restore it with a strong hand. For this purpose I have sent ahead these men who now stand before you to reconnoitre. They will investigate the situation carefully and report back to me faithfully. Help them as messengers of your Lord and in their persons fulfil your duties as a vassal of their Lord. And may he for his honour, the salvation of your soul, and the health and peace of your kingdom, bring you safe and happy to a good and peaceful end" (*Letters*, 141–42; *PL* 182, cols. 224C–225A [#92]).

104. Writing to King Henry I of England, Bernard says: "We are on the threshold of the city, delivery is at the gates, justice is on our side; but the Roman soldiers cannot live on such fare. So we try to please God with the justice of our cause and cower the enemy with our arms, but we lack the bare necessities of life" (*Letters*, 209; *PL* 182, cols. 292B–293A [#138]).

105. "To his most loving father and lord, the Supreme Pontiff Innocent, the humble devotion of Brother Bernard. The opposition of Cremona has hardened, their prosperity is their undoing; the Milanese have become arrogant, their over-weening self-confidence deceives them. I am undone and my efforts are frustrated by those who put their trust in horses and chariots. I was sadly leaving when I received some consolation from you. Although the trials I endure for the sake of Christ are many, so also are the consolations I receive through him. When I received your welcome letter my heart was gladdened by the assurance it gave of your safety, of the misfortunes of the enemy, and of the successes of our allies. But when I came to the sad conclusion, my joy was a little damped. Who would not fear your anger? I admit

{he gives the} first Sermons on {the} Canticle of Canticles {in}

---

that it is reasonable, and therefore all the more to be feared. My opinion is that what has not yet been accomplished, should be done; but in God's good time. Then you can just as readily do what you intend, and perhaps with less risk. By intemperate action, how soon could all you have accomplished with these people by the mercy of God, and at the cost of so much labour on the part of yourself and your servants, be reduced to nothing! And it would be surprising if such an action were to please him who exalts mercy over justice. Unhappy the lot of that bishop who has been transferred to Ur of the Chaldees from a sort of paradise, 'to have dragons for his brothers, and ostriches for his company.' What can he do? He would like to obey you, but the beasts of Ephesus bare their teeth at him. Very prudently he is trying to disguise his sentiments for the time being, but only to incur thereby the very much more fearful wrath of yourself. On all sides he is beset by difficulties; unless he should find it more satisfactory to be without a people than without a lord, since he very properly prefers the favour of his Pope to his See of Milan. Can you doubt his loyalty? If any evil-minded person has tried to suggest to you the contrary, he only proves himself disloyal by spitefully persecuting with venomous tongue a man of excellent character. I implore you, most loving father, to have consideration for this most loyal servant of yours, for the work that has only just been started, for this newly planted tree; I beg you to spare the people who have only lately attached themselves to you and to remember the benefits which, as you rightly say, you have only recently conferred upon them. Remember, dear lord, those words of your Lord: 'I have been coming to look for fruit on this fig tree for three years, and cannot find any.' You have waited scarcely three months, and yet you are already preparing the axe! If you had waited already three years, we would still be entitled to expect a faithful servant of the Lord to wait yet a fourth. Therefore I say: Let it be for this year and permit him to whom you have entrusted the sterile ground of Milan, to dig it about with the spade of penance, to dung it with his tears, so that he can induce it to bring forth fruit" (*Letters*, 205–6; *PL* 182, cols. 520C–521D [#314]).

106. To the Cistercian abbots meeting in General Chapter: "Weak in body and (God knows) anxious of heart I write to you—a wretched man, born to labour, but yet your brother. Would that I might merit to have the Holy Spirit, in whose name you are come together, as my advocate to impress upon your hearts the misfortunes from which I suffer, to portray to your loving eyes the picture of myself sad and on my knees before you. It is not my prayer that he should create in you a new spirit of pity, for I know how habitual to you is that virtue. But I do pray that you may understand from

Advent, after his return to Clairvaux for a quiet interval. {In} 1136

---

the bottom of your hearts how badly I need your pity. Then I am sure tears would well up from the fount of your love, and that with sighs and groans you would storm the gates of heaven so that God should hear you and have pity on me and say: 'Go back to your brothers, you shall die amidst your own and not amidst strangers.' I am afflicted by so many labours and worries that life itself often becomes a burden to me. To speak in a human way because of my great weakness, I desire to be spared until I can return, so that I shall not die until I am with you. For the rest, dear brothers, 'amend your lives and your likings' and determine and observe what is good, what is honest, and what is wholesome; but above all endeavour to preserve unity in the bonds of peace, and so the God of peace will be with you" (*Letters*, 213; *PL* 182, cols. 302B–303A [#145]).

107. To the monks of Clairvaux: "My soul is sorrowful and will not be comforted until I return to you. What consolation can there be for me in this evil hour, in this land of my exile? There is only yourselves. Wherever I am, your dear memory never leaves me. But for this very reason your absence is all the more hard to endure. Unhappy am I to be doomed to an exile ever prolonged! In the words of the Prophet, 'Hard was my hurt to bear and these have added to it,' who separate me from you. The exile from God, which we all endure while we are in the body, is hard enough to bear; but added to this I have to endure an exile from you which almost renders me impatient with my lot. To be involved for so long in the vanity of everything here, to be shut in by the rotten feculence of the body, to remain still bound by the bonds of death and still subject to sin, to be for so long without Christ, this is a continual affliction, a wearisome suspense. I had but one remedy for all this, a truly heaven-sent gift, and it was the sight, instead of God's glorious countenance which is as yet hidden from us, of you who are his holy sanctuary. From this it seemed an easy passage to that glorious sanctuary for which the Prophet sighs when he says: 'One request I have ever had of the Lord, let me claim it still, to dwell in the Lord's house my whole life long, gazing at the beauty of the Lord, haunting his sanctuary.' What more can I say? How many times has not that one comfort of mine been frustrated! Unless I am mistaken this is the third time that my sons have been torn from me, weaned before their time. I am prevented from rearing the sons I have 'begotten in the Gospel.' I am obliged to leave my own to undertake the cares of others. I do not know which is the more painful: to be taken away from the former or to be saddled with the latter. O good Jesu, 'for very misery my strength ebbs away, my frame is wasted, and my years are but sighs.' For me 'death is more welcome than life,' only let it be amongst my

{the} first sermons on {the} *Cantica* {were} sent to Bernard ({a}

own brethren, my own family, my own dear sons! As everyone knows, it is sweeter, safer, and more natural to die thus. It were a loving act 'to give me some respite, some cooling breath of comfort, before I go away and am known no more.' If it please my Lord, let my sons be allowed to close the eyes of their father, albeit I am not worthy to be their father; let them be present at my last end and console my passing away; if it should seem good to thee, let my soul be lifted up on the wings of their prayers to the company of the blessed; let my poor body be buried by their hands amongst the bodies of the poor. If I have found favour in thy eyes, grant this my one great desire for the sake of the prayers and merits of my brethren. Yet not my will, but thine be done. 'I do not wish to live as my own master or die as my own master.' As I have told you of my sorrows, it is right that I should also mention my consolations. First, it is for God's sake that I am suffering all this grief and misfortune; it is for the cause of him for whom all things live. Whether I wish it or not, I cannot but live for him who has purchased my life by laying down his own; for the merciful judge who is able and willing to reward on that last day the sacrifices we have made for him. If I should fight his cause unwillingly, it will only be by his dispensation that I am doing so, and I shall be a wicked servant; but if willingly, then I shall have glory. It is this thought that gives me some respite amidst my troubles. And it is true to say that, for no merits of my own, he has given my labours a happy issue; I can tell from many things that 'the grace he has given me has not been without fruit,' something of which you will probably know. I should like to tell you, for your consolation, how necessary my presence here is or was at this juncture, were it not that it would savour of boasting. It is better that you should learn this from others. Sorrowfully and reluctantly, weak and sickly, and (I must admit) ever haunted by the wan spectre of pale death, I have bowed before the urgent request of the Emperor, the command of the Apostolic See, the prayers of the Church and of secular princes, and suffered myself to be dragged to Apulia. Pray for the peace of the Church, pray for my health, pray that I may see you again, live with you, and die with you. So live that your prayers may avail. Pressed for time and with ebbing strength, my words are broken by tears and sobs, as our dear brother Baldwin, who has taken this letter down for me, can testify. He has been called to serve the Church in another sphere and in another post. Pray for him, because he is my only comfort now and my spirit finds great refreshment in his company. Pray for our lord the Pope who cherishes myself and all of you with fatherly affection. Pray for the lord Chancellor who is like a mother to me, and for all those who are with him . . . my lord Luke, my

Carthusian) (read Letters 153,[110] 154[111]); {he is} absent, briefly, to

---

lord Chrysogonus, and Master Ivo, who are as brothers to me. Brothers Bruno and Gerard are with me and they too beg you to pray for them" (*Letters*, 214–15; *PL* 182, cols. 300B–302B [#144]).

108. To Pope Innocent, on the murder of Prior Thomas of St. Victor: "To his most loving father and lord, Innocent, by the grace of God Supreme Pontiff, the entire devotion and service, for what it is worth, of Bernard, the unworthy Abbot of Clairvaux. A wild beast has devoured Joseph and, unable to meet the attacks of our dogs, it has fled to you, they say, for protection. The wretch must be mad to think that he, a wanderer and fugitive on earth, can find a refuge just where he should have most cause for fear. The scoundrel! Does he think that the seat of supreme justice is a den of thieves or a lair of lions? Does he seek refuge with the mother whose son he has butchered, does he dare to appear before his father, still licking his chops, his jaws still red with the blood of their son? Yet if he should ask to do penance, it should not be denied to him. But if he should only ask for a hearing, let him receive the answer that Moses gave to the people when they were worshipping the molten image, or that Phinees gave to the fornicating Israelite, or that Mattathias gave to the man who sacrificed to devils or, to take examples from nearer your home, let him hear from you what Ananias heard from the blessed Peter, or what the Saviour said to the money changers in the temple. Do we not know that the sins of some men go before them to judgement? Does not the voice of your brother's blood cry out against him to heaven? I believe that the spirit of our martyr, whom he has brutally killed during the last few days, with the souls of all the others who have been slain, is crying out with a strong voice from beneath the altar and demanding a vengeance all the more urgently for his blood having been poured forth so recently. Do you ask, wretch, 'Was it I who killed him?' No, not you, it is true, but your people on your account. Whether by your designs, God shall see and judge. If you have any excuse, you whose teeth are spears and arrows, you whose tongue is a sharp sword, then the Jews are not to be blamed for the death of Christ, for they were careful to keep their hands off him. When the archdeacon found his cupidity restrained by blessed Thomas, a lover and protector of justice, so that he could no longer levy the illegal exactions which, on the score of his archidiaconate, he had been in the habit of doing for some time, he hated him so much that with bloodthirsty intent he was wont to threaten that he would murder him. There are now many witnesses of this, and they should not be ignored. Let the archdeacon say, if he can, what else than this his nephews had against him that they should have laid their murderous hands upon him, a holy man of God. If this man

Poitiers, otherwise at peace in {the} monastery. {In} 1137 {he is}

---

who is the cause, instigator, and also (as everyone suspects) the plotter of this crime; if, I say, this man should go unpunished by the Holy See (which, with unbelievable audacity, is just what he is hoping for) it will be an enormous incitement to other evils in the Church. One of two things would then have to follow: either no one noble or powerful according to the world could be admitted to ecclesiastical honours, or the clergy would have to be permitted everywhere to use their holy office for unworthy purposes, for fear that if anyone, fired by zeal for God's glory, should try to restrain them, they would be immediately butchered by the swords of soldiers as an upholder of justice. And then what would become of the spiritual sword, ecclesiastical penalties, Christian law and order, reverence for the priesthood, and finally the fear of God, if through terror of the secular power, no one should dare to so much as whisper against the effrontery of the clergy? Could there be any worse disorder, anything more unworthy of the Church, than that anyone should claim for himself ecclesiastical dignities by virtue of brute force and not of a holy life? Judge this man, my lord and father, as it shall seem good to you, but let your judgement be such as to benefit the Church and assure security, not only for the present time, but for future generations. Let coming generations know not only of the crime that was done in our times, but also of the punishment that rapidly followed. Otherwise, if the poison should creep through the body without the antidote being administered, it is much to be feared that it will destroy many, and may God forbid this!" (*Letters*, 232–34; *PL* 182, cols. 315B–319A [#158]). This letter and the following one are evidently referred to here as exemplifying what James calls "*the confusion occasioned by the schism*" (*Letters*, 232).

109. To Pope Innocent on the murder of Archibald, sub-dean of Orleans: "The voice of the blood of the Sub-Dean of Orleans increases in strength! Alas now, in the words of the Prophet, 'bloodshed never ends, but it begins again' and cries out to you with a strong voice from France. The blood cries out, I say, and lifts up its voice in a cry strong enough to shake the very palace of heaven, piteous enough to soften even a heart of stone. What are you about, O friend of the Bridegroom, guardian of the bride, and shepherd of Christ's sheep? Do you believe it is enough to think out a remedy for such a fearful, such an unheard-of disease as this? Certainly it is necessary to find something that will heal the wound that has been lately inflicted on the Church and act as a deterrent for the future, but it must also be applied. Gird your thighs with a sword, most powerful one! The destruction will not cease until Phinees rises up and makes amends. If the strength of the Church should spare these two, I mean John and Theobald Notier, by whom innocent

again in Italy (February)—called there by Innocent; {an} illness

---

blood has been shed, if not by their own hands, certainly by their consent, and perhaps by their design, who cannot see what must follow? How many amongst the clergy would the impunity of these men help to high preferment against all right and justice, not for their good lives, but for fear of their armed friends. A new disease must be met with a new remedy. Many think that it would be a good thing and most beneficial if you should cut these men off from all ecclesiastical dignities, so that they may be deprived of what they have and prevented from rising to others" (*Letters*, 234; *PL* 182, cols. 320B–321A [#161]).

110. To Bernard, Monk of the Chartreuse-des-Portes-en-Bugey: "You earnestly entreat me and I firmly refuse you, but only because I want to spare myself, not because I scorn you. I wish I could compose something worthy of your zeal and intelligence. I would give you my very eyes, even my life, were I able to, my most dear friend, for I especially have every reason to love you spiritually in Christ with all the power of which I am capable. But how can I find the ability, let alone the leisure, to do as you ask? It is not as though you were asking me to do some little thing that would be quite easy and ordinary. You would not be so insistent were it only a small matter. Your many letters, and the vehemence which animates them, are a clear enough indication of how serious you are in the matter and what great store you lay by it. And the more anxious I feel you to be, the more diffident do I become. Why so? Simply because I do not want to bring forth an absurd mouse in return for your great hopes. This is what I so much fear, and this is the reason for my delay. It is not surprising that I should fear to give you what I should blush to see published. I am most unwilling to produce what I should regard as more fit for contempt than for publication. Who would wish to give anyone something that it would shame him to give and be no advantage to receive? I willingly give you what I have, but I am not so willing to lose it. Everyone knows how disappointing it is to receive something small when something great has been expected. And what is received with disappointment is not given but lost. 2. It is your endeavour, as a man of leisure and freedom, to seek on all sides fuel for the fire that burns within you, so that you may burn the more, and thus fulfil the words of the Lord to you: 'What would I but that it be kindled?' I have nothing but praise for this, but I beg you to look where you may not be disappointed {in receiving. You are mistaken if you think you can find anything in me to satisfy you. It is I who should beg from you. I know very well that it is more blessed to give than to receive, but only if the gift is creditable to the giver and useful to the receiver, such a gift as I doubt whether I have got to give. Were I to

of Gerard {is} cured by {the} prayer of Bernard; {a} conference of pope and emperor at Bari goes badly; in September, Bernard and Innocent are at Monte Cassino with the German army camped

---

give you what I have, I am afraid that you would feel ashamed to have asked for it, and would regret having received it. But still, perhaps it would be better for you to make your own excuses for me, that your own eyes should provide you with evidence of the truth of what I say. And so I will accede to your importunity, so that you may have no doubts about my insufficiency. It is a matter between friends. I will not try any more to spare my modesty, I will forget my own foolishness in trying to satisfy your demands. I am having copied a few sermons I wrote recently on the first verses of the Song of Solomon, and as soon as they are ready I will send them to you. When I have the time, when Christ sees fit to calm the storm of cares that beset me, I shall continue with them, but you must encourage me. I send my devoted greetings to my lord and father, your Prior, and to your other brethren, and I humbly beg them to remember me before God" (*Letters*, 228–29 [#159]; *PL* 182, cols. 312A–313B).

111. To the Same: "My dearest Bernard, I cannot hide my sorrow nor can I disguise from you any longer the grief which I suffer. I have not forgotten my long-standing promise to you, I have for long had the firm intention and great desire to pass by you, so that I may see again those whom my soul loves and, in their company, find consolation for my journey, relief for my labours, and healing for my sins. But in punishment for my sins it has come about that regretfully I find that I am not able to do so. I acknowledge this not as a fault, but as a punishment for my faults. I beg you to understand, man of God, that it is not at all that I do not care for my friends, nor is it that I am lazy or negligent in the matter, but simply that I am prevented by the work of God which I cannot ignore. My vexation gnaws at me like a worm, and my grief is ever with me. I am troubled enough on other accounts but, I must confess, on none so much as on this. It vexes me more than all the labours of my journey, than the discomfort of the heat, than the anxiety of my responsibilities. Now that I have exposed my wound to my friend, it is your business to have pity on me and relieve me by sharing my burden. I implore your prayers, and the prayers of the holy men with whom you live. I am sending you the sermons on the beginning of the Song of Solomon, as you have asked me to do and as I have promised. When you have read them, I beg you to write as soon as you conveniently can and tell me whether you think I should continue with them or not" (*Letters*, 230 [#160]; *PL* 182, col. 313BD).

at the bottom of the hill; Bernard's health is bad; {at the} end of the year {are} fruitless conferences with Roger of Sicily in Apulia; Bernard returns to Rome in December. {In} 1138 Anacletus dies, but there is a new antipope; but the latter gives in, and in May the schism is ended, thanks to the work of Bernard; {in} June, Bernard returns to France, only to find more trouble in {the} diocese of Langres; Bernard, sick in bed at Clairvaux, dictates letters to end the affair (Geoffrey de la Roche becomes bishop); {the} dedication of Clairvaux's new church (the second one) {and} the death of Blessed Gerard {also occur this year}.

{The} *Fourth Period*. {In} 1139, {during} Lent, {Bernard preaches his} Sermons on Psalm 90;[112] Bernard refuses election as Archbishop of Rheims; {following the} visit of St. Malachy, {a} movement for {a} foundation in Ireland {begins}. {In} 1140 relations with Suger of St. Denis {develop}; the problem of Peter Abelard {intensifies} (Letter 239[113]) (condemnation of Abelard {is made on} July 16); Bernard founds his thirty-fifth daughter house in Sicily; a monk of Clairvaux, Stephen, becomes a cardinal. {In} 1141 {occurs the} intervention of Clairvaux in the affair of York; relations {develop} with Robert Pullen (Letter 205[114]); {the year also sees the} death of Guy and {of} Humbeline. {In} 1142, Mellifont, {Clairvaux's} fortieth daughter house, {is} founded in Ireland; Bernard writes *De Precepto et Dispensatione*.[115] 1143 {is a} difficult year: Bernard, intervening in conflicts between Louis VII and {the} archbishop of Bourges, and in another affair concerning the pope, is bitterly reproved by both pope and king; {the} pope says he intervenes too much in politics; war {breaks out} between {the}

---

112. *In Psalmum XC, "Qui Habitat," Sermones XVII* (*PL* 183, cols. 185B–234C).

113. *Letters*, 317–20 (to Pope Innocent); *PL* 182, cols. 354A–357A [#189].

114. *PL* 182, cols. 372C–373A (*Letters*, 344–45 [#271]); Robert Pullen was a scholar who became the first English cardinal and refounded the schools at Oxford; this letter is written to the bishop of Rochester concerning Bernard's recommendation that Pullen spend some time studying in Paris; for a letter to Pullen himself, see *Epistola* 362 (*PL* 182, cols. 563A–564B) (*Letters*, 386–87 [#316]).

115. *PL* 182, cols. 859D–894C.

Count of Champagne and {the} King of France; {the} York affair {is} also hot; Arnold of Brescia {is} active—Bernard opposes his activities. {In} 1144 (Letter 305 to Peter the Venerable—read {this} letter, #2[116]) {Bernard} declares he is through—{he} will no longer leave his monastery; but in June, at St. Denis, he negotiates peace between {the} King of France and his enemies. 1145 {sees the} election of Eugene III; Bernard {is} in Languedoc, fighting the Albigenses. {In} 1146 {there is a} Roman rebellion, partly fomented by Arnold of Brescia; Eugene, in France at the request of King Louis VII, appeals for {a} crusade; Bernard opens preaching for {the} crusade {on} 31 March: {there is} tremendous enthusiasm; in {the} fall St. Bernard preaches {the} crusade in Flanders,

---

116. "I welcomed your letter with open hands. I have read it and re-read it greedily and gladly, and the more often I read it the better pleased I am. I must say I enjoy your fun. It is both pleasantly gay and seriously grave. I do not know how it is you are able to be both gay and grave, so that your fun has nothing about it of frivolity, and your dignity loses nothing by your gaity. You are able to keep your dignity so well in the midst of your fun that those words of the holy man might be applied to you: 'I smiled on them though they were never so ill at ease, and the encouragement of my glance never failed them.' So you see I have answered you, and now I think I am entitled to demand more than you promised! It is only right that you should know how things are going with me. I have decided to stay in my monastery and not go out, except once a year for the general chapter of Abbots at Cîteaux. Here, supported by your prayers and consoled by your good will, I shall remain for the few days that are left to me in which to fight, 'until the time comes for me to be relieved at my post.' May God be merciful and never alienate his mercy or your prayers from me. I am broken in body and have a legitimate excuse for not going about as I used to do. I shall sit still and hold my peace, so that perhaps I may experience something of that inner sweetness of which the Prophet sings: 'If deliverance thou wouldst have from the Lord, in silence await it.' And, so as not to appear the only one to make fun of me, I suppose you will not now dare to reproach me with my silence and, in the way you have, to call it sloth! As a matter of fact I think Isaias has more suitably and properly called it 'the service of righteousness'; and, inspired by God, he also says, 'In quietness and in confidence lies your strength.' Commend me to the prayers of your holy brethren at Cluny having first, if you think fit, greeted them from me as the servant of them all" (*Letters*, 37–76; *PL* 182, cols. 397B–398B [#228]).

then in the Rhineland, then {in} Switzerland; {on} 24 December, {at the} Diet of Spires, with difficulty {he} persuades {the} emperor to take up the cross with his knights (December 28). {In} 1147 (January, February) {he} travels back up the Rhine {and} returns to Clairvaux with sixty postulants; {at the} Council of Étampes, Bernard designates Suger as regent in {the} absence of Louis VII; {he is} again in Germany {for the} departure of the crusaders; Clairvaux now has fifty foundations. {In} 1148 Eugene III {is} at Clairvaux; Bernard travels about with him.

{The} *Fifth Period.* 1149 {sees the} failure of the Second Crusade; Bernard writes the *De Consideratione*[117] for Pope Eugene III. {In} 1150 a new crusade {is} prepared—Bernard {is} named by {the} Council of Chartres to lead it, {and} this decision is ratified by EUGENE III, but this project was defeated by the abbots of the Order, who persuaded Eugene to call it off (?) (Letters {256}, {364}, 408[118]); Bernard writes {his} *Life of St. Malachy*;[119] Bernard {is} betrayed by his secretary Nicholas (read Letter 354, p. 431[120]);

---

117. *PL* 182, cols. 727A–808A.

118. The marginal addition reads "Letters 257, 214, 408"; 257 is apparently an error for *Ep.* 256 (*PL* 182, cols. 463C–465A; *Letters*, 470–72 [#399]), written to Pope Eugene in 1150 to urge another crusade to retake the Holy Land after the failure of the Second Crusade but refusing to lead it himself; n. 214 has no relevance to this matter either in the numbering of the Latin text or of the English—somehow it must have been a mistranscription for *Ep.* 364 (cols. 568C–570A; *Letters*, 469–70 [#398]), written the same year to Peter the Venerable to encourage him to attend the Council at Chartres concerning plans for a new crusade; the third reference is a correct number, but referring to the English translation (*Letters*, 477–78; *Ep.* 380 [cols. 583D–584A]), a letter to Abbot Suger of Saint-Denis about the troubles in the East. See also *Letters*, 472–73 [#400] (not included in *PL*), written to Peter the Venerable after the Council at Chartres, which Peter did not attend, and encouraging him to come to a follow-up meeting at Compiègne.

119. *PL* 182, cols. 1073A–1118A.

120. To Pope Eugene: "I am in danger from false brethren. Many forged letters have gone out under a forgery of my seal. And, what I fear may have happened, these forgeries are said to have reached even you. This is why I

{he} travels in Brittany and Normandy. {In} 1151 {Bernard has a} consultation with Peter the Venerable, in {a} quarrel between {the} Benedictines of Gigny and {the} Cistercians of Miroir over tithes (Cistercians were exempt); Bernard negotiates between King Louis VII and the Count of Anjou at Paris; {the} death of Suger {occurs}. {In} 1152, Bernard {is} at Cluny over the Miroir quarrel[121] (read Letter 353[122]); {the} *De Consideratione* {is} finished;

---

have rejected my old seal and am, as you see, using a new one for the future, containing both my image and name. Do not any longer accept the other seal as coming from me, except in the case of the Bishop of Clermont to whom I gave a letter sealed with that seal before I had had this one made" (*PL* 182, col. 491A [#284]).

121. Because the Cluniac Abbey of Gigny had lost revenue from tithes from the Cistercian Abbey of Miroir, now exempted by the pope from paying them, some of the Gigny monks invaded Miroir and did extensive damage, for which they were ordered to pay compensation.

122. To Pope Eugene: "In the hope of reaching a peaceful settlement I met the monks of Gigny at Cluny. We worked hard for peace, but nothing came of our endeavours except the ruin of our hopes. We repeated the instructions you gave in your letter about the payment of compensation and the restitution of what had been taken away, but all to no purpose. The damage was very great for, not to go into details, one whole abbey was destroyed and the cost of rebuilding it is estimated at not less than thirty thousand *solidi*. They thought that this was too much for them to pay. Since we had lost so much I was prepared to forgo full compensation, but the sum they offered was so trivial that the venerable Abbot of Cluny, whose efforts on behalf of peace have been more kind than successful, did not think it worth our while to accept it. And so no agreement was reached because the compensation they offered was so absurdly small. They said that certain evil-minded persons among them had done this thing and that they should see to it, that it was no concern of theirs. This is an absurd excuse. It is notorious in the whole neighbourhood that the outrage was committed by the men of the monastery, that some of the monks were present at the time, and that all consented to it. Up to the present I have not heard of any one of them being opposed to it. The abbot himself has openly refuted and condemned this sort of shuffling by declaring that a monastery is entitled to require full compensation for any damages that it may suffer from another. We await the last word in this matter from you, for it has been more than clearly proved

{following the} episcopal election at Auxerre, Bernard heads a commission to see that everything is legal (see Letter 280[123] and 282[124]); {the} death of Theobald Count of Champagne {takes place}; {by the} end of the year, Bernard {is} fatally ill. {In} 1153, Bernard travels to Metz to make peace, {then} returns to Clairvaux for the last time; the rest of the year, he is dying; in this year his seventieth foundation is made; Clairvaux has 164 daughter houses (counting those that came over from Savigny, Obazine, etc.); {there are} over 700 monks and brothers at Clairvaux; {on} 20 August, Bernard dies, about 9 AM. {In} 1174 (18 January) Bernard {is} canonized.

## The Earlier Works of Saint Bernard

The best thing to do with St. Bernard is to read him together and explain what he is trying to do. A mere "course on" St. Bernard is practically useless in our monasteries. It is of no avail to know the list of the books he wrote or even the main themes he treated, nor even to know the outlines of his theological thought. These matters are helpful only when they serve to clarify a reading of St. Bernard that helps us to share in his experience and his worship, which were those of his time. Hence we will, at this point, take a few characteristic works in some detail. We must remember our objective: to enter into the *mind* of Bernard as a saint and genius, and as a writer; to see him as an example of the religious sensibility of the twelfth century with its deep *sense of the sacred*, {its} sense of the *reality of mystery*, {the} capacity to *reach sacred reality through symbol*, in which the invisible and visible are

---

that it can only be settled with a strong hand" (*Letters*, 430; *PL* 182, cols. 489B–490A [#283]).

123. *PL* 182, cols. 485A–487B (*Letters*, 424–26 [#347]); this is Bernard's third letter to Pope Eugene III on this matter; see also *Epistolae* 275 (*PL* 182, cols. 480B–481B) and 276 (cols. 481B–482C) (Letters, 422–24 [##346, 345]).

124. *PL* 182, cols. 488A–489B (*Letters*, 426–27 [#348]); this letter is written to King Louis of France concerning the election.

brought together (*collatio*). It will help us to remember that we lack this sense of the sacred to a great extent; in proportion as we recover it we may learn to appreciate St. Bernard. The key to St. Bernard's experience is this: (a) the sense of the gap between the created and transcendent; (b) the realization that the divine mystery is made accessible to us in a simple figure, or in the humble *historia*[125] of Scripture, or in the rites of the common life and worship; (c) the self-transcending "leap" of exultation at this sense of presence; (d) {the} expression of it in creative poetic forms, considered as *demonstratio* ("showing"). The whole point of *demonstratio* is that there is not logical continuity but simultaneous presence in contrasting likeness, due to an act of God's merciful love revealing Himself. The strength of the *demonstratio* is diminished in proportion as one tends to despise and neglect the humble external sign and treat it as worthless. One must attend to it in its existential presence, for only here do we contact the invisible mystery (cf. Chenu: *La Théologie au Douzième Siècle*, p. 182[126]). Another term—*translatio*—{refers to} accepting the

---

125. I.e., the narrative itself.

126. "[L]e symbole fait appel, pour l'efficacité de son transfert, à une matière dont la réalité ne se dissolve pas dans le processus de signification, que ce soit la réalité des éléments naturels, que ce soit la réalité de l'histoire en typologie biblique, que ce soit la réalité du matériau en action liturgique. Sur plusieurs points, les maîtres du xiie siècle réagirent fermement en faveur de cette loi des valeurs symboliques: ces valeurs ne jouent que dans la mesure où la *res* garde consistence sous le *signum*. A tourner la réalité en pur figure, la tropologie s'anémie elle-même. Ce fut là, nous le verrons, la grande opération, non seulement exégétique, mais théologique, menée par Hugues de Saint-Victor, revendiquant la nécessité première, du *fundamentum* avant l'*allegoria*, la vérité de l'*historia* avant les *tropi*" (Marie-Dominique Chenu, OP, *La Théologie au Douzième Siècle* [Paris: J. Vrin, 1957], 181–82); ET: "The symbol, in order to effect the transference for which it is the vehicle, calls for matter which does not disappear in the process of signifying, such, for example, as the reality of the natural elements, or the reality of history in biblical typology, or the reality of the material used in a liturgical action. On many counts the masters of the twelfth century responded wholly in favor

symbol {while} rejecting that in the symbol which is *unlike* God {but} keeping that which is common to both and thus "passing over" (by {an} act of love) to God. {There are} two dangers: (a) excessive *spiritualization*—leaving the reality of the symbol behind; (b) excessive *materialization* of the symbol—allegorization, verbalism, not going on to reality.

1. *Homilies on the Missus Est* (*De Laudibus Virginis Matris*).[127]

One of the earliest, most characteristic and most carefully composed of the works of St. Bernard is this group of four homilies on the Virgin Mother. (Note: what is a *homily*? from *omilos*—gathering.) *The Preface*: {it is} the fact that there is a preface which explains that this is a literary work, and not something preached for any special need of the brethren. Because he is ill, he cannot follow all the community exercises (*non valeo sectari conventum*[128]—this means something different from "community exercises"[129]—terms are important!). What would be the difference in meaning between "assisting at community exercises" and "*sectari conventum*"? The term *conventum* implies the "coming together" of the people of God at the call of God Himself, to hear

---

of this law of symbolic values: these values emerge only in proportion as the *res* retains its integrity while functioning as *signum*. In turning reality into nothing but a figure, tropology weakens itself. Such an insistence underlay the great exegetic and theological undertakings of Hugh of Saint-Victor, who asserted the prior necessity of the *fundamentum* before *allegoria*, of the truth of *historia* before *tropi*" (Marie-Dominique Chenu, OP, *Nature, Man, and Society in the Twelfth Century*, trans. Jerome Taylor and Lester K. Little [Chicago: University of Chicago Press, 1968], 132–33).

127. "[The angel Gabriel] was sent" (Luke 1:26) ("On the Praises of the Virgin Mother") (*PL* 183, cols. 55C–88A).

128. Col. 55C.

129. See *St. Bernard's Sermons for the Seasons and Principal Festivals of the Year*, trans. A Priest of Mount Melleray [Ailbe Luddy, OCSO], 3 vols. (1921–1925; Westminster, MD: Carroll Press, 1950), 1:53: "At present, however, being prevented by bodily illness from joining in the community exercises, I am able to enjoy a little leisure, which . . . I shall endeavour to turn to the best account."

His word and praise Him. Cenobitic life means much more when we think of it in this light than {if it is} merely explained in terms of "community exercises" carried out as a matter of formal duty and at which "one must assist"—doubtless with good dispositions. His motives: *devotio jubet . . . quod saepe animum pulsavit*.[130] He is inspired, moved, urged interiorly by devotion, commanded by devotion, to speak in praise of the Virgin Mother, especially on a definite *lectio evangelica*,[131] the *"historia"* of the Annunciation. All these terms mean something special. *Lectio* implies the public reading of the gospel in the liturgy, {a} solemn {event}. *Historia* {is} not just {a} "story" or "history" in our sense. It is the literal statement of the mystery according to the hallowed and familiar words of the gospel account, the starting point for contemplative exposition, or moral exposition, or personal meditation, etc. (cf. the Nativity gospel from Luke in {the} Christmas liturgy[132]). With St. Bernard, {it is} not merely a personal meditation, though his love is involved: his experience is not absent, but it is the Church's experience. Much of what he writes is drawn directly from the Fathers. It comes out in the form of a homily that should by rights be read or preached in the *"conventu"* (in community) and shared with the brethren, having the *"historia"* in mind.

HOMILY 1 (Luke 1:26-27): he quotes the verses.[133] In patristic preaching, the words would have been sung by an ordained

---

130. Col. 55C ("devotion orders . . . what has often knocked at the soul").

131. Col. 55C, which reads: *"lectione evangelica"* ("gospel reading").

132. The reference is evidently to Luke 2:15-20, the gospel for the second or dawn Mass on Christmas, rather than to Luke 2:1-14, the gospel for Midnight Mass; specifically Merton seems to be referring to v. 19: "But Mary kept all these words, pondering them in her heart."

133. *"Missus est angelus Gabriel a Deo in civitatem Galilaeae, cui nomen Nazareth, ad Virginem desponsatam viro, cui nomen erat Joseph, de domo David: et nomen Virginis Maria"* (col. 55D) ("[And in the sixth month], the angel Gabriel was sent from God into a city of Galilee, called Nazareth, to a virgin espoused to a man whose name was Joseph, of the house of David; and the virgin's name was Mary").

lector, then commented on by the bishop. Bernard is conscious of the tradition which gives the abbot the bishop's teaching role in his own *"conventus."* Homily 1.1 (cols. 55–57): this should be studied in detail. It gives us deep insight into what St. Bernard is trying to do, how he regards this *"historia,"* what the word of God means to him, how he listens to it and responds to it, and what is the meaning of such a response. We will find first of all that this is quite unfamiliar to our modern way of thinking, reading, studying, and yet it fills a *most profound need*, especially in monasteries, and so it is very important to try to recreate the experience of Scripture heard and commented in the twelfth-century *conventus* of Clairvaux. He immediately asks a question: why all these names, one after the other? the messenger who is sent; the Lord by whom the messenger is sent; the spouse of the Virgin; the family (of David) to which they belong; the town and district where the message is delivered. The Evangelist NOLUIT NOS NEGLIGENTER AUDIRE *quod tam diligenter studiit enarrare*.[134] {Note the} relationship {between the} *narratio (historia)*[135] and the *"auditor"*[136] (who will of course become a *"factor verbi"*[137]). The *historia* in a certain sense lacks its meaning, indeed does not even truly exist (precisely as *historia*) outside this situation where it is spoken and heard. The *historia* {is important} not for its own sake, but for the sake of the *"auditus"*[138] which makes it *verbum fidei*[139] and leads to *obedientia fidei*.[140] If neither a leaf falls from the tree nor a sparrow to the ground without the will of the Father, "am I to think that from the lips of the Holy Evangelist there should flow a superfluous word [comment on *superfluum diffluere verbum*]

---

134. Col. 56C ("did not wish us to listen negligently to what he so diligently made an effort to relate").
135. Col. 56C.
136. "listener".
137. "doer of the word" (James 1:22).
138. "hearing".
139. "word of faith" (Rom. 10:8).
140. "obedience of faith" (Rom. 1:5, 16:26).

ESPECIALLY IN THE SACRA HISTORIA OF THE WORD [*sacra historia Verbi*]? I think not. All are filled with supernal mysteries and each one is overflowing [here *redundantia*, not *diffluere*] with heavenly sweetness—provided only that they have a DILIGENTEM INSPECTOREM who knows how to suck honey from the rock and oil from the hardest stone."[141] He then backs this up with a quote from Joel 3:18 (*in illa die stillabunt montes* etc.[142]) and Isaias 45:8 (*Rorate coeli*[143]). {What is the} import of these quotes? They are the substance of the mystery itself, a poetic expression for the mystery of the Incarnation, which is to be experienced in our hearts by faith. It is a poetic expression of the mystery of revelation, an "unction" of the earth with heavenly sweetness: (a) Christ {is} the *mons coagulatus* and *mons pinguis*[144] on Whom mercy and justice meet;[145] (b) the evangelist (Luke) {is} a *mons non modicus, mellifluo eloquio*,[146] like a *mons aromatum* (a forest of spice-bearing trees) moved by the south wind and the sun, giving forth a

---

141. "*putem ego de ore sancti Evangelistae superfluum diffluere verbum, praesertim in sacra historia Verbi? Non puto. Plena quippe sunt omnia supernis mysteriis, ac coelesti singula dulcedine redundantia; si tamen diligentem habeant inspectorem, qui noverit sugere mel de petra, oleumque de saxo durissimo*" (col. 56C).

142. Col. 56D, which reads: ". . . *stillarunt* . . ." ("In that day the mountains shall drop down [sweetness]").

143. Col. 56D, which reads: "*quando rorantibus coelis desuper, nubibusque pluentibus justum, aperta est terra laeta germinans Salvatorem*" ("Drop down dew, ye heavens, from above, and let the clouds rain the just: let the earth be opened, and joyfully bud forth a savior").

144. Col. 56D, which reads: "*montem coagulatum et pinguem*" (Ps. 67[68]:16) ("A curdled mountain, a fat mountain").

145. Col. 56D, which reads: "*misericordia et veritas obviaverunt sibi, justitia et pax osculatae sunt*" (Ps. 84[85]:11) ("Mercy and truth have met each other: justice and peace have kissed").

146. Cols. 56D–57A, which reads: "*inter caeteros montes non modicus . . . suo mellifluo . . . eloquio*" ("among other mountains not a low one, . . . with his eloquence sweet as honey").

heavenly odor of sweetness.¹⁴⁷ He concludes: "WOULD THEN THAT GOD WOULD NOW ALSO SEND FORTH HIS WORD AND MELT THESE [spices] FOR US AND MAKE THE WORDS OF THE GOSPEL UNDERSTANDABLE FOR US: may they then become in our hearts more desirable than gold and very precious stones, and may they become more sweet than honey and the honeycomb."¹⁴⁸ ({As an} example, this is like putting grains of incense ["words"] on a hot coal ["{the} presence of love"] and getting sweet smoke.)

To understand Bernard, we must understand the *symbolic* mentality of the Middle Ages ({the} twelfth century at least). A symbol *signifies*—it does not *explain*. It points to an invisible and sacred reality which we attain not by comprehension but by love and sacred awe, {by an} initiation to a higher world, and {by} the gift of ourselves. For St. Bernard, scriptural symbols are effective in the same way as sacraments: if we attend to them seriously, *they impart grace*. {Recognize the} difference between St. Bernard and St. Thomas—{they have} two entirely different approaches to God. St. Bernard {draws near} to God as Word—through created and written (or spoken) "words," culminating in *sweetness* ({an} experience of love): Gustate *et videte!*¹⁴⁹ St. Thomas {draws near} to God as *Being*—through created "beings," culminating in *certitude* ({an} experience of truth): *Intellegite!*¹⁵⁰ (In this connection, see *Sermo 18 in Cantica*, n. 6.¹⁵¹)

---

147. *"veluti perflante austro, atque e vicino sole radiante justitiae, quaedam ex eo spiritualia profluxerunt aromata"* (col. 57A) ("from which flowed forth certain spiritual fragrances, as though the south wind was blowing through and from nearby the sun of justice was shining").

148. *"Utinam et nunc Deus emittat verbum suum, et liquefaciat ea nobis; . . . et fiant nobis intelligibilia verba evangelica: fiant in cordibus nostris desiderabilia super aurum et lapidem pretiosum multum, fiant et dulciora super mel et favum!"* (col. 57A).

149. "Taste and see" (Ps. 33[34]:9[8]).

150. "Understand!"

151. *PL* 183, cols. 862B–863A, which follows a section on being nourished by the food and drink of good works and prayer that brings gladness, and emphasizes the centrality of love infused by the Holy Spirit and then poured out in service to God and other people.

Homily 1.2ff.: St. Bernard's exegesis of the "names" follows the procedure of the grammarians in the schools of liberal arts of the twelfth century—going back also to the *Etymologies* of St. Isidore,[152] etc. {Note} the meaning and power of names—the relation of name to essence—this has something to do with the intellectual climate of the twelfth century—the conflict in the schools between *nominalism* and *realism*. However St. Bernard is apart from this. {He has} a kind of biblical and existentialist approach, {a} phenomenology of revelation. The "reality" of which Bernard speaks is not the "idea" but the divine *Spiritus* and man spiritualized in Christ. Instead of the dichotomy between *name* and *idea* (essence, reality) Bernard is concerned with *letter* and *spirit, figure* and *realization*. {Regarding} *the Angel Gabriel*—what does Bernard mean by an *angel*? He is very definite. Angels have an important role in the divine economy (see *In Cantica*, 5.6;[153] *De Consideratione*, 5, chaps. 3, 4, 5[154]):

a) Angels have "spiritual bodies," intelligible bodies, which are not for their own use but serve them in their communications with us. This means that when Gabriel "comes" to Mary, there is real local motion. Are these bodies *natural* to angels? He recognizes a difference of opinion in the Fathers, but seems to believe angelic bodies are natural.[155] For St. Bernard, God alone

---

152. Isidore of Seville, *Etymologiarum Libri XX* (*PL* 82, cols. 73A–728C).

153. *PL* 183, cols. 800D–801A; this section is part of the longer discussion throughout this sermon (cols. 798D–803B) about the angels' need for a body in order to communicate the divine message to humanity.

154. *PL* 182, cols. 790A–795C; in this book Bernard considers that which is above humanity, God Himself and the angels: he distinguishes three approaches to the truth that is above—opinion, which has no certainty, faith, which depends on authority, and understanding, which relies on reason (c. 3); he considers the question of whether the bodies of angels are intrinsic to them or merely functional to be a matter of opinion, the fact of their understanding to be a matter of understanding, the names of the various orders of angels and their roles to be on the level of opinion rather than faith or certain understanding, and sees in each order a manifestation of and participation in a particular attribute of God (cc. 4–5).

155. See *In Cantica*, 5.7 (*PL* 183, col. 801BC).

is truly and perfectly incorporeal. He says angels *accept* bodies which are useless to them, but from God, for our sakes. Whether or not this is sound doctrine, it contains a deep insight into Bernard's own spirituality and his "mind." It has definite implications for monks.

b) As against Denis,[156] he holds that *all* the angels, even the highest, can be sent directly on missions for salvation of men (Hebrews 1:14), but the lower are ordinarily sent by the higher;[157] and all work through sensible media because God alone acts directly and immediately on the soul.

c) They are at once *brothers* and *servants* (the higher beings in order of love *serve* the others). They prepare us for the visits of the Word, inspiring us to do penance, to pray, etc., helping us to fight or avoid temptation. In this he makes an original contribution. *Gabriel* {means} *fortitudo Dei*.[158] He examines the appropriateness of the name and of the messenger: Christ is the true *virtus Dei*[159] and *fortitudo Dei*, "*substantive*."[160] The angel is the power of God only *nuncupative*.[161] What is the point of this? That

---

156. See Pseudo-Dionysius, *The Celestial Hierarchy*, 9.2, 10.2, 13 (J. P. Migne, ed., *Patrologiae Cursus Completus, Series Graeca* [*PG*], 161 vols. [Paris: Garnier, 1857–1866], vol. 3, cols. 260AB, 273AB, 300B–308B; ET: Pseudo-Dionysius, *The Complete Works*, trans. Colm Luibheid [New York: Paulist Press, 1987], 170–71, 173–74, 176–81); the first two passages present the idea of revelations being transmitted through the descending hierarchy of angelic beings and transmitted to humans by the angels proper; the third explains the apparently contrary scriptural teaching that Isaiah was purified by a seraph as meaning either that an angel was exercising a "seraphic" role by cleansing the prophet's lips by fire (etymologically related to "seraph") or that through the revelation of an angel the prophet was raised up to a vision of even the highest level of the angelic hierarchy as the ultimate source of his purification.

157. N. 2 (*PL* 183, col. 57A).
158. Col. 57A ("the strength of God").
159. Col. 57C ("Power of God") (1 Cor. 1:24).
160. Col. 57C ("substantially," "by nature").
161. Col. 57C ("according to a manner of speech").

The Cistercian Fathers and Their Monastic Theology    57

the Incarnation is a work of God's power, the strong man armed (the devil) is evicted by one stronger than he. In reading a passage like this we go astray if we try to regard the "name" of Gabriel as scientifically explaining anything. It is an occasion to draw attention to the mystery of the Incarnation, to a special aspect of that mystery. He might have chosen some other aspect: he just felt this one was important. He adds, Gabriel is the strength of God, either because this is fitting for his mission, or else in order to strengthen the Virgin "lest she be terrified by the novelty of the miracle,"[162] as well as strengthening St. Joseph (this means he thinks Gabriel is the angel concerned in Matthew 1:20). {In} n. 3 {he says of} Nazareth, "*Interpretatur flos.*"[163] What does he do with this? He goes back to the promises made to the patriarchs and says they were "seeds." The "flowering" of the seeds are the *magnalia Dei*, the great works of God in the exodus, etc. ("*in figuris et {aenigmatibus} per totum iter in deserto*";[164] "*deinceps in visionibus et vaticiniis prophetarum*"[165]), and all the history of Israel until Christ. Christ Himself is the fruit which has replaced this flowering. PRODEUNTE FRUCTU, FLOS DECIDIT, QUIA VERITATE APPARENTE IN CARNE, FIGURA PERTRANSIIT (58).[166] Hence what have we here? Not an explanation, but again he takes occasion from a word to proceed to what he believes to be the reality of the Mystery of Christ. {In} n. 4, *flos decidit* {signifies that} the Jewish dispensation is finished: {there is} no temple, no priesthood; all has been replaced by Christ, the reality.

Summary of this first part of the sermon: he talks about the mystery of the Incarnation as a manifestation of strength and

162. "*de miraculi novitate ne expavesceret*" (col. 57C).
163. Col. 57D ("It means flower").
164. Col. 58A ("in signs and mysteries through the whole journey in the desert").
165. Col. 58A ("finally in the visions and predictions of the prophets") (copy text reads: "*aenigmatis*").
166. Col. 57A ("Once the Fruit has come forth, the flower falls away, because once the Truth has appeared in the flesh, the sign passed away").

power, divine power, in the world subject to evil, and he talks about the presence of Christ, the fulfillment of the prophecies, as the *reality* which has replaced all outward forms and figures. He is therefore saying that through such forms and figures as we have, principally in the Scriptures, we must learn to penetrate to this supreme reality in mystery.

NN. 5–9[167] {provide} *moral and ascetic lessons* from the humility and virginity of Mary. Virginity is praiseworthy, but humility more so. Virginity is counseled, but humility is commanded. If you cannot be a virgin, you can at least be humble. He who is without virginity can still please God by his humility, but without humility even the Virgin Mary would not have been pleasing to God; and though her virginity was pleasing to God, it was her humility that caused her to conceive the Word, because if she had not been humble, the Holy Spirit would not have rested upon her (see Isaias 66:2). The obedience of Jesus to Mary teaches us the greatest humility and obedience. "As often as I wish to be placed in command over men, I desire to go ahead of my God and therefore I do not really know the things of God" (60).[168] Here again, we can say that St. Bernard is doing what he did above: penetrating from external signs to the inner mystery of our life in God. Virginity and purity may be signs of sanctity, but humility and obedience are closer to the essence. The deepest reality in the moral and ascetic life is participation by love in the total obedience and humility of Christ.

*St. Bernard's Mariology in the Homilies on {the} Missus Est*: at this point it may be worthwhile to consider the modern discussions that have surrounded this topic of St. Bernard's "mariology":[169]

---

167. Cols. 58D–61B.

168. "*Quoties enim hominibus praeesse desidero, toties Deum meum praeire contendo: et tunc vere non sapio ea quae Dei sunt.*"

169. Merton relies here particularly on Henri Barré, cssp, "Saint Bernard, Docteur Marial," *Saint Bernard, Théologien* (*Analecta Sacri Ordinis Cisterciensis* 9 [1953]: 92–113).

1. St. Bernard had a tremendous reputation in the late Middle Ages as a writer who gave expression to an unusual fervor and insight when writing about the virginal motherhood of Mary and her virtues, her place in Christian spirituality. This reputation is justified, and so too is the sobriquet *"citharista Mariae"*[170] that was given him (cf. the image of the troubadour). There is no question of the fact that St. Bernard was regarded as a *great authority* on Mary, as the one who summed up in his writings *all the early traditions* and expressed them with the greatest eloquence and fervor.

2. As a result of this, a great deal of medieval Marian writing was ascribed to St. Bernard. Also, many Marian *legends* were associated with his name. Gradually a kind of "image" was built up of Bernard as one whose entire body of writing was centered on the mystery of Mary. In this sense, the term *citharista Mariae* became a distortion. ({There is a} relatively small amount of writing about Mary in Bernard: *De Laudibus* and seven other sermons;[171] many of his sermons on Marian feasts have nothing to do with her. In quantity, he writes less on Mary than Rupert of Deutz, for instance.)

3. As a feature in this image, the phrase *"de Maria numquam satis"*[172] was ascribed to St. Bernard, {and} not only taken to mean

---

170. "the lute-player of Mary"; see Pierre Pourrat, *Christian Spirituality*, vol. 2, *In the Middle Ages*, trans. S. P. Jacques (1927; Westminster, MD: Newman, 1953): "Bernard has also been called the singer of Mary, *citharista Mariae*, literally the *musician* of Mary; for it may well be called a music which he makes heard when he sings the glories of the Queen of heaven."

171. See Barré, "Saint Bernard, Docteur Marial," 95.

172. "About Mary [one can] never [say] enough" (see Barré, "Saint Bernard, Docteur Marial," 100: "Jamais . . . il n'aurait écrit ce fameux *De Maria nunquam satis* qu'on lui prête, ou, tout au moins, il ne lui aurait pas donné ce sens excessif qui n'est que trop courant" ["He would never have written that famous '*De Maria nunquam satis*' which is attributed to him, or at least would never have given it that excessive interpretation that is only too prevalent"]).

that one could never tire of praising Mary, but in the far more questionable sense that one should never fear to extend beyond all measure the greatness of her prerogatives, removing all limits. This phrase was never written or said by St. Bernard, according to any reliable historical record, and as to the exaggerated meaning attributed to it, this is quite contrary to the actual mind of St. Bernard as reflected in his caution about the Immaculate Conception, in the Letter (174) to the canons of Lyons.[173] There he said clearly that *caution* was the most important thing in dealing with new developments in Marian doctrine, and he felt that the Immaculate Conception was a rash novelty.

4. Other legends, for instance the legend of the "stain on the white cowl" of Bernard (because of his failure to support the celebration of the Feast of the Immaculate Conception) complicate the issue. This is pure legend ({coming from} Nicholas of St. Albans, in {a} letter to Peter de Celle[174]—not to be confused with Nicholas of Clairvaux[175]). {This is} the negative reaction to the "image."

5. However, the myth of Bernard as the *Doctor Marianus* par excellence has come down and been received with favor in modern times, with the result that exaggerated and distorted ideas of his mariology have been entertained. He is treated as THE great Marian doctor of the Middle Ages: actually he is but one of many, and he adds little or nothing to the doctrine taught

---

173. *PL* 182, cols. 332D–336C (*Letters*, 289–93 [#215]).

174. *Epistola* 172 of the correspondence of Peter of Celle (*PL* 202, cols. 623CD–624D); see Barré, 101, who summarizes the story heard and reported by Nicholas of a laybrother at Cîteaux who had a vision of Bernard dressed in white clothing with a dark spot on the breast; asked for the reason, Bernard replied that it was due to his writing against the Immaculate Conception.

175. See also C. H. Talbot, "Nicholas of St. Albans and Saint Bernard," *Revue Bénédictine* 64 (1954): 83–117, who provides detailed descriptions of the two monks, clearly demonstrating that they were two different people (83–87).

not only by the great Fathers but by those closer to his own time, such as Fulbert of Chartres, Rupert of Deutz and St. Anselm. It is wrong to imagine that St. Bernard somehow outdistanced all of these and introduced new insights unknown to them. He made use of the traditional material common to them all. He is treated as a professional mariologist, and this is an anachronism. There were no such specialists in his day and he would barely have understood the concept of a specialized "mariology" in our modern sense of the word. In order to defend this "image" of St. Bernard as a great mariologist, some have resorted to futile expedients, to whitewash his reputation concerning the Immaculate Conception. They try to claim Letter 174 is not by Bernard, or that he was merely against the celebration of the feast as inopportune, not opposed to the doctrine of the Immaculate Conception. In actual fact, St. Bernard was simply a conservative and a traditionalist who, like others of the same type, feared to accept a new development in thought which was not clearly *evident* in the Fathers.

6. However, when all this has been said, we must not go to the other extreme and simply assume that St. Bernard's writings on Mary are without real significance, and that their effect was a kind of collective delusion. The whole thing is not a mere myth. St. Bernard was a great Marian writer, but we must not look for the wrong things in his writing. He is NOT an originator of new developments in Marian doctrine. He is a conservative, a traditionalist, a witness to the commonly accepted doctrines generally accepted by the whole Church in his time. He is not a technical doctor, but a preacher and a mystic who takes the traditional materials of Marian thought and expresses them with an extraordinary fervor and love. He has the *mystic's insight* into the realities in question, and his treatment is profoundly religious and filled with literary quality. He says things that have been said before, things that others have said with great fervor also. But he adds special *personal* qualities of his own. He *does* emphasize in a very personal and unique way Mary's *mediation* of grace. {For} example, {see} the most famous passage in the *Homilies on the Missus Est*

(Hom. 2.17)—read:[176] on "the virgin's name was Mary," and the

176. "*In fine autem versus,* Et nomen, *inquit,* Virginis Maria. *Loquamur pauca et super hoc nomine, quod interpretatum* maris stella *dicitur, et matri Virgini valde convenienter aptatur. Ipsa namque aptissime sideri comparatur; quia, sicut sine sui corruptione sidus suum emittit radium, sic absque sui laesione virgo parturit filium. Nec sideri radius suam minuit claritatem, nec Virgini Filius suam integritatem. Ipsa est igitur nobilis illa stella ex Jacob orta, cujus radius universum orbem illuminat, cujus splendor et praefulget in supernis, et inferos penetrat: terras etiam perlustrans, et calefaciens magis mentes quam corpora, fovet virtutes, excoquit vitia. Ipsa, inquam, est praeclara et eximia stella, super hoc mare magnum et spatiosum necessario sublevata, micans meritis, illustrans exemplis. O quisquis te intelligis in hujus saeculi profluvio magis inter procellas et tempestates fluctuare, quam per terram ambulare; ne avertas oculos a fulgore hujus sideris, si non vis obrui procellis. Si insurgant venti tentationum, si incurras scopulos tribulationum, respice stellam, voca Mariam. Si jactaris superbiae undis, si ambitionis, si detractionis, si aemulationis; respice stellam, voca Mariam. Si iracundia, aut avaritia, aut carnis illecebra naviculam concusserit mentis, respice ad Mariam. Si criminum immanitate turbatus, conscientiae foeditate confusus, judicii horrore perterritus, barathro incipias absorberi tristitiae, desperationis abysso; cogita Mariam. In periculis, in angustiis, in rebus dubiis, Mariam cogita, Mariam invoca. Non recedat ab ore, non recedat a corde; et ut impetres ejus orationis suffragium, non deseras conversationis exemplum. Ipsam sequens non devias: ipsam rogans non desperas: ipsam cogitans non erras. Ipsa tenente non corruis; ipsa protegente non metuis; ipsa duce non fatigaris; ipsa propitia pervenis: et sic in temetipso experiris quam merito dictum sit,* Et nomen virginis Maria. *Sed jam modice pausandum est, ne et nos in transitu claritatem tanti luminis intueamur. Ut enim verbis apostolicis utar,* Bonum est nos hic esse *(*Matth. xvii, 4*): et libet dulciter contemplari in silentio, quod laboriosa non sufficit explicare locutio. Interim autem ex devota scintillantis sideris contemplatione, ferventior reparabitur in his quae sequuntur, disputatio*" (cols. 70B–71A). ("At the end of the verse it says, 'And the Virgin's name was Mary.' Let us say a few words also about this name, which is said to mean 'Star of the Sea,' and is applied very suitably to the Virgin Mother. For she herself is very aptly compared to a star, because just as a star sends out its ray without detriment to itself, so did the Virgin bring forth her Son without harm to herself. And as the ray does not diminish the brightness for a star, neither does the Son diminish the integrity for the Virgin. Therefore she herself is that noble star arisen out of Jacob, whose ray illumines the whole world, whose splendor both shines forth in heaven and penetrates the nether world; pervading the world, and warming souls more than bodies, it fosters virtues and burns out vices. She herself, I say, is the bright and outstanding

invocation of Mary: *respice stellam, voca Mariam.*[177] This trope goes back to Christian antiquity, to a Pseudo-Jerome (*PL* 30:535[178]) as well as to Paschasius Radbertus, Fulbert of Chartres, Peter Damian

---

star, raised up as indispensable above this great and spacious sea, shining with merits, luminous with examples. Oh, whoever you are that recognize yourself in the flux of this age to be floating among storms and tempests more than walking on solid ground, do not turn your eyes away from the radiance of this star, if you do not wish to be submerged by storms! If the winds of temptations arise, if you are rushing upon the rocks of tribulations, look up at the star, call upon Mary. If you are tossed about by the waves of pride, of ambition, of detraction, of jealousy, look up at the star, call upon Mary. If anger, or avarice, or the attractions of the flesh strike the little ship of your soul, look to Mary. If in turmoil from the enormity of your offenses, bewildered by the foulness of your conscience, terrified by a dread of judgement, you begin to be swallowed up by the depths of sadness, the abyss of despair, think of Mary. In dangers, in difficulties, in situations of doubt, think of Mary, call upon Mary. Do not let her disappear from your lips nor disappear from your heart; and so that you may obtain the benefit of her prayer, may you not abandon the example of her way of living. Following her, you do not get lost; asking her, you do not despair; thinking of her, you do not stray. Holding fast to her, you do not fall; under her protection, you do not fear; with her leading you, you do not become weary; through her favor you reach your goal; and so you experience in yourself what is justly said, 'And the Virgin's name was Mary.' But now we should briefly pause so that we may reflect in passing on the brightness of so great a light. To use the words of the apostle, 'It is good for us to be here' [Matt. 18:4]: it is pleasing to contemplate sweetly, in silence, what labored speech does not suffice to explain. Meanwhile, from devout contemplation of this shining star, the consideration of those things that follow will be more fervently invigorated.")

177. "Look at the star, call upon Mary."

178. *In Evangelium secundum Matthaeum*, c. 1, v. 18: "*Sonat Maria, stella maris, quia stella dulcis est, mare amarum est; sic Maria in mare mundi fuit inter peccatores velut stella maris: quia ut . . . stella viros ad portum adducit, si sequantur illam: sic Maria in mundo ubi natus est Christus, qui omnes ad vitam ducit, si sequantur illum*" ("Mary means Star of the Sea, because a star is sweet and the sea is bitter; so in the sea of this world Mary was in the midst of sinners like a star of the sea; for as a star leads men to port if they follow it, so in the world is Mary when Christ was born, Who leads all to life if they follow Him"); Barré dates this author to the seventh or eighth century (111).

and Odilo of Cluny. Let us look at some of the texts, *first* Paschasius Radbertus: *Stella maris, sive illuminatrix Maria, inter fluctivagas undas pelagi, fide ac moribus sequenda est, ne mergamur undis diluvii; sed* per eam illuminemur *ut Christum natum ex ea pro salute totius mundi credamus (PL* 120:94).[179] This is all that is given. The essential idea is present, but not developed. Second, Fulbert of Chartres (Sermon on {the} Nativity of {the} Blessed Virgin [*PL* 141:322]) develops the "mystical meaning" of the name Mary, which means *stella Maris*: *Oportet universos Christicolas, inter fluctus hujus saeculi remigantes, attendere maris stellam hanc, id est Mariam, quae supremo rerum cardini Deo proxima est* [he compares her to the pole star] *et respectu exempli ejus cursum vitae dirigere. Quod qui fecerit non jactabitur vanae gloriae vento etc.* . . . *sed prospere veniet ad portum quietis aeternae.*[180] St. Odilo of Cluny (*PL* 142:1003) {treats the topic in his} *Sermo 4 De Incarnatione Dominica*: this whole Christmas sermon of St. Odilo is about stars. St. Gregory the Great is called to witness that the writers of the Bible are like the stars of the Pleiades. Then {he} especially embarks on the *praedulcis interpretatio*[181] of the "most noble"[182] Name of Mary, which means not only *Stella Maris* but *Domina*.

> *Consequens etenim est ut Dei Genitrix et semper Virgo Maria maris stella vocetur, quia sicut illi qui inter fluctus maris exercitatione navigii laborant, stellis sibi auctore Deo famulantibus, ad*

---

179. *Expositio in Evangelium Matthaei*, c. 1 ("The Star of the Sea, that is, Mary the light-bearer, in the midst of the surging waves of the sea, should be followed in faith and in behavior, so that we may not be submerged by the waves of the flood; but through her may we be enlightened in order to believe Christ, born from her for the salvation of the whole world").

180. *Sermo 4 De Nativitate Beatissimae Mariae Virginis* ("All Christ-worshippers, rowing among the billows of this age, should pay attention to this star of the sea, that is, Mary, who is nearest to God the supreme pivot point of reality, and should direct the course of life in accord with her example. The one who does this will not be tossed about by the wind of vainglory, etc., . . . but will successfully come to the port of eternal repose").

181. Col. 1003B ("most sweet interpretation").

182. *"Hujus nobilissimi nominis"* (col. 1003B).

*portum quietis venire desiderant . . . etc. ita . . . necesse est ad contemplationem istius stellae aciem mentis dirigat, per cujus meritum et gratiam posse se ab omni periculo liberari non dubitat. Stellae enim, ut scitis, divino nutu ordinantur . . . etc.* [{note the} informal, conversational tone]. *Et haec nostra stella splendida et matutina, adhuc incumbentibus ignorantiae tenebris et jam jamque Deo propitio deficientibus, praeparabatur, ut per illam ad nos procederet sol justitiae Christus Deus noster . . . Ex qua [Maria—stella] illa claritas, illa lux illudque lumen, Verbum caro factum ad nos processit.*[183]

In other words, this is an example of a rhetorical *trope*, treated diversely by various authors. Most of these examples are in the familiar style of a sermon of an expository nature. St. Bernard treats the same theme with passion and ardor, and in fact develops and deepens every aspect of the theme, so that for him Mary is not merely an "example" but actually a source of light and grace, acting in our souls: *fovet virtutes, excoquit vitia.*[184] And of course, with the rhythmic repetition of the *"respice stellam, voca Mariam,"* we have a really original exhortation *to appeal directly to her* in all our needs. His conclusion is characteristic: *Et sic in temetipso EXPERIRIS QUAM MERITO DICTUM SIT et Nomen Virginis Maria.*[185]

---

183. Cols. 1003C–1004A, which reads: ". . . *Deo auctore* . . ." ("It is in fact logical that the Mother of God and ever-virgin Mary be called 'Star of the Sea' because, just as those who labor amidst the waves of the sea in the working of a ship desire, through the assistance of the stars created by God, to come to the port of repose, etc., so . . . is it necessary to direct the attention of the soul to the contemplation of this star, through whose merit and grace one does not doubt to be able to be freed from every danger. For stars, as you know, are ordered by the divine will, etc. And this our splendid morning star was being prepared for those already oppressed by the darkness of ignorance and those falling away right now from the gracious God, so that through it Christ our God, the Sun of justice, might come forth to us. . . . From this [Mary—the star] that brightness, that light, that lamp, the Word made flesh, has come forth to us").

184. Col. 70C ("it fosters virtues and burns out vices").

185. Col. 71A ("and so you experience in yourself what is justly said, 'And the Virgin's name was Mary'").

{Consider the} *development of the trope by St. Bernard*. The *essence* is not new, but there is a very real originality in devotion and insight: (1) {the} comparison of starlight and {the} virgin birth "without detriment to itself";[186] (2) Mary communicates warmth to souls, fosters virtue, burns out vice, illuminating the whole universe; (3) {the} implication that every trial should drive us to prayer and refuge in her; (4) never suffer her name to leave our lips or our heart; (5) *experiencing* the power of Mary in our lives; (6) silent contemplation of Mary.

*Summary*—{the} salient characteristics of St. Bernard's Marian writings: they are traditional, but they do deepen and in some sense develop the mystical insight into the *personal implications* of the traditional doctrine, as far as DEVOTION to Mary is concerned. Bernard's characteristic is a really powerful and personal development of Marian DEVOTION. The aspects of Marian doctrine which he contemplates are still the most ancient and traditional ones, especially the *virginal motherhood* of Mary. He still sees the mystery of Mary as inseparable from the mystery of the Incarnation and as an important aspect of that mystery. He does not separate the Mother from the Son. He contemplates the virginity of body and the humility which is the corresponding virginity of Mary's soul. {He puts} great emphasis on her humility as playing a positive role in the Incarnation. He emphasizes Mary's *act of choice* in her response to the angel, her freedom as perfected by virginity of spirit. He emphasizes the fact that in the Incarnation, through the humility of Mary: *Sapientia vincit malitiam*.[187] Mary was a most pure creature, in her humility, {and}

---

186. "*sine sui corruptione*" (col. 70C).

187. "Wisdom overcomes malice" (Wis. 7:30) (*De Laudibus Virginis Mariae*, 2 [PL 183, col. 62D, which reads: "*vicit*"]; *De Diversis*, 14 [PL 183, col. 574D]; *In Cantica*, 82 [PL 183, col. 1180D]; *In Cantica*, 85 [PL 183, col. 1192A]). See Merton's discussion in his article "The Sacrament of Advent in the Spirituality of St. Bernard": "One of the key ideas in the Mystical Theology of St. Bernard is his summary of the whole work of Redemption in the phrase *Sapientia vincit malitiam*. Man lost the taste, the experiential knowledge, of

is a perfect instrument of the divine wisdom, re-establishing the order of love in the sinful universe disrupted by malice and self-love, pride. *In other places*, St. Bernard emphasizes Mary's compassion and mystical martyrdom with her Son on Calvary (*Dominica infra Octavam Assumptionis*, n. 14, 15[188]). He speaks of the great mystical love of Mary, the "wound of love" in her heart. But note that she plays almost no part at all in his commentary on the Canticle. He emphasizes imitation of Mary's virtues, and service of Mary as a kind of chivalric self-consecration to "Our Lady" (this expression {is} not original with St. Bernard—it goes back to Carolingian times). He emphasizes above all the *mediation* of Mary (Sermon on the Nativity: *De Aquaeductu*[189]). This is perhaps the most personal and original contribution of St. Bernard to Marian devotion. For St. Bernard, as for Ambrose Autpert, Mary is the ideal of all monks and the source of unfailing help for all who seek to serve God in the monastic life: "*Maria regula*

---

divine things (*sapida scientia*) in the fall. Adam's sin was primarily that form of pride which is so subtly analyzed by St. Bernard as *curiositas*. Now in this work of reparation, divine Wisdom seeks to blot out every trace of evil. In order to do so most perfectly, it restores man to his former dignity in the same way in which he lost that dignity: through a woman. *Si {vir} cecidit per feminam non erigitur nisi per feminam*. It is through Mary that we are 'reformed unto wisdom.' It is over her that the Spirit of God broods, most lovingly in the accomplishment of His sublimest work, preparing to restore to man his lost taste for spiritual things by giving him, for his food, the Word Himself, incarnate, as the Fruit of this virginal flower. From this text it is obvious that Mary is at the very heart of Cistercian mysticism. She is the Mother of our contemplation because she is the Mother of Jesus in us" (Thomas Merton, *Seasons of Celebration* [New York: Farrar, Straus & Giroux, 1965], 84–85; the Latin sentence is taken from the second homily on the *Missus Est*, n. 3 (col. 62C), which reads: ". . . *jam non erigitur* . . . ["If man fell through a woman he is not raised up now except through a woman"]; "*vir*" is misprinted as "*via*" in the text).

188. "Sermon for the Sunday within the Octave of the Assumption" (*PL* 183, cols. 437B–438C).

189. *PL* 183, cols. 437D–448B.

*monachorum*" (Autpert[190]). Hence it is understandable that Pope Pius XII in *Doctor Mellifluus* proposes St. Bernard to all as a model of Marian devotion and piety.[191] However, it is an exaggeration to treat him as a *unique originator* in Marian theology, as if he alone in the Middle Ages had discovered Mary: see also St. Anselm, St. Odo of Cluny, Fulbert of Chartres, Eadmer.

## 2. DE DILIGENDO DEO

This is perhaps the most important of St. Bernard's short treatises. It should be read and meditated by every monk. More than any other single work of his, it gives the deepest understanding of his thought, and it also gives us the key to the theology and spirit of the Cistercian writers of the twelfth century. At this point it would be good to go back briefly to what was said by Pius XII in *Doctor Mellifluus*: Pius XII, moved not only by theological but above all by pastoral considerations, emphasized the importance of St. Bernard's teaching on love as *most necessary*, spiritually, in the world today. It is of course most necessary of all for monks, and particularly for Cistercians whose function in the Church is to live the monastic life as a "school of charity"[192]

---

190. "Mary the rule of monks" (Ambrose Autpert, "*Sermo in Laudibus Beatae Mariae*," in Jacques Winandy, *Ambroise Autpert: Moine et Théologien* [Paris: Librairie Plon, 1953], 94; a longer version of this sermon on the Nativity of the Virgin, erroneously attributed to Alcuin, a contemporary of Ambrose, is found in *PL* 101, cols. 1300–1308 [see Winandy, 85]). In his essay "The Humanity of Christ in Monastic Prayer," Merton identifies Ambrose as the Abbot of the Monastery of St. Vincent on the Volturno and a spiritual heir of St. Gregory the Great and calls him "a Benedictine master of the eighth century who is less well known than he deserves to be" (Thomas Merton, *The Monastic Journey*, ed. Brother Patrick Hart [Kansas City, MO: Sheed, Andrews & McMeel, 1977], 104).

191. *Last of the Fathers*, 112–15 and 86–89 (Merton's commentary).

192. The term is used by William of St. Thierry in *De Natura et Dignitate Amoris*, 9.26: "*Haec est specialis charitatis schola, hic ejus studia excoluntur, disputationes agitantur, solutiones non ratiocinationibus tantum, quantum ratione et ipsa rerum veritate et experientia terminantur*" (*PL* 184, col. 396D) ("This is a special school of charity; here its studies are developed, its disputations are

in which they become perfectly like to Christ by love, through the action of the Holy Spirit. (Reread here several passages from *Doctor Mellifluus* in *Last of the Fathers*, p. 102 [bottom], 103, 104.[193])

---

engaged in, its solutions are reached not so much by rationalizing as by reason and the truth of reality itself and by experience"). See Étienne Gilson, *The Mystical Theology of Saint Bernard*, trans. A. H. C. Downes (New York: Sheed & Ward, 1940), c. 3: "Schola Caritatis" (60–84), where the term is used to describe the monastic instruction of St. Bernard and of the early Cistercians generally.

193. "Hence, that divine love which burned so mightily in the Doctor of Clairvaux must be re-kindled in the hearts of all men, if we desire the restoration of Christian morality, if the Catholic religion is to carry out its mission successfully, and if, through the calming of dissension and the restoration of order in justice and equity, serene peace is to shine forth for a worn and anguished humanity. May those who have embraced the Order of the Mellifluous Doctor, and all the members of the clergy, whose special task it is to exhort and urge others to the fervor of divine love, be most ardently inflamed with that love which ought always to unite us most perfectly with God. In our own day, more than at any other time—as we have said—men need this divine love; family life needs it; the whole of human society needs it. Where it burns and urges souls on to God, Who is the supreme goal of all mortals, all other virtues wax strong; when, on the contrary, it is absent or has died, then tranquillity, peace, joy, and all other genuine good things gradually disappear or are completely destroyed, since they flow from Him who 'is love.' Of this divine charity no one, perhaps, has spoken more excellently, more profoundly, or more ardently than Bernard: 'The reason for loving God,' as he says, 'is God; the measure of this love is to love without measure.' 'Where there is love, there is no labor, but delight.' He admits having experienced this love himself when he writes: 'O holy and chaste love! O sweet and comforting affection! . . . It is the more comforting and more sweet, the more the whole of that which is experienced is divine. To have such love, means being made like God.' And elsewhere: 'It is good for me, O Lord, to embrace Thee all the more in tribulation, to have Thee with me in the furnace of trial rather than to be without Thee, even in heaven.' But when he touches upon that supreme and perfect love whereby he is united with God Himself in intimate wedlock, then he enjoys a happiness and a peace, than which none other can be greater: 'O place of true rest . . . For we do not here behold God either, as it were, excited with anger, or as

*The Cistercian Theology of Love*: St. Bernard loved *Domina Caritas*[194] as St. Francis loved Lady Poverty. In the writings of the Cistercian Fathers of the twelfth century, and in the writings of students about them at the present time, the central place belongs to the teaching on the love of God, and on the perfect union of love between the soul and God. Since the Middle Ages, no serious doctrinal studies of St. Bernard were attempted. In the early twentieth century the tendency was to *deny* any doctrinal unity in his teaching (Pourrat[195]) or to find only contradictions (Rous-

---

if distracted with care; but His will is proved to be "good and acceptable and perfect." This vision soothes instead of terrifying. It lulls to rest, instead of arousing, our unquiet curiosity. It calms the mind instead of fatiguing it. Here is found perfect repose. The tranquillity of God tranquillizes all about Him, and the contemplation of His rest is rest to the soul'" (quoting 1 John 4:8; *De Diligendo Deo*, c. 50 [*PL* 182, col. 974A]; *Sermo 85 in Cantica*, n. 8 [*PL* 183, col. 1191D]; *De Diligendo Deo*, c. 10.28 [col. 991A]; *In Ps. 90*, 18.4 [*PL* 183, col. 252C]; *Sermo 23 in Cantica*, n. 6 [col. 893AB]).

194. *Epistola* 14 (col. 117B; *Letters*, 50 [#15]) ("Lady Charity"); see Pacificus Delfgaauw, *Saint Bernard, Maître de l'Amour Divin* (Paris: FAC-Éditions, 1994), 16 (this is a published version, identical in text, of Delfgaauw's 1952 dissertation, *Saint Bernard, Maître de l'Amour de Dieu: Étude de Théologie Monastique*, to which Merton evidently had access).

195. "The spirituality of St. Bernard is not remarkable for any particularly new ideas. The Abbot of Clairvaux . . . did not care for speculation; practical knowledge, which taught how to know and serve God, which give to man knowledge of himself and the love of virtue, alone found favour in his sight. Learned mystical theories . . . are not to be sought for in his [writings]. His ideas were those commonly received. . . . St. Bernard was a great mystic. He has not left a synthesis of that part of his spirituality which was concerned with extraordinary states, any more than he has left a theory concerning his asceticism, but the elements of a copious mystical theology are to be found in his writings" (Pourrat, *Christian Spirituality*, 2.18, 20); see Delfgaauw, 18: "P. Pourrat écrivit . . . que la mystique de saint Bernard ne se présente pas sous forme de synthèse: essentiellement pratique, elle ne revêt aucun caractère scientifique" ("Père Pourrat wrote . . . that the mysticism of St. Bernard is not presented in the form of a synthesis: essentially practical, it does not exhibit any scientific character"); Gilson refers to the same statement and says he considers it "to be entirely misconceived" (*Mystical Theology of Saint Bernard*, vii–viii).

selot[196]). Gilson[197] is the first of many to disclose the doctrinal *unity* and the depths of the thought in St. Bernard. His theology is *synthetic* but not *systematic*.[198] (It has profound internal coherence.) As a corollary to this there is a great interest in the *soul* and its faculties, and in its *nature* and its destiny to union.

In the early days of Bernard's abbotship at Clairvaux, when he was visited during sickness by William of St. Thierry, they spent an entire day discussing not only the Canticle of Canticles, the scriptural revelation of the union of the soul with God as Spouse, but also *"de spirituali physica animae"*[199] (*Vita*, 1.1.12a). Treatises on Love tend to be treatises on the soul and vice versa.[200] Le Bail (*DS* 1, 1461f.)[201] classifies as treatises on *love*:

1) *De Gratia et Libero Arbitrio*[202]—{this provides the} psychological basis of his theology of love; the primacy of the will is affirmed. It is a theology of spiritual freedom, based on man's natural being "in the image of God."

2) *De Gradibus Humilitatis*[203]—in reality {this} treats of {the} degrees of love ("truth") because {these are also} degrees of liberation from slavery to self-will, which is opposed to love and

---

196. Pierre Rousselot, *Pour l'Histoire du Problème de l'Amour au Moyen Âge* (Münster: Aschendorff, 1908), 53–54.

197. See Delfgaauw, 18: "C'est le mérite d'Étienne Gilson d'avoir pris position résolument contre l'opinion courante, en montrant . . . la cohérence des fondements théologiques de sa mystique" ("It is the merit of Étienne Gilson to have taken a position firmly contrary to the prevailing opinion in showing the coherence of the theological foundations of his mysticism").

198. See Delfgaauw, 19: "pensée *synthétique*, oui; non, pour autant, *systématique* . . . ."

199. *PL* 185, col. 259B ("about the spiritual nature of the soul").

200. See Delfgaauw, 51: ". . . double traité caractéristique de la literature cistercienne du XIIe siècle: le *De Anima* et le *De Caritate*" (". . . the double treatise characteristic of Cistercian literature of the twelfth century: *On the Soul* and *On Love*").

201. Anselme Le Bail, OCR, "Bernard (Saint)," *Dictionnaire de Spiritualité Ascétique et Mystique* [*DS*], ed. F. Cavallera *et al.*, 17 vols. (Paris: Beauchesne, 1932–1995), 1.1454–99.

202. *PL* 182, cols. 1001A–1030A.

203. *PL* 182, cols. 941A–972C.

to God. Chapter 7 describes {the} union of love with {the} Holy Trinity. The degrees of pride show the perversion of true love by self-will.

3) *De Diligendo Deo*[204]—{this is} made up of *two* essays: (a) {the} reply to Cardinal Haimeric (chap. 1–11)[205] {on} the reasons why we must love God; "returning to God" in Christ; the degrees of love, or stages of the return, culminating in mystical love; (b) repetition[206] of Letter 11 to Guigo:[207] the "Law of God."

4) *The Sermons on the Canticle*,[208] and some other sermons, round out this theology of love and of mystical union, developing the same themes in greater detail and depth, and further exploring implications of the monastic life and the *scriptural and liturgical* dialogue with the Word-Spouse.

*The Liber de Amore*: very often manuscripts of the *De Diligendo Deo* also include two works of William of St. Thierry, ascribed often in the Middle Ages to Bernard: *De Contemplando Deo*[209] and *De Natura et Dignitate Amoris*.[210] It is interesting to read these three works of the two friends together, and to compare them, and to see in what ways they complete each other.

"Theology of Love": there are three principal terms for love in Bernard:[211] AMOR = love as *affectus*, as a sweet and ardent desire, applied chiefly to love of the soul and God, espousals; DILECTIO = love as *consensus*, as rational and spiritual agreement, harmony, peace, joy—most appropriate to fraternal love; CARITAS = love as *amplexus*, love rejoicing in union and wisdom, fruition, delight,

---

204. *PL* 182, cols. 973A–1000B.
205. Cols. 973A–995B.
206. Cols. 995B–1000B.
207. *PL* 182, cols. 108B–115B.
208. *PL* 183, cols. 785A–1198A.
209. *PL* 184, cols. 365A–380B.
210. *PL* 184, cols. 379C–408B.
211. But see Delfgaauw, 74, n. 1, who says "la distinction *amor, dilectio, caritas* . . . n'est pas rigoureuse chez saint Bernard" ("the distinction of *amor, dilectio* and *caritas* is not rigorous in St. Bernard").

praise, gratitude, *fullness, fulfillment*. He says *Deus* caritas *est*,[212] never *Deus est amor*, or *dilectio*. Yet he does speak of *amor* in the sense of consummate love, and *"amplexus"* also (see Epistle 18.2[213]). Modern studies have brought out interesting points on Bernard as a "theologian of love."

1. P. Delfgaauw sees the theology of St. Bernard against the background of the Cistercian movement, "ressourcement" and "intériorité,"[214] and quotes an interesting text of St. Bernard: *plenitudo legis et cordis est caritas*.[215] {Here is the} characteristic search for fullness not only of exterior regularity but of interior realization. Note the element of real *completeness*, unity and wholeness which underlies all Cistercian thought in {the} twelfth century, in spite of apparent divisions (which one might note for instance in {the} *De Contemplando Deo* of William of St. Thierry: Prologue[216]).

---

212. "God is love" (1 John 4:8); for the influence of this verse on St. Bernard, see Gilson, *Mystical Theology of Saint Bernard*, 22–25.

213. *"manna illud absconditum de quo Apostolus, Et vita, inquit, vestra abscondita est cum Christo in Deo (Coloss. III, 3), quia necdum possumus contemplari per speciem, vel plene amplecti per amorem, dedit interim nobis et sapere per fidem, et quaerere per desiderium"* (*PL* 182, col. 121BC) ("Because we cannot yet contemplate the reality nor fully embrace him by love, he feeds us on that hidden manna of which the Apostle says: 'Your life is hid with Christ in God,' allowing us to taste him by faith and to seek him by desire" [*Letters*, 53 (#19)]).

214. Delfgaauw, 15, n. 1 (which reads: "intériorisation").

215. *Sermo 18 in Cantica* (*PL* 183, col. 862C) ("the fullness of the law and of the heart is charity" [Rom. 13:10]); Delfgaauw, 15.

216. *"Noli ergo me in aliena dividere et dissipare, totam me ad te in eum collige: et habebis fruendi copiam, memoriam abundantiae suavitatis ejus eructabis, et in justitia ejus exsultabis. Imo totae ingrediamur, o memoria mea, et omnes affectiones meae, ingrediamur: et memorando, intelligendo et videndo fruamur summo bono, et omnibus bonis ejus. Prorsus penes me est, in amore meo eum invenio; quia certa conscientia amo eum, et amplius et perfectius amare amo et desidero. Totis ergo in eum feramur amplexibus, et osculis incumbamus"* (*Prooemium*, n. 3 [*PL* 184, col. 366AB]). ("Therefore do not divide and scatter me in different directions; gather me completely to yourself in Him, and you will have an abundance

2. Emphasizing this theme of wholeness, Père Delfgaauw notes that the divorce of theology and mysticism has not yet appeared in St. Bernard.[217] He speaks and thinks in the patristic manner. His theology is experienced and his experience enlightens theological study (or rather the reading of the word of God and of the Fathers). This is inevitable in one for whom revelation is summed up as *"Deus Caritas Est."*

3. The condition for the quest for God (his is a Benedictine theology of "seeking God"[218]) is that His image is present in us, in our capacity to love and be loved. The concept of image is *dynamic*, not *static*. {It} is a capacity to move towards union, a disposition to seek union.[219] *The effective quest of union is likeness.* To leave the capacity for union deliberately unfulfilled is the deepest frustration of man's being and of his freedom, and is a caricature of the divine image (see below, Gilson on {the} "Law of Love").

4. Bernard's teaching on man is paradoxical because it goes beyond man's nature. {It is} a theocentric anthropology.[220] The image of God implanted in man's nature is not simply set there

---

of enjoyment, you will put forth the memory of His overflowing sweetness, and you will exult in His justice. Let us enter completely, O my memory, and all my affections, let us enter: and let us enjoy the highest good and all His goods, by remembering, understanding and seeing. He is completely available to me; I find Him in my love; because I love Him with a sure awareness and I love and desire to love Him more fully and more completely. Therefore let us be brought into Him with complete embraces, and let us be close to him with kisses.")

217. Delfgaauw, 15.

218. See *Rule*, c. 58: *"si revera Deum quaerit"* (*The Rule of St. Benedict in Latin and English*, ed. and trans. Justin McCann, OSB [London: Burns, Oates, 1952], 130) ("if [the novice] truly seeks God"); see Delfgaauw, 89.

219. See Delfgaauw, 212: "L'amour bernardin n'est pas autre chose que le mouvement naturel de l'âme vers Dieu" ("Love for Bernard is nothing else but the natural movement of the soul toward God").

220. See Delfgaauw, 213: "L'anthropologie bernardine est *théocentrique*" ("Bernardine anthropology is theocentric").

as a static reflection.²²¹ It comes from God (outside man's nature) and tends to God (outside man's nature). It is for this reason that we must, to be strictly accurate, say that man is made "*in the image of God*" and not just that "man is God's image,"²²² for when the concept of image becomes static, man becomes an idol. The "image" in man is therefore a permanent tendency to self-transcendence.

5. *Magna res est amor*,²²³ and therefore because of his capacity to love, *magna res homo*.²²⁴ Man is great in proportion as he responds to God's eternal and inscrutable and purely merciful love for him. And he does this most perfectly in proportion as he is empty of self.

6. Yet this self-emptying and perfect response which is *pure love* implies an *experience*. It is something that is *lived* and hence apprehended. Hence the culmination of human life is the finding of a higher self outside oneself, in God, transcending the individual nature. The spirit of man united to the Spirit of God finds itself in the source from which it came: that source is love. *Nec animam vivere dixerim quae de illo fonte non hauserit.*²²⁵ Hence we cannot help desiring that source.

---

221. See Delfgaauw, 212: "Le concept de l'image doit se comprendre . . . comme notion dynamique: mouvement vers Dieu, son modèle, sa patrie, dans un communion spirituelle avec lui" ("The concept of the image should be understood as a dynamic notion—a movement toward God, its model, its homeland, in a spiritual communion with Him").

222. See Gilson, *Mystical Theology of Saint Bernard*, 52: "Man is made indefectibly to the image of God. However, he is simply *made* to the image— one alone *is* this Image Itself, namely the Word, because the Word alone is an adequate and subsistent expression of the Father. Albeit therefore man's greatness consists in bearing the image of God, this greatness is nevertheless there by way of gift."

223. *Sermo 83 in Cantica* (cols. 1183B, 1183C) ("Love is a great thing"); Delfgaauw, 16, 150.

224. *Sermo 14 in Psalmum 90* (PL 183, col. 239A) ("Man is a great thing"); Delfgaauw, 16, 150.

225. *De Praecepto et Dispensatione*, 20 (PL 182, col. 893A) ("Nor would I say that the soul is living, which drinks not from that fountain"); Delfgaauw, 16.

7. Bernard is frankly a theologian of *desire*.[226] We must desire God and Him alone. We must purify our hearts of every other desire: *Solus ille desideretur qui solus desiderium replet*.[227] But we must thirst for God with all the power of our being: *ex toto desiderio*.[228] Desire is a habitual state in the spouse, defined as *anima sitiens Deum*.[229]

8. The desire of the soul for God is not selfish:[230] it is created by His own love for the soul, hence it is *an act common to both the soul and God*, and paradoxically, even in selfish love there is still something of the divine love for man, though buried and sullied. It is still a potentiality which can be rescued by response to grace. *Simul accipiens in uno Spiritu unde se praesumet amatum et unde redamet.*[231]

9. Hence the supposed "problem" of carnal love, taken up by Rousselot and answered by Gilson *et al*.[232]

---

226. See Delfgaauw, Part 2, c. 2: "Amour—Désir" (89–107).

227. *Sermo 4 in Dedicatione Ecclesiae* (*PL* 183, col. 528D) ("Let Him alone be desired, Who alone fulfills desire"); this quotation and that immediately following are not found in Delfgaauw's chapter on desire or elsewhere in the FAC edition of his book; perhaps they were present in the original dissertation Merton used and had been inadvertently omitted in the published text.

228. *Sermo 32 in Cantica* (*PL* 183, col. 946C) ("with one's complete desire").

229. *Sermo 7 in Cantica* (col. 807A) ("the soul thirsting for God"); Delfgaauw, 104.

230. See Delfgaauw, 212: "Désir ne veut pas d'abord dire égoïsme, de même que tout amour de soi n'est pas nécessairement amour-propre" ("Desire does not always mean egotism, just as all love of self is not necessarily 'self-love' ").

231. *Epistola* 107 (*PL* 182, col. 247C) ("He receives at the same time and in the same Spirit both the audacity to believe himself loved, and the power to love in return" [*Letters*, 163 (#109)]); Delfgaauw, 213.

232. See Gilson, *Mystical Theology of Saint Bernard*, 37–43.

10. Hence too the central doctrine of Cistercian mystical theology: love IS knowledge[233] when it comes to mystical experience of God.

11. The thesis of P. Pacificus is then: central to St. Bernard's teaching is the idea of charity, in which God and man made in His image are united. This charity is not abstract but is a living experience, *affectus*, a *consensus*,[234] an *amplexus* (NOT *contractus*).[235] Since we have lost our union by unlikeness, the way to return to union is the way of resemblance in and through Christ, by the purification of our love, above all in the *schola caritatis* which is the monastic community. Common life in the monastery leads to common life in God with the Three Divine Persons.

"*The Problem of Love*": other scholars have seen in Bernard not a theology of love but a *philosophical problem of love*. Are there two concepts of love in the twelfth century? (a) *physical*: that love of God and love of self proceed from the same root; (b) *ecstatic*: that love of God is entirely different in its source from love of self. (Note: Landgraf, discussing this in *DS*, Vol. 2, col. 578–579,

---

233. "*Amor ipse, notitia est*" ("Love itself is a kind of knowledge") (St. Bernard, *De Diversis*, 29.1 [*PL* 183, col. 620BC] quoting St. Gregory the Great, *Homily* 27.4 [*PL* 76, col. 1207A]); "*amor ipse est intellectus*" (William of St. Thierry, *Epistola ad Fratres de Monte Dei* [*PL* 184, col. 356A]; *Commentary on the Song of Songs* [*PL* 180, cols. 491D, 499C]; *Disputatio adversus Abaelardum* [*PL* 180, col. 272B]); see Delfgaauw, 80, 201–2.

234. See Delfgaauw, 20: "*affectus, adhaesio, consensus*, termes qui, au fond, désignent la même réalité: une communion de vie avec Dieu" ("*affectus, adhaesio, consensus*—terms which ultimately refer to the same reality: a living communion with God"); see also Delfgaauw, 165.

235. "*Affectus est, non contractus: nec acquiritur pacto, nec acquirit*" (*De Diligendo Deo*, 7.17 [*PL* 182, col. 984D]) ("Love is a commitment, not a contract; it is neither acquired, nor does it acquire, through a bargain"); see Delfgaauw, 27. See also Gilson, *Mystical Theology of Saint Bernard*, 144: "It is not a 'contractus,' but an 'amplexus'"; see also 104, n. 148 for "*amplexus*" as "a Scriptural metaphor indicating ecstasy."

is totally confusing.[236]) Rousselot claimed that St. Bernard's doctrine of love was not consistent. Gilson says if that is true, the whole mysticism of the later Middle Ages will be affected by the error, because of the great influence of St. Bernard's mysticism.[237] What is the *problem of pure love*? The question is: if all our natural tendencies make us prone to love ourselves, how can our nature be ordered to a pure love for God? The first thing is to understand what St. Bernard means by nature: not nature as opposed to grace, but nature as the concrete state in which man was created, in grace. Even after the fall, St. Bernard still does not consider nature apart from grace, for our nature is *ordered to* grace. However, due to the weakness consequent upon the fall, we have to love ourselves first, because if we did not, we would not even subsist. That is, we would not eat, sleep, etc. We have to follow the natural instincts for self-preservation. This is the most elementary form of love, *amor carnalis*.[238] In spite of the fact of *amor carnalis*, man is made in the image of God and is therefore made for union with God. This greatness, this essential dignity of man, his ability to love and be united with God, remains inseparable from his nature. This greatness has been defiled, debased, vitiated by sin. But it remains, and the purpose of life is to restore the divine likeness to the soul which is His image, and then the soul will love Him perfectly and be united to Him. This being given, Gilson shows that there is no contradiction between true self-love and true love of God. They are in the same line, tend to the same end, union with God. Why?

---

236. Arthur Landgraf, "Charité: IV: Le XII$^e$ Siècle: 4. Conception Physique et Conception Extatique de la Charité."

237. Étienne Gilson, *The Spirit of Mediaeval Philosophy*, trans. A. H. C. Downes (New York: Charles Scribner's Sons, 1936), 289; the whole of Gilson's "Appendix: Note on the Coherence of Cistercian Mysticism" (289–303) to his chapter 14, "Love and Its Object," is a response to Rousselot's claim of incoherence in Bernard's presentation, summarized by Merton in what follows; see also Gilson, *Mystical Theology of Saint Bernard*, 239, n. 179 and 240, n. 181 for further commentary on Rousselot's position.

238. "carnal love" (*In Cantica*, 20.6, 8, 9 [*PL* 183, cols. 870A, 871B, 871D]).

> Grant that a being is an image, then the more it resembles the original the more it is faithful to itself. But what is God? He is love; that is to say, being charity by essence He lives by charity. His charity is Himself, therefore it is His life, and in a certain sense we may say it is His Law. Cistercian Mysticism is altogether suspended from a theology of the Trinity of which the central idea would seem to be that God Himself lives by a law and that the law which rules His intimate life is love. The Father generates the Son, and the bond that unites the Son to the Father and the Father to the Son, is the Spirit Who is their mutual love. Charity is thus the bond that assures the unity of the divine life. (p. 298)[239]

He goes on to show that when we, by the Holy Spirit, are united to the Father in and through the Son, then the divine Law of Charity is fulfilled in our own lives; we are perfectly ourselves, and yet we are outside ourselves and lost in God. We have found ourselves at last in Him. *If we do not live by the law of charity* which is perfect freedom, then: (1) we are far from our true selves, and far from God; (2) instead of being free with the freedom of the sons of God, we are bowed under the yoke of slavery to a tyrant, self-will; (3) or, at best, we are mere hired servants of God, serving Him for what we get out of Him, and therefore do not enjoy the liberty of sons and do not have the capacity for perfect love. *If we live by the law of God, then we are "deified":*[240]

> To love God as He loves Himself, that truly is to be one with Him in will, to reproduce the divine life in the human soul, to live like God, to become like God, in a word, to be deified.

---

239. Gilson, *Spirit of Mediaeval Philosophy*, 297–98, which reads: ". . . image, and then . . . its Original . . . the more faithful it is to. . . . He is love: *Deus caritas est* (1 John iv. 8); that is . . . Himself, and therefore . . . law that rules . . . thus, so to speak, the bond . . . ."

240. "*Sic affici, deificari est*" (*De Diligendo Deo*, 10.28 [PL 182, col. 991A]) ("to be thus affected is to be deified"); see Gilson, *Mystical Theology of Saint Bernard*, 130–32, and Thomas Merton, *An Introduction to Christian Mysticism: Initiation into the Monastic Tradition 3*, ed. Patrick F. O'Connell, MW 13 (Kalamazoo, MI: Cistercian Publications, 2008), 63–65.

> The marvel is *that in thus becoming God man also becomes or re-becomes himself,* he realizes his very essence as man in realizing his end, plucks up by the roots the miserable dissimilitude that divided his soul from his own true nature. Losing that whereby it is but partially itself, it finds once more the fullness of its own being, as it was when it came from the hands of God. Where then is the supposed opposition between love of God and love of self? Man is so much the more fully himself as he becomes more fully a love of God for God's sake. (p. 299)[241]

But how do we do this? by perfect conformity to the will of God. In other words, our highest self-interest is to give up our "self" that is opposed to God and separated from Him, and find our true self in union with His will. Self-love in the bad sense is, in fact, what is most opposed to our own good and to our own true self. It cannot produce peace, fulfillment, only fear and slavery and ultimately spiritual death. (Note: this theme of image and likeness is found *everywhere* in the Fathers, especially Origen,[242] Gregory of Nyssa,[243] etc.; Cassian also treats of it.[244]) These are the basic ideas of all Cistercian mysticism and indeed of all mysticism of the Middle Ages.

---

241. Text reads: ". . . the soul from its own . . ." (emphasis added).

242. Merton writes that "Origen bases his asceticism on the fact that man, created in the *image* and *likeness* of God, has lost his likeness to Him, but remains the image of God. *This likeness has to be recovered by grace and love.* St. Bernard took over this doctrine and made it the basis of his teaching" (*Cassian and the Fathers*, 27).

243. See Merton's comments on Gregory's *De Hominis Opificio*: "Man is made in the *image of God*. . . . Man's job in life is to reproduce in the depths of the soul his *divine likeness*. This consists in the right use of his *freedom*" (*Cassian and the Fathers*, 56).

244. See *Conference* 11.7 (*PL* 49, col. 854A): "*Patris imaginem ac similitudinem recipere*" ("to receive the image and likeness of the Father"); see *Cassian and the Fathers*, 111; Thomas Merton, *Pre-Benedictine Monasticism: Initiation into the Monastic Tradition* 2, ed. Patrick F. O'Connell, MW 9 (Kalamazoo, MI: Cistercian Publications, 2006), 57.

BERNARD AND GUIGO: Bernard's first short "treatise" on love is in *Epistola* 11 to Guigo.

A. GUIGO THE CARTHUSIAN:

1. Note with what special respect Bernard addressed Guigo at the beginning of the letter: "To my Fathers revered above all and my friends beloved above all, Guigo . . . and *the other saints* who are with him."[245] As Gilson rightly remarks[246] (*Vie Spirituelle*, Sept. 1934, p. 163): "Bernard is not one of those who goes about distributing diplomas of sanctity, as the Cluniacs knew very well."[247]

2. Bernard's letter was a reply not only to a *letter* but to a *treatise* (Gilson, *loc. cit.*), to the *Meditations of Guigo*: *O quantus in illis meditationibus exardescit ignis!*[248] They had been sent to Bernard as a gift, after a Carthusian had visited Clairvaux and had reported back to Guigo on the holiness of the abbot and community. Wilmart calls the meditations of Guigo the most original work of the period.[249]

3. *Guigo* {was} born about 1083, died 27 July 1137; {he} became Prior of Grande Chartreuse at 27, in 1110, after only three or four years in Grande Chartreuse. {He} wrote "Customs" of the Carthusians {and} wrote {his} *Meditations*, for personal use, about 1110–1116. A few copies were given to select friends about

---

245. "*Inter patres reverendissimis et inter amicos charissimis, Guigoni priori Cartusiensi, caeterisque sanctis qui cum eo sunt*" (*PL* 182, col. 107C) (Merton's translation).

246. Étienne Gilson, "Guigue I le Chartreux: Méditations," *La Vie Spirituelle* 40 (1934): 162–78.

247. "Bernard n'est pas de ceux qui prodiguent les brevets de sainteté . . . les Clunisiens en savaient quelque chose."

248. Col. 108C ("How great must have been the fire burning in your meditations" [*Letters*, 41 (#12)]).

249. André Wilmart, OSB, *Le Recueil des Pensées du B. Guigue* (Paris: J. Vrin, 1936), 9: "Voici, peut-être, l'ouvrage le plus original que nous ait laissé la période vraiment créatrice du moyen âge" ("Here, perhaps, is the most original work that the truly creative period of the Middle Ages has left us").

1120–1122, when Bernard got one. The book was practically forgotten or ignored until {the} fifteenth-sixteenth century. Then the sayings are arranged into chapters (as in Migne, *PL* 153[250]).

4. {At the} *heart of the Meditations* {is} the total dedication of the mind to nature and substantial truth, to see all in this light so as to find true peace in this *source: Sine aspectu et decore, crucique affixa, adoranda est veritas.*[251] (Note: Wilmart's edition is based on three twelfth-century manuscripts, one of which was from Clairvaux and probably a copy of the one sent by Guigo to St. Bernard.[252]) Yet to love the truth for itself is to find perfect peace, for this love unites us with God. *Amato quod amando carere nequeas, id est Deum* (186).[253] We should cling to truth as ants cling to their eggs when their nest is destroyed (221): "One must love truth only, and the peace that comes from truth."[254] Truth is bitter because it opposes all one's pleasure. Notice: his approach is completely existential. Recognition of truth begins with the recognition of our own falsity and misery. *Initium redeundi ad veritatem, displicere sibi in falsitate.*[255] (cf. {the} first degree of truth in *De Gradibus Humilitatis*[256]). On the other hand, *Ignorantia est causa temporalis pacis* (269)[257] ({compare the} Buddhist idea of *avidya*[258]).

---

250. *PL* 153, cols. 601–32.

251. *Meditationes*, n. 5 (Wilmart, 70) ("Without an appearance of beauty, nailed to the cross, Truth is to be adored").

252. Wilmart, 43.

253. Wilmart, 98 ("Love what you cannot abstain from loving, that is, God").

254. "*Sic ama ueritatem et pacem*" (Wilmart, 104).

255. *Meditationes*, n. 162 (Wilmart, 95) ("The beginning of the return to truth is to be displeased with oneself in one's falseness").

256. The first degree of truth is humility—to seek truth in oneself by judging oneself (*De Gradibus Humilitatis et Superbiae*, 3.6 [*PL* 182, col. 944C]).

257. Wilmart, 112 ("Ignorance is the cause of worldly peace").

258. See Thomas Merton, *Zen and the Birds of Appetite* (New York: New Directions, 1968), 82: "Buddhism and Biblical Christianity agree in their view of man's present condition. Both are aware that man is somehow not in his right relation to the world and to things in it, or rather, to be more exact, they see that man bears in himself a mysterious tendency to *falsify* that rela-

*Vide quam te ipsum ignores. Nulla es enim regio tam remota et ignota tibi, de qua facilius credas falsa narranti* (303).[259] The minister of truth must speak only out of charity and not make the truth more bitter than it is already. He must not use truth as a weapon. The root of trouble {is} either (a) receiving truth as an evil; (b) worse still, inflicting truth as an evil, or, correlative to this, seeking truth in so far as it pleases us, using it as a source of pleasure and self-satisfaction. We must seek the truth because it is LIFE to us, even when it seems to put us to death. *Qui vult te laedere, armetur vita tua, id est veritate. Vita enim animae tuae, est veritas. Ergo vulnerat te vita tua, quia mendacio te protegis* (172).[260] The publican was saved by admitting the facts for which the pharisee reproached him in pride and malice (224).[261] When the truth presents itself as our adversary, we find life in *submission* to it, death in *submitting it to ourselves*. True peace has its source only in substantial truths, false peace in appearance and superficial experience, which are subject to change and in which we are vulnerable. *Non ergo, vel quia displicet vel quia placet, dicenda est veritas, sed ut prosit. Silenda est autem tantum ne noceat, sicut lux infirmis oculis* (225).[262] *The whole*

---

tion, and to spend a great deal of energy in justifying the false view he takes of his world and of his place in it. This falsification is what Buddhists call *Avidya*. *Avidya*, usually translated 'ignorance,' is the root of all evil and suffering because it places man in an equivocal, in fact impossible position. It is an invincible error concerning the very nature of reality and man himself. It is a disposition to treat the ego as an absolute and central reality and to refer all things to it as objects of desire or of repulsion. Christianity attributes this view of man and of reality to 'original sin.'"

259. Wilmart, 120 ("See how you do not know yourself. For there is no region so remote and unknown to you, about which you may more easily believe one telling falsehoods").

260. Wilmart, 96 ("One who wishes to harm you may be armed with your life, that is, with the truth. For the life of your soul is truth. Therefore he wounds you with your life, because you protect yourself with a lie").

261. Wilmart, 105.

262. Wilmart, 105 ("Therefore it must be spoken not because it either displeases or pleases, but so that it may benefit. It should be left unspoken only so it will not harm, like light for weak eyes").

*man* saved and possessed by truth—this is his objective. *Si enim nullus in mente motus, nisi veritatis, nullus in corpore, nisi mentis, nullus quoque [in corpore] esset, nisi veritatis, id est Dei* (356).[263] Will-power without knowledge is madness (see 374[264]). *Voluptas bestialis, ex sensibus carnis; diabolica vero, omnis fastus, et invidiae et fallaciae. Philosofica, nosse creaturam; angelica vero, nosse et amare Deum* (203)[265] (cf. 453,[266] {and for} background, Evagrius Ponticus[267]). All suffering comes from self-love and attachment. *Anima humana tandiu in se cruciatur quandiu potest cruciari, id est, quandiu aliquid amat praeter Deum. Deum enim nequit amittere nolens. . . . Nemo enim laeditur nisi a seipso.*[268] Your suffering is an indication of the fact that you have sinned in loving what causes suffering, i.e., a perishable thing, and have turned away from God (254).[269]

---

263. Wilmart, 134 ("For if there is no movement in the mind except that of the truth, and none in the body except that of the mind, there might also be none [in the body] except that of the truth, that is, of God").

264. Wilmart, 141.

265. Wilmart, 101 ("Bestial pleasure is from the senses of the flesh; diabolical pleasure is all pride, both jealousies and deceptions. Philosophical pleasure is to know the creature; but angelic pleasure is to know and love God").

266. "*Hic homo dedit pro laudibus hominum omnia sua, ille pro uoluptate uentris et gutturis. Quis horum peius operatus est? Hoc quidem nescio; sed scio, alterum porcina, alterum diabolica uoluntate actum*" (Wilmart, 162) ("This man gave all his goods for the praises of men, that man, for the pleasure of his belly and gullet. Which of these acted worse? This I really do not know; but I know that one acted like a pig, the other like a devil").

267. See Merton's discussion of Evagrius' teaching on *apatheia*, freedom from the passions (*Introduction to Christian Mysticism*, 100–106), which is "ordered to *gnosis* and love" (105).

268. Wilmart, 149 (n. 399), which reads: ". . . *tam diu iuste . . . quam diu . . . quam diu amat aliquid . . . nolens amittere nequit . . . a se ipso*" (Merton's text corresponds to that in *PL* 153, col. 607B) ("The human soul is tormented within itself justly so long as it can be tormented, that is, so long as it loves anything except God. For one cannot lose God unwillingly. . . . For no one is wounded except by himself").

269. Wilmart, 110.

*Ipsi ergo dolores tui arguunt fornicationes tuas, ita ut non sit opus aliis testibus* (357).[270] *Querit enim amittere, quisquis ea diligit et adquirit, quae retineri non valent* (85).[271] *Non te faciunt adversa miserum, sed ostendunt et docent fuisse* (153).[272] He accepts the reality and value of temporal things, but they are merely "*syllabae quae pereunt suis temporibus Deo modulante,*"[273] and we should not cling to what was said "then" but follow what is being said now. Hence {there must be} detachment and freedom. *Uni ex syllabis magni carminis adhesisti; ideo turbaris, cum canendo procedit {cantor} sapientissimus.*

270. Wilmart, 135 ("Therefore your sorrows themselves testify to your fornications, so that there is no need for other witnesses").

271. Wilmart, 83 ("For whoever loves and acquires things which cannot be retained seeks to lose them").

272. Wilmart, 94 ("Misfortunes do not make you miserable, but they show and teach that you have been").

273. Wilmart, 75 (n. 33), which reads: "*pereunt,—tanquam syllabae suis temporibus, Deo modulante*" ("they perish just like syllables in their own proper time, with God doing the singing"). In his "Note on *The Psychological Causes of War*," Merton writes: "A mediaeval writer of great finesse, Guigo the Carthusian, points out the state of idolatry and alienation of a man who is in all things 'subject to what he himself destroys'—that is to the pleasures and gratifications which the transient and exterior self takes in evanescent things. One might say that this leads us to the crux of the problem: the hope of finding life and joy in the mere *processes* of natural existence leads to the contradiction which tries to *construct* and *create* in acts which have at least an implicitly destructive character. The self-affirmation that springs from 'using up' something or someone else in the favor of one's own pitiable transiency, leads to the outright destruction of others in open despair at our own evanescence. So Guigo says: 'He who loves nothing destructible has no place in himself where he can be wounded by the man of power and he becomes inviolable, since he loves inviolable values as they ought to be loved.' One might add that such a one has no need and no incentive to defend himself violently or to destroy. He does not despise or hate evanescent things. He simply hears them as 'syllables which God utters at their proper time' and passes on" (Thomas Merton, *Faith and Violence: Christian Teaching and Christian Practice* [Notre Dame, IN: University of Notre Dame Press, 1968], 112–13).

*Subtrahitur enim syllaba tibi quam solam amabas* (149).[274] *Nil tibi laboriosius quam non laborare, id est contemnere omnia unde labores oriuntur, universa scilicet mutabilia.*[275] *Facile est iter ad Deum, quoniam exonerando itur* (56).[276] *Quam pulchra ars, vincere in bono malum* (53)[277] (cf. St. Bernard's theme—*sapientia vincit malitiam*[278]—which appears in {a} Homily on Missus Est and in {the} last sermons *in Cantica*—embracing his whole life-work). Guigo's doctrine is not only speculative on this point—it is a true Christian exposition of AHIMSA (non-violent love of truth).[279] *Talis esto erga omnes, qualis erga te veritas extitit. Qualem te sustinuit et amavit, ut meliorem faceret, tales sustine et ama, ut meliores facias* (168).[280] *Positus es quasi signum ad retundenda jacula inimici, id est* ad destruendum malum, oppositione boni (59).[281] *Qui mundum amant, artem qua id quod amant assequantur vel fruantur, laboriose ediscunt. Tu Deum vis assequi, et artem qua adquiritur, id est* retribuere bonum pro malo,

---

274. Wilmart, 93 ("You clung to one of the syllables of the great song; and so you are disturbed when the most wise singer goes on with his singing. For the syllable which alone you loved is taken away from you"); copy text omits "*cantor*".

275. Wilmart, 77 (n. 50) ("Nothing is more laborious for you than not to labor, that is, to scorn everything from which labors arise, namely, all changeable things").

276. Wilmart, 78 ("The way to God is easy, because it is taken by unloading").

277. Wilmart, 78 ("How beautiful an art, to overcome evil by good").

278. See above, n. 187.

279. See Thomas Merton, ed., *Gandhi on Non-Violence: Selected Texts from Non-Violence in Peace and War* (New York: New Directions, 1964), 23: "Ahimsa (non-violence) is for Gandhi the basic law of our being. That is why it can be used as the most effective principle for social action, since it is in deep accord with the truth of man's nature and corresponds to his innate desire for peace, justice, order, freedom, and personal dignity."

280. Wilmart, 96 ("Be toward everyone else just as truth has been toward you. Even as it sustained and loved you in order to make you better, so sustain and love them in order to make them better").

281. Wilmart, 79 ("You are set up as a mark for blunting the spears of the enemy, that is, for destroying evil through the opposition of the good").

*contemnis?* (65).²⁸² The enemy who hates us is a fool, but the devil who uses him as an instrument is clever. Hence we must be gentle to our enemy in order to liberate him, and use caution in response to the spirit of evil (97).²⁸³ Christ did not pray to his enemies to spare him, but to the Father. For all power is from God (101)²⁸⁴ (see also nos. 102, 110, 111, 129, 134, 139, 167, 169, 179, 208, 236, 421, 424, 430²⁸⁵). *Declinare a malo sola veritas novit, et solus ejus amor potest* (120).²⁸⁶ *Neminem odisse potes, nisi tua iniquitate. Nam etiam iniquis optare bonum, sanctorum est* (127).²⁸⁷ *Quomodo enim insania, insaniendo curari potest?* (136).²⁸⁸ *Tibi prodesse possunt etiam aliena mala, si de illis agas quod agendum est* (157).²⁸⁹ *Nec contra aegrum, sed pro aegro, id est contra aegritudinem eius, est medicus; totamque et sufficientem vindictam pro omnibus quae ab eo patitur, salutem eius habet. Neque enim ei aliquid imputat, sed ipsi morbo: et ideo plena est ei ultio, morbi ipsius extinctio* (346).²⁹⁰ *Exul es amore, voluptate, affectu, non loco. Exul es in regione corruptionis, passionum, tenebrarum,*

---

282. Wilmart, 80 ("Those who love the world laboriously learn the art by which they attain and enjoy what they love. You wish to attain God, and do you scorn the art by which He is reached, that is, by returning good for evil?").

283. Wilmart, 84.

284. Wilmart, 85.

285. Wilmart, 85, 87, 90, 91, 96, 97, 102, 107, 155, 157.

286. Wilmart, 88 ("Only truth knows how to turn from evil, and only love for it is able to do so").

287. Wilmart, 90 ("You can hate no one except in your wickedness. For to hope for good even for the wicked is the mark of saints").

288. Wilmart, 91 ("How can raving be cured by raving?").

289. Wilmart, 94 ("Even another's evils can be of service to you if you treat them as you should").

290. Wilmart, 132 ("A doctor is not against a sick man but for him, that is, against his sickness; and he has his health as a complete and sufficient vindication for all which he suffers from it. He does not impute any of it to the doctor, but to the sickness itself; and so the full avenging for him is the extinction of the sickness itself").

*ignorantiae, malorum amorum et odiorum* (61)[291] ({cf. the} Platonic trope—*regio dissimilitudinis*[292]). *Omnia vitia et peccata, quia propter creaturam fiunt, id est, propter ultimum bonum, bonitati creatoris attestantur, id est summo bono* (70)[293] (cf. Bernard: *De Diligendo*[294]). *Novit vera caritas Deum* (83)[295] ({cf.} the Cistercian theme {of} love as knowledge[296]).

CARITAS:

1. *Deus caritas est. Qui ergo caritatem exhibet alicui nisi propter ipsam, Deum vendit, beatitudinem suam vendit. Non enim bene est illi, nisi amando* (89).[297] *Deus caritas est; et ideo qui majus aliquid aut melius caritate habet, aliquid majus et melius Deo habet*[298] (cf. St. Bernard's

---

291. Wilmart, 79 ("You are an exile from love, from pleasure, from feeling, not from a place. You are an exile in the land of corruption, of passions, of shadows, of ignorance, of evil loves and hates").

292. "the land of unlikeness" (*Epistola* 8.2 [*PL* 182, col. 106A (*Letters*, 39 [#9])]; *De Gratia et Libero Arbitrio*, 32 [*PL* 182, col. 1018C]; *De Diversis*, 40.4, 42.2 [*PL* 183, cols. 649A, 661D]); cf. Gilson, *Mystical Theology of Saint Bernard*, c. 2 (33–59), which has this phrase as its title and considers the loss of likeness to God as the result of the Fall, and 224–25, n. 43, which discusses in detail the source and meaning of the phrase in Augustine (*Confessions*, 7.10.16 [*PL* 32, col. 742]) and the Platonic tradition.

293. Wilmart, 81 ("All vices and sins, because they are done for the sake of a creature, that is, for the sake of an ultimate good, witness to the goodness of the Creator, that is, to the highest good").

294. See *De Diligendo Deo*, c. 7, nn. 18–21 (*PL* 182, cols. 985A–987B), in which Bernard shows that rational beings naturally seek what they consider to be most satisfactory to their mind and will and are not content with anything considered less than the best. Since material goods and pleasures are limited and cannot ultimately satisfy, their pursuit is eventually experienced as frustrating and properly points toward the supreme and lasting good, God Himself, the true end of all desire.

295. Wilmart, 82 ("True love knows God").

296. See above, n. 233.

297. Wilmart, 83 ("God is love. Therefore one who shows love to anyone, except for its own sake, sells God, sells his own happiness. For it is not well with him except in loving").

298. Wilmart, 138 (n. 364), which reads: "*Deus enim caritas . . .*" ("God is love; and therefore he who has something greater or better than love has something greater and better than God").

doctrine of pure love[299]—again this is a deeper and subtler idea of the "mercenary";[300] note {the} problem raised by the confusion of *Caritas—Deus* and *caritas—Dei donum*[301]).

2. *Bonum est tibi amari a sanctis, immo ipsis quamprimum hoc expedit.* Ipsi enim te amando sentiunt caritatem quae Deus est. Ipsa itaque dilectio, fit praemium sui (94)[302] (cf. St. Bernard: opening of Epistle 11;[303] *De Gradibus*, second degree of truth,[304] etc.;

---

299. See Gilson's discussion of "pure love" (*Mystical Theology of Saint Bernard*, 140–49), an analysis particularly of *Sermon* 83 on the Songs of Songs.

300. I.e., those who love God for the sake of a reward, as distinguished from the slave, who acts out of fear, and the son, who is motivated by selfless love (see below, pages 91–96, 99–101, 105–6, and *De Diligendo Deo*, 12.34–35, 13.36 [*PL* 182, cols. 995B–997B]).

301. "*Dicitur ergo recte et charitas, et Deus, et Dei donum*" (*Epistola* 11 [*PL* 182, col. 111D]; *De Diligendo Deo*, 12.35 [*PL* 182, col. 996B]) ("It follows that charity can be correctly said to be both God and the gift of God" [*Letters*, 44]).

302. Wilmart, 84 ("It is good for you to be loved by holy people; in fact this is useful for themselves first of all. For by loving you they feel the love which is God. And so love itself becomes its own reward").

303. In his letter to Guigo (*PL* 182, cols. 108B–115B; *Letters*, 41–48 [#12]), Bernard begins by expressing his joy in receiving Guigo's letter and his gift of the *Meditations*, and goes on to say: "I rejoice on my own account and on yours; I congratulate you on your charity, and myself on the profit my soul has derived from it" (*Letters*, 43 [col. 110C]) (these are the words immediately preceding the section of the letter included in the *De Diligendo Deo*). He then explains that "charity is the divine substance itself. And there is nothing new or strange about this, for St. John himself has said, 'God is charity.' It follows that charity can be correctly said to be both God and the gift of God; that charity gives charity; the substance of charity, the quality of charity. When we speak of the giver we mean the substance; when we speak of the gift we mean the quality" (*Letters*, 44 [cols. 111CD; 996B]). See also Merton's comments on the salutation of the letter below, pages 96–98.

304. The second degree of truth, following that of humility and preceding that of contemplation, is charity, expressed in mercy and compassion for one's neighbor: "*Et hic est secundus gradus veritatis, quo eam in proximis inquirunt; dum de suis aliorum necessitates exquirunt; dum ex iis quae patiuntur, patientibus compati sciunt*" (*De Gradibus Humilitatis*, 5.18 [*PL* 182, col. 951C]) ("And this is the second degree of truth, in which they seek it in their neighbors as they move beyond concern for their own needs to those of others;

confusion can be eliminated by making precise the idea that charity is *our likeness* to God and our union with Him).

3. Our true good is not our *propria utilitas* but *prodesse omnibus* (106;[305] cf. 211[306]): (a) *Haec est autem propria uniuscujusque utilitas, omnibus velle prodesse;*[307] (b) *omnibus prodesse velle, ita* ut tales esse velis eos qui tuo non egeant auxilio;[308] (c) *Tanto enim minus agunt quod expedit, quanto propriis utilitatibus videntur intendere;*[309] (d) *Dum enim propriam querit,* quae nulla esse potest, *a communi repellitur, id est a Deo.* Sicut enim omnium hominum una est natura, ita et utilitas.[310] See also 151: Potanda est dilectio gratis, id est propter suam dulcedinem propriam, *tanquam nectar suavissimum,* etiam si omnes insaniant, non vendenda ulla mercede.[311]

4. Love is the common good—it belongs to all. It must not be arrogated by an individual for himself alone (cf. St. Bernard's *voluntas communis*[312]). Amor uniuscujusque hominis, communis

---

from what they themselves have suffered they know how to have compassion on those who suffer").

305. Wilmart, 86 ("our own advantage"; "to be beneficial for all").

306. Wilmart, 102–3.

307. Wilmart, 86 ("To wish to benefit all is an advantage proper to each").

308. "to wish to benefit all so that you wish them to be such as may not act for your assistance."

309. "For they act less because it is suitable than they seem to do for the sake of their own benefit."

310. "While he seeks his own benefit, which can be none at all, he is driven from the common benefit, that is, from God. For as there is one nature for all men, so also there is one benefit."

311. Wilmart, 93 ("Love must be drunk for free, that is, for its own sweetness, like the smoothest nectar; even if others rave, it must not be sold for any price").

312. "*Porro communis voluntas charitas est*" (*In Tempore Resurrectionis*, 3.8 [*PL* 183, col. 286B]) ("Moreover, charity is the common will"); see Gilson, *Mystical Theology of Saint Bernard*, 55, 72–73, 95, 101–2, 135, and below, pages 234–37.

est omnium. *Singuli enim, omnes amare debent.* Qui ergo hunc sibi specialiter exhiberi vult, raptor, et ideo reus contra omnes efficitur (159).[313] {As a} consequence, we must be of advantage and service to our brother, helping him to find truth. *Non hominum superbus dominus, sed utilis socius esse debes. Nec delectari eorum voluptate multiplici, sed utilitate simplici, id est veritate* (175).[314] More than this, *our love is owed to our brother because it is God's gift to him through us. To refuse to love a brother is to rob him of what God has promised him*—namely, our love (see 238[315]). *Non est plene bonus aut beatus, qui aliis non est bonus* (239).[316] The beginning {is} *non concupiscendo*. This enables us to be "chaste" to God and "just" to our brother (258).[317]

5. *Mercenary love*: *Si amas, quia amaris, aut ut ameris, non tam amas quam redamas, amorem pro amore rependens. Cambitor es; recepisti mercedem tuam* (182;[318] cf. 438[319]). Note the bold and powerful description of mercenary love in 241: the *impudens mulier* who

---

313. Wilmart, 94 ("The love of every single person is common to all. For individuals should love everyone. Therefore he who wishes this love to be shown especially toward himself is a thief, and so is made an offender against all").

314. Wilmart, 97 ("You should be not a proud master of men but a useful partner. Do not be delighted in their manifold pleasure, but in an undivided benefit, that is, in the truth").

315. Wilmart, 108.

316. Wilmart, 108, which reads: "*Non est autem plene . . .*" ("He is not completely good or happy who is not good to others").

317. Wilmart, 111 (n. 258) ("by not desiring selfishly").

318. Wilmart, 98 ("If you love because you are loved, or in order to be loved, you do not love so much as you repay love, measuring out love for love. You are a barterer; you have received your reward").

319. "*Vide quomodo uendis amorem et caeteros affectus animi tui ad obolatas et nummatas, sicut in taberna uinum. Rursus attende qualiter emas opiniones et amores ac caeteros affectus siue motus humanorum animorum, ad obolatas et nummatas, sicut in taberna uinum*" (Wilmart, 158) ("See how you sell love and the other affections of your soul for cash and coins, like wine in a shop. Again, notice how you buy the opinions and loves and other affections or movements of human souls for cash and coins, like wine in a shop").

asks her husband to get her lovers—this is like asking God in prayer for things we love more than Him! (cf. 243, 245, 249, 364[320]). Mercenary love {can also be present} in the superior, or "minister of truth": *Prodesse autem hominibus, tuum officium totum.*[321] The master who always wants to be master is not good *because he does not* (by implication) *want his students (disciples) to surpass him* (cf. modern psychology). Semper vult esse morbosos, qui semper vult esse medicus. *Et qui magister, imperitos.* Odit ergo, quos semper tales esse optat (195).[322] The true teacher is one who works in such a way that his own function becomes {unnecessary}.[323] *Qui vero bonus est, contra morbos et imperitiam luctatur, ut pereant.* Ergo et contra officium suum quodam modo, ut pereat (195).[324] But the master *who puts himself between souls and God* is useless and harmful to them (263).[325] On the contrary, he who wants to help another must "put on" the other (*induere*) as Christ put on human nature, and so bring him to God (empathy): *Indue eum prius, quem judicare vis aut corripere. . . . Nam et Christus prius induit hominem quam judicaret* (416).[326] The office of teacher is not so much to make men will the good (this they can do) but *to show them the true good so that they may will it* (see 201[327]). The Christian

---

320. Wilmart, 109, 110, 138.

321. Wilmart, 103 (n. 211) ("to benefit people is your total duty").

322. Wilmart, 100, which reads: "*Semper enim vult . . .*" ("He who always wants to be a doctor wants there always to be sick people. And the one who always wants to be a teacher wants there always to be ignorant people. He therefore hates those whom he always hopes to be such").

323. Copy text reads: "unmercenary," but it seems likely, in light of the quotation that follows, that this is an error on the part of the typist.

324. "He who is indeed good struggles against sicknesses and ignorance so that they may perish. Therefore he is striving also against his own office, in a certain sense, so that it may perish."

325. Wilmart, 111.

326. Wilmart, 154 ("First put on him whom you wish to judge or correct. . . . For Christ too put on man before He would judge").

327. "*Omnes conantur implere quod uolunt, tanquam sint certi, bonum esse quod uolunt. Omnes autem ad hoc reuoca, ut conentur uelle quod oportet*" (Wilmart, 101) ("All try to fulfill what they wish, as if they were certain that what they

is not a defender of the truth but one who is defended by truth. Truth does not need us; we need truth (204): *Non defenditur veritas, sed defendit*.³²⁸ The Master is one who celebrates the "true sabbath"³²⁹ of interior peace. He is not drawn by pleasure or compelled by fear: *"Nec illicitur nec cogitur"* ³³⁰ (cf. 187: true liberty³³¹). *Hic habet se in potestate* (205).³³² Hence he can "give alms"³³³ of himself, and be stern or gentle according as he sees it to be useful to another (205). He is concerned only with the other's good. Mercenary love is "diffused in our hearts by the enjoyment of temporal things" and not by the Holy Spirit (209).³³⁴ At the same time, as these goods perish, they generate fear, as ice makes all that touches it cold (207).³³⁵ Mercenary love is not cured by making one's subjects *unable* to sin (i.e., by removing the opportunity), but by teaching them to be *unwilling* to sin (232).³³⁶ For even when they are physically unable, they can sin in their will. Mercenary love {can be present} in prayer, {with a} loss of spiritual virginity—the "love of forms," that is, the "fruition" of forms by yielding totally to them (249;³³⁷ cf. 333³³⁸). But *Panis, id est veritas,*

---

wish is good. Rather, call them all back to this, that they try to wish what they ought to").

328. Wilmart, 101 ("Truth is not defended, but defends").

329. *"uerum sabbatum"* (Wilmart, 118 [n. 292]).

330. Wilmart, 101 (n. 205) ("He is neither seduced nor compelled").

331. *"nec illici nec cogi potes, quod solum est libertas"* (Wilmart, 98) ("You can neither be seduced nor compelled, which alone is liberty").

332. Wilmart, 101 ("He has himself in his own power").

333. *"de se elemosinam facere"* (Wilmart, 101).

334. *"Per temporalia ergo diffunditur in te"* (Wilmart, 102).

335. Wilmart, 101–2.

336. Wilmart, 106.

337. *"Quacunque forma frueris, ea quasi masculus est tuae menti. Cedit enim et succumbit ei"* (Wilmart, 110) ("Whatever form you enjoy, it is like a male to your mind. For the mind yields and succumbs to it").

338. *"Si haec, quibus in tua mente impressis admiratione et amore—qui cultus soli Deo debetur—succumbis, in aliquo angulo domus seu sculpta seu picta admiratione uel amore seu corporis inclinatione uenerareris, et innotesceret populo, quid de te faceret?"* (Wilmart, 127) ("If you venerated in admiration or love or by bowing the body—worship which is owed to God alone—these things

*confirmat cor hominis, ne succumbat corporum formis* (251).[339] *Potens impotentia, non posse velle malum. Ideo potentissimus [est] Dominus, quia malum velle non potest* (233;[340] cf. 338: *O misera sors, non posse nolle quod obest;*[341] cf. St. Bernard—*De Gratia et Libero Arbitrio*[342]). *Ille amor quo amati sumus ante quam essemus, vel cum inique agebamus, est causa omnium bonorum nostrorum* (271).[343] This is the theme from St. John: [*Deus*] *prior dilexit nos.*[344] *Nil concessum cupiditati, nil vetitum caritati* (276).[345] {This is} a good commentary on St. Augustine's *"ama et quod vis fac."*[346] See 329, on the fact that our love for God should be without limit[347] (cf. the opening of *De*

---

to which you succumb, sculpted or pictured in some corner of your home, which have been imprinted on your mind in wonder and love, and it became known to people, what would they make of you?").

339. Wilmart, 110 ("Bread, that is, the truth, strengthens a person's heart, lest he submit to the forms of bodies").

340. Wilmart, 107 ("It is a powerful powerlessness not to be able to will evil. Thus the Lord is most powerful, because He cannot will evil").

341. Wilmart, 129 ("O wretched lot, to be unable to reject what is harmful").

342. *"Corruit autem de posse non peccare in non posse non peccare, amissa ex toto consilii libertate. . . . Per proprium quippe voluntatem servus peccati factus, merito perdidit libertatem consilii"* (*De Gratia et Libero Arbitrio*, n. 21 [*PL* 182, col. 1013CD]) ("Having lost his freedom of counsel completely, he fell from being able not to sin into being unable not to sin. . . . Having become through his own will the slave of sin, he deservedly lost his freedom of counsel").

343. Wilmart, 113 ("That love with which we were loved before we existed, or when we were doing evil, is the cause of all our good").

344. 1 John 4:10 ("He hath first loved us").

345. Wilmart, 113 ("Nothing conceded to cupidity, nothing forbidden to charity").

346. Augustine, *In 1 Jn.*, 7.8 (*PL* 35, col. 2033, which reads: *"dilige, et . . ."*) ("love and do what you will"); see also the *Commentary on Galatians*, 57: *"Dilige, et dic quod voles"* ("Love, and say what you will") (*PL* 35, col. 2144).

347. *"Taliter ac tantum, qualis et quantus est diligendus est Deus. Est autem aeternus et immensus. Aeternus ergo et immensus est amor, eum quantum et quomodo oportet diligentis"* (Wilmart, 126) ("God should be loved in such a

*Diligendo Deo*³⁴⁸). The good must be sought for its own sake: *Non solum nullum precium debes suscipere ut facias quod oportet, sed etiam nullis adversis quin facias deterreri* (331).³⁴⁹ In this connection he tells a parable of two doctors: one who does all he can for his patient, who dies, and another who does nothing for his patient, who nevertheless recuperates. Which doctor is worthy of payment? ({the} parable {has been} simplified) (349).³⁵⁰ {In} another parable of two doctors, one gives his patient what he thinks is poison, and he is cured. Another gives his patient what he thinks is medicine, and he is poisoned (351).³⁵¹ In this parable he considers the good will or bad will of the doctors. However, in the next meditation (352), he admits: *Duo ergo perficiunt medicum. Voluntas bona, et perfecta scientia.*³⁵² But still, no one can cure everybody, and each doctor is rewarded (by God) for his conscientious care. These parables refer to spiritual direction. {He makes} another comparison: if you put wax and clay in the same sunlight, the wax will melt and the clay will harden. If you set gold before two men, one will desire it for himself, and one will give it to the poor. Hence evil is not in things but in our own minds. *Objects which are presented to us simply show what is inside ourselves* (366).³⁵³ They do not make us evil or good, but manifest the evil or good hidden in us: *Tu quibus conspectis aut imaginatis, quantum movearis attende*

---

way and as greatly as are His own being and greatness. But He is eternal and immeasurable. Eternal and immeasurable, therefore, is the love of the one loving Him to the degree and in the way he should").

348. "*Causa diligendi Deum, Deus est; modus, sine modo diligere*" (*De Diligendo Deo*, 1.1 [*PL* 182, col. 974A]) ("The reason for loving God is God; the way is to love without limit").

349. Wilmart, 127 ("Not only should you accept no payment to do what ought to be done, but you also should not be deterred from doing so by any adversities").

350. Wilmart, 132–33.

351. Wilmart, 133.

352. Wilmart, 133 ("Two things perfect a doctor: good will and complete knowledge").

353. Wilmart, 138–39.

(367).³⁵⁴ {There is also a} negative aspect of mercenary psychology: he who avoids evil out of fear of punishment does not hate the evil itself, {but} he who loves the good *sees that sin itself is punishment*: *Justis autem non aliud est peccare, et aliud puniri. Ipsum utique peccatum atrocissimam poenam ducunt* (404).³⁵⁵ A special study should be made of Guigo's rather more detailed anthropology in the last meditations (464–76):³⁵⁶ these are longer and more developed. They are important as {a} source for St. Bernard's own ideas of man, and we see something of the *"amor carnalis Christi"*³⁵⁷ developed here.

B. Bernard's LETTER {11} to Guigo:³⁵⁸ On the "Law of Charity" (this is n. 12 in Bruno James' translation of the letters³⁵⁹):

1. {It} indicates the part played by friendship in the Cistercian theology of charity. Note the salutation, already remarked on. Why does Bernard call the Carthusians "saints"? Because, characteristically, he experiences them as "mediators" of the fire of charity. They have communicated to him something of an experience of that fire which the Lord came to cast on the earth. Therefore they are close to God, therefore saints. As usual, Bernard bases his statements on an interpretation of his own religious experience. (READ: Bruno James [hereafter BJ]: bottom of p. 41.³⁶⁰) They have greeted him with a *succensa et succendens*

---

354. Wilmart, 139 ("Notice how much you are moved by what has been considered or imagined").

355. Wilmart, 151 ("But for the just it is not one thing to sin and another to be punished. They certainly consider the sin itself the most dreadful punishment").

356. Wilmart, 166–72.

357. See *Sermo 20 in Cantica*, nn. 6–9 (*PL* 183, cols. 870A–872B); see Merton's discussion below, pages 293–95.

358. *PL* 182, cols. 108B–115B; nn. 3–9 incorporated as cc. 12–15 of *De Diligendo Deo* (*PL* 182, cols. 995B–1000B); copy text reads "9".

359. *Letters*, 41–48.

360. "I received the letters of your Holiness with a delight equalled only by my longing eagerness for them. I have read them and mused upon them and they have fired my heart like so many sparks from the fire which the Lord came to spread over the earth. How great must have been the fire

The Cistercian Fathers and Their Monastic Theology 97

*salutatio . . . quasi non ab homine, sed certissime ab illo qui mandat salutes Jacob.*[361] {This} recalls the mystery of the Visitation, implicitly. {A} sacramental concept of friendship {is} implied here. (He speaks specifically of a blessing. Guigo seems to have had a very powerful and concrete sense of what a blessing meant; see some of his other letters: *Lettres des Premiers Chartreux*[362]). {He} apologizes for disturbing their contemplative rest "in the arms of the

---

burning in your meditations to have sent out such sparks as these! Your burning and kindling greeting seemed to me, I confess, to have come, not from man, but from him who 'sent word to Jacob'" (n. 1 [*Letters*, 41–42]).

361. Col. 108CD.

362. *Lettres des Premiers Chartreux*, trans. par un Chartreux, Sources Chrétiennes [SC], vol. 88 (Paris: Éditions du Cerf, 1962), 97–225; see the introductory and concluding sections of Letter 2, to Hugh, the Grand Master of the Templars: "*spiritualium simul et corporalium christianae religionis hostium victoriam plenariam et pacem per Christum Dominum nostrum*" (n. 1 [154]) ("[may you have] a complete victory both spiritual and corporal over the enemies of the Christian religion, and peace through Christ our Lord"); "*Omnipotentissima misericordia et misericordissima omnipotentia Dei, tam in spiritualibus quam etiam corporalibus praeliis, faciat vos semper et felicissime pugnare et gloriosissime triumphare*" (n. 7 [160]) ("May the all-powerful mercy and the most merciful power of God make you always both fight most successfully and triumph most gloriously, as much in spiritual as in physical battles"); the concluding section of Letter 5, to Cardinal Haimeric: "*Deus Pater, qui eduxit de mortuis Pastorem magnum ovium in sanguine Testamenti aeterni, Dominum nostrum Jesum Christum, aptet vos in omni bono, ut faciatis voluntatem ejus, faciens in vobis quod placeat coram se, per Jesum Christum, cui est Gloria in saecula saeculorum, amen*" (Heb. 13:20-21) (n. 10 [194]) ("And may the God of peace, who brought again from the dead the great pastor of the sheep, our Lord Jesus Christ, in the blood of the everlasting testament, fit you in all goodness, that you may do His will; doing in you that which is well pleasing in His sight, through Jesus Christ, to whom is glory for ever and ever. Amen"); the introductory section of Letter 6, to the Council of Jouarre: "*agenda cognoscere, cognita viriliter adimplere per Christum Dominum nostrum*" (n. 1 [200]) ("[may you] know your duty and manfully fulfill what is known through Christ Our Lord"); the introductory and concluding sections of Letter 7, to Peter the Venerable: "*perpetua pace gaudere per Christum*" (n. 1 [206]) ("[may you] rejoice in perpetual peace through Christ"); "*Incolumem vos assiduo virtutum profectu, ad nostrum et totius Ecclesiae gaudium,*

Spouse."³⁶³ But what Bernard does not dare, charity dares, etc. It all started with a charitable report brought back to the Grande Chartreuse by a hermit returning to Guigo with a message. See BJ, p. 43:

> You have listened to him, you have believed him, you have rejoiced in what he said, you have written to me, and thereby you have gladdened me not a little, not only because I have won a place and no small place in your affections, but also because you have shown me something of the purity of your own soul. In a few words you have shown me for certain of what spirit you are.³⁶⁴

This requires little comment. It shows Bernard's deep faith in the communion of saints as a manifestation of the divine love and of the Holy Spirit on the earth, a concrete expression of his love for and faith in the Church. This leads him quite naturally into the exposition of his doctrine, which is identical with what he has experienced, a simple commentary and meditation on his experience.

    2. PRINCIPLE (read {the} beginning of #3 [p. 43]³⁶⁵): *ILLA QUIDEM VERA ET SINCERA EST CARITAS, ET OMNINO DE CORDE PURO, ET DE CONSCIENTIA BONA, ET DE FIDE NON FICTA JUDICANDA PROCEDERE, QUA PROXIMI BONUM AEQUE AC NOSTRUM DILIGIMUS.*³⁶⁶ This principle paral-

---

*clementia divina conservet"* (n. 3 [208]) ("May the divine clemency keep you safe, with continual progress in virtues, for our joy and that of the entire Church"); the introductory section of Letter 9, to the archbishop of Rheims: *"perpetuam salutem et pacem a Domino"* (n. 1 [224]) ("[may you have] eternal salvation and peace from the Lord").

    363. *"inter sponsi brachia"* (col. 109C); Merton's translation.
    364. N. 2.
    365. "I rejoice on my own account and on yours; I congratulate you on your charity, and myself on the profit my soul has derived from it."
    366. Col. 110C, which reads: ". . . *siquidem* . . . *et conscientia* . . . *et fide* . . . *aeque ut nostrum* . . ." ("For that is a true and sincere charity to be attributed entirely to a pure heart and unfeigned faith which leads us to love our neighbours' good as well as our own" [*Letters*, 43]).

lels what is said in the *Meditations* of Guigo on the love of truth *not because it is good for us* but because it is good in itself and for all;³⁶⁷ cf. also in Guigo (n. 321): *Cum vides aut audis aliena mala, respice animum tuum, ut probes quantum ei verae dilectionis erga homines insit.*³⁶⁸

a) He who loves *his own good* (*proprium*) more, or exclusively, shows that he does not have pure love because he loves the good for himself, not for itself.

b) He therefore is unable to obey the prophet and "confess to the Lord because He is good" (cf. St. Augustine on Ps. 53³⁶⁹).

c) {The} degrees of purity of love and *"confessio"* {are} to confess to the Lord because He is POWERFUL (this is for "slaves"); to confess to the Lord because He is GOOD TO US (for "mercenaries"); to confess to the Lord because He is SIMPLICITER BONUS³⁷⁰ (for "sons"). The first two kinds seek their own interest; the third seeks only what please the Father, following the LEX DOMINI IMMACULATA CARITAS,³⁷¹ which seeks God alone.

3. ONLY *CARITAS* CAN COMPLETELY CONVERT THE SOUL. Fear and interested love cannot completely liberate us from love of self and love of the world. *NEC TIMOR NEC AMOR PRIVATUS CONVERTIT ANIMAM. MUTANT INTERDUM* **VULTUM** *VEL* **ACTUM AFFECTUM** *NUMQUAM.*³⁷²
True "conversion" is the inner change of the *"affectus"*—cf. what

---

367. Wilmart, 96 (n. 168).

368. Wilmart, 124 ("When you see or hear evil of another, look to your own soul in order to test how much true love toward people is in it").

369. "*confitebor nomini tuo, Domine, quoniam bonum est*" (*PL* 36, col. 627) ("I will give praise, O Lord, to thy name, because it is good" [Ps. 53[54]:8]).

370. Col. 111A ("Goodness itself" [*Letters*, 43]).

371. Col. 111A, which reads: "*Quam ob rem puto de illa* [i.e., *charitate*] *dictum, Lex Domini, immaculata*" ("On this account I think that the words 'The Law of God is unspotted' refer to charity" [*Letters*, 43]); the quotation is from Ps. 18[19]:8.

372. Col. 111A, which reads: "*Nec timor quippe* . . ." ("Neither fear nor love of self can turn the soul to God; they may sometimes change the aspect or influence the actions of a man, but they will never change his heart" [*Letters*, 43]).

{the} Rhenish mystics say of {the} "ground of {the} soul."[373] The *affectus* of the slave is *"duritia"*: he may do the will of God, but it is against the "hardness of his own will"[374] (this is suggested in Guigo[375]). The *affectus* of the mercenary is *"propria cupiditas,"* or

---

373. In *An Introduction to Christian Mysticism*, Merton discusses the ground of the soul in Eckhart: "The *ground* is the naked, nameless, solitary essence of the soul *flowing directly from God* without medium. . . . The Word being born in the ground of the soul, it is necessary to return to Him by stripping off everything that is exterior to the inmost depth in the soul" (*Introduction to Christian Mysticism*, 200–201); and in Tauler: "The *grund* is called the *mens* and {the} *summit of {the} soul*. It is the place where the image of God is found. . . . It is in and by the *grund* that God is united to us in an ineffable manner. . . . The *gemüt*—or deep will . . . plunges down into the *grund*, to seek God in His image. It is therefore a *dynamic power of conversion to God*, a gravitational force of love, and the inner source of all our activities. It is that *by which we give ourselves* in the deepest sense of the word" (207). See also Merton's journal entry for May 23, 1960: "Tauler—*Gemüt* and the *Grund*—turning the whole desire and strength of the soul to the emptiness, the mirror in which God appears—which is the very mirror being of our being" (Thomas Merton, *A Search for Solitude: Pursuing the Monk's True Life. Journals*, vol. 3, *1952–1960*, ed. Lawrence S. Cunningham [San Francisco: HarperCollins, 1996], 394).

374. *"in sua duritia"* (Col. 111B); Merton's translation.

375. See n. 404 (Wilmart, 151): *"Cum aliquis dolet se commisisse furtum, ob hoc quia incurrit inde opprobrium hominum, non eum paenitet furtum fecisse, sed dolet opprobrium incurrisse. Nec horret aut malum ducit peccare, sed puniri. Iustis autem non aliud est peccare, et aliud puniri. Ipsum utique peccatum atrocissimam poenam ducunt, et ideo nullam iniquitatem impunitam posse esse, eo quod iniquitas ipsa magna poena sit, nichilque peius ea cuique ualeat irrogari; et iccirco ipsam prae omnibus malis cauendam ac fugiendam consent, etiam si nichil aliud mali eam sequatur"* ("When anyone is sorry that he has committed a theft, because of the fact that he has thus incurred the reproach of men, he does not regret having done the theft, but he is sorry for having incurred the reproach. He does not dread or consider it an evil to sin, but to be punished. For the just, however, it is not one thing to sin and another to be punished. Indeed they consider sin itself to be the most dreadful punishment, and therefore no iniquity is able to be unpunished, in that iniquity itself is a great punishment, and nothing worse than that that can be imposed on anyone;

"*proprietas.*"[376] Each of these *affectus* is an *inner law*. The slave is hardened under the law of fear which does not let him relax his grip on himself. The mercenary is *drawn* and lured by his own appetites, and cannot turn to the good as such, even though he may perceive something of it. The Law of sons is the Law of God, which is freedom—entirely from within. Note: the slave does not have *any love* for God; the mercenary *loves God a little*, but *loves himself more*. See the much deeper and subtler notion of mercenary in *Guigo*, meditations #6–8 (Wilmart, p. 70).[377]

---

and for that reason, they believe it should be avoided and fled more than all evils, even if no other evil follow it").

376. Col. 111B, which reads: "*propria cupiditate*" ("only by his greed . . . self-seeking" [*Letters*, 43–44]).

377. "6. *Ad cuius uoluntatem uteris te ipso, ab eo mercedem expostula. Viuendum ergo est ita, ut nichil tibi debeas, quia nichil tibi reddere uales. Opus autem mercennarii tui non maneat apud te, ait Dominus, usque mane. Faciet ergo de te tibi Dominus ultionem. 7. Qui omnia ad suam uoluntatem agit, omnem a se ipso exigat retributionem. Quam cum a se ipso extorquere non poterit, interpellet aduersum se ipsum iudicem iustum Deum. Si ergo te ipsum amares, nunquam eius tibi seruicium dulce esset—id est tui—de cuius mercede desperares. 8. Cur te magis proprium uendicas, quam quemlibet hominum aut agrorum, cum in te nil amplius quam in illis creaueris? Quo iure tibi uendicas quicquam eorum quae non creasti, sicut nec te?*" ("6. Demand payment from him according to whose will you employ yourself. Therefore you should live such that you owe yourself nothing, because you are able to give back nothing to yourself. For 'Do not let the recompense of the hired man remain with you until morning,' says the Lord. Therefore, the Lord will vindicate you for yourself. 7. Let the one who does everything according to his own will claim all retribution from himself. When he is not able to wrest it from himself, let him interpose against himself God the just judge. For if you loved yourself, the service of that—that is, of yourself—would never be sweet to you, and you would despair of being paid for it. 8. Why do you claim more of yourself than of any man or field, since you have created in yourself nothing more than in them? By what right do you claim for yourself anything of those things which you have not created, any more than yourself?")

4. *Ubi proprietas, ibi singularitas . . . ibi angulus . . . ibi sine dubio sordes vel rubigo.*[378] Self-love means necessarily an impure soul. Note this is *not* the conventional Platonism that says "matter" is a source of impurity. {There is} an important distinction: *proprietas* is not necessarily equated purely and simply with matter, {but} rather with the *assertion of one's own will.*

5. *Quod autem Dei est, immundum esse non potest.* That charity is therefore "immaculate" which determines to keep nothing of its own or for itself. *Nil sibi de suo retinere consuevit. Totum profecto quod habet, Dei est: quod autem Dei est, immundum esse non potest.*[379]

6. He then explains why this is called the *"Lex Domini"*— either because it is the Law by which God Himself lives or because *no other can have this as law without a special gift from God. Lex ergo est caritas,* quae Trinitatem in unitate quodammodo cohibet, et colligat in vinculo pacis.[380] And this is the very divine nature itself, for *Deus Caritas est.*[381] Hence {there is} a distinction: *Caritas vel Deus est vel Dei donum.*[382] (Note: this brings us to a technical question in the twelfth century, whether the Holy Spirit was Himself the "virtue of charity" in the soul and personally, immediately carried out the soul's acts of love. Peter Lombard held

---

378. Col. 111B, which reads: *"Porro ubi proprietas, ibi singularitas; ubi autem singularitas, ibi angulus; ubi vero angulus, ibi sine dubio sordes sive rubigo"* ("Where there is self-seeking, there too is self-esteem; where there is self-esteem, there too is private interest; and where private interest makes a corner for itself there rust and filth will collect" [*Letters*, 43–44]).

379. N. 4 (col. 111BC) ("When a man keeps nothing of his own for himself, everything he has is God's, and what is God's cannot be unclean" [*Letters*, 44]).

380. Col. 111C, which reads: *"Lex est ergo, et lex Domini charitas . . ."* ("Charity is therefore a law, and it is the law of the Lord holding together, as it were, the Trinity and binding it in the bonds of peace" [*Letters*, 44]).

381. Col. 111D ("God is charity" [*Letters*, 44]) (1 John 4:16).

382. Col. 111D, which reads: *"charitas et Deus, et Dei donum"* ("charity [is] both God and the gift of God" [*Letters*, 44]).

this.³⁸³ Some of the Cistercians had not yet made the distinction clear. It came out later.) St. Bernard is clear on the point: CARITAS DAT CARITATEM, SUBSTANTIVA ACCIDENTALEM. *Ubi dantem significant, nomen est substantiae; ubi donum, qualitatis.*³⁸⁴

7. HAEC EST LEX AETERNA ET GUBERNATRIX UNIVERSITATIS.³⁸⁵ Charity, selfless love, is built into the very nature of things by God the Creator, for creation resembles the Creator. Compare the meditations of the School of Chartres on creation,³⁸⁶ *Anima Mundi,*³⁸⁷ etc.

383. See Delfgaauw, 144: "Pierre Lombard . . . identifie la charité à l'Esprit Saint" ("Peter Lombard identifies charity with the Holy Spirit").

384. Col. 111D ("charity gives charity; the substance of charity the quality of charity. When we speak of the giver we mean the substance; when we speak of the gift we mean the quality" [*Letters*, 44]).

385. Col. 111D, which reads: ". . . *aeterna, creatrix et gubernatrix* . . ." ("This is the eternal law, the creator and ruler of the Universe" [*Letters*, 44]).

386. See Chenu, *Théologie au Douzième Siècle*, 183: "De même que les artistes qui couvraient les chapiteaux de trèfle, de plaintain, de fougère, aimaient la nature pour elle-même, de même les théologiens chartrains honorent le Créateur dans la dignité de sa création même"; ET: "Just as the artists who covered the capitals with clover, plaintain, and fern loved nature for its own sake, so too the theologians of Chartres paid tribute to the Creator in the respect they showed for his creation" (*Nature, Man, and Society in the Twelfth Century*, 134).

387. See Chenu, *Théologie au Douzième Siècle*, 33: "Il n'est pas étonnant que nous retrouvions au XII<sup>e</sup> siècle l'âme du monde, pièce essentielle de la philosophie cosmique du *Timée*. Nous la retrouvons consacrée dans sa valeur primitive par un concordisme, assez incertain de lui-même d'ailleurs, avec la conception chrétienne d'une présence de l'Esprit dans le monde. . . . En vérité le concordisme était bien extérieur, et il ne devait pas résister à l'examen critique mené tant par les physiciens que par les théologiens. Toujours est-il que l'*anima mundi,* intelligence intérieure du cosmos, opérant sur le corps du monde, lui confère, en réfraction de sa contemplation du Bien, sa vérité, son ordre, sa beauté, sa bonté. L'optimisme intellectualiste de Chartres est à l'opposé d'une interprétation mécaniste de l'univers"; ET: "It occasions no surprise to find here in the twelfth century this doctrine of the world-soul, the essential element of the cosmic philosophy of the *Timaeus*. We find its original import hallowed, brought into relationship—a fairly uncertain one, to be sure—with the Christian conception of the presence of

Meditate on this!—the implicit closeness of *caritas* and *natura*, even though charity is supernatural. Is all nature ordered to the supernatural?

8. Man who does not live according to the LEX CARITATIS MUST THEREFORE LIVE UNDER ANOTHER LAW—HIS OWN LAW. That is to say he "makes a law for himself"[388] by substituting his *propria voluntas* for the "common law" of the universe which is Love. This substitution is "fallen nature." In doing this, he is aping the Creator. He is "creating" a fictitious universe of his own in which his own will is law. Such a creation cannot be anything but fictitious (cf. Guigo, *Meditations*, n. 309[389]).

9. BECAUSE THE LAW OF SELF IS A FICTION, IT IS THEREFORE A BURDEN, because untruth, unreality, is necessarily a burden and a source of constant frustrations, since it implies conflict with

---

the Holy Spirit in the world. . . . In fact, the connection made between the world-soul and the Holy Spirit was wholly superficial and could not stand up under the critical investigation of physicists or theologians. And yet there persisted the idea of a world-soul, an intelligence interior to the cosmos, an agency energizing the physical world and, as it turned from its contemplation of the Good, conferring upon that world its truth, its order, its beauty, and its goodness. The optimistic intellectuality of Chartres stood at the opposite pole from a mechanistic interpretation of the universe" (*Nature, Man, and Society in the Twelfth Century*, 22–23).

388. N. 5 (*Letters*, 44) ("*legem . . . quam ipsi sibi fecerunt*" [col. 111D]).

389. "*Praepara te ad tolerandam legem, quam erga alios ipse exercueris. Legibus enim abs te conditis subiacere cogeris, siue bonis siue malis. In qua autem mensura mensus fueris, in eadem remetietur tibi. Bonas ergo leges et misericordia plenas in alios da, ne si—quod absit—malae fuerint, male sit et tibi, cum eis subiectus fueris. Iudicium enim sine misericordia, ei qui non facit misericordiam*" (Wilmart, 121–22) ("Prepare yourself to endure the law, which you yourself have enforced toward others. For you are forced to be subject to laws established by you, whether good or bad. For in the same measure that you have measured, it will be measured out to you in return. Therefore, give good laws, ones filled with mercy toward others, lest—let it not happen—if they should be bad, it will go badly for you as well when you have been subjected to them. For there is judgment without mercy for one who does not do mercy").

reality. *Grave et importabile jugum super omnes filios Adam* (112;[390] cf. Job 7:20: *Posuisti me contrarium tibi, et factus sum mihimetipsi gravis*[391]). {The} explanation {is that} the fact that we have decreed to be a law to ourselves does not for all that exempt us from God's law and His justice. On the contrary, we are still subjected to it in a new way. We now no longer obey God with freedom and ease, out of love, but as a punishment *we are forced to obey our own law*, which goes contrary to the law of God, and is therefore an insupportable burden. This is an extremely subtle and deeply spiritual analysis. "For this pertained to the eternal and just law of God, that he who did not wish to be sweetly [gently] ruled by God, should be ruled penally [harshly] by himself: and that he who freely threw off the sweet yoke and light burden of charity, *should unwillingly suffer the insupportable burden of self-will*" (112).[392] How this contradicts conventional spirituality! This is certainly one of the most astute pieces of spiritual psychology ever written. It presupposes, however, that in the depths of our nature there is a need to love God. It contains a profound irony: that our own will is the tyrant which rules us "in the place of God," and *is actually the deputy which carries out His justice in punishing us*. We are punished by having what we want. Hence there is in reality no need for God to take "revenge" on us or punish us: *our punishment is itself the fact that we are not ruled by His law*, {so} that we are therefore separated from Him. This burden of our own law is of two kinds: the burden of servile love—the "coercion" of fear; the burden of mercenary love—the "attraction" or allurement of desire. Note: Guigo says (*Meditation #277*): *Id Deus homini praecepit*

---

390. Col. 112A, which reads: "*grave utique et importabile* . . ." ("Alas! what a heavy and insupportable burden is this on the children of Adam" [*Letters*, 45]).

391. Col. 112B ("Why hast thou set me opposite to thee, and I am become burdensome to myself?" [*Letters*, 45]).

392. "*Hoc quippe ad aeternam justamque legem Dei pertinuit, ut qui a Deo noluit suaviter regi, poenaliter a se ipso regeretur; quique sponte jugum suave et onus leve charitatis abjecit, propriae voluntatis onus importabile pateretur invitus*"; Merton's translation.

*amare, quod nunquam potest nimis amare. Id maxime e contrario amat homo, quod nunquam potest vel parum amare.*[393] *Non est praeceptum homini ut faciat sibi beatitudinem, sicut nec Deum, sed ut adquirat non factam, sed aeternam (idem,* 283).[394] Man's self-imposed law is then the law that "he must make himself happy," by idolatrous attempts at fruition in creatures.

10. The LEX FILIORUM[395] {is} expressed in dynamic terms: UT AGAR SPIRITU TUO[396]—*to be moved, impelled, by the Spirit of Love.* To yield to the spirit of freedom is to obey the law of love. Then the Spirit gives testimony to our spirit that we are the sons of God. FOR WE HAVE ONE AND THE SAME LAW WITH GOD. *Dum eadem lex fuerit mihi quae et tibi; sicut tu es, ita et ipse sim in hoc mundo* (112D).[397] Comment?

11. JUSTIS NON EST LEX POSITA.[398] The sons of God have a law, the law of charity. It is by definition not imposed, but freely given and freely accepted out of love. *Nec sine ista lege esse patiuntur.*[399] They will not suffer themselves to be without this law of freedom. Thus it is not said that the just "have no law"[400] but that the law is not "imposed"[401] because it is in fact VOLUNTARIIS EO LIBERALITER

---

393. Wilmart, 113–14 ("God has ordered man to love that which he can never love too much. Man on the contrary loves that above all which he can never or scarcely love").

394. Wilmart, 115 ("Man has not been ordered to make happiness for himself, not like God, but to acquire a happiness not made but eternal").

395. "the law of sons."

396. N. 6 (col. 112C) ("Why am I not led by thy Spirit" [*Letters,* 45]).

397. Col. 112CD, which reads: ". . . *mihi lex fuerit . . . et sicut . . .*" ("While thy law is also mine, . . . as thou art, so also may I be in this world" [*Letters,* 45]).

398. Col. 112D ("The law is not made for the just" [*Letters,* 45]) (1 Tim. 1:9).

399. Col. 112D, which reads: "*nec sine ista patiuntur*" ("neither are they suffered to live without [the law given graciously by the spirit of liberty]" [*Letters,* 45]).

400. "*nec filii sunt sine lege*" (col. 112D) ("neither are the sons of God free from law" [*Letters,* 45]).

401. "*Nec . . . coguntur*" (col. 112D).

DATA, QUO SUAVITER INSPIRATA.[402] This last makes clear what St. Bernard does not quite explicitly say: he still seems to be caught in the apparent contradiction of an "exterior" law that is no longer exterior. But actually it is completely interior to ourselves: *inspirata*.

12. Finally: *Caritas* FULFILLS BOTH THE LAWS OF FEAR AND OF DESIRE. It makes fear chaste; it makes desire ordinate. *Illam temperat, istam ordinat, utramque levigat* (113).[403] The "order" which charity introduces for the transformation of desire is this: the body is loved for the sake of the soul and the soul for the sake of God. *Deus autem propter se ipsum.*[404] But the beginning of all love is in the flesh. Its consummation is in the spirit. This is the great "problem of love" discussed by Gilson and Rousselot.[405] The "degrees of love" are sketched out here, but we will take them in the *De Diligendo*.

DE DILIGENDO DEO—Text

Part 1: *The Reasons for Loving God* (chapters 1–8):

1. God is to be loved because He is God. But what does this mean? What follows is a good model of meditation for a Cistercian. St. Bernard does not enter immediately into a cold, analytical definition of Who God is—"supreme goodness, absolute Being, etc."—and yet we shall see that he does in fact define God as St. John does—*Deus caritas est*[406]—but not in so many words. Rather, making it very concrete, he explains:

2. There can be nothing more just or more fruitful than for us to love God because *He has first loved us*. Who is He that has loved us? The supreme God, Who is pure love.

---

402. Col. 113A ("freely and lovingly accepted by them from him who graciously inspired it" [*Letters*, 46]).
403. N. 7 ("Tempering the one and controlling the other, it eases both" [*Letters*, 45]).
404. Col. 113C ("God [is loved] for His own sake" [*Letters*, 46]).
405. See above, pages 77–81.
406. "God is charity" (1 John 4:8).

3. But who are we, that He has thus loved? His enemies.

4. How much has He loved us? so much as to give Himself completely and totally to us.

5. He has given Himself *gratis*—no ifs—we need to love in order to receive Him, but love is not a condition—it is the gift itself.

God's love for us {is} the reason why we should love Him (*Ipse prior dilexit nos*[407]); that is to say, *He has given us Himself.* St. Bernard divides this up into points: *Quis?*—Who? He Who needs no love of ours: *Vera caritas majestatis non quaerentis quae sua sunt.*[408] *Quibus?*—To whom? to sinners: *Dilexit Deus gratis, et inimicos.*[409] *Quantum?* to the extent of giving His own Son. And if all this is obscure to unbelievers, who have not received the revelation of His love, then let them see how much He has given besides Himself.

Chapter 2: He gives us our daily bread; He gives us breath and air; He gives us light, and eyes; and innumerable other gifts of a lower order. Turning inward to our soul we see that He has given us three special gifts among others. Here we have an outline of Bernard's anthropology. Note: these gifts are evident to *nature* without faith. *Meretur ergo amari propter se ipsum Deus, et ab infideli: qui etsi nesciat Christum, scit tamen seipsum* (II, n. 6 [col. 977]):[410] *dignitas* (man's supreme dignity is his free will—{his} capacity to love); *scientia* (the light to recognize that he has this dignity and that he does not have it from himself); *virtus* (by which he then devotes himself with all zeal to *seek* God who gave him this dignity, and *clings* to Him with all his strength when he

---

407. "He hath first loved us" (*PL* 182, col. 975B ) (1 John 4:10).

408. Col. 975B, which reads; *"vera hujus . . . majestatis, quippe non . . ."* ("The true love of this Majesty not seeking what is for Himself").

409. Col. 975B, which reads: *"Dilexit ergo Deus, et gratis, et inimicos"* ("Thus God has freely loved even enemies").

410. Cols. 977D–980A ("Therefore God deserves to be loved for His own sake, even by the unbeliever, who, even though he does not know Christ, still knows himself").

has found Him, attributing all our good to Him alone).[411] Speaking of *scientia*, St. Bernard stresses the importance of self-knowledge, which *knows our dignity*, knows that *it comes from God*, and knows after that *our state as fallen beings*. Without the knowledge of our dignity, our freedom, the rest is nothing. Without true knowledge of our fallen state, our freedom is dangerous. However, our fallen state is essentially ignorance of our true being in God. Two kinds of ignorance are to be fled at all costs—ignorance of our dignity, {our} freedom, {our} capacity to be more than animals; ignorance of the fact that we owe this dignity to God and that it is His image in us, that it makes us capable of being His sons. To know our dignity but not to know its *source* in God leads to pride. Again *scientia* which only knows our dignity, but not its source, turns outward and becomes *curiositas*,[412] and in fact this is ignorance—a mere conformity to outward objects, without realization of our inner spiritual identity ({cf. the} Hindu concept of *avidya*[413]). It seeks to glory in the gifts of God as if they were our own by right, and without any gift on His part. Sinful man tends to rest in himself as his end instead of directing all his will and all his love to God. Worst of all {is} to seek glory from others for gifts which we have received from God, taking the glory to ourselves. This is vainglory. True glory is in God Who is truth. Vainglory is arrogant and self-sufficient. If all these things should be evident even to the pagans, *yet we Christians have received the*

---

411. Col. 977D ("dignity . . . knowledge . . . virtue").

412. N. 4 (col. 976D); on *curiositas*, the first degree of pride in Bernard's *De Gradibus Humilitatis* (*PL* 183, cols. 957B–963A), see Gilson, *Mystical Theology of Saint Bernard*, Appendix I (155–57); see also Merton's comment in *The Spirit of Simplicity Characteristic of the Cistercian Order. An Official Report, Demanded and Approved by the General Chapter. Together with Texts from St. Bernard of Clairvaux on Interior Simplicity. Translation and Commentary by A Cistercian Monk of Our Lady of Gethsemani* (Trappist, KY: Abbey of Our Lady of Gethsemani, 1948), 105: "*Curiositas* is that vain and illusory knowledge which is really ignorance, because it is the exercise of the intellect not in search of truth but merely to flatter our own self-satisfaction and pride."

413. See above, n. 258.

*greatest of all gifts—Jesus Himself, crucified*. Here St. Bernard speaks of the highest gifts, those of grace.

*God's Gift of Himself in Christ* (c. 3): here we come to one of the central ideas in the spirituality of St. Bernard: contemplation of the merciful love of God in Christ crucified (READ {the} beginning of n. 15 here [col. 983][414]). This is the great remedy for ingratitude and lack of love. For even though theoretically the gifts of our nature, *dignitas, scientia et virtus*, should be quite enough to make us love God more than ourselves, in actual fact they do not suffice without grace. Without grace these gifts are actually never recognized as gifts, and never really known as what they are. Instead of loving God with our whole being, we turn His gifts to our own glory and enjoyment. Hence the mark of the faithful Christian is not only that he recognizes these gifts of nature, but his NECESSARY DEPENDENCE ON CHRIST'S MERCIFUL LOVE as manifested in the Crucifixion. God's "re-making" of fallen man is a greater work than creation. *In primo opere me mihi dedit: in secundo, se: et ubi se dedit, me mihi reddidit. Datus ergo, et redditus, me pro me debeo, et bis debeo* (n. 15 [col. 983]).[415] This necessity of grace is shown by the great love of Christ, as seen in the tremendous contrast between His divine glory and the ignominy He suffered as man. But he also sees it in the greatness of His triumph, and in the renewal of the whole world through the Resurrection of Christ. "The Church is wounded with love be-

---

414. "*Quid retribuam Domino pro omnibus his? Illum ratio urget et justitia naturalis totum se tradere illi, a quo se totum habet, et ex se toto debere diligere. Mihi profecto fides tanto plus indicit amandum, quanto et cum me ipso pluris aestimandum intelligo: quippe qui illum non solum mei, sed sui quoque ipsius teneo largitorem*" ("What return shall I make to the Lord for all these things? Reason and natural justice urge that he [the unbeliever] surrender himself completely to the One from Whom he has all that he is, and that he should love with his entire self. To me, certainly, faith proclaims that He should be loved as much more as I understand He is to be valued above myself, who maintains that He is the giver not only of myself but even of His own self").

415. "In the first work He gave me myself; in the second, Himself: and when He gave Himself, He gave me back myself. Thus given and regiven, I owe myself for myself and I owe it twice."

cause she beholds the Only Begotten Son of the Father carrying His cross, the Lord of Majesty scourged, spat upon, the Author of Life and glory pierced with nails and with the lance, overwhelmed with insults, finally laying down His most precious soul for His friends" (n. 7 [col. 978]).[416] But she sees Him also rising from the dead, she sees the new creation which no longer brings forth merely thorns and thistles, but has flowered with the gifts of grace. The Church is nourished by the fruits which she has culled from the tree of the Cross and refreshed by the flowers of the Resurrection, and these together sustain her ardent love of Jesus, because of the infinite mercy of God. {As a} corollary {he considers} meditation on the life of Christ: *Oportet enim nos, si crebrum volumus habere hospitem Christum, corda nostra semper habere munita fidelibus testimoniis, tam de misericordia scilicet morientis, quam de potentia resurgentis* (n. 9 [col. 979]).[417] This *memoria Christi*[418] is the consolation of our earthly pilgrimage until we enjoy His *praesentia* in heaven.[419] But there is another presence of Christ in us, *now*, in meditation. Meditation is then a means of union with Christ; it is a contemplation with Him, bringing us into His presence. *Ubi suae videlicet aut passionis gratiam, aut resurrectionis gloriam sedula inspicit cogitatione versari,*

---

416. "*Ecclesia . . . ait*, Vulnerata charitate ego sum [The Church . . . says, "I am wounded with love" (Cant. 2:4)] . . . *cernit Unicum Patris, crucem sibi bajulantem; cernit caesum et consputum Dominum majestatis; cernit auctorem vitae et gloriae confixum clavis, percussum lancea, opprobriis saturatum, tandem illam dilectam animam suam ponere pro amicis suis.*"

417. "For if we wish to have Christ as a frequent guest, we ought to have our hearts fortified with faith-filled testimonies of the mercy of His dying as well as of the power of His rising."

418. "the memory of Christ."

419. See Gilson, *Mystical Theology of Saint Bernard*, 81–82: "[note] the very important idea that the *memoria*—and by that let us understand the memory, the sensible recollection of the Passion of Christ—is in us the condition and herald of the *praesentia*, that is to say, in the full sense of the term, of the beatific vision in the future life, but also already of these visitations of the soul by the Word in this life."

*ibi profecto adest sedulus, adest libens* (n. 8 [col. 979]).[420] The mere fact of thinking about Him does not make Him present in this special way: (1) we can enjoy the *thought* of Him—that is one thing; (2) when He sees we like to think of Him, *He gives us a special presence*; (3) we can believe this, and He will be present to us in faith when we think of Him. This is the complete idea of the *memoria Christi* (N.B. an interesting comparison with the argument in St. Anselm's *Proslogion*[421]). St. Bernard then distinguishes between the *monumenta passionis*,[422] the fruits of the old dispensation, which have reached their maturity. But this is still meditation on an old era—*"fructus quasi anni praeteriti."*[423] But "the winter is past"[424] and we live in the new era, that of the resurrection: IN NOVAM SUB GRATIA REVIRISCENTIS AESTATEM . . . *aestivum tempus advenisse cum illo significans*, QUI DE MORTIS GELU IN VERNALEM QUAMDAM NOVAE VITAE TEMPERIEM RESOLUTUS. *Ecce, ait, nova*

---

420. "For where He realizes that the grace of His Passion or the glory of His Resurrection is pondered in diligent meditation, there certainly He is earnestly and willingly present."

421. While the focus of the *Proslogion* is on the existence of God rather than on the redemption, Merton emphasizes in his article "St. Anselm and His Argument" (*American Benedictine Review* 17 [June 1966]: 238–62) that "The real import of Anselm's argument is . . . that it is aimed not against the unbeliever only, but against the unbelief of believers whose God is only a concept and not a transcendent, revealed and intimately personal reality. . . . The light of understanding which shines through being is an epiphany of the God who reveals Himself as the Source of all the intelligibility in all the being created by Him" (242). Thus the recognition of God as "that than which no greater can be conceived" (248) is not a matter of mere logical reasoning for apologetic purposes but an "apophatic sense of 'presence' and of transcendent being" (241) founded on "an intuition of being" (254) that distinguishes between "Pure and Absolute Reality" (254) and contingent beings totally dependent on Being itself. Thus a dynamic of *memoria* and *presentia* similar to that found in Bernard can be discerned in Anselm.

422. Col. 979A, which reads: *"Monumenta siquidem Passionis"* ("the tokens of the Passion").

423. Col. 979A ("like the fruits of a former year").

424. *"Hiems transiit"* (col. 979B) (Cant. 2.11).

*facio omnia. C*UJUS CARO SEMINATA EST IN MORTE, REFLORUIT IN RESUR-
RECTIONE; *ad cujus mox odorem in campo convallis nostrae* REVIRESCUNT
ARIDA, RECALESCUNT FRIGIDA, MORTUA REVIVISCUNT (n. 8 [col. 979]).[425]
This text is important to restore correct perspective on the
Bernardine *amor carnalis* of love of the humanity of Christ. Meditation on the Passion of Christ is important because it shows the
great love of Christ for us, but nevertheless it leads to the realization that we are now in the "new creation" which began with
His resurrection. Meditation on the Passion is relatively meaningless and incomplete without this true perspective. N. 9 is an
extraordinarily dense and rich passage, summing up the whole
economy of salvation. We may quote the following lines, suggesting that the new creation, the world redeemed by Christ, is
to return to paradise. The *"sponsa"* or mystical soul has a very
special place in this paradise.

> With the freshness of all these flowers and fruits, and with
> the beauty of Him who sends forth such a fragrant odor,
> the Father Himself delights in the Son who renews all [*ipse
> quoque Pater in Filio innovante omnia delectatur*] in such a way
> that He says: "Behold the odor of my son like the odor of a
> full field," which the Lord has blessed (Gen. 27:27). Full
> indeed, since from His fullness we have all received. But
> the Spouse all the more familiarly picks flowers and gathers
> fruits for herself just as she likes, and with these she per-
> fumes her inmost conscience so that when the Bridegroom
> enters the bridal chamber of her heart she is sweet and fra-
> grant. (col. 979)[426]

425. "becoming green again in a new summer, through grace . . . showing that summer has arrived with Him who, released from the coldness of
death into the springtime mildness of new life, says, 'Behold, I make all
things new.' The One Whose flesh was sown in death flourishes again in the
resurrection; by His fragrance in the field of our valley, what was dry becomes
green again, what was cold becomes warm again, what was dead revives."
426. "*Horum ergo novitate florum ac fructuum, et pulchritudine agri suavissimum spirantis odorem, ipse quoque Pater in Filio innovante omnia delectatur, ita
ut dicat:* Ecce odor filii mei, sicut odor agri pleni, cui benedixit Dominus
(Gen. XXVII, 27). *Bene pleni, de cujus plenitudine omnes accepimus. Sponsa tamen*

This fragrance consists especially in the living and active faith of our hearts, centered on the great truths of our Redemption (the flowers plucked in meditation). All of these manifest the power and the mercy of God (Ps. 61:12-13[427]):

> Utriusque rei testimonia credibilia facta sunt nimis; Christo utique moriente propter delicta nostra, et resurgente propter justificationem nostram, et ascendente ad protectionem nostram, et mittente Spiritum ad consolationem nostram, et quandoque rediturus ad consummationem nostram. NEMPE IN MORTE MISERICORDIAM, POTENTIAM IN RESURRECTIONE, UTRAMQUE IN SINGULIS EXHIBUIT RELIQUORUM.[428]

Chapter 4 deals with the fact that the *memoria Christi* is only truly a consolation for those who have no other hope but Christ. *Dei ergo quaerentibus et suspirantibus praesentiam, praesto interim et dulcis memoria est, non tamen qua satientur, sed qua magis esurient unde satientur* (col. 980).[429] But this implies suffering and penance in our own lives. The memory of the Passion is of little use if it is only a "memory" or a pious thought. It must also inspire us to follow Christ's example and to "mortify our members which are upon the earth."[430] If we have the courage to mortify our passions and to place our hopes entirely in the Cross of Christ,

---

*familiarius ex eo sibi, cum vult, flores legit, et carpit poma, quibus propriae aspergat intima conscientiae, et intranti sponso cordis lectulus suave redoleat.*"

427. "*Duo haec audivi, quia potestas Dei est, et tibi, Domine, misericordia*" (col. 979C) ("these two things have I heard, that power belongeth to God, And mercy to thee, O Lord").

428. "The testimonies of each of these have become so very credible: for Christ died for our sins and rose for our justification and ascended for our protection and sent the Spirit for our consolation and will one day return for our fulfillment. Surely He showed mercy in His death, power in His resurrection, and both of these in each of the others."

429. "For those seeking and sighing for the presence of God, then, there is meanwhile a sweet memory, by which nevertheless they are not satisfied, but by which they hunger the more for what will satisfy."

430. "*mortificat membra sua quae sunt super terram*" (col. 980D).

then the *memoria Christi* is sweet to us and we look forward to His *praesentia* without trepidation. On the contrary, those who love earthly things find the *memoria Christi* boring and insipid, and at least consciously realize that His *praesentia* will be terrible to them (col. 981). CAETERUM FIDELIS ANIMA ET SUSPIRAT PRAESENTIAM INHIANTER, ET IN MEMORIA REQUIESCIT SUAVITER; ET DONEC IDONEA SIT REVELATA FACIE SPECULARI GLORIAM DOMINI, CRUCIS IGNOMINIA GLORIATUR (n. 12 [col. 981]).[431] In résumé: the effect of the *memoria Christi*, and the anticipation of the light of glory and the *praesentia majestatis*, is rest for the Spouse because it brings freedom from worldly desires, cares and passions, and sets her heart upon one love only—that of Christ. (NOTE the biblical basis for this, in detail: n. 14.[432])

Chapter 7 (n. 17): though we love God without an eye for the reward, this does not mean we will be without reward. *Non enim sine praemio diligitur Deus, etsi absque praemii intuitu diligendus sit* (col. 984).[433] But what is the reward? love itself. In fact, the *purity* of love is the reward of pure love, for pure love is sanctity and union with God (here Bernard is following Cassian[434]). Vacua namque vera charitas esse non potest, *nec tamen mercenaria est*.[435] This is very important. Pure love is not a merely arbitrary act of will on our own part, arrived at by a mental operation and a

---

431. "On the other hand, the faithful soul both sighs deeply for His presence and rests sweetly in recollection; and until it is capable of looking upon the glory of the Lord with unveiled face, glories in the disgrace of the Cross."

432. This section (col. 982D–983A) provides a string of scriptural quotations testifying to the final reward of eternal union with God: Ps. 129[130]:7; Heb. 9:12; Ps. 36[37]:28; Luke 6:38; 1 Cor. 2:9; Phil. 3:20-21; 2 Cor. 4:17-18.

433. "For God is not loved without reward, though He should be loved without concern for a reward."

434. See *Cassian and the Fathers*, 205–6 (on *Conference* 1), and *Pre-Benedictine Monasticism*, 56–57 (on *Conference* 11); both passages mention the importance of this idea for St. Bernard.

435. Col. 984C ("For true love cannot be worthless, but it is not, however, mercenary").

"purification" of intention that abstractly eliminates all thought of "reward." It is objectively and concretely pure. This is because of its very nature as an *affectus*, as a free commitment, not as a *contractus* ({with an} implication of necessity). *Affectus est, non contractus:* NEC ACQUIRITUR PACTO, NEC ACQUIRIT.[436] It is not the result of a "deal." It cannot be so. It does not aim at an exchange, at a *do ut des*[437] contract. *Sponte afficit, et spontaneum facit*[438] (analyze {the} idea of spontaneity); *verus amor seipso contentus est*[439] (analyze {the} idea of contentment); *habet praemium, sed id quod amatur*[440] (translation: it has a reward, but the reward is the fact that love is exercised [this is possible]; or: the reward is that which is loved, the object of love [?]; or: the reward is the fact that the soul is loved [?—unlikely]). The context gives the explanation: "Whatever you seem to love for the sake of something else [*propter aliud*[441]], you love that which is the end to which love tends, not that by which it tends" (i.e., you love the object, not love itself). "Paul does not evangelize in order to eat, he eats in order to evangelize. What he loves is preaching the Gospel."[442] This makes clear that the act itself is its own end. This is a very existential approach. The dynamic of love contains within itself sufficient reason for its existence and is its own fulfillment, because God is love and when we love we are living as He lives, we are like Him, we are participating in His inner life. In the light of this context we see that the proper translation of the disputed text above should be "the reward is in the fact that love is exercised." He then continues: there is no reward for what one does because

---

436. Col. 984D ("It is an affection, not a contract: it neither is acquired nor does it acquire by a deal").

437. "I give so you may give."

438. Col. 984D ("It has its effect freely and makes one free").

439. Col. 984D ("True love is content in itself").

440. Col. 984D.

441. Col. 984D.

442. "*Paulus non evangelizat ut comedat, sed comedit ut evangelizet*" (col. 984D).

he wants to do it, since what he does is its own reward. For instance, one does not reward a hungry man for eating, etc. Hence one does not reward a lover for loving, if the reward is understood as something other than the love itself by which he is united to God Whom he loves. This can appear to us as a very unconventional and even novel idea, which seems to dismiss as irrelevant the whole concept of merit. But when carefully interpreted, it shows that St. Bernard is simply going to the root of the concept. We do not love God for the sake of something *other than* life in God by love. *Quanto magis Deum amans anima, aliud praeter Deum sui amoris praemium non requirit? Aut si aliud requirit, illud pro certo, non Deum diligit* (col. 985).[443] *Ipse dat occasionem, ipse creat affectionem, desiderium ipse consummat.*[444] Comment on these ideas: God is always leading us into situations in which we can love Him. There is none in which we cannot love Him—if it is a good situation, we can thank Him; if it is an evil one, we can cry out to Him for help and seek Him as our refuge. Every situation in which He places us is appropriate for us. Even temptation is appropriate, in order that we may learn the evil that is in us and not trust in ourselves. The love which stirs in our hearts is *created by God*. He awakens in us a need for Him, and He Himself satisfies that need. In everything, then, God is at work to make us love. On our part—*consentire salvari est*[445] (*De Gratia et Libero Arbitrio*). *Ejus amor nostrum et praeparat, et remunerat.*[446] {This is the} true theology of grace! *Se dedit in meritum, se servat in praemium, se apponit in refectione animarum sanctarum, se in redemptione distrahit*

---

443. "How much more does the soul loving God not seek as a reward of his love anything other than God. If he seeks anything else, certainly it is that, not God, that he loves."

444. N. 22 (col. 987B) ("He Himself gives the occasion; He Himself creates the affection; He Himself consummates the desire").

445. C. 1 (col. 1002B) ("to consent is to be saved").

446. Col. 987C ("His love both prepares and rewards ours").

*captivarum.*[447] Here St. Bernard utters one of his most characteristic statements: "Thou art good, O Lord, to the soul that seeks Thee—what wilt Thou be to him who finds Thee?"[448] The consolation of seeking God is a promise and a pledge of finding Him. NEMO TE QUAERERE VALET, NISI QUI PRIUS INVENERIT. VIS IGITUR INVENIRI UT QUAERARIS, QUAERI UT INVENIARIS.[449] Having said all this, having indicated that God leads our love to its consummation, St. Bernard then turns to us. What is our part? First of all, we are the loving subject. What God elevates and transforms with His love is not a mere nonentity. It is our love, *our Human love.*

*Natural Love*: what is love? It is, says St. Bernard, one of the four natural "affections" (love, fear, joy and sorrow) (chap. 8: n. 23[450]). Now the four natural affections *are given us first of all that with them we may serve the Author of nature.* Hence the first commandment: "Thou shalt love the Lord thy God with thy whole heart."[451] St. Bernard here does not distinguish between emotion and will; he simply speaks of the whole being tending towards its object by love, a love which involves both the will and the emotions. A properly ordered love is one in which the emotions are subject to the will and the will is subject to God.

*Carnal Love (amor carnalis*[452]) {is} natural self-love. Since we are creatures, and limited, and God has willed that we take care of ourselves, there is first of all a natural love, of necessity, by which we have to seek to survive; we seek necessary food and

---

447. Col. 987C ("He gave Himself for the sake of merit; He keeps Himself as a reward; He offers Himself as food for holy souls; He sacrifices Himself as redemption of captive souls").

448. "*Bonus es, Domine, animae quaerenti te: quid ergo invenienti*" (col. 987C).

449. Col. 987C ("No one can seek You except one who first has found You. Therefore You wish to be found in order that You may be sought, to be sought in order that You may be found").

450. Cols. 987D–988C.

451. "*Unde et dictum est primum et maximum mandatum:* Diliges Dominum Deum tuum (Matth. XXII, 37), *etc.*" (cols. 987D–988A).

452. Col. 988A.

shelter, etc. It is interesting that St. Bernard realistically begins with this love rooted in our nature—with the love rooted in our psychic automatism, and which cannot be disregarded (for if it is disregarded it will work anyway—but it must be brought under the control of the will). It is very important to note that even *amor carnalis*, when it is ordinate, when it takes care of our just needs, is a service *owed to God* the Author of nature! But we must be careful not to "use the goods of nature to *serve the enemy of nature*"[453]—that is, lust (i.e., concupiscence in general).

*Social Love*: this *amor carnalis is well-ordered* if it limits itself to natural necessity. It is *disordered* if it overflows the limits of necessity, and goes forth to seek luxuries and superfluous comforts for itself. To prevent this disorder, *amor socialis*[454] is commanded us—love of neighbor as self. That means to say that we restrict ourselves to what is necessary for us and help our neighbor to have what is necessary for him, seeing in him our other self, not concentrated entirely on our own self and unable to see anyone else. Here {the} emphasis {is} on {the} OBJECTIVITY OF LOVE. Our "surplus" can go either to our brother (*consors naturae*[455]) or to our own greed (*hostis naturae*[456]). Carnal love is in fact so frail and vulnerable that it can hardly stand by itself and remain ordinate. It quickly degenerates into greed or lust. But carnal love is kept ordinate (i.e., honors God) when it is raised to the level of *social love*. When we deprive our own greed ({the} enemy of nature) and give instead to our brother, our love becomes *temperate* and *just* and is therefore *social*. Supposing that in giving to others, *we ourselves lack necessities*? This is no objection. We must turn to God in confident prayer and He will take care of us.

---

453. "*ne de bonis naturae hosti servias animae, hoc est libidini*" (col. 988B).
454. Col. 988C.
455. Col. 988A.
456. Col. 988B.

To sum up, then, well-ordered natural love is as follows:

1. We provide the necessities of life for ourselves: *ordinabiliter sibi*;[457]

2. By the four cardinal virtues we restrain inordinate appetites, and we live *sociabiliter cum proximo*[458] (*amor socialis*);

3. For this ordinate natural love, obviously grace is absolutely necessary. This natural love is therefore already supernatural. It is obedience to the will of God, the Author of nature. Never forget St. Bernard's respect for nature as an expression of God's will.

4. In order that we may become saints, we must first of all rise to the level of well-ordered natural love from debased self-love and self-will. In order to do this, asceticism, particularly monastic ascesis and obedience, humility, poverty, manual labor, fasting, etc. is necessary.

Note the balance and sanity of this view of things. St. Bernard's mystical and ascetic theology is based on a firm foundation. Very often, today, spiritual writers unconsciously give us the idea that we jump right from fallen nature to the highest kind of supernatural life—no thought is given to restoring the lost balance of our nature, returning to full integration in ourselves, in society, full contact with reality. Grace simply "annihilates" fallen nature and inserts something totally new in its place. But this is false, {and the} result {is} illusion. We imagine we are living a supernatural life and fallen nature is still operating, under the cover of the inefficacious practices and prayers with which we delude ourselves. This is not the will of God. God wills that we advance humbly and quietly one step at a time, slowly but carefully restoring, by obedience to God's will, the order He wills to find in us. All this is included in the "first degree of love."

---

457. *In Festo SS. Petri et Pauli Apostolorum* (*PL* 183, col. 407B, which reads: *"ordinabiliter tibi"*) ("in an orderly way for ourselves").

458. Col. 407B, which reads: *"sociabiliter proximo"* ("sociably with our neighbor").

Therefore the FIRST DEGREE OF LOVE—in which *man loves himself for his own sake*—is a natural love which is well-ordered, which is capable of being elevated by grace. *Below* the first degree is the disordered love of man for himself, self-love, self-will. This is not a degree of love. It has to be corrected before it can be elevated to a higher level by grace. It is not a fit subject for grace, because grace cannot coexist with mortally sinful attachment to self. To say here that man loves himself *ordinabiliter* means that he also loves his neighbor as himself. One might see it as universal man loving himself—Adam loving himself in all men—{the} capacity to become "one Christ loving Himself" (St. Augustine).[459] Without this natural love the mystical body would not be possible.

Preparation for the second degree (*note*—in these degrees, it is very important to understand the *transition* from each one to the next): in practicing *amor socialis* man not only deprives himself of superfluities to give to his brother, *but he may also find himself deprived of necessities*, giving up what he needs for the sake of others. Where then will he find what he needs? He must turn to God, where natural means fail. And they do fail. Hence {there are} three preparations for the next degree of love:

1. We turn to God in confident prayer, asking Him to supply what we need when we have risked our own security for the sake of our brother. {There is a} special presence of God to those who need Him: *Adest libenter in necessariis* (col. 988).[460] *Sponte daturum se pollicetur necessaria, superflua restringenti, et proximum diligenti* (n. 24 [col. 988]).[461] His constant aid shows that while we did not begin to exist without Him, we could not continue in existence without His aid from moment to moment. *Ut cum*

---

459. "*unus Christus amans seipsum*" (*In Epistolam Joannis ad Parthos*, 10.3 [*PL* 35, col. 2055]).

460. N. 24, which reads: "*adsit libenter* . . ." ("He is freely present in times of need").

461. "He promises that He will willingly give whatever is needed to one limiting superfluities and loving his neighbor."

*defecerit homo, et subvenerit Deus, dum homo liberatur a Deo, Deus ab homine, ut dignum est, honoretur* (n. 25 [col. 989]).[462]

2. We realize that we must love our brother in God; otherwise we cannot love him selflessly. If we do not love him in God, we will refuse to make sacrifices for him. In order faithfully to live up to our obligation of *amor socialis*, we need God. If we do not rise to the second degree, we cannot remain on the level of the first.

3. Further, we cannot love our brother in God if we do not love God.

Hence, the SECOND DEGREE OF LOVE {is} *to love God for our own sake*; and this love is arrived at through tribulation, through *constantly experiencing our helplessness* and having recourse to prayer, and then *experiencing the reality of His Providence and His love*. It is through danger and trial that we come to love God. Without them we tend to love only ourselves. With his *frequens liberatio*[463] we come to love Him more than ourselves.

*Passage from the second to {the} third degree of love* (c. 9, n. 26): the value of tribulation and trial lies in this, that we turn more frequently to God and experience His love liberating us. It is hence by experience of our own nothingness and *gratitude for the love of God* that we advance to a purer love for Him. We come by constant experience of His mercy and growing gratitude, to seek Him *for His sweetness* more than for our own need (n. 26 [col. 989]). This is the beginning of religious experience on a deep level. *Gratitude* is the key to the third step, as fraternal *compassion* and the sense of our own {insecurity}[464] were the key to the second. By gratitude, we enter into a deeper experience of God's goodness and thus we begin to love Him for Himself and not for our own sake. We now love Him not just because we have to and because we need Him but because we are spontaneously attracted to Him. Our love is spontaneous and springs up from

---

462. "So that when man has run short, and God has come to his assistance, while man is set free by God, God may be honored, as is proper, by man."

463. Col. 989C ("frequent liberating action").

464. Conjectural reading.

within us, as it were instinctively, not imposed on us from without by necessity.

{The} THIRD DEGREE OF LOVE {is} *Love of God for His own sake: Confitemini Domino quoniam bonus.*[465] This love is now pure, *amor castus, justus* and *"gratus."*[466] *Amat caste*[467] {means} loving God's will for His sake: *casto non gravatur obedire mandato*[468] and *making itself more pure by obeying Him freely*—love not in word but in truth. *Amat juste*[469] {means} embracing God's will because it is right, because He has been so good to us—hence {the exercise of} generosity to repay God for His goodness (cf. St. Anselm[470]).

465. Col. 990A ("Give praise to the Lord, for He is good") (Ps. 117[118]:1).
466. Col. 990A ("pure, just, freely given love").
467. Col. 989D ("He loves purely").
468. Col. 989D ("It is not a burden for the pure to obey a commandment").
469. Col. 989D ("He loves justly").
470. See *Proslogion*, c. 9: *"O misericordia, de quam opulenta dulcedine et dulci opulentia nobis profluis! O immensitas bonitatis dei, quo affectu amanda es peccatoribus! . . . O immensa bonitas, quae sic omnem intellectum excedis, veniat super me misericordia illa, quae de tanta opulentia tui procedit! Influat in me, quae profluit de te!"* (*S. Anselmi Cantuariensis Archiepiscopi Opera Omnia*, ed. Philibert Schmitz, 6 vols. [Edinburgh: Thomas Nelson, 1946–1951], 1:107–8) ("Ah, from what generous love and loving generosity compassion flows out to us! Ah, what feelings of love should we sinners have towards the unbounded goodness of God! . . . Ah, boundless goodness, far beyond all understanding, on me be your compassion which comes from such generosity! Let that which flows from you, flow into me" [*The Prayers and Meditations of St. Anselm*, trans. Benedicta Ward, SLG (New York: Penguin, 1973), 250–51]); *Proslogion*, c. 25: *"Ergo in illa perfecta caritate innumerabilium angelorum beatorum et hominum, ubi nullus minus diliget alium quam seipsum, non aliter gaudebit quisque pro singulis aliis quam pro seipso. Si ergo cor hominis de tanto suo bono vix capiet gaudium suum: quomodo capax erit tot et tantorum gaudiorum? Et utique quoniam quantum quisque diligit aliquem, tantum de bono eius gaudet: sicut in illa perfecta felicitate unusquisque plus amabit sine comparatione deum quam se et omnes alios secum, ita plus gaudebit absque existimatione de felicitate dei quam de sua et omnium aliorum secum. Sed si deum sic diligent toto corde, tota mente, tota anima; et tamen, totum cor, tota mens, tota anima non sufficiat dignitati dilectionis: profecto sic gaudebunt toto corde, tota mente, tota anima, ut totum cor, tota mens, tota anima non sufficiat plenitudini gaudii"* (Schmitz, 1:120) ("So in that perfec-

*Amat grate*[471] {is} a gratuitous love—not in order to gain anything from God but just to praise Him because He is good, seeking our highest reward only in pleasing Him. The "gratuitous" character of love is the transition to the fourth degree.

{The} FOURTH DEGREE OF LOVE {is the} *highest perfection of love* (c. 10.27–29). He begins by announcing that the highest love is paradoxically that in which we love ourselves for God's sake: "*Nec seipsum homo diligit nisi propter Deum*" (990).[472] This is the *mons Dei*,[473] the summit of the mount of perfection. The highest degree of gratuitous love is to love even ourselves in order to please God, and *only* in order to please Him:

a) Is it possible in the present life? only in passing—in rapture: *Vix raro interdum, vel semel*.[474]

b) What are the qualities of this perfect love?

(1) The soul is inebriated with the love of God, forgets itself entirely.

(2) The soul goes out of itself to God and becomes "one spirit" with Him. "To lose thyself as if thou didst not exist, to feel

---

tion of charity of countless blessed angels and men, where no one loves another any less than he loves himself, they will all rejoice for each other as they do for themselves. If the heart of man can scarcely hold the joy that comes to him from so great a good, how will it hold so many and so great joys? In so far as each one loves another, so he will rejoice in the other's good; and as in that perfection of happiness, each one will love God incomparably more than he loves either himself or others, so he will rejoice more and without regard in the happiness of God than in that of himself and of everyone else. But if they love God with their whole heart, mind, and soul, while as yet their whole heart, mind, and soul is not equal to the dignity of that love, truly they will rejoice with their whole heart, mind, and soul, so that their whole heart, mind, and soul will not suffice for the fullness of their joy" (*Prayers and Meditations*, 264–65).

471. "He loves gratefully."

472. Col. 990 B, which reads: ". . . *diligat homo*. . ." ("a man does not love himself except for the sake of God").

473. Col. 990B.

474. Col. 990C, which reads: "*in hac mortali vita raro interdum, aut vel semel*" ("on rare occasions in this mortal life, or only a single time").

thyself not at all, to be emptied of thyself and almost as it were annihilated, this is the life of heaven, not human living."[475] St. Bernard does not really mean that we cease to exist. We are lost in God mystically, not ontologically. We remain our autonomous selves, but our mind and will are so absorbed in the love of God that we seem to have no interests or concerns of our own and we are in fact totally taken up with the superabundant love of God which transcends all human modes and limitations. We are out of ourselves. Our love is God's love, and our knowledge is His knowledge. Hence our limitations are drowned and overwhelmed in the inrush of His divine Spirit, and we no longer know ourselves, but only His love. As he says in the *Sermons on the Canticle*: *Qui amat, amat et aliud novit nihil*.[476]

(3) In what sense do we then love ourselves for His sake? (n. 28). God has made all things for His own sake. When we are perfectly conformed to His will, we will therefore will ourselves for His sake. "We then have no desire that either we ourselves or anything else should exist except because He has willed it—seeking nothing but His will, not our own pleasure."[477]

## II. St. Bernard and Cluny—The *Apologia*—1123

*The Controversy between Cîteaux and Cluny*: this plays an important part in the early life of the Order and contributed something to the formation of the Cistercian spirit. It is unfortunate that the spirit of the Order crystallized out in an atmosphere of

---

475. "*Te enim quoddammodo perdere, tanquam qui non sis, et omnino non sentire teipsum, et a teipso exinaniri, et pene annullari, coelestis est conversationis, non humanae affectionis*" (col. 990C).

476. *Sermo 83 in Cantica* (col. 1182D) ("He who loves, loves and knows nothing else").

477. "*sic nos quoque nec nosipsos, nec aliud aliquid fuisse, vel esse velimus, nisi aeque propter ipsum, ob solam videlicet ipsius voluntatem, non nostram voluptatem*" (col. 991A). For an extensive discussion of this fourth degree, see pages 374–80 below.

polemics, which gave it a permanent militancy and aggressiveness. This distracts attention from the main purpose of our life and leads us to concentrate too much on the justification of certain points of observance. It even leads to a warped idea of the essence of our life. The definition of the Cistercian ideal as the *"literal* observance of the *Rule"* is a consequence of this warped perspective. It is much too narrow a view. But in any case, study of this controversy *on both sides* is very important.

*Letter 1 of St. Bernard*:[478] we can see something of St. Bernard's attitude toward Cluny in his First Letter, to Robert of Châtillon, after the latter had left Clairvaux for Cluny. It is a fiery and passionate letter. Here St. Bernard contrasts the life of the Benedictines with that of the Cistercians and accuses the Cluny monks of infidelity and tepidity. The tone throughout is passionate, because the letter was dictated by one burning under a sense of outraged justice. He felt that he and his monastery had been wronged. This must also be seen in the context of Bernard's other "vocational" letters. They form an interesting and important group, especially those concerning cases of *transitus* from Benedictine monasteries to ours, and vice versa.[479]

*Analysis of Letter 1*: {it is} the "first shot" in the battle between the White and Black monks. Robert is Bernard's *cousin* (sometimes called nephew because {he was} so much younger). He has gone from Clairvaux to Cluny without permission, though {he was already} under vows. {The} pretext {was that} he had been "given" to Cluny as a child. {The actual} reason {was that} the life has been too severe, and apparently there has been a personal conflict with Bernard (see n. 2). {N.} 1:[480] note the dramatic, personal, emotional tone. Bernard takes this departure as a very personal insult and injury. There is no question (nn. 1–2) that this is a matter of personal conflict. Robert has left partly "to get away

---

478. *PL* 182, cols. 67D–79C.
479. See below, pages 224–33.
480. Cols. 67D–71A.

from Bernard" (READ n. 1[481]). N. 2:[482] Bernard admits his share of the blame. Both must correct themselves and Robert must return. Bernard will no longer be severe. *N. 3*: Bernard recognizes the need for gentleness. Robert really needs to be led by love, not by austerity, severity and the law of fear. Here we have a recognition of a conflict within monasticism and in Bernard himself—the conflict between love and fear, spirit and letter. This is also invoked in the debate—by Cluny and Cîteaux equally, but more

---

481. "Long enough, perhaps too long, have I waited, dearest Robert, for the Lord that he might deign to touch your soul and mine through yours, moving you to salutary regrets for your error and me to joy for your deliverance. But seeing myself still disappointed of my hope, I can no longer hide my sorrow, restrain my anxiety, or dissemble my grief. And so, against all the laws of justice, I who have been wounded am forced to recall him who wounded me; who have been spurned, him who spurned me; who have been smitten, him who struck the blow. In short I must cast myself at the feet of him who should cast himself at mine. Sorrow is not careful to count the cost; is not ashamed; does not nicely weigh the pros and cons; is not fearful for its dignity; respects no rules; it cares only that it has what it would be without, or lacks what it would have. 'But,' you will say, 'I have hurt no one, spurned no one. Rather have I, spurned and repeatedly hurt, sought only to fly my oppressor. Whom can I have hurt, if I have only avoided being hurt? Is it not wiser to yield to the persecutor than to resist him? To avoid him who strikes than to strike back?' Quite so; I agree. I am not writing to dispute with you, but to remove the grounds for dispute. To fly persecution implies no fault in him who flees but in him who persecutes. I do not deny this. I shall overlook the past. I shall not ask why or how the present state of affairs came about. I shall forget old injuries. To act otherwise were better calculated to open than to heal wounds. I am concerned with what lies closer to my heart. Unhappy man that I am who have not you by me, who cannot see you, who am obliged to live without you for whom to die would be to live, and to live without whom is no better than death! So I do not ask why you left me, I only grieve that you do not return; I do not blame your going away, I only blame your not coming back. Only come and there will be peace; return and there will be satisfaction. Return, I say, return, and I shall sing in my heart, 'My brother who was dead has come to life again; was lost and is found'" (*Letters*, 1–2).

482. Col. 71AD.

by Cluny. *Nn. 3–4*:[483] the "fall" of Robert {is} compared to the fall of Adam. The part of the devil {is} played by the grand prior of Cluny. Note the arguments of the grand prior: "God does not want suffering."[484] To lead another by the path of suffering can be a work of love!—to *lead*, not to *drive*. *N. 5*[485] {describes} the triumphant return to Cluny, {with its} merrymaking over the sinner ({and} implicit comparison with the Prodigal Son). *N. 6*:[486] Rome supports Cluny and decides in favor of their claim: "A soul for whom Christ died must be lost to please Cluny"[487]—Bernard has his own definite question about who is right and who is wrong, regardless of a rescript from Rome!! (READ top of p. 5—James ed.[488]). *N. 7*:[489] Christ will come and give true judgement.

---

483. Cols. 71D–72C; 72C–73B.

484. " 'When,' he asked, 'was God pleased with our sufferings' " (*Letters*, 4).

485. Col. 73BC.

486. Cols. 73C–74A.

487. *Letters*, 5.

488. "In the meantime representations were made at Rome. The authority of the Holy See was cajoled. And to make sure that the Pope would not refuse his assent, it was suggested to him that this youth while still a child had been oblated at Cluny by his parents. There was no one present to refute this nor was it anticipated that there would be. Judgement was pronounced on the case in the absence of the judged. Those who had done the injury were upheld, the plaintiffs lost their suit, the defendant was absolved without making satisfaction. And this far too indulgent sentence of absolution was confirmed by a cruel ordinance whereby the hesitating and doubtful youth was confirmed in an ill-advised stability and security. The gist of the rescript, the sum of the judgement, the whole significance of the suit was nothing more than that the robbers could keep their spoils and that those who lost thereby must keep silent. And withal a soul for whom Christ died must be lost to please Cluny. So another profession is made, what will not be kept is vowed, what will not be performed is proposed: and since the first sin has been made void, in the second transgression is doubled, and sinning there is sin beyond measure" (*Letters*, 4–5).

489. Col. 74AC.

*Nn. 8–9*[490] (READ[491]): *the Canonical issue*—Bernard says that the

---

490. Cols. 74C–75A; 75A–76A.

491. "8. Let them see and judge which has the most force: the vow a father makes on behalf of his son, or the vow a son makes on his own behalf, especially when it is a vow of something better. Let your servant and our law-giver, Benedict, judge which is the more in order: a vow made for a child when it is too young to know anything about it, or the vow he afterwards makes for himself when he realizes and understands what he is doing, when he is of an age to speak for himself. However there is no doubt that the boy was only promised to Cluny without any formal oblation, for the petition prescribed by the *Rule* was not made by his parents, nor was his hand bound in the altar cloth, and the offering made before witnesses. They point out the land which, they say, was made with the child and for him. But if they received him with the land how was it they kept the land and not the child? Can it be that they prized the land more than the child? If he had been oblated what was he doing in the world? A nursling of God, why was he exposed to the maw of the wolf? You yourself, Robert, are a witness that you entered our Order from the world and not from Cluny. You implored to be admitted, you begged and besought, but, much against your will, your entrance was put off for two years on account of your tender age. When this time had been allowed patiently to pass and without evasion, at last with prayers and (as you will remember) with many tears you besought the long awaited mercy, and were granted the admission you had sought for so long. You were tried in all patience for a year according to the *Rule*, living perseveringly and without complaint. After the year had passed you, of your own free will, made your profession and then, for the first time, you put off the attire of the world and were clothed in the habit of Religion. 9. You foolish boy! Who has bewitched you to break the vows which adorned your lips? Will you not be justified or condemned out of your own mouth? Why then are you so anxious about the vow your parents made and yet so regardless of your own? It is out of your own mouth and not out of the mouth of your parents that you will be judged. Of your own vow, not of theirs, will you be called to render an account. Why does anyone try to bamboozle you with an Apostolic absolution, you whose own conscience is bound by a divine sentence, 'No one putting their hand to the plough and looking back is fit for the kingdom of God'? Would they persuade you that you have not looked back who say to you, 'Well done!' My son, if sinners shall entice you, consent not to them. Believe not every spirit. Be at peace with many, but let one in a thousand be your counsellor. Gird yourself, cast off your seducers, shut

vow made by Robert on his own initiative annuls the vow made by his father for him, especially because this is a vow to live a higher and better life (p. 7, top). Discuss this question. Bernard's arguments are very solid. (Robert had in fact entered Cîteaux from the *world*.) Robert should consult his own conscience. To embrace an easier life is to apostatize. *Nn. 10–11*[492] {focus on} the injury done to Bernard by Cluny. They cannot save Robert (READ {the} classic passage, top of p. 8[493]). *N. 12*[494] {presents} the remedy: with determination and courage, Robert can overcome his weak-

---

your ears to flatterers, search your own heart, for you know yourself best. Listen to your conscience, examine your intentions, consider the facts. Let your conscience tell you why you left your monastery, your brethren, your own place, and myself who am related to you by blood, but even more closely by spirit. If you left so as to lead a harder, higher, and more perfect life, fear not, you have not looked back, rather you can glory with the Apostle, saying, 'Forgetting what I have left behind, intent on what lies ahead, I press on with the goal in view.' But if it be otherwise, be not high minded but fearful because (you must pardon my saying this) whatever you permit yourself in food, unnecessary clothes, idle words, vain and curious travel in excess of what you promised when you were with us, is without any doubt to look back, to equivocate, to apostatize" (*Letters*, 6–7).

492. Cols. 76AB; 76B–77B.

493. "Does salvation rest rather in soft raiment and high living than in frugal fare and moderate clothing? If warm and comfortable furs, if fine and precious cloth, if long sleeves and ample hoods, if dainty coverlets and soft woolen shirts make a saint, why do I delay and not follow you at once? But these things are comforts for the weak, not the arms of fighting men. They who wear soft raiment are in kings' houses. Wine and white bread, honey-wine and pittances, benefit the body not the soul. The soul is not fattened out of frying pans! Many monks in Egypt served God for a long time without fish. Pepper, ginger, cummin, sage, and all the thousand other spices may please the palate, but they inflame lust. And would you make my safety depend on such things? Will you spend your youth safely among them? Salt with hunger is seasoning enough for a man living soberly and wisely. If we eat before we are hungry, then we must concoct mixtures with more and more I know not what far-fetched flavours to arouse our greed and stimulate our flagging appetites."

494. Cols. 77B–78B.

ness, especially {through} manual work. {Here is the} *apologia* for Cistercian austerity (READ[495]). *N. 13*[496] {is an} exhortation comparable to Jerome[497] (READ p. 9[498]): {It is a} greater victory to return

495. "But what, you say, is to be done if one cannot live otherwise? Good. I know you are not strong, that you would now find it difficult to support a harder way of life. But what if you can act so as to make yourself able to do so? I will tell you how it could be done. Arouse yourself, gird your loins, put aside idleness, grasp the nettle, and do some hard work. If you act thus you will soon find that you only need to eat what will satisfy your hunger, not what will make your mouth water. Hard exercise will restore the flavour to food that idleness has taken away. Much that you would refuse to eat when you had nothing to do, you will be glad of after hard work. Idleness makes one dainty, hard work makes one hungry. It is wonderful how work can make food taste sweet which idleness finds insipid. Vegetables, beans, roots, and bread and water may be poor fare for one living at his ease, but hard work soon makes them taste delicious. You have become unaccustomed to our clothes and now you dread them as too cold in winter and too hot in summer. But have you not read, 'They that fear the frost, the snow shall fall upon them'? You fear our vigils, fasts, and manual labour, but they seem nothing to anyone who considers the flames of hell. The thought of the outer darkness will soon reconcile anyone to wild solitudes. Silence does not displease when it is considered how we shall have to give an account of every idle word. With the picture before our eyes of that weeping and gnashing of teeth the difference between a rush mat and a feather bed seems small enough. If we spend well all the night enjoined by the *Rule* in psalmody, it will be a hard bed on which we cannot sleep. If we labour with our hands as much during the day as we are professed to do, rough indeed will be the fare we cannot eat" (*Letters*, 8).

496. Cols. 78B–79C.

497. See Merton's discussions of Jerome's letters on monastic renunciation to Heliodorus (#14 [*PL* 22, cols. 347–55]) (*Cassian and the Fathers*, 67–69) and to Rusticus (#125 [cols. 1072–85]) (*Pre-Benedictine Monasticism*, 164–69).

498. "Arise, soldier of Christ, I say arise! Shake off the dust and return to the battle. You will fight more valiantly after your flight, and you will conquer more gloriously. There are many soldiers of Christ who have begun valiantly, stood their ground well, and finished by conquering, but few who have returned to the battle after they had fled, thrown themselves once more

and win after flight. Later, in the *Apologia*, St. Bernard renews the

---

into the thick of the danger from which they had escaped, and put to flight the foe from whom they had run. A thing is the more precious for being rare, so I rejoice that you can be one of those who are the more glorious for being so scarce. But if you are still fearful, I ask you why you should be afraid where there is no cause for fear, instead of where you have every reason to tremble. Do you think that because you have forsaken the front line the enemy has forsaken you? Far from it. He will follow you in flight more readily than he would fight you when striking back. He attacks you more willingly from behind than he would strive with you face to face. Can you sleep unarmed without anxiety in the morning hours when it was at that time that Christ rose from the dead? Do you not know that unarmed you are both more fearful and less to be feared? A multitude of armed men surround the house, and can you still sleep? Already they are scaling the ramparts, swarming over the barriers, pouring in at the rear. Would you be safer alone or with others? Naked in bed or armed in camp? Get up, arm yourself, and fly to your fellow soldiers whom you have forsaken by running away. Let the fear that drove you away also bring you back. Is it the weight and discomfort of arms that you shun, feeble soldier? Believe me when an enemy is at hand and darts begin flying a shield seems none too heavy, and a helmet and corselet are not noticed. Everything seems hard at first to someone coming suddenly from darkness into light, from leisure to labour. But when you have got away from your former habits you will soon get used to the labour. Practice soon makes perfect. What seemed difficult at first presently becomes quite easy. Even the bravest soldiers are apt to tremble when they first hear the bugle summon to battle, but after thay have closed with the enemy hope of victory and fear of defeat soon inspires courage. Surrounded by a company of single-hearted brethren, what have you to fear? What have you to fear at whose side angels stand and whom Christ leads into battle encouraging his friends with the words, 'Fear not, I have overcome the world.' If Christ is with us, who is against us? You can fight with confidence where you are sure of victory. With Christ and for Christ victory is certain. Not wounds, nor falls, nor bruises, nor (were it possible) can a thousand deaths rob us of victory, if only we do not forsake the fight. Only by desertion can we be defeated. We can lose the victory by flight but not by death. Happy are you if you die in battle for after death you will be crowned. But woe to you if, by forsaking the battle, you forfeit at once both the victory and the crown. May Christ save you from this, dear son, for at the last judgement you will incur a greater penalty on account of this letter of mine if, when you have read it, you do not take its lesson to heart" (*Letters*, 8–10).

contrast between Cluny and Cîteaux and makes the same criticisms of Cluny in greater detail, attacking the splendor and lavishness of the monastery and other evidences of what he considers a worldly and lax spirit.

Letter One and the second half of the *Apologia* are frequently quoted, but we must remember that in the first half of the *Apologia*, St. Bernard also had a great deal to say about certain Cistercians and criticizes a false rigidity and austerity which is mistaken by some White Monks for the true religious spirit. Whenever we read an ancient document, we must be careful to make sure we read *what it says*, not just what we think it ought to say. For this we have to read *everything* and weigh all the statements made in the light of their context. We must also find out something about the background. If we do not read objectively and carefully, our idea of what we read will be nine-tenths fantasy.

In order to understand the attitude of St. Bernard toward Cluny, we must first of all take note of his relations with *Peter the Venerable*. Peter the Venerable became abbot of Cluny in 1122 after a short period of decline under Abbot Pontius. But before Pontius, under St. Hugh, Cluny had been one of the outstanding monasteries of the Christian world, for its observance and fervor. About 1123, when many Cistercians were attacking Cluny and its observance, Peter the Venerable wrote a very humble and peaceful letter to St. Bernard, listing those accusations and humbly asking the advice of the Abbot of Clairvaux on the points mentioned. St. Peter Damian, Camaldolese hermit and no less austere and uncompromising a reformer than St. Bernard, had compared Cluny to a *"paradise watered by the four rivers of the gospels, a garden of delights, a spiritual region in which earth and heaven meet and a spiritual arena in which frail human nature battles against the powers of the air"* [499] (quoted by Mabillon [Migne, 182:897]). St. Peter Damian also asserted that at Cluny, the Holy Spirit truly presided

---

499. "*Paradisum, quatuor Evangeliorum fluentis irriguum, hortum deliciarum, spiritualem campum, ubi coelum ac terra congreditur, ac velut arenam certaminis, ubi, spiritualis more palaestrae, caro fragilis adversus potestates aereas colluctatur*" (*Epistolae*, 6.4).

over the formation of the monks, and in particular he praised their silence.[500]

*Two Early Letters of Peter the Venerable to St. Bernard* (from his *Letters*: Book I, n. 28 [*PL* 189, col. 112ff.]; Book II, n. 17 [*PL* 189, col. 321ff.]). (A note on Cluny: Cluny represents the monastic idea of Charlemagne—a great monastery exempt from episcopal control, directly under the pope and working in close cooperation with the emperors; a center of liturgical worship and official devotions for the empire; a center of economic prosperity and power, highly centralized and conservative; a center of reform for the Church; {this is a} *clerical* monasticism: the monastery is a nursery of bishops—the monks, being clerics, do not engage habitually in manual labor; a center of Christianizing influence in society: Cluny originated the idea of the "truce of God"— periods of peace interrupting wars. Peter the Venerable oriented Cluny away from the empire. He succeeded Pontius, who resigned because of failure of his [economic] administration, but who nevertheless occupied Cluny by force during the absence of Peter. Pontius dies in prison in Rome {in} 1127.) The letter of 1123 is found in Migne: *PL* 189, col. 321ff. (*Letters*, 2.17). It is full of charity and concern for healing divisions. An *earlier* letter is a cold and formal list of arguments.

1. *Letter* 1.28 (*PL* 189, col. 112ff.) {is} a detailed outline of the Cistercian accusations against the Benedictines. {The} *basic charge* {is that} the Benedictines are not keeping their vows, are not faithful to the *Rule*. They have substituted their own traditions for those of the Monastic Fathers. *Details* {include the following}: (a) the usual questions of fasting, clothing etc. are raised; (b) other points: the Benedictines have no novitiates; candidates are admitted to profession without training; they receive back fugitives and apostates more than three times; they do no manual labor; they have parish churches, collect tithes, etc.; (c) trifling points— some of the accusations go into trivial details: the abbot does not

---

500. "*conversatione et Ordine non adinventionis humanae studium, sed Spiritus sancti magisterium inesse asserit*" (*Epistolae*, 6.5 [*PL* 182, col. 897B]).

have a list of the tools of the monastery; those who say the office outside of choir do not say it kneeling; the abbot does not eat with the guests; the porter is not an old man and doesn't answer *Deo gratias* every time someone knocks at the door; the monks do not prostrate before every guest that arrives, etc. Then he gives a résumé of the Benedictine replies. {The} *basic charge* {is that} the Cistercians are Pharisees, separating themselves and putting themselves above others. They do not keep the degrees of humility: the monk should esteem himself below all others. They are singular. They have changed the color of the habit (black = {the} color of humility and penance, {and} goes back to St. Martin). {The} *Benedictine apologia* {is that} in following their superiors and the changes approved by the Church, they are following monastic obedience. "Love God and do what you will" (St. Augustine).[501] Note that in his defence Peter the Venerable repeatedly appeals to charity as against "formalism" and "rigidity." In *principle*, his appeal is good, but in practical application it is sometimes faulty. This is an example to show, in practice, {that} the appeal to "love" may in fact be simply a justification of weakness and laziness or unwillingness to make a necessary effort demanded by genuine charity. {With regard to} *novices*, to receive candidates immediately is Christlike charity (117) (the Apostles followed Christ immediately). It is for the salvation of their souls (150). {As for} *apostates*, {they} receive them back repeatedly, {for the} *Rule* says, "Let all things be so disposed that souls may be saved."[502] {As for} *clothing*, the *Rule* prescribes clothing according to climate and leaves the decision to the abbot; *fur coats*? after all, God made "garments of skins for Adam and Eve [!] and they were symbols of penance, too!"[503] (121) (see other scriptural arguments for

---

501. "*Hinc beatus Augustinus:* Habe, *inquit*, charitatem, et fac quidquid vis" (cols. 118D–119A); see above, n. 346.

502. "Sic, *inquit*, abbas omnia temperet atque disponat, ut animae salventur" (col. 119B); see *Rule*, c. 41, which reads: ". . . *Et sic omnia . . . qualiter et animae salventur*" (McCann, 98).

503. "Fecit, *inquit*, Deus Adam et uxori ejus tunicas pelliceas, et induit eos (Gen. II). . . . *pro poenitentia*" (col. 121C).

*"pelliceae"*—col. 122[504]); *femoralia*? more Scripture arguments {are provided} (123[505]). {With respect to} *food*, the *Rule* provides for differences according to need, circumstances of work, climate, etc. ({he} quotes Augustine against the Manichaeans[506]). {As for} *manual work*, the *Rule* says that monks must *not be idle*. The Benedictines spend the majority of their time in prayer, and this is better than work (129). He argues about the "impossibility" of monks making their living by manual labor: "living on vegetables, they have no strength"[507] to work (144). It is also "unfitting"[508] for monks to do manual labor, he says. They are dedicated to the service of the sanctuary and must not be degraded by vile occupations (145). It is legitimate for monks to own villages, because once they are in the hands of monks they are dedicated to God and become, as it were, "oratories" (145). It is good for monks to have serfs because serfs are better treated on monastic property: they are regarded as brothers. Behind this we see the real issue—economic injustice, defence of the feudal *status quo* with its "advantages" and rationalization of the "religious value" of an outdated economic setup. (Notice: the Cistercians soon found themselves in much the same kind of position, even though they continued to work.) He appeals to a tradition that St. Maurus and his monks, having had their needs supplied without work, spent all their time in spiritual exercises. Yet he was glorified by miracles. Later, {the} reception of tithes, etc. {is} justified by {the} fact that monks continually praise God (141–42). Furthermore, he adds that if the Cistercians insist that the Cluniacs ought to pros-

---

504. Reference is made to Heb. 11:37 (prophets dressed in skins); 4 Kings [2 Kings] 1:8 (Elijah); Matt. 3:4; Mark 1:6 (John the Baptist); as well as to St. Benedict in Gregory the Great's *Life*.

505. "undergarments"; reference is made to the linen underclothing of the priests in Exod. 28:40-43 and the properly clothed body in 1 Cor. 12:23.

506. Augustine emphasizes that everything should be governed by charity (col. 126CD).

507. "*oleribus et leguminibus fere nullas vires corpora dantibus.*"

508. "*indecens*" (col. 144D).

trate before all the guests and wash their hands, they would be doing this from morning to night and would not have time to do anything else (130–31). *Other details*: this letter reveals important facts about Cluniac observance and their way of interpreting the *Rule*. Guests sometimes ate at the abbot's table in the community refectory (133). {With regard to the} salutation of brethren, in regular places they bowed in silence. Outside regular places, the junior said *Benedicite* when bowing (133). The gate is normally left open except when the brethren are asleep, and then the various gates are kept by family brothers (134). Cluny has an indult from Urban II permitting the reception of monks from other monasteries in spite of the opposition of their previous superiors (137) because Cluny was held by the Church to be a monastery of exemplary fervor and observance. The question of *exemption* comes up (137–38): the Cistercians accuse Cluny of being "under no bishop."[509] They reply: "We are under the Bishop of Rome.[510] *Huic soli specialiter obedimus.*"[511] {There are} details on {the} history of exemption (139) and economic background (142ff.). Monks as advocates in lawsuits {are discussed} (147): why should they not fight for truth when the martyrs died for the truth (!!). *Principles*: after all these details and arguments, some having value and others without much force, Peter the Venerable sets down his principles:

1. The commandments of God cannot be changed, but certain ecclesiastical rules can be changed or dispensed. No change in essentials has been made by Cluny. The changes are all in accidentals, where change is allowed for the sake of charity. The *Rule* of St. Benedict is subject to change (in accidentals) under the higher rule of charity (148–49).

---

509. "*proprium episcopum habere refugimus*" (col. 137A) ("we avoid having our own bishop").

510. "*Quis enim rectior, quis verior, quis dignior Romano episcopo episcopus potest inveniri*" (col. 137A) ("For what bishop can be found more proper, more authentic, more worthy than the bishop of Rome").

511. "To him alone we are obedient in a particular way" (col. 138A).

2. *Rectitudo regulae charitas est.*[512] Their vows bear most of all on the *rectitudo regulae*. Hence changes made for the sake of charity do not affect their fidelity to the vow, even though not in accord with the letter of the *Rule*. *Si charitas excluditur, rectitudo excluditur . . . necesse est ut Regula destruatur* (149).[513] *Unum et solum charitatis officium humanam salutem modis omnibus quaerere* (155).[514] *Quia igitur mutata sunt quaedam in Regula, charitas fecit* (157).[515]

3. Saints, like Gregory the Great, made accidental changes. Were they wrong? (152). But we may be permitted to disagree with his application of the principles. How do you reply to the following? (a) It is charity to the novice to shorten his time of temptation and keep him from falling back into the world by letting him make vows at once, or after a few weeks, or six months (150); (b) *Vestibus vero pelliciis eadem charitatis Regula nos ideo vestit ut corpus a frigore, anima defendatur a murmure* (150);[516] (c) there is more love in prayer than in work: *Melius est orare quam arborem secare* (151).[517] *Only in the last lines of the letter does he approach the real point—the fact that the Rule counsels the monk to greater generosity and sacrifice* (158): *Licet hoc Regula non jubeat, monet tamen ut monachus ad meliora transeat* (158).[518] Peter the Venerable insists (rightly): *Quod si tantum monet, non compellit* (158).[519] He says that the Cistercians are wrong to *compel* men to take a more austere

---

512. Col. 149C, which reads: "*Rectitudo autem Regulae . . .*" ("The ordering principle of the *Rule* is charity").

513. Col. 149C, which reads: "*Si ergo charitas . . .*" ("If charity is excluded, order is excluded. . . . It is inevitable that the *Rule* be destroyed").

514. Cols. 155D–156A ("The one and only duty of charity is to seek human salvation in all ways").

515. "Therefore because certain things in the *Rule* have been changed, charity has done it."

516. "The same rule of charity clothes us in fur garments in order that the body may be protected from the cold, the soul from murmuring."

517. "It is better to pray than to cut down a tree."

518. "Granted that the *Rule* does not order, it nevertheless instructs the monk to pass on to better things."

519. "But if it only instructs, it does not compel."

course and argues that some austerities are so imprudent as not even to be advisable. The Cistercians, depriving monks of warm clothes, make them murmur, or leave the monastery, or destroy their health so they can no longer serve God (157). *Nam quod regionis poscit frigiditas, poscit necessitas. Quod necessitas hoc plane et charitas* (157).[520] *Dei igitur et Regulae mandato contradicit, qui monachos pelliciis uti non debere dicit* (157–58).[521] As we read this letter today we are bewildered by a multitude of apparent sophistries and we wonder how Peter could really have believed all this. We do not realize the power of habitual association, custom and environment. *His principles are perfectly sound*, and St. Bernard not only agreed with them but adopted them. *His practice was dubious* and he himself made a serious reform at Cluny.

Letter 2.17 deplores the controversy over details of observance {and} again cites the principle of charity, the one great rule. There can and should be various customs in various places, but all should be one in charity and not be divided on account of customs. He is no longer criticizing the Cistercians but saying each should follow his own (order's) way to God. What matters is purity of intention in either case (329). Why argue about such things as {the} color of the habit? *Noli, noli, oro te, frater, si ovis Christi esse cupis, vario de vellere causari* (333).[522] (In this letter he refers to his voyage in Spain and the translation he has had made of the *Coran* [339], {and} gives information about Mohammed.)

Many Benedictines began to accuse St. Bernard of being the spearhead of all the Cistercian attacks against Cluny, which was not true. Bernard was urged by his friend William of St. Thierry to deny these charges and state the real position, and this he did in the *Apologia*. To us the second half of the *Apologia* hardly reads like a peacemaking document. It is typical of the passionate

---

520. "For what the coldness of a region demands, necessity demands. What necessity demands, this clearly charity does as well."

521. "Therefore one who says monks should not use fur garments contradicts the command of God and of the *Rule*."

522. "Do not, I beg you, brother, do not make a pretext of the diverse color of wool, if you wish to be a sheep of Christ."

sincerity of St. Bernard, who says just what he has on his mind and does not always trouble to qualify or soften his judgements. But remember that the *Apologia* does begin with high and sincere praise of the Order of Cluny. To read only the second half of the *Apologia* is to be very unjust not only to Cluny but also to our Father St. Bernard, because this puts *him* in an unfavorable light. Note at the same time, however, that Peter the Venerable was *equally scathing* in a letter he himself wrote to the Benedictine abbots of his time, and so St. Bernard's accusations must have been well-founded. Note also that as a result of his contact with St. Bernard, Peter the Venerable drew up new statutes to "encourage mortification." [523] Further, in regard to St. Bernard's condemnation of the pomp of Cluny, note the Lateran Council in 1123 said the same thing of abbots (the council was strongly against the aspiration of abbots to pontifical regalia, etc.) (see {*St Bernard*}, p. 198[524]). A Benedictine abbot replied to the *Apologia* in a manuscript preserved at Oxford and pointed out among other things: "It is said in the *Rule* that a monk should not write letters, and you have sent letters full of cutting criticism and malice and mockery all over the wide world" ({*St Bernard*}, p. 200).[525] The

---

523. "Il en arrive aux décrets concernant le régime alimentaire. Pour 'augmenter, ne serait-ce qu'un peu, la mortification,' il remet en vigueur la loi de l'abstinence continuelle de viande et il fixe les jours eu jeûne" (Jean Leclercq, OSB, *Pierre le Vénérable* [Paris: Éditions du Fontenelle, 1946], 149) ("He then comes to the decrees concerning regulations about food. In order to 'increase, even if only a little, mortification,' he reinstitutes vigorously the law of continual abstinence from meat and he establishes the days for fasting"); the actual text reads simply: "*licet parvum abstinentiae incrementum*" (n. 11 [*PL* 189, col. 1029A]) ("it allows for a small increase in abstinence").

524. See "Bernard et l'Ordre de Cluny," in Commission d'Histoire de l'Ordre de Cîteaux, *Bernard de Clairvaux* (Paris: Éditions Alsatia, 1953), 193–217; the copy text reads: "*St Bernard et Son Temps*," a completely different collection.

525. "*Item in regula quoque precipitur quod monachus non mittat litteras vel eulogias. Tu vero per amplum terrarum orbem pitteras non qualescumque sed satiricas et viciis et derisionibus . . . (plenas edidisti)*"; this is from the *Riposte* attributed, erroneously, to Hugh of Amiens.

*Apologia*, however, had good results in general—it led to the convocation of a general chapter of Benedictines in the province of Rheims (non-Cluniac) while Peter the Venerable also convoked his own priors and instituted reforms. Further, the Benedictines carried out these reforms with great courage, even though the reforms were criticized by the papal legate, Matthew of Albano, a Benedictine. Other aspects of the conflict between the two monastic families {include}: (a) conflicts over tithes—the battle between Miroir and Gigny;[526] (b) Cistercian intervention in episcopal elections (v.g. York[527]). These are not matters of regularity or spirituality and they do not concern us here. Let us turn to the *Apologia* itself.

*Outline of the* Apologia *itself*:

1. St. Bernard defends himself and blames the excessive and combative severity of certain Cistercians. {In the} Prologue, and chapters 1–6, {he writes that} some Cistercians tend to forget the *spirit* of the *Rule*. This is evident in their criticism of Cluny. {Then} there is a transition—a question of principle (chap. 7): the monastic life is not a matter of the letter only or of the spirit only, but of *both letter and spirit*. In reality you cannot have one without the other. This is the key to the whole issue.

2. Criticisms of Cluny: in general, Cluny has failed by neglecting the letter of the *Rule* to a point where essentials have been cast aside and the spirit is no longer alive in their observance: (a) Cluny encourages intemperance, lack of mortification; monastic values are subverted; souls are endangered; especially is this true in the matter of food and drink: fasting has been forgotten; so has poverty; (b) the fault lies largely with the superiors, who themselves live in luxury and emulate the splendor of bishops and lords of the Church; (c) it is especially scandalous that the churches and monasteries of Cluny are so lavish and splendid when the poor are starving at the gates (there has been a famine in 1123–1124). Here St. Bernard particularly criticizes the love of

---

526. See *Letters*, 428–29 [#353].
527. See *Letters*, 259–84 [##187–208, with a substantial headnote].

*art* and display in certain Benedictine churches, not because he is against art as such, but because he believes that display and pomp are foreign to the true spirit of monastic simplicity without which prayer cannot be what it ought to be. Bernard is for contemplative prayer without images, centered on {the} revelation of Christ in His word. "Seeing" may interfere with "hearing," which is more interior.

*Estimate of Bernard's Criticism*:

1. We are to assume that it is in general fair, and not exaggerated, since both Peter the Venerable and other Benedictines agreed with him and initiated a reform. If there is any exaggeration it is more or less rhetorical and would be understood in the circumstances. St. Bernard had a vivid imagination and a very fluent pen.

2. But if his accusations are correct, then the *Apologia* was a necessary and salutary document. The fundamental obligation of monks is to separate themselves from the world—*a saeculi actibus se facere alienum*.[528] Their function in the Church is to lead an "angelic" life by prayer and mortification, a life of perfect renunciation, a totally new life in Christ. But according to St. Bernard, the Black Monks tended to excuse and even encourage a life which by its useless comforts, its pomps and luxury, fomented pride, intemperance {and a} worldly spirit and frustrated the whole purpose of the monastic life. This was definitely not true of Benedictinism as such but it was true of certain monasteries. *St. Bernard is careful to exonerate the average monk who is in good faith*. He is criticizing the spirit and the general level of observance accepted as good by Cluny. He is criticizing a whole outlook and attitude.

3. Furthermore, St. Bernard's criticism was not mere partisan feeling. He was not simply defending his own order against other

---

528. *Rule*, c. 4 (McCann, 26) ("make ourselves strangers to the ways of the world": Merton's translation in Thomas Merton, *The Rule of Saint Benedict: Initiation into the Monastic Tradition* 4, ed. Patrick F. O'Connell, MW 19 [Collegeville, MN: Cistercian Publications, 2009], 122).

orders, but he was defending the *purity of monasticism* against corruption from either kind of extreme—from the extreme literalism and rigidity of some Cistercians as well as from the lax tendencies of certain Benedictines. He even felt that he was defending the purity of Cluny itself against corruption from within. It was because Bernard had an intense and passionate love for the *reality of the monastic ideal*—something that was not just a concept to be loved but something to *be lived and put into practice*. He saw the real necessity for true monks in the Church of God. He was thinking of the Church and of souls—the souls of the monks themselves. There is no doubt whatever that in the Middle Ages the monastic spirit sometimes became so feeble that monks were in danger of losing their souls and perhaps did lose them. This can happen at any time, but history teaches that there was a dangerous laxity in some quarters in the Middle Ages.

4. We must remember not to apply these standards of St. Bernard too literally today. The situation is no longer quite the same; at best there might be a remote analogy. But it is for us to remember, as individual monks, that it is necessary to keep a high ideal of mortification and of charity at the same time. We must deny ourselves if we are followers of Christ. There must be, in the world, men of penance and prayer, and our renunciation must be a fact, and not just a word. The *Apologia* reminds us of this. We must never forget it.

*Some details of the* Apologia:

1. *Charges against the Cistercians*: these lessons give us solid and sober principles to guide us in our attitude towards other orders. We must never pretend we are better than others. This conflict is a "scandal" in the Church and Bernard seeks first of all to remove the stumbling block by admitting {that} some Cistercians are wrong. In substance, St. Bernard says: "We Cistercians are accused of crawling out of our caves, dressed in rags, to insult the holy Benedictines, the light of the world. Here we are, not so much wolves in sheep's clothing as fleas and moths. If this is true, then we are pharisees, boasting of our austerity of life. What will be the use of our mortifications and labors if we

lack charity towards other religious families? Indeed, if in this life alone we hope in Christ we are of all men the most miserable" (c. 1, n. 1 [col. 899]).[529] There may be a vein of satire in all this, but the substance is serious. St. Bernard squarely faces the real danger of pharisaical pride, which would rob our austere observance of merit. This raises the whole question of sincerity and purity of intention, which is brought into doubt by the aggressive criticism of others. This being the case, then those who boast and condemn others have found a "hard way to hell";[530] St. Bernard laments, could we not have taken the broad and easy path? Why all this fasting on earth if we are to be in hell afterwards? Here again he is serious. He faces *the danger to souls*: we can be damned for lack of charity. He then utters his "woes": *Vae pauperibus superbis*;[531] *Vae portantibus crucem et non sequentibus Christum*;[532] *Quomodo intra praesepium Domini simulatrix arrogantia se coarctat*;[533] *Quid facit superbia sub pannis humilitatis Jesu?*[534] (This is interesting especially because it shows that the Cistercian Fathers considered

---

529. "*scilicet miserrimi hominum, in pannis et semicinctiis, de cavernis, . . . gloriosissimo Ordini vestro derogare, sanctis qui in eo laudabiliter vivunt, . . . mundi luminaribus insultare: Itane sub vestimentis ovium, non quidem lupi rapaces, sed pulices mordaces, imo tineae demolientes. . . . Si ita, inquam, pharisaica jactantia caeteros homines, et (quod superbius est) nobis meliores despicimus, quid nobis prodest tanta in nostro victu parcitas et asperitas, in vestitu notabilis illa vilitas ac diversitas, in opera manuum quotidiana desudatio, in jejuniis et vigiliis jugis exercitatio, totius denique vitae nostrae singularis quaedam atque austerio conversatior? . . . Nonne si in hac vita tantum in Christo sperantes sumus, miserabiliores sumus omnibus hominibus?*"

530. "*non inveniebatur nobis via . . . tolerabilior ad infernum*" (col. 899C).

531. Col. 899D, which reads: "*vae iterum . . .*" ("Woe likewise to the proud poor").

532. Col. 899D, which reads: "*vae iterum . . . crucem Christi . . .*" ("Woe likewise to those carrying the cross of Christ and not following Christ").

533. Col. 900A ("How does arrogant pretension squeeze itself into the manger of the Lord?").

534. Col. 900A, which reads: "*quid enim facit . . .*" ("What is pride doing under the swaddling clothes of the humility of Jesus?").

our life of austerity a special form of union with the infant Christ, a living of the mystery of the Divine Infancy, which would be impossible without humility and faith and abandonment and littleness, the very essence of our spirit according to this—a most important observation. Note too that it is the pomp and worldly greatness of Cluny that he condemns most. What he is defending is the spirit of humility and littleness, essential to the monk.)

*St. Bernard's own defence of himself* (chaps. 2–4):[535] he has never attacked Cluny but always honored it. He praises the Cluniac life. Cluny is a nursery of saints (2.4 [col. 900]). {He} thanks them for their hospitality, is glad of their prayers {and} speaks of his many friends in the order. There should be peace among all orders. The unity of many orders in one Church is compared to Joseph's many-colored coat, the seamless garment of Christ. It is necessary that there be diversity in the Church; the Holy Spirit is the Master of His gifts, and there are many vocations because this is the will of God (see Eph. 4). Some are called to Cluny, others to Cîteaux, others to the regular clergy, others to the secular, others to the married state. But all form one Church, because all are united by charity. But if each vocation envies and derides the other, they all become worthless, because {they are} no longer united in Christ. St. Bernard adds that he praises and loves all orders and belongs to all by his love, though only to one by his vows (see n. 8 [col. 903]). He parenthetically expounds a great principle, later to be taken up by St. Thérèse of Lisieux:[536]

---

535. Cols. 900C–901A; 901B–903A; 903A–904D.

536. See *Story of a Soul: The Autobiography of St. Thérèse of Lisieux*, trans. John Clarke, OCD (Washington, DC: Institute of Carmelite Studies, 1976), 196: "I am the *Child of the Church* and the Church is a Queen since she is Your Spouse, O divine King of kings. The heart of a child does not seek riches and glory (even the glory of heaven). She understands that this glory belongs by right to her brothers, the angels and saints. Her own glory will be the reflected glory which shines on her Mother's forehead. What this child asks for is Love. She knows only one thing: to love You, O Jesus. Astounding works are forbidden to her; she cannot preach the Gospel, shed her blood;

if he has greater admiration, in charity, for the work of others, he will gain more merit for that work than the work he does himself if the latter lacks charity (4.8 [903]).

*Chapters 5–6*[537] {discuss} *detractors*. Those who despise and detract others wish to set up their own standard of justice, and thus withdraw from the justice and mercy of God (5.10 [905]). Those who think they alone are keeping the *Rule* had better remember the parable of the Pharisee and Publican (*id*.). Seeing the mote in their neighbor's eye (a tendency to laxity), they do not see the beam in their own (pride, detraction) (*id*., 11 [905]). "But," one might object, "our accusations are true."[538] Bernard admits the accusations are true but says it makes no difference. The Kingdom of God consists in interior virtues, and to detract another out of pride and uncharitableness is worse than lax observance. The exterior and corporal observances of the *Rule* are second to the interior and spiritual precepts: humility, obedience, charity. *Melior est pellibus involuta humilitas quam tunicata superbia* (6.12 [906]).[539] He adds {that} it is better to eat meat, with discre-

---

but what does it matter since her brothers work in her stead and she, *a little child*, stays very close to the *throne* of the King and Queen. She *loves* in her brothers' place while they do the fighting." See also Thérèse's May 9, 1897 letter to Père Adolphe Roulland (*Collected Letters of Saint Thérèse of Liseiux*, trans. Frank J. Sheed [New York: Sheed & Ward, 1949], 332): "Leaving to great souls, great minds, the fine books I can't understand, I rejoice to be little, because 'only children, and those who are like them, will be admitted to the heavenly banquet.' I am so happy that 'in the Kingdom of God there are many mansions', for if there were but the one, the description of which and the way to which seem to me incomprehensible, I could not get in. All the same I should like to be not too far from *your mansion;* in consideration of your merits, I hope the good God will grant me the grace to share in your glory, just as on earth the sister of a conqueror, though she lack all natural gifts, does, in spite of her poverty, share in the honours paid her brother."

537. Cols. 904D–905D; 905D–907A.

538. See n. 12 (cols. 905D–906A).

539. Col. 906B, which reads: "*melior sit* . . ." ("Humility wrapped in furs is better than pride in tunics").

tion, than to stuff yourself with beans to satiety: "With a belly full of beans and a heart full of pride we condemn foods cooked in meat fat."[540] It is better to drink a little wine, for the sake of health, than to glut yourself with water. In other words he lays down the principle that food and drink are not in themselves evil. What is good is virtue; what is bad is vice—no matter where they are found. In short, St. Bernard indicates that where there is backbiting and calumny and envy and anything tending to discord in the Church, there is a worldly and fleshly spirit, no matter how ascetic the monks may appear to be.

2. *The Great Principle* (c. 7[541]): here he is in complete agreement with Peter the Venerable and indeed follows him:

a) He concludes therefore that since the spiritual element in the *Rule* is greater than the exterior and bodily, one who transgresses the spiritual precepts sins worse than he who neglects the bodily ones. Note that this depends on the assumption that the laxists are only lax and not also themselves proud. This is a hypothesis which evidently Bernard later sets aside. However, remember that Peter the Venerable was indeed a very humble man though his observance was less strict, and Bernard may have had him in mind when he wrote chapter 6.

b) If you hold that the *Rule* must be kept so literally that no dispensation is to be admitted, then you yourself are not keeping the *Rule*, which admits and supposes the need for dispensation in individual cases.

c) However, if the letter is secondary, it is not to be cast out altogether. If different observances are legitimate, in themselves, they must nevertheless accord with the essence of the *Rule* and not discard penance altogether.

d) If Bernard will now turn to the abuses of Cluny, it is precisely to defend Cluny itself, the "Order" of Cluny against the individuals who corrupt that order (7.15 [908]).

---

540. "*Repleti deinde ventrem faba, mentem superbia, cibos damnamus saginatos!*" (col. 906C).
541. Cols. 907A–908B.

148     *The Cistercian Fathers and Their Monastic Theology*

3. *Criticism of Cluny*: it is one thing to permit dispensation, as the founders of Cluny rightly did. But one must distinguish between rightful dispensations in case of need and *wholesale mitigation reaching the point of abuse*. Bernard charges that such wholesale mitigation is evident almost everywhere in the Benedictine abbeys, especially in the matter of food and drink, clothing, equipage for travel and monastic buildings. Bernard says that this has gone to such a point that *monastic values are completely subverted*, and that vice has acquired the name of virtue. Poverty is called avarice, sobriety is called boorishness, silence is considered uncharitable melancholy. *Laxity is called discretion; extravagance is called liberality; dissipation rates as good fellowship*; softness and luxury are called simplicity and cleanliness. Beneath it all is a *false notion of charity*—those who encourage one another in these vices are thought to be charitable. But this is the opposite of charity, because it brings souls into danger: *"How can you call it discretion to give everything to the body and nothing to the soul?"* (8, n. 16 [908]).[542] {With regard to} true discretion—St. Anthony had this: he gave priority to the soul over the desires of the body. {Bernard} contrasts the charity of the ancient hermits with the triviality of monastic recreations (READ #19 [col. 910][543]). {This is

542. *"quaeve discretio totum dare corpori, et animae nihil?"* (col. 908D).
543. *"Quis in principio, cum Ordo coepit monasticus, ad tantam crederet monachos inertiam devenire? O quantum distamus ab his qui in diebus Antonii exstitere monachi! Siquidem illi cum se invicem per tempus ex charitate reviserent, tanta ab invicem aviditate panem animarum percipiebant, ut corporis cibum penitus obliti, diem plerumque totum jejunis ventribus, sed non mentibus transigerent. Et hic erat rectus ordo, quando digniori parti prius inserviebatur: haec summa discretio, cum amplius sumebat quae major erat: haec denique vera charitas, ubi animae, quarum charitate Christus mortuus est, tanta sollicitudine refocillabantur. Nobis autem convenientibus in unum, ut verbis Apostoli utar,* jam non est dominicam coenam manducare *(I Cor. XI, 20). Panem quippe coelestem nemo est qui requirat, nemo qui tribuat. Nihil de Scripturis, nihil de salute agitur animarum; sed nugae, et risus, et verba proferuntur in ventum. Inter prandendum quantum fauces dapibus, tantum aures pascuntur rumoribus: quibus totus intentus, modum nescias in edendo"* ("In the beginning, when the monastic order began,

followed by the} classic description of meals at Cluny (#20 [col. 910][544]). He admits, however, that most of the monks make use of these mitigations in good faith; they accept what is given to them but are not attached; they are willing to follow another observance if called upon to do so; they seek above all to keep peace with their brethren. The *real blame belongs to a few* who impose this manner of life upon the others (8.18 [909]). Here St. Bernard reconciles the two halves of the *Apologia*. It is true that the monks of Cluny are in general good, but it is also true that their observance ought to be more strict. Carefully note how he qualifies! His chief complaint is that in the Benedictine monasteries there is a more "fleshly" attitude toward the monastic life. He has nothing against "humanism," but when humanism

---

who might have believed monks would fall into such idleness? Oh, how different are we from these who were monks in the days of Anthony! If on occasion they visited one another out of love, they took hold of the bread of souls with such eagerness that, having completely forgotten about food for the body, they generally passed the entire day with their stomachs, but not their minds, fasting. This was the proper order, when the more worthy part was served first. This is the highest discretion, when what was greater was taken care of more amply; this, finally, is true love, when souls, for love of whom Christ died, were cared for with such great solicitude. But when we come together in assembly, to use the words of the Apostle, it is now not to eat the Lord's supper (1 Cor. 9:20). There is certainly no one who asks for the heavenly bread, no one who bestows it. Nothing about the Scriptures, nothing about the salvation of souls is considered; but trifles and laughter and words are put forth into the wind. While eating, the throat is fed with food to the same degree as the ears are with gossip; completely absorbed in this, you may know no moderation in eating").

544. Bernard describes a multi-course meal, meatless but with two separate fish servings, in which, rather than simple, natural preparation, unusual flavors are added to attract the palate even when hunger has been satisfied, and the appearance of the food is designed to be attractive to the eye. The variety of eggs, for example, soft, hard, scrambled, fried, roasted, even stuffed, served alone or with other dishes, keeps meals from being ordinary and repetitive, but unlike the eye and the palate the stomach ends up being more overburdened than simply satisfied.

brings with it a relaxation that amounts to a *cult* of comfort, luxury and display, then he denounces it, and rightly. It is not a question of forbidding legitimate dispensations and adaptations, but Bernard accuses Cluny of re-orientating the whole monastic life from spirit to flesh, to worldly and human values. This frustrates the basic monastic obligation of *conversio morum*.[545] The *Rule* declares that in the matter of dispensations, the weak should *accept with humility what they should never desire but what their superior declares necessary for them*. But when the spirit of the *Rule* is perverted, then mitigation itself assumes the place of the *Rule* itself and *is desired as if it were virtue*. This desire for mitigation *as if it were a higher spiritual good* is what St. Bernard attacks as a perversion. But he will always permit necessary relaxations in particular cases where they are really called for. Chapter 9[546] {focuses on} *intemperance*—gluttony. St. Bernard points to the austere fasts of the early monks, commending at the same time their discretion in breaking their fasts for a higher motive, namely charity. Here, he says, is the right order. This is his principle (9.19 [col. 910]). But whereas the monks of the desert broke their fast and conversed of spiritual things with guests, the monks of Cluny, he says, stuff themselves with many foods at the same time exchanging gossip and rumors and feeding the mind with trivial news and jokes. This he takes to be symptomatic of their worldliness (910). (N.B. in this connection, see the table talk of St. Anselm with his monks [Eadmer, *Vita Anselmi* (Southern), p. 73, 74 etc.][547]). {He provides} details: {as for} food, though meat

---

545. The Benedictine vow of "conversion of manners" (for a discussion see Thomas Merton, *The Life of the Vows: Initiation into the Monastic Tradition* 6, ed. Patrick F. O'Connell, MW 30 [Collegeville, MN: Cistercian Publications, 2012], 274–311).

546. Cols. 909D–912B.

547. Eadmer, *The Life of St. Anselm, Archbishop of Canterbury*, ed. and trans. R. W. Southern (London: Thomas Nelson & Sons, 1962), c. 11: "How he employed his tongue as an instrument of spiritual melody during meals," in which Anselm responds to a monk who was concerned that he has been assigned by his abbot to engage in business dealings with the world, by comparing human life to the workings of a mill, in which those concerned

is avoided, fish courses follow one another in profusion; too great a care is taken in the preparation of tasty food, and this pandering to the pleasures of taste leads to excessive eating. Care is even taken to make the food *look* attractive. {With regard to} drink, there is too much wine drunk, and the wine is too well prepared (namely he attacks the custom of certain monasteries where wine mixed with honey is served on feast days). The monks are so full of wine that they fall asleep after dinner, or if they can get to the night office with throbbing heads, *"non cantum sed planctum potius extorquebis"* (911).[548] Other abuses {include the fact that} those who do not need meat and are perfectly well get themselves put in the infirmary so as to have meat, thus endangering their souls; and they make use of canes to give the appearance of being sick. {As for} clothing, etc. (c. 10[549]), not content with dressing for protection against the cold, vanity prompts them to seek novelty and luxury in clothing, {with} special materials, and lack of poverty in bedclothes is another abuse (blankets of special fur, etc.). Reproaching them in all this for lack of poverty and pointing to the example of the first Christians who shared all they had and lived with *"cor unum et anima una,"*[550] St. Bernard diagnoses the source of the trouble.

{His} *diagnosis* {is as follows}:

1) {The} *first reason* for these abuses {is the} loss of interior spirit. Unable to find peace and contentment with the kingdom of God within, vain monks have abandoned their own interior sanctuary to go and seek consolation in external things. And so: "But when you go to buy a cowl, you run from city to city, you visit all the fairs, you enter the houses of all the merchants, you

---

only with worldly gain lose their entire stock of flour, others weakened by various vices preserve only some of their stock of flour, but obedient monks, so long as they do not work for vainglory, receive their full reward; Eadmer provides this discourse as a typical example of Anselm's informal teaching at meals.

548. Col. 911A ("you will drag forth not a song but a lament").
549. Cols. 912B–913C.
550. Col. 913A ("one heart and one mind") (Acts 4:32).

turn all their stock upside down, you unfold huge amounts of cloth, you feel it with your fingers, you submit it to close scrutiny, you take it over to the window and look at it in the light of the sun. If it is the least bit coarse, or if the color does not have just the right shade, you reject it; but if it is really fine cloth and of the most perfect color, then no matter what the price you must posssess it" (col. 913).[551] He comments, from the treasure of the heart our actions speak: a vain heart bears fruit in exterior vanity. *Non tanto curaretur corporis cultus, nisi prius neglecta fuisset mens inculta virtutibus* (col. 913).[552]

2) *The second reason* for these abuses is that the superiors, instead of doing their duty and seeing that infractions are corrected, are themselves worse than the others and more infected with this worldly spirit (n. 27 [913–14]). He portrays an abbot travelling with enough retinue for two bishops (col. 914). He has seen one with sixty horsemen in his train. {He} portrays them travelling with all their fancy bedding, table-ware, clothes, etc. "They have but to go four leagues from the monastery, and they take all their furniture with them; you would think they were going off to wage a long military campaign or to cross a desert where the necessities of life could not be found. Could they not use the same vessel to pour water over their hands and to drink wine out of? Couldn't they get along with the light of a lantern, instead of taking a whole candlestick, and that of silver or gold?" (col. 914).[553]

---

551. "*At tu quando cucullam empturus lustras urbes, fora circuis, percurris nundinas, domos scrutaris negotiatorum, cunctam evertis singulorum supellectilem, ingentes explicas cumulos pannorum, attrectas digitis, admoves oculis, solis apponis radio; quidquid grossum, quidquid pallidum occurrerit, respuis; si quid autem sui puritate ac nitore placuerit, illud mox quantolibet pretio satagis tibi retinere.*"

552. "Care of the body would not be attended to so much if the mind, untrained in virtues, had not first been neglected."

553. "*Vix denique quatuor leucis a sua quispiam domo recedit, nisi cum tota supellectili sua, tanquam sit vel iturus ad exercitum, vel transiturus per desertum, ubi non valeant inveniri necessaria. Annon posset eodem vasculo et aqua manibus*

*Inordinate splendor in decoration of churches*: however grave these other abuses may seem in the eyes of St. Bernard, he feels that the lavishness with which the monks decorated their monasteries and churches was a far worse abuse: "*Haec parva sunt, veniam ad majora*"[554] (opening of chap. 12[555]). {As for} St. Bernard's attitude toward Romanesque art, it should be properly understood. In the first place, it would be wrong for us today to take literally the same attitude as St. Bernard. The circumstances have changed. St. Bernard's renunciation of aesthetic values for something higher is not possible if you do not first possess the capacity to enjoy those values. For one who has no capacity to judge or enjoy good religious art, to reject it all in the same terms as St. Bernard would be sheer pharisaism and the rejection of what he does not appreciate or understand. At the same time, without puritanism (St. Bernard was not a puritan[556]), we should realize the force of St. Bernard's criticism: he is aiming at a *higher value*, a spiritual value, in which artistic values are not destroyed but sublimated, and the proof of this is to be found in the aesthetic quality of Cistercian architecture. This quality is in fact very high and very pure. It would be harmful and vain to reject *all* consideration for such values—we would end in a scandalous cult of ugliness which would bear witness to our spiritual mediocrity. Here are some of St. Bernard's criticisms: they bear not directly on art as

---

*vergi, et vinum bibi? Annon posset ardens lucere lucerna, nisi in tuo quod portas candelabro, et hoc aureo, vel argenteo?"*

554. "These are small things: I am coming to greater."

555. Cols. 914C–916B.

556. In *The Spirit of Simplicity* Merton writes: "Writers like G. C. Coulton, who have called this reaction on the part of the Cistercians 'puritanism,' cannot justify their use of that term, at least in the strict sense. The puritans would never have admitted the concepts of monastic poverty and the mystical life with which this spirit of simplicity was essentially connected. Cf. Etienne Gilson, *Mystical Theology of St. Bernard*, p. 233" (*Spirit of Simplicity*, 45, n. 48); see Gilson, *Mystical Theology of Saint Bernard*, 233, n. 97, responding to G. G. Coulton, *Five Centuries of Religion*, 4 vols. (Cambridge: Cambridge University Press, 1923–1950), 1:300.

such but {on} art *as display*, art not precisely as a spiritual activity, but rather *as a sign of worldliness and wealth*.

1. He blames the inordinate size of the basilicas, {a} size not required by the need to accommodate people: *supervacuas latitudines*.[557] {This is} useless space. (It may be replied that in fact "space" is very important and an aid to devotion—Cistercian architecture itself proved this.)

2. He blames the lavish sculpture and the "curious painting"[558]—it is not sculpture or painting as such that he blames, according to the letter of the words here, but the fact that they can be "lavish and curious."[559] Neither lavishness nor curiousness is a quality of true art. His reason for blaming them {is that} they are a distraction from true prayer. This too can be disputed in fact. Consider for example the sculptured doorways of Vézelay, Autun, etc.—these have a profoundly spiritual and mystical quality; they are religious art in this highest possible sense and not mere curiosities. Bernard admits that all this "may be" for the honor and glory of God.[560] The issue here is "lavishness for God." {According to} the Benedictine view, the sanctuary should be splendid in the highest degree, as a sign of the hidden spiritual splendor of the divine King enthroned in the midst of His people. Bernard argues: the sanctuary is full of gold but Christ is starving in His members, the poor, outside the basilica—always a cogent point![561] Again a distinction {must be made}: all these works of art may be very well for bishops and their cathedrals, but do they belong in a monastery, whose church is not frequented by people

---

557. Col. 914C ("superfluous widths").
558. "*curiosas depictiones*" (col. 914C).
559. "*sumptuosas . . . curiosas*" (col. 914C).
560. "*fiant haec ad honorem Dei*" (col. 914C).
561. See Gilson, *Mystical Theology of Saint Bernard*, 74: "The 'luxury for God' of the Cluniacs was also in its own way a very Christian sentiment, beautiful in itself, and an inexhaustible source of beauty; but one of the essential reasons that provoked St. Bernard's indignation was that in pouring out silver and gold for the ornamentation of their churches they left Christ to suffer in the person of those that wanted bread."

at large? He argues that monks have come to the desert to leave sensible things, and consequently art etc. have no place in the monastery. Gilson has remarked, however, that though the Cistercians abandoned plastic arts in the time of St. Bernard (when the *Apologia* was written manuscripts were still richly illuminated at Cîteaux), still St. Bernard's style remains lavish, ornate, rich, artistic.[562] In conclusion, he adds caustically that perhaps all this art is necessary to extort contributions from the faithful (*ergo* the churches of the Black Monks were frequented by the faithful after all—perhaps this too is an objection in Bernard's eyes, for he concludes: "No doubt, being mixed up with the gentiles we have continued to serve their graven idols" [915][563]).

3. St. Bernard's main argument is that all this art is a product not of true interior life but of avarice and love of the things of the world, inordinate in monks: it is not the love of art that is a sign of avarice, but the love of money, according to Bernard, is the occasion for all this art. Again, it is not the art as such that he criticizes but the avarice with which he believes it to be connected. "This art is in fact an investment of money, which pays off with interest. Money is spent here in order that it may be multiplied; it is poured out in order that there may be a plenitude of it. By the view of such sumptuous works, by the sight of so many vanities, men are stirred up to make offerings rather than to pray.[564] *Sic opes opibus hauriuntur, sic pecunia pecuniam trahit*" (915).[565] And again he concludes: *Fulget ecclesia in parietibus, et in*

---

562. "In spite of all his formidable asceticism St. Bernard was no puritan when it came to literature. The walls of his monasteries were bare, but his style was not bare. . . . These Cistercians have renounced everything save the art of good writing; each and all of these hardy ascetics carried in his bosom a humanist who by no means wanted to die" (Gilson, *Mystical Theology of Saint Bernard*, 63; see also 233, n. 97).

563. "*An quoniam commisti sumus inter gentes, forte didicimus opera eorum, et servimus adhuc sculptibilibus eorum.*"

564. "*Tali quadam arte spargitur aes, ut multiplicetur. Expenditur ut augeatur, et effusio copiam parit. Ipso quippe visu sumptuosarum, sed mirandarum vanitatum, accenduntur homines magis ad offerendum quam ad orandum.*"

565. "Thus riches are drawn by riches; thus money attracts money."

*pauperibus eget* (col. 915).⁵⁶⁶ {As for} art in the cloister, he laments expense for "these vile monkeys, these mad lions, these monstrous centaurs, these half-men and spotted tigers, these fighting soldiers and trumpeting hunters. Under one head you see many bodies, and on one body many heads. Here we have an animal with the tail of a snake, there a fish with the head of an animal. . . . Dear God, if we are not ashamed of such nonsense, why do we not lament the waste of money?" (916).⁵⁶⁷ Such subjects are of course characteristic of the Romanesque.

*Conclusions*: St. Bernard returns to his original tone and hopes that he has not already said too much, hopes also that what he has said will not cause more trouble and scandal. He hopes however that the strict Cistercians will cease their detractions, and that the less strict Benedictines will tighten up a bit. Let each one hold to the good which he possesses and not judge the other. If some can lead a stricter life, let them not be uncharitable or envious of those who have more latitude. And let those whose rule is easier give credit to the stricter ones without trying rashly to imitate them. Those who have chosen a stricter life cannot without fault descend to a less strict level, but those who need more latitude would be rash to try to go beyond their strength. He is not encouraging Benedictines to fly to the Cistercian observance. He has seen too many do so with scandal to their own monastery and without edification in their new home, their change being prompted rather by levity and impatience than by a desire for higher perfection. *Securius est ut perseveremus in bono quod coepimus, quam quod incipiamus ubi non perseveremus* (918).⁵⁶⁸

---

566. "The church glows in its walls, and is needy in its poor."

567. "*Quid ibi immundae simiae? quid feri leones? quid monstruosi centauri? quid semihomines? quid maculosae tigrides? quid milites pugnantes? quid venatores tubicinantes? Videas sub uno capite multa corpora, et rursus in uno corpore capita multa. Cernitur hinc in quadrupede cauda serpentis, illinc in pisce caput quadrupedis. . . . Proh Deo! si non pudet ineptiarum, cur vel non piget expensarum?*"

568. Cols. 917A–918A, which reads: "*securius est tamen ut . . .*" ("It is safer for us to persevere in the good that we have begun, rather than to begin something when we might not persevere").

*The Cistercian Fathers and Their Monastic Theology* 157

{The} Effect of {the} Apologia—Reform of Cluny by Peter the Venerable:

1. An "encyclical letter" (*Loquar an sileam*[569]) {was written} to all the priors of the Cluniac houses by Peter (*Letters*, Bk. VI, n. 15 [*PL* 189, col. 418]); {it was} written {in} 1150. {He} strongly blames {the} complacency of Cluny. A reform is needed! On one point he goes beyond St. Bernard: *he condemns abuse in the eating of meat*—even in times of fast and abstinence! He depicts the monks "like hawks or vultures,"[570] flying wherever there is the smoke of a kitchen or the smell of something frying or roasting (419). "Beans, cheese, eggs and even fish are now found nauseating. Only the cauldrons of Egypt are pleasing. Roast or well-broiled pork, hares and rabbits, the best goose from the flock, chickens and all four-footed things, every kind of domestic fowl covers the tables of the holy monks. Yet even these have now become unpleasing. . . . Royal and exotic delicacies are now in order. The sated monk can now eat only stag or venison or wild boar, or bear meat from the forest. The woods must be combed, hunters are in demand. Pheasants, partridges and doves are to be taken by the trapper's skill, lest the servants of God die of starvation" (col. 419).[571] He roundly condemns meat-eating monks for infidelity to their vow (of obedience to the *Rule*). He says that this is *one of the points of the Rule that cannot be changed* (as far as monks in good health are concerned) (420). Hence he counters the argument that it is a valid tradition and adaptation. "Hear me, thou crow-monk, and be not angry that I give thee

---

569. "Shall I speak, or remain silent?"
570. "*ut milvi et vultures*" (col. 419A).
571. "*Faba, caseus, ova, ipsi etiam pisces, jam in nauseam versi sunt. Solae ollae Aegyptiorum placent. Assus aut elixus porcus, juvenca pinguis, ciro grillus et lepus, anser ex anserum grege electus, gallinae, et prorsus omne quadrupes, aut volatile domesticum, sanctorum monachorum mensas operiunt. Sed viluerunt jam et ista. . . . Ad regales et peregrinas delicias transitus factus est: satur monachus, jam non nisi caprea, cervo, apro, vel urso agresti vesci potest. Lustranda sunt nemora, venatoribus opus est. Aucupum arte phasiani, perdices, turtures capiendi sunt, ne servus Dei fame pereat.*"

this name. How dost thou differ from a crow, or a buzzard, a bear or a wolf? These birds and beasts hunger for bloody foods, and make no distinction of day from day or hour from hour. So thou also, etc." (422).[572] This is an unusual letter, and it must not be taken out of context or exaggerated. It shows however that Peter had largely come around to St. Bernard's point of view! It echoes the *Apologia*.

2. In a special Chapter of 1132 at Cluny, Peter and two hundred priors institute a reform in the statutes of Cluny. Dom Leclercq (*Pierre le Vénérable*, p. 150–51[573]) points out the wise spirit of this reform. It introduces austerity in certain points, but in others it reduced complication and pressure of work or multiple observances in order to *simplify* to some extent the monk's life. Many useless or outdated customs are suppressed. He also tries to reorganize the *economic* life of Cluny. In *PL* 189, col. 1025ff.,[574] we have the *Statuta* of Peter the Venerable—a collection of the changes made in the Cluniac observance under his rule. The Prologue says he is compiling this collection twenty-four years after becoming abbot—therefore in 1146. It undoubtedly gives us the spirit and letter of the reforms carried on by Peter the Venerable:

a) *In the Prologue, he returns to his general principle*: certain unchangeable laws come from God Himself. Other *changeable*

---

[572]. "*Audi, corvine monache; nec irascaris quia te sic nomino. In quo enim differs a corvo, in quo a vulture, in quo ab urso, in quo a lupo? Inhiant volucres illae aut ferae sanguineis dapibus; nec dies a diebus, nec horas ab horis in vescendo discernunt. Sic, ut video, et tu . . . .*"

[573]. He mentions changes in regulations regarding washing, traveling, shaving, all designed to "free religious from absurd routines" ("*à libérer les religieux de routines absurdes*"); reintroduction of manual labor, but taking place within the confines of the cloister to minimize contact with the secular world; establishing reasonable age parameters for the clothing ceremony (20) and ordination (25); eliminating non-monastic "familiars" from Cluniac houses; reducing the number of feasts at which the great candelabra is lit; excluding seculars from certain areas of churches in order to preserve the privacy of the monks for certain exercises.

[574]. *Statuta Congregationis Cluniacensis*, cols. 1025A–1048A.

laws are made by men in His name. These latter can and should be changed, because with time they lose their usefulness, their meaning, or their reason for existing. The things that belong to the essence of virtue are unchangeable. Those which are merely aids to the practice of virtue should be changed when they do not adequately fulfill their function (*Quae verae virtutis sunt, numquam mutanda sunt; quae vero adjumenta virtutum, pro congruentia rerum, personarum, et temporum utilitate dispensanda sunt* [1025][575]). Charity, humility, chastity, etc. can never be dispensed. Fasting, vigils, manual labor, etc. can vary according to circumstances. His changes have been made with the consent of the chapter and in accordance with the tradition of Cluny.

b) *The office*: {he} cuts down {the} inordinately long pause at {the} mediant of {a} psalm verse[576] {and} restores more importance to {the} Sunday office (over feasts of saints).[577] {The} Feast of {the} Transfiguration {is} to be celebrated with special solemnity.[578] Emphasis {is placed} on {the} conventual Mass.[579] {There is} less use of {a} huge candelabra in the basilica[580] (criticized by Bernard).

c) *Fasting and abstinence*: {he} cuts down on {the} use of *meat* at feasts.[581] Strict observance of abstinence from meat {is} imposed.[582] {The} monastic fast {is} to be observed.[583]

d) *Clothing*: certain restrictions {are imposed} in {the} use of showy furs and other brightly colored materials.[584]

---

575. "What pertains to true virtue must never be changed; what are actually aids to the virtues should be arranged according to usefulness proper to the objects, the persons and the times."
576. N. 1 (col. 1026B).
577. Nn. 2–3 (cols. 1026C–1027B).
578. N. 5 (col. 1027C).
579. N. 6 (col. 1027D).
580. N. 52 (col. 1039CD).
581. N. 11 (col. 1029AC).
582. N. 12 (col. 1029CD).
583. N. 14 (cols. 1029D–1030B).
584. Nn. 16–18 (cols. 1030C–1031B).

e) *Silence* {is} to be stricter in {the} infirmary than it was;[585] recreations {are} cut down;[586] useless speaking {is} castigated (1037[587]).

f) *Other points*: general care {is taken} to cut out useless or merely external formalities (cf. n. 26 [col. 1033]); *novices* {are to have} at least *one month's* novitiate (to give less time would be imprudent, as one could not test their vocation) (1036[588]); *some manual labor*—housework, etc.—{is to be undertaken}, but "out of sight of seculars."[589] When a brother is whipped, his shirt must be removed lest it be damaged by the whips (1043[590]); brethren {are} to guard the dormitory because of stealing of clothes, etc. (1044[591]).

### III. DE CONVERSIONE

*Preamble: Student Life in Twelfth-Century Paris—Intellectual Life in Paris*:

1. The mid-twelfth century is a time of *awakening*. {There was a} sense of *progress*, {and} hence {also} conflict between progressive and traditional elements.

2. Progressive elements enter into contact with *Moslem thought* and discover Aristotle, Greek medicine, etc., through {the} intermediary of Arabic manuscripts. (N.B. Peter the Venerable has "agents" at Toledo translating Arabic texts; they were working in 1142.) Also the progressives *learn and translate Greek*. {The} influence of *mathematics and {the} sciences* {is evident} ({e.g., the} discovery of zero), {as well as the} influence of {the} newly discovered *Organon* of Aristotle ({the} logical works). {There was extensive} commercial expansion (the word "check" has an Arabic origin {which is} curious and worthy of investigation: {it is} con-

---

585. N. 19 (cols. 1031C–1032A).
586. N. 21 (col. 1032B).
587. N. 42 (col. 1037CD).
588. N. 37 (col. 1036BC).
589. "*remoto conspectu saecularium*" (n. 39 [col. 1037A]).
590. N. 63 (col. 1043AB).
591. N. 69 (col. 1044CD).

The Cistercian Fathers and Their Monastic Theology    161

nected with *chess* and *checkers*—Persian games; the English exchequer, {the} finance department of the Norman kings, met in a board room with a checkered table cloth on which counters represented sums of money.) (For Peter the Venerable and Arabic translations, read {the} quote from Daniel of Morley in Le Goff, *Les Intellectuels du Moyen Age*, p. 23.[592]) {The} importance of *critical*

---

592. "*La passion de l'étude m'avait chassé d'Angleterre. Je restai quelque temps à Paris. Je n'y vis que des sauvages installés avec une grave autorité dans leur sièges scolaires, avec deux ou trois escabeaux devant eux chargés d'énormes ouvrages reproduisant les leçons d'Ulpien en letters d'or, avec des plumes de plomb dans la main, avec lesquelles ils peignent gravement sur leurs livres des astérisques et des obèles. Leur ignorance les contraignait à un maintien de statue mais ils prétendaient montrer leur sagesse par leur silence même. Dès qu'ils essayaient d'ouvrir la bouche je n'entendais que balbutiements d'enfants. Ayant compris la situation, je réfléchis aux moyens d'échapper à ces risques et d'embrasser les 'arts' qui éclairent les Écritures autrement qu'en les saluant au passage ou en les évitant par des raccourcis. Aussi comme de nos jours c'est à Tolède que l'enseignement des Arabes, qui consiste presque entièrement dans les arts du quadrivium, est dispensé aux foules, je me hâtai de m'y rendre pour y écouter les leçons des plus savants philosophes au monde. Des amis m'ayant rappelé et ayant été invité à rentrer d'Espagne, je suis venu en Angleterre avec une précieuse quantité de livres. On me dit qu'en ces régions l'enseignement des arts libéraux était inconnu, qu'Aristote et Platon y étaient voués au plus profond oubli au profit de Titus et de Séius. Ma douleur fut grande et pour ne pas rester seul Grec parmi les Romains, je me suis mis en route pour trouver un endroit où apprendre à faire fleurir ce genre d'études . . . Que personne ne s'émeuve si traitant de la création du monde j'invoque le témoignage non des Pères de l'Église mais des philosophes païens car, bien que ceux-ci ne figurent pas parmi les fidèles, certaines du leurs paroles, du moment qu'elles sont pleines de foi, doivent être incorporées à notre enseignement. Nous aussi qui avons été libérés mystiquement de l'Égypte, le Seigneur nous a ordonné de dépouiller les Égyptiens de leur trésors pour en enrichir les Hébreux. Dépouillons donc conformément au commandement du Seigneur et avec son aide les philosophes païens de leur sagesse et de leur éloquence, dépouillons ces infidèles de façon à nous enrichir de leurs dépouilles dans la fidélité*" (Jacques Le Goff, *Les Intellectuels au Moyen Âge* [Paris: Éditions du Seuil, 1957]) ("A passion for study had driven me from England. I remained for some time at Paris. I saw there only savages, installed with grave authority in their scholars' chairs, with two or three stools before them, loaded with enormous books reproducing the lessons of Ulpien in letters of gold, with lead pencils in their hands, with which they gravely marked asterisks

scientific thought, as opposed to dogma proposed by authority, {increased}.

3. *Enthusiasm for the new intellectual life* (READ John of Salisbury in {a} letter to Thomas à Becket [1164] [Le Goff, p. 28];[593] also

---

and obols in their books. Their ignorance restricted them to the appearance of a statue, but they pretended to show their wisdom by their very silence. Whenever they tried to open their mouths, I heard only the babbling of infants. Having understood the situation, I reflected on the ways of escaping from these risks and of embracing the 'arts' which illuminate the Scriptures otherwise than having a nodding acquaintance in passing or avoiding that through summaries. As, in our day, it is at Toledo that the teaching of the Arabs, which consists almost entirely in the arts of the quadrivium, is presented to throngs, I hastened to get myself there to listen to the teachings of the most learned philosophers in the world. When some friends called me back and I was invited to return from Spain, I came to England with a precious quantity of books. I was told that in these regions the teaching of the liberal arts was unknown, and that Aristotle and Plato were doomed to the deepest neglect, in favor of Titus and Seius. My sorrow was great, and in order not to remain the only Greek among the Romans, I set out on a journey to find a place to learn to make this kind of study flourish. . . . So that no one would be disturbed when discussing the creation of the world, I cited not the Fathers of the Church but the pagan philosophers, because although they are not included among the faithful, certain of their words, from the moment they are filled with faith, should be incorporated into our teaching. The Savior has ordered us also, who have been mystically liberated from Egypt, to despoil the Egyptians of their treasures in order to enrich the Hebrews. So let us, in conformity with the commandment of the Lord and with his assistance, despoil the pagan philosophers of their wisdom and their eloquence; let us despoil these infidels so as to enrich ourselves, in fidelity, with their spoils").

593. "*J'ai fait un détour par Paris. Quand j'y ai vu l'abondance de vivres, l'allégresse des gens, la considération dont jouissent les clercs, la majesté et la gloire de l'église tout entière, les diverses activités des philosophes, j'ai cru voir plein d'admiration l'échelle de Jacob dont le sommet touchait le ciel et était parcourue par des anges en train de monter et de descendre. Enthousiasmé par cet heureux pèlerinage j'ai dû avouer: le Seigneur est ici et je ne le savais pas. Et ce mot du poète m'est venu à l'esprit: Heureux exil que celui qui a cet endroit pour demeure*" ("I made a detour through Paris. When I saw the abundance of provisions, the happiness of the people, the consideration which the clerics enjoyed, the

Philip of Harveng[594]).

4. Reaction to the new intellectual life: contrast the Cistercian emphasis on the monastery as the *Schola Christi*[595] (cf. {Bernard's} letter to Henry Murdac [James translation, #107][596]). Peter of

---

majesty and glory of the entire Church, the various activities of the philosophers, full of admiration I believed I was seeing Jacob's ladder, whose top touched heaven, and which was traversed by angels ascending and descending. Enthused by this happy pilgrimage, I had to avow: The Lord is here, and I did not know it. And this word of the poet came to mind: A happy exile is he who has this place to live").

594. "*Poussé par l'amour de la science te voilà à Paris et tu as trouvé cette Jérusalem que tant désirent. C'est la demeure de David . . . du sage Salomon. Un tel concours, une telle foule de clercs s'y presse qu'ils sont en voie de surpasser la nombreuse population des laïcs. Heureuse cité où les saints livres sont lus avec tant de zèle, où leurs mystères compliqués sont résolus grâce aux dons du Saint-Esprit, où il y a tant de professeurs éminents, où il y a une telle science théologique qu'on pourrait l'appeler la cité des belles-lettres!*" ("Impelled by the love of knowledge, there you are at Paris, and you have found that Jerusalem which so many desire. It is the dwelling-place of David . . . of the wise Solomon. Such a throng, such a crowd of clerics gathers there, that they are well on the way to outnumber the laity. Happy the city where the sacred books are read with so much zeal, where their complicated mysteries are resolved thanks to the gifts of the Holy Spirit, where there are so many eminent professors, where there is so much theological knowledge that one could call it city of the humanities") (28–29).

595. "school of Christ" (St. Bernard, *Sermo 121 de Diversis* [PL 183, col. 743B]).

596. "To his dear friend Henry Murdac, health, and not only in this life, from Bernard, styled Abbot of Clairvaux. What wonder if you are tossed about between prosperity and adversity since you have not yet gained a foothold on the rock. But if you have sworn and are determined to keep the just commandments of the Lord, neither prosperity nor adversity can sever you from the love of Christ. Oh if you only knew, if only I could explain to you! 'Such things as were never known from the beginning, as ear never heard, eye never saw, save at thy command, thou, O God, hast made ready for all that await thy aid.' I hear, brother, that you are reading the Prophets; think you that you understand what you read? If you do, you will perceive that it is to Christ which they refer. And if you would grasp him, you will do so sooner by following him than by reading of him. Why seek the Word

Celle, a friend of both St. Bernard and John of Salisbury, {writes}: "O Paris, you knew well how to ravish and deceive souls! The nets of vice, traps of evil, the arrows of hell destroy the innocent in your streets. . . . Happy, on the other hand, is that school where Christ teaches to our hearts the word of eternal wisdom, and where without labor or courses we learn the way of eternal life. We buy no books, we pay no professor, we have no embroiled disputes, no sophisms; the solution of every problem is easy, and

---

amidst written words, when in the flesh he stands before your eyes? He has long since left his hiding place in the Prophets and appeared unto the Fishermen. Like a bridegroom from his bridal bed he has leapt from the shady coverts of the mountain sides and run into the open pastures of the Gospels. Let him who has ears to hear, hear him crying out in the Temple: 'Whosoever thirsts, let him come to me and drink,' and: 'Come unto me, all ye who labour and are burdened, and I will refresh you.' Are you afraid that you will break down where Truth himself has promised to refresh you? Certainly if the 'dark waters from the clouds of the air' please you so much, you will be more than delighted with the clear water that springs from the fountains of the Saviour. If you could but once taste for a moment the 'full ears of corn on which Jerusalem feasts' how gladly would you leave the dry husks for Jewish hacks to gnaw! If I could but have you as my fellow in the school of piety of which Jesus is the master! If only I might submit the vessel of your heart when it has been purified to the unction which teaches all things! How gladly would I share with you the warm loaves which, still piping hot, fresh, as it were, from the oven, Christ of his heavenly bounty so often breaks with his poor! Would that when God sweetly deigns to shed on his poor servant a drop of that heavenly dew which he keeps for his chosen, I might presently pour it forth upon you and in turn receive from you what you feel! Believe me who have experience, you will find much more labouring amongst the woods than you ever will amongst books. Woods and stones will teach you what you can never hear from any master. Do you imagine you cannot suck honey from the rocks and oil from the hardest stone; that the mountains do not drop sweetness and the hills flow with milk and honey; that the valleys are not filled with corn? So many things occur to me which I could say to you that I can hardly restrain myself. But as it is for prayers and not a sermon that you have asked me, I will pray God that with his laws and his commandments he may open your heart. Farewell" (*Letters*, 155–56; *PL* 182, cols. 241–242C [#106]).

we learn the reasons for all things" (Le Goff, p. 25[597]). Discuss this!

5. Reasons for the opposition? See the *Goliards* ({who are} like Beatniks): they are the result of a *new {mobility}*[598] *in urban society of the age* (also {of the} Crusades)—wanderers, nonconformists, rebels, loving wine and gambling, denying {the} moral teaching of the Church.[599] (Serlo of Wilton, {an} English Goliard, repents and becomes a Cistercian.[600]) ({For} background, see Sedulius Scotus—sixth century[601]).

597. "O Paris, que tu sais ravir et décevoir les âmes! Chez toi les filets des vices, les pièges des maux, les flèches de l'enfer perdent les coeurs innocents . . . Heureuse école au contraire que celle où c'est le Christ qui enseigne à nos coeurs la parole de sa sagesse, où sans travail ni cours nous apprenons la méthode de la vie éternelle! On n'y achète pas de livre, on n'y paie pas de professeur d'écriture, là nul embrouillamini des disputes, nulle intrication des sophismes, la solution de tous les problèmes y est simple, on y apprend les raisons de tout."

598. Copy text reads: "*nobility.*"

599. See Merton's comment that a "sense of being transported with praise came to life in the monasteries of the early Middle Ages: but perhaps after the years it was deadened (and then we get the bawdy and despairing songs of the wandering, lost, beat monks, the Goliards)" (Thomas Merton, *Conjectures of a Guilty Bystander* [Garden City, NY: Doubleday, 1966], 122).

600. In a September 1, 1956, journal entry (*Search for Solitude*, 77), Merton refers to Helen Waddell's discussion of Serlo of Wilton (see Helen Waddell, *The Wandering Scholars*, 6th ed. [New York: Henry Holt, 1932], 141–43).

601. For Sedulius Scotus (or Sedulius of Liège, where he lived after leaving Ireland), see Waddell, *Wandering Scholars*, 65–69, who notes that Sedulius and the leader of the Goliards, the "Arch Poet, three hundred years later, . . . are at one on the superiority of verse well-soaked" (66; on the Arch Poet, see chap. 7 [161–76]), though she also points out his excellent scholarship (67–68); Sedulius actually lived in the ninth century (fl. 848–74) (298); he is perhaps being confused here with the fifth-century Roman poet Sedulius (ca. 450). See also Waddell's edition and translation of *Mediaeval Latin Lyrics*, 5th ed. (London: Constable, 1948), which includes eight of Sedulius's poems (118–25); she notes that the same monastery "that kept the single manuscript of his verse that has come down to us kept also the Archpoet's: and their souls likewise are garnered in one place" (315).

The University of Paris did not yet exist, but the Left Bank ({the} "Latin Quarter") was largely occupied by students of the great schools of Notre Dame, St. Victor and St. Genevieve.[602] *St. Victor*, founded by William of Champeaux outside the city in 1108, was originally a group of hermits; William retired there to seek peace and abandon the world of scholarship and debate. Students followed him, and William took up teaching again there in the country. *St. Genevieve*, founded by Abelard, {a} pupil of William, {became the} center of new philosophical thought—conceptualism, midway between the nominalism of Roscelinus and the realism of William of Champeaux (see histories of philosophy)—discussing the problem of *universals*. The school of *Notre Dame* remained strongly traditional. *St. Victor*, also traditional, under the guidance of Hugh of St. Victor, became a center of speculative mysticism. The great striving of the Victorines was to explain the knowledge of God that is gained by love and by union with Him. (The Victorine School will be discussed elsewhere.) *St. Genevieve*, under Abelard, was {the} most radical of the three. He used reason as an instrument to analyze faith, but as a *critical* instrument; not that he intended to undermine faith as such, by reason, but that he believed that traditional theology, basing itself on dogmatic affirmations, was not really understood and was accepted blindly without understanding. Abelard wanted to explain and demonstrate by reason the truths which faith accepted as dogmas. This attempt had a great popular appeal, and without realizing the danger, Abelard did in fact substitute reason for faith and did in fact fall into error. (Note: Abelard was also something of a Goliard—{he} wrote popular Goliardic verse.[603] His affair with Heloise was also well known.)

---

602. See Williams, Preface to *Of Conversion*, vi–vii.
603. These poems, which are not extant, were evidently more courtly than Goliardic: see Gilson, *Mystical Theology of Saint Bernard*, 158.

*The Case of Peter Abelard*—"the first professor," "the knight of dialectic," "the first modern intellectual":[604] here we must digress and give some details about Abelard, one of St. Bernard's chief adversaries. We cannot understand St. Bernard completely without knowing Abelard. At the same time, we cannot know Abelard if we merely look at him through the eyes of the Cistercians. The double myth of Abelard: (a) the nineteenth century venerated him as one of the "first rationalists" and an apostle of free thought (not to mention free love), then "used" him against medieval concepts of theology, authority, etc.; (b) the conventional Catholic view {considered} Abelard as a rebel, a rambunctious intellectual, devoured by intellectual pride, seeking only the gratification of his ambitions and lusts, unfaithful to his vocation and duties of state. Neither of these myths gives us contact with the real Abelard. He is much more complex than that. There is a little of both in him. He is to some extent a proud, ambitious, restless, even rebellious man. But there is also in him great intellectual brilliance. He made a very real intellectual contribution to his times. He also struggled with his own passions and made serious efforts to do the right thing in marrying Heloise. Later he strove earnestly to find his place as a monk and finally he did die a holy death as a monk at Cluny, after admitting his errors. He has a very clear, very strong and traditional monastic doctrine which we will discuss. It is important for twelfth-century monasticism.

*Life of Abelard*:[605] {he was} born near Nantes {in} 1079. As a student in the schools he was ambitious, aggressive {and} vain; {he} loved to hold sway over crowds of students and to attract them to his own teaching; he loved to fight and to overcome other masters. {As for} his affair with Heloise, it was a cold-blooded act in search of experience. Heloise was very beautiful, {the} seventeen-year-old niece (or daughter?) of Canon Fulbert. Abelard

---

604. "*la première grande figure d'intellectuel moderne . . . le premier professeur . . . le chevalier de la dialectique*" (Le Goff, 40).

605. For these details Merton relies on Étienne Gilson, *Héloïse and Abélard*, trans. L. K. Shook (London: Hollis & Carter, 1953), 1–19.

seduced her deliberately, but then she responded with great passion, and the affair became one of dramatic love. It is a quasi-legendary "love affair." Let us understand it aright:

a) Abelard was not a loose-living man, chasing women. This was the only one in his life. He was however somewhat akin in spirit to the Goliards at one point. His love songs were famous ({they} are now lost; his hymns only have survived).

b) Abelard was only a cleric, not in major orders, and he was free to marry. Often he is treated as though he were a fallen priest or monk. He became a monk only *after* the affair.

c) The problem of their marriage (see Gilson[606]): here we must emphasize the nobility of their love on the human plane and the depth of the issues involved. We can have no part with the sneers of those who only regard this as a lustful adventure of a cleric. Abelard wanted to marry Heloise in order to have her forever as his own and also in order to fulfill his obligations to her and their child that would be born of her (characteristically they named the child Astrolabe), {and} also to pacify the anger of Fulbert. Heloise was opposed to the marriage on intellectual grounds and for the sake of Abelard's career. She felt that for him to marry was just making himself ridiculous; he could "never be another St. Jerome or Seneca"[607] if he married and lived among the cries of babies. It is not that he would never become a priest or prelate, but {that} he was demeaning himself—it was unworthy of his genius (she believed). "He was cutting himself off from the heroes of the spiritual life and all hope of return would, from that moment, be denied him" (Gilson, p. 22). This has a background in the humanism of the twelfth century. Heloise was a well-read student. Theophrastus, {in} *De Nuptiis*, says a wife prevents a man from attending to philosophy.[608] What Heloise wanted was for Abelard to dedicate himself totally to philosophy and the highest things of life, not to her. Gilson points out the

---

606. Gilson, *Héloise and Abélard*, 20–36 (chap. 2).

607. Gilson, *Héloise and Abélard*, 22, which reads: "so long as Abélard was free he could still become, if not a St. Jerome, at least a Seneca."

608. See Gilson, *Héloise and Abélard*, 23–24.

self-sacrificing nobility of her love: "Abélard was unworthy of Héloise and on the plane of human love he always lagged behind her" (p. 34[609]). After {an} all-night vigil together in church (with Fulbert present) they were secretly married, but when Fulbert made the marriage known, Heloise denied it and went to a convent. Then Fulbert had armed men attack and mutilate Abelard at night in his lodgings. Abelard then retires to St. Denis as a monk but does not settle down, and soon gets into a row with the entire community by asserting that the legend of St. Denis[610] was a fabrication and had no basis in fact. Later Abelard retires to solitude near Troyes {and} founds the Paraclete, to which Heloise herself comes; she becomes abbess while Abelard goes to Brittany to be abbot of a small monastery where the monks try to kill him when he tries vainly to reform the monastery. In 1131 the Paraclete is approved by Innocent II (see Abelard's monastic letters and "Rule" below). Abelard continues to direct Heloise by letter. This is the spiritualization and development of their earthly love, raised to a higher plane. Abelard regards his mutilation as a grace and a liberation from the flesh and admits that it was pride that led him into sin, yet at the same time he in no way repudiates his love for Heloise and accepts it fully as part of the providential plan of his life, for the sanctification of them both. We must see in what a spirit of faith their love continued. To Heloise Abelard writes: "*Accede et tu, inseparabilis comes, in una gratiarum actione, quae et culpae particeps facta es et gratiae*" (*PL* 178, col. 207).[611] They should be united in thanksgiving, for they have been united both in sin and in pardon: *Deus clementer disposuit*

---

609. Text reads: "Never does he more clearly show that he was unworthy of Héloise, nor how much, on the plane of human love, he always lagged behind her."

610. The legend was that Paul's disciple Dionysius the Aeropagite (see Acts 17:34) was identical to the reputed third-century Bishop of Paris and martyr St. Denis: see *Epistola* 1 (*Historia Calamitatum*) (*PL* 178, cols. 153B–155B); see also Le Goff, 47.

611. *Epistola* 5 ("come too, in a single act of thanksgiving, my inseparable comrade, who became a partner both in fault and in grace").

*in uno duobus consulere, quos diabolus in uno nitebatur extinguere* (col. 208).[612] {Here is a} deeply Christian sense of providence {and} mercy. He says that due to their marriage she has been saved from the world, though his intention had been just to save her for himself. She does not take willingly to convent life, but Abelard, in this more "religious," works hard to persuade her. He tries to teach her by a life of prayer and meditation to love Christ her true spouse. *Amabat te ille veraciter, non ego* (col. 210).[613] And he urges her to accept their common trials in gratitude and love: *Accipe itaque, soror, accipe, quaeso, patienter quae nobis acciderunt misericorditer* (210).[614] In dedicating his book of sermons to her, he speaks of her as *Mihi quondam in saeculo chara, nunc in Christo charissima; in carne tunc uxor, nunc in spiritu soror, atque in professione sacri propositi consors* (col. 379).[615] His *Confessio Fidei* (Letter 17 [PL 178:375]) retracts errors: *Nolo sic esse philosophus, ut recalcitrem Paulo. Non sic esse Aristoteles, ut secludat a Christo.*[616] See his beautiful prayer for himself and Heloise (col. 212[617]). In

---

612. Cols. 207D–208A, which reads: "*ipse, inquam, clementer . . .*" ("He Himself mercifully arranged to look after two people together, whom the devil strove to annihilate together").

613. "He Himself, not I, loved you truly."

614. "Accept therefore, sister, accept patiently, I beg, what has mercifully happened to us."

615. "Once dear to me in the world, now most dear in Christ; then wife according to the flesh, now sister according to the Spirit, and partner in the profession of religious life."

616. "I do not want to be a philosopher so that as a consequence I am at odds with Paul, nor to be an Aristotle so that it separates me from Christ."

617. "*Deus, qui ab ipso humanae creationis exordio femina de costa viri formata nuptialis copulae sacramentum maximum sanxisti, quique immensis honoribus vel de desponsata nascendo, vel miracula inchoando nuptias sublimasti, meaeque etiam fragilitatis incontinentiae utcunque tibi placuit olim hoc remedium indulsisti, ne despicias ancillulae tuae preces, quas pro meis ipsis charique mei excessibus in conspectu majestatis tuae supplex effundo. Ignosce, o benignissime, imo benignitas ipsa; ignosce et tantis criminibus nostris, et ineffabilis misericordiae tuae multitudinem culparum nostrarum immensitas experiatur. Puni, obsecro, in*

a beautiful letter after Abelard's death, Peter the Venerable says

---

*praesenti reos, ut parcas in futuro. Puni ad horam, ne punias in aeternum. Accipe in servos virgam correctionis, non gladium furoris. Afflige carnem, ut conserves animas. Adsis purgator, non ultor; benignus magis quam justus. Pater misericors, non austerus Dominus. Proba nos, Domine, et tenta, sicut de semetipso rogat Propheta* (Psal. xxv, 2). *Ac si aperte diceret: Prius vires inspice, ac secundum eas tentationum onera moderare. Quod et beatus Paulus fidelibus tuis promittens, ait, Potens est enim Deus, qui non patietur vos tentari supra id quod potestis, sed faciet cum tentatione etiam proventum ut possitis sustinere* (I Cor. x, 13). *Conjunxisti nos, Domine, et divisisti quando placuit tibi, et quo modo placuit. Nunc quod, Domine, misericorditer coepisti, misericordissime comple. Et quos a se semel divisisti in mundo, perenniter tibi conjungas in coelo. Spes nostra, pars nostra, exspectatio nostra, consolatio nostra, Domine, qui es benedictus in saecula. Amen*" ("God, who from the very beginning of human creation, when woman was formed from the rib of man, sanctified the great sacrament of the nuptial bond, and who elevated marriage with immeasurable honors by being born of one who was betrothed, or by the beginning of Your miracles; who once also provided this remedy for the incontinence of my frailty, in a way that pleased You, do not despise the prayers of Your handmaid, which I pour out in the sight of Your majesty as a suppliant for my own excesses and those of my beloved. Forgive, O most gracious One—or rather graciousness itself—forgive our great offenses, and may the ineffable vastness of Your mercy deal with the multitude of our faults. I beg You, punish the culprits in the present, so that You may spare them in the future. Punish in time, so that You may not punish in eternity. Take up the rod of correction upon Your servants, not the sword of wrath. Afflict their flesh so that You may save their souls. May You be present as a purifier, not as a punisher; be merciful more than just; a merciful Father, not a stern Lord. Probe us, Lord, and test us, as the prophet asks for himself (Ps. 25[26]:2), as if he said openly: 'Prove me, O Lord, and try me.' This is what the blessed Paul promises to Your faithful, when he says: God is faithful, Who will not suffer you to be tempted above that which you are able: but will make also with temptation issue, that you may be able to bear it' (1 Cor. 10:13). You have joined us together, Lord, and You have separated us, when it pleased You, and in what manner it pleased You. Now, Lord, most mercifully complete what You have mercifully begun, and those whom You have once separated on earth, unite forever to Yourself in heaven. Lord, our hope, our portion, our expectation, our consolation, Who are blessed forever and ever. Amen").

to Heloise that Christ reserves Abelard to be reunited to her after the resurrection: *in Adventu Domini tibi per ipsius gratiam {restituendum} reservat (PL {189}*, col. 352)[618]—this because of the strength of their love, *in divinae charitatis vincula*.[619]

*Intellectual Problems Dealt with by Abelard*:

a) {The} *problem of meaning*, especially in connection with the "universals." What about Abelard's "conceptualism"? "Things" are not universal. The concept is given a universal meaning by reference to that in things which they have in common. In theology, the question of meaning comes up in the *Sic et Non*.[620] What meaning is to be sought in the conflicting teaching of the Fathers? How does one arrive at "right" and "wrong" in theology? {through a} critical discussion of the meaning of terms used. In this consists his "rational approach" to theological teaching. *Nihil potest credi nisi primitus intellectum*.[621] However this leads him into real error in {his} dialectical approach to mystery of the Trinity, {which was} condemned at {Soissons} {in} 1121. {Note the} ambiguity of {the} condemnations—he knows that his enemies are merely trying to silence him.

b) *Theology*: he is the first to construct a theological system. Hitherto theology was *"doctrina sacra"* and *"sacra pagina."*[622] He reduces it to a *summa* and not a collection of glosses and explanations. {He} divides it into three parts: (a) faith and mysteries, especially the Holy Trinity; (b) sacraments; (c) charity. {He} places

---

618. Text reads: ". . . *Domini, in voce archangeli, et in tuba Dei descendentis de coelo, tibi . . .*" ("in the coming of the Lord, in the voice of the archangel, and in the trumpet of God coming down from heaven, He keeps him to be restored to you through His own grace") (copy text reads: *"reservendum"*; volume number left blank).

619. Col. 352B, which reads: *"divinae charitatis vinculo"* ("in the bond of divine charity").

620. *PL* 178, cols. 1339A–1610A.

621. *Epistola* 1 (*Historia Calamitatum*) (*PL* 178, col. 142A) ("Nothing can be believed unless first it is understood"). Copy text erroneously refers to Sens rather than Soissons below.

622. "sacred doctrine"; "the sacred page" (i.e., scriptural commentary).

great emphasis on the philosophers (pagans) and on reasoning about the Holy Trinity, {with} not enough understanding of the importance of revelation. The question of *faith* is therefore central, and he seems to water down the idea of faith and its certitude. Gilson says, "the legend of Abelard the free-thinker"[623] is now exploded, and Knowles adds: "He was never a rationalist in the modern sense."[624] However, his definition of faith as *existimatio non apparentium*[625] is ambiguous and insufficient. This is a faith without real certitude. Hence also his treatment of the mystery of the Trinity by reasoning was weak and confusing. It was considered dangerous, and in fact he used heretical terminology. In his discussion of the motives of the Incarnation he was also ambiguous and was condemned. The ambiguity was in the terms with which he rejected the idea that the devil had acquired a *right* to a payment for man in the redemption—properly expressed by St. Anselm (*Cur Deus Homo*).[626] Abelard horrified William of

---

623. David Knowles, *The Evolution of Medieval Thought* (New York: Vintage Books, 1962), 122, citing Gilson, *Histoire de la Philosophie Médiévale* (Paris: 1945), 281 (apparently a reference to Gilson's *La Philosophie au Moyen Âge des Origines Patristiques à la Fin du XIV$^e$ Siècle* [Paris: Payot, 1944]).

624. Knowles, *Evolution of Medieval Thought*, 122, which reads: "Abelard was never a rebel against the authority of the Church, and never a rationalist in the modern sense."

625. *Introductio ad Theologiam*, 2.3 (*PL* 178, col. 1051D) ("opinion about things that do not appear").

626. "St. Anselm first of all rejects the conservative Augustinian thesis that Adam's sin had somehow given the devil real *rights* over the human race, and that the 'price of redemption' had consequently to be paid to the devil, in order that man might be ransomed. At the same time, St. Anselm did not go to the other extreme, reached by a more modern and liberal theology, of saying that there was in fact no atonement and no redemption at all, an answer which solves the problem by dismissing it altogether. . . . In being merciful to man, God is certainly paying no debt to the devil, and the redemptive death of Christ on the Cross is offered not to appease the forces of evil, but to do full honor to the infinite Life and Truth which are one with God Himself, and thus to overcome death" ("St. Anselm and His Argument," 257). See also Merton's "Reflections on Some Recent Studies of St. Anselm"

St. Thierry by saying that the "Son of God did not become man in order to liberate men."[627] Obviously this statement in itself is heretical. The context shows Abelard meant "to liberate man *from a power which the devil had acquired over him by right*,"[628] so that the devil would have been unjustly treated if Christ had liberated man by power or in some other way (*PL* 180:269–270). However, Abelard used careless and provocative language. William himself agrees that the devil had no right over man but did have power: "*Potestas a diabolo est in hominem* non iure acquisita, sed nequiter presumpta, *et a Deo iuste permissa, qua homo servus ejus factus est a quo superatus est*" (*Disputatio adversus Abaelardum*, c. 7 [*PL* 180, col. 271]).[629] The question is: does Abelard deny not only the rights of the *devil* but also his *power*? And also, *does not Abelard completely empty the dogma of Redemption of its objective character and reduce it to a subjective act of love on Christ's part*? He rejects the ideas of *sacrifice* and *satisfaction* (stressed by St. Anselm[630]).

---

(*Monastic Studies* 3 [1965]: 221–34), in which he comments: "It is true that St. Anselm is quite free of every trace of that primitive doctrine of the 'rights of the devil,' traces of which are still found in Augustine," which he goes on to describe as "the old idea that by original sin the devil had acquired a strict right over fallen man and that the price of man's Redemption therefore had to be paid to the devil. In other words the death of Christ is thus regarded not only as a satisfaction owed to divine justice but also in some way owed to diabolical power!" (231).

627. "*nec Filius Dei, ut hominem liberaret, carnem assumpsit*" (as cited by William of St. Thierry, *Disputatio adversus Abaelardum*, chap. 7 [*PL* 180, col. 269D]).

628. "*Sed, ut nobis videtur, nec diabolus unquam in homine habuit jus aliquod*" ("But, as it seems to us, the devil did not have any right over man") (as cited by William, col. 269D).

629. "Power over man was acquired by the devil not by right, but was wickedly usurped, and was justly permitted by God, through which man became the slave of him by whom he was overcome."

630. The satisfaction theory of the atonement, by which the sacrificial death of Christ, fully human and fully divine, pays the infinite debt of humanity contracted by sin against the divine honor, is developed in Anselm's *Cur Deus Homo?* But Merton emphasizes that this theory is properly understood not merely as a juridical transaction but as a synthesis of justice and

c) *The Problem of Freedom and Sin*: earlier ethical thought had stressed the objective evil that was done in sin. Abelard stresses the subjective intention, perhaps excessively. He is interested in analysis of *consent* and *intention* and concentrates on the *inner motives* of the sinner. In the *Scito Teipsum*[631] he distinguishes

---

love in Christ's free self-gift. "This concept, that emphasizes above all the liberty of Christ, His spontaneity in sacrificing His life to the Father, thereby to restore the violated order to the universe by *putting man back in his original place* among the angels, is far from the quasi-materialistic view that considers the destruction of the humanity of the Son both necessary and sufficient to appease the Father! . . . Anselm exclaims: 'It was not that the Father compelled this Man [Christ] to die by His command, but that the Son spontaneously did that which He understood was pleasing to the Father and profitable to man.' . . . The sacrifice of the Son was not a blind submission to an arbitrary and incomprehensible will, having infinite power over Him. It was perfectly free, clear-sighted, spontaneous choice, and what was pleasing to the Father in this sacrifice was not so much the shedding of physical (albeit infinitely precious) Blood, as the supreme generosity of the love which such obedience implied. Anselm emphasizes that this sacrifice was not something that the Father could justly demand of His Son. . . . This again is crucial to Anselm's concept of the divine honor: the 'honor' of God does not reside in His infinite power to exact every form of blind submission to an arbitrary will, but in the perfect concord of transcendent justice and love, expressed in the joyous liberty of the sacrifice accepted by the Son for the glory of the Father's love and for the salvation and happiness of men. . . . It is not a question of God's honor being repaired by the punishment of sin in Christ's death, though that death is indeed a perfect satisfaction for all the sins of the world. But here we see that God's honor demands, above all, man's salvation and restoration—a fact which is overlooked by those who see only the 'juridical' aspect of Anselm's doctrine. Anselm makes it quite clear that the satisfaction given to God for man's sin was not something that God required for Himself alone but rather for mankind and for the beauty of His cosmos. . . . Hence the honor of God that is wounded by sin and demands satisfaction is seen to be nothing other than His infinite Goodness and loving concern for man His creature. . . . Where sin dishonors God, is then, in refusing to recognize and accept His will in the order of creation and in the truth where He has made us stand" ("Recent Studies," 229–30).

631. *PL* 178, cols. 633A–678A.

between vice and sin (cf. St. Anselm, Letter 285 to Conon[632]). Vice is not sin but the inclination to sin. The fact that a man by temperament may be inclined to lust does not make him *ipso facto* a sinner; sin is not in the inclination but in the act. *"Nec tamen in ipso hoc peccant quia tales sunt, sed pugnae materiam ex hoc habent, ut per temperantiae virtutem de se ipsis triumphantes coronam percipiant"* (PL 178:635).[633] Evil is in the *pravus consensus*,[634] because it implies *contemptus Creatoris*,[635] despising His will (col. 636). However, he gets into errors in this area also, through ambiguity, {espousing a} Pelagian concept of freedom. {With regard to} *authority*, speaking of bishops who out of anger or love of power impose unjust penalties, he concludes that what Christ said to the apostles about the power of binding and loosing does not apply to such bishops. He was condemned because the language in which he said this could clearly be interpreted to mean that the power of binding and loosing was given *only* to the apostles, not to their successors.

*Summary*:

> Look at him [Abelard] how we will, and when full weight has been given to the impression of restlessness, vanity and lack of spiritual depth given by his career and some of his writings, Abelard remains, both as a teacher and as a thinker, one of the half-dozen most influential names in the history of medieval thought. As a master of unrivalled powers of attraction he did much to raise the intellectual level of the

---

632. *S. Anselmi Opera Omnia*, 4.204: *"De his tribus . . . illa est levior, quae in solo opere est, quia non fit nisi per ignorantiam; et tamen vitium est, quia corrigendum est"* ("Of these three [forms of pride] that is less serious which is in the act alone, because it is not done except through ignorance; nevertheless, it is a vice, which must be corrected").

633. "Nevertheless, they do not sin in this, that they are such, but from this they have matter for battle, so that triumphing over themselves through the virtue of temperance, thay may receive the crown."

634. Col. 635D, which reads: *"in consensum . . . pravum"* ("wicked consent").

635. Col. 636A ("contempt of the Creator").

schools of his day, and by his lengthy sojourns in Paris, did more than any other single teacher to ensure the primacy of the city as a centre of student life. Prince and paladin of dialecticians, he made of the "arts" a discipline of high intellectual content, besides originating a theory of epistemology that was to have a great future. It was no fault of his that the dialectic of his day was outmoded by the rediscovered Aristotle, and that theological speculation based upon it not only shocked contemporaries, but failed to attract posterity. As a theologian, he was the first to see his subject as a whole, and to conceive the possibility of a survey or synthesis for his pupils, thus taking an important part in fixing the method of teaching. Finally, and perhaps most significantly, he approached theological and ethical problems as questions that could be illuminated, explained and in part comprehended by a carefully reasoned approach, and still more by a a humane, practical attitude which took account of difficulties and of natural, human feelings, and he endeavoured to solve problems of belief and conscience not by the blow of an abstract principle, but by {a} consideration of circumstances as they are in common experience. Abelard failed to become a much-cited authority by reason of his double condemnation and the attacks of celebrated adversaries, but his ideas lingered in the minds of his disciples, and many of them came to the surface, unacknowledged, in the golden age of scholasticism. It would be difficult to instance any other theologian, accused so often and justifiably of error, who has given so much of method and matter to orthodox thought. Yet despite all this, Abelard falls short of the highest achievement. In logic and dialectic, he came too early to enjoy the complete legacy of Aristotle, and he practised a logic that was soon to fall out of favour. In theology, he lacked both the constructive power and the depth of spiritual insight that informed an Augustine, an Anselm, a Bonaventure and an Aquinas. While they enriched and deepened the exposition of the Christian mysteries, Abelard could only explain and criticize on the lower level of human wisdom and experience. On that level, and as a teacher and master who for forty years could draw a multitude with his magic wand, Abelard was unsurpassed; his only rival, in a field that bordered on his own, was the great abbot of Clairvaux. (David Knowles, *Evolution of Medieval Thought*, pp. 129ff.)

*William of St. Thierry and Abelard*: quotations from William's *Disputatio adversus Abelardum* (*PL* 180) show us that William is a better theologian, more conversant with the Bible and the Fathers than Abelard, who relies more on arguments from reason and is too impatient with what he considers to be the ambiguities of traditional theology. William, besides objecting to the obvious errors of Abelard, objects also and above all to the *spirit* and *attitude* of Abelard. It is the *mind* of Abelard that disturbs William more than the particular statements made by him. He objects to the turbulent, agitated, combative and "proud" character of Abelard's thought, because it is totally alien to the monastic spirit. Typical is William's reaction to Abelard's statements on the motives of the Incarnation:

1. He finds {that} Abelard's reasonings are *insensitive to the spiritual mystery of God's love in the Incarnation*, and repeatedly accuses Abelard of "ingratitude."[636]

2. He is not against Abelard's admiration for Plato altogether, but adds that Abelard is always trying to give Plato a Christian interpretation—while he is not equally benign towards the gospel. *Platonem cum legit, ubi eum intelligit,* sensum in eo philosophicum magnifice praedicat *et extollit, ubi vero non intelligit, vel secundum spiritum hujus mundi secus eum aliquid dicere deprehendit, in meliorem semper partem interpretari conatur.*[637] (William wishes Abelard could read the gospel *"eadem benevolentia"*[638]) (*PL*

---

636. C. 7: *"homo ingratus"* (col. 269C).

637. "When he reads Plato, where he understands him, he wonderfully proclaims and extols the philosophical meaning in him; but where he does not understand him, or when he perceives that he is saying something inadequately according to the spirit of this world, he always tries to interpret in a better sense."

638. Col. 270C, which reads: *"ea benevolentia . . . qua Platonem legit"* ("With that benevolence with which he reads Plato").

180:270). Bernard is much more blunt about Abelard's Platonism: *Ubi dum multum sudat, quomodo Platonem faciat christianum, se probat ethnicum* (*Tractatus adversus Abaelardum*, c. 4 [*PL* {182}, col. 1062]).[639]

3. Abelard *lacks {a} sense of mystery* and respect for it. {Concerning} the Redemption, {William writes}: Difficilis quaestio est, non agitanda in tumultu, sed pie et humiliter quaerenda in spiritu. *Ipsum etenim est* sacramentum . . . *justitia vero quae per fidem est in sanguine ejus*, non nisi in spiritu apparet quibusdam spiritualibus. *In quo tamen qui amat non laborat*, quia ipse ei amor intellectus est, qui sensum Christi habet (I Cor. II), *sicut Apostolus se dicit habere, qui bonum gratiae justificationis sentiendo in Christo Jesu, in semetipso etiam hoc ipsum meretur* sentire, *nequaquam illud valens* sentire *in semetipso, nisi prius pleno illuminante fidei sensu* sentiat *in Christo* (*PL* 180:272).[640] {Note here} William's favorite idea: *amor ipse est intellectus*.[641] Note the inordinate emphasis on *sensus*[642]—the idea appears five times in a few lines. William is opposing the reasoning of Abelard with the "*sensus Christi*"[643]—

---

639. "While he sweats heavily trying to make Plato a Christian, he proves himself to be a heathen" (copy text reads: "184").

640. "This is a difficult question, that should not be stirred up in a disorderly way, but sought reverently and humbly in spirit. For it is itself a mystery. . . . For the justice which there is through faith in His blood does not appear except in spirit, to certain spiritual people. In this, however, the one who loves does not labor, because for one who has the mind of Christ (1 Cor. 2), as the Apostle says he has, love itself is understanding; by experiencing the good of justifying grace in Christ Jesus, such a person merits to experience this very thing within himself, by no means able to experience it within himself unless he first experienced it in Christ by a full illuminating sense of faith."

641. The phrase also is used by William in the *Epistola ad Fratres de Monte Dei* (*PL* 184, col. 356A) and in his *Commentary on the Song of Songs* (*PL* 180, cols. 491D, 499C); see also the similar phrase "*amor ipse, notitia est*" ("Love itself is a kind of knowledge") in St. Gregory the Great, *Homily* 27.4 (*PL* 76, col. 1207A), quoted by St. Bernard, *De Diversis*, 29.1 (*PL* 183, col. 620BC).

642. "feeling"; "experience"; "mind".

643. "the mind [or experience] of Christ".

not only faith but mystical experience. (How valid is this opposition, this appeal to what is basically subjective and unverifiable?) {There are} further amplifications of this theme by William: *Videt* [!] *autem etiam in hac vita Filium hominis in regno suo quicunque, Regnum Dei effectus, et fidei intellectu et amoris affectu, et vitae effectu manens in Christo, ipsumque habens in se manentem, secundum Apostoli praeceptum, novit eum sanctificare in corde suo. Haec fides testimonium est illud fidele, sapientiam praestans parvulis, contemplans in sacramentis suis justitias Domini rectas, recta "laetificantes corda; praeceptum Domini lucidum, illuminans oculos" (Ps. 18); timorem Domini sanctum permanentem in saeculum saeculi; "judicia Domini vera justificata in Semetipsa" (ibid.), super omnia quae desiderantur desiderabilia, ut intelligantur; super omne quod dulce est dulcia, cum intelliguntur. In hac fide, cum habetur . . . nulla quaestio, nulla haesitatio, sed fruens tantum affectus* (272D).[644] *Res quippe Dei est, cujus proprium est amari, in hoc maxime dignoscitur, quod quidquid de eo est, amore maxime intelligitur* (273B).[645]

St. Bernard in his *Tractatus de Erroribus Abaelardi* (PL 182:1053ff.), the letter to Innocent II demanding condemnation of Abelard, {writes}: *Quomodo ergo fidem quis audet dicere aestimationem, nisi qui Spiritum istum nondum accepit, quive Evangelium*

---

644. "Whoever sees even in this life the Son of Man in His kingdom, having himself been made the kingdom of Christ, abiding in Christ by the understanding of the faith, and by the affect of love, and by the effect of his life, having Christ Himself abiding in him, according to the instruction of the Apostle, has learned to sanctify Him in his heart. This faith is that faithful witness providing wisdom to little ones, contemplating in His mysteries the upright justice of the Lord, 'rejoicing upright hearts; the clear precept of the Lord, illuminating the eyes' (Ps. 18); the holy fear of the Lord, abiding for ever and ever; 'the true judgements of the Lord, justified in themselves' (*ibid*.), desirable above all things that are desired, so that they may be understood; sweet above all that is sweet when they are understood. In this faith, when He is possessed . . . there is in it no question, no hesitation, but only love that enjoys" (text reads: ". . . *regnum Christi effectus*, . . . *nulla in ea quaestio* . . .").

645. "Certainly this matter is of God, whose essence is to be loved; this is recognized most particularly in this, that whatever is from Him is understood above all by love."

*aut ignoret, aut fabulam putet?* (1061).[646] Academicorum *sint istae aestimationes quorum est dubitare de omnibus, scire nihil* (1062).[647] (This is simply a condemnation of {Abelard taken from} William of St. Thierry's *Disputatio,* cap. 1 [col. {250}].[648]) In attacking Abelard's doctrine on the Redemption he is much more violent than William and pushes the *ad personam* argument to the limit. William says Abelard lacks a spiritual sense of the Christian mysteries. Bernard says Abelard is in the power of the devil, "the very power which he denies!"[649] Non potes gratias agere cum redemptis, qui redemptus non es [!!]. *Nam si redemptus esses, Redemptorem agnosceres, et non negares redemptionem. Nec quaerit redimi, qui se nescit captivum* (1064).[650] However, Bernard accumulates conclusive scriptural arguments that man was *liberated* by the redeeming death of Christ.[651]

*Conclusion*: St. Bernard says that this power of the devil over men was *just*—i.e., a *right*—he returns to the ancient position (col. 1065) which has been abandoned by the Church (*Dictionnaire*

---

646. "How then does someone dare to say [faith is] an opinion, unless he is one who has not yet received the Spirit, or either does not know the Gospel or considers it a fable?"

647. "Those are the opinions of the Academicians, to whom it belongs to doubt about everything, to know nothing."

648. "*opiniones academicorum sint aestimationes istae, quorum sententia est nihil credere, nihil scire, sed omnia aestimare*" ("those opinions are the attitudes of the academicians, whose stance is to believe nothing, to know nothing, but to have an opinion about everything") (copy text reads: "249").

649. "*Non enim vis ut diabolus in hominem habeat, vel habuerit potestatem. . . . Quod minime negares et tu, si non esses sub manu inimici*" (cols. 1063D–1064A) ("You do not wish that the devil has, or has had, power over man. . . . Even you would scarcely deny this, if you were not under the hand of the enemy").

650. "You who are not redeemed cannot give thanks with the redeemed. For if you had been redeemed, you would recognize your Redeemer and would not deny the redemption. He who does not know that he is a captive does not seek to be redeemed."

651. He cites Ps. 106[107]:2–3, 6 (glossed by John 11:51-52 and Job 40:18); 2 Tim. 2:26; John 14:30; Luke 11:21; Matt. 12:29; Luke 22:53; Col. 1:13; John 19:11 (cols. 1064A–1065A).

*de Théologie Catholique*, vol. 13, col. 1946).[652] *Discat ergo [Abelard] diabolum non solum potestatem,* sed et justam *habuisse in homines. . . . Caeterum etsi justam dicimus diaboli potestatem, non tamen et voluntatem. . . . Hoc ergo* diaboli quoddam in hominem jus, etsi non jure acquisitum, sed nequiter usurpatum; juste tamen permissum.[653] However, Bernard tries to modify his declaration slightly: *Sic itaque homo juste captivus tenebatur, ut tamen nec in homine, nec in diabolo illa esset justitia, sed in Deo* (1065)[654]—a rather ambiguous position. What precisely does it mean? simply that God gave the devil power over man, for his punishment (i.e., he is, as Abelard says, merely a jailer[655]); does it follow that the devil had *rights* over man? St. Thomas settles the question by distinctions (*Summa*, III, q. 49, a. 2[656])—{a} last reminiscence of the old doctrine dying out: ad. 1: [{Diabolus}] iuste permittebatur *nocere hominibus;*[657] ad. 2, 3: the *objective* power of the Passion was {the} only protection against the devil, who still has power *"semper tamen per passionem Christi est paratum hominibus remedium se habendi contra nequitias daemonum, etiam tempore Antichristi"* (ad. 3).[658]

---

652. J. Rivière, "Redemption," *Dictionnaire de Théologie Catholique*, 15 vols. (Paris: Letouzey et Ané, 1908–1950).

653. "Let him learn, then, that the devil has had not only power, but a just power, over men. . . . And yet, even if we call the power of the devil just, still we do not also call his will so. . . . Therefore, this sort of right of the devil over man, even if not acquired by right but wickedly usurped, has nevertheless been justly permitted."

654. "Thus man was justly held captive, so that there might be that justice, neither in man nor in the devil, but in God."

655. *"carcerarius"* (col. 1063A).

656. *Sancti Thomae Aquinatis Doctoris Angelici Ordinis Praedicatorum Opera Omnia, secundum Impressionem Petri Fiaccadori Parmae 1852–1873 Photolithographice Reimpressa*, 25 vols. (New York: Misurgia, 1948), 4:217–18.

657. Aquinas, *Opera Omnia*, 4.218 ("The devil was justly permitted to harm humans") (copy text reads: *"diabolum"*).

658. Aquinas, *Opera Omnia*, 4.218, which reads: ". . . *se tuendi contra* . . ." ("However, through the Passion of Christ a remedy has always been prepared for humans for guarding against the evil deeds of the demons, even in the time of Antichrist").

{In} 1140, {at the} Synod of Sens, Abelard {was} condemned. He was denounced by William of St. Thierry (*PL* 182, col. 531[659]). He would have settled peacefully but was pushed into debate by his friend Arnold of Brescia (a Roman revolutionary). Instead of debating with him, Bernard meets privately with the bishops beforehand and arranges to have Abelard arraigned. The debate does not take place; instead Abelard finds himself on trial for heresy, with the bishops sitting in judgement on him. Feeling that they have already decided against him, and claiming that the synod did not have the proper authority, Abelard appealed to Rome. However, Bernard and the bishops were very energetic in the court of Rome, and before Abelard could manage to get a hearing, he was condemned as a heretic and silenced by Innocent II. He submits and retires to Cluny (see *Fidei Confessio* [*PL* 178][660]). ({As an} interesting note {on} ecclesiastical censorship at {the} time of Abelard, it was the condemnation of Abelard at Sens that gave impetus to repressive censorship, denunciation of books, and their solemn condemnation, as a regular procedure: see {the} article by G. B. Flahiff: "Ecclesiastical Censorship of Books in the Twelfth Century" in *Mediaeval Studies*, IV [1942][661]).

---

659. *Epistola* 326, addressed to St. Bernard and Bishop Godfrey, and included among the letters of Bernard (summarized but not translated in *Letters*, 314, following a helpful summary of the controversy [312–14]).

660. *Epistola* 17 (cols. 375C–378A).

661. G. B. Flahiff, "Ecclesiastical Censorship of Books in the Twelfth Century," *Mediaeval Studies* 4 (1942): 1–22, points out that the "case of Abelard, the first one in the twelfth century and the most resounding one throughout its length, is especially significant for it occupies historically a key-position in regard to the attitude adopted towards heretical teaching" (2), and that opposition to Abelard, which began more with regard to his person than to his doctrine but which gradually came to center both on his dialectical method and its doctrinal results, led to "his two condemnations, at Soissons in 1121 and at Sens in 1140" (3); according to Abelard himself, at Soissons (mislabeled Sens in the text), "the legate was persuaded to condemn the book [on the Trinity] and order it to be burned by the author's own hand, not because of proven error but solely, it is said, because he had taught this book publicly and allowed copies to be made without it being approved by the Pope or by the Church" (4), though Flahiff questions whether this

*The Last Days and Death of Abelard*: {see the} Letter of Peter the Venerable (IV, *Ep*. 28 [*PL* 189, col. 347ff.]) to Heloise:

1. Concerning Heloise herself, Peter the Venerable praises her learning, first secular, then her finding of the "true philosophy"[662] in her conversion to religion. As {a} nun, "You have made a far better exchange of studies. You have traded logic for the Gospel, physics for the Apostle, Plato for Christ, the academy for the cloister. You have done this as a wholly philosophical woman [*Tota jam et vere philosophica elegisti*]. Having conquered your enemies you have snatched from them the treasure of Egypt, and passing through the desert of this exile you have built for God a precious tabernacle in your heart" (col. 348).[663] As abbess, she is a *discipula veritatis*[664] and at the same time *magistra humilitatis*.[665] He numbers her among the "fighting women"[666] praised by the Old Testament (Deborah, etc.). He concludes: "Would that our Cluny had acquired you, would that the joyous prison of Marcigny

---

account, which suggests that official ecclesiastical approval of a text was required before lecturing from it, was a general norm or a unique case as proposed by Abelard's opponents; in the aftermath of Sens, the pope ordered Abelard's "books to be burned wherever they were to be found," and "the whole procedure in this case turned out to be one exclusively of repressive censorship of books and followed the pattern that became standard. Certain writings, without being sought out by ecclesiastical authorities, are cited to them nevertheless as suspect of heresy; they are officially, sometimes even solemnly, examined and condemned for their false teaching; whereupon the pope confirms the sentence, once more on the evidence of the books themselves, and orders these to be burned in all their existing copies" (5).

662. "*vere philosophica*" (col. 348A).

663. "*longe in melius disciplinarum studia commutasti, et pro logica Evangelium, pro physica apostolum, pro Platone Christum, pro academia claustrum, tota jam et vere philosophica mulier, elegisti. Eripuisti victis spolia hostibus, et thesauris Aegyptiacis per hujus peregrinationis desertum transiens, pretiosum in corde tuo tabernaculum Deo erexisti.*"

664. Col. 349A ("a disciple of truth").

665. Col. 349A ("a teacher of humility").

666. *Ductrices . . . exercitus Domini*" (col. 349BC) ("leaders of the army of the Lord").

[*jucundus Marcinianensis carcer*] had imprisoned you with the other handmaids of Christ who there await the freedom of heaven" (350).[667] (N.B. there were recluses at Marcigny. In the *Life of Christina of Markyate* [Talbot, p. 126[668]] it is said that they wanted the English recluse to transfer to Marcigny to add glory to that place; note {the} use of "*carcer*" in {the} *Life of Christina*.[669])

2. However, if Cluny has not gained Heloise, it has Abelard. He is to Cluny a treasure more precious than any gold or precious stone. Peter refers to Abelard as "*illo tuo saepe ac semper cum honore nominando, servo ac vere Christi philosopho magistro Petro.*"[670] Peter praises the sanctity of Abelard in his last days: *Cujus sanctae, humili ac devotae inter nos conversationi*,[671] especially his humility. He is another Martin, another Germanus. He was outstanding for his poverty and simplicity in clothing, food, etc. {as well as} his love of reading and prayer. Though silenced, he received permission to teach at Cluny and taught the brethren. *Mens ejus, lingua ejus, opus ejus, semper divina, semper philosophica, semper eruditoria meditabatur, docebat, fatebatur.*[672] He became ill {and} was

---

667. "*Utinam te Cluniacus nostra habuisset! utinam te jucundus Marciniaci carcer, cum caeteris Christi ancillis libertatem inde coelestem exspectantibus inclusisset!*"

668. *The Life of Christina of Markyate, a Twelfth-century Recluse*, ed. and trans. C. H. Talbot (Oxford: Clarendon Press, 1959); Merton mentions that he is reading this work and that he "find[s] it marvelous" in a March 14, 1964, journal entry (Thomas Merton, *Dancing in the Water of Life: Seeking Peace in the Hermitage. Journals*, vol. 5, *1963–1965*, ed. Robert E. Daggy [San Francisco: HarperCollins, 1997], 90).

669. "*In hoc ergo carcere Rogerus ovantem sociam posuit*" ("In this prison Roger placed his happy companion") (*Life of Christina*, 102/103).

670. Col. 350C, which reads: "*de illo tuo, de illo, inquam, saepe . . .*" ("of him who was yours, of him, I say, to be called often and always with honor the servant and truly the philosopher of Christ, Master Peter").

671. Col. 350CD ("whose holy, humble and devout conduct among us").

672. Col. 351B ("His mind always contemplated what was divine, his tongue always taught what was philosophical, his work always witnessed to what was scholarly").

sent to {the} Priory of St. Marcel at Châlons. There Christ came and found him *"vere vigilantem"* (col. 352)[673] *et ad aeternas nuptias, non ut fatuam, sed ut sapientem virginem evocavit.*[674] He received the last sacraments with great devotion, and later his body is taken to the Paraclete. The document absolving Abelard of formal heresy is sent by Peter the Venerable and suspended on his tomb. Finally Peter will try to obtain a prebend for their child Astrolabe, in Paris [*Letters*, IV.21 and 22 [col. 429][675]).

*Monastic Doctrine of Abelard (Letter* VIII [*PL* 178:258ff.[676]]):

{In his} introduction he sums up the monastic life—*summa religionis monasticae*[677]—{as} "To live continently and without property and to observe silence above all" (*silentio maxime studere*) ({258}).[678] (Much is said about obedience later; obedience is implied here under interior chastity and poverty. Discuss this!) Chastity of body {means} no lascivious act or word; of soul {means} (a) no consent to impurity; (b) no pride. {The} context shows that this formula means carrying the cross of Christ (cf. {the} Cistercians: *formula perfectae paenitentiae*[679]). The spirit of chastity implies also fidelity to one's total dedication to God. For instance he praises the *casta voluntas*[680] of a recluse who was so devoted to silence that she never received visitors and would not even make an exception for St. Martin when he wished to visit

---

673. "truly keeping watch."

674. Col. 352A, which reads: *"ad aeternitatis nuptias . . ."* ("and He called him to the wedding of eternity, not as a foolish but as a wise virgin").

675. The first (cols. 427B–428A) is a letter from Heloise to Peter the Venerable that mentions both the document and the request for Astrolabe; the second (cols. 428A–429A) is Peter's reply.

676. Cols. 255D–326A.

677. Col. 258A, which reads: *"religionis monasticae summam"* ("a summary of monastic religious life").

678. *"continenter, et sine proprietate vivatur, ac silentio maxime studeatur"* (col. 258A; copy text reads: "259").

679. "formula of perfect penitence" (*Exordium Magnum*, 1.1 [*PL* 185, col. 997B]).

680. Col. 265A, which reads: *"castam . . . voluntatem"* ("chaste will").

her (col. 265; cf. {the} quote from St. Jerome, Ep. 51;[681] the example of this recluse is also cited by St. Ailred, *De Institutione Inclusarum*, n. 6 [Sources Chrétiennes, p. 56][682]). Abelard adds: *Haec revera de contemplationis suae lectulo surgere dedignata vel verita, pulsanti ad ostium amico parata erat dicere: "Lavi pedes meos, quomodo inquinabo illos?"* (col. 265).[683] {With regard to} poverty, "Having left all things, we follow the naked Christ in nakedness"[684] (*nudum Christum nudi sequimur* [Jerome[685]]) when we renounce earthly possessions, the love of our carnal relatives, our own will. (Here obedience is included as a form of interior poverty and indeed as a certain perfection of the spirit of poverty.) *Ut non nostro vivamus arbitrio, sed praelati nostri regamur imperio, et ei qui nobis loco Christi praesidet tanquam Christo penitus pro Christo subjiciamur.*[686] Note {that} this is based on traditional scriptural texts: Luke 10:16 (he who hears you hears Me); Luke 14:26 (to hate one's own soul is to refuse to follow our own will); Luke 9:23 (If any man would come after Me let him take up his cross); John 6:38 (I did not come to do My own will). Commenting on these texts, {he writes}: *terrena delectatio*[687] consists essentially in fulfilling our own will even if we have to labor and struggle to do it. Hence renouncement of earthly joy is equivalent to renouncing our own will. The heart

---

681. The story is originally told by Sulpicius Severus in his *Dialogues*, 2.12 (*PL* 20, cols. 209C–210B), and repeated not by Jerome himself but by a Pseudo-Jerome (*Epistola* 42.10 [*PL* 30, cols. 300D–301A]).

682. Aelred de Rievaulx, *La Vie de Recluse; La Prière Pastorale*, ed. and trans. Charles Dumont, SC 76 (Paris: Editions du Cerf, 1961), Part 1, n. 6.

683. "Having in fact scorned or feared to arise from the bed of her contemplation, this woman was prepared to say to a friend knocking at the door: 'I have washed my feet, how shall I defile them?' (Cant. 5:3)."

684. "*relictis omnibus nudum Christum nudi sequimur*" (col. 258C).

685. Jerome, *Epistola* 125 (*PL* 22, col. 1085).

686. Col. 258C ("so that we may live not according to our own will but may be ruled by the command of our superior, and may be completely subjected, as to Christ, for the sake of Christ, to the one who presides over us in the place of Christ").

687. Col. 259B ("earthly enjoyment").

of the matter {is to} renounce {one's} appetite for *domination* in order to be truly free. "What else is bearing the cross but to allow things to be done against our own will?"[688] Later, speaking of obedience to {the} deaconess after she has given a decision at a council meeting, even if one's own views seem better, Abelard quotes Augustine: "He sins much who disobeys his prelate in anything, even though he may choose something better than is commanded him" (283).[689] Abelard comments: "*Multo quippe melius est nobis* bene facere, *quam* bonum facere."[690] *Bene fit quod per obedientiam fit, etiamsi quod fit bonum esse minime videatur* (283).[691] (The last part is excessive! But {the} context corrects it.) For superiors, however, he insists on reasonable commands: *reason must always be preferred to custom,* if they conflict. *Numquam consuetudo rationi praeponatur, nec unquam aliquid defendatur, quia sit consuetudo, sed quia ratio; nec quia sit usitatum, sed quia bonum; et tanto libentius excipiatur, quanto melius apparebit* (284).[692] To act otherwise is to be a Judaizer. Christ said not "I am Custom" but "I am Truth"[693] (cf. Tertullian, Augustine, etc.—see {the} quotes from Augustine on this point [284][694]). To renounce our-

---

688. "*Aut quid est aliud crucem ferre . . . nisi contra voluntatem nostram aliquid fieri*" (col. 259B).

689. "*Multum peccat qui inobediens est suis praelatis in aliquo, si vel meliora eligat quam ea quae sibi jubentur*" (Abelard references the *Confessions*, but this sentence does not appear there).

690. "It is certainly much better for us to do well than to do good."

691. Col. 284A, which reads: "*Bene vero fit quidquid per obedientiam fit . . .*" ("Whatever is done through obedience is truly done well, even if what is done seems to be least good").

692. "Let custom never be preferred to reason, and never let something be defended because it is a custom, but because it is reasonable, nor because it is familiar, but because it is good; and it may be accepted the more freely, the more it appears better."

693. "*Ego sum, inquit,* Veritas (Joan. xiv, 6). *Non dixit: Ego sum consuetudo.*"

694. Augustine cites Cyprian and declares that preferring custom to truth is either hostile to other people or ungrateful to God; Abelard notes the example of Peter yielding to Paul, who was proclaiming the truth, and

selves and all ambition is to renounce all proprietorship, interior as well as exterior, and embrace the common life of the apostles ({he} refers to Acts 4:32[695]).

{With respect to} *silence*, he emphasizes the word *silentium studere* (*Rule* of St. Benedict, chap. {42}[696]). It is more than just *silentium habere*.[697] *Studere* {is} *vehemens applicatio animi—nulla studiose agimus nisi* volentes vel intenti (260).[698] (Comment!) He quotes the story of St. Anthony and the old man who came with the talkative hermits in the boat. "They are good but they leave the stable door open and anyone can come in and steal the donkey."[699] {The} donkey {is the} mind, which should be "tied to the manger of the Lord and eat from it."[700] *Sacrae se meditationis in eo quadam ruminatione reficiens.* {. . .} Cogitatione Deo loquimur sicut verbis hominibus (260).[701] N.B. Abelard foresees that the nuns will communicate by signs in great silence, but otherwise by necessary words.

*Solitude*: besides his teaching on silence, Abelard has a thoroughly traditional doctrine on solitude. The usual Scripture texts

---

quotes from the fourth book of Augustine's *De Baptismo*, which rejects an appeal to custom against reason and truth and what has been revealed by the Holy Spirit.

695. Col. 259C.

696. McCann, 100 ("to be diligent in silence") (chapter number left blank in text).

697. "*Plus quippe esse constat silentio studere quam silentium habere*" ("It certainly consists more in being devoted to silence than in keeping silence").

698. Text reads: "*Est enim studium vehemens applicatio animi ad aliquid gerendum. Multa vero negligenter agimus vel inviti, sed nulla studiose nisi volentes vel intenti*" ("For study is the the intense focus of the mind on doing something. We do many things negligently or unwillingly, but we do nothing studiously unless we are willing and attentive").

699. "*Boni sunt siquidem, sed habitatio eorum non habet januam* [does not have a door]. *Quicunque vult, intrat in stabulum, et solvit asinum*" (*Verba Seniorum*, Book 4, c. 1 [*De Continentia*] [*PL* 73, col. 864D]).

700. "*Quasi enim ad praesepe Domini anima nostra ligatur.*"

701. "refreshing itself there by some ruminating on sacred reflection. . . . We speak to God by reflection as we do to men by words."

are brought forward: Christ in the desert (col. 262); God leading the Chosen People into the desert. One can serve Him with all purity only in the desert. *Patenter docuit quantam ejus singularitas solitudinem pro nobis amet, cui purius in ea vacare possumus* (262).[702] The classical term *Deo vacare*[703] comes in several times. He alleges the example of the early Desert Fathers. *Tumultum saeculi et plenum tentationibus mundum fugientes,* ad quietem solitudinis [another traditional term] lectulum suae contemplationis [*id.*] *contulerunt, ut videlicet* Deo possent sincerius vacare (262).[704] He returns to the *lectulum contemplationis* and the *lectulum sponsae* in column 305. He goes back to the sons of the Prophets whom Jerome took to be the first monks (Jerome, *Ep.* 4:13[705]); these ad solitudinis secretum [another traditional term] *se transtulerunt, praeter fluenta Jordanis casulas suas constitutentes*[706] (Qumran?). Hence, though "the place does not sanctify"[707] a monk, solitude has very definite reasons to support it: *Multas tamen praebet opportunitates ad religionem facilius observandam; multa religionis auxilia ex eo consistunt* (262).[708] Further "tropes" {are provided}:

702. "He clearly taught how much solitude His withdrawal cherishes for us, in which we are able to devote ourselves more purely to Him."

703. "to be free for God, to be occupied with God alone."

704. "Fleeing the tumult of the age and a world full of temptations, they carried the bed of their contemplation to the quiet of solitude, so that they could more sincerely devote themselves to God."

705. "*nostri duces filii Prophetarum, qui habitabant in agris et solitudinibus, et faciebant sibi tabernacula prope fluenta Jordanis*" ("our guides are the sons of the prophets, who used to dwell in the fields and solitary places, and to pitch their tents near the streams of the Jordan") (*Ep.* 58.5, to Paulinus [*PL* 22, col. 583]).

706. "They brought themselves to the secret of solitude, setting up their huts beyond the stream of the Jordan."

707. "*Quamvis locus non salvet*" (col. 262A).

708. Text reads: ". . . *observandam, et tutius muniendam* [and more safely protected]. . . . *auxilia vel impedimenta* [or hindrances] . . ." ("nevertheless it provides many opportunities for observing religious life more easily . . . and many aids to religious observance depend on it").

the monk is the "wild ass"—*onager* (cf. Gregory, *Moralia in Job*, on Job 39:5[709]); the "wild ass is the monk who, freed from the bonds of secular life, has gone over to the tranquil liberty of the solitary life" (262)[710]—i.e., he roams freely in the desert and is not tamed by man. He contrasts the quite solitary life of the monk with the busy life of the priest in towns, again taking the same line as Jerome (*Ep.* {14}).[711] The monk stands before God and is hidden from men: *Et nos ergo, ut coram Domino stare, et ejus obsequio parati magis valeamus assistere, tabernacula nobis erigamus in solitudine, ne lectulum nostrae quietis frequentia hominum concutiat, quietem turbet, ingerat tentationes, mentem a sancto evellat proposito* (263).[712] This is supported by classic stories: Arsenius—*fuge, tace, quiesce* (263).[713] A recluse who refuses to see St. Martin is praised (264—see above). {In} contrast, {there is} criticism of the monks of the twelfth century, who would build big guest houses "to draw men to them";[714] who rejoice in the presence of bishops and their court, and build special accommodations for them. Whole towns

709. *PL* 25, col. 770D.

710. "*Onager . . . monachus est, qui saecularium rerum vinculis absolutus ad tranquillam vitae solitariae libertatem se contulit.*"

711. In his letter on monastic renunciation to Heliodorus, n. 8 (*PL* 22, cols. 352–53), Jerome contrasts the vocation of the monk with that of the priest, declaring that his advice to Heliodorus to flee into solitude is not a denigration of the clergy, whose pastoral duties are quite different from those of the monk (copy text reads: "15").

712. "Therefore, so that we may be able to stand in the presence of the Lord and be better prepared to show allegiance to Him, let us set up tents for ourselves in solitude, lest the throngs of men jostle the bed of our rest, disturb our quiet, bring on temptations, and draw the mind away from its holy profession."

713. *PL* 73, col. 858AB; see Thomas Merton, *The Wisdom of the Desert: Sayings from the Desert Fathers of the Fourth Century* (New York: New Directions, 1960), 29 (n. xii), where Merton translates "*Fuge, tace, quiesce*" as "fly, be silent, rest in prayer."

714. "*saeculi potentes . . . asciscunt*" ("they draw in the powerful of the age").

have arisen around the monasteries: *et sic ad saeculum redierunt, imo ad se traxerunt saeculum* (265).⁷¹⁵ Hence {they have} much labor and trouble, which comes paradoxically from the desire for an easier life. The monastic life is "harder" in proportion as it becomes "easier." It becomes a servitude binding them to "ecclesiastical as well as secular powers." *Dum otiose appetunt vivere, et de alieno victitare labore, ipsum quoque monachi, hoc est solitarii nomen pariter amiserunt et vitam* (265).⁷¹⁶ Thus they are *miseriis maximis implicati*.⁷¹⁷ He attacks the wandering monks who cannot bear even the relaxed regularity of the cloister and wander about in twos and threes, or alone ({this is the} language of St. Benedict's *Rule*⁷¹⁸) *sine aliqua observatione regulae victitantes,* TANTO SAECULARIBUS DETERIORES *sunt hominibus, quanto a* propositione *sua amplius apostatantur* (265).⁷¹⁹ {He notes} the irony of the fact that the places where they live are called "obediences."⁷²⁰ {In} conclusion, solitude {is} all the more necessary for those who are weak. It is a protection.

*Obedience*: {he stresses} its necessity: *sicut in castris saeculi, ita et in castris Domini*.⁷²¹ We will naturally be interested in Abelard's concept of obedience since he has an established reputation as a rebel. In point of fact, he has the traditional *concept* of obedience:

1. There is one superioress at the Paraclete: *una omnibus praeest* matrona (266).⁷²² He argues from Scripture, classical lit-

---

715. "and so they have returned to the world, or rather have drawn the world to themselves."

716. Text reads: ". . . *appeterent* . . ." ("while they seek to live at leisure and to subsist from the labor of others, they have lost the very name of monk, that is, of a solitary, and likewise the life").

717. Col. 265C, which reads: "*se miseriis maximis implicantes*" ("entangling themselves in the greatest miseries").

718. "*bini aut terni aut certe singuli*" (*Rule*, chap. 1 [McCann, 14]).

719. "Living without any observance of a rule, they are that much worse than worldly men the more they are unfaithful to their profession."

720. Col. 265D.

721. Col. 266B ("As in the camp of the world, so also in the camp of the Lord").

722. Text reads: ". . . *praesit* . . ." ("one matron presides over all").

erature, lives of saints and St. Jerome that there should be one superior, to avoid confusion and division: *in nave unus gubernator* (Jerome).[723]

2. He emphasizes the ascetic and educational function of monastic obedience: *Nulla ars sine magistro discitur* (Jerome).[724]

3. He describes obedience correctly: *una matrona, ad cujus considerationem et arbitrium omnes reliquae omnia operentur*.[725] (Note {the} use of the word *matrona*, implying {a} married woman.) {The} qualities of obedience {entail that} no one is to resist her exteriorly; no one is to murmur interiorly against her commands (266). {The} *matrona* {is} an elderly married woman—see her place in sponsoring *recluses* ({cf. the} rite of reclusion according to Busch[726]—fifteenth century). It can be said that his notion of obedience is quite correct, but that at this point he does not go into the spirituality of obedience. However, he does speak of the structure of the community and the different officers. At the head is the *matrona* (also called *diaconissa* and *abbatissa*[727]). Under her command are the *officiales*:[728] portress, cellaress, *vestiaria*,[729] infirmarian, chantress, sacristan. The rest who have no special job are simply called *claustrales*.[730] Finally there are the *conversae: saeculo*

723. Col. 267B ("in a ship there is one pilot") (Jerome, *Epistola* 125 to Rusticus [*PL* 22, col. 1080]).

724. Col. 267B, which reads: "*Nulla . . . ars absque . . .*" ("No art is learned without a master") (*PL* 22, col. 1080).

725. Col. 266BC, which reads: ". . . *considerationem atque arbitrium . . .*" ("one matron, according to whose decision and judgement all the others are to carry out everything").

726. See Francis D. S. Darwin, *The English Mediaeval Recluse* (London: SPCK, 1944), 72, which describes a service of enclosure for a new recluse in which a "devout and wealthy matron" acts as "a sort of sponsor"; the source is the *De Reformatione Monasteriorum*, ed. Karl Grube (Halle: Otto Hendel, 1886), 2.42, of Jan Busch (d. ca. 1480), an Augustinian canon who had charge of three anchoresses in Germany.

727. "*diaconissam, quam nunc abbatissam nominant*" (col. 267D) ("the deaconess, whom now they call the abbess").

728. Col. 267D.

729. Col. 267D ("wardrobe mistress").

730. Col. 267D.

*renuntiantes, obsequio monialium se dicarunt, habitu quodam religioso, non tamen monastico.*[731] The *claustrales* are like the knights in an army, the *conversae* like infantry—*pedites* (268). As to the *diaconissa*, he takes rules from St. Paul on widows (1 Tim. 5:3-11, etc.), {and} emphasizes that she should have had experience of marriage (*unius viri uxor*[732]) and should be of mature years (268). It is desirable that she be educated but not essential, as she must teach by example above all (269). He quotes from {the} Desert Fathers on the relative unimportance of learning, if virtue and example are present (269). {He stresses the} importance of virtue in the superior, and not election according to social prestige (269). He goes on for several columns on this subject, lest the superior be living as a noble, apart from the community and in constant contact with the nobility. {This was} a real abuse in {the} Middle Ages. {He} wants monasteries of nuns to be provided for and cared for by neighboring monasteries of men, rather than by seculars (277, 278). He goes into great detail about the work of the various officers, {which is} historically interesting (col. 277ff.). For example, {he writes of} the *chantress*: "She provides for the choral functions and sets in order the divine offices, and she shall be charged with teaching what is necessary to know about singing and reading, *also what is needed for writing and dictating*. Let her have care of the common box of books [*armarium*], give out the books and take them back, have care for the work of copying books. She shall order the sitting in choir and provide seats, and will appoint those who are to sing and read. On Saturdays she will draw up a list to be read in chapter for the weekly officers."[733] (Hence she

---

731. Cols. 267D–268A, which reads: "*Conversae, autem, quae etiam saeculo* . . ." ("the lay sisters, who have also renounced the world, dedicate themselves to service of the nuns, in a sort of religious, though not monastic, habit").

732. Col. 268A ("a wife to one man").

733. "*Cantrix toti choro providebit, et divina disponet officia, et de doctrina cantandi vel legendi magisterium habebit, et de eis quae ad scribendum pertinent vel dictandum. Armarium quoque librorum custodiet, et ipsos inde tradet atque suscipiet, et de ipsis scribendis vel aptandis curam suscipiet, vel sollicita erit. Ipsa ordinabit quomodo sedeatur in choro, et sedes dabit, et a quibus legendum sit vel*

must be literate.) *Ipsa etiam post diaconissam toti disciplinae providebit* (278).[734] {Concerning} the *infirmarian*, {he writes that} great care is to be taken of the sick both in body and soul. As to the body, Abelard lays down {the} axiom: *infirmis non est lex posita*.[735] {The sick are to have} baths, meat, etc., care in medicines, bleeding and so on (278). For the soul, the infirmarian must dispose things so that the sick, *and especially the dying, may be preserved from occasions of sin*, and especially care is to be taken about silence, lest sins of the tongue occur carelessly. His dispositions regarding death and burial show tender concern and respect for the human person (279). {There is} a beautiful section on the *vestiarian*, quoting and applying to her Proverbs 31[736] (the *mulier fortis*[737]). {Note the} historical interest of this section: she is in charge of sheep-shearing, tanning leather, and *even looks after the novices until they are* received into the community (279). {Likewise note the} historical interest of all that is said about the *cellaress*, *portress*, etc. {The} portress is in charge not only of watching the door, admitting only those who should be admitted {and} dealing with the poor, but also "keeping rumors out"[738] of the convent. But if she hears news that ought to be known, she discreetly conveys it to the deaconess (280). Great poverty and simplicity are prescribed for the *oratory* (281); {he is} almost Cistercian in simplicity here. No statues {are} allowed, {only a} simple cross with {an} image of {the} Savior painted on it. He is especially solicitous for the nuns to get adequate sleep, and allows them to get back to rest after vigils if necessary, especially in summer. "*Maxime namque somnus lassatam recreat naturam*, et patientem

---

*cantandum providebit, et inscriptionem component Sabbatis recitandam in capitulo, ubi omnes hebdomadariae describentur*" (cols. 277D–268A).

734. "She herself, after the deaconess, will oversee the whole system of discipline."

735. Col. 278B ("The law was not put in place for the sick").

736. "*Quaesivit lanam et linum, et operata est consilio manuum suarum*" (col. 279C) ("She hath sought wool and flax, and hath wrought by the counsel of her hands" [Prov. 31:13]).

737. "strong woman" (Prov. 31:10).

738. "*verum etiam rumores penitus excludere*" (col. 280C).

operis reddit, et sobriam conservet et alacrem [sc. *monialem*]" (282).⁷³⁹ {There are} several columns denouncing wine (288–92). His conclusion {is that the} *sponsa Christi vinum fugiat pro veneno* (291).⁷⁴⁰ In fact, he goes on with more columns generally concerned with abstinence, but it is still wine he has in mind, and he legislates as to how little wine they may have (in col. 296). {He} permits it for the sick. In community the wine that is drunk must be at least one-fourth diluted with water (296). He permits meat once a day (299) but encourages abstinence and fasting of particular nuns, with {the} blessing of obedience. {He discourses} on the reading of Scripture (306ff.) {and} reproves the training of nuns so that they only sing correctly and pronounce words correctly in choir without understanding what they mean. They only "bleat like sheep" (308)⁷⁴¹ but derive no spiritual nourishment from their office. {He} reproves monastic formation of the time as "education of the tongue and not of the heart" (311).⁷⁴²

*St. Bernard's Attitude to {the} Intellectual Life*:

1. It was not purely hostile and negative. He favored scholars and encouraged them—v.g., John of Salisbury, Robert Pullen. He was a close friend of Hugh of St. Victor and William of Champeaux. He favored and encouraged Peter Lombard. He did not attack philosophy and theology as *such*, but he feared modern movements and he feared what seemed to go with them.

2. Bernard strongly disliked scholastic dispute and felt a great repugnance for the arguments of the great doctors, surrounded as they were by the clamor and applause of factions. All this was using science for personal glory and ambition, while

---

739. "For sleep refreshes weary nature the most, gives it back the ability to endure work, and keeps it sober and alert" (Merton suggests that the object of the last two verbs is "nun" understood, but it is more likely still "*naturam*").

740. "Let the bride of Christ avoid wine like poison" (Jerome, *Epistola* 22 [*PL* 22, col. 399]).

741. "*quasi ovium balatus.*"

742. "*nec cor instruere, sed linguam student.*"

Bernard thought knowledge should bear fruit in charity and union with God (hence his agreement with the Victorines).

3. He feared above all the spirit of libertinism and revolution, which deliberately attacked Church authority. He especially feared Abelard.

*The Sermo de Conversione*: when Bernard was in Paris in 1140, the bishop unexpectedly asked him to preach a sermon to the students. Confronted by this unusual audience, vividly aware of the strange conditions in which they lived—the independence, libertinage, atmosphere of vice—he at first refused, but then consented to speak to them. It is an earnest plea that they abandon the occasions of sin in which they lived. However, the special note of urgency in the sermon comes not merely from the fact that student life in general was a bit wild, but because this was the year of Bernard's conflict with Abelard—the Council of Sens was held at Pentecost {in} 1140. This sermon was in part, then, a general protest against the influence of Abelard and against all that Abelard stood for. It is not known whether the sermon was given before or after the council, and there is nothing in it that deals directly with dogmatic errors. The sermon is directed rather at the atmosphere of moral licence which accompanied the intellectual revolution of the twelfth century. Among those who heard the sermon were Peter Lombard and Geoffrey of Auxerre, who was then a pupil of Abelard, and followed St. Bernard to Clairvaux with many others. Twenty-three in all entered Clairvaux and made their profession the following year.

*The Theme of the Sermon*: St. Bernard's purpose is to counteract sterile intellectualism, a life that is lived entirely in the mind, and has little effect in changing one's morals. We are called to contemplate and love and be united with the Truth, but this involves our whole being, our whole person; {it} is a spiritualization of our whole life, until everything is penetrated and possessed by truth. Furthermore, Truth is not merely an abstraction but a Person—the Incarnate Word. To enter into this intimate and spiritual communion with the Truth of God in Christ, it is not sufficient to spend one's whole life in "studying without ever learning anything,"[743] or wasting one's time and gifts in sterile dialectics: what is demanded is a *metanoia*, a conversion, a change of heart—a change that takes place deep in one's being and reorientates the whole course of one's life—away from the world, towards the Kingdom of God. This is evident from the fact that the intellectuals St. Bernard was addressing lived disedifying lives, while talking about the Truth.

This sermon falls into two halves, plus a conclusion:

1. Chapters 1–9,[744] in which conversion itself is described and discussed. How does it take place? What are the struggles involved? How are the problems solved? What are the chief helps?

2. Chapters 10–18:[745] once the soul is determined to lead a new life, how does it progress in good and ascend towards perfection? How do the virtues help the soul to become strong in good? How are the powers of the soul restored and set in order? What are the various stages of the ascetic and mystical ascent to union with God?

3. St. Bernard ends with a brief indication of the nature of perfection and union—the perfect restoration by charity of the divine likeness in the soul, created in God's image, and closes by reproving the laxity of the clergy (19–22[746]). In these three parts we find the traditional "three ways"—purgative, illuminative, union.

*Details of the Treatise*:

{As for the} opening lines—what are they here for? to hear the Word of God. Word {is used} in the sense of *will*. To hear the Word means to *do* what God wills. And what He wills is "conversion": *Voluntas ejus conversio nostra* (834);[747] and *conversio = humili-*

---

743. This phrase is not found in the *De Conversione*.
744. Nn. 1–19 (*PL* 182, cols. 833B–844D).
745. Nn. 20–31 (cols. 845A–852B).
746. Nn. 32–40 (cols. 852B–856D).
747. "Our true life is found only through conversion" (Williams, *Of Conversion*, 1).

*tas:*⁷⁴⁸ *effici sicut parvulus.*⁷⁴⁹ St. Bernard then treats of the *power of God's word*—preached by those sent by Christ, the Word is not "heard" unless grace itself speaks in the depths of the conscience. *Conversio animarum opus divinae vocis est non humanae.*⁷⁵⁰ He speaks of the conversion of the apostles, and of Peter's fruitless efforts until he casts the net "at Christ's word"⁷⁵¹ and catches a great number of fish. St. Bernard adds: *Utinam jactemus et nos hodie in hoc verbo rete,*⁷⁵² announcing that he is fishing and *they* are the fish (835). Let them listen to God speaking in their heart with His power!

He tries to awaken them to a consciousness of the great power of the voice of God, for when this voice is heard, it changes our lives completely. And he goes on to say that God speaks to all, but not all are capable of hearing Him, not because it is hard to hear Him, but because in the perversity of our hearts we allow ourselves to be occupied with things that shut out the sound of His words. How is this? We fly from the silent sanctuary of our own soul so as not to hear the voice of Truth speaking within us (836). He adds that we labor *not* to hear the voice of God. In itself the voice is very plain, but we are constantly laboring to stop our ears against it. If we remain simple and open, we will certainly hear (n. 3 [835]). The voice of God is at the same time a light which illumines the dark recesses of our *memoria*⁷⁵³ and brings us face to face with our acts and motives in their reality. It shows us our heart stamped with the *amara signa*⁷⁵⁴ left by our evil acts.

---

748. "Conversion = humility."

749. Col. 835A, which reads: "*efficiamini sicut parvuli*" ("to become like little children" [Matt. 18:3]).

750. N. 2 (col. 835B) ("conversion of souls is the work of the Divine, not of the human voice" [Williams, *Of Conversion*, 2]).

751. "*in verbo Domini*" (col. 835C) ("at the Lord's word" [Williams, *Of Conversion*, 2]).

752. "Today may we too cast the net at his word" (Williams, *Of Conversion*, 2).

753. Col. 836B ("memory").

754. Chap. 3, n. 4 (col. 836C) ("thoughts of its bitterness" [Williams, *Of Conversion*, 6]).

This is the book of conscience, written with the inexorable pen of truth. It is like a stomach which should hurt because of the bitter poisons that are in it! (836). Sin is really a form of self-hatred destroying our whole being, both soul and body (4.5 [837]). ({This has} interesting implications for psychosomatic illness.) Note how he tells sinners that they are ruining themselves needlessly, not simply that they are defying authority of law, etc. He then speaks of the *nature of the conscience* (c. 5[755]) and shows how a perverted conscience makes us insensitive to what hurts and kills the soul. The perverted conscience is that which is entirely taken up with exterior things and loses its sensitivity to spiritual values. The man who does not know himself, {who} does not feel the sting of conscience, is totally *obsens sibi*, and is in a "far country," in *longinquam profecta est regionem*[756]—the *regio dissimilitudinis*;[757] {he} must come to himself and realize that he has eviscerated his own being by sin. This evisceration {is} like a spider catching flies (pleasure, etc.); he spins out of his own innards the web of sin (837). Most important is to see what we are doing: *redire ad cor*.[758] Rather than flying from the pain of the "worm"[759] that bites and gnaws within our soul, we should be glad *to feel that gnawing in this life when it is possible for the worm to be killed*. But the sinner seeks only to anaesthetize himself so that he will not feel the gnawing of the worm, and as a result, if he dies with the worm living in his soul, he will have to suffer the torments of its gnawing throughout eternity (c. 5). But in this life, if we face the fact of our sinfulness and resolutely embrace the suffering that this causes, God Himself will give us grace and strength to overcome the evil that is in us. But we must *face it*. Only penance is a valid remedy for the pain caused by a bad conscience (838). The *struggle* for conversion is graphically represented in chapter 6. Conver-

---

755. N. 7 (cols. 838C–839B).
756. Chap. 4, n. 5 (col. 837D) ("it has gone away into a far country" [Williams, *Of Conversion*, 9]).
757. *De Diversis*, 42 (*PL* 183, col. 661D) ("the land of unlikeness").
758. "*Redite . . . ad cor*" (col. 835D) (Isa. 46:8).
759. "*vermis*" (chap. 5, n. 7 [col. 838CD]).

sion is by no means easy—it is an agony—a wrestling with ourselves. In fact they "who give their minds to conversion are more gravely tempted"[760] (READ p. 13 of Watkin Williams' translation[761]).

1. First of all it is useless to embrace pious practices as long as we do not give up our real sins. For instance, fasting is useless when we still continue to be attached to our anger and injustice. But we must make *all our members* and faculties fast from evil and do good. This is not easy, especially in the beginning.

2. The reason sees that all this must be done, and it decrees that a conversion must take place. But the members and senses of the body all protest unanimously against all this, and run to the "flesh"—the mistress of the house—who is "lying sick in bed"[762]

---

760. Williams, *Of Conversion*, 31, which reads: ". . . are the more . . ." (chap. 11, n. 22 [col. 346BC]).

761. "Again the voice from heaven (*Matt.* xvii, 5 *and par.*) speaks. Now it says: Thou hast sinned; cease from sinning. And this [is] what it tells of. Long has the overflowing cesspit been poisoning the whole house with its intolerable stench; vain is it for thee while still the filth flows in to pump it out, to repent while as yet thou dost not cease to sin. For who can look favourably upon the fasts of men who fast for strife or for contention and smite with impious fist, while in them are found their own wills and their own pleasures? Not such is the fast which I have chosen, says the Lord (*Isa.* lviii, 3 sqq.). Shut the windows, watch the approaches, bar the openings with care; and so at last, when no fresh filth comes in, thou wilt be able to purge out the old. The man, in his ignorance of spiritual discipline, thinks that he can easily fulfil these commands. Who, he says, is to prevent me from paying less obedience to my members? Accordingly he imposes fasting upon gluttony; he forbids drunkenness. He orders the ears to be stopped from hearing blood (*Isa.* xxxiii, 15); the eyes to be turned aside from beholding vanity (*Ps.* cxviii, 37); the hands to be stretched out rather to give in pity than to get in avarice. Forbidding robbery, he may wish perhaps to give these members work to do: *He that stole, let him now steal no more: but rather let him labour, working with his hands the thing which is good, that he may have something to give to him that suffereth need (Eph.* iv, 28)" (Williams, *Of Conversion*, 13–14) (chap. 6, n. 8 [col. 839BC]).

762. "*quae paralytica jacet in domo*" (col. 839D) ("who now lies at home paralyzed" [Williams, *Of Conversion*, 14]).

(as a result of grace). This shrew of a wife immediately jumps out of bed and begins fighting back.

> Whereupon the little old woman leaps forth in her fury, forgetful of all her weakness. With dishevelled locks, with torn garments, with naked breast, scrabbling at her ulcers, gnashing the teeth in her parched mouth, infecting the very air with her poisonous breath, she exclaims: Why is not the reason ashamed of such an attack, such an onslaught upon the wretched will? Is this, says she, all your conjugal fidelity? Is this the way you feel for me when I suffer so much? Hitherto you have spared to add grief to my wounds (*Ps.* lxviii, 27). It seemed to you, I suppose, that something ought to be taken from my rich dowry! But what is left when you have done what you propose? You have simply inflicted this added grief upon a poor worn-out creature. And you know how once you honoured my every whim! Would that now, by good chance, the threefold ill of this dreadful disease from which I suffer befel you and not me! Forsooth I am voluptuous, I am inquisitive, I am ambitious; and with this threefold ulcer there is in me no wholeness from the sole of my foot to the crown of my head (*Isa.* i, 6). Accordingly my gullet—my obscene parts—since it is necessary again to take account of my members one by one—have been given over to pleasure. For the wandering feet, the undisciplined eyes are servants to curiosity. The ear and the tongue indeed serve vanity; while through the ear the oil of the sinner makes fat my head (*Ps.* cxl, 5), with the tongue I myself supply the defects in other men's praises of me. For it gives me great pleasure both to receive praise from other people and, when I can opportunely do so, to report this praise to someone else, being anxious to be talked about by myself as well as by others. It is to this disease especially that your skill is wont to bring the greatest relief.
> 
> To continue—to the hands themselves, which always have freedom of movement, we do not assign any particular work, but it is sometimes to vanity, sometimes to curiosity, sometimes to pleasure that they do their so painstaking service. Despite of this, however, none of these members has ever been able, even in one single respect, to give me

satisfaction; for neither has the eye its surfeit of seeing, nor the ear of hearing (*Eccles.* i, 8). Ah, would indeed that at times the whole body were an eye to see with, or that all the members were turned into a gullet to eat with! Is this then the fragment of consolation which you give me, that however hard I may beg for a thing, you try to take it away from me? So she spoke, and going off furious and indignant she cried: I hold on and long shall I do so. (chap. 6)[763]

(Compare medieval morality plays! v.g., *Everyman*.[764]) The violence of this reaction stuns the reason, which is now forced to admit that the work of conversion is not going to be easy: the *memory* is full of evil, the *will* is languid and inert, and there is little hope of resisting the flesh, now up in arms:

> And now its very plight brings understanding to the reason (*Isa.* xxviii, 19); now the difficulty of its undertaking begins in some degree to dawn upon the mind; now the supposed facility of recovery begins to vanish. For the reason sees the memory to be full of filthiness; it sees this and that filth to be more abundantly pouring in; it sees the windows themselves wide agape for the entrance of death (*Jer.* ix, 21) and quite impossible to be shut. It sees that the will, although still ruling, is but a languid lady, from whose ulcerated wounds there flows a wealth of bloody matter. Finally the soul sees itself contaminated through no other channel than its own body, yet from no other source than itself. For it is thus with the soul; as there is the memory which is befouled, so there is the will which befouls. In a word, the soul itself in its entirety is nothing else than reason, memory and will. But now, as things are, the resourceless reason is found to be, as it were, blind in that it has not hitherto seen all this; to be altogether feeble in that even what it does recognize

---

763. Williams, *Of Conversion*, 15–16 (n. 10 [cols. 840AD]).

764. The anonymous late fifteenth-century morality play about the human person who is summoned by Death, and who searches in vain for companions to accompany him, until after repentance and forgiveness his good deeds are freed from bondage and go with him to the grave and ultimately to salvation.

it does not possess the strength to correct. The memory too is as utterly filthy as it is fetid; and the weak will is running all over with horrible ulcers. And, to leave out of account nothing which belongs to the man, the very body is rebellious, and every single member is a separate window by which death enters into the soul, and incessantly the confusion grows worse (chap. 6).[765]

Note: the full conversion of the soul is a conversion of the *mind*, the *will*, and the *memory* in that order.

3. St. Bernard however says that this condition is no cause for discouragement. On the contrary, "*Who is poorer in spirit than the man who nowhere in his own spirit finds any place to lay his head?*"[766] (chap. 7) and above all "HE WHO FINDS NO PLEASURE IN HIMSELF MAY PLEASE GOD, AND HE WHO HATES HIS OWN HOUSE, MAY BE ENTERTAINED IN A HOUSE OF GLORY"[767] (cf. *Letters of St. Thérèse*[768]). This is a basic principle—from the evil that afflicts us we can hope to draw good and salvation by turning to God. Misery can make us blessed, not by itself, but because it humbles us, opens our hearts to receive the mercy of God, keeps us from trusting in ourselves and opens us entirely to the action of grace,

---

765. Williams, *Of Conversion*, 16–17 (n. 11 [cols. 840D–841A]).

766. Williams, *Of Conversion*, 18 (col. 841B).

767. Williams, *Of Conversion*, 18, which reads: ". . . and that he who hates his own house, a house indeed full of dirt and discomfort, may be entertained . . ." (col. 841B).

768. See Thérèse's Christmas 1896 letter, written as though from the Blessed Virgin, to her sister Céline (Sr. Geneviève): "If you are willing to bear serenely the trial of being displeasing to yourself, you will be to me a pleasant place of shelter; you will suffer, of course, for you will be outside the door of your own home; but have no fear, the poorer you are, the more Jesus will love you" (*Collected Letters*, 303). In his biography of Mother Berchmans, Merton quotes the original French and provides a translation of a slightly different (edited) version of this passage as it was included (transposed into another, earlier letter) in early editions of Thérèse's autobiography *Story of a Soul* (Thomas Merton, *Exile Ends in Glory: The Life of a Trappistine, Mother M. Berchmans, O.C.S.O.* [Milwaukee: Bruce, 1948], 160).

if we are only *meek* in our will. "It is not misery, but compassion, which makes a man blessed; yet the proper object of compassion is misery. At least then let this misery make thee blessed, so that a low estate may be the road to humility."[769] It is not necessary to have a strong will, but we must be *meek and pliant, submitting to the divine action* (841), *willing to be guided, taught and commanded*.

4. Here we realize that St. Bernard is enumerating the beatitudes; we have seen the soul must be *poor* and *meek*. We will see another in chap. 11: blessed are they who *mourn*—that is, those who suffer constant temptation because of the fact that they are striving to make progress, mourning for the fact that there is no consolation save in hope (READ Williams' translation, p. 32[770]).

---

769. Williams, *Of Conversion*, 18, which reads: ". . . object for compassion . . ." (col. 841C).

770. "But would that such a one would turn away from ungodliness, and beware of the terrible abyss of which it is written: *The wicked man, when he is come into the depth of sins, contemneth* (*Prov.* xviii, 3). Indeed his case demands the most powerful remedies; and he is beset by dangers unless with much concern he strives to follow the advice of the physician and to obey his precepts. Temptation is tempestuous; it is nigh to bringing about despair unless he takes courage, and turns his attention to taking pity upon his own soul, and listens to the voice which says: *Blessed are they that mourn, for they shall be comforted* (*Matt.* v, 5). Let him mourn abundantly, for the time of mourning has come; his plight is sufficient to absorb continual tears. Let him mourn, but not without submission to the Divine will, not without prospect of consolation. Let him consider that no relief is to be found for him in himself, but that all things are full of misery and desolation; let him consider that there is no good thing in his flesh (*Rom.* vii, 18), nay rather, that this wicked world (*Gal.* i, 4) holds naught else than vanity and affliction of spirit (*Eccles.* i, 14; ii, 11, 17; iv, 16). Let him consider, I say, that neither within, nor beneath, nor around is there consolation for him, that so at length he may at some time learn that it is to be sought above and hoped for from above. Yet, let him mourn, bewailing the while his own grief (*Job* x, 20); let his eyes pour out water (*Ps.* cxviii, 136), and let not his eyelids rest in sleep (*Prov.* vi, 4). Verily the eye, which was before in darkness, is purged by tears and its sight is made keen, so that it may be able to gaze into the brightness of serenest light (*Act. App.* xxii, 11)" (n. 23 [cols. 846C–847A]).

Note at the end of chapter 7: "Thy will is thy Eve."[771] *The great task is conversion of the will* (in its deepest sense) (cf. Jung's idea of *animus* and *anima*[772]). *Meekness* = a gentle and reasonable asceticism, not trying to force the will by violence, but bringing the will into peaceful subjection to reason and spirit. Chapter 8[773] {presents} more on the harm done by vice. Note: "I know not what harder lot I could invoke for him who, shunning grateful quietude takes delight in the restlessness of curiosity, than that he should always attain the object of his search" (W. Williams, p. 21).[774] Conclusion: the reason demonstrates that there is *no genuine joy* in sensual pleasure. On the contrary it is a great labor without fruit.

Here the transition takes place—we pass over to the way of progressives {and learn} *the means of ascending* and becoming delivered from a life of sin:

1. {The} basic importance of the *Presence of God* (chap. 9[775]) and fear of judgement (chap. 9) {is emphasized}.

2. *Reason bids the will consider the delights of the spiritual garden of virtue and a pious life* (chap. 12ff.) as contrasted with the desert and wasteland of fruitless effort to find joy in sin (chaps. 8–9). Here the *conversion of the will* begins. (READ chaps. 12–13 [Williams, pp. 33–35][776]). In other words, *virtue must be made attractive*, there

---

771. Williams, *Of Conversion*, 19 (col. 841D).

772. In C. G. Jung's psychology, the masculine and feminine dimensions of the psyche that must be accepted and integrated in developing a mature, fully individuated personality.

773. Nn. 13–17 (cols. 841D–844A).

774. N. 14 (col. 842B).

775. Nn. 18–19 (col. 844AD).

776. "Chapter XII. Henceforward then he would do well to raise his eyes to the heavens, to look forth through the lattice (*Cant. Cant.* ii, 9), to follow with full intent the guiding star; yea, let him, zealous as the Wise Men, seek the True Light by the glitter of the sky (*Ps.* xxxv, 10). For he will find a wondrous place in which to pitch his tent (*Ps.* xli, 5), where man may eat the Bread of Angels (*Ps.* lxxvii, 25); he will find the paradise of pleasure planted by the Lord (*Gen.* ii, 8); he will find a garden of flowers most delight-

must be a *positive hope* of something better, a real *promise of solid*

---

ful, an abode of refreshment; and he will say: O that the poor will would but listen to my voice, that it might enter in and behold these good things and visit this place. Here truly will it find richer rest, and also will it less disquiet me as it will be the less disquieted itself. For he speaks the truth who said: *Take up my yoke upon you . . . and you shall find rest to your souls* (*Matt.* xi, 29). Believing this promise he addresses somewhat kindly the irritated will, and with a certain show of cheerfulness accosting it in a soothing tone may say: Let your indignation cease entirely; it is not I who am able to offend you; it is your own body; it is your own self; there is no reason for you to be afraid; there is nothing which you need fear. But let it be no matter for surprise if more bitter than ever is the will's reply: Your many cogitations have made you mad (*Acts* xxvi, 24). Meanwhile let the reason wait quietly until, speaking of one matter after another, at a time convenient it may remark: To-day I happened upon a most beautiful garden, a very pleasant place, where it would be good for us to be (*Matt.* xvii, 4 *and par.*). For it is indeed harmful for you to be tossed upon this bed of sickness, this painful pallet; with a heavy heart to be grieving in your chamber (*Ps.* iv, 5). The Lord will be at hand to him who seeks him, to the soul which hopes in him (*Lam.* iii, 25). He will attend to suppliant vows, and to his words will he give power (*Heb.* iv, 12). He will move strongly the will's desire, that it may long wistfully not alone to see this place, but step by step to enter and therein abide (*John* xiv, 23).

Chapter XIII. But it is not to be thought that this paradise of inward pleasure is material. It is not with the feet, but with the affections that a man enters therein; and what commends it to thee is not the abundance of the trees of earth, but the delightful and fair planting everywhere of spiritual virtues. It is an enclosed garden where a sealed fountain derives into four heads (*Cant. Cant.* iv, 12) and from one vein of wisdom fourfold virtue flows. There also spring most glorious lilies, and when the flowers appear there is heard the voice of the turtle-dove (*Cant. Cant.* ii, 12). There the ointment of the spouse yields its most fragrant odour, and the rest of sweet smells pervade when the north wind has fled and the south wind blows gently (*Cant. Cant.* i, 11; iv, 16). There in the midst is the tree of life (*Gen.* ii, 9), that apple-tree of the Song of Songs, more precious than all the trees of the wood, whose shadow refreshes the spouse and whose fruit is sweet to her taste (*Cant. Cant.* ii, 3). There shines the fair beauty of continence and the vision of pure truth irradiates the heart's eyes; moreover to the ears the most sweet voice of the inward consoler brings joy and gladness (*Ps.* l, 10). There, as it were, *happiness and peace*. The soul cannot go on struggling when it has nothing but a purely negative spirituality. St. Bernard realizes the necessity for optimism and joy based on faith and above all on Christian hope. It is useless to urge souls on to good without giving them any motives for hope in God; this only ends in discouragement. This hope is not remote, not only in distant heaven, but even in this life there is joy to be tasted in the fruits of true charity. These are tasted not by *scientia* but by *conscientia*.[777] Here then is the next beatitude—{to} *hunger and thirst* (for the life of virtue and its rewards) with a certitude of being filled (848). For,

---

is wafted to the nostrils of hope the very pleasant odour of a fruitful field which the Lord has blessed (*Gen.* xxvii, 27). There a foretaste of the incomparable delights of charity is eagerly enjoyed, and, the thorns and briars by which it once was torn now cut away, the mind anointed with pity in good conscience is at rest. And these are not to be reckoned amongst the rewards of eternal life, but as the wages of our bodily warfare; nor do they belong to what is promised to the Church in the future, nay rather, to what is promised to her now (1 *Tim.* iv, 8). For this is that hundredfold reward in this world which is set before those who despise the world (*Matt.* xix, 29). Thou dost not need that any word of mine should commend it to thee; what it is the Spirit alone reveals (1 *Cor.* ii, 10). Thou hast no cause to consult the written page, seek rather experience. Man knows not the price of wisdom; wisdom derives from within; nor is its sweetness found to be that of those who live sweetly upon earth (*Job* xxviii, 12, 13 and 18). Forsooth thou wilt not see how sweet the Lord is, unless thou has tasted his sweetness. *Taste*, says the Scripture, *and see that the Lord is sweet* (*Ps.* xxxiii, 9). The new name, which no man knows save only he who receives it, is hidden manna (*Apoc.* ii, 17). It is not learning but unction which teaches it (1 *John* ii, 20 and 27), neither does science but conscience understand it. It is a holy thing; it is pearls (*Matt.* vii, 6); he who began both to do and to teach (*Acts* i, 1) will not do what he himself forbids. Yet he no longer accounts as dogs and swine those who renounce their former sins and wickednesses; he even consoles them, saying by the word of the apostle: Such some of you were. But you are washed: but you are sanctified (1 *Cor.* vi, 11). Only let the dog beware that he return not to his vomit, and the sow that she return not to her wallowing in the mire (2 *Pet.* ii, 22)" (nn. 24–25 [cols. 847A–848C]).

777. "knowledge"; "conscience".

as St. Bernard points out, experience teaches that the goods of this world never satisfy, but only produce satiety and loathing. But the goods of the spirit do indeed satisfy our hunger: but this is learned only by experience—by doing good. It is not sufficient to think good thoughts and to approve the better course; one must actually do good before he experiences the satisfaction of the spiritual life. *Hunger and thirst for justice marks the conversion and purification of the will.* Chapter 13, on the spiritual paradise, is important, {with its} allusions to the joy of virtue and the *spiritual senses*. *Experience alone* teaches all this.

3. The soul is now making progress (chap. 15[778]). The body is to some extent subject to the reasonable will, and the fountain of evil has been partly dried up. The will has been purified and rectified in part: but now *the memory must be purified*. This is the "most difficult task" (read p. 41[779]). How is this done? by the word of the mercy of God which takes *away the defilement of sin*.

---

778. N. 28 (cols. 849C–850A).

779. "And now that the will has been changed, the body brought into subjection to it (1 *Cor.* ix, 27), the fount of evil having been to some extent dried up and the opening stopped, there still remains the third and most difficult task, that, namely, of purging memory, of pumping out the cesspit. For how shall my life escape from my memory? Suppose that some piece of thin, poor parchment has absorbed the writing of a scribe, by what art can it be erased? The stain is not superficial, it is ingrained. In vain should I try to remove it; I should tear the parchment before the wretched writing was got rid of. For perhaps entire forgetfulness might destroy the memory itself, so that, my reason lost, I should no longer remember what I had done. It remains then to ask: What keen edge can effect the scouring of my memory without destroying it? Surely it is alone the word living and powerful and more penetrating than any double-edged sword (*Heb.* iv, 12), which puts away thy sins. Some Pharisee may murmur and say: Who can forgive sins save God alone (*Mark* ii, 7)? Yes, but he who speaks that word to me is God, and none other will be compared with him, who found out all the way of discipline, and gave it to his servant Jacob and to Israel his beloved after that he was seen upon earth and dwelt with men (*Baruch* iii, 36 *sqq.*)" (n. 28 [cols. 849C–850A]).

Note {that} St. Bernard does not demand that our sins be entirely blotted out from our memory. *But when we are confident of forgiveness, in humble trust, then they no longer fester like a wound but become a source of compunction and greater trust.* "His pardon blots out sin, not indeed so that the memory of it is destroyed, but that what formerly was wont alike to be in the memory and to defile the memory, henceforth is in the memory in such a way as not to defile it at all. . . . Take away condemnation, take away fear, take away confusion [and full remission of sins does all this] and not only will [our sins] not be against us, but *they will work with us for good* in order that we may give devout thanks to him who has remitted them" (Williams, p. 42[780]). Here it would be well to recall what is said about the *amor carnalis Christi* (Canticle, Sermon 20.4-7)[781] and the *memoria Christi*.[782] The memory is pure when the recollection of past sin begets tears of compunction. It is once again the all-important point of being able to turn our deficiencies into material for building—this cannot be done unless we let go, abandon our pride and place ourselves confidently in the hands of the divine mercy. Hence the next beatitude—*Blessed are the merciful* (chap. 16[783]). And mercy begins at home. M‍ISERERE ERGO ANIMAE TUAE, QUI DEUM TIBI VIS MISERERE (850).[784] We must first of all repent, be reconciled with ourselves, find peace within, and then we can begin to be merciful to others. St. Bernard understands the most important fact that feelings of self-hatred and resentment of our own limitation pour themselves out in resentment and criticism of others, and we cannot be charitable to others unless we are first content with our own poverty. We cannot accept others as they are unless we accept ourselves and strive to

---

780. N. 28 (col. 850A) (emphasis added).
781. See above, pages 78, 118–19, and below, pages 293–95.
782. See above, pages 111–15.
783. N. 29 (col. 850BD).
784. "Have mercy then upon thine own soul (*Ecclus.* xxx, 24), thou who wouldst that God should have mercy upon thee" (Williams, *Of Conversion*, 43).

love God with our present limitations. Cf. the first two degrees of truth (*Degrees of Humility*)[785] (READ translation, p. 43[786]). The merciful can then pray honestly: "*Dimitte nobis debita nostra sicut et nos*" (trans. p. 44[787]). "*Give alms, if thou canst not of thy worldly substance, then of thy good will, and all things shall be pure;* not only will the reason be enlightened and the will corrected, but the very memory also will be clean" (850).[788] Then we come to the next beatitude, Blessed are the clean of heart. This is an important consideration—*the memory is purified by mercy*—peace with ourselves, compassion for others, disinfects the memory. The memory of sin remains, but it is now clean and productive, the wound no longer festers, and we begin a salutary convalescence. Note especially that the purification of the memory by no means consists in putting out all thoughts of the flesh, or of our past sins, least of all their humiliating qualities! But this in fact is what the "unmerciful" soul most seeks to avoid. He tries to run away from

---

785. The first two degrees of truth are humility and charity (*De Gradibus Humilitatis*, nn. 6–18 [PL 182, cols. 944B–951C]); for an extensive discussion, see below, pages 360–69.

786. "Already now a befitting response is made to him who prays for the Divine mercy: *Blessed are the merciful: for they shall obtain mercy* (*Matt.* v, 7). Have mercy then upon thine own soul (*Ecclus.* xxx, 24), thou who wouldest that God should have mercy upon thee; wash thy bed every night, remember to water thy couch with tears (*Ps.* vi, 7). If thou takest compassion upon thine own self, if thou dost toil with groaning (*Ps.* vi, 7) in thy repentance—this is the first step in showing mercy—then indeed thou wilt find mercy. If thou art, perhaps, a great and grievous sinner, and seekest great mercy and a multitude of pities (*Ps.* l, 3), then do thou strive to enlarge and multiply the mercy which thou showest. Thou hast been reconciled to thyself, for, in that thou wast an enemy to God, thou didst grave injury to thyself (*Job* vii, 20). Peace then having now been restored in thine own house, it needs that it be extended towards thy neighbours, in order that last of all even God himself may kiss thee with the kiss of his mouth (*Cant. Cant.* i, 1) and, as is written, having been reconciled thou mayest have peace with God (*Rom.* v, 1)" (n. 29 [col. 850BC]).

787. Col. 850C ("Forgive us our debts as we forgive our debtors").

788. Col. 850D (emphasis added).

the truth about himself and about others, and the sins in his memory are constantly boiling and fermenting, producing all kinds of evil.

4. However (see chap. 17;[789] trans. p. 46), *the period of convalescence is a further period of severe purification*, and St. Bernard's terms here suggest that it is something akin to the nights of St. John of the Cross (St. Bernard talks little about interior darkness and passive purification—but this is one place where he seems to do so). "Let no one therefore think himself to be cleansed because he has escaped from the cesspit; nay rather, let him know that he is now in need of much purification, that not merely must he be washed with water, but *he must be purged and tried by fire.*"[790] The *pure in heart*, passing through a salutary darkness (851), are actually seeing God *per speculum in aenigmate*.[791] {A} comparison {is made to} a wounded eye: the foreign body is removed lest the eye remain in darkness. {There is a} suggestion of two darknesses: (a) soothing; (b) bitter. *Perfection* {is associated with the beatitude} Blessed are the peacemakers. He starts with three kinds of peacemakers: (a) those who render good for good, *and wish to hurt nobody*; (b) those who do not render evil for evil, *but suffer injury patiently*; (c) those who render good for evil {and thereby} *win the souls of those who wrong them.* The first possesses peace, to an extent; the second keeps peace; but the third is a true peacemaker. He is truly a son of God; *grateful for his own reconciliation, he reconciles others to the Father.* This is the peak of the spiritual life (note here the implications: the highest level of the spiritual life is fruitful for souls—{it} brings other souls to God besides our own). Note what he says in chapter 19[792] (translation, p. 50): "Woe

---

789. N. 30 (cols. 850D–851C).

790. Williams, *Of Conversion*, 46, which reads: ". . . to be forthwith cleansed . . . but he must be purged . . ." (emphasis added) (n. 30 [col. 851C]).

791. Col. 851C ("by means of a mirror in a riddle" [Williams, *Of Conversion*, 46]).

792. Nn. 32–33 (cols. 852B–853C).

unto the sons of wrath, who feign themselves mediators of peace"[793]—i.e., those of the clergy who have not listened to the voice calling to conversion.

{Bernard's} *final exhortation* {focuses on} the scandal given by the sins of the clergy. When he has reached the point of talking of the truly apostolic soul, the truly priestly soul, detached from evil, humble, compassionate, purified, and a peacemaker, St. Bernard suddenly turns to the sins of the clergy, comparing the sinful priest to Judas, to the Pharisees who have the key of knowledge and do not enter in, or allow others to enter. What sins does he mean in particular? First of all he names *worldly ambition*—{a} particular abuse of the time; men sought priesthood and benefices for political and human prestige and for wealth. In utter selfishness they usurped the office of peacemaker without any concern for souls or even for virtue itself, and none for the honor of God. They had no compunction, no compassion, no humility, and many had not been called by God to the priesthood. "On all sides men run to ordination,"[794] but they are not good priests; there is quantity but not quality. . . . Nor is there lacking serious immorality in their ranks (854). "These not only do not appease the wrath of God, but provoke it."[795] In chapter 21[796] he seriously urges them to do penance and to live a life appropriate to their calling—not to fear to give themselves at last to God. The last chapter (22[797]) reminds them of their duty not only to be good priests and lead good lives, but also to preach and tend their flock (although in this time the bishops were the ones who did the preaching) and even to suffer persecution in defence of their flock.

---

793. Williams, *Of Conversion*, 50 (col. 853A).
794. Williams, *Of Conversion*, 53, which reads: ". . . to the sacred orders" (n. 34 [col. 853D]).
795. Williams, *Of Conversion*, 55, which reads: "For such men . . . but they provoke him the more" (n. 36 [col. 854C]).
796. Nn. 37–38 (col. 855AD).
797. Nn. 39–40 (cols. 855D–856D).

Conclusion:

1. We note above all how St. Bernard is consumed with zeal for the truth. If clerics are supposed to belong to God, let them be what they are supposed to be, men of God. Let them be authentic, not a mere sham. Let there be reality in the Christian life.

2. St. Bernard spends most of the sermon going into details of the psychological reality of the spiritual life—exactly what happens when one seeks to leave the world and follow Christ. This is all based on experience, and the whole sermon is an appeal to Christian experience, not just to concepts and abstract principles. The principles are there, strong and clear, but embodied in experience.

3. St. Bernard is uncompromising in his assertion that the cleric and monk should aim at the highest perfection of love. This implies a total purification and leads to fruitfulness for souls and for the Church.

4. Although he frankly points out and condemns the abuses in clerical life he does not do so until he has fully exposed the positive side of the spiritual life and shown the beauties of the Christian vocation to sanctity. His condemnation is not violent; it is moderate, though complete and frank; and manifestly his words are inspired by the most sincere charity, zeal for the glory of God and for the welfare of Holy Church. They are truly the words of a saint.

## IV. DE PRAECEPTO ET DISPENSATIONE

A reply to monastic questions raised by Benedictine monks of St. Pierre at Chartres.

1. *Monastic Obedience*: the first question asked by the Benedictines of Chartres is one which is fundamental for the solution of the other questions proposed by them. "Are the prescriptions of the *Rule* of St. Benedict to be regarded as PRECEPTS [therefore binding under sin] or {as} counsels?" (*PL* 182, col. 861);[798] and

---

798. "An monasticae Regulae instituta praecepta sint, an consilia duntaxat."

then, perhaps are "SOME of the prescriptions precepts, and others, counsels?"[799] St. Bernard's consideration of the question is detailed and subtle, and it is woven throughout the whole treatise. We may attempt a brief summary in very few points:

1) To vow to live under the *Rule* of St. Benedict is to oblige oneself to live according to the *Rule*. About this there is no doubt (cap. 1 [col. 861–62]).

2) The *Rule* includes some points which even God cannot change ({the} precept to love God above all), some which God alone can change, and *some which can be dispensed by men*. In this distinction, St. Bernard is separating the precepts of divine law in the *Rule* from the *observances, about which our question mainly revolves*.

3) *The purpose of the observances is charity*. When the observances do not promote the perfection of charity, or in some way accidentally stand in the way of it, they can be changed by the superiors—but these are not allowed to change the observances at will. There must be an objective reason for making the change (cap. 2.5 [col. 863]).

4) The religious is bound to observe everything in the *Rule*, but not every violation of the *Rule* is a serious fault. He distinguishes *peccatum*—by which he means here a fault of negligence or weakness, which is not serious—and *crimen*—a fault proceeding from bad will, which can be serious ([col. 870] cap. 8).

5) *Peccata* against the *Rule* are more or less unavoidable, but they are allowed by God for a purpose, namely to humble us and make us use the remedies prescribed by the *Rule*. Here we come close to the concept of "penal law."[800] He says {that} in practice one who violates the observances *does not sin unless at the same time he neglects the prescribed remedy* (penalty) (col. 879).

---

799. "*an certe quaedam sint deputanda imperiis, quaedam pro consiliis reputanda*" (col. 862A).

800. For this concept, which refers to rules that do not bind under pain of sin but for which there is a moral obligation to perform assigned penance for violations, see *Life of the Vows*, 48, 230, 232.

6) What are these *peccata*? Examples {would include} a violation of silence when a word bursts out unintentionally. But it is clear that {a} deliberate violation of silence for St. Bernard—*ex contemptu*—is a *crimen*, that is to say, a sin. {Is it} mortal??? That would be an extreme judgement, except in very grave matter, with grave scandal, etc.

7) In summary, St. Bernard certainly seems to believe that in infractions of our most notable observances, like silence, fasting and so forth, there can be real sin, perhaps serious sin, if there is formal disobedience to the *Rule*, and that other kinds of transgression out of weakness and inadvertence are not really to be regarded as sins, but as faults of frailty which we have come to the monastery to correct. There is no possibility of foisting on St. Bernard an opinion that the *Rule* can be observed or not according to the discretion of the individual!

*Points on Obedience* from *De Praecepto et Dispensatione*:

{In} chapter 6 {Bernard writes that} perfect obedience is not obedience which confines itself within the limits of what can be commanded by vow. That is negative, "inert and servile"[801] obedience, which always stops to question the superior's right to command, examines the command, judges it and rejects it if it is at all inconvenient. *Imperfect obedience does not really want to obey*; it simply wants to avoid the consequences of disobedience. *Perfect obedience* is so ardently desirous of obeying ({it} loves {the} "*bonum obedientiae*"[802]) that it goes beyond obedience and becomes love. *Not content* with the mere limits of the letter of the law, it seeks to go beyond. (Imperfect obedience welcomes the limit with relief and satisfaction.) But this does not mean doing more than the superior wills—i.e., what he does not will. {It is} *more generous—largiori voluntate fertur in latitudinem caritatis* (868).[803] When we

---

801. "*inerti et servili*" (col. 868A).

802. "the good of obedience" (col. 870A), quoted from *Rule*, chap. 71 (McCann, 158).

803. "it is elevated into the breadth of charity by a more generous will."

*The Cistercian Fathers and Their Monastic Theology* 217

hold back and set limits to our gift of our own will, we are in fact restricting our liberty and our ability to give, for liberty is proportionate to love in the doctrine of St. Bernard. But this gift is *qualitative*—more according to the will of {the} superior? {It is} more spontaneous on our part. *How does the perfect religious obey? spontanea vigore;*[804] his soul is *"liberalis et alacris"*;[805] *modum non considerans;*[806] {it is} always ready to love, not constrained by necessity. This obedience purifies the heart and makes it ready for contemplation. He seeks to obey even when it is impossible (cf. *Rule*, {c.} 68); *transire alacriter votum et obedire in omnibus* (868).[807] This is a perfect imitation of the obedience of Jesus, made obedient unto death. *Remarks*: it is by our obedience that our real generosity is measured, and not by our efforts to assert our own preferences and follow our own attractions in spiritual things. True and perfect obedience is not possible without a real renunciation of self. Pretended obedience soon reaches limits, since it is not a real giving up of our own will. Real obedience is never totally easy; it always costs some kind of sacrifice. Only after the complete sacrifice of our will has been made does real obedience become easy. There are innumerable ways in which we refuse obedience and justify ourselves. St. Bernard will show us some of them. The real point is: *do we really want to obey?* If in point of fact we only want to obey in those things which suit us and please us, and refuse obedience when it is a real sacrifice, then it can be said that we have no effective will to obey, and our vow (though not violated) is something of a pretense. Such is the opinion of

---

804. "spontaneously, with vigor" (though this is presented as a phrase, in the text there is a comma after *"spontanea,"* which must modify the understood subject, *"obedientia,"* rather than the masculine ablative *"vigore,"* with which it does not agree in gender).

805. Text reads: *"vigore liberalis alacrisque animi"* ("with the vigor of a generous and cheerful mind").

806. "paying no attention to a limit".

807. Text reads: ". . . *alacriter etiam votum* . . ." ("even gladly to go beyond the vow and obey in everything").

St. Bernard: "Whenever this perfect obedience is interrupted, it becomes disobedience, a sin, a transgression, a prevarication."[808]

*Degrees of obedience*: (1) it is good to obey for fear of hell, even though this is to some extent servile—at least it is better than disobeying! (2) it is better to obey out of love for God; (3) *the most perfect obedience is that which unites our will and judgement with the will and judgement of the superior*: *cum eo animo injunctum opus recipitur, quo et praecipitur* (870).[809]

This is important—it is a question of *evaluating things as the superior evaluates them*. St. Bernard does not demand that we take exactly the same speculative view of things to be done, but that we carry them out in practice with the same evaluation as is set upon them by the superior, giving greater attention to what is essential in his eyes, but not neglecting what is slight. The reason? The superior is to be obeyed as if he were God. *Obedientia quae majoribus praebetur, Deo exhibetur* (*Rule*, c. 5,[810] quoted by St. Bernard [{col. 873}]).[811] The principle here is that the will of the superior is the deciding factor where God's will is otherwise not known. Sometimes the superior merely enforces the known will of God, for instance when he insists on something already clearly stated in the *Rule*. But at other times, things which are indifferent, or good in themselves, become evil as soon as they conflict with the will of the superior. Hence "Whenever a superior commands in the name of God, as long as it is not certainly displeasing to God, [it] is without doubt to be accepted fully as commanded by God Himself" (873).[812] {An} objection {may arise}: suppose the superior

---

808. "*Haec ergo quoties interrumpitur, inobedientia dicitur, et peccatum, et transgressio seu praevaricatio*" (col. 868C).

809. "when the work imposed is received in the same spirit in which it is commanded."

810. McCann, 34.

811. "The obedience which is given to superiors is shown to God" (copy text reads: "875").

812. "*Quamobrem quidquid vice Dei praecipit homo, quod non sit tamen certum displicere Deo; haud secus omnino accipiendum est, quam si praecipiat Deus.*"

is mistaken as to what is pleasing to God? St. Bernard replies: what is that to you? You are not responsible. It is the office of the superior to decide what is the will of God, where the will of God is not quite clear, or to interpret it when it is not clear enough, and our responsibility is then to accept his manifestation of clarification, and not to analyze or criticize his views (873).

*Signs of Imperfect Obedience* (cap. 10, n. 23 [874]): it is manifestly not easy to accept the superior's judgement of an uncertain case when it seems to us that God's will might be quite different from what the superior has decided. *The difference between good and bad religious lies not in the absence or presence of difficulty*, but in the way each one handles the difficulty. But for the imperfect monk, the difficulties are endless and insupportable. He creates difficulties even where there are none, because he does not really want to obey. The presence of innumerable difficulties, even where the monk is consciously sincere, shows that there is at least a fundamental weakness on the point of obedience. However, we must remember that there are often other factors at work too. The monk may have a bad training and a false view of obedience, and in a word may be suffering from a badly formed conscience. The monk who does not really obey has the following characteristics: (a) his love is not perfect, and his will is weak; (b) therefore he discusses and analyzes every command; he has to thrash the whole thing out before he can act—in reality he is hoping to find reasons for not obeying; (c) he sticks at every point (*haerere ad singula*[813]) {and} won't move forward—{this is} an illusory cautiousness, again seeking motives for evasion; (d) he demands an explanation for everything; there are some who appear to be obedient and think themselves so, but who in fact require everything to be explained in minute detail, when it is already obvious, perhaps unconsciously "playing for time"; (e) they suspect every injunction for which they do not immediately see the reason—in a word {they are} always on the alert for some infringement of their precious "liberty," which is in fact a slavery to self-love. In

---

813. Col. 874B.

a word, they "never obey willingly unless they are told to do something that they like" (874).[814] The effects of this kind of obedience {are that} *it makes everything hard. "The yoke of Christ is insupportable unless it is borne with the Spirit of Christ"* (874),[815] and we cannot be lifted up by the Holy Spirit unless we really renounce our own will and abandon ourselves by a generous gift, to God's love and God's will. The gift is *demanded by our profession*. If we do not make it, it is our own fault, says St. Bernard. We ought to have weighed the matter before taking vows.

*Is it possible to keep the whole Rule without offense?* The Benedictines of Chartres complained to St. Bernard that there were in fact so many things commanded in the *Rule* that it was impossible not to sin against obedience somewhere along the line by breaking a rule. St. Bernard replied:

1. First of all, when one views the precepts of the *Rule* as a kind of trap, it is because one has not yet tasted the love of God, and one is infected with legalism born of fear (c. 13 [878]).

2. He agrees that it is difficult to keep the *Rule* faithfully all one's life and to be for many years obedient to superiors. But this is what one must weigh carefully when planning to make monastic vows: *Qui potest capere capiat*.[816]

3. Finally and most important of all, we must *properly understand our obligation*. NO ONE VOWS TO BE ACTUALLY PERFECT IN OBEDIENCE. If he did, then the monastic life would indeed be impossible. If one promised by vow that he would never again offend in anything, he would be guilty of the greatest presumption, and would certainly commit sacrilege against such a vow (879). If the *Rule* aimed to impose such an obligation, it would certainly not correct sin but only increase it. NEMO, SI CAUTE PROFITETUR, POLLICETUR SE ULTRA IN NULLO TRANSGRESSURUM (n. 32

---

814. "nec unquam libenter obedire, nisi cum audire contigerit quod forte libuerit."

815. "Christi quippe jugum et onus est, et omnino importabile, nisi Christi aeque spiritui."

816. "He that can take, let him take it" (Matt. 19:12) (col. 879B).

[879]).[817] To understand our vow correctly, we must distinguish between two kinds of rules: *praecepta* and *remedia*.[818] To vow obedience according to the *Rule* is then not to vow never to break the *Rule* in anything, but to order one's life under a superior, within the framework set up by the *Rule* in an effort to remedy one's inevitable failings. Within the framework, we embrace both *precepts* and *remedies*. This means that we *try to keep the precepts* as faithfully as we can. However, since human frailty is inevitable, if we do fail in something, the failure is not imputable to us if we make use of the *remedies* foreseen by the *Rule*: that is to say, if *we admit our fault* (accusing ourselves), *accept a penance* if one is imposed, and *try to do better* next time. Thus in actual fact, a person may commit many faults against the *Rule*, and fail in many respects, but if he has good will and sincerely makes use of the normal remedies, *he is not accounted either disobedient or irregular*, and he certainly does not sin against his vow (33 [879]). These principles are of the greatest importance to protect us against a rigid and scrupulous formalism that makes the true development of the religious soul impossible, because it does not accord with reality. St. Bernard says: "I would say that he only has violated his vow . . . *who has contemned both the precept and the remedy*" (879).[819] "But I would say that he is fully secure [in regularity and obedience] who even though at times he may go beyond the limits of obedience, does not reject the counsel of penance."[820] (That is to say, {he} is humble enough to admit and correct his fault when he becomes aware of it.) "It is easy to find

---

817. "No one, if he makes his profession thoughtfully, promises that he will never transgress in anything."

818. "*Partienda est proinde nobis in duo universa haec observatio regularis, in Precepta videlicet, et Remedia*" ("The entire observance of the *Rule* should be divided for us into two—that is, precepts and remedies").

819. "*Solum itaque censuerim fregisse votum . . . qui et praeceptum contempserit, et remedium.*"

820. "*Nam illum sane dico securum, qui etiamsi interdum obedientiae limitem praeterit, consilium non respuit poenitentiae.*"

the cure for our tendencies to disobedience, and we find this cure in the *Rule* itself, provided that our offense is not aggravated by contempt"[821] (which would make us despise the remedies in the *Rule*) (880). He concludes that those who think that the *Rule* obliges us never to violate any point under any pretext have a false conscience and are living in an occasion of constant scandal in the religious life. In other words, they are heading for the frustration and ruin of their vocation to love God. They are, as we would say, perfectionists, and do not understand the reality of religious observance which in fact takes into account our weakness and frailty and makes use of them for the purpose of our sanctification, under the mercy of God.

2. *Some points on stability* (*De Praecepto*, cap. 16[822]): in discussing stability, let us first of all remember: (1) our vocation is a special gift of God—a pledge of eternal life, a sign of predestination; (2) we must accept it with love, gratitude and reverence; (3) we must correspond—and pray to persevere; (4) we must studiously avoid everything that would be an obstacle to generous cooperation with God's call (i.e., for instance paying too much attention to human frailties or deficiencies in the community); (5) love of stability is a great help in perseverance. The question {is}, in what cases is it *permissible or worthwhile* to change one's stability?

A. The general principle {is that} *when one has vowed a good, one is never permitted to abandon it for a lesser good*. (Valid dispensation in the case of a vow presupposes that the circumstances of the case make it no longer possible for the good to which the vow obliges us to be fully attained—and that the good of charity must be sought elsewhere more effectively.) Hence stability cannot be changed unless *a greater good* will result from the change. But since stability in the monastery is a great help to virtue and perfection, instability will never be a greater good than stability. One may never legitimately change stability merely in order to descend

---

821. "*facilis cura ejus invenitur in Regula, si quidem sit transgressio absque contemptu.*"

822. Cols. 885A–888C.

to an easier life (*remisso descensui*[823]); to win an argument with superiors (*contensioso decessui*[824]); to gratify unstable nature (*vago et curioso discursui*[825]); or for any motive of inconstancy (n. 44 [885]).

B. *Practical applications* (remember that in general it is a great temptation, when one is well-established, to seek to go elsewhere):

(1) In a regular and well-ordered monastery, no monk has the right to leave even for a higher life without the permission of his superior (n. 45 [885]). (This seems strange to us, but before the present Code,[826] one was permitted to leave to embrace a higher life even without his superior's permission.)

(2) If a monk has left his monastery and found a better one, then he should not return to his first monastery.

(3) No one is permitted to leave a strict monastery in order to enter a more relaxed one. St. Bernard regards this (loosely) as "apostasy" (885).[827] (However, St. Thomas does not agree with this. According to him[828] it is not only permissible but praiseworthy for a religious who cannot keep a strict rule to

---

823. "a negligent descent".

824. "a contentious departure".

825. "unsettled and inquisitive wandering".

826. See Canon 632: "*Religiosus nequit ad aliam religionem, etiam strictiorem, vel e monasterio sui iuris ad aliud transire sine auctoritate Apostolicae Sedis*" (*Codex Iuris Canonici*, ed. Petrus Cardinalis Gasparri [New York: P. J. Kenedy & Sons, 1918], 183) ("A religious may not transfer to another order, even a stricter one, or from one monastery with its own jurisdiction to another, without the authorization of the Holy See").

827. "*ad inferiora jam vel remissiora . . . nequaquam apostabit*" ("by no means shall he apostasize to an inferior or more negligent [monastery]").

828. "*Tertio, propter infirmitatem vel debilitatem; ex qua interdum provenit quod non potest aliquis arctioris religionis statuta servare posset autem servare statuta religionis laxioris. . . . In tertio casu etiam est necessaria dispensationis*" ("Thirdly, on account of illness or weakness, due to which it happens that someone is unable to observe the rules of a more strict religious life but would be able to keep the rules of a less rigorous order. . . . In the third case a dispensation is also needed") (*Summa Theologiae, Secunda Secundae*, q. 189, a. 8 [*Opera Omnia*, 3.664]).

transfer to some order where he can keep the rule. In such a case he should seek a dispensation. This presupposes a real inability to keep the rule, not just lack of generosity.)

(4) In any case, according to the *Rule*, no abbot can receive a monk from another known monastery without the permission of the abbot of that other monastery.

C. *The particular question of Benedictines who want to become Cistercians*:

(1) St. Bernard's answer {is} NON CONSULO:[829] he does not advise it, at least not without the permission of his abbot. This is to be balanced against St. Bernard's own practice in various cases (see for instance letters 33, 34, 35[830]). He often did not hesitate to receive Benedictines even against the protest of an irate abbot.

(2) Reasons for *not* transferring from Cluny to Cîteaux {include the following}: (a) because it is a scandal for the monks who remain behind {and} makes them restless; (b) it is not prudent to leave something certain for something doubtful—*certa pro dubiis relinquere tutum non est*;[831] the monk can be a good Benedictine, but can he be a good Cistercian? (c) {the} danger of levity; (d) it is not a valid objection to say (as the founders of Cîteaux said!!!!) that one is not really keeping the *Rule* in a monastery of Cluny—no, says Bernard, we do not vow to keep the *Rule* but to live according to the *Rule*, and the observances of Cluny are a legitimate interpretation of the *Rule*: "*Boni usus a Regula non discordant*" (n. 47 [886]).[832] Indeed, he appeals to the eighth degree of humility, which says that we should live according to the customs of our own monastery. In practice, however, if a monastery is so lax that one is not living a regular life, St. Bernard would certainly permit the monk to go to a stricter monastery.

*Some Letters of St. Bernard on Transfer and Change of Stability*: before considering the strong and classical letters of exhortation

---

829. N. 46 (col. 886A) ("I do not advise it").
830. *Letters*, 65–69; *PL* 182, cols. 136A–140D (##32–34).
831. "It is not safe to leave what is certain for what is doubtful."
832. "good customs do not depart from the *Rule*."

urging men of the world to enter the monastery (note: this will be done elsewhere[833]), let us look at a few samples of ordinary letters about the routine business of deciding vocations, recommendations and advice concerning vocations, and especially regarding transfer to another monastery. (The references, for simplicity's sake, will be given according to the English translation of Bruno James [Chicago, 1953]: *Complete Letters*.) {In} Letter 461 (p. 518),[834] he urges a Benedictine abbot to accept two novices who did not have the strength to persevere "*in our Order*" (note {the} different connotation of *Ordo noster*), and he adds, "be not in a hurry to profess them."[835] {In} Letter 460,[836] to a Cistercian prior, {Bernard is} recommending a boy be met in Châlons who did not want to become a knight but a soldier of Christ (READ pp. 517–18[837]). Letter 463[838] {is written} to an abbot, to receive back a fugitive brother who promises to amend his ways, recommending leniency and relaxation of rules on fugitives (discuss these rules). Letters 33, 34 {and} 35 {were written} concerning the monk Drogo, who had left St. Nicasius to become a Cistercian, but probably did not persevere; {the first is} to an abbot, Jorannus, who eventually left the Benedictines to become a Carthusian:

---

833. No discussion of these letters is included in these conferences.

834. *PL* 182, col. 638BC (#442).

835. Text reads: "These young men have good wills but not the physical strength necessary for our Order; . . . . But do not be in any hurry to profess them . . ."

836. *PL* 182, col. 638AB (#441).

837. "I found the young man who is bringing you this letter awaiting me at Châlons. When he saw me he asked me with great diffidence and simplicity to receive him into our Order and make a monk of him. He explained that Thomas of Marla, whose shield-bearer he had been, wished to make him a knight in the service of the world, but that he preferred the service of Christ, and for this reason sought refuge with us. Consult some of your brethren and, if they should approve and you see fit, receive him and put him to the test."

838. *Letters*, 519 (*PL* 182, col. 639C [#445]).

a) {Letter} 33[839]—to Jorannus, the abbot of St. Nicasius, angry at the transfer of Drogo without his blessing. He says he would not have received Drogo. (Evidently Drogo entered Pontigny.) Bernard consoles the abbot but tells him to accept God's will (READ par. 2, p. 66[840]). {Note} the anecdote: "Wherever he is, if he is good, he is mine" (comment). {He} refers to his own case, and the departure of Robert to Cluny,[841] {and} ends by advising another Brother Hugh to stay where he is {and exercise} perseverance (67).

b) {Letter} 34[842]—to Hugh, abbot of Pontigny. {Here we see} Bernard as politician! He has written a previous letter to Hugh, prompted by Abbot Jorannus and the archbishop of Rheims. He tried to word it politically to cover the following ground: (1) he knew that Drogo wanted to be a Cistercian, is glad that Drogo is a Cistercian but, while possibly doubting he will persevere, hopes he will do so; (2) he knows the abbot is angry, and knows he has a right to be angry, and to make trouble for Pontigny; (3) he fears that he himself may be suspected of complicity, and so to clear himself he writes a strong letter to Hugh; (4) but he hoped

---

839. *Letters*, 65–67 (*PL* 182, cols. 136A–138B [#32]).

840. "So that you may not be drowned in this horrid storm, so that you may not be swallowed up in the depths, so that the mouth of the insatiable pit may not close over you, do you in humble prudence take care that you are not overcome by evil, but rather overcome evil by good. And overcome you will if you put your hope in God and patiently await the issue. If Brother Drogo should be brought to his senses either by his fear of you or by the difficulty of what he has undertaken, well and good; but if not, then for your own good you must 'bow down under the strong hand of God' and not kick against the ruling of heaven, because what is of God cannot be undone. You should try to control your stirrings of anger, however justified they may be, by remembering that saying of one of the saints who, when some of the brethren were provoking and reproaching for not recalling a brother who had gone to another monastery in defiance of him, replied: 'Not at all. Wherever he is, if he is good, he is still mine.'"

841. *Letters*, 1–10 (#1); see above, pages 126–33.

842. *Letters*, 67–68 (*PL* 182, cols. 138B–139D [#33]).

Hugh would have had the sense to read between the lines!!! Was St. Bernard a little bit devious in this? Bruno James remarks he was certainly "human."

c) {Letter} 35[843]—note the totally different tone of the letter to Drogo! First {he expresses} effusive affection, then unusual praise, in addition to which Jorannus is now alluded to as a Pharisee, and Drogo is encouraged not to pay attention to his complaints, even though in 34 Bernard admits them to be perfectly justified. {The} real purpose of this letter {is} to urge Drogo to stay at Pontigny, making it clear there is no intention of getting him to Clairvaux.

Letter 67,[844] to {the} bishop of Lincoln, informing him that one of his clerics wants to enter Clairvaux, {is} a gracious and clever letter. Canon Philip, on pilgrimage to Jerusalem, has found his vocation at Clairvaux: "Your Philip has found a short cut to Jerusalem" (READ par. 1, p. 91[845]). The monastery {is presented} as "Jerusalem," where one is *no longer in exile* (contrast {the} theme of exile and *peregrinatio*), {emphasizing the} relationship

---

843. *Letters*, 68–69 (*PL* 182, cols. 139D–140D [#34]).
844. *Letters*, 90–92 (*PL* 182, cols. 169A–170C [#64]).
845. "I write to tell you that your Philip has found a short cut to Jerusalem and has arrived there very quickly. He crossed 'the vast ocean stretching wide on every hand' with a favourable wind in a very short time, and he has now cast anchor on the shores for which he was making. Even now he stands in the courts of Jerusalem and 'whom he had heard tidings of in Ephrata he has found in the woodland plains, and gladly reverences in the place where he has halted in his journey.' He has entered the holy city and has chosen his heritage with them of whom it has been deservedly said: 'You are no longer exiles or aliens; the saints are your fellow citizens, you belong to God's household.' His going and coming is in their company and he has become one of them, glorifying God and saying with them: 'We find our true home in heaven.' He is no longer an inquisitive onlooker, but a devout inhabitant and an enrolled citizen of Jerusalem; but not of that earthly Jerusalem to which Mount Sinai in Arabia is joined, and which is in bondage with her children, but of that free Jerusalem which is above and the mother of us all."

of the monastic community and the heavenly Jerusalem: "He is no longer an onlooker but a devout inhabitant," etc. Discuss this monastic conception of the Church and its effect. READ par. 2 (p. 91)[846] {on} Clairvaux and the heavenly Jerusalem: "conformity of life" {and} "spiritual affinity"; rest, not in vision but in true peace; temporal matters {are} then dealt with. {In} paragraph 3, "So much for Philip"—and now an exhortation to Alexander the Magnificent: death may come unawares.

*To the Abbot of Anchin—Letters 68,*[847] *69:*[848] Godwin, one of the best monks of Anchin, leaves to enter Clairvaux, evidently without permission (not strictly required), and {his} abbot was angry. Godwin died, and {the} abbot relented. Bernard praises his mercy, then defends his own action (READ par. 3, p. 93[849]). His course of

---

846. "And this, if you want to know, is Clairvaux. She is the Jerusalem united to the one in heaven by whole-hearted devotion, by conformity of life, and by a certain spiritual affinity. Here, so Philip promises himself, will be his rest for ever and ever. He has chosen to dwell here because he has found, not yet to be sure the fulness of vision, but certainly the hope of that true peace, 'the peace of God which surpasses all our thinking.' But this blessing, although he has received it from on high, he wishes to have, and is indeed quite sure that he does have, with your good will, because 'a wise son maketh the father glad.' He begs you of your fatherly love, and I unite my prayers with his, that the arrangement he has made for his creditors to have his prebend, may be allowed to stand, so that he may not become (God forbid) a defaulter and breaker of his covenant, and his daily sacrifice of a contrite heart be unacceptable because a brother has something against him. He also begs that the house which he has built for his mother on Church lands with the ground which he has assigned to it, may remain hers so long as she lives. So much for Philip."

847. *Letters*, 92–94 (*PL* 182, cols. 170D–173B [#65]).

848. *Letters*, 94–95 (*PL* 182, cols. 173B–174B [#66]).

849. "And so your very affection for your son excuses him, but what reasons can you have, my father, for excusing me? What adequate satisfaction can I make to you? What satisfaction can you ask of me for the great injury I have done you in receiving your son when he left you? What can I say? If I tell you that I did not take him in (and would that I could say this without sin), it would be an obvious lie. If I admit that I received him, but

action: (1) he did not invite Godwin to enter Clairvaux; (2) he suggested that he return to Anchin {and} tried to persuade him {to do so}; (3) only when Godwin insisted, Bernard took him, since perhaps he is sent by God; (4) {he} recognizes that he has been wrong in the sense that he has offended this abbot, and asks pardon.

Letter 69 {is written} to {the} abbot of St. Medard, {asking him} to intercede with {the} abbot of Anchin for him. {It provides a} further statement of his view: "Whether it be just or unjust, I ought not to ignore resentment against me."[850] It is therefore a "scandal" that has to be removed. {What is the} solution of the "case"?

*The Monks of Flay*: contrast Letters 70[851] {and} 71[852] with the above. Here Bernard is much more nonchalant, {and} even seems to us in some sense cynical about it (actually he is not). A monk of Flay comes to Clairvaux, Bernard receives him, the former

---

maintain that it was right for me to have done so, I would seem to be excusing myself. If I take the safer course and admit that I have done wrong, there is a question of how far I have done wrong. I do not say in self-defence, 'Who would not have taken him in?' I say, 'Who would have turned that holy man away when he was knocking on the door or would have sent him off when he had been received?' Who can tell whether God was not satisfying my need from your abundance by sending me one out of your many good religious to be at the same time a comfort to me and a credit to you, for the Scriptures tell us that a wise son is a credit to his father. I did not try to anticipate his wishes by inviting him to come, I did not attempt to lure him away from you. God knows that, on the contrary, when he was imploring me to take him in I would not do so before I had first tried to persuade him to return to you. Only when he refused to return, and then only grudgingly, did I give way to his importunity. If I am at fault for receiving a good man, a stranger, and alone, and for receiving him in the way that I did, it is the only time I have offended you by such a fault and it would therefore not be unbecoming in you to forgive it, seeing that it is not lawful for you to refuse pardon even to one who has fallen seventy times seven."

850. *Letters*, 94.
851. *Letters*, 95–96 (*PL* 182, cols. 174B–176C [#67]).
852. *Letters*, 97–99 (*PL* 182, cols. 176C–179A [#68]).

abbot protests {and} appeals to {the} *Rule*, chapter 61. Apparently {he} upbraided Bernard somewhat bitterly. Instead of following the line above, Bernard says: (1) your sorrow is not supernatural, perhaps; (2) *Rule*, chapter 61 says {that} one must not receive a monk from a known monastery—"Your monastery may be well known, but not to us";[853] (3) we have never heard of you, or of your religious observance and way of life; (4) the line of action taken {was that Bernard} refused to admit the monk {and} tried to persuade him to return to his monastery, but he lived as a hermit nearby for seven months, then renewed {his} request, and they took him in when they learned that in his own monastery the abbot was "using him as a doctor" (READ p. 96, middle[854]); (5) "We did not compel him to enter and we will not force him to leave. He says that if we drive him out he will not return to you but will go still farther away."[855] {There were} further invectives: they accuse him of violating not only the *Rule* but the canons and natural law. He retorts that he has given refuge to a poor monk seeking a decent life. They say he is receiving an excommunicate. He replies they did not excommunicate the monk until they knew he was received at Clairvaux. {Here there

---

853. *Letters*, 95.

854. "Then he told us that his abbot used him not as a monk but as a doctor; that he forced him to serve or rather used him to serve not God but the world; that in order to curry favour with the princes of this world he was made to attend tyrants, robbers, and excommunicated persons. And he told us that when he suggested to his abbot both in private and publicly that all this was a source of danger to his soul, no attention was paid to him, so that finally, with the advice of experienced men, he left, not so much his monastery as the occasions of sin, not so much his holy religion as his unholy way of life. When he had told us all this he once more begged us to open to his knocking and admit him for the safety of his soul. And when we saw his constancy and heard the reasons for his leaving the monastery and could discover nothing against him, we granted him admission, proved and approved him, admitted him to profession, and now regard him as one of ourselves."

855. *Letters*, 96.

is a} renewal of {the} argument about the "unknown monastery" (READ par. 2[856]). He would be glad if any of his monks could find greater perfection elsewhere ({the} implication {being} that this is not possible). If they promise the monk can return and have peace in the cloister (not being {a} doctor), it is an admission that he did not have peace before, etc., etc. (READ n. 4, p. 99[857]).

856. "The only grounds for enquiry between us, the only thing that remains to be discovered, is whether he was rightly received by me. You for your part, as you cannot deny that a monk may be lawfully received from an unknown monastery, contend that you are not unknown to me. I deny this, but you will not believe me. And so, as you will not believe my simple word, I affirm it again by oath. By the very Truth, which is God, I assure you that I have not known you and do not know you. Your letters are from persons quite unknown to me, and my letters to you are to unknown persons. I have experienced vexation and worry from you, but I have had no experience of you who vex and worry me. So as to prove me guilty of feigned ignorance you bring forward the irrefutable argument that I must know you because I have inscribed the name of your abbot and monastery upon my letters, as if to know the name of a thing were the same as to know the thing itself. By this reasoning it would be a great thing for me to know the names of the angels Michael, Gabriel, and Raphael because by the very sound of the words I would be blessed with a knowledge of the blessed spirits. By this reasoning I must have profited not a little by hearing the names of Paradise and the third heaven from the Apostle, because, although I have not been rapt there with him, from the very names themselves I should be able to know the secrets of heaven, and words unspeakable which it is not lawful for men to utter. And how foolish I must be, for although I know the name of God yet I continue to groan and sigh with the Prophet, saying, 'I long, Lord for thy presence,' and 'When shall I come and stand in the presence of my God?' and 'Smile upon us, O God, and we shall find deliverance.'"

857. "Cease, therefore, brothers, cease worrying your brother about whom you have no cause to worry, unless indeed (and may such a thing be very far from you!) it is your own interests and not the glory of God you are seeking, your own satisfaction in your brother's return and not the salvation of his soul. As you say he was always a rolling stone with you and, contrary to his state and the commands of his abbot, spending the money he made from the practice of his art upon himself, if you love him you ought to rejoice now that by the mercy of God he is cured. For I bear witness that never now

*Case of a scandalous canon*—Letter 81:[858] should a Premonstratensian canon who has given public scandal leave his order and do penance in Clairvaux? Bernard recommends that he do penance in another house of his own order, because the sin became public before it was confessed and repented. If it had been confessed secretly, then it would have been the duty of the superior to keep the man in that house and to cure him there.

*Another argument over {a} transfer—Letter 328 to Hugh, Abbot of Prémontré*:[859] the Abbot of Prémontré is very angry and threatens to break with Clairvaux after {a} long friendship. Bernard protests this is unjust. {The conflict is over} the reception of Br. Robert of Prémontré to Clairvaux. {The} usual approach {is taken}: Bernard has explained his reasons openly {and} will do so again. Robert was at first refused and told to return to Prémontré. This was repeated over the course of "many years." He persuaded many others who wanted to transfer to remain at Prémontré. Robert was received with the support of the pope (at his "command") and with the understanding that his superiors were permitting it. Another brother, Fremund, {was} received with the consent of {the} abbot but not of {the} chapter—{but the} consent of {the} chapter {was} not needed. {Also discussed is the} affair of {the} buildings at Basse-Font (nn. 6–7); READ n. 8: {the} burning of a hut built by {the} brothers of Prémontré on

---

does he wander abroad but, peacefully persevering in the monastery, he lives without complaint among poor men the life of a poor man. So far from having betrayed the faith he first pledged with you, he has now ratified it; together with obedience and conversion of manners, without which he is deceived who trusts in his stability, he now keeps that faith whole and entire. So I beg you, brothers, calm your anger and stop worrying me. But if you will not, then do what you like, write what you like, abuse me as much as you like, charity suffers all things, beareth all things. And for my part, I am determined that from henceforth I shall love you with a pure love, treat you reverently, and regard you as friends."

858. *Letters*, 118–20 (to Abbot Luke of Cuissy) (*PL* 182, cols. 199C–201B [#79]).

859. *Letters*, 403–8 (*PL* 182, cols. 453A–458D [#253]).

{the} property of Igny.⁸⁶⁰ {There is also discussion of the} interdict on St. Follian's (Premonstratensian) monastery (see pp. 406, 407).

The offering of {a} child, and {his} subsequent personal vocation, {is discussed in} Letter 419.⁸⁶¹ {This is the} same juridical problem as raised in Letter 1 (Robert of Châtillon at Cluny). The personal decision of the monk is what decides his vocation, not the offering made by his parents in his infancy (read par. 2: "Do not stifle the Spirit"⁸⁶²).

---

860. "Then you complain of me because a lay-brother of Igny burnt down a hut of your brethren at Braine. What a hut it was too! A mere shelter of boughs where the brother, who looked after the crops in the field, might find shade. It was not burnt from malice but for the very good reason that it was on a field which belonged to the brethren at Igny and occupied land which it was necessary to cultivate. The place was hardly worth two pence and, unless I am mistaken, the Abbot of Braine has already received satisfaction for it, so that he makes no complaints whatsoever and has no reason to do so. But if he has not received satisfaction, I am ready to see that he does as soon as I know. And likewise with regard to the Abbot of Longpont, as soon as I heard your complaint that he was intending to build on your territory I forbade him to do so, and I believe that he has given up the project, but if he has not I will see that he does as soon as I know for certain."

861. *Letters*, 487–88 (to Leonius, Abbot of St. Bertin) (*PL* 182, cols. 585A–586C [#382]).

862. "But so that the sacrifice I offer you may be reasonable and the honour I pay you well considered, I must be prudent and cautious for 'dearly the kingly heart loves justice.' Therefore concerning that matter about which you wrote to me I answer that I dare not and you ought not to hinder a man who would do good. For how should we answer the Apostle when he says: 'Do not stifle the spirit'? It would not be safe for you to stifle what you could not light again if you tried. And where does that other saying come in: 'Everyone has his own vocation, in which he has been called'? Thomas has been called. It was not I who called him, but he 'who can raise up the dead to life and send his call to that which has no being, as if it already were.' This thing has come about, not by men nor through men, but by God. It is not man who has done it, but God who works on the hearts of men that he may incline them to his will. I say that this is the Lord's doing and therefore it ought to be not only wonderful in our eyes, but also unalterable. What is man that he should presume to counsel the Lord and his Spirit? He who

### Sermon III {for} Paschal Time

*Common and Proper Will*: in order to understand St. Bernard's doctrine on love and obedience, indeed on the whole meaning of the monastic life, we must understand that charity means *union of wills with God*—the renunciation of self. What do these expressions signify in St. Bernard? Sometimes spiritual writers seem to believe that all spontaneity is nothing but self-will, and that to do the will of God is, in the end, to act passively and without "will" at all on our own part. This would be grossly un-Christian. To love means to *will* what is willed and loved by the Beloved. But what is the will of God? What is our own self-will? How can we tell which is which? *Self-will (voluntas propria)* is the perversion of man's inborn capacity to love. It is the "twisting back upon self of a charity which has degenerated into cupidity" (Gilson,[863] p. 55). This turning back of our capacity to love upon ourselves and away from God and our brother, is the "hidden ulcer that consumes us" (*idem*). *Characteristics of self-will* {are that it} (1) {is} directed to self, not to others, not to God; (2) refuses to share love—{it} wants to get, not to give; (3) seizes upon the good things of God for itself, without gratitude or acknowledgement; (4) tends even to deny God, the author and giver of all goods. The disorders of self-will flow from *attachment to our own judgement (proprium consilium)*: "The more we are wedded to our own opinion . . . the worse we are and the more we believe ourselves righteous. There is no disposition of soul that more easily brings with it an illusory sense of righteousness, for it sins not by lack of zeal, but by lack of knowledge. . . . True, it exalts righteousness—not God's however, but its own" (Gilson, p. 57). This attachment to our own judgement is the great *destroyer of unity and peace* in the Church and in monastic communities. It is basically idolatry and revolt against God. This disease of the judgement

---

seeks his lost sheep knows what he is seeking and where to seek it. And he knows too from whence to call him and where to place him so that he may not be lost again. But do not try to pull down again a man whom God has set up, and do not try to trip up a man whom God is helping to climb."

863. Gilson, *Mystical Theology of Saint Bernard*.

corrupts the will and leads to attachment to our own will. This in turn makes self-knowledge impossible and imprisons the soul within its own illusions and attachments. The soul is wretched and helpless, and tormented by restlessness is unable to find peace in anything, yet will not turn to the truth, or face the truth about itself. Where is the remedy?

{In} *Sermon III {for} Paschal Time*[864]—on Naaman's seven baths in the Jordan—{Bernard teaches that} the remedy for all the "leprosy" of our soul is in the mysteries of Christ, particularly in the Passion and Resurrection. We are purified from the leprosy of attachment to worldly goods by the poverty of Jesus in His Incarnation (if we love that poverty and unite ourselves to Him). From attachment to sensual pleasure {we are} purified by the Passion of Jesus, as also from the "leprosy of impatience and murmuring, by His humility and silence before His tormentors."[865] *But the worst leprosy is that of the heart, which is twofold— self-will (propria voluntas) and attachment to our own judgement (proprium consilium).*[866] What are these? St. Bernard defines them: *voluntas propria* is "that will which is *not common to God and other men, but is purely and simply our own.*"[867] This is one of the best and clearest definitions of self-will. It enables us to understand the real nature of self-love, and not to go wrong by thinking that everything that gives us satisfaction is somehow wrong. Self-will is not what pleases ourselves, or attracts our own desires, or gratifies ourselves. That we may be pleased or gratified is secondary or accidental. What matters is *whether or not the gratification*

---

864. *PL* 183, cols. 288C–292C.

865. "*Cum enim adversi quidquam contigerit, murmuramus, et impatientiae verbum tanquam leprae sanies effluit. Sed ab hac mundamur, si illum attendimus, qui tanquam ovis ad occisionem ductus est, et non aperuit os suum*" (col. 289C) ("When something negative has happened, we murmur, and a word of impatience flows forth like the suppuration of leprosy. But we are healed of this if we are attentive to the One who was like a sheep led to the slaughter and did not open His mouth").

866. N. 3 (col. 289D).

867. "*Voluntatem dico propriam, quae non est communis cum Deo et hominibus, sed nostra tantum.*"

*and pleasure at the good is capable of being shared with God and other men, or not. Self-will* is that will which is "not common." *Common will*, charity, shares a universal good, a real good, with God and with others. Its good is not diminished by being shared. It is therefore united to others in love. It is, in fact, LOVE. The common will and the common good are the same: they are love. Wherever there is real love, that reaches out to God and to other men and excludes none, then *we cannot have self-will*. As soon as we exclude others and love the good for our own sakes, without sharing, then we have self-will. The distinction depends not so much on the object as on our *real intention*. Self-will, then, acts not for God, not for our brethren, but for self alone: QUANDO QUOD VOLUMUS, NON AD HONOREM DEI, NON AD UTILITATEM FRATRUM, SED PROPTER NOSMETIPSOS FACIMUS (n. 3 [289])[868]—i.e., we do it for ourselves to the *exclusion of* the good of another. What is the test: the *intention* to *satisfy the inner movements of our own soul*. NON INTENDENTES PLACERE DEO ET PRODESSE FRATRIBUS SED SATISFACERE PROPRIIS MOTIBUS ANIMORUM (*idem*).[869] This is directly opposed to charity. It is the enemy of God. It is the food for the flame of hell. CESSET VOLUNTAS PROPRIA ET INFERNUS NON ERIT (*idem* [290]).[870] He illustrates—the sufferings which we undergo flow from the fact that we have to bear what is contrary to our will, what we "don't want." As soon as we accept what is contrary, and embrace it as the will of God, our will is "common" and the basic suffering of opposition to Him is removed. In proportion as we cannot fully accept, we suffer. But the rebellion of our senses and emotions need not disturb the inner peace of the abandoned will; these are not "will" but "*corruptio voluntatis*"[871] (*idem*). We can have peace in spite of them. On the contrary, if we cling to our own will, the whole world itself will never satisfy us. Not only that, but self-will attacks God

---

868. "when we do what we want, not for the honor of God, nor for the benefit of our brothers, but for the sake of ourselves alone."
869. "not intending to please God or benefit the brothers, but to satisfy the personal movements of souls."
870. "Let self-will cease, and there will be no hell."
871. "the corruption of the will."

in order to justify itself. It seeks in effect to "destroy" Him by trying to subvert His order, and deny His truth. {With regard to} *proprium consilium*, like self-will, which prefers our own private gratification to the good of all, our own judgement is not mere judgement, but *the judgement to which we cling in opposition to everyone else*. It is obstinacy in holding to one's own views and refusing to be guided or advised by anyone else. QUAE MAJOR SUPERBIA QUAM UT UNUS HOMO TOTI CONGREGATIONI JUDICIUM SUUM {PRAEFERAT,} TANQUAM IPSE SOLUS HABEAT SPIRITUM DEI (n. 4 [290]).[872] {The} *remedy* {is} the humility and obedience of Jesus. Jesus, though He was Wisdom Itself, gave up His own views in order to be subject to Mary and Joseph. Even though He was infinitely wise, He judged it better to embrace the common view rather than to maintain His own (n. 4 [291]). Jesus in the Garden of the Agony renounced His own desires, though they were good and perfect, in order to fulfill in His passion what was good for us and pleasing to His Father. The obedience of Jesus Crucified is the most perfect example of the "common will"—what was pleasing to the Father, to Jesus Himself, and salutary for us.

### A NOTE ON CONTEMPLATION AND MYSTICAL THEOLOGY

Before we approach the sermons of St. Bernard on the Canticle of Canticles, let us consider what is meant by "mystical theology" and clear the way of obstacles that might prevent us from arriving at a proper understanding of St. Bernard and his doctrine.

1. There is nothing explicit in the gospels or the Apostolic Fathers about such things as "contemplation" or "mystical theology" considered as separate departments of theology or of the life of prayer. Everything is centered in the mystery of Christ, and it is clear that the Christian who lives "in Christ" will come to have a very deep experience of the reality of this life (cf. for instance chapters 14–17 of St. John's Gospel).

---

872. "What greater pride is there than that one person prefers his own judgement to that of the whole community, as though he alone had the Spirit of God?" (copy text reads: "PRAEFERT").

2. For the Greek Fathers, "mystical theology" and "contemplation" are two ways of saying the same thing. The term "contemplation" is borrowed from Greek philosophy. Both terms mean the hidden knowledge of God by experience, the "passive" illumination of the soul by the divine light "in darkness." To be precise, *theology* (*theologia*) refers to the highest contemplation of God, in Himself, the Triune God. *Contemplation* (*theoria*) refers rather to the contemplation of God in creatures, and in the action of His Providence in the world, in the "economy" of man's salvation (therefore above all in the Scriptures).

3. The Latin Fathers—St. Augustine, St. Gregory, St. Bernard, etc.—do not consider themselves "mystical theologians" in the modern sense. For them, theology as such is a *wisdom* (*sapientia*) which culminates in experience of the reality of the dogmas revealed by God. The perfect theologian is one who is a contemplative and has an experiential realization of the mysteries of faith rather than just a book-knowledge *about* God and the mysteries of faith.

4. In the late Middle Ages, and in the Renaissance and later, "mysticism" comes to be separated from dogma (in the decline of scholasticism). Dogma is the technical apparatus proper to the doctors in the schools. Mysticism is the province of the "mystics"—contemplatives set apart from the theologians, and in opposition to them. This is exemplified in St. John of the Cross and St. Teresa, who make a kind of profession of contemplation, and they write about mystical experience as such, *ex professo*, and nothing else. Here mystical theology becomes the study of the life of prayer and union, etc., etc. It tends even to become a summary of the techniques by which one can dispose himself to ascend the degrees of the spiritual life, under the guidance of grace.

5. In the eighteenth century, after many violent reactions against contemplatives and the contemplative life, and after the sensational effects of extraordinary mystics and their revelations (v.g., St. Margaret Mary), mysticism becomes identified with the *extraordinary and even charismatic* graces given by God in exceptional cases. Mystical theology then becomes *the study of these exceptional cases*. The true idea of contemplation is then obscured

and forgotten, and "mysticism" becomes something rare and suspicious, from which the average man must flee and which even saints will not necessarily experience.

6. In modern times—{the} twentieth century—there has been a *revival of the study of mysticism and of contemplation*, with a renewal of the traditional emphasis on the more "ordinary" forms of contemplation which can (according to many theologians) be regarded as the "normal" development of the life of grace. In our time, contemplation has once again become a center of interest and of discussion. Much has been written about the subject, from many different points of view. As a result: (a) contemplation has once again become "known," at least to some; (b) but at the same time, the multitude of books and varying opinions has created a certain amount of confusion, and one feels that much of what has been said and written has been sterile and misleading.

7. What are some of the *modern approaches to mystical theology*?[873]

a) Phenomenology: *Poulain*[874] studies the "symptoms" of different degrees of prayer, with numerous quotes from "the mystics." This descriptive method is really a technique for "placing" various states of prayer, classifying them and then applying an appropriate prescription. But it is *not theology*, however useful. Unfortunately, while useful for a director, this book tends to make some monks examine themselves, analyze their own degree of prayer, etc., and in the end, for some, the "contemplative life" is simply a struggle to hoist themselves from one degree of prayer to another. But the contemplative life is not to be regarded as a greenhouse in which plants are forced on to the higher degrees. Such a conception is in fact disastrous to the true spirit of contemplation.

---

873. For a more detailed discussion of this topic, see *Introduction to Christian Mysticism*, 19–38.

874. Augustin-François Poulain, sj, *Des Grâces d'Oraison* (1901; 10th ed., Paris: Beauchesne, 1922); ET: *The Graces of Interior Prayer: A Treatise on Mystical Theology*, trans. Leonora L. Yorke Smith (St. Louis: B. Herder, 1950).

b) {The} speculative method {of} *Garrigou-Lagrange*,[875] etc.: these theologians develop a *scholastic and Thomistic theory* of the place of contemplation in the Christian life. This theory states that the graces of mystical prayer are the result of special inspirations of the Holy Ghost working according to the gifts of understanding and wisdom, and since the gifts are part of the Christian's normal equipment, received at baptism, contemplation should therefore be considered a normal development of the life of grace. Other theologians differ and present other opinions, but again in a scholastic framework.

c) Patristic: a return to the study of the theology of the Fathers, with emphasis on their view of the mystical life, or rather with emphasis on the *wholeness* of their theology in which mysticism and dogma are not separated but integrated in theological wisdom—for instance, Dom Anselm Stolz,[876] Dom Cuthbert Butler,[877] Gilson,[878] Daniélou,[879] etc., etc. *This is our tradition, as monks. This is where we ought to make our acquaintance with mystical theology.*

d) Popularizations: in addition to the above categories, we must cite the numerous works which combine one or other

---

875. Reginald Garrigou-Lagrange, OP, *Perfection Chrétienne et Contemplation selon S. Thomas d'Aquin et S. Jean de la Croix*, 2 vols. (Paris: Éditions du Cerf, 1923); ET: *Christian Perfection and Contemplation according to the Teaching of St. Thomas Aquinas and St. John of the Cross*, trans. Sr. M. Timothea Doyle (St. Louis: Herder, 1937); see also Reginald Garrigou-Lagrange, OP, *Les Trois Âges de la Vie Intérieure, Prélude de Celle du Ciel* (Paris: Éditions du Cerf, 1938); ET: *The Three Ages of the Interior Life, Prelude of Eternal Life*, trans. Sr. M. Timothea Doyle (St. Louis: Herder, 1947–1948).

876. Anselm Stolz, OSB, *Theologie der Mystik* (Ratisbon: Friedrich Pustet, 1936); *Théologie de la Mystique* (Chevtogne: Éditions des Bénédictins d'Amay, 1947); ET: *The Doctrine of Spiritual Perfection*, trans. Aidan Williams, OSB (St. Louis: Herder, 1938).

877. Dom Cuthbert Butler, *Western Mysticism: The Teaching of SS. Augustine, Gregory and Bernard on Contemplation and the Contemplative Life*, 2nd ed. (London: Constable, 1926).

878. Gilson, *Mystical Theology of Saint Bernard*.

879. Jean Daniélou, SJ, *Platonisme et Théologie Mystique: Doctrine Spirituelle de Saint Grégoire de Nysse*, rev. ed. (Paris: Éditions Montaigne, 1953).

of the above types in an effort to bring mysticism to the level of the ordinary religious and the faithful. An example {is} Dom Vital Lehodey's *Ways of Mental Prayer*,[880] or popularizations of the Carmelite School (Fr. Eugene, *I Want to See God*,[881] etc.). These partake somewhat of Poulain, St. Teresa, Garrigou-Lagrange and the Fathers. Again the emphasis seems to be mostly on the degrees of the spiritual life and what to do in order to ascend them effectively. (I leave on one side the studies of purely extraordinary mystical phenomena.)

8. *Contemplation in the Church Today*: what are the fruits of the above studies? How can we evaluate what has been done so far in the twentieth century? Let us be tentative, frank and simple. What follows is simply a matter of opinion, necessarily open to much qualification and correction:

a) There is a certain superficial knowledge of "contemplation" and the "mystical life" spread abroad among *some* priests, *some* religious and *some* of the faithful. These may or may not cling, in bewilderment, to some school or other, some opinion or other. In any case they have a vague knowledge of the degrees of prayer and perhaps a guilty feeling that they ought to be ascending all these degrees, but cannot quite explain why they never get around to doing so. (Very often this takes the form of fixing the blame for the lack of contemplatives on this or that abuse: for instance, the fewness of contemplatives in Cistercian monasteries may be blamed on "relaxations" and "irregularity.")

b) There are *relatively many who attain to the lower degrees of contemplative prayer*. (Whether or not this has been helped by the things said about it is not clear—one thing is probable: reading about contemplation has helped many to understand that it is not so remote and strange as they at first thought, and they have been able to recognize graces that otherwise would have passed unobserved.)

---

880. Vital Lehodey, *The Ways of Mental Prayer*, trans. A Monk of Mount Melleray (Dublin: M. H. Gill, 1924).

881. Marie-Eugène de l'Enfant-Jésus, *I Want to See God: A Practical Synthesis of Carmelite Spirituality* (Chicago: Fides, 1953).

c) It has become clear that a desire for the contemplative life (in the sense of the mystical life) and for graces of prayer is altogether permissible, if one has the right dispositions and is willing to cooperate with the grace of God.

d) On the other hand the multitude of writings has tended to *water down* the true notion of contemplation until the most insignificant of consolations are hailed as "contemplative prayer." For some writers, it would seem that any consolation in prayer, any tendency to remain in loving attention to God, is a "mystical grace." Hence there exists among religious a kind of comfy, armchair contemplation which is little more than a spiritualization of bourgeois ease, and does not represent a real abandonment of self into the hands of God.[882] (This on the other hand does not mean that one can become a contemplative by building up the number of one's penitential practices. The point I am making is that entrance into the mystical life implies a true *metanoia*, a complete inner change. This change may be *prepared* by certain graces, consolations of affective prayer and prayer of "simplicity" so-called. But to indulge in these things without having crossed the frontier of *metanoia* is not the real mystical life, even though these graces may be to a great extent passively "infused.")

e) The mystical life of the Church in our time does, in fact, consist to a great extent of *extraordinary and charismatic* gifts, either separated from or combined with graces of contemplation properly so called (v.g., apparitions of Our Lady, etc.).

9. *Contemplatives in our monasteries* should not be rare (says the *Spiritual Directory*[883]). In fact, they seem to have been quite

---

882. See Thomas Merton, "Contemplation in a Rocking Chair," in Thomas Merton, *Early Essays, 1947–1952*, ed. Patrick F. O'Connell, Cistercian Studies [CS], vol. 266 (Collegeville, MN: Cistercian Publications, 2015), 91–102 (originally published in *Integrity* 2, no. 11 [August 1948]: 15–23).

883. "These graces [the state of quiet and of mystical prayer] form a worthy consummation to such a life if it should please God to grant them. This ordinarily happens only after a long and laborious period of prayer and of severe trials. These favors should not be rare in a penitential order such as ours" ([Vital Lehodey, ocso,] *A Spiritual Directory for Religious* Translated from the Original French Text *"Directoire Spirituel à l'Usage des Cister-*

rare up until recently, even in Europe. The lower degrees of contemplative prayer are common in our monasteries today, or, to put it better, our monks quite frequently have just the kind of prayer-life one would expect from sons of St. Bernard. One finds the kind of prayer described in the Sermons *in Cantica*, or the treatises *De Contemplatione* of the Middle Ages, where the "degrees" are not too clearly differentiated as yet. *This is to be regarded as good and satisfactory. It is a sign of the blessing of God.* Many monks reach contemplation quite early. Do they progress? I think it can be said that they progress in ways that are not easy to follow and which *do not conform to the clear outlines laid down in the books*. The progress is usually in the direction of exterior ordinariness and colorlessness, with a great deepening of interior simplicity and sincerity and a kind of disappearing into the ways of God, a "getting lost." This is the normal way for monks, and it would be wrong to look for a skyrocket ascent from prayer of quiet to prayer of union, to {the} night of the soul to mystical espousals and marriage. *Failures* are sometimes spectacular. It is not infrequent for novices and young religious to receive evident graces of prayer and yet to have their vocation collapse under them. {What are the} reasons? Perhaps their system was too weak to stand the kind of "graces" they were getting. Lack of preparation and foundation are another reason. Confusion brought about by aimless reading and direction may be a contributing factor—also {an} inability to persevere in the monastic life as it now is. The big trouble would seem to be that these monks *become involved in themselves*. A taste for contemplation makes them plunge into themselves and lose contact with reality. Many give up whatever remains to them of humility and common sense and end up in disaster. {There are} a large number of cases of what St. Teresa called "melancholy"[884]—again an instance of the fact that "many

---

*ciens de la Stricte Observance*" by a Priest of New Melleray Abbey, Peosta, Iowa [Trappist, KY: Abbey of Our Lady of Gethsemani, 1946], 36).

884. See *The Interior Castle*, Sixth Mansions, chap. 3 (*The Complete Works of Saint Teresa of Jesus*, trans. and ed. E. Allison Peers, 3 vols. [New York: Sheed & Ward, 1946], 2:279).

are called but few are chosen."[885] But we must not be too sure where the blame is to be laid. Perhaps after all no one in particular is to "blame." Who can tell? Perhaps after all the confusion of modern life and the complexities of the modern temperament imply certain deficiencies which make a lifelong contemplation impossible for many.

*Conclusion*: the great helps to the contemplative life are obvious—they are the virtues of the monastic life itself—humility, detachment from ourselves, renunciation of our own will by obedience and docility, mortification, patience, meekness, charity; above all, not taking ourselves too seriously and concentrating on ourselves and what happens to us, and how we get along—but above all looking at Jesus, loving Him, doing His will, as it is manifested in objective reality. It is essential to avoid inordinate subjectivity and a purely individualistic approach to contemplation. Contemplation is the spiritual experience and awareness of life in Christ, of life in the Church which is the Body of Christ. The approach to contemplation should not be merely psychological and ascetic but above all theological and sacramental. Above all contemplation implies obedience to the Holy Spirit, not only in our heart but speaking in and through the Church (*sentire cum Ecclesia*[886]).

### V. The Mystical Doctrine of St. Bernard's Sermons on the Cancticle of Canticles

*Preface*: all that we have studied of St. Bernard's so far, though important, is really secondary. His great work, the one that is most typical of him, that contains the fullness and variety of his teaching and reflects the real depths of his experience, is

---

885. Matt. 22:14.
886. "to experience or think with the Church"; the phrase was coined by Ignatius of Loyola in his *Spiritual Exercises*: see "Rules for Thinking with the Church" in *The Spiritual Exercises of St. Ignatius*, trans. Anthony Mottola (Garden City, NY: Doubleday Image, 1964), 139–42.

the series of Sermons on the Canticle of Canticles.[887] Let us first reflect on the reasons for the very special importance of these sermons:

1. *If we want to find the full flowering of St. Bernard, we must look for it here.* The sermons were written and preached during the last, most mature and most productive period of his life. They also reflect his final development: his doctrine reaches its climax in the final sermons, preached just before his death. Here we have the essence of his teaching, and all its various aspects are shown in the whole series of sermons.

2. Since St. Bernard is in fact the one who resumed in himself all that is most important and most characteristic in Cistercian mysticism, it is evident that the Sermons on the Canticle of Canticles are the most important single source for Cistercian mystical doctrine and Cistercian spirituality. Note that in these Sermons:

    a) St. Bernard was giving his monks at Clairvaux the *formation he believed they needed*—indeed the formation which the Holy Spirit Himself inspired him to give them.

    b) He was also preaching to them the *doctrine for which they thirsted*. It was indeed thirst for this doctrine which filled the Cistercian monasteries in St. Bernard's time—his preaching was then the response to the *need for intimacy with God*, the desire for an *inner experience of divine things.*

    c) It was not only a doctrine, but a life: for his teaching in these sermons is drawn from his own life and his own experience, as well as from that of his monks. Hence, in the sermons on the Canticle of Canticles, we have *not only a theoretical exposition of spiritual doctrine, but a living expression of the spiritual experience that was common in the Cistercian monasteries of the twelfth century.* This was what St. Bernard himself lived, felt, experienced in his own prayer-life, and this too was the prayer-life of his monks.

    d) This being the case, and since the Holy Spirit raised up St. Bernard for this very purpose, if we apply ourselves to study

---

887. *Sermones in Cantica Canticorum* (PL 183, cols. 785A–1198A).

and to *prayer* above all, and try to penetrate into the heart of this living doctrine, we will surely receive *special graces* to share in the spiritual experiences of St. Bernard and the early Cistercians, though in our own way. This grace would seem to be something we have every right to expect by the very fact that we are called to live as sons of St. Bernard and as Cistercian contemplatives. Indeed the Holy Father, in *Doctor Mellifluus*, not only encourages Cistercians to live by St. Bernard's doctrine of love, but tells them it is their duty to do so.[888]

3. In addition, we must remember that the Sermons *in Cantica* are a great work of art, one of the masterpieces of the Latin medieval literature. St. Bernard, besides being a saint, was also a genius and an artist. In studying these sermons we also learn to appreciate something of the literary art of the twelfth century, and this in turn increases our understanding of the other arts at that time—and of the whole age.

4. The Sermons *in Cantica* are a fine example of Patristic Theology—in which St. Bernard, "the Last of the Fathers," echoes many of the great Fathers of the Eastern and Western Church, notably, Origen, St. Augustine, St. Gregory of Nyssa, St. Ambrose, etc.

5. In these sermons St. Bernard, as a doctor of the Church, gives us a whole theology of the spiritual life, that is to say, not a treatise in mystical and ascetical theology considered as a separate study, apart from dogma and moral, but rather an elucidation of the mysteries of the faith from the point of view of personal experience. St. Bernard's Sermons *in Cantica* are really a theology of the great mysteries of the Incarnation and Redemption in so far as the faithful participate in them by the action of the Holy Spirit, and particularly in so far as these mysteries become a matter of experience for monks elevated by the Spirit of Christ to a high degree of pure love by union with the Incarnate Word. Here St. Bernard teaches us what must be the term and fulfillment

---

888. *Last of the Fathers*, 103.

of the mysteries of the Incarnation and Redemption in the souls of those who are united with Christ by divine grace. These sermons show the way to the perfect realization of the fullness of the divine life in the souls of the elect, the members of the mystical Christ.

6. We might add that these sermons have a special importance in teaching us about the character and the life of St. Bernard himself, as well as giving us many insights into the history of the Order and of the time. St. Bernard never feels himself bound to follow a strict plan and often digresses to talk about something that is of immediate interest to himself and to his monks at the moment. Hence we not only learn his thoughts and experiences in prayer, but we also catch glimpses of his troubled time, with its schisms and heresies; we see details of St. Bernard's own busy and devoted life; we share in his grief at the death of his brother Bl. Gerard and learn about the sanctity of the latter—etc., etc.

7. Above all, let us not forget that the Sermons *in Cantica* are a great panegyric on the life and spiritual vitality of Holy Church. The Song of Songs is the song of the Church, the Bride of Christ. Not only that, but the voice of the Bridegroom unites itself and harmonizes with the voice of the Bride—for the sermons are a tissue of quotations from the Sacred Scriptures inspired by the Spirit of God.

*St. Bernard's Mysticism*: it is very important that we understand St. Bernard's point of view as a mystical doctor. If we get a wrong idea of his "mysticism" we will misunderstand his language and go perhaps very far astray. This is especially important if we are to understand rightly St. Bernard's view of the monk's *call to the mystical life*.

a) St. Bernard, like all the Fathers, is a speculative mystic. That is to say, he is a true theologian. He is not studying *mysticism* but the *mystery of our union with God*. The two may sound like the same thing, but they are poles apart. *To study "mysticism" is to study mystical phenomena and experience as such, or to study and compare mystical doctrines.* But to study the mystery of the soul's union with God is to enter into the great mystery of the Incarnation and

Redemption as a theologian who, enlightened by the Holy Spirit and guided by the Church, seeks to give us the teaching of the Church on that union. In other words, it is to show how our union with God is really a prolongation of the Incarnation, an effect intended by God when the Word became incarnate. It is to see how charity is the bond between the soul and God, and only after that to explain in what sense and to what degree this charity which unites us with God also gives us an experience of God. St. Bernard, the speculative mystic, studies how the charity "which is poured forth in our hearts by the Holy Spirit Who is given to us"[889] both unites us with God and makes it possible for us to "experience" divine things.

b) Consequently, when St. Bernard invites us to the heights of the mystical union with God, he is inviting us to the *perfection of charity*. When he is inviting us to the mystical marriage, he is inviting us to pure love for God. But this pure love unites the soul to God so that they are really one (not just morally or psychologically). But St. Bernard is not speaking of visions and revelations or other psychophysical effects which *may accompany* mystical marriage. Compare *St. Teresa, Interior Castle*, 8.2 (2, p. 334): "When granting this favour for the first time, His Majesty is pleased to reveal Himself to the soul through an *imaginary vision* of His most sacred Humanity, so that it may clearly understand what is taking place."[890] Many mystics see the Mystical Marriage as a ceremony in which they receive a ring etc., or an exchange of hearts. St. Bernard says nothing of this, and seems to ignore it completely. It is by no means necessary for Mystical Marriage. {See also} St. Margaret Mary, Letters 133 (p. 227 ff.—read pp. 227-28[891]): she is "altogether overcome by the sovereign splendor of

---

889. Rom. 5:5.

890. Emphasis added.

891. "Feeling myself altogether overcome by the splendor of this sovereign Majesty before Whom I had prostrated myself, I mentioned to Him several holy souls who would cooperate faithfully with His plans. But He said: 'I want you and no one else, and I want you to consent to My desire.'

this sovereign Majesty" (no doubt this is not yet marriage!); she is "quite overcome and in tears"—"He so showered His grace on me that I did not know myself anymore" (preparation for the marriage) (p. 228). He is "always present with me" (cf. St. Bernard). Read especially p. 228, bottom:[892] "This divine presence evokes

---

Quite overcome and in tears, I replied that He knew I was a criminal, that victims ought to be innocent, and that I would do only what my superior ordered. He agreed to this but kept on insisting, and I kept on resisting, because of the great fear that these extraordinary ways might withdraw me from the pure spirit of my vocation. I resisted Him in vain, however, for He gave me no rest until under obedience He made me immolate myself to all His desires. He wanted me to hand myself over as a victim sacrificed to every kind of suffering, humiliation, contradiction, pain, and contempt, with no other purpose than the accomplishment of His designs. I did so. He told me He knew my fears and promised, as I think I have already told you, to so accommodate His graces to the spirit of my rule, to the obedience due my superiors and to my own weakness and infirmity that there should be no conflict in anything. After that He so showered His graces on me that I did not know myself any more. This only served to increase my fears and forced me to insist that He would never allow to appear in me outwardly anything but what would make me more vile, abject and contemptible in the eyes of men. He promised. I made a retreat sometime afterwards, during which I received many graces from His wonderful liberality and mercy. Of these I need not speak. I shall say only that it was then His goodness showed me most of the graces He had determined to give me, especially those connected with His lovable Heart. Thereupon I prostrated myself and asked Him to be so good as to give these graces to some faithful soul who would know how to correspond with them. He knew well, I told Him, that I would only be an obstacle to His designs. But He gave me to understand that it was for that very reason He had chosen me, so that I might not be able to attribute anything to myself. He Himself would make up for what was wanting in me" (Letter, dated November 3, 1689, to Fr. Croiset, *The Letters of Saint Margaret Mary Alacoque*, trans. Clarence A. Herbst, SJ [Chicago: Regnery, 1954]).

892. "This divine presence evokes from me such great reverence that when I am alone it gives me no rest unless I am prostrate or on my knees, like a little bit of nothingness before this Omnipotent One. This infinite grandeur encompasses me with Its power and so takes possession of mine

from me such great reverence'; and p. 229, bottom: "I saw His divine Heart as on a throne of flames" etc.[893] St. Bernard, however, in Sermon 83 *in Cantica* gives us the essentials, but not the accidentals:

> The return of the soul is its conversion, that is, its turning to the Word; to be reformed by Him and to be rendered conformable to Him. In what respect? In charity. It is that conformity which makes, as it were, a marriage between the soul and the Word, when, being already like unto Him by its nature, it endeavours to show itself like unto Him by its will, and loves Him as it is loved by Him. And if this love is perfected, the soul is wedded to the Word. What can be more full of happiness and joy than this conformity? What more to be desired than this love, which makes thee, O soul, no longer content with human guidance, to draw near with confidence thyself to the Word, to attach thyself with con-

---

and of my whole body and soul that I think I can say that I no longer have any power over myself, for He acts in me independently of me. I am powerless to resist Him, although the fear of being deceived often makes me do all in my power to do so. It is all in vain. He leaves me no liberty at all whenever it so pleases Him. But He does give me profound peace, a joy, a satisfaction, an ardent desire to be conformed to the suffering, humble, hidden, and lowly life of my Savior. And that in such a way that contempt, poverty, sorrow, and humiliations are the delicious meat with which He continually nourishes my soul. It no longer has a taste for any other. All my pleasure in this land of exile is that of having every kind of suffering found on the cross, deprived of every other consolation except that of the Sacred Heart" (228–29).

893. "After that I saw this divine Heart as on a throne of flames, more brilliant than the sun and transparent as crystal. It had Its adorable wound and was encircled with a crown of thorns, which signified the pricks our sins caused Him. It was surmounted by a cross which signified that, from the first moment of His Incarnation, that is, from the time this Sacred Heart was formed, the cross was planted in It; that It was filled, from the very first moment, with all the bitterness, humiliations, poverty, sorrow, and contempt His sacred humanity would have to suffer during the whole course of His life and during His holy Passion."

stancy to Him, to address Him familiarly and consult Him upon all subjects, to become as receptive in thy intelligence as fearless in thy desires? This is the contract of a marriage truly spiritual and sacred. And to say this is to say little; it is more than a contract, it is embracement (*complexus*). Embracement surely, in which perfect correspondence of wills makes of two one spirit. Nor is it to be feared that the inequality of the two who are parties to it should render imperfect or halting in any respect this concurrence of wills; for love knows not reverence. Love receives its name from loving, not from honouring. Let one who is struck with dread, with astonishment, with fear, with admiration, rest satisfied with honouring; but all these feelings are absent in him who loves. Love is filled with itself, and where love has come it overcomes and transforms all other feelings. Wherefore the soul that loves, loves, and knows nought else. He who justly deserves to be honoured, justly deserves to be admired and wondered at; yet He loves rather to be loved. They are Bridegroom and Bride. What other bond or constraining force do you seek for between spouses than to be loved and to love? . . . God says: If I be Father, where is My honour? He says that as a Father. But if he declares Himself to be a Bridegroom, will He not change the word and say: If I be Bridegroom, where is My love? For he had previously said: If I be Lord, where is My fear? God, then, requires that He should be feared as Lord, honoured as Father, but as Bridegroom loved. Which of these three is highest and most to be preferred? Surely it is love. Without it fear is painful and honour without attraction. . . . Neither of these will He receive if it be not seasoned with the honey of love. Love is sufficient by itself, it pleases by itself, and for its own sake. It is itself a merit, and itself its own recompense. Love seeks neither cause nor fruit beyond itself. Its fruit is its use. I love because I love; I love that I may love. Love, then, is a great reality. It is the only one of all the movements, feelings, and affections of the soul in which the creature is able to respond to its Creator, though not upon equal terms, and to repay like with like. For example, if God is wroth with me, may I similarly be wroth with Him?

Certainly not, but I shall fear and tremble and implore pardon. . . . But how different is it with love! For when God loves, He desires nought else than to be loved, because He loves us for no other purpose than that He may be loved, knowing that those who love Him become blessed by their love itself. . . . Love that is pure is not mercenary; it does not draw strength from hope, nor is it weakened by distrust. This is the love of the Bride, {because all that she is is only love. The very being of the Bride} and her only hope is love. In this the Bride abounds; with this the Bridegroom is content. He seeks for nothing else; she has nothing else. Thence it is that He is Bridegroom and she is Bride. This belongs exclusively to a wedded pair, and to it none other attains, not even a son. The Bridegroom's love, or rather the Bridegroom who is Love, requires only love in return and faithfulness. Let it then be permitted to the Bride beloved to love in return. How could the Bride not love, she who is the Bride of Love? How could Love not be loved? Rightly then does she renounce all other affections, and devote her whole self to Him alone Who is Love, because she can make a return to Him by a love which is reciprocal. For even when she has poured her whole self forth in love, what would that be in comparison to the ever-flowing flood of that Fountain? Not with equal fullness flows the stream of love from the soul and the Word, the Bride and the Bridegroom, the creature and the Creator. What then? Shall the desire of her who is espoused perish and become of no effect, because she is unable to contend with a Giant who runs His course, to dispute the palm of sweetness with honey, of gentleness with the lamb, of brilliance with the sun, of love with Him Who is Love? No. For although, being a creature, she loves less, because she is less; nevertheless if she loves with her whole self, nothing is wanting where all is given. Wherefore, as I have said, to love thus is to be wedded (*nupsisse*); because it is not possible to love thus and yet not to be greatly loved, and in the consent of the two parties consists a full and perfect marriage (*connubium*). Can anyone doubt that the soul is first loved, by the Word, and more dearly? Assuredly it is both anticipated in loving and surpassed. Happy the soul whose favored lot it is to be prevented with the benediction of a delight so great. Happy the soul to which is granted to experience the embracement (*complexus*) of such sweetness, which is nought else than a love holy and chaste; {a love sweet and delightful; a love as serene as it is sincere;} a love mutual, intimate, powerful, which not in one flesh, but in one spirit joins together two, and makes them no more two, but one, according to St. Paul: "He that is joined to God is one spirit" (*Cant.* 83,[894] the whole sermon, compressed). (Quoted in Butler, *Western Mysticism*, 111–13[895])

Here we have the essentials, but not the accidentals: (a) perfect mystical conformity to the Word; (b) by love that makes their two wills one, not morally only but *mystically*; (c) a transformation that produces complete resemblance and indeed identity of the soul's love and God's love: two beings, but one action; (d) the soul is guided and moved in all things by the Word. BUT, as Butler makes abundantly clear,[896] terms like *ecstasy* and *rapture* in St. Bernard, along with "visits of the Spouse" etc., are not to be taken in the sense of *psycho-physical phenomena*. Ecstasy for him is *spiritual* and implies no bodily effect {or} alienation of the senses. Visits of the Spouse also {imply} no vision, no revelation. ST. BERNARD EXPLICITLY DENIES AND EXCLUDES THESE FROM HIS INTENDED MEANING.

> The love of the heart is in a certain sense carnal, in that it chiefly moves the heart of man towards the flesh of Christ and what Christ in the flesh did and said. The sacred image of the God-Man, either being born or suckled or teaching or dying or rising again, is present to one in prayer, and must needs stir up the soul to the love of virtue. But although such devotion to the flesh of Christ is a gift, and a great gift, of the Holy Ghost, nevertheless I call it carnal in comparison with that love which does not so much regard the Word which is Flesh, as the Word which is Wisdom,

---

894. Cols. 1134B–1138D.
895. Phrases in braces omitted by eyeskip.
896. Butler, 115–19.

which is Justice, which is Truth, which is Holiness (*Cant.* xx. 6, 8).[897]

In this knowing of Jesus and Him crucified, while abiding in His wounds, and contemplating gladly the things which relate to Him, Incarnate and in His Passion . . . I do not suppose that in this vision there is presented to the senses any images of His Flesh or of His Cross, or any other kinds of likenesses of our weak flesh; for in these respects "He hath no form nor comeliness." But that the soul beholding Him now pronounces Him fair and comely, shows He appeared to her by means of a nobler vision . . . a vision certainly sublime and sweet (*Cant.* 45.4, 6).[898]

As often as you hear or read that the Word and the soul converse together or behold each other, do not imagine that so to say bodily words pass between them, or that bodily images of those conversing are seen. Think rather that the Word is a spirit and the soul is a spirit, and they have tongues of their own by which they speak to one another and indicate their presence. The tongue of the Word is the favour of His condescension, and the tongue of the soul is her fervour (*ibid.*, 7).[899]

When with eager mind we ponder His testimonies and the judgements of His Mouth, and meditate on His law day and night, we should know for certain that the Bridegroom is present and is speaking to us, that we may not be wearied by our labours, being rejoiced by His words (*Cant.* 32.4).[900]

[In the union of the soul with God] the Word utters no sound, but penetrates; It is not full of words, but full of power; It strikes not on the ears, but caresses the heart; the form of its Face is not defined, and it does not touch the eyes of the body, but it makes glad the heart, not with charm of colour, but with the love it bestows. (*Cant.* 31.6)[901]

---

897. Butler, 118; cols. 870AB, 871B.
898. Butler, 118–19; cols. 1001B, 1002A.
899. Butler, 119; col. 1002D.
900. Butler, 119; col. 947CD.
901. Butler, 119; col. 943C.

If then we would profit by St. Bernard, we must:

1. Remember his own qualifications, and take what he says spiritually and not "carnally." We would do immense harm to ourselves and turn ourselves aside from the true end of our vocation, we might indeed endanger our whole vocation itself, if we begin concentrating on psycho-physical side-effects of possible graces of prayer. We *must avoid* a hankering after special "feelings" of the presence of God or apprehensions of the "voice" of the Beloved in a physical sense, as well as other feelings or impressions of "heat," light and so forth which register themselves as it were physically in one way or another. What St. John of the Cross says about this would be fully approved by St. Bernard, where for instance St. John condemns attachment to "successive locutions" (*Ascent*, 2.29, 4 [vol. 1, pp. 210, 211, and his conclusion on p. 212][902]). "We must therefore *not* apply the understanding to that which is supernaturally communicated to it [even to a genuine locution that comes from God!!!] BUT SIMPLY AND SINCERELY APPLY THE WILL TO GOD WITH LOVE."[903] Explanation: if we apply our natural understanding etc., to these things, the graces (if such they be) that come to us will then be *modified* according to our own nature, temperament, character, and may even be perverted and twisted beyond recognition, and the soul will go completely astray led by its own activity, and "all will be merely natural and most erroneous and unworthy."[904] {The} principle {is that} anything that can be seen, heard, felt, understood in this life is not a proximate means of union with God, *but faith alone is such a means.*

2. If we understand St. Bernard thus, we will understand him correctly and we will strive in all things to purify our love, by obedience, by HUMILITY (the great sign of a genuine soul of prayer!) and this in turn will lead us to a greater ordinariness, a

---

902. St. John of the Cross, *The Ascent of Mount Carmel*, 2.29.4–7 (*The Complete Works of Saint John of the Cross*, ed. and trans. E. Allison Peers, 3 vols. [Westminster, MD: Newman Press, 1946]).

903. *Ascent*, 2.29.7 (Peers, *John of the Cross*, 1.212) (emphasis added).

904. *Ascent*, 2.29.7 (Peers, *John of the Cross*, 1.212).

greater sense of our own unworthiness and lowliness, a disinclination to compare ourselves with others or to be too occupied with ourselves, together with a greater zeal for true charity and humble devotion of ourselves to duty and to the WILL OF GOD expressed in ordinary everyday life, particularly through superiors, brethren and providential events.

*The Sermons*: we owe the Sermons *in Cantica* to the years of leisure which St. Bernard enjoyed after the settlement of the schism of Anacletus. Returning to Clairvaux in 1135, and relatively undisturbed until 1137, he began at that time to preach the series of sermons to his monks. The biographer of St. Bernard, Arnold (Ernaldus) of Bonneval says: "The man of God, finally able to enjoy some moments of leisure, rested from his labors by giving himself to other occupations. He retired into a hut made of branches and there gave himself up to the meditation of the things of God. And suddenly in this humble retreat, so like that which witnessed the birth of the Savior, the Canticle of love presented itself to him with all the delights of the spiritual wedding feast."[905] (N.B.: note the presence of a hermitage at Clairvaux!) It is probable that the first sermons on the Canticle were preached in Advent 1135 (St. Bernard having returned from Italy in November). Sometimes the sermons followed one another from day to day. St. Bernard frequently ends a sermon promising to finish the same matter "tomorrow." At other times there must have been long interruptions between them. The first *twenty-three sermons* are preached between 1135 and 1137. Then there was an interruption of about a year, and the series began again on his second return from Rome in 1138. Forty more sermons were then spread out between 1138 and 1146; during his period of great activity he nevertheless receives many "visits from the Bridegroom."[906] In

---

905. "*Nactus vero Vir Dei aliquod quietis tempus, aliis se negotiis occupavit, et secedens in casulam pisatiis torquibus circumtextam, solus meditationibus divinis vacare disponit. Et repente occurrunt ei in diversorio humili, quasi ad praesepe Domini consistenti, amatoria Cantica, et spiritualium fercula nuptiarum*" (*Vita Prima*, II.6.40 [*PL* 185, col. 291B]).

906. See *In Cantica* 57.4, 74.3-6 (*PL* 183, cols. 1052A, 1140A–1142A).

these sermons he continues to talk of the nature of mystical experience, but also of the relation of action and contemplation, with, be it noted, a certain emphasis on the superiority of the apostolic life. The last twenty sermons, belonging to the final years of his life, speak mostly of the heights of spiritual marriage—the marriage of the Church with the Word, the marriage of the Word with the individual soul.

*St. Bernard and the Scriptures*: we cannot really appreciate the sermons on the Canticle, or any of St. Bernard's other works, unless we fully realize that his attitude toward the Scriptures is different from our own. In modern times, there has been an increasing emphasis on the literal sense of Scripture, and rightly so. The spirit of scientific and rationalistic criticism has made necessary a careful, objective study of the Scriptures, in the light of textual, linguistic, literary and other problems. These problems did not occupy St. Bernard and the Fathers at all. They assumed that the literal sense was fairly clear, and did not question the authority of the Vulgate in any way. Starting from the Vulgate, considered to be the last word in textual perfection, they tried to plumb the *spiritual depths* of the word of God. St. Bernard certainly would have considered himself an exegete of the Scriptures, but his idea of an exegete would probably not correspond too well with our own. To understand St. Bernard's view of Scripture, we must go back to Cassian's Fourteenth *Conference, on "Spiritual Science"*—that of Abbot Nesteros.[907] This is in reality a conference on the contemplative life, for which we are prepared by ascetic purification. Here are the main points:

1. The monk who has left the world and purified his heart by the works of the "active life" (of virtue and self-denial) is ready to seek God in the Scriptures. No other preparation can help a man really to penetrate the inner meaning of the Sacred Book. "It is impossible for a soul that is even slightly occupied with worldly distractions to merit the gift of knowledge, or to become

---

[907]. *PL* 49, cols. 953B–988B; for a discussion of this conference, see *Cassian and the Fathers*, 114–15, and in greater detail, *Pre-Benedictine Monasticism*, 45–51.

a fruitful recipient of spiritual understanding, or even to persevere tenaciously in the labor of reading" (Conf. 14.9).[908]

2. This contemplative insight into Scripture does not come from study alone (application is absolutely necessary—*acedia* makes it impossible for the soul to enter into the Scriptures) but is above all a *gift of the Holy Ghost*. Those who are not taught by the Holy Spirit are able to see only the outer surface of revelation, and cannot penetrate to the inner meaning. Pride and self-complacency, vain preoccupation with their own gifts, is what prevents seemingly "learned" souls from receiving true insight into the Scriptures.

3. "Spiritual knowledge" implies first of all an understanding of the *literal* (historical) sense of Scripture, but this is only the beginning. True *"scientia"* is the understanding of the *spiritual senses* of the sacred text—tropological, allegorical and anagogical. In other words, true contemplative reading of the Scriptures is an infused and divinely given understanding of the way the texts all point to Jesus Christ as to the center of all revelation, how they show us more or less how we must live to be united to Him and to have Him living in us, and how we are all tending to our last end, the Kingdom of God, the glorification of Christ in His Church, the Heavenly Jerusalem.

This is exactly how St. Bernard looks at it. This is precisely what he is trying to do in the sermons on the Canticle of Canticles. Jesus has come to unite us mystically to Himself, by His Holy Spirit. Everything in Scripture points to this union of Christ and His Church—and with the individual soul. St. Bernard will point out *how* the text of the Canticle does this, and he will do so by letting the Holy Spirit speak through him. How? by letting his own heart speak, by seeing the Scripture in the *light of his personal experience* of God that has been granted to him in his own reading of the Scriptures, by the action of the Holy Spirit. But this reliance on his own experience is not arbitrary and independent. St. Bernard's understanding of the Scriptures follows closely the

---

908. "*Impossibile namque est animam quae mundanis vel tenuiter distentionibus occupatur, donum scientiae promereri, vel generatricem spiritualium sensuum, aut tenacem sacrarum lectionum fieri*" (col. 966B).

tradition of the Fathers and is entirely inspired by the way in which the Church herself makes use of the Scriptures in her liturgy. In a word, St. Bernard's commentary on the Canticle is then an elaboration of what he himself has found, by experience, in the sacred text, after having entered into it guided by the Church and by the tradition of her Fathers and Doctors. In doing so, he himself speaks as a doctor of the Church.

TEXTS: to illustrate St. Bernard's attitude towards the Scriptures, read {the} *beginning of Sermon 73* (Mount Melleray trans., vol. 2, 363[909]). The literal sense is the "portion of the Jews."[910] Instead of studying the letter alone, St. Bernard will seek out in

---

909. "But as for me, following the counsel of the Lord, I will search for the treasures of spirit and life hidden in the profound depths of these inspired utterances. This is my inheritance, because I am a believer in Christ. Why should I not endeavour to find the wholesome and savoury food of the spirit beneath the unprofitable and unpalatable letter, as the grain amongst the chaff, the meat in the shell, or the marrow in the bone? I will have nothing to do with this letter which when tasted savours of the flesh, and when swallowed brings death. Nevertheless, that which lies concealed in it is of the Holy Ghost, for 'by the Spirit (it) speaketh mysteries,' as the Apostle bears witness. But Israel is content to hold the veil of the mysteries, instead of the mysteries themselves, which are hidden beneath. Wherefore? For no other reason than that the 'veil is still upon his own heart.' Hence to him belongs the sound of the word, but the signification thereof is mine. And so whilst the Scripture in the letter ministers death to the Jew, it becomes for me a source of life in the spirit. For 'it is the spirit that quickeneth,' that is, by giving understanding. Is not understanding life? 'Give me understanding that I may live,' cries out the Psalmist, speaking to the Lord. Understanding does not remain outside in the letter; it does not stick fast in the surface; it is not satisfied to grope its way by the touch of exterior objects, like a blind man. Rather it explores the profound deeps, whence it is accustomed to extract and to bring up with insatiable avidity the most precious spoils of sacred truth. Hence it can say with the Psalmist, 'I will rejoice at Thy words, as one that hath found great spoil.' It is thus, my brethren, that the 'kingdom of heaven suffereth violence, and the violent bear it away'" (*St. Bernard's Sermons on the Canticle of Canticles*, trans. A Priest of Mount Melleray [Ailbe Luddy, ocso] [Dublin: Browne and Nolan, 1920], 2.363–64) (cols. 1134C–1135B).

910. Luddy, *Sermons on the Canticle*, 2.363 ("*Hic litterae tenor, et haec Judaeorum portio*" [n. 1 (col. 1134D)]).

the depths of the revealed text "spirit and life": IN PROFUNDO SACRI ELOQUII GREMIO SPIRITUM MIHI {SCRUTABOR} ET VITAM.[911] He will have nothing to do with the "letter": *Nihil mihi et litterae huic.*[912] (He would not deny that the literal sense is the gateway to the spiritual sense—he merely means that he will not stop at the letter.) The letter, without any further meaning, brings death: *gustata carnem sapit, glutita mortem affert*[913] (this would be true, for instance, if we read the Canticle *merely as a human love story* and nothing else). But there is something more in the "letter"—hidden beneath the outer shell is an inner kernel of life-giving spiritual food. This is placed there by the Holy Spirit. Both the Jew and the Christian hear the same words: for one they are a source of death and for the other a source of life. What is the difference? To us, because we have *faith*, the Spirit gives *understanding*, and this *understanding* is "life for our spirit." *Spiritus est qui vivificat: dat quippe intellectum. An non vita intellectus?*[914] The spiritual understanding breaks in with eager hunger to seize upon the real inner meaning and to be nourished by it. Later, comparing the Jews to the elder son in the parable of the prodigal,[915] he shows the importance of entering into the *banquet of Charity*. {In} *Sermon 7 in Cantica*,[916] in the famous passage on the divine office, he speaks of the necessity of thinking about what we sing in order to enter into the inner meaning. Hence it is not entirely the work of the Holy Ghost. We must cooperate with grace. Just as food tastes good in the mouth, the psalms must be *tasted in the heart*.

---

911. N. 2 (col. 1134D) ("I will search for the treasures of spirit and life hidden in the profound depths of these inspired utterances") (copy text reads "*scrutabo*").

912. Col. 1134D ("I will have nothing to do with this letter").

913. Col. 1134D ("which when tasted savours of the flesh, and when swallowed brings death").

914. Col. 1135A ("For 'it is the spirit that quickeneth,' that is, by giving understanding. Is not understanding life?").

915. N. 2 (col. 1135B).

916. N. 5 (col. 809AB).

St. Bernard's understanding of Scripture is not a mere matter of *lectio divina*[917] in private—the lights that are given come frequently in choir where with the brethren united as one body in the monastic *Ecclesia*, chanting to God as a member of Christ, he is most frequently enlightened by the light of Christ. If the soul is to taste the psalms interiorly, one must not neglect to "chew with the teeth of understanding."[918] Just as honey is contained in the honeycomb, so devotion is contained within the letter. The letter is wax; it is but a container. The true sweetness comes from the spiritual meaning thus contained. {In} *Sermon 74 in Cantica* {he writes}: "Let us, my brethren, proceeding with simplicity and caution in the exposition of a sacred and mystical utterance, accommodate ourselves to the usage of Holy Scripture, which, in our human words, 'speaketh wisdom in a mystery' "[919]—simple and powerful words that do not come out clearly in the English translation: (1) in *our words* ({in} human words, God hides His divine mystery); (2) in *our affections*—the sacred text gives a *figure or picture of God* and at the same time *makes Him present within us* (*Deum dum figurat insinuat*[920]); (3) in *sensible realities*—familiar to us, as though in chalices, Scripture gives us to drink *of the unknown and invisible things of God*. These texts show us clearly enough what is St. Bernard's attitude towards the Scripture. This is what he aims to find in the Canticle of Canticles.

917. "sacred reading"; for an extensive discussion of *lectio*, see Thomas Merton, *Monastic Observances: Initiation into the Monastic Tradition* 5, ed. Patrick F. O'Connell, MW 25 (Collegeville, MN: Cistercian Publications, 2010), 149–53, 155–56, 165–69; see also Thomas Merton, "*Lectio Divina*," *Cistercian Studies Quarterly* 50, no. 1 (2015): 5–37.

918. "*terere . . . quibusdam dentibus intelligentiae suae*" (col. 809A).

919. Luddy, *Sermons on the Canticle*, 2.374, which reads: ". . . this exposition . . . wisdom hidden in . . ." ("*Nos autem in expositione sacri mystiqueque eloquii caute et simpliciter ambulantes, geramus morem Scripturae, quae nostris verbis sapientiam in mysterio absconditam loquitur*" [n. 2 (col. 1139C)]).

920. Col. 1139C ("which commends the Divinity to our love by investing him with human affections [*nostris affectibus*]" [Luddy, *Sermons on the Canticle*, 2.374]).

NOTE: Dom Leclercq, OSB has a brief, useful article in the *Collectanea* (Jan. 1957)[921] aimed especially at helping beginners and novices to make their first acquaintance with St. Bernard. He makes the following points:

1. Our aim {is} not only to understand St. Bernard but to cultivate a taste for him.

2. In doing this, we should choose a certain *order*, beginning with the easier works like *De Diligendo*, *De Praecepto et Dispensatione*, *De Conversione*, *De Gradibus Humilitatis* and some of the letters. Read the Sermons after this introduction. The Sermons on the Canticle of Canticles should come last.

3. Read also other writers who are like St. Bernard, {who} have the same kind of outlook: {e.g., the} *Golden Epistle* of William of St. Thierry,[922] St. Ailred's *Spiritual Friendship*.[923]

4. Our way of reading is important—you cannot read St. Bernard the way you read the newspaper or the *Readers' Digest*. *Lectio divina* implies leisure, patience, not just seeking out the important passages where everything is concentrated, but being able to follow the author through bypaths without feeling that one is "not getting anywhere." Yes, the bypaths *do* get somewhere; and they help us get in a state of mind which is free and peaceful because detached. One must know how to *taste* and *enjoy*. One must let the writing *refine* our spirit. One should read in Latin, if possible.

5. Background reading {should include} the Fathers {and} books of monastic spirituality.

---

921. Jean Leclercq, OSB, "Comment Aborder S. Bernard," *Collectanea Ordinis Cisterciensium Reformatorum* 19 (1957): 18–21.

922. *PL* 184, cols. 307A–380B; ET: William of St. Thierry, *Golden Epistle* (*A Letter to the Brethren at Mont Dieu*), trans. Theodore Berkeley, OCSO, Cistercian Fathers [CF], vol. 12 (Kalamazoo, MI: Cistercian Publications, 1976).

923. *PL* 195, cols. 659A–702B; ET: Aelred of Rievaulx, *Spiritual Friendship*, 2nd ed., trans. Lawrence C. Braceland, ed. Marsha Dutton, CF 5 (Collegeville, MN: Cistercian Publications, 2010).

## The Sermons in Cantica

We now turn to the sermons themselves.

1. The Desire for Contemplation: *"Osculetur me osculo oris sui"*[924]—Sermons 1–8. St. Bernard spends eight sermons commenting on the opening line of the Canticle. This is typical of his leisurely approach. In fact, it is so leisurely that the modern reader may go through these eight sermons without any sense of direction or purpose and without getting anything but a few unconnected thoughts and impressions. Actually, the whole doctrine of the Sermons *in Cantica* is pretty well sketched out here, in broad outlines. In these first sermons he treats of the *desire of mystical union*, and explains the *nature of that union*. He also shows briefly *how that union is possible*. These topics will be treated over again in various ways throughout the series. Especially in the final sermons (82ff.[925]), he will give the finishing touches to his doctrine on the Mystical Marriage. Again and again he will talk of the desire for union, and the vicissitudes of the mystical life which make that desire stronger and more pure. He will frequently return to explanations of that union, and describe it now from one point of view, now from another, and in many sermons he will discuss the relations of action and contemplation. Above all, he will develop the one great theme which is mentioned in passing in these first sermons, namely the union of Christ and the Church.

*A General View of the First Eight Sermons*: Sermon 1 begins with a prologue to the whole work. The Canticle of Canticles is called a *sacrum theoricumque sermonem* (n. 3).[926] It is the song of nuptial union, of peace, the union of Christ and the Church. It is a hymn of joy and gratitude, and from the first he appeals to their own *experience* to help them understand what this is about. But he

---

924. *In Cantica* 1.5 (col. 787A) (Cant. 1:1) ("Let him kiss me with the kiss of his mouth" [Luddy, *Sermons on the Canticle*, 1.4]).

925. Cols. 1177A–1198A.

926. Col. 786A ("discourse on holy contemplation" [Luddy, *Sermons on the Canticle*, 1.3]).

insists that this canticle can only be understood by those who are advanced in the spiritual life. *Sermon 2*[927] begins with the ardent desire of the patriarchs and prophets for the *Incarnation*. In this great mystery God and Man are united in One Person. The infusion of knowledge of this great mystery is the *osculum*[928] which the soul desired—knowledge of God by union with Christ in whom God and Man are one. *Sermon 3*[929] {considers that} if all experience of God in Christ is an *osculum*, there are nevertheless degrees of intimacy in this experience. The threefold ascent to perfect union is symbolized by the kiss of the feet, of the hands and of the mouth. Note that all are in some sense regarded as unitive. But one must be careful to ascend by degrees with true humility and inner purity of heart; otherwise one will not reach union with God. *Sermon 4*[930] becomes more technical and bewildering to the modern reader. To explain his statement that we kiss the "hands and the feet"[931] of God, he shows that there is nothing of the body in God and talks about the different kinds of spiritual beings—angels and men and even lower animals—all of them "spirits" that in some way "need the use of a body."[932] *Sermon 5*[933] {shows that} God is the One Spirit Who is infinitely above everything corporeal. The angels, according to Bernard, need some kind of a "body" (spiritual) in order to "be present" among other created beings. As for the animal spirit, it depends entirely on the body for its existence. Between the angel and the beast is man, by nature spiritual and bodily at the same time—by original sin he has fallen below the level of the beasts; by grace he can be raised to union with God. *Sermon 6*[934] {teaches that} the

---

927. Cols. 789D–794A.
928. "kiss."
929. Cols. 794A–796C.
930. Cols. 796C–798D.
931. "*manus vel pedes*" (n. 4 [col. 797D]).
932. "*liquet omnem creatum spiritum . . . corporeo prorsus indigere solatio*" (*In Cantica*, 5.6 [col. 800D]) ("it follows that every created spirit requires the agency of bodily members" [Luddy, *Sermons on the Canticle*, 1.36]).
933. Cols. 798D–803B.
934. Cols. 803B–806D.

*Incarnation* of the Word of God is what this union of man and God is: *In carne et per carnem facit opera non carnis sed Dei* (6.{3}).[935] We have known God in Christ. But since Jesus has ascended into heaven, He still continues to work invisibly and to "go about doing good"[936] among men, with the two feet of justice and mercy. His presence in the soul is then marked by fear (of judgement) and hope (of mercy). Note that the three sermons (4, 5, 6) have arisen out of the difficulty that God does not have "feet" that we can kiss (the first degree of the three which Bernard proposed to ascend in Sermon 3). In reading St. Bernard, we tend to lose sight of the objective and get lost in digressions, but if we keep our mind on what he is trying to do, everything will be more clear and more understandable. {In} *Sermon 7*[937] he returns to the theme of union. Very briefly he skips over the "kiss of the hands"[938] and turns to mystical union, the kiss of the mouth. In this very important sermon he defines mystical union as a union of wills and spirits in which the soul is perfectly united with God to the point of spiritual identification (not metaphysical!) by *pure love*. Who is the Spouse? *anima sitiens Deum* (7.2),[939] distinct from the *mercenarius*, the *discipulus*, the *filius*[940] (here {there are} four degrees of love, reminding us of the *De Diligendo Deo*[941]). He then proves how only the Spouse, of all these four, is united with God. For the Spouse loves, and God is love. God is the principle of love, and love fully returns to its principle only by loving for the sake of loving. When the soul is a "Spouse," seeking nothing but

---

935. Col. 804AB ("For whilst in the flesh He did not the works of the flesh, but the works of God" [Luddy, *Sermons on the Canticle*, 1.43]) (copy text reads: "6.2").

936. "*pertransit et nunc, benefaciendo*" (n. 7 [col. 805D]) (Acts 10:38).

937. Cols. 806D–810C.

938. N. 1 (cols. 806D–807A).

939. Col. 807A ("the soul that thirsts after God" [Luddy, *Sermons on the Canticle*, 1.49]).

940. Col. 807A ("mercenary . . . disciple . . . son" [Luddy, *Sermons on the Canticle*, 1.50]; Merton omits mention of the slave here).

941. *De Diligendo Deo*, 8.23–10.27; see also 12.34-35, 13.36 (*PL* 182, cols. 987D–990D, 995B–997B); see above, pages 118–25, 99–101, 105–6, and below, pages 374–80.

love, not any other reward—not liberty, not an inheritance, not knowledge—then it has all things in common with the Beloved. Pure love has three qualities: it is chaste (*amat caste*[942]) because it seeks nothing but the Beloved; it is holy (*amat sancte*[943]) because it is not fleshly but spiritual; it is ardent (*amat ardenter*[944]) because it is so inebriated with love that it forgets the Majesty of God and aspires to union with Him by a holy daring. Such a soul has manifestly come forth from the *cella vinaria*[945] (of which more later). (Note: love comes forth from God and leads back to God. For God is love. Not so fear, reward, etc.) St. Bernard concludes: *O quanta amoris vis! Quanta in spiritu libertatis fiducia! Quid manifestius quam quod perfecta charitas foras mittit timorem* (7.3).[946] There follows a passage on the divine office which is not really a digression. It is, in effect, to the angels that the Spouse souls say *"osculetur me"* etc.,[947] and the angels are present to us above all in choir, when we sing to God in the sight of the angels. Hence the office is the place where the soul learns true love and is most proximately prepared for union with the Word—by an understanding of the spiritual sense of the psalms, which understanding is taught us by the angels who are present with us in praising God. *Laudem ergo cum coeli cantoribus in commune ducentes, utpote cives sanctorum et domestici Dei, psallite sapienter.*[948] The purity of our praise de-

---

942. N. 3 (col. 807C) ("She loves with a pure love" [Luddy, *Sermons on the Canticle*, 1.51]).

943. Col. 807D ("She loves with a holy love" [Luddy, *Sermons on the Canticle*, 1.51]).

944. Col. 807D ("She loves with an ardent love" [Luddy, *Sermons on the Canticle*, 1.51]).

945. Col. 807D ("the 'wine-cellar'" [Luddy, *Sermons on the Canticle*, 1.51]) (Cant. 1:3; 2:4).

946. Col. 808A ("Oh, how mighty is the power of love! How great confidence in liberty of spirit! What can be plainer than that perfect love 'casteth our fear'?" [Luddy, *Sermons on the Canticle*, 1.51]) (1 John 4:18).

947. N. 8 (col. 810B) ("Let him kiss me . . ." [Luddy, *Sermons on the Canticle*, 1.56]).

948. N. 5 (col. 809A) ("Since therefore it is your privilege to sing the praises in common with the heavenly choristers, as being fellow-citizens

pends on purity of heart and of intention. {In} *Sermon 8*,[949] here finally is the essence of his teaching. The other seven sermons have been nothing but a preparation for the eighth, which contains all the doctrine he promised from the first paragraph of Sermon 1. What is this *osculum* which the Spouse seeks, and which is true union with God? *It is the Holy Spirit* Who proceeds from the Father and the Son and is the union of the Father and the Son. To be "kissed" by God is simply to receive the Holy Spirit, and to be united to the Father in the Son: *Osculari ab osculo . . . non est aliud nisi infundi Spiritu Sancto. . . . Petit audenter dari sibi osculum, hoc est Spiritum illum, in quo sibi et Filius reveletur et Pater. . . . Spiritum qui Patris Filiique imperturabilis pax sit, gluten firmum, individuus amor, indivisibilis unitas* (8.2-3).[950] This union is a union of *knowledge*—of God one and Triune, the Father being known in the Son, and the Son with the Father in the Holy Spirit. The Spirit Himself is also known where the Father and the Son are known. *It is above all a union of love*—a knowledge of God that is without love is not from the Holy Spirit. *Revelatio, quae per Spiritum sanctum fit, non solum illustrat ad agnitionem, sed etiam accendit ad amorem.*[951] For the knowledge of God produced by the Holy Spirit is above all knowledge of His supreme goodness and love for us (manifested in the Incarnation and Redemption). Hence the knowledge of God by love is penetrated through and through with a spirit of praise and gratitude. The knowledge

---

with the saints and domestics of God, 'sing ye wisely' " [Luddy, *Sermons on the Canticle*, 1.54]) (Ps. 46[47]:7, 8).

949. Cols. 810D–814D.

950. Col. 811BC, which reads: ". . . *Petit ergo audenter . . .*"; the final quotation actually concludes n. 2 and precedes the second quotation ("to be kissed with that Kiss, namely, to receive an infusion of the Holy Spirit. . . . Hence she boldly asks a kiss, that is, the Holy Spirit, in Whom are revealed both the Father and the Son. . . . the Divine Spirit, Who is the imperturbable Peace of the Father and Son, the everlasting Bond, the undivided Love, the indivisible Unity" [Luddy, *Sermons on the Canticle*, 1.60]).

951. N. 5 (col. 812B) ("the revelation which is made by the Holy Spirit not only communicates the light of knowledge, but also enkindles the flames of love" [Luddy, *Sermons on the Canticle*, 1.62]).

which is puffeth up,[952] on the contrary, is cold and proud, born of curiosity and self-will, seeking only to penetrate the secrets of God for the sake of knowing them, and for the satisfaction of the mind. However, *knowledge is essential*. We cannot go to the other extreme, and think that union with God can exist in a soul that has zeal without knowledge and discretion. Blind fervor and zeal are not the signs of a spouse united to the Word, for the Spirit of wisdom and understanding not only enkindles the fire of love but the light of knowledge: *habet omnino et unde accendat lumen scientiae, et unde infundat saporem gratiae* (8.6).[953] *In osculo isto nec error locum habet, nec tepor* (*idem*).[954] The *osculum*, which is the Holy Spirit, introduces us by knowledge and love into the deep inner mystery of God, and gives us possession of the secrets of His love for us. This possession is not a matter of human striving, but of divine gift. It is realized not in achievement but in *peace and rest* above and beyond all understanding. The Spirit of God in our hearts produces a peace and a joy which is the spirit of sonship in which we cry *Abba*, Father[955]—that is to say we share the love of Jesus for the Father; or Jesus, by His Spirit, loves the Father in us. And this in turn is proof that the Father loves us as He loves His own Son. *Ipsa paterno se diligi praesumat affectu, quae eodem se Spiritu, quo et Filius, affectam sentit. . . . In Spiritu Filii filiam cognosce te Patris, sponsam Filii vel sororem* (8.9).[956]

---

952. 1 Cor. 8:1.
953. Col. 813A ("[the Spirit] has wherewith to light the lamp of knowledge and to infuse the sweetness of devotion" [Luddy, *Sermons on the Canticle*, 1.64]).
954. Col. 813B ("With it error and coldness are alike incompatible" [Luddy, *Sermons on the Canticle*, 1.64]).
955. N. 9 (col. 814C) (Gal. 4:6).
956. Col. 814C ("let him feel assured of the love of the Father, for he has the testimony of his own conscience; he is led by the same Spirit as the Son. . . . In the Spirit of Christ thou canst recognise thyself as the daughter of the Father and as the spouse and sister of the Son" [Luddy, *Sermons on the Canticle*, 1.67]).

2. The Anointing of the Soul: *Contrition, Devotion and Mercy*—Sermons 9–12. At the beginning of Sermon 9,[957] St. Bernard returns for three paragraphs to the literal sense. This is usually the sign that he intends to move on to another section of the Canticle and to another theme, or rather to another aspect of the same theme which runs through all these sermons. In point of fact, from Sermon 9 to Sermon 22 we have a series of instructions on what we should call the *illuminative life*. There are, of course, references to the beginner's way of penance and contrition and there are brief views into the land of contemplation, but in these sermons St. Bernard generally deals with the operations of the Holy Spirit in the soul which correspond to the second degree of truth in the *Degrees of Humility*.[958] It is not yet pure love, to which he has introduced us in Sermons 7 and 8, but rather the anointing of the soul that prepares the way for pure love. Here we find a more detailed discussion of "devotion" and fervor in gratitude to God, {along with} trust in God {and} love of God for Himself alone. We are in the same area as that which is covered by the third degree of love in the *De Diligendo Deo*.[959] Most important is the relation of fraternal charity to contemplation, which keeps recurring all through these sermons: not only in the dealings of the abbot, the contemplative and father of souls, with his sons, but also in the relation of the monks to one another. In the anointing of the soul by the Holy Spirit, there is no process more fruitful and important than the *grace of compassion* which enables us to understand and sympathize with the failings of others and with their troubles, and to make their troubles our own, so that we become all things to all men and bear our brothers' burdens.

*The line of thought* {is as follows}: after sketching out the framework into which he will fit his spiritual interpretation,

---

957. Cols. 815A–819C.

958. *De Gradibus Humilitatis*, n. 18 (*PL* 182, col. 951BC); see the discussion below, pages 369–71.

959. *De Diligendo Deo*, n. 26 (*PL* 182, cols. 989C–990A); see the discussion above, pages 122–24.

St. Bernard announces in a brief paragraph what will later be his main theme; but then, as usual, he leaves it and enters into a long digression. The theme he announces is this: no soul would aspire to union with God if it did not have some *experience of the divine mercy* (Sermon 9.5). (The patience of God and His mercy in receiving the sinner {are considered as the} two "breasts.") This is just announced in passing, but we shall see that this is the very essence of the doctrine of the ointments and the "milk of divine consolation" (*ubera tua meliora vino, fragrantia unguentis optimis*[960]). To avoid confusion we must note that St. Bernard applies the allegory of "breasts" now to God, now to the Spouse, now to the spiritual father (or mother!!) entrusted with consoling the monks. In general, the theme is this: the very heart of the illuminative way is *mercy*, the experience of the divine mercy, response to the mercy of God by gratitude and confidence in our own hearts, and by compassion for our brothers. He then starts out as if to attack this theme; the advance must be *interior*, he says; it is far more profitable for the interior life to be carried forward by spiritual consolation and the sense of God's mercy truly experienced in the heart than to be driven by the discipline of a superior. He means that mere *exterior* compulsion will never make us saints, though of course discipline and obedience are essential. But they are only the beginning. Unless the soul *interiorizes* its striving to do good, and allows itself to be guided inwardly by grace, spiritual growth is impossible. *Pinguedo gratiae, quae de tuis uberibus fluit, efficacior mihi est ad spiritualem profectum, quam mordax imprecatio praelatorum* ({*In*} *Cant.* 9.6).[961] This allusion to the discipline of the abbot is not just accidental: we shall see that it leads in fact to a secondary theme which runs in counterpoint to the first,

---

960. N. 4 (col. 816C, which reads: "*meliora sunt ubera tua vino, . . .*") ("Thy breasts are better than wine, smelling sweet of the best ointments" [Luddy, *Sermons on the Canticle*, 1.71]) (Cant. 1:1-2).

961. Col. 817D ("The oil of divine grace that flows from Thy Breasts is more useful to me for my spiritual progress than are the reproofs, wine-like in their pungency, of my human superiors" [Luddy, *Sermons on the Canticle*, 1.74]).

especially later where he talks about action and contemplation (Sermon 18). He continues, then, to develop the idea of *devotio*; but the question of the interior life of the abbot, the *praelatus*, who guides souls to union with God, immediately comes to the fore. This is St. Bernard's own problem, and we see that he is speaking from his heart, and thinking out loud on his own interior life all through this group of sermons; and indeed he tends to do so throughout the entire series. *Devotion* in prayer is very often the fruit of *generosity in spite of dryness* (9.7). But when the consolations of prayer have been received, there is a test to know whether they are genuine: in the Spouse of God, consolation is not given for herself alone; it is to be *shared with others*. "Do not insist too much on the joys of contemplation," he declares, "for the fruitfulness of preaching is of greater value" (9.8).[962] He is giving his own personal solution to a problem which distressed him deeply as an abbot and Father of souls. He knew that it was his duty, when God called, to devote himself to others rather than merely to be piously selfish and taste the grace of prayer for his own happiness alone. This text has to be balanced against others where he shows clearly that the monk must not presume to leave contemplation for action unless it is clearly the will of God—i.e., unless he is clearly called by charity or obedience. We shall see this theme of action and contemplation discussed in greater detail in Sermon 18.

St. Bernard here goes on to make two important remarks about the life of the Father of souls: (a) it is fatal to make someone a director of others if he is not himself mature in the spiritual and contemplative life (10.1[963]); (b) those who seek themselves instead of the souls entrusted to them are greatly to be blamed, especially if they seek only their temporal comfort and material prosperity (10.3[964]). However, he who is mature in the contemplative life and thus fitted to direct others receives much light and grace in

---

962. "*Noli ergo nimis insistere osculis contemplationis; quia meliora sunt ubera praedicationis*" (col. 818C) (Merton's translation).

963. Cols. 819C–820A.

964. Col. 820BD.

prayer with which he is able to do two things above all—to *encourage* others and to *console* them with paternal sympathy. This emphasis is very important. St. Bernard insists on these positive qualities, and not on the spiritual father's ability to humiliate and mortify and crush and dissect those entrusted to him! These are not the work of a true spiritual father, though punishments and correctives may sometimes be required. In general, throughout Sermons 9 and 10, St. Bernard seems to be talking of the consolations of God in so far as they reach the soul through the ministrations of the spiritual father. Without explicitly announcing that this will be his viewpoint, it is the viewpoint that he actually takes. In 10.4[965] he returns to the work of the Holy Spirit in the soul of the contemplative who is being prepared for divine union. Here he begins his discussion of the *three anointings*:

(1) *Penance*: "There is an ointment which the soul compounds for itself, when it is caught in many sins . . . it gathers together its sins, crushes them in the mortar of conscience, cooks them over the fire of sorrow etc." (10.5)[966] (cf. *De Conversione*[967]). This is the first sacrifice that God asks of us, and without it the others will not be pleasing. The soul is thus anointed and softened and consoled by humility and compunction, and the sweet odor of this ointment even rejoices the angels (10.6[968]).

(2) *Devotion*: St. Bernard strongly insists that we cannot confine ourselves to this first anointing. It is not sufficient preparation for union with the God of love. The elements from which the second ointment is made are not of this world—they must be sought in heaven, in the goodness of God Himself. They are found in *gratitude* for all God's goodness to us, *trust* in His mercy,

---

965. Cols. 820D–821A.
966. "*Est ergo unguentum, quod sibi conficit anima multis irretia criminibus . . . colligat, congerat, conteratque in mortariolo conscientiae multas ac varias species peccatorum suorum, et intra aestuantis pectoris ollam simul omnia coquat igne quodam poenitentiae et doloris*" (col. 821A) (Merton's translation).
967. See above, pages 197–214.
968. Cols. 821B–822A.

and the ointment of *devotio* is applied most of all in divine praise (Sermon 11.1–2[969]). All through Sermon 11 he develops motives for gratitude to God and ways of stirring up fervent devotion. This reminds us of the early chapters in *De Diligendo Deo*, where he talks of the motives for loving God.[970] One of the greatest sources of *devotio* for St. Bernard is meditation on the fact that God will be all in all. In a word, *devotio* comes from a constant meditation on the whole mystery of God's love for us in Christ, a love which extends to labors and sufferings (which were not in themselves strictly necessary) in order that He might win our love for Him (cf. 11.7).

(3) *Pietas* (fraternal compassion): it is important to notice the gradation of the three ointments. The highest is not *devotio* (devoted gratitude to God) but *pietas*—merciful and compassionate love for our neighbor. This "ointment" "far excels the other two" (*ambobus longe antecellit*[971]). What is it made of? the needs and limitations and miseries and sufferings of others. "Such materials may seem contemptible, but the ointment that is made of them is beyond all price. It has great healing power, for it is written: Blessed are the merciful for they shall obtain mercy."[972] How are these materials compounded together? with the oil of mercy, over the fire of charity. What are the effects of this ointment in the soul? the joy which is known only by the merciful. Mercy is for St. Bernard the great reality of the spiritual life. How close to the gospel! In order not to misunderstand St. Bernard, we must look closely at the psychology of fraternal compassion. It is by no means a condescending and self-satisfied philanthropy, a kind of benevolent paternalism. It is something far more genuine. It

---

969. Cols. 826B–827C.

970. *De Diligendo Deo*, nn. 1–22 (*PL* 182, cols. 974A–987D); see above, pages 107–18.

971. 12.1 (col. 828A) (Merton's translation).

972. "*Despicabiles videntur species istae; sed est super omnia aromata unguentum, quod ex eis conficitur. Sanativum est: beati enim misericordes, quoniam ipsi misericordiam consequentur*" (col. 828B) (Matt. 5:7) (Merton's translation).

involves real self-sacrifice, real putting of others before ourselves, feeling their sorrows as our own, bearing the burdens of others, suffering with them, and not merely making their sufferings an occasion for self-complacent vanity in ourselves. St. Bernard is not talking about anything self-complacent or sentimental, but of the vital and fruitful activity of one who really loves others and shoulders their burdens with them. Such a one must have the following qualities—{being} ready to sympathize, prompt in bringing aid, preferring to give rather than to receive (in reality this is neither common nor easy, although the counterfeit is common enough—i.e., the giving that costs nothing and looks good in the eyes of the world), always ready to forgive, almost impossible to make angry, absolutely refusing to get even, and in all things regarding the needs of the brother as one's own (see 12.1[973]). Such a monk has the main quality which is the secret of progress in the mystical life, "a soul lost to itself, utterly forgetful of itself, all things to all men"[974]—*tamquam vas perditum*,[975] *so dead to self that one lives for all* (cf. 12.1[976]). This is the key to the mystery. As long as one is shut up within himself, he remains poor and limited. But when charity takes possession of him, then he becomes, as it were, infinite, he loses his limitations, and in Christ he lives in all men and all times. He can no longer be confined merely to himself. He is free; you cannot stop him from loving or make him a prisoner. The rest of Sermon 12 is taken up with scriptural examples of men who possessed this gift—St. Paul, Job, David, Joseph, etc.

3. THY NAME IS OIL POURED OUT: the Missions of the Son and of the Holy Spirit—Sermons 13–18: the *leitmotif* of these sermons is announced in the first paragraph of Sermon 13, in the very first sentence: ORIGO FONTIUM ET FLUMINUM OMNIUM MARE EST, VIRTUTUM ET

---

973. Col. 828A.

974. "*sic te omnibus omnia faciens*" (col. 828C) (1 Cor. 9:22).

975. Col. 828C ("as 'a broken vessel'" [Luddy, *Sermons on the Canticle*, 1.101]) (Ps. 30[31]:13).

976. "*sic denique mortua tibi, ut vivas omnibus*" (col. 828C).

SCIENTIARUM DOMINUS NOSTER JESUS CHRISTUS.[977] As all waters are drawn up from the sea and rain down on the land and return to the sea in the rivers, so all spiritual good in man comes from Jesus and returns to God in and through Him. Again, the mystery of the Incarnate Word is central, and the culmination of this thought is found in Sermon 15, on the *Name of Jesus*. Once again, we have to be on the alert and recognize the theme which St. Bernard (according to his custom) announces, then apparently abandons for several pages. What follows, apparently a long digression, is in fact the chief moral consequence of the above statement: the necessity of *gratitude*. The theme of gratitude is so preponderant in these early Sermons *in Cantica* that we cannot help noticing that it is, as it were, the keynote of St. Bernard's spirituality. It is the source of that *joy* which is also so characteristic of him, and makes his mysticism eminently a mysticism of light, and his spirituality in every way positive and consoling. In this he is simply echoing the gospels.

Sermon 13.2-7[978] {focuses on} *the pharisaical spirit*. This apparent digression is in reality significant. It is continued in Sermon 14,[979] almost throughout the whole sermon. St. Bernard is making a point which he deems essential for the understanding of what is to follow in Sermon 15 (on the name of Jesus). The Holy Name is light, food, medicine; it is as "oil poured out,"[980] a source of all good and consolation, only if it means to us what it means in itself. Jesus is SAVIOR. Without any merit on our part, purely out of love for us, God has sent His only begotten Son into the world to save us. Our response can be nothing else but gratitude and joyful acceptance by total abandon of ourselves to

---

977. Cols. 833D–834A, which reads: ". . . *Dominus Jesus Christus*" ("As the ocean . . . is the source of all rivers and fountains, so is our Lord Jesus Christ the Well-Spring of all virtue and knowledge" [Luddy, *Sermons on the Canticle*, 1.114]).

978. Cols. 834B–838C.

979. Cols. 839A–843C.

980. "*oleum effusum nomen tuum*" (14.3 [col. 840C]) (Cant. 1:2).

His love. But this is not the spirit of the Jews, that is to say of the Old Law. They were not able to recognize the *absolute gratuity* of the salvation offered to man by God; they could not accept the gift of grace except on their own terms—as something they had merited by their own justice and their own goodness. The Pharisees gave thanks, indeed, but they were not praising the Lord; they were only praising themselves (13.2[981]); and this was proved by the fact that they *despised others* (hence {the} intimate connection between what has gone before, the ointment of *pietas*). In despising others, they did not recognize that others had simply received less than they, through no fault of theirs; in priding themselves, they failed to see that they had received more through no merit of their own, and that comparisons were meaningless (assuming that they had indeed received more!). St. Bernard is as usual very subtle in his psychology in these paragraphs. Read him closely and think carefully what he means. It is a very delicate analysis of the psychology of pride. In a word, then, the pharisaical spirit is one of *ingratitude, masking as gratitude and love for God, selfishness and conceit masking as religion*. It is detected infallibly as contempt for others who are less gifted and less virtuous. We see why this apparent digression is in fact a subject of great importance in the spirituality of St. Bernard (cf. also the Christmas sermons of Bl. Guerric[982]).

Sermon 14 continues the same theme: the Pharisee demands justice; the faithful Christian asks *mercy*. Both receive what they desire. "The synagogue is strong; she does not care for a light burden or an easy yoke. She is healthy; she has no need of a physician, nor of anointing by the Holy Spirit. She trusts in her law: let it save her if it can" (14.2).[983] This is the reverse of the coin of *pietas*—we learn by implication that our mercy towards those

---

981. Cols. 834B–835B.

982. *PL* 185, cols. 29B–46D: ET: *The Christmas Sermons of Bl. Guerric of Igny*, trans. Sr. Rose of Lima, introductory essay by Thomas Merton (Trappist, KY: Abbey of Gethsemani, 1959).

983. "*Sed Synagoga fortis est, non curat onus leve nec jugum suave. Sana est, non est ei opus medicus, nec unctio Spiritus. Confidit in lege, liberet eam si potest*" (cols. 839D–840A) (Merton's translation).

who are suffering, and to sinners and the unfortunate (with whom we are *one*—all in the same boat!) makes us like Christ who loves us precisely for our misery and our need of Him, and not for our virtues and our own justice. Note that like most of the Fathers, St. Bernard makes the Jews the "type" of all that is wrong in the spiritual life. After emphasizing the gratuity of salvation, St. Bernard nevertheless makes it clear that his doctrine is not quietism. There is a difference between the *perfect* soul, who is the Spouse, who has entered within to the secret banquet with the Beloved, while the others remain outside, waiting to enter (14.4-5[984]). Those outside are the *adolescentulae* (the "young maidens").[985] They are not yet perfect, not yet ready for the Mystical Marriage. Hence there *is* some work, some action, which makes a difference between perfection and mere virtue. *All* believe firmly in the mercy of God and hope for His mercy and love Him, but the Spouse is characterized by a *more complete confidence*, the fruit of *pure love*, which is possible only to those who have abandoned all other love but that of God. In other words, this presupposes perfect detachment. St. Bernard adds that the example and the influence of the perfect (those whose love is really pure) is one of the principal means by which God reaches the hearts of the imperfect. In the good lives of the saints His Name is as "oil poured out" upon all the faithful (14.6[986]).

Sermon 15[987]—The Holy Name of Jesus: in Jesus, God, known to the saints of the Old Law as a just God and a terrible God of power, has finally revealed Himself as kind and merciful. Hence it is in Jesus that the Name of God becomes consoling and encouraging. The "outpouring" of the "Name" of Jesus as "oil" means: (a) the visible mission of the Word in the Incarnation; (b) the revelation of that mission; (c) His invisible mission in our hearts. The whole world responds to this with praise and thanksgiving. For St. Bernard, this phrase of the Canticle sums up all

---

984. Cols. 841A–842A.
985. Col. 841D, which reads: "*adolescentularum.*"
986. Col. 842AD.
987. Cols. 843D–848C.

the meaning of our divine worship: thanksgiving and praise to the hidden God Who, out of love for us, has given Himself entirely to us in Jesus. The effects of the Presence of Jesus in the world—of the "Name" of Jesus {are}: {LUCET}—{it is the} light of faith, when *preached*; PASCIT—{it} gives strength, repairs our weakness, gives savor to life, when *meditated*; {UNGIT}—{it} is a healing medicine {that} counteracts the bad effects of sin {and} heals sin itself, when it is *invoked*.[988] All this is contained within the Holy Name of Jesus (READ 15.6[989]). The *reality* that is in the divine

---

988. N. 5 (col. 846C) ("for lighting, for food, and for healing" [Luddy, *Sermons on the Canticle*, 1.142]) (copy text reads: "LUCIT . . . UNGET").

989. "Whence, think you, that great light of faith, and as sudden as great, throughout the whole world, except from the preaching of the name of Jesus? Was it not by the refulgence of this name that God called us 'into His marvellous light,' to whom thus illuminated, and contemplating the Light by this light, St. Paul truly says, 'You were heretofore darkness, but now light in the Lord'? This is the name which the same Apostle was charged to 'carry before the gentiles, and kings, and the children of Israel.' He bore this name about as a lamp. With it he illuminated his native land, crying out everywhere, 'The night is passed, and the day is at hand. Let us, therefore, cast off the works of darkness, and put on the armour of light. Let us walk honestly as in the day.' And he directed the gaze of all to the Candle on the Candlestick, by everywhere preaching 'Jesus and Him crucified.' Oh, with what splendour this light shone forth and dazzled the eyes of all beholders, when, flashing like the lightning flame from Peter's mouth, it strengthened the corporeal 'feet and soles' of one person physically lame, and enlightened the eyes of many others, who were spiritually blind! Surely it glittered with fiery scintillations when the same Peter pronounced the words, 'In the name of Jesus Christ of Nazareth, arise and walk.' But the name of Jesus is not merely light. It is food as well. Do you not, my brethren, experience an increase of strength as often as you recall it? What can so enrich the soul that reflects upon it? What can so reinvigorate the weary mind, fortify the virtues, engender good and honourable dispositions, foster holy affections? Dry is every kind of spiritual food, which this oil does not moisten. Insipid, whatever this salt does not season. If thou writest, thy composition has no charms for me, unless I read there the name of Jesus. If thou disputest or conversest, I find no pleasure in thy words, unless I hear there the name of Jesus. Jesus is honey in the mouth, melody in the ear, jubilation in the heart. Yet not alone

Person of the Incarnate Word is communicated to us as though by a sacrament in the Name of Jesus. Meditation and love of the Holy Name is as it were a prolonged spiritual communion. It is

---

is that name light and food. It is also medicine. Is any amongst you sad? Let the name of Jesus enter his heart; let it leap thence to his mouth; and lo! the light that radiates from that name shall scatter every cloud and restore tranquillity. Has some one perpetrated a crime, and, moreover, abandoning hope, is rushing in desperation towards 'the snare of death'? Let him but invoke this vivifying name, and straightway he shall experience a renewal of courage, and a revival of confidence. What hardness of heart, common as it is with some, what torpidity of sloth, what rancour of spirit, what weariness of disgust has ever been able to resist the potent influence of this all-saving name? What exhausted fountain of devotional tears has not, at the invocation of the name of Jesus, sent forth a fuller and a sweeter flood? Who ever, when trembling with terror in the presence of danger, has not immediately felt his spirits revive and his fears departing as soon as he called upon this name of power? Who ever, agitated and buffeted by the billows of doubt, has not perceived his mind to be suddenly illuminated with the clear light of certitude, the moment he invoked this illustrious name? Who ever, overwhelmed by misfortune, and already on the point of succumbing, has not been strengthened in mind by an infusion of fortitude when he pronounced this helpful name? For this name is the sovereign remedy for all those various maladies and languors of the soul. By using it thus we may test the truth of the promise, 'Call upon me in the day of trouble; I will deliver thee and thou shalt glorify Me.' There is nothing so efficacious as the name of Jesus for restraining the violence of anger, depressing the swellings of pride, healing the smarting wound of envy, curbing the passions of the flesh, extinguishing the fire of concupiscence, tempering the thirst of avarice, and banishing every unlawful desire. For when I name the name Jesus, I call to mind a Man Who is 'meek and humble of Heart,' Who is kind, sober, chaste, and merciful, and perfect in all goodness and sanctity, and Who is, at the same time, the great Almighty God, Who restores me to health by His example, and strengthens me by His help. All this sounds in my ear whenever I hear the name of Jesus. I find models for my imitation in His Humanity, and assistance to copy them in His Omnipotence. The examples of His mortal life I use as medicinal herbs which I prepare with the assistance of His divine power, and so make for myself an efficacious restorative such as no human physician can compound" (Luddy, *Sermons on the Canticle*, 1.142–45) (cols. 846C–847C).

a remedy of all our spiritual ills (cf. 15.7[990]). By the constant invocation of the Holy Name, *all our senses and actions* become directed to Jesus and centered on Him. By means of this name, we are *raised from spiritual death* like the child raised by Eliseus. The Jews could not be vivified by the message of the prophets, which was no more than the staff laid on the dead child by Eliseus' servant. For St. Bernard, the Holy Name is a *principal instrument* by which God acts in our lives to produce all good in our souls and to transform us by the vivifying effect of His grace.

Sermon 16[991] continues the above themes, comparing the action of the Risen Humanity of Jesus in our lives to the action of Eliseus on the dead child. In our supernatural life it is as if we had the Lord Himself stretched out upon us and influencing all our faculties, and we respond to this influence with seven "spasms" or "gasps"[992] which Bernard allegorically interprets. In this allegory he speaks of the various effects of grace in the soul, especially effects of compunction and "confessions."[993] The theme of this sermon may be boiled down to the virtue of true humility which manifests the life of Christ in our souls.

Sermon 17[994] pursues the same theme—the effects of the grace of Christ in our souls, particularly {in} the *discernment of spirits*. How can we tell the action of the Holy Spirit from the action of our own spirit or of the evil one?

a) Is this important? *Id plane periculosissime ignoratur.*[995] It is something we really need to know, to avoid gross self-deception. Bernard's idea is not so much that we should cultivate this discretion in order to feel complacent and self-satisfied when the Holy Spirit is present. Still less does he encourage this introspection in order to foster illusions of omniscience and infallibility

---

990. Cols. 847C–848C.

991. Cols. 848C–855B.

992. "*Et oscitavit . . . puer septies*" (n. 3 [col. 850B]) (4 Kings [2 Kings] 4:35).

993. "*ex voce confessionis*" (n. 8 [col. 852C]).

994. Cols. 855B–859B.

995. N. 1 (col. 856D) ("[It] would manifestly be attended with the gravest peril" [Luddy, *Sermons on the Canticle*, 1.164]).

about our inner life. Why do we need to know the movements of the Holy Spirit? Without this knowledge, *we do not desire Him when He is absent; we do not glorify Him when He is present.* This simple phrase speaks volumes.

b) When the Spirit is absent, then we may doubt of the truth. We should not be surprised. It is nothing new for a spiritual person to be in the dark, and to hesitate about which way to choose. This is not the danger; but the real danger is to embrace error for truth—*sapere falsitatem*.[996] When the Spirit is present, then there is no doubt, and no hesitation. He brings *non solum veritas sed certa veritas*.[997] He speaks with certitude and evidence we cannot reject (if He speaks plainly). But when he speaks in silence, it is more difficult. We must learn to interpret His silence itself as speech to us (17.3).

c) Our task then {is} "to distinguish between what is clear and what is doubtful, and not to declare that the doubtful is clear or the clear doubtful" (17.4).[998] This is itself a gift of the Holy Spirit—without His gift we cannot make this distinction. 17.7 contains a beautiful hymn of gratitude to God for His mercy to us in guiding us by His own Spirit (READ: Luddy translation, p. 172[999]).

---

996. Col. 857C ("to embrace voluntarily what is false" [Luddy, *Sermons on the Canticle*, 1.166]).

997. Col. 857C ("There succeeds to them not simply truth, but the certain assurance of truth" [Luddy, *Sermons on the Canticle*, 1.167]).

998. "*Distinguendum sane inter manifesta et dubia, nec illa scilicet adduci in dubium, nec ista temere affirmari*" (col. 857A) (Merton's translation).

999. "Thanks to Thee, Father of the fatherless, and Defender of the orphans, 'a curdled mountain, a fat mountain' has imparted to us its heat. 'The heavens dropped (dew) at the presence of the God of Sinai.' Oil has been poured out. Thy name has been spread abroad—the name which the enemy enviously begrudged to us, as he did us to it. That name, I say, has been spread abroad, extending even to the hearts and lips of little ones. For 'out of the mouth of infants and sucklings' it has 'perfected praise.' Then, 'the sinner shall see and shall be angry.' But as his anger is implacable, so shall the fire be inextinguishable 'which is prepared for the devil and his angels.' 'The zeal of the Lord of hosts will perform this.' How Thou lovest me, O my God, my Love! how Thou lovest me! Everywhere Thou art

Sermon 18[1000]—ACTIVE AND CONTEMPLATIVE LIVES: continuing the same subject, the action of the Holy Spirit in our souls, St. Bernard distinguishes between the *charismatic gifts* granted to some for the salvation of others and the graces given us for our own sanctification. Here again, discretion is necessary: we must not pour out the secret treasure of grace which is indispensable for our own sanctification, and we must not retain for ourselves the charisms that have been given us for others. *Caution* is required. Here St. Bernard makes the celebrated distinction between the "canals" and "reservoirs" (READ 18.2-3—Luddy translation, p. 175: [1001] SI SAPIS, CONCHAM TE EXHIBEBIS ET NON

---

mindful of me! Everywhere Thou are zealous for my salvation, not alone against the pride of men, but even against the pride of exalted angelic spirits! Both in heaven and on earth 'Thou, O Lord, dost judge them that wrong me, dost overthrow them that fight against me.' Everywhere Thou art my defence! Everywhere Thou art my support! Everywhere Thou dost appear at my right hand! For these things 'in my life I will praise the Lord; I will sing to my God as long as I shall be'" (Luddy, *Sermons on the Canticle*, 1.171–72) (col. 858CD).

1000. Cols. 859B–863A.

1001. "Yet, with regard to these graces, both interior and exterior, we must be on our guard against two temptations. These are, on the one hand, to give away what we have received for ourselves, and, on the other, to retain for ourselves what has been entrusted to us for the benefit of our neighbours. Certainly, you incur the guilt of keeping what belongs to another, if, whilst full of virtues, and adorned exteriorly with the endowments of wisdom and eloquence, through fear or sloth, or influenced by indiscreet humility, you seal under a useless, I should rather say, criminal silence, the 'good word,' which might have subserved the progress of many. Of such we read in Proverbs, 'He that hideth up corn shall be cursed among the people.' On the contrary, you waste and squander what you should keep for yourselves, when, without waiting for a complete infusion of the Spirit, you are impatient, although not more than half full, to empty yourselves out upon others. Thus you transgress the law which forbids us to plough with the first-born of the cow, or to shear the first-born of the sheep. I mean to say, you deprive yourselves of the life and health which you are communicating to others; because, whilst trying to serve your neighbours without purity of intention, you are but inflating yourselves with the wine of vainglory or inoculating yourselves with the poison of cupidity, or exposing to loss your own lives

CANALEM[1002]). The principle is: the sharing of contemplation with others presupposes that we are able to overflow and grant them of our surplus. Our apostolate, like our contemplation itself, must

---

by fostering the swelling of the deadly abscess of pride. Wherefore, my brethren, if you be wise, you will make yourselves to be reservoirs rather than conduits. The difference between a conduit and a reservoir is this, that whereas the former discharges all its waters almost as soon as received, the latter waits until it is full to the brim, and only communicates what is superfluous, what it can give away without loss to itself. Remember that a curse has been pronounced against him who deteriorates the lot which has been transmitted to him. And lest you should despise my counsel, attend to one who is wiser than I. 'A fool,' says Solomon, 'uttereth all his mind; a wise man deferreth and keepeth it till afterwards.' Yet we have in the Church to-day many conduits and but very few reservoirs. So great is the charity of those through whom the celestial streams of knowledge are communicated to us, that they want to give away before they have received. They are more willing to speak than to listen. They are forward to teach what they have not learned. Although unable to govern themselves, they gladly undertake to rule others. For my part, I think that, with regard to one's own salvation, no degree of charity is so necessary as that which Solomon proposes to us, where he says, 'Have pity on thy own soul, pleasing God.' If I have but a very small stock of oil for my own use, do you consider I ought to give that little away, and keep nothing for myself? But I want all I have for my own anointing, nor will I share it with others, except at the bidding of a prophet, like the widow of Sarepta at the word of Elias. And should some of those 'who think of me above that which they see in me, or hear anything of me,' persist in demanding a share of my oil, they shall get this answer: 'Lest, perhaps, there be not enough for us and for you, go ye rather to them that sell, and buy for yourselves.' But you may tell me, 'Charity seeketh not her own.' No, indeed, but do you know why? She 'seeketh not her own' because, no doubt, nothing of her own is wanting to her, and so needing to be sought. Who seeks for that which he already possesses? Charity is never without 'her own,' that is, without what is necessary for her own salvation. Not only has she what is requisite in this respect, but she has it in superabundance. She wishes to abound first unto herself, that she may also abound unto others. She keeps a sufficiency for herself, so that she may be wanting to none. For charity that is not full is not perfect" (Luddy, *Sermons on the Canticle*, 1.175–78) (cols. 859D–860D).

1002. N. 3 (col. 860A) ("if you be wise, you will make yourselves to be reservoirs rather than conduits" [Luddy, *Sermons on the Canticle*, 1.176]).

be God-like, it must proceed from a certain fullness. *Disce et tu nonnisi de pleno effundere, nec Deo largior esse velis* (18.4).[1003] {Note the} importance of receiving, of listening, of waiting. The point is largely psychological: he is warning his monks against the restless activism which avoids silence and solitude, which neglects the long process of organic development that is necessary for the light of God to gain full possession of a soul. His imagery must not lead us to conceive grace as a commodity, a thing (oil) poured into our souls. It is rather a condition of being attuned to God Who is present within us. The first reverberations of our being to the presence of God make a deep impression and we "feel" as if we had much to communicate. But if we violate the laws of living growth, and neglect the long periods of silent growth which God Himself demands of us, we will lose our contact with Him. In Sermon 18:5–6,[1004] St. Bernard again gives a rapid sketch of the various degrees of the interior life, this time in function of a love that builds up to an apostolic and charismatic mission. The soul must first be healed and cleansed of sin—a time of *compunction and penance*. Then it must be nourished, fortified and refreshed by the food of good works and the refreshing potion of prayer. This "wine of the spirit"[1005] makes us *forget carnal pleasures* (a point worthy of note—necessary in the ascent to "pure love"). The "sick man"[1006] being thus nourished, there is time for *convalescence*, and this rest and convalescence is *contemplation*. It follows upon the *sudores actionis*[1007] (the active life in the ascetic sense of purification and illumination). Features of this contemplation and rest (cf. Luddy translation, p. 181 ff.) {are that}: (a) the soul "dreams" of God {and} sees Him in the darkness and

---

1003. Col. 861B ("Learn to belch forth of thy fulness, and do not desire to be more generous than God" [Luddy, *Sermons on the Canticle*, 1.179]).
1004. Cols. 861C–863A.
1005. "*vinum spiritus*" (n. 5 [col. 862B]).
1006. "*aegrotus*" (n. 6 [col. 862B]).
1007. N. 6 (col. 862B) ("painful fatigues of action" [Luddy, *Sermons on the Canticle*, 1.181]).

"sleep" of contemplation,[1008] and not face to face (he does not imply imaginative day-dreaming here); (b) in this mysterious presence of God, there are *brief intuitions of love which give us rapid and transient contacts* with {the} God of love—God is not *seen* but sensed: *raptim et quasi sub quodam coruscamine scintillulae transeuntis, tenuiter vix attacti inardescit amore.*[1009] This kindling, as by a spark, is very important; for here is enkindled the fire of love without which our apostolate will be sterile and cold (cf. St. John of the Cross, *Spiritual Canticle*[1010]). When the soul has thus been enkindled, though the burst of "flame" may pass, there remains

1008. "*Dormiens in contemplatione Deum somniat*" (col. 862B) ("But whilst she thus slumbers in the peace of prayer, she sees God, as in a dream" [Luddy, *Sermons on the Canticle*, 1.181]).

1009. Col. 962BC ("in a passing way, and by the light of a sudden and momentary blaze of glory, so great a flame of love is enkindled in her" [Luddy, *Sermons on the Canticle*, 1.182]).

1010. See *Spiritual Canticle* (second recension), stanza 25 ("In the track of thy footprint The young girls run along by the way; / At the touch of a spark, at the spiced wine, Flows forth the Divine balsam"): "5. In the first two lines we have explained how the souls in the track of the footprint of the Beloved run along by the way by means of exercises and outward works; now in these last lines the soul describes the exercise which these souls perform inwardly with the will, moved by two other favours and inward visits which the Beloved grants them, which she here calls the touch of a spark and spiced wine; and the inward exercise of the will which results from these two visits and is caused by them she calls the flowing forth of Divine balsam. With respect to the first point, it must be known that this touch of a spark which she mentions here is a most subtle touch which the Beloved inflicts upon the soul at times, even when she is least thinking of it, so that her heart is enkindled in the fire of love just as if a spark of fire had flown out and kindled it. Then, with great rapidity, as when one suddenly awakens, the will is enkindled in loving, desiring, praising, giving thanks, doing reverence, esteeming and praying to God with savour of love. These things she calls the flowing forth of Divine balsam, which, at the touch of the sparks, issue forth from the Divine love which struck the spark, which is the Divine balsam, that comforts and heals the soul with its fragrance and substance" (Peers, *John of the Cross*, 2.323; virtually the same material is found in the first recension, stanza 16.4 [2.97]).

a steady burning fire of true spiritual zeal. {There is a} *"plenitudo dilectionis"*:[1011] *Talis amor zelat.*[1012] Features of this zealous and mystical love for souls {include}: (a) it is appropriate to one who is a friend of the Bridegroom, that is to say, who is no longer seeking his own interests but those of Christ; (b) it makes one a *"fidelis servus et prudens,"*[1013] worthy to be placed in charge of the Lord's household—hence *fidelity* and *prudence* are essential to it; (c) this love, in addition to its purity, nourishes and strengthens the soul {and} fills it to overflowing with a deep spiritual action that reaches out to others; it has transforming power, and is immensely fruitful: *Hic nutrit, hic fervet, hic ebullit;*[1014] (d) hence it can freely and without danger pour itself out to others: *hic jam securus effundit, exundans et erumpens, ac dicens:* Quis infirmatur, et ego non infirmor? Quis scandalizatur, et ego non uror?[1015] Again, note the characteristically Bernardine touch. Pure love is built on a foundation of solid fraternal charity which bears the burdens of another because it has the strength (i.e., the purity) to do so. The purity St. Bernard speaks of here is *real unselfishness* and not a self-complacent and angelistic feeling of purity, or feeling of faultlessness. It implies not merely a condition of one who is spiritually "beautified" and made pretty, but one who is indeed spiritually strong, with a *really strong love*. St. Bernard is not being puritanical: he is simply practical, as the Cistercian architects of the twelfth century were practical. He wanted to build a solid edifice on a firm foundation, and make sure that

---

1011. Col. 862D ("the fulness of love" [Luddy, *Sermons on the Canticle*, 1.183]).

1012. Col. 862C ("Such a love is full of zeal" [Luddy, *Sermons on the Canticle*, 1.182]).

1013. Col. 862C ("the faithful and wise servant" [Luddy, *Sermons on the Canticle*, 1.182]) (Matt. 24:45).

1014. Col. 862C ("Such a love fills up the soul's capacity; it waxes hot and boils over" [Luddy, *Sermons on the Canticle*, 1.182]).

1015. Col. 862C ("Then it may securely pour itself out, overflowing and overleaping its bounds and crying aloud: 'Who is weak and I am not weak? Who is scandalized and I am not on fire?'" [Luddy, *Sermons on the Canticle*, 1.182]) (2 Cor. 11:29).

the thing would stand. Another characteristic of this true zeal {is that} it is also *without vanity*: *Non est quo se immisceat vanitas, ubi totum occupat charitas.*[1016] Here is *true fullness*. The soul is filled with reality, with God Himself, for God is charity, and to be filled with God is to fulfill the law of God, for charity is both *plenitudo legis et cordis*[1017]—it objectively fulfills the law, and subjectively brings complete peace and happiness to the heart. This fullness is the complete work of the Holy Spirit, the *infusio*[1018] of sanctifying grace upon which must follow the other work, the *effusio*[1019] of charismatic graces, also His work in us for souls—and this means miracles, etc.

4. THE LOVE OF THE YOUNG MAIDENS for the Spouse— Sermons 19–20: these two sermons are especially important for novices. It is in fact to the "young maidens"—the beginners that follow the Bride as her escort and seek the Spouse after her example—that St. Bernard explicitly addresses these words. Sermon 19 serves as an introduction to the real theme, developed in Sermon 20, which is one of St. Bernard's most beautiful and most practical writings—on the love of Jesus Christ in His Humanity and Divinity. {In} *Sermon 19*[1020] St. Bernard begins with the literal sense of the verse {on which} he is about to comment (Cant. 1:2: *propterea adolescentulae dilexerunt te nimis*[1021]). The Spouse is speaking, and because of the graces of prayer given to her, therefore the other less advanced souls are also stirred up to a more ardent love of the Bridegroom. (St. Bernard speaks of course of himself and his community.) {In nn.} 2–5,[1022] he speaks of the love of the

---

1016. Col. 862C ("There is no room for vanity in the soul where all is charity" [Luddy, *Sermons on the Canticle*, 1.182]).

1017. Col. 862C ("For charity is the fulfilling of the heart no less than of the law" [Luddy, *Sermons on the Canticle*, 1.182]).

1018. Col. 862D.

1019. Col. 862D.

1020. Cols. 863A–867A.

1021. Col. 863A ("Therefore young maidens have loved Thee" [Luddy, *Sermons on the Canticle*, 1.184]).

1022. Cols. 863C–865C.

angelic hierarchies for the Word. This is interesting, but somewhat beside the point. {N.} 7 {asks}: who are the *adolescentulae*? those who are still "infants" in Christ and have need of milk rather than solid food. Their love for the Spouse is vehement indeed, but perhaps inordinate and ill-directed. St. Bernard here speaks of the *inordinate zeal of beginners*. READ n. 7:[1023] "You who

1023. "Thus all the angelic choirs love according to their several capacities. But the 'young maidens,' with less understanding, have also less capacity, and are altogether unable to attain to things so high, for they are but 'little ones in Christ,' requiring to be fed with milk and oil. Hence it is on the breasts of the Spouse that they must find the motives of their love. The Spouse possesses the oil poured out, the perfume of which arouses in the hearts of the 'young maidens' a desire to 'taste and see how sweet the Lord is.' And seeing them inflamed with love, she turns to her Beloved, and says, 'Thy name is as oil poured out, therefore, young maidens have loved Thee exceedingly.' What is it, my brethren, to love exceedingly? It is to love greatly, passionately, ardently. Or perhaps in the spiritual sense of the words, the Holy Ghost conveys an indirect reproof to some amongst you who are beginners in the religious life, censuring that indiscreet zeal, or rather that 'exceedingly' obstinate imprudence of theirs, which I have so often in vain endeavoured to repress. To such I say, you are unwilling to be content with the common life. You are not satisfied with the regular fasts, with the solemn vigils, with the ordinary observance of discipline, with the clothes and food I provide for you. You prefer what is private to what is common. Why do you thus resume charge of yourselves after having once and for all committed that responsibility to me? For, lo! you have again taken as your superior, in place of me, that self-will, which, as your conscience bears witness, has betrayed you into so many offences against God. By it you are taught not to spare nature, not to listen to reason, not to follow the counsel or the example of the seniors, not to submit to my authority. Are you not aware that 'obedience is better than sacrifice'? Have you not read in your Rule that whatever is done without the sanction and consent of the spiritual father shall be attributed to vainglory and shall merit no reward? Have you not read in the Gospel the example of obedience set by the Boy Jesus for the imitation of all other youths who aspire after holiness? For when He had remained behind in Jerusalem, and declared that it was necessary for Him to be about His Father's business, yet, as His parents would not consent to His staying longer, He did not disdain to follow them to Nazareth, the Master obeying

have but recently come to the monastery," he says, are the ones to whom this spiritual sense of the text is to be applied. He speaks of his difficulty is curbing their *minus {discretam} vehementiam*[1024] and indeed their *intemperantiam nimis obstinatam*.[1025] {It is the} duty of {a} good director to curb indiscreet zeal—novices do not always mean what they say—or know what they say. This emphasis on discretion and obedience places St. Bernard squarely in the Benedictine tradition, the true and sound monastic doctrine going back to Cassian (cf. Conference 2[1026]) and reflected later on by St. John of the Cross (see "faults of beginners" in *Dark Night of the Soul*, especially the chapter on spiritual gluttony and the

---

His disciples, God obeying man, the Word, the Wisdom of the Father obeying a poor artisan and his consort! Nor is this all. The inspired narrative goes on to say, 'And He was subject to them.' How long will you be wise in your own conceits? God commits and subjects Himself to mortals, and will you still walk in your own ways? You did indeed receive a good spirit, but you have made an ill use of the gift. I am now afraid lest that good spirit should depart from you and one that is wicked succeed, who will strive to deceive you with the outward appearance of virtue, so that having begun in the Spirit you may end in the flesh. Do you not know that the angel of darkness frequently 'transformeth himself into an angel of light'? God is Wisdom and wills us to love Him, not alone sweetly, but wisely as well. Hence the Apostle speaks of 'your reasonable service.' Believe me, if you neglect the knowledge of truth, the spirit of error will have no trouble in misdirecting your zeal. For that cunning enemy can find no more efficacious means of expelling the love of God from your hearts than by causing you to walk in it without caution or reason. Wherefore I am thinking of proposing to you certain canons of conduct which those who love God may find it worth their while to put in practice " (Luddy, *Sermons on the Canticle*, 1.191–93) (cols. 865D–867A).

1024. Col. 866A ("that indiscreet zeal" [Luddy, *Sermons on the Canticle*, 1.191]) (copy text reads: "*discretum*").

1025. Col. 866A, which reads: "*intemperantiam prorsus nimium obstinatam*" ("that 'extremely' obstinate imprudence" [Luddy, *Sermons on the Canticle*, 1.191]).

1026. *PL* 49, cols. 523B–558A; see Merton's discussion of this conference in *Cassian and the Fathers*, 220–26.

one on spiritual pride[1027]). In résumé, St. Bernard reproaches them for the following reasons: *Non vultis esse communi contenti vita,*[1028] in fasting, vigils, etc. *Privata praefertis communibus*[1029]—the natural urge to prefer what one has chosen for oneself. He asks: "Why did you come here and put yourselves under our care if you intend to be your own directors and run your own lives? Behold, that *same self-will which led you so often to offend God, you now take as your Master in the spiritual life*. It is self-will that teaches you not to spare your nature, not to listen to reason, not to pay attention to the counsel and example of the seniors, and not to obey your abbot."[1030] He holds up to them the example of obedience of the Child Jesus. He reminds them of the *Rule* (telling them that their penances are only vanity if performed outside obedience). "How long will you be wise in your own eyes? God entrusts Himself and subjects Himself to mortal beings, and you still go your own way?"[1031] He then makes an *important distinction*: true, this fervor *may have begun* with the grace of the Holy Spirit, but self-will can mix itself with true spiritual fervor and corrupt it. This is a constant danger—the more so as the subject feels that the beginning was indeed good. But: *Bonum receperatis spiritum,*

---

1027. St. John of the Cross, *Dark Night of the Soul*, Book 1, cc. 1–7 (Peers, *John of the Cross*, 1.350–70); spiritual gluttony is treated in chap. 6 (364–68) and spiritual pride in chap. 2 (352–56).

1028. Col. 866A ("you are unwilling to be content with the common life" [Luddy, *Sermons on the Canticle*, 1.191]).

1029. Col. 866B ("You prefer what is private to what is common" [Luddy, *Sermons on the Canticle*, 1.191]).

1030. *"Qui vestri curam semel nobis credidistis, quid rursum de vobis vos intromittitis? Nam illam, qua toties Deum, conscientiis vestris testibus, offendistis, propriam scilicet voluntatem vestram, ecce nunc iterum magistram habetis, non me. Illa vos naturae docet non parcere, rationi non acquiescere, non obtemperare seniorum consilio vel exemplo, non obedire nobis"* (col. 866B) (Merton's translation).

1031. *"Quousque vos sapientes estis in oculis vestris? Deus se mortalibus credit et subdit; et vos in viis vestris adhuc ambulatis?"* (col. 866C) (Merton's translation).

*sed non bene utimini eo.*[1032] {In} conclusion, INDISCREET ZEAL IS THE BEST MEANS BY WHICH THE ENEMY CAN TAKE AWAY TRUE LOVE FROM OUR HEARTS (868D).

Sermon 20[1033]—ON THE LOVE OF JESUS: the conclusion of the last sermon is, in effect, that self-love is incompatible with spiritual perfection. Hence the problem of the spiritual life is to get rid of self-love and self-will and to cultivate true love of God. How? The way of true love is here set forth for us simply and positively by St. Bernard. Jesus Himself is our model. He is the way. It is He that we must love as He has loved us. The way to "perfection" is not the love of an abstraction but the love of a person. Without the love of Jesus, no perfection is possible, all spirituality is illusory. *Qui non amat Domino Jesus, anathema sit* (1 Cor. 16:22).[1034]

N. 1: Jesus is our life, our light, our very being—hence our obligation to love Him. Supernaturally, it is by charity that we live, exist and think "in Christ." If we do not love Him, we are supernaturally dead. *Dignus plane est morte, qui tibi, Domine Jesu, recusat vivere, et mortuus est: et qui tibi non sapit, desipit: et qui curat esse nisi propter te, pro nihilo est, et nihil est.*[1035] We belong to God; we have been made for Him. If we desire and seek to live for ourselves rather than for Him, we begin to fall into nothingness. St. Bernard has this very acute sense of supernatural reality, on which the whole Christian and monastic life is based. We too must build on this. Without this insight into the fact that our life

---

1032. Col. 866C ("You did indeed receive a good spirit, but you have made an ill use of the gift" [Luddy, *Sermons on the Canticle*, 1.192]).

1033. Cols. 867A–872B.

1034. N. 1 (col. 867A) ("If any man love not our Lord Jesus Christ, let him be anathema" [Luddy, *Sermons on the Canticle*, 1.194]).

1035. Col. 867A ("Evidently, he is unworthy to live at all, whoever, O Lord Jesus, refuses to live for Thee. Yea, he is already dead! And whoso has no understanding of Thee, is only a fool. And he that desires to exist save only for Thee, is to be esteemed as nothing, for nothing he is indeed" [Luddy, *Sermons on the Canticle*, 1.194]).

"in Christ" is our only true life, and without the realization of what this life implies, we will be monks in appearance only—living for ourselves and therefore living in illusion. Since we are, however, not perfectly united to Christ, we always have cause to lament the fact that most of our life has been wasted and lost. But to recognize this fact with compunction and trust, and to resolve for the future to give ourselves entirely to God—this is our duty.

So far, he has considered the *creation* of man, in the Word, as the reason for loving the Word Incarnate. In n. 2 he passes on to the Redemption. *Super omnia, inquam, reddit amabilem te mihi, Jesu bone, calix quem bibisti, opus nostrae redemptionis. Hoc omnino amorem nostrum facile vindicat totum sibi.*[1036] St. Bernard here contemplates the infinite love of God for us in Christ, Who gave Himself for us when we were not even His friends but His enemies. *Ipse prior dilexit nos* (1 Jn. 4:10)—a basic idea in St. Bernard.[1037]

N. 3: *the Love of Christ for us*. Here St. Bernard considers Christ's love for us, and he will later go on to show that His love must be the model for our love for Him, which must possess the same qualities. D*ilexit dulciter*[1038]—by taking on our human nature: this means first of all a *tender* and *human* love—implying

---

1036. Col. 867C ("What makes Thee, O good Jesus, amiable to me above all things is the chalice Thou didst drain for us, the work of our Redemption. This easily attracts to Thee all the love of our hearts" [Luddy, *Sermons on the Canticle*, 1.195]).

1037. In the *De Diligendo Deo*, Bernard's starting point for loving God is that God first loved us: "*quia ipse prior dilexit nos*" (c. 1.1 [*PL* 182, col. 975B]), and he repeats these words in chapter 6, summarizing his argument thus far: "*Hic primum vide, quo modo, imo quam sine modo a nobis Deus amari meruerit; qui (ut paucis quod dictum est repetam) prior ipse dilexit nos*" ("See here first how God merits to be loved—without limit—for (repeating in few words what has been said) He Himself loved us first" [chap. 6.16 (col. 983D)]); see Gilson, *Mystical Theology of Saint Bernard*, 22–25 for the foundational importance of 1 John 4 in Bernard's teaching.

1038. Col. 868A, which reads: "*Dilexit autem dulciter, sapienter, fortiter*" ("His love for us is sweetly tender, and wise, and strong" [Luddy, *Sermons on the Canticle*, 1.196]).

all St. Bernard's doctrine of *compassion* and *mercy; sapienter*—but the love of Christ for us, though *human*, was not "carnal," was without the weakness of human nature, leading to sin, was a "prudent" love on the level of *reason* and of the Spirit: *in carne quaesivit, dilexit in spiritu;*[1039] *fortiter*—above all, the love of Christ was more powerful than death, for He underwent death on the Cross for our sakes: *Adjutor fortis*[1040]—*redemit in virtute.*[1041] These qualities complete one another to produce a *perfect spiritual love*.

N. 4: *Our love for Jesus. Disce, O Christiane, a Christo quemadmodum diligas Christum* (cf. Luddy translation, 198).[1042] He then rings the changes on the three ideas of *dulciter, sapienter et fortiter*:

a) *dulciter*—the *amor carnalis Christi*—this is very important. Note that the tender and human love of the soul for Jesus Christ is not an invention of St. Bernard; it goes back even to the Desert Fathers. He simply reminds us that without this human and tender affection, which is intimately personal and real, we cannot go on to higher things in the spiritual life. At the same time, this tender and human love is *not in itself enough*. Very often St. Bernard is misunderstood, and his doctrine is made to mean the opposite of what he intends, by those who think he believes that *human affection for Jesus felt to be present as a personal reality* is the whole story in love for God and spiritual perfection. No, it is only the beginning, and if it is not completed by the other qualities, it is *insufficient*. The need for *amor carnalis* {means that} it is necessary that we have a sensible and human affection for Christ to give our sensible nature a way of spiritualizing its action, and to deliver us from the otherwise overwhelming attractions of sense.

---

1039. Col. 868A ("those whom He sought in the flesh, He loved in the Spirit" [Luddy, *Sermons on the Canticle*, 1.197]).

1040. Col. 868B ("a powerful Helper" [Luddy, *Sermons on the Canticle*, 1.197]).

1041. Col.868A ("He . . . redeemed in His power" [Luddy, *Sermons on the Canticle*, 1.197]).

1042. Col. 868C ("O Christians, learn from Christ how you ought to love Christ" [Luddy, *Sermons on the Canticle*, 1.198]).

It is necessary to protect us from *ambition* and *sensuality*: *vincat dulcedo dulcedinem*.[1043] It gives us strength to prefer Jesus to every sensible pleasure or temporal good that is not willed by Him (871). It gives us *fervor*. St. Bernard does not despise the emotions. They have their place in the spiritual life. But they are secondary and must be spiritualized. This fervor is love of the *heart*. We cannot leave the heart out of the spiritual life and go to God purely coldly and intellectually. This is not fully human, and Bernard has full respect for the human nature created by God in order to be sanctified by His grace. Every part of that human nature must be sanctified. We must indeed love with our "whole heart": *toto et pleno cordis affectu* (869).[1044] The love of the apostles for Jesus before His Ascension and before Pentecost was of this character—it was tender and human, but it had serious limitations. As it was, it would have ultimately hindered their spiritual interests and their salvation itself. *Expedit vobis ut vadam*.[1045] In n. 6, St. Bernard gives a good and thorough description of *amor carnalis* (READ n. 6—Luddy 201–202[1046]). {He} defines it: "It is that

---

1043. Col. 869A ("Let sweetness be overcome by sweetness" [Luddy, *Sermons on the Canticle*, 1.199]).

1044. N. 4 ("with the full and entire affection of your hearts" [Luddy, *Sermons on the Canticle*, 1.199]).

1045. N. 5 (col. 869C, which reads: ". . . *ut ego vadam*") ("It is expedient for you that I go" [Luddy, *Sermons on the Canticle*, 1.200]) (John 16:7).

1046. "And take notice that the love of the heart is, in some sense, carnal, because it tends to turn the hearts of men towards the Flesh of Christ, and towards His example and precepts, given in the flesh. One that is filled with this love is easily affected by every discourse on such subjects. There is nothing he more willingly hears, more attentively reads, more frequently calls to mind, more affectionately ponders. With this love, as with the fat of the 'fatted calf,' he enriches his holocausts of prayer. He has before his mind, as he prays, the sacred image of the God-Man, in the manger, or on His mother's breast, or teaching, or dying, or rising from the tomb, or ascending into heaven. Every such representation must necessarily urge his soul to the love of virtue, or help to repress the carnal passions, put temptations to flight, and extinguish evil desires. To my thinking, this appears to have been one of the main reasons why the invisible God willed to appear in visible flesh, and as Man to converse amongst men, that, namely, He might draw

love which moves the heart of man to love the flesh of Christ and those things which Christ did in the flesh."[1047] {Its} *effects* {are} consolation and fervor: the soul loves to hear Jesus spoken of, to read about Him; {it} prays with ardent zeal {and} easily imagines Jesus in His various mysteries and has Him present in one or other of them most of the time. Aided by this "presence" of Jesus, it overcomes temptations and pacifies desires of the flesh. This was the main reason, says St. Bernard, why Jesus became incarnate—to win to Himself the love of carnal man who had no other way of loving than a human and sensible way. (Note that *carnalis* in this context does not mean evil or sensual, but rather "sensible.") This love is in itself *spiritual* and a "great gift of the Holy Spirit"[1048] (871).

b) *Sapienter—amor rationabilis Christi*:[1049] but a higher love is altogether necessary, or the limitations of *amor carnalis* will be detrimental to the soul in the long run. *Amor carnalis* is *dulcis sed seducibilis*.[1050] A love that depends on feeling is subject to serious danger of error. We will eventually tend to judge by our feelings

---

all the affections of carnal men, who knew how to love only in a carnal manner, first to a salutary love of His own Flesh, and thence lead them gradually to a more spiritual love of His Divinity. Was not the former the degree of charity in which they still stood, who said, 'Behold we have left all things and followed Thee'? Surely we must admit that it was the love of Christ's sensible presence alone that had led them to leave all things, since they could not listen patiently to a single word about His saving Passion and death before the events, nor afterwards witness even the glory of His Ascension without oppressive sorrow. This is what He Himself meant when He said, 'Because I have spoken these things to you, sorrow hath filled your heart.' Thus, it was as yet only by the power and the grace of His own presence in the flesh that He had withdrawn them from all other love according to the flesh" (Luddy, *Sermons on the Canticle*, 1.201–3) (col. 870AC).

1047. "*Et nota amorem cordis quodam modo esse carnalem, quod magis erga carnem Christi, et quae in carne Christus gessit vel jussit, cor humanum afficiat*" (col. 870A).

1048. "*magnum donum Spiritus*" (n. 8).

1049. "the rational love of Christ."

1050. "sweet but susceptible to being seduced."

and not according to reality. To save us from the danger, we must love *rationabiliter*, with *discretion*, with clear and detached judgement. This love is a love not merely of the flesh of Christ, but of the TRUTH and LIGHT of Christ: *ne seducaris . . . lucescat tibi veritas Christus* (868).[1051] It is not enough to have the fervor and zeal born of a tender personal love for Jesus. This zeal must be *guided* and formed by *"scientia."*[1052] (We shall see later[1053] how St. Bernard returns to this subject of discretion and illuminated zeal. He is an enemy of blind zeal, which causes disaster in the spiritual life.) We must love God not only with our whole heart but with *our whole mind*. It would seem that if in St. Bernard's time it was necessary to place a special emphasis on the human and tender love of the heart of Christ, the average devout person is not likely to overlook this in our day. At least it is a theme which is heavily stressed in modern spirituality. It would seem rather that in our day we ought to throw more emphasis on the *rational* love of Christ as truth, and the *strong* love that is perfectly spiritual and purified to the point of martyrdom. The proper province of *amor rationalis* is the life of virtue and illumination. (It corresponds to the *pietas* we discussed above in Sermons 9–12.) It takes care of *industria seu judicium rationis*[1054]—good works and discretion (868). It loves *tota rationis vigilantia et circumspectione* (869).[1055] It loves not so much *Verbum caro*, as *Verbum sapientia*, *Verbum justitia*, Verbum veritas, *Verbum pietas*, etc. (871).[1056] It no longer is content merely with "feeling" certain sentiments of devotion and love at the thought of Jesus suffering on the Cross, but it *puts into effect*

---

1051. N. 4 ("If you would not be led astray . . . Christ, Who is truth, must enlighten your minds" [Luddy, *Sermons on the Canticle*, 1.198]).

1052. "knowledge" (col. 868D).

1053. See below, Appendix V, pages 340–46.

1054. Col. 868D ("the activity or judgement of our reason" [Luddy, *Sermons on the Canticle*, 1.199]).

1055. "with all the vigilance and circumspection of your understanding" (Luddy, *Sermons on the Canticle*, 1.199).

1056. N. 8 ("not so much the flesh of the Word as the Word under the aspect of Wisdom, of Justice, of Truth, of Sanctity, of Piety, of Power" [Luddy, *Sermons on the Canticle*, 1.204–5]).

good works which spring from the truth of Christ. It is marked by zeal for justice and truth, discipline of morals, sanctity of life. IT IS GUIDED IN ALL THINGS BY PRINCIPLES OF FAITH AND BY THE MIND OF THE CHURCH and not merely by human feelings, however sure and however right, for the mysteries of Christ.

c) *Fortiter*: the last and most important love, that makes our hearts truly spiritual, that loves God with "all our strength," is the *amor fortis*, without which even *amor rationalis* is imperfect and incomplete. Without *amor fortis*, the soul is liable to succumb under the trials and difficulties of life, and fail to measure up to the perfect love of God. It is not enough to have good will and live according to principles of faith; one must also be prepared to suffer and to die for love of Jesus. But this perfect love is a supreme gift of the Spirit. With this *amor fortis* the soul has not only fervor and light but *constancy* and the ability to stand firm and resist evil in all its forms, not by our own power but by the power of God. Without this *amor fortis*, Peter swore that he would go to death with Christ, but afterwards denied Him. But after Pentecost, when he had received the gift of the Spirit, Peter was glad to suffer something for the love of his Master. "And if such great power of the Holy Spirit comes to help you so that no pressure of trials or tortures or even the threat of death itself makes you desert justice, then you love with all your power and your love is truly spiritual" (872).[1057]

5. "*TRAHE ME*"—Sermons 21–22: {these are} two sermons of relatively lesser importance—they deal with trials and weaknesses in the spiritual life. St. Bernard starts with a problem: it is the Spouse who says "*trahe me.*"[1058] Is it then necessary even for the Spouse to be "drawn," as it were, by force after her Beloved? If so, this is not a question of unwillingness or lack of zeal on her part, but simply of the incapacity of a created being to respond

---

1057. "*Quod si etiam adjuvantis Spiritus vigor tantus accedat, ut nulla vi laborum vel tormentorum, sed nec mortis metu justitia unquam deseratur; in hoc etiam tota virtute diligitur, et est amor spiritualis*" (Merton's translation).

1058. Col. 872B ("Draw me" [Luddy, *Sermons on the Canticle*, 1.207]) (Cant. 1:3).

perfectly, of its own accord, to the Love of God. "I know that I cannot reach Thee unless I follow Thee; but I cannot even follow Thee unless I am helped by Thee; hence I pray Thee; to draw me after Thee" (21.2).[1059] From what follows, there emerges a subtle psychological point: we must follow Christ, and in following Him we discover our own infirmities and weaknesses. Hence it is that so many do not even want to follow Him—*cupientes consequi sed non et sequi* (21:2).[1060] In talking of the trials of those who follow Christ, St. Bernard uses the term *vicissitudo*.[1061] This sermon and the following give insight into his meaning. This is the state of those who, faithful to the Bridegroom and even far advanced in the spiritual life, nevertheless continue to experience the ups and downs inevitable for all; they often feel themselves, as it were, completely abandoned, tepid and useless. This should not be a cause for anxiety; one should humble himself, face reality, pray trustfully, and continue in the dark until help comes. *The rule of action to follow* {is}: in the time of consolation, do not get too self-confident; in time of desolation, do not give way to discouragement. And recognize that even our trials and temptations, even our failures and weaknesses, are instruments by which the Beloved seeks to draw us after Him (21.11[1062]).

Sermon 22[1063] is unusually objective. The ointments of the Bridegroom, whose sweet odor draws us after Him, are not now merely subjective experiences, but objective graces and virtues present in the Incarnate Word—effects of the mystery of the

---

1059. "*scio . . . me nequaquam posse pervenire ad te, nisi gradiendo post te; sed neque hoc quidem, nisi adjutam abs te; ideoque precor ut trahas me post te*" (col. 873B).

1060. N. 2 (col. 873D) ("They would wish to overtake without the labour of pursuing" [Luddy, *Sermons on the Canticle*, 1.210]).

1061. "change, alternation"; see *In Cantica*, 31.1 (col. 940C), 32.2 (col. 946C); the expression is also found in Guerric of Igny, *In Festo Benedicti, Sermo* 4.5 (*PL* 185, col. 115B) and in Gilbert of Hoyland, *In Cantica*, 25.5, 27.7, 30.1, 31.2 (*PL* 184, cols. 133A, 144D, 155B, 161B); see Gilson, *Mystical Theology of Saint Bernard*, 143–44 and 241, n. 215, for a discussion of this term in Bernard.

1062. Cols. 877B–878A.

1063. Cols. 878A–884A.

Incarnation in the world, for instance the "mercy of God" which has gone forth from Christ into the whole earth.[1064] It is a sign of spiritual life to respond to the sweet odor of this mercy, a sign of spiritual death not to be affected by it in the least, to have no love for Jesus. {In} 22.9 {he points out} the diversity of gifts, and of vocations. Not all respond alike to the odor of the same mystical ointments. Some are moved to piety, and their piety (we would say today) centers on the Passion of the Savior. The most perfect of these are the martyrs. Others are penitents, moved with the hope of pardon. Still others "are aflame with zeal for wisdom."[1065] Again, others, inspired above all by all the virtues and life of Christ, seek above all to imitate Him by their virtuous lives. It is, of course, merely a question of emphasis. In all, Christ must be wisdom, justice, sanctification and redemption. We must seek all virtue, strength, wisdom and prudence in Him.

6. THE CELLARS OF THE SPOUSE—Sermon 23:[1066] this is one of the most important of the whole series, packed with material; it sums up the first group of sermons and is the culminating point of St. Bernard's early maturity. He had reached this point when he left to combat the schism of Peter de Leone.[1067] There is much here about the interior life and about contemplation, drawn from St. Bernard's own experience. Where then are the Spouse and young maidens "running"? to the "cellars" of the Spouse—*loca redolent penes Sponsum, plena odoramentis, referta deliciis*.[1068] We must get St. Bernard's image—cool, dark, underground storerooms, smelling of wine, spices, oils, etc.—images for the riches

---

1064. "*misericordia Domini plena est terra*" (n. 8 [col. 881B] ("the earth is full of the mercy of the Lord" [Luddy, *Sermons on the Canticle*, 1.228]) (Ps. 32[33]:5).

1065. "*vehementius studiis flagrare sapientiae*" (n. 9 [col. 582]).

1066. Cols. 884A–894A; see also pages 380–89 below.

1067. I.e. the antipope Anacletus II (see above, pages 35–44).

1068. N. 1 (col. 884B, which reads: "*loca quaedam redolentia . . .*") ("the Bridegroom's sweet-smelling promptuaries . . . filled with odoriferous fruits of the soil, replenished with all manner of delights" [Luddy, *Sermons on the Canticle*, 1.234]).

and gifts stored away for us in the mystery of God's love from which all good comes to us. In the spiritual life, we must always be animated by *hope* of entering into the good things of God in sharing in His gifts, not for the sake of the gifts but for His sake Who loves us—the greatest of all gifts being to love Him with no thought of any other reward but love. The "gifts" in these cellars will help our love to become more pure. *Quae amat ardentius, currit velocius, et citius pervenit* (23.1).[1069] *Charitas sponsae non quiescit.*[1070] Her more ardent zeal means that she enters herself into the cellars of the Spouse, and the "young maidens"[1071] who cannot enter with her nevertheless receive divine gifts through her. Again St. Bernard is thinking of his own vocation, and his relation to his monks.

*Contemplation {comes} through the senses of Scripture*, {including} the moral sense. The garden where the young maidens tend to remain is the literal sense; the cellars is the moral sense (for progressives); the *cubiculum* {is} the spiritual sense (for contemplatives). There are three cellars, he says: they will summarize the ascetic life for him—again. But we must be on our guard. This is not just another lineup of "three degrees" in arbitrary fashion. There is more. There is a deep teaching on the relation of *asceticism to human nature*. We find ourselves confronted with a theme which St. Bernard treats more like the Greek Fathers than like post-Tridentine mysticism and theology. Bernard here is *on the side of nature*. Nature is not something evil that has to be destroyed by the ascetic life, or merely something infirm that has to be healed and corrected by the ascetic life. It is a great good, which has to be *fully restored* by asceticism in order that it may attain the end destined for it by God, divinization in union with the Word. The ascetic life makes possible, in the lives of individ-

---

1069. Col. 884B ("[she] runs more swiftly because she loves more ardently, and so reaches her destination more speedily" [Luddy, *Sermons on the Canticle*, 1.234]).

1070. Col. 884C ("The charity of the Spouse is not at rest" [Luddy, *Sermons on the Canticle*, 1.235]).

1071. "*adolescentulae*" (col. 884B).

*The Cistercian Fathers and Their Monastic Theology* 301

uals, the restoration of human nature in Christ and its divinization.

a) *Disciplina*:[1072] the first step {is that} the individual must learn to live *sub alio*.[1073] He must renounce the fatal independence and license of a false individualism, and return to vital contact with society by submission to others who are more advanced, more united with God, more clear-sighted, more endowed with grace. He must become a *discipulus*.[1074] He must learn from others, must obey, must submit, must follow. Why? because by original sin the *bonum naturae*,[1075] which is equal in all, becomes the object of inordinate love in the individual, who strives to exalt himself above others. To cure this, he must learn to submit and humble himself, to renounce self-will and *insolentia morum*[1076]—hence the special importance of the Benedictine *Rule*. "The good of nature which he had lost by pride, he will finally regain through obedience, so that he will learn to live at peace with others by natural affection and not through fear of punishment."[1077] This is very important, with its clear echo of the *Rule* (prologue[1078] and chapter 7[1079]) and its emphasis on the fact that the common life restores our natural capacity for love and affection, which is intended to

---

1072. N. 6 (col. 886D).

1073. Col. 886D ("under others" [Luddy, *Sermons on the Canticle*, 1.240]).

1074. Col. 887A ("disciples" [Luddy, *Sermons on the Canticle*, 1.240]).

1075. Col. 887A, which reads: "*bono naturae*" ("natural perfection" [Luddy, *Sermons on the Canticle*, 1.240]).

1076. Col. 287A ("the wantonness of our manners" [Luddy, *Sermons on the Canticle*, 1.241]).

1077. "*bonumque in se naturae, quod superbiendo amiserat, obediendo recipiat; dum solo jam naturali affectu, non metu disciplinae, cum universis naturae suae sociis*" (col. 887A).

1078. "*ut ad eum per obedientiae laborem redeas, a quo per inobedientiae desidiam recesseras*" ("that by the labour of obedience thou mayest return to him from whom thou hast strayed by the sloth of disobedience") (McCann, 6/7).

1079. "*Ergo his omnibus humilitatis gradibus ascensis, monachus mox ad caritatem Dei perveniet illam quae* perfecta foris mittit timorem" ("Then, when all these degrees of humility have been climbed, the monk will presently

serve the purposes of God in uniting us in one Body by supernatural love. But before we can love supernaturally, we must be able to love naturally—St. Bernard would insist on this. Supernatural union with our brethren in community life can never be achieved by crushing and destroying the natural power to love—or at least not according to St. Bernard's way of looking at things. All that has to be done away with is the *selfish* and *self-centered* love which actually is not natural, according to his view.

b) *Natura*: after the soul has been taught and formed by living *sub alio*, it can once more live according to its nature. {This is an} important idea: ascetic discipline aims at restoring man's nature as it came from the hands of God—in what sense? It is man's nature to love. Purified of selfishness by discipline, he can now go out to others and love them unselfishly. This, for St. Bernard, is *natural*, and good, and necessary for sanctity. The life according to nature is the life in which we live *cum alio*,[1080] in which one learns to be a *socius*[1081] rather than just a *discipulus*. While the life of *disciplina* is bitter and hard, this is hard and consoling and pleasant. (*Ecce quam bonum et quam jucundum habitare fratres in unum.*[1082]) "*Quasi unctus* [by the *bonum naturae* of good fraternal affection] *redditur homo suavis et mitis, homo sine querela, neminem circumveniens, neminem concutiens, neminem laedens, nemini se superextollens aut praeferens, insuper et libenter communicans in ratione dati et accepti*" (n. 6 [887]).[1083] This, we now realize, is a familiar theme with St. Bernard. Here we see it in a

---

come to that perfect love of God which casts out all fear") (McCann, 48/49) (1 John 4:18).

1080. Col. 886A ("with others" [Luddy, *Sermons on the Canticle*, 1.240]).

1081. "companion."

1082. Col. 887B ("Behold how good and pleasant it is for brethren to dwell together in unity, like precious ointment on the head!" [Luddy, *Sermons on the Canticle*, 1.241]) (Ps. 132[133]:1).

1083. "This unguent renders a man sweet and mild, makes him such that he never complains, never overreaches, never strikes or otherwise injures anybody, never boasts or prefers himself to anyone, and, moreover, he enters gladly into the kindly intercourse of friendship which consists in the interchange of all good offices" (Luddy, *Sermons on the Canticle*, 1.242).

particular light. The moral consequences are always the same. One cannot begin the interior life without renouncing self, but mere negative renunciation is not enough. We must cultivate the *positive* side of the ascetic life: gentleness, charity, kindness, meekness, non-violence and pure affection—*humanitas*.

c) *Gratia*: his choice of a title for the third stage (*cella vinaria*:[1084] *gratia*) seems at first sight arbitrary, but if we recall the theme of Sermon 18 we will see that it is not arbitrary at all. This degree is that in which one learns to be a *superior*—*praeesse*[1085]—and according to St. Bernard superiorship and *apostolica* cura animarum[1086] calls for special graces and gifts from God, a special charity which goes "out of itself" and "is lost to itself" in order to think of others before itself. We might be inclined to think, according to a certain modern approach, that it takes more grace to submit, less grace to live in affection with others according to the standards of Christ. There is grace in the life of the *discipulus*, more in the life of the *socius*, most of all in the life of the *magister*.[1087] (However, it is not necessarily grace which makes one *aspire* to be a superior—cf. passages where St. Bernard condemns those who seek prelacy for selfish motives.) The *magister* is said to be introduced into the *cella vinaria* because there he has drunk of a charity and fervent zeal, without which one cannot rightly take charge of other souls. This is the *cella gratiae*[1088] because, though all three require grace, this requires the *fullness of grace*.

*The spiritual sense* {focuses on} the CUBICULUM (n. 9f.),[1089] {symbol of} CONTEMPLATION. St. Bernard now considers the *call to contemplation*. (We pass over the apparent discrepancy with Sermon

---

1084. Col. 885C, which reads: "*cellam vinariam*" ("wine-cellar" [Luddy, *Sermons on the Canticle*, 1.242]) (Cant. 2:4).

1085. N. 7 (col. 887D) ("to govern" [Luddy, *Sermons on the Canticle*, 1.242]).

1086. "the apostolic care of souls."

1087. Col. 887A.

1088. Col. 887D, which reads: "*cellam . . . gratiae*" ("the cellar of Grace" [Luddy, *Sermons on the Canticle*, 1.243]).

1089. Col. 888D ("bedchamber" [Luddy, *Sermons on the Canticle*, 1.244]).

18, where contemplation is required as a prerequisite for the life of an abbot.)

a) The diversity of vocations: not all are called to the same "mansion" in the interior life. The choice depends not so much on us as on Him Who has chosen us. "It is not given to all to enjoy, in the same place, the delightful and secret presence of the Spouse."[1090] Each one advances only as far as his merits permit. But only the Spouse is admitted to the *cubiculum*.

b) What is and is not the *cubiculum*: St. Bernard distinguishes, following his own experience. The *cubiculum* must be both *secret and a place of rest*:

(1) *Intellectual contemplation* admits us to a secret and delightful contemplation of the ways of God—a place of *lights*, but *not of rest: minime quietus*.[1091] There is labor, and effort, and seeking, and "studying"; there is fatigue and restlessness. This is not true contemplation; it is not the *cubiculum*.

(2) *The dark night—locus terribilis*[1092]—{brings} a terrifying realization of God's inexorable justice, of His condemnation of the reprobate. St. Bernard speaks again from experience, lets us see something of the saint's *horror of sin*. He is shattered by it, crushed by the spectacle of evil in the world, {even} in prelates and princes of the Church—it is especially this contradiction between the holiness of their state and the unholiness of their lives that afflicts St. Bernard. Here we have no ordinary "dark night" but the affliction and horror of soul which was part of his own vocation as a reformer of society and of ecclesiastical life in his time. He is thinking especially of the pride, avarice, sacrilege, simony and callous indifference of prelates to truth and justice— in some sense a much greater scandal than the sins of the godless.

---

1090. "*Non omnibus uno in loco frui datur grata et secreta sponsi praesentia*" (col. 889A).

1091. N. 11 (col. 890A ("very far from quiet" [Luddy, *Sermons on the Canticle*, 1.248]).

1092. N. 12 (col. 890C) ("place [which is] terrible" [Luddy, *Sermons on the Canticle*, 1.249]).

(In our own time the evil of the Nazis and the injustice and hypocrisy of the Reds might be the basis for a corresponding sense of the mystery of evil.) *Terribilis est locus iste, et totius expers quietis, totus inhorrui, si quando in eum raptus sum.*[1093] St. Bernard feared because he had to some extent identified himself with the rest of sinful humanity, and seeing the open evil in other prelates, dreaded lest the roots of the same evil be hidden in himself. Yet St. Bernard concludes that this place of fear introduces one into contemplation: *locus Dei est iste.*[1094] It is the house of God and gate of heaven.[1095] Why is this place the "beginning of wisdom,"[1096] and not intellectual contemplation? *Ibi instruimur,* hic afficimur.[1097] It is a passive and quasi-experiential knowledge of the holiness of God, arrived at indirectly through the experience of the mystery of evil. TUNC PRIMUM DEUS ANIMAE SAPIT, CUM EAM AFFICIT AD TIMENDUM, *non cum instruit ad sciendum. Sapit tibi potens Deus, quia* TIMOR SAPOR EST (n. 14 [892]).[1098] This is typical of St. Bernard. The beginning of wisdom is not *curiositas* and mere intellectual effort, all from the top of the head; wisdom is a knowledge that has its roots in the heart, and possesses man's whole being, not just his brain.

---

1093. N. 13 (col. 891B) ("Terrible in truth is this place, and entirely incompatible with the quiet of repose. I shudder all over, whenever I enter it" [Luddy, *Sermons on the Canticle*, 1.250]).

1094. Col. 891C, which reads: "*Dei locus et iste*" ("even this is a place of God" [Luddy, *Sermons on the Canticle*, 1.251]).

1095. Cf. Gen. 28:17.

1096. "*Initium . . . sapientiae*" (col. 891D) (Ps. 110[111]:9).

1097. N. 14 (col. 891D), which reads: ". . . *instruimur quidem, sed hic* . . .") ("There our minds are instructed, here our wills are affected" [Luddy, *Sermons on the Canticle*, 1.251]).

1098. Text reads: ". . . *sciendum. Times Dei justitiam, times potentiam; et sapit tibi justus et potens* . . ." ("it is only then the soul begins to relish God, when she is inspired with the fear of Him, not when she is instructed in the knowledge of Him. You fear the divine justice, you fear the divine power, and hence . . . fear gives savour" [Luddy, *Sermons on the Canticle*, 1.252]).

(3) *True contemplation* {is the} *locus quietus:*[1099] this is true contemplation, where God Himself is experienced, passively, in rest and in deepest secrecy. It is above all an *experience of God's mercy*. This is necessary, in view of what has gone before. If one saw the justice of God and did not experience that mercy overcame justice, one could hardly rest in God. Furthermore it is a place of security, in a mercy which is not fickle and unstable but endures forever. It is an awareness of God's will, as it were, pressing down on us with His mercy so that we are truly His and cannot doubt of it. STAT SENTENTIA PACIS SUPER TIMENTES EUM ([892] n. 15).[1100] Here God is seen in peace and quiet, because He Himself brings peace and quiet to our souls. *Quiescens et quietus cernitur Deus.*[1101] He pours into our hearts peace, confidence, assurance, love. He pacifies all curiosity, all striving of the mind, all strain, all agitation of the interior and exterior senses. TRANQUILLUS DEUS TRANQUILLAT OMNIA; ET QUIETEM ASPICERE, QUIESCERE EST (n. 16 [893]).[1102] So great is the power of God over the soul here that there are *no longer any distractions*, no desires, no anxieties, no cares. This then is the *cubiculum*—the place of true peace. But unfortunately one does not remain there for long: *Heu, rara hora, et parva mora!*[1103]

[This series on the Sermons *in Cantica* was discontinued here.]

1099. N. 16 (col. 892B, which reads: *"verae quietis locus"*) ("place of true rest" [Luddy, *Sermons on the Canticle*, 1.255]).

1100. "[There] stands fixed . . . His decree of mercy 'upon them that fear Him'" (Luddy, *Sermons on the Canticle*, 1.253).

1101. Col. 892B ("the Lord appears truly tranquil and at rest" [Luddy, *Sermons on the Canticle*, 1.253]).

1102. "The tranquillity of God tranquillises all about Him, and the contemplation of His rest is rest to the soul" (Luddy, *Sermons on the Canticle*, 1.255).

1103. N. 15 (col. 892B) ("But all too rare that privilege, alas! And all too short-lived" [Luddy, *Sermons on the Canticle*, 1.253]).

# {Appendices I–VII}

## Appendix I

*Haec est generatio quaerentium Dominum.*[1]

St. Bernard, {in} Sermons 37 and 38 *De Diversis*,[2] sees the joy and gladness hidden in the monastic life. {The} background of *Sermo* 37 {is that} Bernard finds the community weary and distracted with the labors of the harvest (sometimes they did not even have conventual Mass in harvest time) and he is filled with consolation because in the community at work he beholds the mercy and love of God. (We must cultivate the gaze of faith, which sees God in the community life, as our Fathers did. Then we will love our monastery.) For St. Bernard, in these sermons, the beauty of the monastic life consists in the fact that the monks are men who are not only sought by God, and saved without realizing fully the immensity of His love, but they also seek Him in return—they realize their vocation. This fact that they seek Him is proof that they have already found Him.[3] They could not seek Him unless they had found him. (Apply this to our monastic community: all are seeking—all have to some extent found.) "The Word may indeed be possessed without being sought, but He

---

1. J. P. Migne, ed., *Patrologiae Cursus Completus, Series Latina* [*PL*], 221 vols. (Paris: Garnier, 1844–1865), vol. 183, col. 640A ("This is the generation of them that seek the Lord") (Ps. 23[24]:6).

2. Cols. 639D–644A, 644A–645C.

3. "*Nemo te quaerere valet, nisi qui prius invenerit*" ("No one is able to seek You except one who has already found You") (*De Diligendo Deo*, 7.22 [*PL* 183, col. 987C]).

cannot be sought without being possessed"[4] (n. 4), because He comes first with His graces and produces in us the desire for Him. "He hath first loved us!"[5] Hence the greater our desire for Him, the closer we really are to Him. *Certissima mihi probatio et indubitabile argumentum, quia habetis quem sic quaeritis, et in vobis habitat, qui tam valide trahit vos ad se ipsum*[6] (n. 4). This desire for God is expressed above all in fervor in keeping the *Rule*, devoting oneself to the *"conversatio monastica"*[7] (in particular the manual labor in {the} harvest). {It} also {includes} desires for prayer, solitude, intimacy, zeal for silence, humility, etc. Hence St. Bernard wants his monks to know "what a spirit they have received from God"[8]—the spirit of the apostles, the prophets, the angels. {For} example, {he says of} the prophetic spirit: *Ambulare in spiritu, ex fide vivere, quae sursum sunt quaerere, non quae super terram. Oblivisci quae retro sunt, et extendi in anteriora, ex magna parte prophetare est*[9]—to live already in heaven, to see already the *"dies Domini"*[10] (n. 6). But we must persevere in our quest for God. {It is} not enough to seek Him only in moments of sensible fervor. This is not true "simplicity"—it is "duplicity":[11] double-mindedness (n. 9). {The} persevering search for God {is a} pledge of salvation: *Quaeramus veraciter, quaeramus frequenter, quaeramus perseveranter: ut nec pro illo quaeramus aliud* [{the} Cistercian vocation to con-

---

4. "*Et is quidem non quaesitus haberi forsitan potest; non habitus autem quaeri omnino non potest*" (col. 641A).

5. 1 John 4:10.

6. Col. 641C ("For me this is the most certain proof and indubitable argument that you have Him Whom you seek, and that He Who draws you to Himself so strongly dwells within you").

7. Col. 641C, which reads: *"forma ista conversationis"* ("that form of religious life").

8. "*qualem spiritum accepistis, spiritum qui ex Deo est*" (n. 5 [col. 641C]).

9. Col. 642B ("To walk in the spirit, to live from faith, to seek those things which are above, not those things which are on earth; to forget those things which are behind, and to stretch toward what lies ahead—this is in great part what it is to be a prophet").

10. Col. 642C, which reads: *"diem Domini"* ("the day of the Lord").

11. *"simplicitatem . . . . duplicitatem"* (col. 643C).

templation] *nec cum illo aliud* [for God alone, not for any work with God] *sed nec ab illo ad aliud convertamur.*[12]

*Sermo 38 De Diversis*: the last sermon of St. Bernard might have suggested to the monks that those who were inundated with sensible consolation were truly seeking God, not the others. Here he makes clear that we are truly seeking God even (and especially) when we seek Him without consolation, in poverty, and still retaining some involuntary faults and imperfections, or even bad habits which we struggle to overcome. The text of the sermon {is} "All things work together for the good of those that love God."[13] He begins: "WE SEEM TO BE POOR, AND INDEED WE ARE; BUT IF WE HAVE RECEIVED THE SPIRIT FROM GOD, TO KNOW THE THINGS THAT ARE GIVEN US FROM GOD, GREAT GLORY AND GREAT POWER HAVE BEEN GIVEN TO US"[14] (n. 1). Comment: so great is our power as sons of God, which is given us by faith, and by receiving Jesus (John 1), that all things are made subject to us: *An non filiorum Dei potestas est ista, quando etiam nobis serviunt universa?*[15] Then he confronts the objection of some who may say, "let others glory in God; they are fervent; they are true sons. I am poor and a beggar, lacking in filial love, without any true devotion."[16] He replies: we are promised hope through patience and the consolation of the Scriptures (Romans 15:4); we are not promised perfect peace—that is for heaven. *Affectus quem quaeris, pax*

---

12. Col. 643D ("Let us seek truthfully, let us seek repeatedly, let us seek with perseverance, so that we may not seek anything instead of Him, nor seek anything along with Him, but may not be turned from Him to anything else").

13. "*Diligentibus Deum omnia cooperantur in bonum*" (col. 644A) (Rom. 8:28).

14. "*Pauperes quidem videmur, et sumus: sed si spiritum qui ex Deo est accepimus, ut sciemus quae a Deo donata sunt nobis; magna ab eo gloria magna nobis est collata potestas*" (col. 644A).

15. Col. 644A ("Is not the power of the sons of God this: when all things serve us?").

16. "*Glorientur certe de potestate filiorum Dei, in quibus filialis erga eum fervet amor, viget affectus . . . ego vero mendicus sum et pauper, carens affectu filiali, expers dignae devotionis*" (col. 644B).

*est, non patientia; in patria est, non in via; nec eos qui ejusmodi sunt opus est consolari.*[17] Then (n. 2) he goes on to say we are of those *"qui secundum propositum vocati sunt sancti"*[18]—we are saints, *non secundum meritum, sed secundum propositum, non secundum affectionem, sed secundum intentionem.*[19] {It is} folly to expect perfect untroubled sanctity in this life, says St. Bernard. *Illam enim quam putas sanctitatem nec ipse quidem Paulus, corruptibili adhuc gravatus corpore, arbitrabatur se comprehendisse.*[20] Sanctity in this sense is therefore the following: "To propose in your heart to decline from evil and seek good, to hold to what you have and progress to what is better. If at some time you have acted less well, as human frailty leads us to do, {you are} not to remain in this bad way, but to repent and to correct it as far as you can":[21] *eris sine dubio sanctus et tu*[22] (n. 2, end). For such ones, all things cooperate together unto good. All evils can turn to our good: those that we DO (*culpa*), by leading to compunction; those that we SUFFER (*poena*) can keep us from sin.[23] How? *Perfecte sentire onus peccati*[24]—to *feel* {the} burden of our sins is to do penance for them, in loving acceptance and trust and {a} spirit of penance and compunction—meaning

---

17. Col. 644B, which reads: "*Affectus enim ille quem . . . sunt, a Scriptura opus . . .*" ("That experience that you are seeking is peace, not patience; it is in the homeland, not on the way; this is not what is needed to comfort those who are in such a condition").

18. Col. 644C ("to such as, according to his purpose, are called to be saints") (Rom. 8:28).

19. Col. 644C ("not according to merit, but according to purpose, not according to feelings, but according to intention").

20. Col. 644C ("For not even Paul himself, still weighed down by a corruptible body, thought that he had attained to what you think to be holiness").

21. "*Et ut ergo si proposueris in corde tuo declinare a malo et facere bonum, tenere quod coepisti, et proficere semper in melius; sed et si quid aliquando minus recte egeris, ut est humana fragilitas, non in eo persistere, sed poenitere, et corrigere quantum praevales*" (col. 643D).

22. Col. 644D ("without doubt even you will be holy").

23. N. 4 (col. 645A) ("fault . . . punishment").

24. Col. 645B, which reads: ". . . *perfecte senserit* . . ." ("perfectly to feel the burden of sin").

confidence. Quisquis enim perfecte senserit onus *peccati, et animae laesionem, exteriorem utique aut parum sentiet, aut ex toto non sentiet corporis poenam, nec reputabit laborem, quo peccata noverit deleri praeterita, futura caveri.*[25]

## *Appendix II*

SELF-WILL AND DISOBEDIENCE (from *Isaac of Stella*'s Third Assumption Sermon [*PL* 194, Sermon 53[26]]).

"There are some fools so great that, after they have renounced their own will and promised obedience to men, yet nevertheless in many things quarrel daily for the sake of their own will. And in many things they murmur against God, rebelling against His ordinances, since they desire to have free disposition of themselves, resisting the authority constituted by Him."[27] This is all in contrast to Mary, who says, in the words of the Psalms, *"in voluntate tua deduxisti me."*[28] Submission to the divine will is the only way to glory and salvation. Men prefer their own liberty, and this is the source of all struggle and unrest and captivity. They not only want to guide themselves, but they want to bend everyone else to their own will.

> Thus and thus will we do, they say. At this time we will do this, and at another time we will do that. And what is madder still, they want to teach all others, and they want everything to be carried out according to their own will. Thus and thus, they say, should things be done. But when,

---

25. Col. 645BC ("For whoever perfectly feels the burden of sin and the wound of his soul, either at least will scarcely feel outward pain, or will not completely feel bodily punishment, nor mind the effort by which he knows past sins to be wiped out and future ones avoided").

26. Cols. 1870B–1872C.

27. "*Et nescio qui stulti, et maxime, qui propria voluntate abdicata, professi sunt obedientiam hominibus, pro sua voluntate quotidie litigant, et in multis contra Deum murmurant, et ejus ordinationi repugnant, dum potestati quae est ab ipso rebellant, sui dispositores esse cupientes*" (col. 1871BC).

28. Col. 1871B ("by thy will thou hast conducted me" [Ps. 72[73]:24).

on the contrary, things are done just the opposite, they murmur, backbite, judge and condemn. See how far have sunk those men who ought to be doing all things at the behest of another; men who disdain to be led by others; their own guides, their own destroyers.[29]

The source of all conflict and social division is self-will. "The stubborn man, obstinate in his own will, is rightly blamed by all. And yet from this source flow all controversies, from this arise all lawsuits and contentions. Each man fights for what seems good to him, and he defends against others who want something different, the things that please him and that he desires. Among men this may at times be excused by some show of justice: but against God all disobedience is nothing but impiety."[30] He now turns to those who openly or implicitly resist God's will and His Providence. "To Him as Author, Ruler and Judge, all must subject themselves with a humble will: for if today they do not consent to do this, they are nevertheless compelled to submit by servile necessity."[31] This is the key to the problem of liberty in obedience. Obedience to God is simply adaptation to reality—the consent to conform to what *is*. If we insist on acting as if reality were other than it is, and try to force it to be so, then we are compelled against our will and judgement to submit to reality unwillingly. But if we submit to the will of God, our life is a life of joy and

---

29. "*Sic et sic, inquiunt, faciemus; et tunc hoc, et tunc illud; et quod adhuc dementius est, alios omnes docere volunt, et ad suam voluntatem omnia actitari. Sic et sic, inquiunt, facere deberent. Cumque secus aliquid fit, murmurant, detrahunt, judicant, et condemnant. Ecce quo demersi sunt, qui ad alienum imperium omnia facere debent, et ab aliis deduci contemnunt; sibi ductores, sui praecipitatores*" (col. 1871C).

30. "*Homo procax, et in voluntate sua obstinatus, jure ab omnibus vituperatur; et tamen hac sola occasione omnis controversia nascitur, omnis lis et contentio gignitur. Ideo enim quisque contendit, quia quod sibi videtur, et placet, et vult, contra alium qui aliud vult, defendit. Et hoc inter homines aliquando nonnullam potest vel justitiam vel excusationem habere, contra Deum vero sola impietas est omnis inobedientia*" (col. 1871CD).

31. "*Huic etenim omnium Auctori, Rectori et Judici omnes subjici debent humili voluntate; quod etiam si nolunt, faciunt servili necessitate*" (col. 1871D).

gratitude, liberty and peace. *In voluntate tua deduxisti me. Pie dixit [Maria] qui pie obedivit; pie gratias agit ei, qui eum utiliter deduxit*[32] (i.e. in following God's will she followed what was best for her). Then, the reason {is given} why God's will is the source of all our good: *Tenet Dominus electos suos fortiter, deducit utiliter, suscipit feliciter. . . . Suscipit in coelis, a quo suscipitur in terris.*[33]

## Appendix III

### DE REQUIE SPIRITUALI[34]

To make profession as a Cistercian is to enter upon an angelic life, with Mary the Queen of Angels and Saints, assumed into Heaven. The "contemplative" ideal of our Order is expressed in concrete terms by the Fathers of the Order. They do not speak so much of the contemplative life (sometimes they do, but in that sense it is a life of infused contemplation restricted to a few within the Order) but they insist that all in the Order are called to spiritual rest in God by a life of faith and union with the Incarnate Word. Mary assumed into heaven is not only the Queen of the Cistercian Order but the model and "rule" of the monks— *Maria regula monachorum.*[35] The theme is found everywhere in our Fathers. Let us examine it in two places—Bl. Guerric's Third Sermon for the Assumption[36] and Baldwin of Ford's Tract *"De*

---

32. Col. 1871D, which reads: ". . . *voluntate igitur tua . . . obedivit, qui pie . . .*" ("You have led me in Your will. Thus piously speaks the one who obeyed piously, the one who gives thanks piously to Him Who has led him profitably"). (Merton refers these words to Mary, though the masculine pronouns presuppose a more general reference.)

33. Col. 1871D, which reads: *"Tenet enim Dominus . . ."* ("For the Lord holds His chosen ones firmly, leads them profitably, receives them blessedly. . . . He receives in heaven the one by whom He is received on earth").

34. "On Spiritual Rest".

35. Ambrose Autpert, *"Sermo in Laudibus Beatae Mariae"* (see above, page 68, n. 190).

36. *PL* 185, cols. 193D–197B.

*Requie Caelesti"* (*PL* 204:411ff.). Both are commentaries on *"In omnibus requiem quaesivi."* [37]

1. *Bl. Guerric's Third Assumption Sermon*: he opens by saying that the Feast of the Assumption brings them not only a welcome rest from harvest labors; but by celebrating the rest of the Mother of God they find recreation and joy of spirit in contemplating the joys of eternity that are before them. This has a direct relation to their labors in this life, for by labor they are sowing what they will reap in the rest of heaven. Hence spiritual rest for the Cistercian Fathers does not mean avoiding labor, but the grace to work with such peace and faith and hope that in our labors we already rest in the foretaste of heaven. *Fructus hujus laboris, illa requies erit: requies a labore, merces pro labore, cujus etiam recordatio vires reparat in labore* (193).[38] Our rest {is} a *"memoria"* [39] of the rest to come to us. This "faith" which gives us rest in labor is an actual contact with the person of the Word Incarnate—as he puts it, it makes us "rest under the wings of Jesus." [40] This contact with Christ in faith not only refreshes and strengthens us against temptation but renews our strength for our labors. When we have great faith, and great desire to find Christ and be united with Him in heaven, we are able to rest in all things, while the man who lives for himself and by his own will finds rest in nothing (194). *Outside of Jesus, Who is the center of everything, there is no rest*. Compare the hub of a wheel: when we are on the outer rim, we turn and whirl with every movement of the wheel. There is no rest. But when we are in the center, then no matter how the wheel of life may turn, we are always at rest (194): *In circuitu impii*

---

37. *PL* 185, col. 193D; *PL* 204, col. 441C ("In all these I sought rest") (Sir. 24:11).

38. Cols. 193D–194A, which reads: ". . . *recordatio fideles vires* . . ." ("The fruit of this labor will be that rest: rest from labor will be the reward for labor, even the remembrance of which restores the strength of the faithful in labor").

39. Col. 194A, which reads: *"memoriam"*.

40. *"sub umbra alarum Jesu"* (col. 194A) ("under the shadow of the wings of Jesus").

*ambulant*[41] (this theme {is} also developed by St. Bernard in his Sermons on Psalm 90[42]). He asks who it is that thus speaks, saying:

41. N. 2 (col. 194D) ("The wicked walk round about") (Ps. 11[12]:9).

42. See the opening section of the twelfth sermon *In Psalmum XC*, "*Qui Habitat*": "*Si meminiistis, hesterno sermone vias daemonum praesumptionem diximus et obstinationem, nec tacuimus quare id diceremus. Possumus tamen, si necessarium iudicatis, vias eorum via adhuc alia investigare. Nam, etsi omnimodis eas occultare laborent, multipliciter eos prodit Spiritus sanctus, multipliciter in Scripturis sanctis declarat semitas iniquorum. Legimus siquidem de eis omnibus, quoniam in circuitu impii ambulant (Psal. XI, 9). Legimus de eorum principe, quoniam circuit quaerens quem devoret* (I Petr. *v, 8). Quod et ipse fateri cogitur in praesentia majestatis, cum inter filios Dei astans et unde veniat requisitus: Circuivi, ait, terram, et perambulavi eam* (Job *I, 7). Dicamus itaque vias ejus, circuitionem et circumventionem: ista enim ad nos, illa utitur in se ipso. Semper ille extollitur, sed dejicitur semper: superbia ejus ascendit semper, semper humiliatur. Numquid non circuitus iste? Qui enim in circuitu ambulat, proficiscitur quidem, sed proficit nihil. Vae homini qui sequitur hunc circuitum, qui nunquam a propria voluntate recedit. Si conaris avellere, paululum sequi videbitur, sed in dolo. Circuitus est, aliunde reditum parat, non ab ea penitus abducetur. Satagit undique, undique fugitat, haeret tamen semper propriae voluntati*" (PL 182, col. 231BD) ("If you recall, in yesterday's sermon we spoke of the ways of demons— presumption and obstinacy—and we were not silent about why we spoke of this. Still, if you consider it necessary, we can consider their ways in another fashion. For, even though they work to conceal them in every way, the Holy Spirit brings them out in many ways, and in the holy scriptures in many ways He declares the paths of the wicked. Indeed we read of them all that 'The wicked walk round about' [Ps. 11:9]. We read of their prince that 'he goeth about seeking whom he may devour' [1 Pet. 5:8]. He himself was forced to admit this in the presence of the Divine Majesty when standing among the sons of God he was asked where he came from: 'I have gone round about the earth, and walked through it' [Job 1:7].Therefore let us call his ways a circuit and a circumvention—the latter as pertaining to us, the former to himself. He is always being raised up, but always being cast down: he always rises in his pride, and is always humiliated. Is that not a circuit? For whoever walks in a circuit is indeed setting out, but is not reaching the end. Woe to the one who follows this circuit, who never moves away from his own will. If you try to pull him back, he seems to follow for a little way, but in guile. It is a circuit: he gets ready to return from somewhere, but he will not be led away from it at all. He bustles around every which way, he flits about hither and yon, but still he always sticks to his own will").

"In all things I have sought rest"?[43] He answers: it is the voice of God's wisdom; it is the voice of the Church and the voice of Mary and of every wise soul. The wisdom of God the Father teaching us the "discipline of heaven" teaches us this wisdom and this rest in Christ. Like Mary, in whose flesh the Wisdom of the Father found rest (*qui creavit me requievit in tabernaculo meo*[44]), {he} has in turn found rest in the bosom of the Father. How? by seeking rest in all her actions on earth, by seeking Christ, and finding Him, in everything. In this she is our pattern. Wisdom goes about the streets, crying out to the sons of men. Unless Wisdom can find rest in our hearts, we will never find rest in heaven (195). How does Wisdom find rest in us? if we are *humble*. "Upon whom shall I rest but upon the humble and quiet man" (Is. 66:2).[45] *In plenitudine humilitatis requievit etiam corporaliter omnis plenitudo divinitatis* (196).[46] The Wisdom of God finds rest in us when we are charitable to one another, when we see Him in the poor and receive Him in the poor and the guests. (Hospitality {is} important in monastic life.) The Wisdom of God rests in us when we are working for Him. Guerric has beautiful thoughts on labor. While the impious man is always restless, carried about by every wind of doctrine {and} is at {the} mercy not only of his own whims but of those of others, the man who works will be quiet. (Here he is commenting on 1 Thessalonians 4:11 etc.) *Opus est onus, quo veluti pondus navibus, ita quies et gravitas inquietis additur cordibus, sed {et} exterioris hominis fundatur atque componitur status* (196).[47]

43. N. 3 (col. 195A).
44. Col. 195B, which reads: "*Qui creavit me, creatus ex me, requievit in tabernaculo corporis mei*" ("He Who created me, having been created from me, rested in the tabernacle of my body").
45. "*Super quem autem requiescam, inquit, nisi super humilem, et quietum*" (n. 4 [col. 196A]).
46. "In the fullness of humility the whole fullness of divinity rested even bodily."
47. Col. 196D, which reads: ". . . *sed exterioribus* . . ." ("Work is a burden by which, like ballast in ships, quietude and seriousness is thus added to restless hearts, but the state of the outer man is also made secure and peaceful").

*Omnes ergo pariter sic operam demus, {ut quieti simus,} ut in quiete nostra semper in meditatione aeternae quietis occupemur, ac desiderio illius ad omnem parati laborem inveniamur* (197).[48] It is precisely this liberty of spirit that comes from generosity and self-forgetfulness that enables us to find rest in all things, because we are ready for everything. Faith shows us how we can please God and find Christ in all things, and thus we are upset by nothing, but accept all gladly and lovingly, do all things willingly, in order to rest in Christ.

2. *Baldwin of Ford's Tract: De Requie Caelesti*—more exactly, *De Requie quam sibi et nobis Christus quaesivit et paravit*.[49] He begins as does Guerric by listening to the voice of Wisdom saying "In all things I have sought rest."[50] "The Wisdom of God in which all things were created and all were restored"[51] says that all His works have been done with a view to rest. Who is the Wisdom of God? Christ, {Who} in Himself {is} perfect peace and rest, {the} unchanging perfection of His love for the Father and of the Father's love for Him. *In omnibus quae ab initio operatus est propter nos, requiem sibi quaesivit, in nobis, et in se nobis* ({442}).[52] For all the things He has done outside of God have been done in order that He might glorify man in God, and glorify God in man, so that God might rest in man, being perfectly pleased with man (image—likeness) and man might rest in God, loving all God's will and separated in no way from God. *In the Creation*, God "worked" without "labor."[53] This was to be man's pattern—to

---

48. "Let us all alike therefore do our best so that we may be at rest, so that in our rest we may always be absorbed in the meditation of eternal rest, and through the desire for that may be found prepared for every labor" (copy text omits: "*et*"; "*ut quieti simus*").

49. Col. 441B ("On the Rest which Christ Sought and Prepared for Himself and for Us").

50. "*In his omnibus requiem quaesivi*" (col. 441C).

51. "*Sapientia Dei, in qua instaurata et restaurata sunt omnia*" (col. 441C).

52. "In all things that He carried out from the beginning for us, He sought rest for Himself in us, and for us in Himself" (cols. 441C–442C) (copy text reads: "412").

53. "*operans, et non laborans*" (col. 442C).

produce good things, to cooperate in the creative action of God, without labor, hardship, sweat, frustration, failure—to rest in his labor. *After the Fall*, in the heart of fallen man God labors, and yet cannot work. Baldwin bases this on two quotes from Isaias: {in} 1:14, it is "labor" and weariness for God to "bear" the vain sacrifices of men:[54] "My soul hateth your new moons and your solemnities; they are become troublesome to me, I am weary of bearing them"; and in Isaias 43, God says: "Thou hast wearied me with thy sins."[55] But God seeks rest in us when we rest from our sins (*quiescite agere perverse*[56]), when we become humble, when we fear Him; this is the beginning of wisdom and rest for own souls, and it is the beginning of God's rest in us. *In the Incarnation*, God rested in the "Tabernacle of the Humanity of Christ."[57] *After the Redemption*, Christ seeks and finds rest in us by faith, hope and charity. He finds rest in the individual and in the community. Baldwin here brings up the theme of the iniquitous man never resting, not knowing where to find rest. But the just man looks to the true place of rest—*in haereditate Domini morabor*[58]—and Israel is the Lord's inheritance. It is the Church that is the tabernacle and resting place of the Lord. We allow the Lord to rest in the community and in our own hearts when we are truly united by deep fraternal charity. Wisdom lives in us when we are one with Christ, and we all share our rest and joy in Him. *Ecce hic est requies, in haereditate scilicet Domini . . . . Haereditas Domini quaenam est, nisi congregatio sanctorum?* (446).[59] It is by our obedience and humility that we make this possible (446). {It is the} unity of the common life that is the manifestation

---

54. "*Laboravi sustinens*" (col. 442D).

55. "*praebuisti mihi laborem in iniquitatibus tuis*" (col. 443A).

56. Col. 443A ("cease to do perversely") (Isa. 1:16).

57. "*Tabernaculum autem suum dicit assumptam humanitatem*" (col. 444B) ("He says His tabernacle is His assumed humanity").

58. "I shall abide in the inheritance of the Lord" (Sir. 24:11); cf. col. 446B, which reads: "*in haereditate Domini commorari*" ("to rest in the inheritance of the Lord").

59. "Behold, here is rest, that is, in the inheritance of the Lord. . . . What is the inheritance of the Lord, if not the assembly of the saints?"

of the mystery of the Kingdom of God, and a type of the life of heaven. *Unitas socialis vitae figura est et significatio quaedam illius supernae societatis, ubi per amoris communionem quae propria sunt singulorum inveniuntur communia omnium* (448).[60] Hence we have entered the monastery (Israel) and left the world (Egypt) because in Egypt there is not true rest. And in Israel, among the elect, we must sink deep roots of charity (*in electis meis mitte radices*[61]). Our monastic life draws all its strength from these roots which make us part of the community of the elect—an unshakable charity, love for God that cannot be broken by temptation or turned into cupidity, and love for neighbor that cannot be shaken by temptations to resentment and hostility. We must persevere in this love unto the end. This is the real purpose of our profession. He closes by considering the various sources of trouble and temptation that can threaten our peace: the instability of human nature itself; the trials that come with the passage of time, when all things change and conditions are modified; our own malice, temptations, selfishness; the weakness and faults of others. All these are sources of distraction and temptation. They make us realize our weakness, they make us humble, they make us desire true rest as a gift of God, and show us that we cannot attain it merely by our own powers.

> O rest, where art thou and where shall I find thee? I know that I shall not find thee, unless thou come to me. Lord God, thou alone art the rest of souls, and there is no peace for us, in all our misery, except through Thee and in Thee . . . . Make in me Thy Tabernacle, and rest in me that I might rest in Thee. For Thou dost rest in us by making us rest. Work therefore in me that I may love Thee before all and above all; that I may seek nothing outside of Thee, nothing except for Thy sake; then I will have peace, and there will be rest

---

60. Cols. 447D–448A ("The unity of social life is a figure and a kind of signification of that society on high where, through a communion of love, those things which are proper to individuals are found to be common to all").

61. Col. 448D ("put down roots in my elect") (Sir. 24:13).

in my heart from evil desires, from the malice of my heart like birds with grievous bitings[62] etc. (see col. 450).

## Appendix IV

ST. BERNARD'S LENTEN SERMONS[63] (*In Capite Jejunii in Quadragesima*—Excluding the Special Series on *Psalm 90*).

THE SPIRITUALITY OF LENT ACCORDING TO ST. BERNARD: St. Bernard's *Lenten Sermons* reflect, first of all, a characteristically Cistercian preoccupation with truth, authenticity. The spiritual combat, especially fasting, the *militia christiana*,[64] and the special desire for mortification and penance which is emphasized in Lent, is the sign of a true monk and of a true Christian. The founders of Cîteaux sought, in their poverty, simplicity, austerity, labor and solitude, to live the Gospel, put on the "new man," and be united with Christ (*"pauperes cum paupere Christo"* [65]). St. Bernard sees Lent in exactly the same light.

{It is a} GIFT. *The Lenten fast is a gift* consecrated and blessed by Jesus Himself, and given to us that we may share in His mortification, His Passion, and thus share in the joy of His resurrec-

---

62. "*O requies, ubi es, et ubi te inveniam! Scio, quia non inveniam te, nisi tu venias ad me. Domine Deus, tu solus es requies animarum, et non est pax nobis a tota miseria ista, nisi per te, et in te. . . . Fac in me tabernaculum tuum, et requiesce in me, ut requiescam in te. Hac est enim requies tua, operatio requiei nostrae. Operare ergo in me, ut ante omnia et super omnia diligam te; ut nihil cupiam extra te, nihil nisi te, vel propter te: et erit mihi pax, et erit mihi requies in corde meo, a cupiditate mala, a malitia cordis mei, a curis tam multis, tam malis, tam acerbis, quae cor meum devorant* [from so many, so evil, so bitter cares, which devour my heart], *sicut aves morsu amarissimo*" (col. 450AB) (line probably lost by eyeskip).

63. *PL* 183, cols. 167C–186A.

64. Col. 167D, which reads: "*tempus militiae Christianae*" ("the time of Christian military service").

65. "poor with the poor Christ" (*Exordium Parvum*, c. 15 [*Nomasticon Cisterciense, seu Antiquiores Ordinis Cisterciensis Constitutiones A.R.P.D. Juliano Paris* . . . Editio Nova, ed. Hugo Séjalon (Solesmes: E Typographeo Sancti Petri, 1892), 63, which reads: "*cum paupere Christo pauperes*"]).

tion and in His glory. Those who receive the Lenten fast with fervent devotion, as a gift of Jesus, are true monks and true Christians. They are the ones who fast with perfect dispositions (see below), and thus give glory to God and are truly delivered from the law of self-love. (*N.B.* all Christians fasted until vespers in {the} twelfth century—cf. Sermon 3, n. 1[66]). *Qualis ille est, non dicam monachus, sed Christianus, qui minus devote jejunium {suscipit,} quod ei tradidit ipse Christus?* (Serm. 3, n. 2).[67]

{It is a} SACRAMENT. This gift is a "sacrament" in the same way as we have seen that Advent comes to us as a "sacrament";[68] that is to say, it is a mystery which accomplishes our union with Christ in proportion as we enter into it with the dispositions inspired by His Holy Spirit. In giving us the Lenten Fast, Jesus gives us the graces and merits of His own sufferings, enables us to enter into union with Him by participation in these: in the "sacrament" of Lent, as in that of Advent, Jesus gives us *Himself.* {The} difference between *Lent* and *Advent* {is that} Advent concentrates on the mystery of Christ present in the world by His Incarnation, Lent on the mystery of Christ still suffering in the world in His Mystical Body. In either case the sacrament is fundamentally the same—Christ in the world: the union of men with the Father, through Him. The *difference* is in the *manner* of the union, the *means* offered to union, the *devotio*, the motives which draw us to union with the Father in Jesus, by the Holy Spirit. *Tota devotione suscipite quadragesimale jejunium, quod non sola abstinentia*

---

66. Cols. 173D–175B.

67. Col. 175C ("What sort of—I shall not say monk, but Christian—is he who receives less devoutly the fast which Christ Himself handed on to him?") (copy text reads: "*suscepit*").

68. See Merton's article "The Sacrament of Advent in the Spirituality of St. Bernard," in Thomas Merton, *Seasons of Celebration* (New York: Farrar, Straus & Giroux, 1965), 61–87, in which he traces the idea of Advent as "the *sacramentum*, the *mysterium* of which St. Paul writes to the Ephesians. It is the 'sacrament' (or 'mystery') of the divine will, according to the design which it pleased Him to form in Christ, to be realized in the fullness of time, *to unite all things in Christ*" (63); see *Sermo 1 in Adventu Domini*, n. 1 (*PL* 183, col. 35C: "*magnum aliquod sacramentum*").

*commendat, SED MULTO MAGIS SACRAMENTUM* (Serm. 3, n. 1).[69] *Comment*: (1) It is because Lent is a sacrament, a "gift," a holy gift, the gift of Jesus Himself, that we must receive it with "all devotion"— "*tota devotio*"—{a} complete, integral response: we shall see what that means; (2) the *sacramentum*, the mystery, and our response of *devotio*, is much more important than the fast itself; the fast is only a means to the end—charity, union with Jesus; (3) because the Lenten fast is common to all Christians, and unites all in Jesus, it is a particular sign of the unity of the faithful in the Mystical Body of Christ; it is an expression of the common obligation of all to share in the sufferings of Christ in order to participate in the glory of His resurrection: *Quidni commune sit Christi jejunium omnibus Christianis? Quidni caput suum membra sequantur? . . . Non est magnum si compatiatur membrum capiti, cum quo et glorificandum est. Felix membrum, quod huic adhaeserit per omnia capiti, et sequetur illud quocunque ierit* (Serm. 1, n.1).[70] *Comment*: our fasting is also an expression of monastic virginity—separation from all worldly pleasures—union with Christ alone, following Him in His sufferings—refusing Him nothing. The allusion, "following Him wherever He goes," is clear—in the liturgy for {the} Common of Virgins[71] (cf. Apocalypse 14:4[72]).

---

69. Col. 173D ("With complete devotion undertake the Lenten fast, which not only abstinence, but much more the sacrament, recommends").

70. Cols. 167D, 168C ("Why should not Christ's fast be common to all Christians? Why should the members not follow their Head? . . . It is not great if the member suffers together with the Head, with whom it is also to be glorified. Happy the member which will cling through all things to this Head, and will follow Him wheresoever He goes").

71. See the third stanza of the vespers hymn for the common of virgins, "*Jesu, corona Virginum*": "*Quocumque pergis, Virgines / Sequuntur, atque laudibus / Post te canentes cursitant, / Hymnos dulces personant*" (2.9-12) ("Wherever You go, the virgins / Follow, and with praises / They run after You, singing; / They make the sweet hymns resound") (*Breviarium Cisterciense Reformatum*, 4 vols. [Westmalle, Belgium: Typis Cisterciensibus, 1951], Pars Hiemalis etc., 108*).

72. "*qui sequuntur agnum quocumque abierit*" ("These follow the Lamb whithersoever he goeth").

{It is a} TRANSFORMATION, {a} *"conversio."* The fruitful participation of the monk in the Lenten Fast is marked not by exterior observance but by INTERIOR TRANSFORMATION. St. Bernard calls this "conversion"—*conversio*—a complete "turning" of our whole being with all its faculties to God, and hence a complete aversion from inordinate and worldly values. It forms the subject of the Second Ash Wednesday Sermon ({cf. the} Ash Wednesday liturgy: *convertimini ad me in toto corde vestro in jejunio et fletu et planctu, et scindite corda vestra, non vestimenta vestra* [Joel 2:12-13][73]). This conversion, St. Bernard says, is the "mystery of the Kingdom of God."[74] To know the secret of this interior conversion is to enter into the mystery of the Kingdom of God which Jesus reveals only to His friends. His enemies after all were great fasters and penitents—the pharisees—but their observance was exterior; their values were natural and corrupted with pride and self-interest, and therefore, although the "Kingdom of God was in the midst of them" (Luke 17:21), they were unable to recognize it. It was a scandal to them. They had eyes and did not see; they had ears and did not hear (Psalm 134:16-17). After asking, "How is it that we can turn to God when God is everywhere,"[75] St. Bernard answers: "*SECRETUM EST, QUOD SOLIS CREDATUR AMICIS. MYSTERIUM REGNI DEI EST.*" What is the mystery? "*NISI CONVERSI FUERITIS ET*

---

73. "Be converted to me with all your heart, in fasting, and in weeping, and in mourning. And rend your hearts, and not your garments" (*Missale Romanum: Ex Decreto Sacrosancti Concilii Tridentini Restitutum: S. Pii V, Pontificis Maximi, Jussu Editum: Aliorum Pontificum Cura Recognitum: a Pio X Reformatum et Benedicti XV Auctoritate Vulgatum*, 4th ed. [New York: Benziger, 1944], 64–65; *Missale Cisterciense: Reformatum juxta Decretum Sacrorum Rituum Congregationis Diei 3 Julii 1869* [Westmalle: Ex Typographia Ordinis Cist. Strict. Obs., 1951], 54).

74. "*Mysterium regni Dei est*" (col. 171C).

75. "*Quid sibi vult . . . quod praecipit Dominus, ut convertamur ad eum? Ubique enim est, et replet omnia, et nihilominus complectitur universa*" (col. 171C) ("What does it mean . . . that the Lord teaches us to turn to Him? For He is everywhere, and fills all things, and embraces no less than the entire world").

*EFFICIAMINI SICUT PARVULI, NON INTRABITIS IN REGNUM COELORUM"* (Serm. 2, n. 1; cf. Matt. 18:3).[76]

{It is} HUMILITY. The key to transformation, *conversio*, is humility. Without humility we are not united to Him who is meek and humble of heart, and therefore we cannot be taught by Him, cannot be drawn into His manner of life, cannot be transformed in Him. All our other works, without humility, are a ridiculous waste of time. By humility St. Bernard means not merely a low intellectual estimate of ourselves; he means a complete self-emptying, and complete self-renunciation, in order to abandon and subject ourselves totally to the action of God's love, to God's will, and to our brethren for the sake of God. Even in Lent, St. Bernard surprises us by recalling to mind Jesus as a "little one"[77]—another indication that Christmas is the mystery which sets a peculiar stamp upon the whole Cistercian spirit: the Incarnation and Divine Infancy is, *par excellence*, the source of Cistercian spirituality. "*Ad parvulum converti necesse est.*"[78] We must be converted; we must turn to Him Who is a Little One, that we may learn from Him Who is meek and humble of heart: it was for this reason that He was given to us as a Little One. *The way of humility makes fasting joyful and easy.* St. Bernard started out by reminding us of our obligation to receive the Lenten fast with fervor {and} devotion, and therefore with joy. In this he is only echoing the gospel of Ash Wednesday,[79] in which Jesus tells us that when we fast we must anoint our heads and give outward expression to joy, as opposed to the public emaciation and long faces of the pharisees. *Est caput istud mens interior, quae tunc ungitur in jejunio, cum spiritualitur delectatur in eo* (Serm. 1, n. 6).[80]

---

76. Col. 171C ("This is the secret which is entrusted to friends alone. It is the mystery of the Kingdom of God. . . . Unless you be converted and become as little children, you shall not enter into the kingdom of heaven").

77. "*parvulum*" (col. 172B).

78. Col. 172B, which reads: "*ad hunc parvulum . . . converti necesse sit*" ("It is necessary to be converted to this little child").

79. Matt. 6:16-21 (*Missale Romanum*, 65; *Missale Cisterciense*, 55).

80. Col. 171A, which reads: "*Est autem caput . . .*" ("This head is the interior self, which is anointed in the fast when it delights in it spiritually").

This obligation is confirmed by the fact that our gifts must all be offered to God with joy, since He loves a "cheerful giver."[81] But the devil strives to disturb our peace, in Lent, by *fears, anxieties, cowardice*. He does this in order to make us sad, to diminish the merit of our fast and thus to break down our interior resistence and reduce our spiritual strength by fasting, which ought normally to build up our spirit. *Hoc enim quantum potest laborat adversarius noster, ut holocaustum nostrae devotionis pinguedine vacuetur, ut et minus acceptum sit Deo, et conscientia nostra in spirituali gaudio minus exhilaretur: sicque de pusillanimitate tolerantiae, etiam conscientiae pusillanimitas generetur* (Serm. 3, n. 1).[82] *Comment*: (1) note that the real sacrifice of Lent is our devotion, our interior joy, not the mere exterior fast; (2) however, the exterior fast has a definite relation to this joy. If we lose heart and diminish our fasting without reason, this will have an effect on our interior dispositions, and the joy of our devotion will evaporate. The interior and exterior are therefore closely connected. It would be completely false to suppose that a *merely interior* sacrifice will be sufficient for our Lent. We must give up exterior things, we must deny ourselves in one way or another, and in fact, as we shall see, we must "fast from all vices"[83] and renounce many other legitimate pleasures besides those of food.

One of the essentials of the Lenten spirit is compunction, sorrow for sin, "tears" of desire for heaven. Hence the interior joy of Lent is rooted in real sorrow, real "rending" of the heart. It is not a superficial human cheerfulness nourished by compromise and self-indulgence. The joy of Lent is only genuine if it springs from real self-sacrifice. Here again, St. Bernard is interested

---

81. 2 Cor. 9:7.

82. Col. 175A ("Our adversary labors as much as he can so that the holocaust may be emptied of the richness of our devotion, and so may be less acceptable to God, and that our conscience may be less exhilarated with spiritual joy: and thus from faintheartedness of endurance a faintheartedness of conscience may be generated as well").

83. *"jujunandum est longe amplius a vitiis, quam a cibis"* ("Fasting should be far more from vices than from food") (*Sermo* 2.4 [col. 173B]).

only in the "real thing." He seeks nothing but the truth, the true *"forma* conversionis" (Serm. 2, n. 2).[84] But in what way does humility (the *"forma conversionis"*) make sacrifice easy and joyous? {There is} no doubt of the fact that St. Bernard believes it does so. NIHIL VERO FACILIUS VOLENTI, QUAM HUMILIARE SEMETIPSUM (Serm. 2, n. 1).[85] {Note the} *context*: this surprising phrase occurs in an important paragraph where St. Bernard analyzes the psychology of suffering in his usual vein—the source of all suffering is self-will (cf. Serm. 3 *in Paschal Time*[86]). "If the way to God were a way of exaltation and might [*via sublimitatis*], and if that were the road by which the salvation of God were shown to us, how many things men would do to exalt themselves! How cruelly would they lay one another low, and trample one another under foot! How boldly they would push on and struggle to raise themselves upwards upon the heads of other men! Certainly, he who seeks to outstrip other men in competition finds many difficulties, has many rivals, suffers from many who contradict him and from many who climb up against him from the other side. But nothing is easier than to humble ourselves" (Serm. 2, n. 1).[87]

JOY IN LENT: the joy which makes our Lenten fast pleasing to God has its origin above all in our union with Christ. This joy is a virtue, an act or effect of charity, and is opposed to the *"tristitia"* which is an effect of self-love and lies, with self-love at the root of all vice. See St. Thomas, *Summa*, II-II, q. 28: *Tristitia quae est vitium causatur ex inordinato amore sui* (II-II, q. 28, a. 4,

---

84. Col. 172C ("pattern of conversion").

85. Col. 172B ("But nothing is easier for one who is willing than to humble himself").

86. Cols. 287C–292C; for a discussion of this sermon, see above, pages 234–37.

87. *"Si forte sublimitatis esset via proposita, et illic iter quo ostenderetur salutare Dei, quanta facerent homines ut exaltarentur? Quam crudeliter invicem sternerent, invicem conculcarent! Quam impudenter reperent, manibusque et pedibus conarentur in altum, ut imponerent sese homines super capita aliena! Et certe qui contendit supergredi proximos, multas inveniet difficultates, multos habebit aemulos, multos patietur contradictores, ascendentes equidem ex adverso: nihil vero facilius est volenti, quam humiliare semetipsum"* (col. 172AB).

ad. 1).[88] *Caritas autem est amor Dei, cujus bonum immutabile est quia ipse est sua bonitas, et ex hoc ipso quod amatur, est in amante per nobilissimum sui effectum, secundum illud* 1 Joan. 4:16. *Qui manet in caritate in Deo manet et Deus in eo. Et ideo* spirituale gaudium quod de Deo habetur ex caritate causatur (II-II, q. 28, a. 1).[89] *De Deo potest esse spirituale gaudium dupliciter, uno modo secundum quod gaudemus de bono divino in se considerato; alio modo secundum quod gaudemus de bono divino, prout a nobis participatur (ibid.,* ad. 3).[90] However, as we shall see, the joy of Lent is compatible with, and indeed demands, a certain "*tristitia,*" a sorrow which is also an effect of love, and which laments the obstacles to our perfect love for God: these obstacles are our sins, our exile in the present life, the sins of the world, etc. See St. Thomas again (*Summa,* II-II, q. 28, a. 2): *Haec autem participatio [in bono divino] potest impediri per aliquod contrarium, et ideo ex parte gaudium caritatis potest haberi admixtionem tristitiae, prout secundum aliquis tristatur de eo quod repugnat participationi divini boni vel in nobis, vel in proximis quos tamquam nosmetipsos diligimus.*[91] St. Bernard

---

88. *Sancti Thomae Aquinatis Doctoris Angelici Ordinis Praedicatorum Opera Omnia, secundum Impressionem Petri Fiaccadori Parmae 1852–1873 Photolithographice Reimpressa,* 25 vols. (New York: Misurgia, 1948), 3:119 ("Sadness which is a vice is caused by an inordinate love of self").

89. Aquinas, *Opera Omnia,* 3.117 ("Charity, then, is the love of God, Whose good is unchangeable because He Himself is His own goodness, and from this very fact that He is loved, He is in the one who loves Him by His most excellent effect, according to 1 John 4:16: *He who abides in charity, abides in God and God in him.* And therefore spiritual joy, which is received from God, is caused by charity").

90. Aquinas, *Opera Omnia,* 3.117 ("There can be spiritual joy with regard to God in two ways: in one way according to which we rejoice in the divine good considered in itself; in another way according to which we rejoice in the divine good in as much as it is shared by us").

91. Aquinas, *Opera Omnia,* 3.118, which reads: ". . . *ex hac parte . . . habere permixtionem . . . prout scilicet aliquis . . . nosipsos . . .*" ("This sharing, then, can be hindered through anything opposed to it, and therefore, from this position, the joy of charity can have an admixture of sadness, in as much as one is saddened by that which resists a sharing of the divine good, either in us or in our neighbors. whom we love as ourselves").

shows that the joy of the Christian soul is a participation in that anointing of joy, the Holy Spirit, poured out upon Christ (the Anointed) as Head of the Church, and flowing down upon all those who are united with Him. The soul that does not cherish and foster the divine life within itself by penance, soon learns that the "root of bitterness,"[92] which had been cut out by baptism, tends to grow back (Serm. 1 *in Capite Jejunii*, n. 1). But the soul that rejects all inordinate love of earthly things finds joy even in suffering, because of the realization that it is united with Jesus by charity and shares in His sufferings for mankind (Serm. 1 *in Capite Jejunii*, n. 2). Here again, the joy in fasting is a sign of the union of members in Christ. *"Ipsa [caritas] est, per quam omne corpus per nexus et juncturas crescit. Hoc glutinum bonum . . . . per [quod] bonum et jucundum est habitare fratres in unum"* (Serm. 1 *in Capite Jejunii*, n. 2).[93]

JOY AND SORROW (cf. St. John of the Cross, *Maxim* 54[94]): the paradox of "joy in sorrow," joy in penance, which is the mystery of Lent, is to be sought in *authenticity* and *charity*. Where charity is genuine, we rejoice in doing penance: and the explanation is, as we have seen above, that joy in God and sorrow at evil, at what stands as obstacle between us and God, are simply aspects of charity. The two chief vices of those who fast with wrong motives are *vanity* (or hypocrisy), and *impatience* (or rancor) (Serm. 1 *in Capite Jejunii*, n. 6[95]). *Vanity* {is} an impure intention, {a} lack of truth, of authenticity. *Rancor* {is a} hardening of heart against

92. *"radix amaritudinis"* (col. 168D).
93. Col. 169AB, which reads: *"Ipsa enim est . . . per quam bonum est et . . ."* ("It is charity itself through which the whole body grows through its sinews and joints. This is the good glue . . . through which it is good and pleasant for brothers to dwell together in unity") (Ps. 132[133]:1).
94. "It is not the will of God that the soul allow aught to trouble it, or suffer trials; if it suffer them in the adversities of the world, this comes from the weakness of its virtue; for the soul of the perfect man rejoices in that which causes the imperfect soul affliction" (*The Complete Works of Saint John of the Cross*, ed. and trans. E. Allison Peers, 3 vols. [Westminster, MD: Newman Press, 1946], 3.247).
95. Col. 171AB.

our brethren; {it} is united with jealousy, and springs from selfishness. In order to get rid of hypocrisy we must purify our intention ("wash the face"[96]—that is, the conscience), and in order to get rid of hardness of heart we must anoint the *"mens interior"*[97]—the summit of the soul—with deep and sincere joy in our fasting. That means we must rejoice in what humbles us and deprives us of what we naturally desire. *Mens interior ungitur in jejunio cum spiritualiter delectatur in eo* (*idem*).[98] This "anointing" must be produced by compunction, which first softens our heart and takes away its bitter desire to rejoice in superiority over others. It teaches us to be sorry for our own hypocrisy, our own selfishness. Compunction transfers our sorrow from the good of others (their ability to do greater things than we ourselves) to our own evil dispositions. Thus it changes evil sorrow into good sorrow. Compunction produces humility and humility leads to charity by which we rejoice not at our own false good (our apparent triumph in fasting), but at the real good of our own souls and of others. Thus compunction leads to charity which brings with it, inseparably, a joy in good, above all *a joy in the divine good of grace, participated {in} by us and by other men*. This means, in practice, rejoicing at the grace to see our own nothingness: therefore, joy in compunction, joy in sorrow; *and it means rejoicing in the gifts of others*, which is charity. *Debes in dilectione Christi fraternis congaudere prosperitatibus* (Serm. 2 *in Capite Jejunii*, n. 3).[99] This joy, which comes from the interior anointing of the soul by compunction, humility and charity, is *produced in us by the action of Jesus "teaching and forming" the soul* which is in His school, for the monastery is a *"schola Christi."*[100] This joy is the effect of an

---

96. *"Faciem tuam lava"* (col. 171A) (Matt. 6:17).
97. Col. 171A.
98. See page 324, no. 80 above.
99. Col. 173A, which reads: *"Debes et in . . ."* ("You should rejoice together in the love of Christ at the good fortune of brothers").
100. St. Bernard, *Ep.* 320 (*PL* 182, col. 525C); *Ep.* 385 (*PL* 182, col. 588A); *In Nativitate S. Joannis Baptistae* (*PL* 183, col. 397D); *De Diversis*, 121 (*PL* 183, col. 743B).

interior grace, flowing down upon us from the Head of the whole Body, Jesus, the *Magister mansuetudinis et humilitatis* (*idem*, n. 2).[101] Spiritual joy is the sign that we are being taught by Jesus.

THEOLOGY OF LENTEN JOY: there is a special theological reason for this Lenten joy. This joy of charity is the expression in us of the supernatural vitality of love which unites us to God in Christ. It is the *overflowing of the life of grace which is common to all those who are united in one Mystical Body*. It is the joy of the Holy Spirit, the expression of the liberty of the sons of God and of their common inheritance of the good things of God. St. Thomas says[102] that the joy of charity is twofold: on the one hand it rejoices in the fact that God Himself is infinitely good. It delights in the goodness of God for *His* own sake. On the other hand it rejoices in that goodness in so far as we have a share in it. But the second joy cannot exist without the first. The reason is obviously because the goodness of God is God Himself, and God is Love. We cannot share in His Life unless we share in His infinitely selfless Love. *We cannot receive from God unless we somehow give to God, because the love we receive is the ability to give, and we cannot receive it except by giving ourselves to Him*. The more we give ourselves, the more of His charity do we receive, because our gift of ourselves is produced by charity and brings more charity. It is the expression of the divine life in our souls. The joy of Lent, which is the joy of emptying ourselves and giving ourselves, purified by compunction, to God in a total *conversion* of our being to Him, gives us a participation in the love of the Father for the Son. That is to say, it gives us a share in the "anointing of joy"[103] which is the Holy Spirit, and which the Heavenly Father has poured out upon Jesus, and which has run down to the hem of His garment to the least members of His Mystical Body (Serm. 1 *in Capite Jejunii*, n. 2). St. Bernard says: "The Father anointed the Son beyond all others, pouring out upon Him all the gifts of benignity, meekness and

---

101. Col. 172B, which reads: *"mansuetudinis et humilitatis magistrum"* ("the Master of gentleness and humility").

102. See page 327, no. 90 above.

103. *"oleo laetitiae"* (col. 169B) (Ps. 44[45]:8).

kindness, filling Him superabundantly with mercy and compassion. He sent Him to us and showed Him to us full of grace and love" (*idem*, n. 3).[104] Jesus comes to us, pouring out His love into our hearts. But He asks a return of love. Thus anointed by the Father He asks to be anointed by us, because only in this way will He be able to give us a share in His divine life. *Ad fontem unde exeunt flumina revertuntur, ut iterum fluant* (*idem*).[105] St. Bernard explains this: "Christ does not ask you to give back the love He gave you as though He Himself had lost something in giving His love to you; *He does so because you would otherwise lose what you should wish to return to Him.*"[106] In returning love to Him our love lives. If we try to hold on to it for ourselves (for instance, in the form of consolation in which we can take complacency), then it is lost to us. Love is only kept by being given away.[107] St. Bernard continues: "Thus the waters of a river, if they stand still, become corrupt, and overflowing their banks they are pushed back [towards their source]. In the same way the stream of grace will stop if it does not flow back to its source. Not only does the ungrateful man receive no increase but even what he has received turns to his disadvantage. SIC GRATIARUM CESSET DECURSUS UBI RECURSUS NON FUERIT" (Serm. 2 *in Capite Jejunii*, n. 4).[108] How? Pour back love in *gratitude* and *praise* (hiding from human glory).

---

104. "*Unxit . . . Pater Filium prae participibus suis, accumulans super eum universa charismata benignitatis, mansuetudinis et suavitatis, abundantius eum replens visceribus misericordiae et miserationis. Unctum denique misit ad nos, quem nobis exhibuit plenum gratiae et miserationis*" (col. 169D).

105. Col. 169D, which reads: "*Ad fontem enim unde . . .*" ("unto the place from whence the rivers come, they return, to flow again") (Eccl. 1:7).

106. "*Non vero, ut minus habens, quod dederat Christus repetit: sed ne tibi pereat quidquid ad eum referre volueris*" (cols. 169D–170A).

107. See the title of the opening chapter of Thomas Merton, *No Man Is an Island* (New York: Harcourt, Brace, 1955): "Love Can Be Kept Only by Being Given Away" (3).

108. "*Siquidem etiam fluminis aqua, si stare coeperit, et ipsa putrescet, et inundatione facta superveniens, repelletur. Sic plane, sic gratiarum cessat decursus, ubi recursus non fuerit: nec modo nihil augetur ingrato, sed et quod acceperat vertitur ei in perniciem*" (col. 170A).

LENTEN COMPUNCTION: the joy of Lent is necessarily connected with sorrow. In fact, paradoxically, it flows from sorrow. Both the joy and the sorrow of Lent are two different aspects of one thing: that charity which unites us to God the Father, in Christ, by the bond of the Holy Spirit. On the one hand, charity rejoices to be united with Christ even in suffering. On the other, the same charity laments the obstacles to its perfect fulfillment, weeps over our infirmities and sins, and strives to make amends for them, especially in the season of Lent. However, penance and compunction can never be confined entirely to Lent. This is another way in which Lent is a "sacrament." It shows us, as we have seen, the mystery of our union with Christ by a total *"conversio"* in humility and abnegation. But it is also a *"sacramentum"* or symbol of the whole life of man on this earth. It reminds us that our whole life must be a struggle to overcome sin, and to arrive at union with God by self-denial and charity. *What is compunction?* It is a grace by which God draws us to Himself, causing in us *sorrow* for what we have done, *aversion* from what we are, *fear* of what we may yet become, a complete *conversion* of our whole being to God in *desire* and *supplication.* This awakens in us *confident hope* of pardon (cf. transformation), and *joy* in the goodness of God which is already tasted in this hope. (*Hardness of heart,* on the contrary {brings} *joy* in evil, *complacency* with ourselves, *fear* of losing objects of satisfaction, *desire* for more pleasure and self-satisfaction {and} *aversion* from spiritual values and from all that humiliates us.) N.B.—liturgy is a school of compunction: {we} learn compunction from the *psalms,* {from the} *crucifix,* {from} *Jesus in the Blessed Sacrament. Quadragesima est non solum pars, sed et sacramentum totius temporis hujus* (Serm. 3 *in Capite Jejunii,* n. 4).[109] In this sacramental aspect also, Lent is to be accepted with great fervor, in order that it may sanctify our whole life; that is to say, in order that the whole life of the monk may be penetrated with the spirit of sacrifice which is characteristic

---

109. Col. 176A, which reads: "*Quadragesima . . . quae non solum pars, sed et sacramentum est totius . . .*" ("Lent is not only a part, but is also a sacrament of this entire time").

above all of Lent. *Continuanda enim nobis est quadragesima cunctis diebus miserae hujus vitae (idem*, n. 3).[110] In his search for the authentic spirit, which he finds exemplified in Lent as well as in Advent, and indeed in all the seasons of the Church year, St. Bernard concludes that our Lent is really valuable if it impresses a kind of "spiritual form" upon our whole monastic life. This spiritual form is the integral conversion of man's whole being. We have already discussed this, and will return to it again presently (Serm. 2 *in Capite Jejunii*, n. 2[111]).

COMPUNCTION IS A SOURCE OF STRENGTH: meanwhile St. Bernard reminds us that there is one bread which we must not deny ourselves in Lent: it is the bread of tears. It alone can be our strength on the hard journey. *Sed est panis a quo vos jejunare nolo, ne forte deficiatis in via: et si nescitis, panem dico lacrymarum* (*idem*, n. 4).[112] *Compunction is a source of strength*. Why? *because it liberates us from the shackles of attachment*. It clears away obstacles. It helps us to cast aside all useless baggage. Tears are our strength in the monastic life, if they are tears which proceed from love of God and which, by a true spirit of remorse and penance, lead to the transformation of our interior life. It would therefore be uncharitable to foster in monasteries a false human joy based on compromise with weakness and even with imperfection and with vice. This is a shallow joy which belongs to the world and not to the cloister. It cannot bring true peace to the heart of the monk or of the Christian. We cannot rejoice in God if our hearts have settled down and made peace with the desires and attachments which are opposed to our union with God. We must therefore seek the "rending of heart,"[113] the interior sorrow, the peaceful anguish of compunction which liberates us from attachment and

---

110. Col. 175D ("For us Lent must be continued all the days of this wretched life").

111. Col. 172BD.

112. Col. 173B ("But there is a bread from which I do not wish you to fast, lest perhaps you may faint along the way: and if you do not know, it is, I say, the bread of tears").

113. "*scindite corda vestra*" (col. 173C) (Joel 2:13).

sets us free to fly to the God of peace. UT IN TOTO CORDE CONVERTARIS.[114] Above all, our love must lead to the gift of our whole heart to God.

Let us now examine in some detail St. Bernard's description of the right and wrong way to enter into the mystery of Lent. The distinction is clear: it is brought before us by the epistle of Ash Wednesday,[115] where the Prophet Joel tells us to rend our hearts and not our garments. The true, interior observance of Lent is, as we have seen, a total "conversion" of our whole being to God. This conversion is a kind of form, a stamp of truth, which authenticates the Lenten observance of the true monk, and gives evidence that he is united to Christ by charity. Without this interior *conversio*, exterior fasting, penance and prayer are useless. They are pure formalism. They are not pleasing to God and they do nothing to sanctify the soul. On the contrary, they harden the soul, embitter it, dry up the springs of charity. But above all this false, exterior asceticism leads to illusion and blindness of soul. Those who give themselves over to purely exterior practices, perhaps even in a spirit of competition with one another, measuring their success by the attention which they attract, and by the complacency which they feel within themselves, are hypocrites. They destroy the truth in themselves, and become a living lie. Their conversion is only an "appearance." *Forma conversionis est ista, non veritas, vacuam virtute gerens speciem pietatis. Miser homo, qui totus pergens in ea quae foris sunt, et ignarus interiorum suorum, putans se aliquid esse, cum nihil sit, ipse se seducit* (Serm. 2 in Capite Jejunii, n. 2).[116] The greatest tragedy of monastic formal-

---

114. Col. 172D, which reads: ". . . *corde tuo convertaris*" ("Be converted to me with all your heart") (Joel 2:12).

115. See page 323, n. 73 above.

116. Col. 172C, which reads: "*Forma siquidem conversionis . . . aliquid se esse . . .*" ("This is the outward form of conversion, not the reality, bearing the appearance of piety, empty of virtue. Wretched man, who proceeds completely into those things which are exterior, and, ignorant of his own inner life, thinking himself to be something when he is nothing, undermines himself").

ism is that it deceives only those who practice it. The deception cannot have any real effect on the outside. Even worldlings can recognize fake piety and pharisaism by a sure and mysterious instinct. It is a great scandal to those who might possibly love God, but who are convinced by the spectacle of false piety and formalism that all religion is only an empty form. I here translate two passages from the Ash Wednesday Sermons: "Looking only at the outward surface of his life, the formalist believes that all goes well with him, and does not feel the hidden worm that gnaws out everything within. He still has his tonsure. He has not put off the habit of religion. He keeps the rule of fasting. He sings psalms at the appointed hours. But *'his heart is far from me,'* says the Lord" (Serm. 2 *in Capite Jejunii*, n. 2).[117] "The hypocrite puts on a long face: that is to say, he goes in for singular and unusual practices. He does not anoint his head: that is to say, his heart is far from Christ; and he takes delight in the vain marks of human favor. Rather it is himself that he anoints, in order that he may spread abroad the fragrance of his own self-complacency" (Serm. 1 *in Capite Jejunii*, n. 5).[118]

ST. BERNARD AND ST. JOHN OF THE CROSS ON THE GIFT OF OURSELVES TO GOD: to give our hearts to God means to give all the desires, hopes, fears, joys and sorrows of our heart to God. It means the subjection of all the passions of the soul to reason and, through reason to faith, and thus to the pure love of God alone. St. Bernard gives us this traditional doctrine in a passage that is echoed almost word for word by St. John of the Cross in the *Ascent of Mount Carmel*:

---

117. "*Exteriorem quippe superficiem intuens, salva sibi omnia suspicatur, non sentiens vermem occultum, qui interiora corrodit. Manet tonsura, vestis necdum mutata est, jejuniorum regula custoditur, statutis psallitur horis;* sed cor longe est a me, *dicit Dominus* (Marc. VII, 6)" (col. 172CD).

118. "*hypocrita magis exterminat, dum singularia magis et inusitata sectatur. Sed nec caput ungit, cujus affectio elongatur a Christo, et vanis favoribus delectatur. Ungit potius semetipsum, ut propriae fragrantiam opinionis respergat*" (col. 170C).

St. Bernard, Serm. 2 *in Capite Jejunii*, n. 3: "The whole heart is found in these four passions [desire, fear, joy, grief]. It is in these that I would have you seek the meaning of the truth that we must be converted to God with our whole heart. Let thy love [desire] be converted to Him, so that thou desirest nothing but Him, or for His sake. Let thy fear be converted to Him, for every fear is perverted if it fears something other than Him, or on account of Him. Thus also let thy joy and thy sorrow be converted to Him. This will take place if thou grievest or rejoicest only in relation to Him."[119]

St. John of the Cross, *Ascent of Mount Carmel*, Bk. iii, c. 16, n. 2: "The strength of the soul consists in its faculties, passions and desires, all of which are governed by the will. When these faculties and desires are directed by the will toward God, and turned away from all that is not God, then the strength of the soul is kept for God and thus the soul is able to love God with all its strength. . . . These passions are four, namely: joy, hope, grief, and fear. These passions, when they are controlled by reason with respect to God, so that the soul rejoices only in that which is purely the honour and glory of God, and hopes for naught else, neither grieves save for things that concern this. It is clear that the strength and ability of the soul are being directed toward God and kept for Him. For, the more the soul rejoices in any other thing than God, the less completely will it centre its rejoicing in God; and the more it hopes in aught else, the less will it hope in God; and so with the other passions."[120]

---

119. "*Totum enim cor in his quatuor affectionibus est; et de his accipiendum puto quod dicitur, ut in toto corde tuo convertaris ad Dominum. Convertatur proinde amor tuus, ut nihil omnino diligas nisi ipsum, aut certe propter ipsum. Convertatur etiam ad ipsum timor tuus; quia perversus est timor omnis, quo metuis aliquid praeter eum, aut non propter eum. Sic et gaudium tuum, et tristitia tua aeque convertantur ad ipsum. Hoc autem ita fiet, si nonnisi secundum eum doleas, aut laeteris*" (cols. 172D–173A).

120. Peers, 1.259–60, which reads: ". . . Now when . . . faculties, passions and desires. . . . These affections and passions . . . concern this, neither fear aught save God alone, it is clear . . ."

Note that St. Bernard and St. John of the Cross tell us not to annihilate passion but to change its course, redirect it to God, *submerge* it in the stream of grace which flows from God and leads to God, and purifies all that it touches. {The} *wrong way* {is to} try by effort of will to *force out* joy and sorrow, {to try to} keep them from the soul altogether. {The} *right way* {is to} *convert* joy from false to true, {to} convert sorrow from false to true. {*For*} *instance* {if one feels} anger at another person {or} sorrow at his domineering over us, change sorrow's object: lament {the} harm his anger does him, and rejoice at {the} good of our own humiliation—try to destroy evil in him by charity. St. Bernard tells us how to follow out the practical consequences of this truth. The rending of the heart (*scindite corda vestra* [121]) means the work of *detachment, brought about by pure faith*—renouncing what we see for what we do not see, on the authority of God's word. *Quis in vobis est, cujus voluntas circa unum aliquid solet obstinatior inveniri? Scindat cor suum gladio spiritus, quod est verbum Dei . . . . NON EST CONVERTI AD DOMINUM IN TOTO CORDE, NISI SCISSO CORDE.* {. . .} *Spiritus Domini multiplex (Sap. 7:22) non potest sequi multiplicem sine multiplici scissione.*[122] Hence complete detachment, complete plasticity, makes us ready for everything God wills. If we desire nothing but what He wills, we desire everything that He wills, no matter what. *PARATUM [cor meum] AD ADVERSA, PARATUM AD PROSPERA: PARATUM AD HUMILIA, PARATUM AD SUBLIMIA; PARATUM AD UNIVERSA QUAECUMQUE PRAECEPERIS.*[123] This liberty, freedom of the perfectly detached soul, is the same thing that we find in St. John of the

---

121. Col. 173C ("rend your hearts") (Joel 2:13).

122. Cols. 173D–174A, which reads: ". . . *Aliquis non est . . . multiplex, ait Sapiens . . . non potest . . .*" ("Who is there among you whose will is usually found more stubbornly fixated on some one thing? Let him rend his heart with the sword of the Spirit, which is the word of God. . . . No one is converted to the Lord with all the heart unless the heart has been rent. . . . The Spirit of the Lord is manifold [Wis. 7:22] . . . . and one cannot follow the manifold Spirit without a manifold rending").

123. Col. 174A ("[A heart] ready for adversity, ready for prosperity; ready for the lowly, ready for the lofty; ready for everything whatsoever You might command").

Cross. This freedom is the true fruit and grace of Lent, the "*mysterium*" which makes God known to His friends.

## Appendix V

"ORDINAVIT IN ME CARITATEM"[124]

After considering the idea of the total conversion of our whole being to God by love, which is the theme of St. Bernard's Lenten sermons, it is well to see his deepest treatment of this subject: the *ordinatio caritatis*,[125] which is one of the big functions of Cistercian theology to define and determine. We are called to union with God in which all our powers are consecrated to Him; all our desires are centered on Him. Our nature is made for love, for God. It is created to be elevated by His grace. The monastery is a *schola caritatis*,[126] in which our fallen nature is reformed by grace, the *imago reformationis*[127] is perfected, until our lost likeness to God is recovered in perfect charity. The practical problem which St. Bernard faces, and which is not so clearly treated by

---

124. *In Cantica*, 49.1 (*PL* 183, col. 1016C) ("He set in order charity in me") (Cant. 2.4).

125. N. 5 (col. 1018B) ("the ordering of charity").

126. "school of charity" (see Gilson, *Mystical Theology of Saint Bernard*, chapter 3, "Schola Caritatis" [60–84]; the phrase is taken from William of St. Thierry, *De Natura et Dignitate Amoris*, 9.26: "*Haec est specialis caritatis schola, hic ejus studia excoluntur, disputationes agitantur, solutiones non ratiocinationibus tantum, quantum ratione et ipsa rerum veritate et experientia terminantur*" [231, n. 85; *PL* 184, col. 396D] ["This is a special school of love; here its studies are perfected, its disputations carried on, its conclusions reached not so much through abstract reasoning as through an intuitive grasp and direct experience of the truth of reality"]; see also St. Bernard, *De Diversis*, 71 [*PL* 183, col. 743B]: "*In schola Christi sumus, in quo duplici doctrina erudimur; quia aliud per seipsum ille unus et verus magister docet, aliud per ministros. Per ministros timorem; per seipsum, dilectionem*" ["We are in the school of Christ, in which we are educated by a twofold teaching, for the one true Master teaches one thing by Himself, another through His ministers—through ministers, fear; through Himself, love"]).

127. "the image of reformation."

St. John of the Cross (who gives the *solution* rather than the problem itself—and who perhaps had arrived at a more perfect experience of the solution than St. Bernard)—this problem is: (1) TO WHAT EXTENT *IN PRACTICE* CAN ALL THE POWERS OF THE SOUL BE ORDERED AND CONSECRATED TO GOD IN THIS LIFE? (2) WHAT IS THE PERFECTION OF CHARITY? IS IT A PERFECTION THAT IS MERELY *WILLED*, OR IS IT ALSO *EXPERIENCED*? (3) TO WHAT EXTENT IS OUR CALL TO PERFECTION *DETERMINED* OR *HELPED* BY A SENSIBLE ATTRACTION? We merely discuss St. Bernard's treatment of the problem in his own terms, without comparing it with other treatments (for instance, that which sees the whole problem in the light of active or passive prayer, the control of the active or contemplative gifts, etc.). They do not throw light on St. Bernard's text, and are better left out. Sermons 49 and 50 *in Cantica* are on a quite different level. The contrast between them throws much light on St. Bernard as a person. In Sermon 49,[128] it is a regular, thoughtful ascetic conference on the interior life, an objective series of reflections on the function of *discretion* in keeping our movements of fervor in order. It is clear, dispassionate, on the level of most of his monks, but in the middle of it St. Bernard soliloquizes on his own problems, and a whole new aspect of the *ordo caritatis* dawns on him. The thoughts of the saint, now on a more personal, and therefore a more practical and experiential level, immediately get very deep. He tries without full success to define a profound personal problem, and to work out the relation between the *duty* which keeps him occupied with things of immediate material importance, less valuable in themselves, and the *love* which draws him to things of greater objective value—the things of the spirit, his own interior life. His attempt to sketch this problem is unsatisfactory—it is an impromptu reflection, which he breaks off half-finished, in order to return to it again. The next day, instead of going on with something else he had planned, he returns to the question (having thought it out more deeply), and treats it (to his own satisfaction) on an entirely new level—profound speculation, deep psychology,

---

128. Cols. 1016C–1020C.

in which he is completely involved as a person: he not only thinks the problem out, he *lives* it out for his monks, and probably only the minority understood what he was talking about. Here St. Bernard is most original and most himself—{and} also most profound.

SERMON 49 *IN CANTICA*: the theme {is that} God introduces the fervent soul sometimes into the *cella vinaria*[129] of contemplation, or at least of fervent affective prayer. St. Bernard describes this kind of prayer (n. 3 [col. 1017]), but it does not concern us here. Emerging from the *cella vinaria*, full of spiritual consolation, the contemplative finds himself full of zeal, but this zeal has to be *regulated by discretion*. {In his} first statement of the *ordo caritatis* St. Bernard is merely looking at "experienced love" (*caritas*) from the commonplace angle—the sensible fervor of devout prayer—mystical prayer, no doubt—which is not to be taken as the guide and basis of our activity, but still demands to be regulated by the standards of *reason* guided by the light of faith. {The} sense of the line is then {that} God "orders" the movements of fervent love in the soul by the influence of discretion: in what does this order consist; why is it necessary; what are its advantages? The saint then remarks that this ordering of charity is necessary not only for the individual, but is carried out by the action of the Holy Spirit throughout the whole Mystical Body of Christ (Sermon 49, n. 5[130]). {Note} the importance of *discretion*, its function in the interior life of a contemplative ({a} mystic perhaps). "*IMPORTABILIS ABSQUE SCIENTIA ZELUS EST.*"[131] {The} use of {the} terms *zelus*, *aemulatio*,[132] etc. refer to the ardent zeal for good produced in us

---

129. Col. 1016C, which reads: "*cellam vinariam*" ("the cellar of wine") [*St. Bernard's Sermons on the Canticle of Canticles*, trans. A Priest of Mount Melleray [Ailbe Luddy, ocso] (Dublin: Browne and Nolan, 1920), 2.56]).

130. Cols. 1018B–1019A.

131. Col. 1018B, which reads: "*Importabilis siquidem absque . . .*" ("Zeal without knowledge is a thing insupportable" [Luddy, *Sermons on the Canticle*, 2.60]).

132. Col. 1018B ("rivalry").

as a result of graces of prayer. The seat of this zeal is in our nature; its source is in grace. The terms might be translated as sensible fervor, ardent zeal for the glory of God, etc., etc. This zeal is the fruit of real grace, but it remains the fervor of "beginners," in the language of St. Bernard and St. John of the Cross (READ *Dark Night*, Bk. i, c. 1, nn. 2–3[133]—note: *Dark Night* is St. John's treatise

133. "2. It must be known, then, that the soul, after it has been definitely converted to the service of God, is, as a rule, spiritually nurtured and caressed by God, even as is the tender child by its loving mother, who warms it with the heat of her bosom and nurtures it with sweet milk and soft and pleasant food, and carries it and caresses it in her arms; but, as the child grows bigger, the mother gradually ceases caressing it, and, hiding her tender love, puts bitter aloes upon her sweet breast, sets down the child from her arms and makes it walk upon its feet, so that it may lose the characteristics of a child and betake itself to greater and more substantial occupations. The loving mother is like the grace of God, for, as soon as the soul is regenerated by its new warmth and fervour for the service of God, He treats it in the same way; He makes it to find spiritual milk, sweet and delectable, in all the things of God, without any labour of its own, and also great pleasure in spiritual exercises, for here God is giving to it the breast of His tender love, even as to a tender child. 3. Therefore, such a soul finds its delight in spending long periods—perchance whole nights—in prayer; penances are its pleasures; fasts its joys, and its consolations are to make use of the sacraments and commune of Divine things. In the which things spiritual persons (though taking part in them with great efficacy and persistence and using and treating them with great care), commonly find themselves, speaking spiritually, very weak and imperfect. For since they are moved to these things and to these spiritual exercises by the consolation and pleasure that they find in them, and since, too, they have not been prepared for them by the practice of earnest striving in the virtues, they have many faults and imperfections with respect to these spiritual actions of theirs; for, after all, everyone's actions correspond to the habit of perfection attained by him. And as these persons have not had the opportunity of acquiring the said habits of strength, they have necessarily to work like feeble children, feebly. In order that this may be seen more clearly, and likewise how much these beginners in the virtues lack with respect to the works in which they so readily engage with the pleasure aforementioned, we shall describe it by reference to the seven capital sins, each in its turn, indicating some of the many imperfections

on the "ordination" of charity): "such a soul finds its delight in spending long periods—perchance whole nights—in prayer; penances are its pleasures; fasts its joys," etc., etc. (p. 351). But this fervor is full of *imperfection*, because they are moved to these exercises *not by reason but by blind appetite* ("by the consolation and pleasure which they find in them"). See also c. 2, n. 2: "In these persons the devil often *increases the fervour and desire* to perform these works . . . so that their pride and presumption may grow greater. . . . for all these works are not only valueless to them, but even become vices in them" (p. 352).[134] Read {the} context—n. 3.[135] See also especially p. 364: St. John of the Cross

---

which they have under each heading; wherein it will be clearly seen how like to children are these persons in all they do. And it will also be seen how many blessings the dark night of which we shall afterwards treat brings with it, since it cleanses the soul and purifies it from all these imperfections" (Peers, 1.350–52).

134. Text reads: ". . . fervour that they have and the desire to perform these and other works more frequently, so that . . . . For the devil knows quite well that all these works and virtues which they perform are not . . ." (emphasis added).

135. "Sometimes, too, when their spiritual masters, such as confessors and superiors, do not approve of their spirit and behaviour (for they are anxious that all that they do may be esteemed and praised), they consider that they do not understand them, or that, because they do not approve of this and comply with that, they are themselves not spiritual. And so they immediately desire and contrive to find some one else who will fit in with their tastes; for as a rule they desire to speak of spiritual matters with those who, as they understand, will praise and esteem what they do, and they flee, as they would from death, from those who disabuse them in order to lead them into a safe road—sometimes they even harbour ill-will against them. Presuming thus, they are wont to resolve much and accomplish very little. Sometimes they are anxious that others shall realize how spiritual and devout they are, to which end they occasionally give outward evidence thereof in movements, sighs and other ceremonies; and at times they are apt to fall into certain ecstasies, in public rather than in secret, wherein the devil aids them, and they are pleased that this should be noticed, and are often eager that it should be noticed more" (Peers, 1.353).

mentions {the} importance of DISCRETION.[136] St. Bernard is describing the same "zeal" without so much emphasis on its potential imperfections. Nevertheless, he says clearly: (1) without discretion this zeal becomes fruitless (*minus efficax, minusque utilis*[137]), and often harmful (*plerumque autem et perniciosus*[138]); (2) without discretion this zeal quickly becomes a *vice*; (3) the zeal itself is simply a *passion* aroused indeed by grace, a natural instrument of grace, but *without discretion it frustrates grace, and even destroys nature itself*: "*Tolle hanc, et virtus vitium erit, ipsaque affectio naturalis in perturbationem magis convertetur, exterminiumque naturae*" (col. 1018D).[139] *Discretio*, a function of the virtue of prudence, but also of the *gift of knowledge*, teaches us to adapt means to ends and to do the right thing at the right time and in the right way (cf. Sermon 2 *in Tempore Resurrectionis*, n. 6,[140] where he shows how discretion "ordinates" fraternal charity {and} teaches {a} right balance between mercy and correction). See especially {*In*} *Cantica* 23, n. 8,[141] where he shows how discretion and charity necessarily complement one another. By charity he means "*affectus*" *caritatis*, "*fervor*"

---

136. C. 5.2, 3: there is no explicit mention of discretion here, but St. John refers to those who "become irritated at the sins of others, and keep watch on those others with a sort of uneasy zeal," as well as those "who are vexed with themselves when they observe their own imperfectness, and display an impatience that is not humility; so impatient are they about this that they would fain be saints in a day. . . . Some souls, on the other hand, are so patient in this matter of the progress which they desire, that God would gladly see them less so."

137. Col. 1018C ("instead of being efficacious or useful" [Luddy, *Sermons on the Canticle*, 2.61]).

138. Col. 1018C ("generally turns out to be extremely pernicious" [Luddy, *Sermons on the Canticle*, 2.61]).

139. "Take away this, and virtue becomes vice. Take this away, and the very affections implanted in us for the perfection of our nature, turning aside from their destiny, begin at once to work for the disturbance and the ruin of our nature" (Luddy, *Sermons on the Canticle*, 2.61–62).

140. Cols. 285D–286A.

141. Col. 888AD.

*caritatis*.[142] Their union is elevated by contemplation (*cella vinaria*) to complete contempt of self (*miro Spiritus sancti magisterio*[143]). Discretion is here called *mater virtutum*[144] (col. 888). "*Virtus discretionis absque charitatis fervore jacet, fervor vehemens absque discretionis temperamento praecipitat*" (*ibid*.).[145] Discretion alone produces nothing; {it} *sees* but does not *do*; {it is} theory without practice—*jacet*—{it is} inert, dead, sterile. *Fervor caritatis* alone wastes energy; {it} ruins us; {it} exhausts nature; {it is a} futile expense of {the} good natural power to love; {it} dissipates our power; {it is} spiritual fornication in sensual prayer and avaricious works. *Discretion prevents* the above "corruption." The two together *collect* all {the} powers of {the} soul and drive them towards God. Discretion harnesses and guides {the} energy generated by fervor. St. Thomas uses discretion in the same sense: "*Discretio quae ad prudentiam pertinet, est genetrix et custos et moderatrix virtutum*" (*III Sent*., 33, 2.5.c.)[146] (language borrowed from Cassian[147]). Also, St. Thomas {says}: Salt in {the} sacrifices of {the} Old Law signified discretion (I-II, q. 102, a. 3, ad. 14): "*Sal offerebatur quia impedit corruptionem putredinis; sacrificia autem Dei debent esse incorrupta; et etiam quia in sale significatur discretio sapientiae vel*

---

142. See *Sermo* 49, n. 4 (col. 1018B): "*contemplationis excessus . . . in affectu . . . in fervore*" ("ecstasy of contemplation . . . in affection . . . in fervor").

143. Col. 888C ("under the admirable direction of the Holy Ghost" [Luddy, *Sermons on the Canticle*, 1.244]).

144. Text reads: "*matrem virtutum*" ("the virtue which is mother of all the others" [Luddy, *Sermons on the Canticle*, 1.244]).

145. Text reads: "*Virtus sequidem . . . jacet, et . . .*" ("Without the fervour of charity, discretion is unfruitful and sluggish; whilst, unless tempered with discretion, the impetuosity of fervour easily induces precipitation" [Luddy, *Sermons on the Canticle*, 1.244–45]).

146. Aquinas, *Opera Omnia*, 7.366 ("Discretion, which belongs to prudence, is the mother and guardian and governess of the virtues").

147. *Conf*. 2.4 (*PL* 49, col. 528C): "*Omnium namque virtutum genetrix, custos moderatrixque discretio est*" ("Discretion is the mother, the guardian and the governess of all virtues").

*etiam mortificatio carnis.*"[148] {See} also {the} fuller treatment {in} *Lectio* I in *Cap.* XII *Epistola ad Romanos.*[149] Discretion applies the right measure in exterior actions, by which they are ordered to fulfill the ends of charity (here used in the strict sense as {a} theological virtue in the will, without the implications suggested by St. Bernard).

*The Functions of Discretion* (Serm. 49 *in Cant.*, n. 5): it is a *vigilantior scientia,*[150] an alert and prudent awareness of practical and spiritual values, which comes into play especially in times of fervor, in order to counteract the repercussion of grace on the passions—the fervor of "passionate" charity: *zelum supprimat* (sensible fervor); *spiritum temperet* (natural action of the will); *caritatem ordinet* (supernaturalized love—using {the} force of desires).[151] {The} precise distinction between these three {is} not clear, but {it is} safe to say that *zelus* is more a sensible fervor, *spiritus* a natural action in the will, and *caritas* the virtue of charity in so far as it enlists in its aid the supernaturalized "passion" of the soul. By regulating the *passions of the soul,* bringing our desires (however holy) under the control of reason enlightened by faith, discretion comes to govern and perfect *all the virtues.* It gives them *order,* which produces *"modus"*[152] *(measure); beauty; permanence,* {which} gives *"perpetuity."*[153]

{In} SUMMARY, {the} practical norms for discretion {are as follows}: the function of discretion is to prevent us from acting out

---

148. Aquinas, *Opera Omnia*, 2.384-85, which reads: *"Sal autem . . ."* ("Salt, then, was offered because it prevents the corruption of putrefaction; sacrifices to God should be incorrupt; and also because in salt is signified the discernment of wisdom, and the mortification of the flesh as well").

149. Aquinas, *Opera Omnia*, 13.120-22.

150. Col. 1018C, which reads: *"vigilantiori . . ."* ("the light of knowledge should proportionately increase" [Luddy, *Sermons on the Canticle*, 2.61]).

151. Col. 1018C, which reads: *". . . ordinet charitatem"* ("To moderate zeal, to regulate fervor, and to set charity in order" [Luddy, *Sermons on the Canticle*, 2.61]).

152. Col. 1018C, which reads: *"modum."*

153. *"etiam et perpetuitatem"* (col. 1018C).

of *passion* (even though the passion be holy), rather than according to reason and faith. In order that we may not be blinded and lose merit and act from natural motives when we think we are guided entirely by zeal, we must use discretion to *mortify* the instinct to act for the sake of the pleasure (however spiritual) the action produces in us. For this end, see St. John of the Cross, *Maxim* 42: "Blessed is he that puts aside his pleasure and inclination and regards things according to reason and justice in order to perform them"[154] (cf. {also} *Maxim* 41[155] and 43[156] [Peers, III, p. 246]; also 69[157] [p. 248]; also *Cautions*, nn. 16,[158] 17[159] [Peers, III, pp. 225, 226]).

---

154. Peers, 3.246.
155. "Enter into account with thy reason to do that which it counsels thee on the road to God, and it will be of greater worth to thee with respect to thy God than all the works that thou doest without this counsel and than all the spiritual delights that thou seekest."
156. "He that acts according to reason is like one that eats of substantial food, and he that is moved by the desire of his will is like one that eats insipid fruit."
157. "Though thou perform many actions, yet thou shalt make no progress in perfection if thou learn not to deny thy will and to submit thyself, losing all anxiety concerning thyself and thine own interests."
158. "The second caution is that thou never fail to perform any good works because of the lack of pleasure or sweetness that thou findest therein, if it be fit that they should be done in the service of Our Lord; neither perform thou them only for the sweetness and pleasure that they give thee. On the contrary, it behoves thee equally to perform these and others that are distasteful to thee, for otherwise it is impossible for thee to gain constancy and overcome thy weakness" (Peers, 3.225–26).
159. "Let the third caution be that the spiritual man must never in his exercises set his eyes upon that which is delectable in them and thence derive attachment to them, and perform them for this reason only; neither must he flee from that which is displeasing to him in them, but rather he must seek that which is toilsome and distasteful. In this way he bridles his sensual nature; and if thou do otherwise thou wilt neither lose the love of thyself, nor wilt win and attain the love of God" (Peers, 3.226).

*The* EXTERIOR *order of charity*: read St. Paul, 1 Corinthians 12:12 to {the} end;[160] especially *Ephesians* 4:2 ff.: 3. Eager to preserve the unity that the Spirit gives you . . . you are one body with a single spirit . . . The same Father Who is above all things and pervades all things . . . each has received his own special grace dealt out to him by Christ's gift ["*secundum* MENSURAM *donationis Christi*"— {the} Vulgate preserves {the} idea of order]; 11: Some He has appointed to be apostles . . . they are to *order* the lives of the faithful . . . BUILD UP THE FRAME OF CHRIST'S BODY UNTIL WE ALL REALIZE

160. "For as the body is one, and hath many members; and all the members of the body, whereas they are many, yet are one body, so also is Christ. For in one Spirit were we all baptized into one body, whether Jews or Gentiles, whether bond or free; and in one Spirit we have all been made to drink. For the body also is not one member, but many. If the foot should say, because I am not the hand, I am not of the body; is it therefore not of the body? And if the ear should say, because I am not the eye, I am not of the body; is it therefore not of the body? If the whole body were the eye, where would be the hearing? If the whole were hearing, where would be the smelling? But now God hath set the members every one of them in the body as it hath pleased him. And if they all were one member, where would be the body? But now there are many members indeed, yet one body. And the eye cannot say to the hand: I need not thy help; nor again the head to the feet: I have no need of you. Yea, much more those that seem to be the more feeble members of the body, are more necessary. And such as we think to be the less honourable members of the body, about these we put more abundant honour; and those that are our uncomely parts, have more abundant comeliness. But our comely parts have no need: but God hath tempered the body together, giving to that which wanted the more abundant honour, that there might be no schism in the body; but the members might be mutually careful one for another. And if one member suffer any thing, all the members suffer with it; or if one member glory, all the members rejoice with it. Now you are the body of Christ, and members of member. And God indeed hath set some in the church; first apostles, secondly prophets, thirdly doctors; after that miracles; then the graces of healing, helps, governments, kinds of tongues, interpretations of speeches. Are all apostles? Are all prophets? Are all doctors? Are all workers of miracles? Have all the grace of healing? Do all speak with tongues? Do all interpret? But be zealous for the better gifts. And I shew unto you yet a more excellent way."

OUR COMMON UNITY THROUGH FAITH IN THE SON OF GOD. . . . WE SHALL REACH PERFECT MANHOOD, THAT MATURITY WHICH IS PROPORTIONED TO THE COMPLETED GROWTH OF CHRIST, etc., as opposed to the *disorder* of those who are tossed about by every wind of doctrine. Read 5:15-16: follow truth in a spirit of charity and so *grow up into a due proportion with Christ* . . . On Him all the body depends . . . it is ORGANIZED, etc. {The} same idea was brought out by Pius XI in *Ad Catholici Sacerdotii*—{the} unity of priests with bishops {in} carrying out assigned functions, etc.[161]

{In} SUMMARY, Scripture teaches us that the Holy Spirit, pouring out charity in our hearts, brings each of us special graces fitting to fulfill our own individual functions in the Church. Hence the "ordering" of charity by discretion, which mortifies our urge to act on "holy" impulses, extends beyond ourselves, and has reference to the unity and development of the whole Church. *In practice*, this means a discreet balance between *individual attraction* and the *guidance of authority*. Where authority is misused, everything goes dead. {There is} exterior order, but no interior life. Where attraction is deified, {there are} heresies and schisms {along with} false mysticism, ending in sterility.

ST. BERNARD {considers the} exterior order in the *Church* and in the *Cistercian monastery*:

1 {With regard to} the Church (Serm. 49 *in Cant.*, n. 5), he quotes Ephesians 4:11-12 and comments: "It is fitting that all these be bound together by charity and fitted together into the unity of the Body of Christ: but this can by no means be done if their charity is not ordered. FOR IF EACH ONE IS CARRIED AWAY BY IMPULSE ACCORDING TO THE MOVEMENT OF HIS OWN SPIRIT AND RUSHES OFF TO EVERYTHING THAT CATCHES HIS FANCY, without heeding the judgement of reason, all will become discontented with the office assigned to them, and all will strive together to

---

161. Pope Pius XI, *Ad Catholici Sacerdotii* (*The Catholic Priesthood*) (December 20, 1935) (*Acta Apostolicae Sedis* 28 [January 2, 1936]: 5–53).

fulfill the same functions, producing not unity but rather confusion."[162]

{2.} *"Ordo caritatis" in the Cistercian Monastery*—a few remarks on Sermon 3 *for the Assumption*:[163]

n. 1: a very important idea running through the whole sermon {is that} we have to know whether we are Martha, Mary or Lazarus, because (n. 1) {there is a} big difference. Martha *uses the body and material things* as the means by which she "receives the Lord into her house,"[164] while for Mary the body, etc. are rather an "impediment,"[165] and she receives the Lord into her spirit. Hence *discretion* has different functions in each case, and the attraction in each case is of a different quality. In determining our vocation, *discretion* enables us to distinguish between *four* kinds of *attraction (fervor)*: (1) *natural*, produced by *emulation* of others around us; (2) *natural*, produced by emulation in reverse, *reacting against* others in implicit protest; (3) *natural*—good attraction—{as an} expression of our deepest needs (grace usually builds on this); (4) *supernatural*, {which} *may* or *may not* take nature into account— here obedience to superiors and docility to {one's} director {is} very important.

n. 3: he says explicitly that the *ordinatio caritatis* in the monastery assigns the proper place to all *three* vocations: ACTIVE (Martha); CONTEMPLATIVE (Mary); PENITENT (Lazarus). There are

---

162. "*Oportet autem ut hos una omnes charitas liget, et contemperet in unitatem corporis Christi: quod minime omnino facere poterit, si ipsa non fuerit ordinata. Nam si suo quisque feratur impetu secundum spiritum quem accepit, et ad quaeque volet indifferenter, prout afficitur, et non rationis judicio convolarit; dum sibi assignato officio nemo contentus erit, sed omnes omnia indiscreta administratione pariter attendabunt, non plane unitas erit, sed magis confusio*" (cols. 1018D–1019A) (Merton's own translation, here and in the following quotations).

163. *PL* 183, cols. 421C–425B; Merton makes frequent reference to this sermon in his essay "Action and Contemplation in St. Bernard," in *Thomas Merton on St. Bernard*, Cistercian Studies [CS], vol. 9 (Kalamazoo, MI: Cistercian Publications, 1980), 23–104.

164. "*excepit illum in domum suam*" (col. 421D) (Luke 10:38).

165. "*impedimento*" (col. 422A).

two important factors to be considered in the ordination of these three levels:

a) (n. 2) It would be a disorder in the community if the actives had the upper hand, and if the contemplatives were carried away with a desire to get into action, not appreciating the higher value of their own vocation. "Blessed is the house, and happy always is that community in which Martha complains of Mary. But for Mary to envy Martha would be altogether unworthy and indeed unlawful, etc."[166]

b) (n. 4) The same applies to Lazarus. The contemplatives and the penitents must not of their own accord get themselves appointed to activity. This would be deordination. "Those who have no office entrusted to them must either sit at the feet of the Lord with Mary, or indeed confine themselves with Lazarus within the precincts of the tomb etc."[167]

*Special Points*: (1) (nn. 5–6) rules to be observed by those who engage in active works: discretion must keep them from being carried away *"propriis motibus animorum,"*[168] for thus all their offering will be spoiled and corrupt; (2) read n. 7, {a} description of the "best part"—that of Mary.[169]

---

166. *"Felix domus, et beata semper congregatio est, ubi de Maria Martha conqueritur. Nam Mariae Martham aemulari prorsus indignum, prorsus illicitum est"* (col. 422B).

167. *"Quibus enim nulla credita est dispensatio, administratio nulla commissa, his omnino sedendum erit, aut secus pedes Jesu cum Maria, aut certe cum Lazaro intra septa sepulcri"* (col. 423C).

168. "by the movements proper to their souls" (col. 424A).

169. *"Quibus ita sollicitis circa frequens ministerium, videat Maria quemadmodum vacet, et videat quoniam suavis est Dominus. Videat, inquam, quam devota mente, quam tranquillo sedeat animo secus pedes Jesu, providens eum semper in conspectu suo, et verba ex ore ejus excipiens, cujus et aspectus delectabilis, et eloquium dulce. Diffusa est enim gratia in labiis ejus, et est speciosus forma prae filiis hominum, imo etiam super omnem gloriam angelorum. Gaude et gratias age, Maria, quae partem optimam elegisti. Beati enim oculi qui vident quae tu vides, et aures quae merentur audire quod audis. Beata plane, quae venas susurrii divini percipis in silentio, in quo utique bonum est homini Dominum exspectare. Simplex esto, non tantum sine dolo et simulatione, sed et absque multiplicitate occupationum, ut*

St. Bernard's Personal Problem (Sermon 49 *in Cantica*, nn. 6–8[170]): {this is a} soliloquy of St. Bernard on the problem of *ordinatio caritatis* in the active life of a superior who, nevertheless, feels himself drawn above all to contemplation. In this soliloquy he only sketches out the problem, and the situation is not quite clear. He will clarify and resolve it in Sermon 50. {He provides a} STATEMENT OF THE PROBLEM (Serm. 49 *in Cantica*, n. 6): what is the meaning of *ordinatio caritatis* in his own case, as a Father of souls? What he seems to be saying in this difficult passage is {that} he must first of all *give himself entirely to the work* Jesus has

---

*tecum sit sermocinatio ejus, cujus et vox dulcis, et facies decora. Unum cave, ne abundare incipias in sensu tuo, et velis plus sapere quam oportet sapere: ne forte dum lucem sectaris, impingas in tenebras, illudente tibi daemonio meridiano, de quo non est hujus temporis disputare. Nam Lazarus quo devenit? ubi posuistis eum? Sorores alloquor, quae sepelierunt fratrem praedicatione et ministerio, exemplo et oratione. Ubi ergo posuistis eum? Absconditus est fossa humo, sub lapide jacet, non facile invenitur"* (cols. 424D–425B) ("While those are thus busy about much serving, let Mary see how to spend her free time, and let her see that the Lord is sweet. Let her see, I say, how with a devoted mind and tranquil spirit she may sit at the feet of Jesus, keeping Him always in her sight and receiving the words of His mouth, Whose countenance is lovely and Whose speech is sweet. For grace is poured out on His lips, and He is handsome beyond the sons of men, indeed beyond all the glory of the angels as well. Rejoice and give thanks, Mary, who have chosen the best part. For blessed are the eyes that see what you see, and the ears that deserve to hear what you hear. Truly blessed, who receive the veins of the divine whisper in silence, in which it is certainly good for a man to wait for the Lord. Be simple, not only without guile and simulation, but also far from all multiplicity of occupations, so that His conversation, and His sweet voice, and His lovely face, may be with you. Beware of one thing, not to begin to overflow in your sense, and desire to taste more than it is proper to taste—lest by chance while you are pursuing the light, you rush into darkness, inveigled by the noonday devil, about whom there is not time to consider. For where has Lazarus come? Where have you put him? I am addressing his sisters, who have buried their brother with proper words and action, with story and prayer. Where then have you put him? He has been hidden away in a hole in the earth; he lies beneath a stone; he is not easily found").

170. Cols. 1019A–1020C.

designated for him (*ut sic mihi curae sint universae quae sunt ipsius*[171]). He must therefore *give first place to what most intimately concerns this duty* (*ut tamen quod mei potissimum . . . officii esse constiterit id ante omnia curem*[172]). But he must also *reserve his esteem for what is best and highest in itself* (contemplation). It is not *ordered* charity to love anything more than his duty. It is only *partly ordered* charity to love his duty, and yet not to rejoice in the progress of others more than his own. It is *perfectly ordered* charity to give himself entirely to his duty and yet to recognize that the greatest thing of all is contemplation, which perhaps he himself cannot enjoy while he sees others advancing in it. *Perfect order* {is to be} *entirely* given to duty, and *entirely* committed to his contemplative ideal. What is the SOLUTION to this problem? Can it be that God merely demands the sacrifice of what the saint himself would prefer? Is the solution that God makes us renounce an ideal for what is less perfect? Can we do so with a good conscience? *It is because he loves God above all that he gives himself entirely to God's will to bring others to love of Him, at the same time desiring nothing for himself but perfect union with God.* {The} same standards apply to activity which is not *cura animarum*.[173]

SERMON 50 IN CANTICA[174]—ORDINAVIT IN ME CARITATEM:[175] AFFECTIVE AND EFFECTIVE CHARITY: the "order" of charity is easy enough to determine in the abstract. In the concrete circumstances of life the problem is not so easily solved, because it is not merely a question of regulating our "attractions" and "aspirations" and "fervor" by the norms of "discretion" so that we arrive

---

171. Col. 1019A ("So should I keep faithful watch over all His interests" [Luddy, *Sermons on the Canticle*, 2.62]).

172. Col. 1019A, which reads: ". . . *propositi seu officii esse . . .*" ("but in such a way that what I recognise as belonging most particularly to my duty and office, should have my first attention" [Luddy, *Sermons on the Canticle*, 2.62]).

173. "the care of souls."

174. Cols. 1020C–1025A.

175. N. 1 (col. 1020D) ("He set charity in order in me" [Luddy, *Sermons on the Canticle*, 2.67]) (Cant. 2:4).

at the attainment of an ideal. There may seem to be a direct opposition between our duty and our ideal. This ambivalence would not be so painful if the *duty* and the ideal were not at the same time expressions of the same divine vocation, inseparable from that vocation, clear expressions of the will of God. {The} *solution of the problem* {is that} there are *two* charities to be ordered, and they must be balanced together. PERFECT BALANCE {is} PERFECTION. Perfection does not consist in pursuing *one* of these loves to the limit {and} neglecting the other. *Effective charity* {is imaged as a} horizontal line ({the} order of execution). It is regulated by the law of *necessity* {and} takes {the} world as it is, {with} our miseries and our needs. These cannot be ignored. {It is the} *"veritas caritatis"*:[176] it gives first place to what is first in the order of necessity—for example, bodily needs, love of enemies, etc.; {it} deals with what is urgent: the "emergencies" of this present life—after that, more lasting interests. Discretion here consists in ordering our activity, our dealings with immediate needs, to eternal ends. Effective charity is therefore ACTIVE (*"actualis"*[177]). This is what is above all *commanded*. It is the way by which we are to *merit* eternal life (*mandatur ad meritum*[178]). *Affective charity* {is the} vertical line ({the} order of intention). This charity sees values as they are in themselves—eternally in God—hence it places God first, contemplation first. {As an} *example* of {the} *contrast* between {these} two charities, if I am praying in church and the place catches fire, *actualis caritas* faces the necessity and tries to put out the fire, but *affectualis caritas*[179] is still able to recognize the primacy of contemplation over fire-fighting. Affective charity, though it can exist on earth, is only perfected in heaven, where there is no more

---

176. N. 6 (col. 1023B, which reads: *"charitatis veritas"*) ("the truth of charity" [Luddy, *Sermons on the Canticle*, 2.74]).

177. Title (col. 1020C, which reads: *"actuali"*) ("effective" [Luddy, *Sermons on the Canticle*, 2.67]).

178. N. 1 (col. 1021A) ("enjoined as the principle of merit" [Luddy, *Sermons on the Canticle*, 2.68]).

179. Title (col. 1020C, which reads: *"affectuali"*) ("affective" [Luddy, *Sermons on the Canticle*, 2.67]).

*necessitas.*[180] {As a} PRINCIPLE, it would be contrary to truth, to reality, and therefore an illusion and {a} sin ({since} true love {must be} based on truth), to try to live in this life exclusively on the vertical line of *affectualis caritas*. Why? Return to {the} ideas of discretion in Sermon 49. To judge all things by *affectio* in this life would be in fact, to DESCEND BELOW THE LEVEL OF REASON AND TO BE GUIDED NOT BY GRACE, WISDOM, CONTEMPLATION, BUT MERELY BY THE APPETITES OF THE FLESH—*propriis motibus animorum.*[181] Hence it follows that *actualis caritas* purifies the soul, and enables us to enter fully and perfectly and without illusion into the *affectualis caritas* which calls us to perfect union with God. {What is the} reason why? BECAUSE *"ACTUALIS CARITAS"* TRAINS US TO LOVE THE TRUTH IN ITS CONCRETE REALITY, not only in its ideal and speculative expression. Trained by *actualis caritas* in the experience of true values that are of a lesser order, we can go on to the EXPERIENCE (not speculation) of the highest values in their own concrete reality. Sermon 50 *in Cantica*, therefore, simply repeats the same argument that is more clearly and fully developed in *De Gradibus Humilitatis* ({the} Three Degrees of Truth[182]). THE SOLUTION of the problem is centered in nn. 4–6 of Sermon 50: the *key* is *"AFFECTUS RATIONALIS."*[183] The two orders of charity are not in fact completely separate. It would be false to say that *affective love* consisted in loving what is good but what is beyond our reach, while *effective love* consists in doing what we do not relish, merely out of a sense of duty, and with a total sacrifice of all attraction, relish and satisfaction. The *affective* order coincides with *effective* charity in so far as by discretion we learn to direct our love to God as He is concretely found in the requirements of the present situation, especially in the service of our neighbor, even though at the sacrifice of contemplation—{cf.} n. 4: "I do

---

180. "*hominum necessitates*" (n. 5 [col. 1023B]) ("the necessities of men" [Luddy, *Sermons on the Canticle*, 2.73]).

181. "by the movements proper to their souls" (col. 424A).

182. See the discussion below, pages 359–74.

183. "*affectio . . . quam ratio regit*" (col. 1022) ("An affection which is obedient to the rule of reason" [Luddy, *Sermons on the Canticle*, 2.70–71]).

not say that we must be without affection and that we must set our hands to our work with a dry heart."[184] Indeed, there is a sinful lack of "affection" (Romans 1:31). {It is} false to caricature the monastic life as a complete sacrifice of all consolation, as a continual Calvary, in which we always do what we hate, and always sacrifice everything that attracts us, so that we go on from day to day like the living dead and carry out *all* our duties with frozen-faced automatism, through sheer force of will. This is not St. Bernard's idea.

There are *three affections* which can be the source of our activity. One is *completely evil* and must always be eliminated: *carnal affection* cannot be subject to {the} law of God (Romans 8:7); we can never be guided by this, {which is the} source of all illusions. {There is a} danger of mistaking this for "grace." Another is *perfectly good* and totally attractive, but it belongs to heaven rather than earth, and here below is found only in rare moments of contemplation. It is the affection of *"Wisdom"*:[185] this *affectus sapientialis*[186] guides and moves *amor affectualis*; it moves us to act by the very experience of the goodness of God—the action is rather a rest in Him, the reception of His inflowing into the soul. This *sapientia* does two things: (1) it completely wipes out every trace of carnal affection; (2) it is the reward which is promised to the intermediate *rational affection*—it is, in fact, our union with God. The "*AFFECTUS RATIONALIS*" which lies in between the two is the one by which we work out our sanctification. THIS IS THE "AFFECTION" WHICH HAS TO BE ORDERED BY DISCRETION—THIS IS THE "*CARITAS*" THAT HAS TO BE SET IN ORDER (not solely, but principally). The *affectus sapientialis* is already in order. When the two loves, affective and effective, are perfectly coordinated, perfection is reached. This perfection depends entirely on the subjection of our affections to *reason* in the work of effective charity.

---

184. "*Neque hoc dico, ut sine affectione simus, et corde arido solas moveamus manus ad opera*" (col. 1022A).

185. N. 4 (col. 1022AB).

186. "the affection of wisdom" (the term is not actually used here).

## Appendix VI

SELECTIONS from ADAM OF PERSEIGNE[187] on *SILENCE* (from *Letter* 29 [Migne, *PL* 211, col. 688ff.])

*Aderit disputanti de silentio amica silentii Trinitas, quae et ex ore infantium et lactentium suas laudes perficere consuevit. Quicunque sub discipuli forma* Verbi incarnati frequentat auditorium, *eo debet diligere et servare silentium, quo in magistrum {sibi eligit} Dei Verbum. Magister enim humilium Christus, non modo ea ratione Verbum Patris dicitur,* quod sit voluntas ejus omnipotens, sed ideo etiam dicitur Verbum, quod semper requirat auditum. *Qui audit, auscultat; qui auscultat, silet; qui silet et audit, alieni audientiam praestat.* SEMPER IGITUR PATER EXIGIT A CREATURA RATIONALI SILENTIUM, CUI SEMPER LOQUITUR TALE VERBUM. *Nam Verbi hujus ineffabilis generatio sola est creaturae rationalis eruditio, cui sola spiritalis infantia eo exhibet reverentiam debitae audientiae, quo feriatam custodit innocentiam in silentio et quiete.* SEMPER LOQUITUR NOBIS PATER, DUM SEMPER VERBUM INEFFABILE GENERAT, ET AD AETERNUM EJUS ELOQUIUM CONTINUUM DEBET CREATURA SILENTIUM. VERBUM AUTEM OMNIPOTENS COGNOSCITUR, NEC INTELLIGERE, NEC DILIGERE, QUI AB EO NON METUIT AUDITUM CORDIS ADVERTERE: *unde scriptum est, Vir linguosus non dirigetur in terra* (Psalm 139); *in terra quippe non dirigitur qui, divini rationem eloquii percipere, aut intelligere non meretur. Id autem non meretur vir linguosus, qui* dum in lingua et lingua loquitur minima, quid Verbi Spiritus in linguis igneis deferat [non] experitur. VIDES QUANTUM TOTA TRINITAS APPROBET SILENTII DISCIPLINAM. PATER *silentium diligit, quia, dum de substantia sua coaeternum sibi Verbum ineffabiliter*

---

187. On Adam, see Thomas Merton, "The Feast of Freedom: Monastic Formation according to Adam of Perseigne," in *The Letters of Adam of Perseigne*, vol. 1, trans. Grace Perigo, Cistercian Fathers [CF] vol. 21 (Kalamazoo, MI: Cistercian Publications, 1976), 3–48; this is a somewhat expanded version of "Christian Freedom and Monastic Formation," *American Benedictine Review* 13 (September 1962): 289–313, which is itself a longer version of the article "La Formation Monastique selon Adam de Perseigne," *Collectanea Ordinis Cisterciensium Reformatorum* 19 (January 1957): 1–17.

*generat et proponit, procul dubio {ad} hujus arcani intelligentiam intentam {cordis aurem requirit}. . . . VERBUM quoque ipsum non immerito sibi fieri silentium exigit, quia, dum thesauros sapientiae et scientiae omnes in se custodit, ad illos quasi nostris auribus inculcandos, quasi quamdam linguam nobis non ignotam nostram humanitatem suscepit . . . . SPIRITUS etiam Verbi summam sibi obedientiam fieri voluit, dum Verbum abbreviatum, et ideo magis obscurum, quasi per quasdam glossas exponens, se in linguis igneis revelavit; nam glossae linguae interpretantur. Spiritus enim sanctus de obscuritate Verbi abbreviati, id est usque ad servi formam exinaniti, quasi quamdam expositionem fecit, dum tanti mysterii causas ipsius Verbi discipulorum tam evidenti dispersione linguarum impressit.*[188] *Quod autem diligat*

---

188. Col. 688AD, which reads: "*Aderit itaque disputanti . . . CORDIS AUDITUM . . . nobis linguam . . .*" ("Thus to one discoursing on silence will be present the friend of silence, the Trinity, which is accustomed to perfect His praises from the mouth of babes and of sucklings. Whoever is regularly in attendance in the role of disciple in the hall of the incarnate Word should love and keep silence, in as much as he chooses for himself the Word of God as master. For Christ, the Master of the humble, not only is called the Word of the Father for the reason that He is His omnipotent will, but also is called the Word because He is always seeking to be heard. The one who hears listens carefully; the one who listens carefully is silent; the one who is silent and hears gives hearing to another. Therefore the Father always requires silence from a rational creature, to whom such a Word is always speaking. For the ineffable generation of this Word is the only instruction of the rational creature, for whom only spiritual infancy provides the reverence of the listening that is owed, in as much as it guards unoccupied innocence in silence and quiet. For the Father is always speaking to us while he is always begetting the ineffable Word, and the creature owes continuous silence to His eternal eloquence. But one who does not fear to turn away from Him the listening of his heart is known neither to understand nor to love the omnipotent Word; thus is it written, 'A man full of tongue shall not be established in the earth' (Ps. 139); he indeed shall not be established in the earth, who does not deserve to perceive or understand the nature of divine eloquence. The man full of tongue does not deserve this, who, while the tongue is speaking trifling things on the tongue, does [not] experience what the Spirit of the Word is bringing forth in tongues of flame. You see how

*Spiritus sanctus silentium testatur Dominus per prophetam: Super quem, inquit, requiescet Spiritus meus, nisi super humilem et quietum? . . .* (Is. 66). U BI *. . .* HUMILITAS ET QUIES, IBI MOTIO SPIRITALIS SILENTII, PAX ET TRANQUILLITAS SOLEMNIZANT, AMICUM EST PACI, AMICUM TRANQUIL-LITATI SILENTIUM, *non potest agi sabbatum cordis, ubi labor labiorum silentii {retundit} disciplinam.*[189] SEPTEM DONA SPIRITUS SANCTI *. . . quasi septem silentia sunt, dum universitatem vitiorum ab animo silere et cessare compellunt. . . . Silentia sunt, quae, dum peccatorum reatus et vitiorum tumultus sopiunt, ad deligenda et diligenda Verbi incarnati mysteria aures cordis idoneas reddunt.* [But above all the Gift of Fortitude produced the silence most favorable to the generation of the Word] *. . . . quia ad illum a regalibus sedibus familiarius venit,*

---

much the whole Trinity approves the discipline of silence. The Father loves silence because, while He ineffably begets and declares from His own substance the Word coeternal to Himself, He requires beyond doubt that the ear of the heart be attentive to the understanding of this mystery. . . . The Word Himself also demands that silence be shown to Him as He deserves, because, while He guards in Himself all the treasures of wisdom and knowledge, He has taken up our humanity as a kind of 'tongue' not unknown to us, in order to inculcate them as it were into our ears. . . . The Spirit of the Word also has willed that complete obedience be shown to Himself, while, setting forth the abridged, and thus more obscure, Word, as though through certain glosses, He revealed Himself in tongues of fire; for 'gloss' is interpreted as 'tongues.' For the Holy Spirit makes, as it were, a sort of explanation about the obscurity of the abridged Word—that is, emptied out all the way to the form of a slave—while, by so evident a distribution of tongues He impressed upon the disciples the causes of so great a mystery as that of the Word Himself") (copy text reads: ". . . *elegit sibi . . . dubio hujus. . . cordia surem requirat . . .*").

189. Cols. 688D–689A, which reads: ". . . *silentium diligat Spiritus sanctus. . .*" ("But the Lord testifies through the prophet that the Holy Spirit loves silence: 'Upon whom,' he says, 'shall my Spirit rest, if not upon the humble and the quiet . . . ?' (Is. 66). Certainly where there is humility and quiet, there is the spiritual motion of silence; peace and tranquillity celebrate; silence is a friend to peace, a friend to tranquillity; the sabbath of the heart cannot be kept where the labor of the lips blunts the discipline of silence") (copy text reads: ". . . *retundat . . .*").

*qui in Spiritu fortitudinis quidquid est puritati contrarium {superat} et prosternit.*[190] [*Silence is necessary for spiritual childhood.*] *Infantes . . . {hujusmodi} non fantes, id est silentes sunt,* qui videlicet salutare Dei cum silentio praestolantur.[191] SILENTIUM EST NON OMNINO NON LOQUI, SED PONERE CUSTODIAM ORI TUO . . . [ut] *quomodo et quando oporteat, ubi et quantum debeas, quid et unde conveniat eloquaris.*[192]

## Appendix VII

QUIES CONTEMPLATIONIS

The "Repose" of Contemplation in St. Bernard: according to St. Bernard, the Cistercian vocation permits contemplative souls to attain the perfection of rest in God by contemplative union with Him. This quiet, interior solitude and silence is a mystical grace. It lasts for all too short a time, but it raises the contemplative above the disturbances which inevitably come from the weakness of the flesh, the necessities of community life, and its activity. We prepare ourselves for it by "quieting" and tranquilizing our souls by self-denial, obedience, humility and charity. To understand the ascent to this rest, read *De Gradibus Humilitatis,*

---

190. Col. 690AB ("The seven gifts of the Holy Spirit . . . are like seven silences, while they compel the totality of the vices to be still and be silent, away from the soul. . . . They are silences which, while they put to sleep the guilt of sinners and tumult of the vices, restore ears of the heart suited to choosing and loving the mysteries of the incarnate Word . . . because [this gift] comes from the royal throne more intimately to one who, in the Spirit of fortitude, overcomes and lays low whatever is contrary to purity") (copy text reads: ". . . *contrarium spernit et . . .*").

191. Col. 689C ("Those of this sort are speechless infants, not speakers; that is they are the silent, namely, those who wait with silence for the salvation of God") (copy text reads: ". . . *hujusmodo* . . .").

192. Col. 690A, which reads: "*Silentium enim est . . .*" ("Silence does not mean not to speak at all, but to put a guard on one's mouth . . . so that you may speak how and when it is appropriate, where and as much as you ought, what is proper and for what reason").

n. 21.[193] *The Three Degrees of Truth* (following the *Twelve Degrees of*

193. "*Dei quippe Filius, Verbum scilicet ac sapientia Patris, primum quidem illam animae nostrae potentiam, quae ratio dicitur, cum reperit carne depressam, peccato captivam, ignorantia caecam, exterioribus deditam; clementer assumens, potenter erigens, prudenter instruens, introrsum trahens, ac mirabiliter utens tanquam pro se vicaria, ipsam sibi judicem statuit, ita ut pro reverentia Verbi cui conjungitur, ipsa sui accusatrix, testis, et judex, contra se Veritatis fungatur officio. Ex qua prima conjunctione Verbi et rationis humilitas nascitur. Aliam deinde partem, quae dicitur voluntas, veneno quidem carnis infectam, sed jam ratione discussam, Spiritus sanctus dignanter visitans, suaviter pugnans* [sic: for *purgans*?], *ardenter afficiens, misericordem facit: ita ut more pellis, quae uncta extenditur, ipsa quoque unctione perfusa coelesti usque ad inimicos per affectum dilatetur. Et sic ex hac secunda conjunctione Spiritus Dei et voluntatis humanae, charitas efficitur. Utramque vero partem, rationem scilicet et voluntatem, alteram verbo veritatis instructam, alteram spiritu veritatis afflatam; illam hyssopo humilitatis aspersam, hanc igne charitatis succensam; tandem jam perfectam animam, propter humilitatem sine macula, propter charitatem sine ruga; cum nec voluntas rationi repugnat, nec ratio veritatem dissimulat, gloriosam sibi sponsam Pater conglutinat: ita ut nec ratio de se, nec voluntas de proximo cogitare sinatur, sed hoc solum beata illa anima dicere delectetur,* Introduxit me Rex in cubiculum suum. *Digna certe, quae de schola humilitatis, in qua primum sub magistro Filio ad seipsam intrare didicit, juxta comminationem ad se factam,* Si ignoras te, egredere et pasce haedos tuos (Cantic. I, 3, 7); *digna ergo, quae de schola illa humilitatis duce Spiritu sancto in cellaria charitatis (quae nimirum proximorum pectora intelligenda sunt) per affectionem introduceretur; unde suffulta floribus, ac stipata malis, bonis scilicet moribus et virtutibus sanctis, ad Regis demum cubiculum, cujus amore languet, admitteretur. Ibi modicum, hora videlicet quasi dimidia, silentio facto in coelo, inter desideratos amplexus suaviter quiescens, ipsa quidem dormit, sed cor ejus vigilat, quo utique interim veritatis arcana rimatur: quorum postmodum memoria statim ad se reditura pascatur. Ibi videt invisibilia, audit ineffabilia, quae non licet homini loqui. Excedunt quippe omnem illam, quam nox nocti indicat, scientiam: dies tamen diei eructat verbum, et inter sapientes sapientiam loqui et spiritualibus spiritualia licet conferri*" (PL 183, cols. 953A–954A) ("Indeed the Son of God, the Word and Wisdom of the Father, when he first found that power of our soul which is called reason weighed down by the flesh, captured by sin, blinded by ignorance, given over to outward things, assumed it mercifully, upraised it powerfully, instructed it prudently, drew it within and employed it marvelously on His behalf as a deputy, set it up as a judge for Himself, so that, out of reverence for the Word to which it is joined, it performs the office of Truth

*Humility* in St. Benedict[194]) {are as follows}:

---

as its own accuser, witness and judge. Humility is born of this first union of the Word and reason. Then the Holy Spirit, condescending to visit another faculty, which is called the will, infected by the poison of the flesh but already judged by reason, and opposing [or: cleansing] it sweetly, endowing it ardently, he brings it under mercy, so that in the manner of a skin which has been treated with oil and is made pliable, it likewise, drenched with heavenly oil, might through its affection be extended even to enemies. And thus from this second union, of the Spirit of God and the human will, charity is created. Each part, that is the reason and the will, the former taught by the Word of truth, the latter filled with the Spirit of truth, that part sprinkled with the hyssop of humility, this part enkindled by the fire of love, is now at last a perfected soul, without spot because of its humility, without wrinkle because of its charity; when neither the will repulses reason nor the reason conceals truth, the Father attaches the glorious spouse closely to Himself, so that neither is the reason allowed to focus on itself nor is the will allowed to dwell on the neighbor, but that blessed soul is delighted to speak of this alone: 'The King has led me into His chamber.' She is truly worthy who, from the school of humility, in which she first learned under her master the Son to enter into herself according to the warning made to her, 'If you do not know yourself, go forth and pasture your herds' (Cant. 1:7)—worthy, then, who from the school of that humility was led through affection, under the guidance of the Holy Spirit, to the storehouse of charity (which is surely to be understood as the hearts of one's neighbors). There, cushioned by flowers, stayed up by apples, that is, by good deeds and holy virtues, she is admitted at last to the chamber of the King, for whose love she languishes. There for a short time, indeed half an hour, while there is silence in heaven, sweetly resting in those desired embraces, she indeed sleeps, but her heart wakes, and in the meantime discovers the secrets of truth, on the recollection of which she will feed afterward when she comes to herself. There she sees what is invisible, hears what is ineffable, which man is not permitted to speak. These things go beyond all that knowledge which night discloses to night; rather, day brings forth this word to day, and among the wise it is permitted to speak wisdom, and spiritual things are allowed to be passed on to the spiritual").

194. *Rule*, chap. 7 (*The Rule of St. Benedict in Latin and English*, ed. and trans. Justin McCann, OSB [London: Burns, Oates, 1952], 36–48); the second half of the *De Gradibus* (nn. 28–56 [cols. 957B–972C]) considers the corresponding degrees of pride as the reversal of the degrees of humility.

1. The *Word* finds reason *weighed down by flesh, captive* to sin, *blinded* by ignorance, and *given over to external things*. The Word delivers reason from this by humility. The conditions described above all produce *activity*. {With respect to the} flesh, {the} more we give in to it, the more we need to "work" to satisfy it. *Sin* {is} a captivity: cf. Pharaoh in *Exodus* {forcing the Israelites to make} bricks without straw[195]—{a} grievous labor with no result except sorrow and shame. The false humility which groans under imperfections and yet tries to defend itself and deny them {is an activity}. {There is a} labor of *fear* that others will recognize them, {a} futile labor of hiding ourselves from ourselves, presenting ourselves to others and to ourselves as we are not. {There is a} terrible labor entailed by constantly trying to silence the voice of our own conscience or to falsify its reports. *Blinded* by ignorance, {we engage in} labor entailed by our mistakes, our useless activities undertaken without foresight, etc. {There is the labor} especially of our own wrong motives, our wrong adaptations to reality. Here physical exhaustion and even sickness result from our inability to see *why* and *how* we act wrongly—making useless mistakes and putting vain efforts into acts based on illusion. *External things* draw us out of ourselves into a field of multiple labors and anxieties. N.B. our true balance does *not* consist in a life completely dissociated from external things. It would be disastrous to attempt such a theory. It means *independence* of externals is so far as we *control* them, and they do *not* control us. But {the} first way to control them is to simplify our life and get rid of useless possessions and occupations. But all these labors come in the last analysis from a futile battle *against* truth—{a} flight from truth in ourselves and in our own lives. Read Genesis 3:7-8:[196] {this is the} typical pattern—Adam and Eve, realizing

---

195. See Exod. 5:7.
196. "And the eyes of them both were opened: and when they perceived themselves to be naked, they sewed together fig leaves, and made themselves aprons. And when they heard the voice of the Lord God walking in paradise at the afternoon air, Adam and his wife hid themselves from the face of the Lord God, amidst the trees of paradise."

their insufficiency and nothingness, hide from God {and} no longer rest and delight in His presence, as they were created to do. Paradise is no longer paradise for them—God {is a} source of anxiety, not of peace. So too, God would gladly walk with us in the "evening" of our works and good activities and our prayer. But seeking ourselves, we flee from Him, and we *labor* to hide ourselves from Him Who is our rest. This labor comes from the "beam"[197] of pride in our eye (*De Gradibus*, n. 15). What happens when you get a grit in your eye—worse still, a splinter! The peace and health and quiet of reason {is} restored by the Word—but note this: USING REASON ITSELF AS HIS VICAR. {The} way to rest {is} by good activity, {by} self-knowledge, {by} judging ourselves. {The} steps of this activity (*De Gradibus*, 21[198]) {are}: reverence for the word (Truth) *to which it is joined*; it acts as *prosecutor, witness* and *judge*; in doing so it *unites itself* with Truth, but in doing so it BEGINS TO REST; {the} mind cannot help resting in truth—{it} is made for that! In this rest {the} Word *gently lifts up spirit* from flesh, *strengthens* against sin, prudently instructs against ignorance, and turns to internal things.

2. The *Holy Spirit* comes and delivers the *will* from its rebellion against reason and its inability to keep peace with other men. Here {are} more sources of struggle and labor, done away with by {the} second degree of Truth—charity, which learns *compassion* and makes the will free and supple, able to resist selfishness and prepared to be united to God. The KEY TO THIS SECOND DEGREE OF TRUTH is a *"flight from Justice to Mercy"* (see especially *De Gradibus*, n. 18[199]). The reason, enlightened by truth and humility, sees itself as distasteful to itself and displeasing to God. Hence with hunger and thirst for justice, {it} strives to do penance, to execute justice upon itself. But having done all penance, they see that penance alone is insufficient—{this is a} very important transition. Then "they FLEE FROM JUSTICE TO MERCY,"[200] thus escaping

---

197. "*trabe*" (col. 949D).
198. Cols. 953A–954A.
199. Col. 951BC.
200. "*de justitia ad misericordiam confugiunt*" (col. 951C).

"willfulness" (*studium*), changing it to *gemitum*.[201] This flight from justice to mercy delivers them from arrogance, pride, the labor of judging others and thinking about faults of others, {the} bitter slavery to the labor of constantly comparing self with others in order to maintain the distinction: "I am not like other men" (*De Gradibus*, n. 17).[202] {It} delivers {them} from *proprium consilium*.[203] Compassion smoothes out the "roughness," {the} harshness of soul that is tough with itself and not yet merciful to others: "The will is now GRACIOUSLY VISITED, GENTLY PURGED, ARDENTLY ENERGIZED AND MADE MERCIFUL BY THE HOLY GHOST, so that like a skin which is anointed and stretched, divinely anointed, it is extended in affection even to its enemies"[204] etc. This too is a *union with God*—{the} soul becomes merciful with His mercy, and they thus "know the truth, needy and naked and weak."[205] It is Jesus Whom I love in the weakness and imperfection of my brother. LOVE FOR THE SPIRITUALLY UNDERPRIVILEGED {is} a greater work of mercy than corporal almsgiving. In {the} active life the two often coincide. The soul is now *"propter caritatem sine ruga."*[206] The inevitable harshness and narrowness of one who is merely penitent {is} washed away (cf. Dom Séjourné, "Les Inédits Bernadins du Manuscrit d'Anchin,"[207] {in} *Saint Bernard et son Temps*, Vol. II, Appendice {C},[208] pp. 271–73). The soul fallen in sin "rests" in a

---

201. N. 19 (col. 952A) ("groaning").

202. *"Non sum sicut caeteri hominum"* (col. 951AB) (Luke 18:11).

203. "one's own counsel" (*Sermo in Tempore Resurrectionis*, 3.3 [PL 183, col. 289D]); for a discussion, see Gilson, *Mystical Theology of Saint Bernard*, 56–59; for Merton's discussion of this sermon, see above, pages 234–37.

204. *"Aliam deinde partem, quae dicitur voluntas . . . Spiritus sanctus dignanter visitans, suaviter pugnans, ardenter afficiens, misericordem facit: ita ut more pellis, quae uncta extenditur, ipsa quoque unctione perfusa coelesti usque ad inimicos per affectum dilatetur"* (col. 953B).

205. "ne . . . egentem, nudam et infirmam veritatem ignorant" (col. 952A).

206. Col. 953C ("because of charity without wrinkle").

207. Dom Séjourné, OSB, "Les Inédits Bernardins du Manuscrit d'Anchin," *Saint Bernard et Son Temps*, 2 vols. (Dijon: Académie des Sciences, Artes, et Belles-Lettres, 1929), 2:248–82.

208. Text reads: "B."

sick-bed of "sloth" and "anxiety."[209] *Anxiety* makes the soul fear to get up and labor for true virtue—a labor which means that the will must impose penance on the *body*. The eight Beatitudes raise the soul from this sick-bed to rest in contemplation. *The hunger and thirst for justice* is decisive here. {The} spirit of *fortitude* does what could not be done by *fear* or *piety*. Armed by fortitude, {the} intellect "kicks the will out of bed" (p. 272).[210] Doing penance, the will begins to taste and see that the Lord is sweet.[211] Then the will is more definite about making {the} body serve reason and faith. Then *mercy*, inspired by the spirit of *counsel*, goes beyond the work of penance and accomplishes the rest of the soul's purification. After this the soul breathes easier; the labor is sweet and light. *Mercy* and *penance* have prepared the way for {the} repose of contemplation—*the end of this monastic vocation*—and purification of spirit from all images. *Munda cor, exoccupa te ex omnibus, esto monachus, id est singularis, unam pete a Domino, hanc require: vaca et vide quoniam ipse est Deus. {Sicque}, ubi per spiritum intellectus cor mundaveris, mox per spiritum sapientiae Deum videbis, Deoque perfrueris* (273).[212] {In} summary, three purifications *lead* to rest in God: (1) penance—{the} spirit of fortitude—hunger and thirst for justice—purifies {the} will and body; (2) mercy—{the} spirit of counsel—purifies {the} depths of *"memoria"* from all sin; (3) understanding purifies {the} memory from all *images*. However, beware of *false compassion*. *"Misericordia"*[213] must come *after* *"esuries justitiae,"*[214] hunger for justice. {A} wrong order {is} ex-

---

209. *"voluntas . . . aegra et morbida iacebat in lecto desidiae, coaegrotat et coanxiatur"* ("the will lay sick and infected in a bed of idleness, made ill and anxious") (2.271).

210. *"suscitans eam a lecto desidiae."*

211. Cf. Ps. 32[33]:9.

212. "Purify the heart; empty yourself of everything; be a monk, that is, unified; seek one thing from the Lord, ask for this: be at rest and see that He is God. And so, when you have purified the heart through the spirit of understanding, you will soon see God through the spirit of wisdom, and you shall enjoy God" (copy text reads *"Seque"*).

213. Matt. 5:7.

214. Matt. 5:6.

emplified in Adam's "compassion" for Eve—neglecting justice to God. {We} must first do the penance we *owe* to God before mercifully being lenient to weakness to others; otherwise we risk falling into a kind of league of tepidity, an alliance of injustice, condoning one another's vices (for {the} false compassion of Adam, see Sermon 1, *All Saints*, n. 11[215]). But {see} also {the} *false justice* of Adam (*ibid.*, n. 12[216]). Adam should have taken blame on himself and interceded before God for the weakness of woman. Instead, {he} throws all {the} blame on Eve (Genesis 3:12). *Quomodo, pro dolor omnia confudisti! Perniciose misericors, ubi severus esse debueras; et perniciosius crudelis, ubi misericordiam impendere {oportebat} (PL* 183:460).[217] (For {the} idea of *sine ruga*[218]— there is still a wrinkle in the compassion of {the} saints in heaven, desiring us to be with them [*All Saints*, 3:2[219]]; {cf. the} rest of Jesus in all [*id.*, 3:3;[220] cf. also Baldwin of Canterbury, *De Requie*][221]). Finally, the true rest of the soul is not merely in mercy and piety, but {in} understanding and wisdom. We go beyond preoccupations with brethren to find God in interior solitude. This is not necessary for all, but *absolutely necessary for some*. Even when you love {the} brethren, the community can sometimes seem like a desert. Thirst for the strong living God. Thirst for wisdom in silence and depths beyond communication with others. The will of God—{the} common will—leads into the desert, for those whom He has chosen. St. Thomas says {that} charity is shown by {the} will to labor for the brethren, but *much more* by {the} will to

---

215. *PL* 183, cols. 458D–459C.

216. Cols. 459C–460B.

217. "Alas, such sorrow—how you have mixed everything up! Perniciously merciful when you should have been severe, perniciously cruel when it was proper to show mercy" (copy text reads: *"impendere debueras"*).

218. "without wrinkle" (Eph. 5:27).

219. Cols. 469B–470A.

220. Col. 470AD.

221. Baldwin of Canterbury, *Tractatus Quintus, De Requie quam Sibi et Nobis Christus Quaesivit et Paravit* (*PL* 204, cols. 441C–452B); see above, pages 317–20.

leave all things of this life for contemplation.²²² {It is} most important that we understand this second degree. It is also a degree of *joy* and *freedom*. Our thesis {is that} the *joy*, *freedom* and *rest* of contemplation are inaccessible in any high degree or with any kind of habitual frequency, to those who have not set their own nature at rest within itself by humility and obedience, and who have not recovered their natural and spontaneous joy of peace with {the} brethren, achieved by a life of self-sacrifice, meekness, compassion, gentleness, modesty, etc.—all of these being expressions of a deep and tender and personal love for one's brethren. Note that this is the work of grace re-establishing a certain NATURAL goodness and harmony in our souls, the necessary preparation for progress towards a more *supernatural* state of love and prayer. The result here {is} *supernatural* in *mode*, *natural* in its *term*. In contemplation {it is} supernatural both in the end and in the means, or in the mode of attaining the end.

222. See *Summa Theologiae, Secunda Secundae*, q. 187, a. 2: "*status religionis est ordinatus ad perfectionem charitatis consequendam; ad quam quidem principaliter pertinent Dei dilectio, secundario autem dilectio proximi. Et ideo religiosi praecipue et propter se debent intendere ad hoc quod Deo vacent. Si autem necessitas proximis immineat, eorum negotia ex charitate agere debent*" ("the religious state is ordered to reaching the perfection of love, which is principally found in the love of God, and secondarily in the love of one's neighbor. Therefore religious should above all and for its own sake strive to be available to God. If however the need of one's neighbors is urgent, out of love they should work for their concerns") (*Opera Omnia*, 3.642); *Secunda Secundae*, q. 188, a. 2: "*religionis status ordinatur ad perfectionem charitatis, quae se extendit ad dilectionem Dei et proximi. Ad dilectionem autem Dei directe pertinet contemplativa vita, quae soli Deo vacare desiderat; ad dilectionem autem proximi pertinet vita activa, quae deservit necessitatibus proximorum: et sicut ex charitate diligitur proximus propter Deum, ita etiam obsequium delatum in proximos redundat in Deum*" ("the religious state is ordered to the perfection of love, which includes the love of God and of neighbor. The contemplative life, which desires to be available to God alone, pertains directly to the love of God; but the active life, which serves the needs of one's neighbors, pertains to the love of neighbor, and as the neighbor is loved for God's sake, out of charity, so also the care bestowed on one's neighbors belongs to God") (*Opera Omnia*, 3.649).

3. "CELLARS" (Sermon 23 *in Cantica*): in *De Gradibus* St. Bernard points out that the Second Degree of Truth brings us, by the Holy Spirit, into the *cellaria charitatis*[223] (cellars: i.e. place of abundance and of quiet, storerooms of good things which we can enjoy, gifts of God opened to us by His bounty). The *cellars of affection* are the hearts of our brethren. Hence these are opened to us as storerooms of plenty, of joy, of sweetness, of consolation, by the Holy Ghost. This must be rightly understood. {It} requires a special vocation, in some sense. Some in {the} monastery are called to a life in which this consolation of selfless fraternal love is the dominant grace. Sermon 22 *in Cantica*, n. 9 says that some in {the} monastery are called especially to *contemplation—studiis flagrare sapientiae*;[224] others to *penance—alios magis ad poenitentiam animari*;[225] others to {a} *life of virtues*—in {a} particular way {to} imitation of Jesus; others to {a} *life of piety—alios ad pietatem passionis memoria plus {accendi}* (882).[226] But see especially Sermon 12 *in Cantica*—the *unguentem pietatis*[227]—a precious ointment made up of the consolations we can offer others. By consoling others, we rest and find our joy in them, in their joy. {Regarding} compassion, {see the comment of} Jacques de Vitry to a friend: "I have a pain in your foot."[228] Taking their sorrows upon ourselves, {we} make a precious ointment out of these elements: *de necessitatibus*

---

223. *PL* 182, col. 953D.

224. *PL* 183, col. 882C ("some more ardent in the pursuit of wisdom" [Luddy, *Sermons on the Canticle*, 1.230]).

225. Col. 882C, which reads: ". . . *poenitentiam spe indulgentiae animari*" ("others more incited to penance by the hope of pardon" [Luddy, *Sermons on the Canticle*, 1.230]).

226. "others more inflamed with love by the memory of His Passion" (Luddy, *Sermons on the Canticle*, 1.230) (copy text reads: "*ascendit*").

227. Col. 828A ("the unguent of Piety" [Luddy, *Sermons on the Canticle*, 1.100]).

228. Jacques de Vitry (c. 1160–1240) was a noted preacher, historian of the Fifth Crusade, friend and biographer of the Béguine mystic Marie d'Oignies, bishop of Acre, and cardinal. The source of this saying has not been located; it is not found in *Lettres de Jacques de Vitry (1160/1170–1240) Évêque de Saint-Jean-d'Acre*, ed. R. B. C. Huygens (Leyden: E. J. Brill, 1960).

*pauperum; de anxietatibus oppressorum; de perturbationibus tristium; de culpis deliquentium; de omnibus miserorum aerumnis* (828B).[229] These are cooked together with the fire of charity and poured out in mercy. Mercy given to another is poured out upon ourselves, and we have the sweet consolation of knowing that we console Jesus.

Summary of the First Two Degrees of Truth (*De Gradibus Humilitatis*, n. 18[230]): {the} *first degree* {is} knowing the truth in ourselves; {it is} produced in us by the Word. {Its} *effects* {are a} sense of our own unworthiness (the things we loved before now become bitter to us; we are displeased with ourselves; we would like to be what we are not, and we aspire to be something that we cannot hope to be by our own power); self-distrust ({the} gift of *fear*); compunction ({we} find consolation in severely judging ourselves); self-contempt; penance; {a} hunger and thirst for justice ({the} gift of *fortitude*). {The} *transition to* {the} *second degree* comes when we realize the inadequacy of penance alone. {Here is} the "flight from justice to mercy" (*de justitia ad misericordiam confugiunt*[231]). {The} *second degree of truth* {is} finding the truth in our brother, by mercy. {It is} produced in us by the Holy Spirit. *Et hic est secundus gradus veritatis, quo eam in proximis inquirunt; dum {de} suis aliorum necessitates exquirunt; dum ex iis quae patiuntur, patientibus compati sciunt*[232] ({the} gift of *piety*, and {of} *counsel*). We reach this degree when we *habitually seek the truth by mercy* even more than by compunction. By these two, our hearts are purified of *ignorance, weakness* and *false zeal*.

---

229. Col. 828AB, which reads: ". . . *delinquentium, et postremo de omnibus quorumlibet miserorum* . . ." ("from the necessities of the poor, the anxieties of the oppressed, the sorrows of the sad, the sins of the guilty, in a word, from all the miseries of all the miserable" [Luddy, *Sermons on the Canticle*, 1.100]).

230. *PL* 182, col. 951BC.

231. Col. 951C.

232. Col. 951C ("And this is the second degree of truth, by which they look for it in their neighbors, while they attend to the needs of others beyond their own, while from those things which they have suffered they know how to be compassionate toward those suffering") (copy text reads: "*se*").

N. 19: *Summary of the Three Degrees*—an ascent to greater and greater peace, {with} fewer obstacles: *ad primum ascendimus per* laborem *humilitatis, ad secundum per* affectum *compassionis, ad tertium per* excessum *contemplationis. In primo veritas reperitur severa; in secundo, pia; in tertio, pura. Ad primum ratio ducit, qua nos discutimus; ad secundum affectus perducit, quo aliis miseremur; ad tertium puritas rapit, qua ad invisibilia sublevamur.*[233] Analyze these expressions—{the} gradation from *ducit* {through} *perducit* {to} *rapit*; {from} *ratio* {through} *affectus* {to} *puritas* = {from} *labor* {through} *affectus* {to} *excessus*. To understand St. Bernard we have to know how to weigh his words and see them in their relation to one another. The term *puritas* here means very much more when we see it as the end of an ascent from *ratio* through *affectus*. This becomes all the more evident in {n.} 20,[234] where he assigns the first degree to the action of the Word, the second to the Holy Spirit, the third to the Father. {The} *action of the Word*, {when He} finds the reason *weighed* down by flesh, *captive* to sin, *blind* with ignorance, *giving itself to external things*, liberates the reason—*clementer assumens, potenter erigens, prudenter instruens, introrsum trahens*[235]—by compunction and humility, in which reason acts as the "vicar"[236] of the Word. Note {that} this rest {is} *achieved by good activity*. {Through the} *action of the Holy Spirit*, {which} finds the will poisoned with the infection of the flesh but already corrected by reason, {the will} remains to be lifted up and strength-

---

233. Col. 952CD ("To the first we ascend through the work of humility, to the second through the feeling of compassion, to the third through the ecstasy of contemplation. On the first, Truth is found to be severe; on the second, caring; on the third, pure. Reason leads to the first, in which we scrutinize ourselves; affection guides us to the second, in which we have pity on others; purity carries us away to the third, in which we are lifted up to invisible realities").

234. Cols. 952C–953A (copy text reads: "note 20").

235. Col. 953B ("assuming it mercifully, upraising it powerfully, instructing it prudently, drawing it within").

236. *"vicaria"* (col. 953B).

ened by the Holy Spirit (otherwise only discouragement can result): *dignanter visitans*[237]—{the} condescending love of God for the soul {is} a "presence" in our mercy and compassion for others; *suaviter purgans*[238]—the purgation is sweet and pleasant, consoling; *ardenter afficiens*[239]—{there is an} inspiration of ardent love—all culminating in mercy. The Second Degree of Truth is a rest in the action of compassionate mercy for others. *Note* that a good religious is not easily disedified. {The} Second Degree of Truth liberates us from the unrest and turmoil and labor produced by reactions to the apparent faults of others. *What happens* {is that} the seeds of the same faults are in ourselves, and when we see them in others, {the} same activity or inordinate passion is stirred up in us {and so} we criticize and condemn—{we} are "scandalized." But {the} psalm tells us: *Pax multa diligentibus legem tuam, et non est illis scandalum.*[240] Rest {is} impossible as long as we are disturbed by faults of others and lose our peace. True peace {is} not found without compassion that *includes, not excludes,* {one's} brother. As a result of this action of the Word and the Spirit, the reason no longer resists truth, and the will no longer resists reason and mercy. {Then} follows the Third Degree, the action of the Father.

4. {The} THIRD DEGREE OF TRUTH {is} contemplation: perfect union with God—as Spouse—in an experience of "glory." *Gloriosam sibi sponsam Pater conglutinat* (n. 21).[241] Rest is here perfect—the soul is no longer aware of itself nor of anyone else. UT NEC RATIO DE SE NEC VOLUNTAS DE PROXIMO COGITARE SINATUR, SED HOC SOLUM ILLA BEATA ANIMA DICERE DELECTATUR, INTRODUXIT ME REX

---

237. Col. 953B.

238. Col. 953B, which reads: "*suaviter pugnans*" (presumably a misprint).

239. Col. 953B.

240. Ps. 118[119]:165 ("Much peace have they that love thy law, and to them there is no stumbling block").

241. Col. 953C ("the Father attaches the glorious spouse closely to Himself").

IN CUBICULUM SUUM.²⁴² This is the description of that *puritas* which knows God alone—the Truth in Himself. {These are the} characteristics of this contemplation, as described in *De Gradibus*, n. 21:

1. It is a union of love with God, the satisfaction of all the desires of the soul, the possession of Him for Whom she has been longing.

2. The virtues and good actions of the soul contribute to the joy of this union (*suffulta floribus, ac stipata malis, bonis scilicet moribus et virtutibus sanctis*[243]).

3. It is a perfect repose in God, a "sleep" in His arms, but does not last long. *Ibi modicum, hora videlicet quasi dimidia, silentio facto in coelo, inter desideratos amplexus suaviter quiescens, ipsa quidem dormit.*[244]

4. But above and beyond this rest and sleep is a higher and transcendent activity, in which the soul contemplates and knows God. We shall see in another conference[245] how St. Bernard calls this a "vigilant" sleep that is full of life—*vigilis vitalisque sopor.*[246] There *can* be a contemplation in which all is so dark that we seem to be utterly idle. But it is often hard to say whether this is contemplation. Those who have *sensus exercitatos* (St. Paul, Hebrews 5) by experience,[247] can tell true contemplation. {There is} some-

---

242. Col. 953C ("neither is the reason allowed to focus on itself nor is the will allowed to dwell on the neighbor, but that blessed soul is delighted to speak of this alone: 'The King has led me into His chamber'").

243. Col. 953D ("cushioned by flowers, stayed up by apples, that is, by good deeds and holy virtues").

244. Col. 953D ("There for a short time, indeed half an hour, while there is silence in heaven, sweetly resting in those desired embraces, she indeed sleeps").

245. See pages 392–93 below.

246. *Sermo 52 in Cantica*, n. 3 (*PL* 183, col. 1031A, which reads: *"vitalis vigilque sopor"*) ("sleep . . . wakeful and life-giving" [Luddy, *Sermons on the Canticle*, 2.94]).

247. *"Perfectorum autem est solidus cibus eorum qui pro consuetudine exercitatos habent sensus ad discretionem boni ac mali"* ("But strong meat is for the

thing in it of an *awakening*, {a} realization of a new world *more real* than the everyday reality of life: (1) sometimes {it is} *seen in and through* ordinary reality; (2) sometimes {it} blacks out all other reality; (3) generally {it is} hard to grasp precisely what it is—{it is} more *real*, but not necessarily more *definite*. {There is a} sense that there is a reality *not seen*, which is infinitely above what is seen, and it is *present* and *living*. *Sed cor ejus vigilat, quo utique interim* veritatis arcana *rimatur . . . .* videt invisibilia, audit ineffabilia, quae non licet homini loqui.[248] This contemplation makes all lower knowledge look like darkness (*nox nocti indicat scientiam*[249]).

5. Above all, it is a pure gift of God, and no effort of our own can raise us to this level (*puritas rapit*[250]) (cf. nn. 22–23[251]).

6. It is secret and, in itself, incommunicable (cf. above). *Tertio ad arcana veritatis rapiuntur et aiunt, secretum meum mihi."* [252] Secrecy {means here a} good instinct to keep quiet about graces. {The} director must know what is going on, must be able to understand. {It is} best if you feel that slight indications are sufficient to make him understand. {There should be a} *sharing* of experience, {without} "irreverence" in dragging it out and explaining {it} according to a text book: {it is a} dead thing then {and} no longer real.

7. In a certain sense, it is an ascent into heaven. {Bernard gives a} long explanation of the fact that the Father is not "sent,"[253]

---

perfect: for them who by custom have their senses exercised to the discerning of good and evil") (Heb. 5:14).

248. Cols. 953D–954A ("but her heart wakes, and in the meantime discovers the secrets of truth . . . . she sees what is invisible, hears what is ineffable, which man is not permitted to speak").

249. Col. 954A ("knowledge which night discloses to night").

250. Col. 952C ("purity carries us away").

251. Cols. 954A–955B.

252. Col. 955B ("In the third they are carried up to the mysteries of truth, and they say, my secret is mine").

253. "*numquam . . . ad terras legitur missus fuisse*" (col. 954C) ("never is it read that He had been sent to earth").

and does not come down, but in contemplation we are raised up to Him. This is a very deep and important point. It shows how thoroughly convinced St. Bernard was that contemplation takes us *entirely out of ourselves*. It is not merely *a rest in ourselves*, not a repose in the grace which we feel within us—such effects might be compatible with the other degrees of truth, with certain visitations of the Spouse short of rapture. But as long as we are aware of ourselves and "in ourselves," we have not reached what he calls true contemplation—*raptus, excessus, puritas amoris*.

QUIES CONTEMPLATIONIS II: Another Text on Contemplation—*The Fourth Degree of Love* (*De Diligendo Deo*, c. 10, n. 27[254]): note the first three degrees: *Amor carnalis—qua homo diligit seipsum propter seipsum*:[255] {we} *love ourselves for ourselves*. {This is} natural love of ourself *and of our fellow man*. In order to really love other men we must love God. Hence {the} second degree {is} *Amor Dei (carnalis) propter nosmetipsos*:[256] {We} *love God for ourselves. Amor Dei justus*[257] {is the} third degree, in which we love God for His own sake {and} obey Him out of love. {We} *love God for Himself. Amor Dei sanctus*[258] {is the} fourth degree—*excessus amoris*[259]—in which we love ourselves for God's sake. {We} *love ourselves for God*. (Note that while it is inadvisable to examine too closely our degree of prayer, these degrees of love are very revealing, and we should certainly sometimes stop to reflect on the quality, fervor and intensity of our love for Him. This favors compunction, gratitude {and} humility, and these are excellent means of purifying our hearts.)

254. *PL* 182, col. 990BD.
255. Col. 988A ("carnal love, in which man loves himself for his own sake").
256. "*Amat . . . propter se*" (col. 989B) ("He loves for his own sake").
257. "*Amat juste*" (col. 989D) ("he loves justly").
258. Col. 991A, which reads: "*O amor sanctus*" ("O holy love").
259. "ecstasy of love"; for a definition of the term *excessus* and its relation to *exstasis*, see Gilson, *Mystical Theology of Saint Bernard*, 237, n. 156; for the influence of Maximus the Confessor on Bernard's use of this term to signify ecstasy, see 26–27; for the conditions of its realization, see 108–11; for the *excessus* of charity in Christ's death on the cross, see 105, n. 149.

Explanation of this *Fourth Degree* ({n.} 28[260]):

1. Why is it necessary? because God made all things for Himself. We must love ourselves for the reason for which we were made, the reason for which God loves us. WE MUST LOVE OURSELVES PERFECTLY BECAUSE WE BELONG TO GOD.

2. Only in this way do we perfectly fulfill the will of God in ourselves—loving ourselves as He loves us, *because* His will is perfectly fulfilled in us. *Ut quomodo Deus omnia esse voluit propter semetipsum, sic nos quoque* NEC NOS IPSOS, NEC ALIUD QUID FUISSE, VEL ESSE VELIMUS, NISI AEQUE PROPTER IPSUM, OB SOLAM IPSIUS VOLUNTATEM, *non nostram voluptatem.*[261] (Note: obviously, this is impossible unless our love is absolutely pure of all selfishness and of every imperfection. He says this is only permanently achieved in heaven, yet we taste something of it in rapture. The detachment St. Bernard speaks of cannot be acquired merely by ascetic effort; it comes with a mystical grace.)

3. We have to taste the pleasure of loving ourselves as God loves us in order to have the highest of all joys, the most complete of all joys, a joy that His will is done *in us*, a joy that finds its reason not in the fact that we are pleased, but in the fact that *He* is pleased, and pleased *with us*. *Delectabit sane non tam nostra, vel sopita necessitas, vel sortita felicitas* QUAM QUOD EJUS IN NOBIS, ET DE NOBIS VOLUNTAS *ADIMPLETA VIDEBITUR* (n. 28 [991]).[262]

4. This *Fourth Degree* is demanded by {the} reverence we owe to God, our Creator and Redeemer. Creation and Redemption (image and likeness) indicate that our being has a certain worth in His eyes. We are precious in His sight, because of *His* goodness, not our own. If we do not fulfill our destiny, His mercy

---

260. Cols. 990D–992A (copy text reads: "note 28").

261. Cols. 990D–991A, which reads: ". . . *aliud aliquid . . . solam videlicet ipsius* . . ." ("Just as God willed all things to exist for Himself, so we also should will that nothing, not we ourselves nor anything else, should have existed or should exist except equally for His sake, on account of His will alone, and not for our pleasure").

262. "Neither necessity satisfied nor happiness attained will delight us so much as that His will in us and for us will be seen to be fulfilled."

is frustrated in us. His mercy must be fulfilled, *have its way in us.* If we did not exist and act, this could not be. Our being, our actions, therefore, become valuable to us in proportion as we love God, and desire His will to be done in us. (N.B. {there can be a} *false desire of death*, out of selfishness.) *Our faults* give God scope for mercy and glory in us. {It} takes high sanctity to see and live this perfectly—as {did} St. Thérèse.[263] This is what we pray for

---

263. See the Epilogue to Thérèse's autobiography (written by her sister Pauline [Mother Agnes]): "She recognized her own limitations clearly, and she accepted all the humiliations of her state of sickness with its weakness, tears, impatience, especially in the presence of a tiresome Sister. When she was corrected for showing impatience with this Sister, she said: '*Oh! How happy I am to see myself imperfect and to be in need of God's mercy so much even at the moment of my death!*' ") (*Story of a Soul: The Autobiography of St. Thérèse of Lisieux*, trans. John Clarke, OCD [Washington, DC: Institute of Carmelite Studies, 1976], 267). Thérèse evidently refers to the same incident in a May 28, 1897 letter to Mother Agnes: "I am glad you saw my imperfection. Ah! What good it does me to have been bad! You have not scolded your little girl, though she deserved it; but the little girl is used to that, your mildness affects her more deeply than stern words; for her you are the image of the good God's mercy. . . . I am happier for having been imperfect than if, upheld by grace, I had been a model of sweetness" (*Collected Letters of Saint Thérèse of Lisieux*, trans. Frank J. Sheed [New York: Sheed & Ward, 1949], 336–37). In a journal entry for July 18, 1948, Merton writes: "Fr. Urban, in a very good sermon . . . told of the Little Flower being glad on her deathbed, not only that she could be judged as imperfect, but that it actually was true. That struck me very deeply. All my desires draw me more and more in that direction. To be little, to be nothing, to rejoice in your imperfections, to be glad that you are not worthy of attention, that you are of no account in the universe. This is the only liberation, the only way to true solitude" (Thomas Merton, *Entering the Silence: Becoming a Monk and Writer. Journals, vol. 2, 1941–1952*, ed. Jonathan Montaldo [San Francisco: HarperCollins, 1996], 219). See also Merton's comments on the influence of this teaching of St. Thérèse on the Trappistine Mother Berchmans: "Now at last Mother Berchmans had discovered that her weaknesses, her stubborn imperfections, the faults that seemed so great in her own eyes, and which had caused her pain for so long—all these things now appeared to her for what they were: fuel to cast upon the fire of God's merciful love that the flames might altogether consume

each day in the *Pater Noster*: *"Fiat voluntas tua sicut in coelo, et in terra."*[264]

*Summary*: St. Bernard leads us to a height of peace and love in which we find ourselves in God and see ourselves from within God, loving ourselves with His love of us, which is also His love of Himself. This also applies to other people, in heaven. *The Fourth Degree of Love is the highest peace, to which we all aspire*: (1) it is the term of all our aspirations and strivings (see {the} Scripture texts {at the} beginning of n. 27: *Factus est in pace locus eius*[265]); (2) it is a foretaste of beatitude, a pledge of sanctity: *"Beatum dixerim et sanctum, cui tale aliquid in hac mortali vita . . . vel semel {. . .} experiri donatum est"* (990);[266] (3) it is a perfect fulfillment of the first commandment (n. 29 [992]); (4) it is really only permanently possessed when we are free from our mortal bodies, for then there is no obstacle to this perfect love of God. Ordinary obstacles {include} *"necessitas corporis, fraterna caritas."*[267] In what sense is "charity" an obstacle? The active exercise of charity cannot be carried on at the same time as we experience the "rapture" of pure love of God. To return from contemplation to action is a descent—but a necessary one. It is willed by God as a fruit and sign of mystical marriage, and increases our merits. In a sense it also further increases our capacity for joy, contemplation, pure love, by a more complete giving of ourselves. The

---

them. . . . God's mercy was infinite; He needed only to be asked, and He would do away with all these failings in His own good time and in His own wise way. Far from causing her discouragement, they would in the future be nothing but motives for hope and for greater trust in the mercy of God" (Thomas Merton, *Exile Ends in Glory: The Life of a Trappistine, Mother M. Berchmans, O.C.S.O.* [Milwaukee, WI: Bruce, 1948], 162–63).

264. "Thy will be done on earth as it is in heaven" (Matt. 6:10).

265. Col. 990B (Ps. 75[76]:3) ("His place is in peace").

266. "I would call him blessed and holy, to whom something such as this has been given to be experienced in this mortal life, even if only once."

267. Col. 990D, which reads: *"carnis necessitas . . . fraterna . . . charitas"* ("The need of the flesh . . . fraternal love").

Fourth Degree of Love is an *"excessus puritatis"*[268]—the same pure love as in the Third Degree of Truth:

1. {It entails} *complete self-forgetfulness. Te enim quodammodo perdere, tamquam qui non sis, et* OMNINO NON SENTIRE TEIPSUM, *et a teipso exinaniri, et paene annullari.*[269] *O pura et defaecata intentio voluntatis! eo certe defaecatior et purior, quo in ea de proprio nil jam admistum {relinquitur} . . . quousque ipsum cor cogitare jam non cogatur de corpore, et anima eidem in hoc statu vivificando et sensificando intendere desinat.*[270] {The} soul {is} no longer in any way weighed down by flesh, just as if it were free of the flesh, {with} no sense of the "self," no reflection on self. Again {we must} stress {the} difference between *moral* and *mystical* self-forgetfulness: moral {means that} by my will, {I} place my own interests behind those of others, so as no longer in some cases even to think of them, but {the} soul is immersed in {the} body and in human relations and in human concerns; mystical {means that the} soul is out of itself in God, {with} no sense of human relations or of itself.

2. {It is} *a completely supernatural love, in which there is nothing left of the human: totum divinum est quod sentitur* (991).[271] SIC OMNEM TUNC IN SANCTIS HUMANAM AFFECTIONEM QUODAM INEFFABILI MODO NECESSE ERIT A SEMETIPSA LIQUESCERE, ATQUE IN DEI PENITUS TRANSFUNDI VOLUNTATEM (991).[272] *Quomodo omnia in omnibus erit Deus, si in homine de*

---

268. "an ecstasy of purity"; see *Sermo 52 in Cantica*, n. 5: "*excessus . . . angelicae puritatis*" (*PL* 183, col. 1031C) ("ecstasy . . . of angelic purity" [Luddy, *Sermons on the Canticle*, 2.95–96]).

269. Col. 990C ("To lose yourself in a way, as though you did not exist, and not to be aware of yourself at all, to be emptied of yourself, and nearly annihilated").

270. Nn. 28, 29 (cols. 991A, 992A) ("O pure and cleansed intention of the will! surely more cleansed and pure, because in it there now remains nothing of the self mixed in . . . until the heart is no longer forced to think of the body, and the soul ceases to provide for the same body in this state by giving it life and sensation") (copy text reads: "*reliquitur*").

271. "what is experienced is completely divine."

272. "Thus, in the saints, it will then be necessary for all human affection to melt from itself in a certain inexplicable way, and be poured utterly into the will of God."

*homine quidquam supererit . . .*[273] *omnino non sentire teipsum* [{see} above] . . . *coelestis est conversationis, non humanae affectionis.*[274]

3. {It is} *an absolutely pure love of God—it is produced and sustained in us by God Himself: in Dei potentia roboretur*[275] (because there is nothing left of self to sustain our love). *Quippe quod Dei potentiae est dare cui vult, non humanae industriae assequi* (992).[276] Therefore {it is} not directly produced by any effort of ours, nor sustained by any technique.

4. *This love effects a complete transformation of the soul in God. Factus sibi* tamquam vas perditum, *totus pergat in Deum, et adhaerens Deo* unus fiat cum eo spiritus (990).[277] (Note: *factus tamquam vas perditum*[278] and *unus fieri cum Deo spiritus*[279] {are} phrases from Scripture, which take on a technical meaning in St. Bernard—{they} always refer to mystical experience.) *Sic affici deificari est*[280] (991; cf. Greek Fathers[281]): like a drop of water in wine, like iron in the fire—our "substance" remains; we are not destroyed, but we are totally elevated to a new mode of existence which is

---

273. Col. 991B ("How will God be all in all if anything of man remains in man?").

274. Col. 990C ("not to be aware of yourself at all . . . is a matter of heavenly encounter, not of human affection").

275. Col. 992A ("it is strengthened in the power of God").

276. "Indeed it belongs to the power of God to give this to whom He wills, not to be attained by human effort."

277. "Having become for himself like a broken vessel, he goes forth completely into God, and clinging to God, becomes one spirit with Him" (text reads: ". . . *sibi ipsi tanquam* . . .").

278. Ps. 30[31]:13.

279. 1 Cor. 6:17.

280. "To be thus affected is to be divinized."

281. Gilson traces Bernard's use of the language of deification specifically to Maximus the Confessor (see *Mystical Theology of Saint Bernard*, 132; also 25–28); for a discussion of patristic teaching on divinization, which includes its influence on the Cistercians, see Thomas Merton, *An Introduction to Christian Mysticism: Initiation into the Monastic Tradition* 3, ed. Patrick F. O'Connell, Monastic Wisdom [MW], vol. 13 (Kalamazoo, MI: Cistercian Publications, 2008), 58–67.

divine. *Manebit quidem substantia, sed in alia forma, alia gloria, alia potentia.*[282]

5. *In its most perfect expression this love requires to be fulfilled in a glorified body.* But before the resumption of the body, the soul "rests" in glory, while the body rests in death (nn. 30–31[283]).

6. *The martyrs tasted this perfect love more perfectly than anyone on earth.* It raised them completely above the sufferings of the flesh (992).

7. *In its most imperfect form, in transient rapture, this love is interrupted by the soul's recall to the body, and by the claims of fraternal charity, the active life. Subito invidet saeculum nequam, perturbat diei malitia, corpus mortis aggravat, sollicitat carnis necessitas, defectus corruptionis non sustinet, quodque his violentius est,* FRATERNA REVOCAT CHARITAS (990).[284]

QUIES CONTEMPLATIONIS III—in the Sermons on the *Canticle of Canticles*:

A. SERMON 23:[285] the "three cellars"[286] and the *cubiculum*.[287] {Situating} *the three cellars* {in} context, {the} beginning of the sermon shows the spouse, the fervent soul, the contemplative soul, animated with {an} ardent desire to enter into the good things of God. *Quae amat ardentius, currit velocius, et citius pervenit.* . . . *Caritas sponsae non quiescit.*[288] The charity of the spouse does not allow her a *false* rest that reposes outside of God. She must

---

282. Col. 991B ("The substance will indeed remain, but in another form, another glory, another power").

283. Cols. 993A–994A.

284. "At once the wicked world is envious, the malice of the day disturbs, the mortal body weighs down, the need of the flesh agitates, the weakness of corruption does not support, and what is more violent than these, fraternal charity calls back."

285. *PL* 183, cols. 884A–894A; see also pages 299–306 above.

286. *"cellas . . . tres"* (n. 5 [col. 886C]).

287. Col. 888D ("bedchamber" [Luddy, *Sermons on the Canticle*, 1.244]).

288. Col. 884BC ("[she] runs more swiftly because she loves more ardently, and so reaches her destination more speedily. . . . The charity of the Spouse is not at rest" [Luddy, *Sermons on the Canticle*, 1.234–35]).

press on to union with Him. Nor does it allow her to neglect her companions, whom she also urges to follow her to the same end. Quietism {is} excluded. Contemplation {is} essentially apostolic, hence the paradox that the charity of the spouse cannot rest—that is, outside perfect *raptus* and *excessus* her charity must be active: before rapture, {in} seeking and desiring union; after rapture, {in} communicating its fruit to others. (This sermon, later than {the} *De Diligendo Deo*, shows no *regret* at having to fall back from contemplation into action.) Sola introducta videor, sed soli non proderit [distinguish: some souls get graces not to be revealed]. *Vestrum omnium est meus omnis* profectus (n. 2 [885]).[289] Then there are several sections devoted to the senses of Scripture in which we find God: in the *literal* sense, as in a garden; in the *moral* sense, as in His storerooms; in the *spiritual* sense, as in the bridal chamber of contemplation.

Note n. 6:[290] {the} *moral* sense {is} divided into three parts: (1) that which teaches us *disciplina* (how to be a *"discipulus"*[291]—{by} humility): note {the} importance of {the} term *disciplina* in {the} sapiential books—formation by obedience, {through} subjection and testing, {with} the *timor* that leads to *sapientia*[292] (*sapor boni*[293]); (2) that which teaches us how to live sociably with others; (3) that which teaches us how to guide others. Compare {the}

---

289. Cols. 884D–885A ("I, indeed, appear to be the only one brought in, but I am not the only one deriving benefit therefrom. For every advantage to me belongs equally to all of you " [Luddy, *Sermons on the Canticle*, 1.236]).

290. Cols. 886D–887B.

291. Col. 886D, 887A ("discipline"; "disciples" [Luddy, *Sermons on the Canticle*, 1.240]).

292. "*Tunc primum Deus animae sapit, cum eam afficit ad timendum, non cum instruit ad sciendum. Times Dei justitiam, times potentiam; et sapit tibi justus et potens Deus, quia timor sapor est*" (n. 14 [col. 892A]) ("it is only then that the soul begins to relish God, when she is inspired with the fear of Him, not when she is instructed in the knowledge of Him. You fear the divine justice, you fear the divine power, and hence . . . fear gives savour" [Luddy, *Sermons on the Canticle*, 1.252]).

293. "a taste for the good."

*Three Degrees of Truth*, and especially the Second Degree (see 887B). The "cellar" of those who guide others is the *cella vinaria*,[294] {since} wine {symbolizes the} zeal of ardent charity.

Note n. 8:[295] the three cellars are three degrees of peace. (Note {the} importance of recognizing our proper cellar, and being there as long as God wills.)

a) *Quam multi sub praeceptore quieti vivunt, quos si jugo absolvas, {videas} non posse quiescere.*[296] Some therefore belong in the first cellar.

b) *Innumeros cernes* simpliciter ac sine querela inter fratres conversari, *super fratres non solum inutiliter, sed et insipienter et nequiter. . . . minime egentes magistro, nec tamen idonei magisterio.*[297] The majority belong to the second group.

c) (The superiors) *Qui* humiliter *praesunt.*[298] (Few are useful superiors, fewer still humble superiors; these latter have peace.) To be both humble and a good superior one must have "discretion," "the mother of virtues"[299] (888B), and one must be inebriated with the wine of charity to the point of complete self-forgetfulness. Note that in this sermon St. Bernard identifies the Spouse of the Word and the abbot. The abbot should be the one

---

294. Col. 885C, which reads: *"cellam vinariam"* ("wine-cellar" [Luddy, *Sermons on the Canticle*, 1.242]) (Cant. 2:4).

295. Col. 888AD.

296. Col. 888A, which reads: ". . . *multi denique sub . . .*" ("How many there are who live a quiet life under the eye of a superior, yet whom, if released from the yoke of subjection, you would find incapable of repose" [Luddy, *Sermons on the Canticle*, 1.243–44]) (copy text reads: *"vides"*).

297. Col. 888AB, which reads: ". . . *minime quidem egentes . . .*" ("How many also do you behold conversing with their equals sincerely and without offence, who, if raised to the rank of superior, would show themselves to be not only useless, but devoid of good sense, and even wanting in probity. . . . They do not indeed any longer need the watchful supervision of a master, but neither are they qualified to act as the masters of others" [Luddy, *Sermons on the Canticle*, 1.244]).

298. Col. 888B, which reads: *"qui et humiliter praesint"* ("who can govern with humility" [Luddy, *Sermons on the Canticle*, 1.244]).

299. *"matrem virtutum discretionem."*

most advanced in prayer, charity and union, *because it is his function to lead others into the ways of Divine Union*. {The} rest of number 8 {provides a} description of the union of fervor and discretion, and other virtues of superiors.

*Summary*: the "three cellars" {are} different realms of peace and quiet. It is most difficult to find peace and quiet in superiorship. Exterior quiet is not possible, usually. Peace depends on being so full of charity as to be "out of oneself" in love for others, therefore completely detached from our interests and plans.

*The Cubiculum: Dixi . . . in theoricae contemplationis arcano regis esse quaerendum cubiculum* (889A).[300] But just as there are many cellars in the King's palace, and not all souls are called to the same ones, so too with His *cubicula*. {There are} various levels of contemplation, not all of them perfectly "quiet." The Father Himself selects those who are to enter the various mansions of contemplation. *Non omnibus in uno loco frui datur grata et secreta sponsi praesentia, sed ut cuique paratum est a Patre ipsius. Non enim nos eum elegimus, sed ipse elegit nos, et posuit nos; et ubi ab eo quisque positus est, ibi est* (n. 9 [889]).[301] *Thomas in latere, Joannes in pectore, Petrus in sinu Patris, Paulus in tertio coelo, secreti hujus gratiam sunt assecuti.*[302] {Note the} importance of each one following his own individual vocation: St. Thomas reaches {the} light of contemplation through faith; St. John, through love of Jesus; St. Paul, *in*

---

300. "I have observed . . . that it is in the privacy of loving contemplation we must look for the King's bedchamber" (Luddy, *Sermons on the Canticle*, 1.246).

301. Text reads: ". . . *uno in loco* . . ." ("Not all are permitted to enjoy in the same chamber the delightful and secret presence of the Beloved, but each in that only which has been prepared for her by the Father. For it is not we that have chosen Him, but He hath first chosen us and appointed us our several places. And wheresoever each has been put by Him, there he ought to remain" [Luddy, *Sermons on the Canticle*, 1.246]).

302. Col. 889B ("St. Thomas obtained the grace of this secret in the Saviour's Side, St. John on His Breast, St. Peter in the Father's Bosom, St. Paul in the third heaven" [Luddy, *Sermons on the Canticle*, 1.246–47]).

*intimo sapientiae*;³⁰³ St. Peter, *in luce veritatis.*³⁰⁴ Each one finds in his "place" the end of his journey, and rests in God.

*St. Bernard now begins to speak of his own experience in contemplation.* These various mansions which he "knows" are not, he admits, the highest and the most secret. (That is, he does not treat them here.) N. 11 {focuses on} "the council chamber" (St. Bernard does not explicitly use this term—it is not yet a *cubiculum.*) *Est locus apud Sponsum, de quo sua jura decernit.*³⁰⁵

This contemplation is intellectual rather than loving. It penetrates truly into the divine decrees. It admires them and takes delight in what it sees. It shares in a divine secret. It sees "what God is doing." It sees how He disposeth all things sweetly. But this involves a certain activity. God it sees, not resting but "working." Hence this is not a place of *rest* in the true sense. Note that in all these degrees St. Bernard is interested above all in an experience not only of what God *is* but of what He *does*—more precisely, WHO He is, as mainfested by what He does. Love penetrates the intimate secrets of the Beloved. *Est locus altus et secretus, sed minime quietus. Nam et ipse, quantum in se est, disponit omnia suaviter, disponit tamen; et contemplantem, qui forte eo loci pervenerit,* quiescere non permittit . . . *rimantem et admirantem* fatigat, et reddit inquietum.³⁰⁶ The "heart watcheth":³⁰⁷ *in vigiliis vero inquietae nihilominus curiositatis ac laboriosae exercitationis pati se fatigationem*

---

303. N. 10 (col. 889B) ("in the profundity of wisdom" [Luddy, *Sermons on the Canticle*, 1.247]).

304. Col. 889B ("in the light of truth" [Luddy, *Sermons on the Canticle*, 1.247]).

305. Col. 890A ("There is in the home of the Bridegroom a certain place where . . . He frames His decrees" [Luddy, *Sermons on the Canticle*, 1.248]).

306. Col. 890AB, which reads: ". . . *locus iste altus . . . Nam etsi ipse, . . . fatigat, redditque. . .*" ("It is a lofty place and a secret, but very far from quiet. For although, as far as depends on Him, He 'disposeth all things sweetly,' still He really does dispose. And He will not suffer the contemplative soul which, perchance, has found her way to this place, to rest there peacefully . . . He wearies and disquiets her in ways no less pleasant than marvellous" [Luddy, *Sermons on the Canticle*, 1.248]).

307. "*cor suum vigilare*" (col. 990B) (Cant. 5:2).

*significat* (890).[308] There is great sweetness in this work, but unrest also, and the soul sometimes would like to escape from the sweetness, and the labor. In this degree of prayer, grace is at work, doubtless a certain mystical grace, but it stimulates an activity within the soul which is not completely passive. {The} intellect sees but does not possess. {There is} light, but not rest, {and there is a} danger of wearing oneself out pursuing this light too far. *"Non igitur locus est iste cubiculi, ubi nequaquam per omnem modum quiescitur"* (890C).[309] This is not the end of the journey, not the terminus of any vocation.

N. 12 {presents the} "Dark Night," in the sense in which it was experienced by a Jeremias. Note that in these degrees of contemplation, we might tend to compare St. Bernard with St. John of the Cross, whereas he himself was probably thinking of his own experience in the light of the experiences of the prophets. Here God is seen in the severity of His judgements. This severity is seen by the soul not in the effects of the judgement, but so to speak from within God. *Est item locus, de quo super rationalem reprobam quidem creaturam immobilis vigilat secretissima et severissima animadversio justi judicis Dei.*[310] St. Bernard is thinking of the terrible judgements of God upon Israel that thought herself just: *in terra sanctorum iniqua gessit.*[311] He seems to have shared something of the experience of Isaias and Jeremias, in regard to the clerics, etc. of his own time. He refers to them here.

---

308. "For she thus signifies that . . . she nevertheless endures fatigue in the watching of her unquiet curiosity and in her painful activity, she signifies that she suffers weariness" (Luddy, *Sermons on the Canticle*, 1.248).

309. "No bedchamber of the King, therefore, can this place be, since the soul therein is not permitted to enjoy perfect repose" (Luddy, *Sermons on the Canticle*, 1.248).

310. Col. 890C ("There is another place, whence is kept an immutable watch over the reprobate rational creatures, by the just vengeance, as severe as it is secret, of the most righteous Judge" [Luddy, *Sermons on the Canticle*, 1.249]).

311. Col. 891A ("In the land of the saints, he hath done wicked things" [Luddy, *Sermons on the Canticle*, 1.250]) (Isa. 26:10).

N. 13 continues the description of this *locus terribilis*.[312] *Habet haec visio tremorem judicii, non securitatem cubiculi. Terribilis est locus iste, et totius expers quietis.*[313] However, this is a *mystical* experience. One is carried into it by "rapture." *Totus inhorrui si quando in eam raptus sum.*[314] It is a *locus Dei: Est tamen locus Dei et iste . . . domus Dei, et porta coeli.*[315]

N. 14: distinguishing this from the previous kind of contemplation, St. Bernard says that true mystical contemplation is found in the *locus terribilis*, not in the former, rather intellectual contemplation of God's judgements. This is a mystical experience produced by *fear*: *Hic sanctum et terribile nomen ejus, et tamquam ingressus gloriae.*[316] It would seem that for St. Bernard, the "beginning of mystical wisdom" is a fear in which we *experience* the greatness and sanctity of God. He stresses the fact that here we are in passive possession of God. In the previous experience we received instruction. Here we are "affected or changed." *Ibi instruimur, hic* afficimur. *Instructio doctos reddit, affectio sapientes.*[317] Here we not only see what God has decreed, but we are moved

---

312. Col. 890C ("place [which is] terrible" [Luddy, *Sermons on the Canticle*, 1.249]).

313. Col. 891B, which reads: ". . . *visio tremorem* [alias, *terrorem*] *judicii* . . ." ("This vision is better calculated to inspire one with the terror of judgement than to suggest the security of a bedchamber. Terrible in truth is this place, and entirely incompatible with the quiet of repose" [Luddy, *Sermons on the Canticle*, 1.250]).

314. Col. 891B ("I shudder all over, whenever I enter it" [Luddy, *Sermons on the Canticle*, 1.250]).

315. Col. 891C, which reads: ". . . *Dei locus* . . ." ("Nevertheless, even this is a place of God . . . the house of God and the gate of heaven" [Luddy, *Sermons on the Canticle*, 1.251]) (Gen. 28:17).

316. N. 13 (col. 891CD) ("His name is holy and terrible, and, . . . as it it were, the vestibule of His glory" [Luddy, *Sermons on the Canticle*, 1.251]).

317. Col. 891D, which reads: ". . . *instruimur quidem, sed hic* . . ." ("There our minds are instructed, here our wills are affected. By being so instructed we become learned; by being so affected we are made wise" [Luddy, *Sermons on the Canticle*, 1.251]).

to comply with His decrees. This obedience and conformity of wills puts us in possession of God and delivers us (at least in this experience) from the danger of the "science which puffeth up."[318] This is an experience of God, in mystical wisdom beginning with fear. *Tunc primum Deus animae sapit, cum eam afficit ad timendum* (892A).[319] "*Sapit tibi justus et potens Deus, quia timor sapor est.*"[320] It is a true experience of God. It bears fruit in humility and in obedience to His will. It is something far above and beyond compunction, it would seem. But it is not a "*locus quietus.*"[321] To resume—not all mystical contemplation is an experience of rest or union. There is a "terrible" contemplation which experiences God in fear but does not rest in Him.

NN. 15–16 {discuss the} "LOCUS SPONSI"[322]—{the} true quiet {of} mystical union. SED EST LOCUS, UBI VERE QUIESCENS ET QUIETUS CERNITUR DEUS (892).[323] Once again, note the objectivity of St. Bernard's contemplation. We do not see God as quiet because the soul is quiet. Our contemplation is not the projection of an interior, subjective effect in our own lives upon God. Our soul becomes quiet when, entering deeper into God, it sees Him more truly as He is. In the "terrible" vision,[324] God is as He is, nor does He change, in Himself, from terrible to quiet. The same God is terrible to those who are opposed to Him, quiet with those who are united to Him. This quiet is produced by the certitude, the experience, of the infinite and eternal mercy of God. It *experiences*

---

318. "*sua scientia inflat*" (col. 892A) (1 Cor. 8:1).

319. "it is only then the soul begins to relish God, when she is inspired with the fear of Him" (Luddy, *Sermons on the Canticle*, 1.252).

320. "You fear the divine justice, you fear the divine power, and hence . . . fear gives savour" (Luddy, *Sermons on the Canticle*, 1.252).

321. "a quiet place."

322. N. 15 (col. 892B) ("the place . . . of the Bridegroom" [Luddy, *Sermons on the Canticle*, 1.253]).

323. "But there is a third place, where the Lord appears truly tranquil and at rest" (Luddy, *Sermons on the Canticle*, 1.253).

324. Col. 891B.

the reality of His decrees to forgive sinners and wipe out sin, and in this experience enters into the very Mercy of God Himself. He *speaks* His mercy to the soul (not a meditation on mercy!). CLARE IBI AGNOSCITUR MISERICORDIA DOMINI AB AETERNO, ET USQUE IN AETERNUM SUPER TIMENTES EUM (892).[325] This is *not* a peace which is based on the sense that *we are just*, that we have deserved no punishment. On the contrary, the terrible vision has dispelled that myth. It sees that all have sinned and need the glory of God (Romans 3:23). *Non peccare, Dei justitia est. Hominis justitia, indulgentia Dei* (892).[326] But it is convinced (in the experience of a hope elevated and strengthened by mystical grace) of the reality of God's mercy—not only on those in general who are to be saved, but on *us*, concretely and particularly, whom He has saved. This experience finds peace, quiet, in the certitude of a hope that already grasps and as it were firmly possesses the "evidence" of our election. *Stat propositum Dei, stat sententia pacis super timentes eum, ipsorum et dissimulans mala et remunerans bona.*[327] The joy and confidence produced by this experience are proportionate to the horror and fear of the other. {There is a} conviction that He will not change. {This is} true contemplation, not speculation—not "understanding" mercy but receiving and experiencing it—how? by *hope* and love. This is the true *cubiculum* (n. 17), based on the unchangeable solidarity of a divine promise. Note how *objective* {it is}, completely above *feelings* of peace. O VERE QUIETIS LOCUS, ET QUEM NON IMMERITO CUBICULI APPELLATIONE CENSUERIM! . . . *Visio ista non terret, sed mulcet; inquietam curiositatem non excitat, sed sedat; nec fatigat sensus, sed tranquillat. Hic vere quiescitur.* TRANQUILLUS

---

325. "There we can plainly see that 'the mercy of the Lord is from eternity and unto eternity upon them that fear Him'" (Luddy, *Sermons on the Canticle*, 1.253) (Ps. 102[103]:17).

326. "God's righteousness is freedom from sin, but the righteousness of man is the forgiveness of God" (Luddy, *Sermons on the Canticle*, 1.254).

327. "The purpose of God stands fixed, as well as His decree of mercy 'upon them that fear Him,' overlooking what is evil in them and rewarding what is good" (Luddy, *Sermons on the Canticle*, 1.253).

*Deus tranquillat omnia: et quietum aspicere, quiescere est.*[328] And he proceeds to say that this peace is undisturbed not only by cares, regrets, anxieties, but even by images of bodily things. {In} *conclusion*, the quiet of contemplation in this sermon is the *quiet of the divine mercy*. It is a participation in the serenity of God, not by the contemplation or apprehension of His Infinite Being resting in Himself, but of His mercy drawing us to Himself. This contemplation is reached not so much through a theological or philosophical concept as through the apprehension of our election (by pure hope and love) as a "fact." It finds rest not merely in mercy abstractly considered as a divine attribute but experienced in its exercise in our own lives.

B. *Sermon 52 on the "Canticle of Canticles"*:[329] {the} title of the sermon ("*De excessu, qui contemplatio dicitur, in qua Sponsus facit quiescere animam sanctam, pro ejus quiete zelans*"[330]) {is an} admirable summary of the sermon, which comments on *Canticles* 2:7: "I adjure you, O you daughters of Jerusalem . . . that you stir not up nor make the beloved to awake, till she please."[331] Contemplation is an *excessus* (ecstasy), or a going out of ourselves, in which we are made to "sleep" to earthly things and passions by the Divine Bridegroom, and in this sleep of ours we are so pleasing to Him that He zealously protects us and will not have us to be disturbed.

---

328. "O place of true rest, and, in my opinion, well deserving to be called a bedchamber! . . . This vision soothes instead of terrifying. It lulls to rest, instead of arousing, our unquiet curiosity. It calms the mind instead of fatiguing it. Here is found perfect repose. The tranquillity of God tranquillises all about Him, and the contemplation of His rest is rest to the soul" (Luddy, *Sermons on the Canticle*, 1.255).

329. Cols. 1029C–1033C.

330. Col. 1029C ("On the ecstasy which is called contemplation, in which the Bridegroom makes the holy soul rest, zealous for its repose").

331. "*Adjuro vos, filiae Jerusalem, per capreos cervosque camporum, ut non excitetis neque evigilare faciatis dilectam, quoadusque ipsa velit*" (col. 1029D).

1. {The} context: in {the} previous sermon (nn. 5–10[332]), he speaks of the Word embracing the spouse with His right arm while His left hand is under her head (1027f.). The left hand and the right arm are two degrees of rest in the presence of the Word, Who comes to strengthen us and support us by His presence, whereas before we have been languishing in trial in His absence. *Felix anima quae {in} Christi recumbit pectore, et inter Verbi brachia quiescit* (Serm. 51.5 [1027]).[333] The passage from one degree of union to another depends in large measure upon *gratitude* (*idem*, n. 6). *Ingratitudo ventus urens, siccans sibi fontem pietatis, rorem misericordiae, fluentia gratiae.*[334] The left hand, according to St. Bernard's allegorical interpretation, is the "fear" of judgement (cf. {the} *locus terribilis* {in the} previous conference), and the right {arm} is the assured hope of heaven. Strictly speaking then, only the second is "rest." The "left hand" is not even "under the head"[335] where there is servile fear; {the} left hand under the head {is the} beginning of repose—where there is love of God and gratitude for His benefits, and fear of offending Him; {the} right arm embraces the spouse when her love is pure, when she loves Him for His own sake, and from this pure love draws perfect confidence of union with Him in heaven ([1028] n. 8). This embrace is a *suavitatis locus*,[336] where the spouse says, *in pace in idipsum dormiam, et requiescam* ([1028] n. 9).[337] (How well this ap-

---

332. Cols. 1027B–1029C.

333. Text reads: ". . . *requiescit*" ("Happy the soul that rests on the Bosom of Christ and reposes in the arms of the Word!" [Luddy, *Sermons on the Canticle*, 2.85]) (copy text omits "*in*").

334. N. 6 (col. 1027D) ("Ingratitude is a burning wind that dries up the fountains of piety, and the dews of mercy, and the springs of grace" [Luddy, *Sermons on the Canticle*, 2.86]).

335. "*laeva . . . sub capite*" (n. 8 [col. 1028C]).

336. Col. 1028D, which reads: "*suavitatis locum*" ("such a height of blissful love" [Luddy, *Sermons on the Canticle*, 2.88]).

337. "In peace in the selfsame, I will sleep and I will rest" (Luddy, *Sermons on the Canticle*, 2.88) (Ps. 4:9).

plies to our Psalm 4 at compline—*singulariter in spe*.[338]) {The} point St. Bernard brings out here is that true hope, and therefore perfect rest, is proportionate to the *purity of our love*. *Donec quis premitur a spiritu servitutis*, PARUMQUE HABET DE SPE, DE TIMORE PLURIMUM: NON EST EI PAX NEQUE REQUIES, FLUCTUANTE NIMIRUM CONSCIENTIA SUA INTER SPEM ET TIMOREM, *maximeque quod a superexcellente timore abundantius crucietur: nam timor poenam habet*.[339] But when perfect love has cast out fear—TOTIS VIRIBUS {EXSURGENS} CARITAS IN ADJUTORIUM SPEI FORAS MITTIT TIMOREM.[340] Then {there is} perfect rest, so {that} the Word would not have the spouse awakened from this rest of pure love, perfect hope—true contemplation being its most perfect expression.

2. Sermon 52 begins: the Word, having taken the spouse in His arms by filling her with pure love and perfect hope, wishes her to rest in His love and *watches over* her rest. St. Bernard sees in this further evidence of the goodness and kindness and condescending mercy of God, which far transcends anything we experience in human love. He cries out, "It is good for us to be here"[341] (considering this truth), for, he says, this gives us insight into the Heart of the Most High. It is a most certain and sure insight since it comes to us from the Holy Spirit Who Himself searches the deep things of God (n. 1 [1030]), and He is the Spirit of Truth. Scripture, then, shows us the unbelievable truth that

338. "[For You, O Lord] singularly [have settled me] in hope" (*Breviarium Cisterciense Reformatum*, 4 vols. [Westmalle, Belgium: Typis Cisterciensibus, 1951], *Pars Vernalis*, etc., 170).

339. Col. 1028D, which reads: ". . . *conscientia inter* . . ." ("So long as the soul is influenced by the spirit of servitude she has but little hope and an excessive amount of fear. For her, . . . there is no possibility of either rest or peace whilst her conscience is thus wavering between security and alarm; and the less so, inasmuch as terror predominates and tortures her above measure, for 'fear hath pain'" [Luddy, *Sermons on the Canticle*, 2.88]).

340. Col. 1029A ("charity, rising up in its might, runs to the help of the sister virtue and 'casteth out fear'" [Luddy, *Sermons on the Canticle*, 2.89]) (copy text reads: "EXURGENS").

341. "*bonum est nos hic esse*" (n. 1 [col. 1030A]) (Matt. 17:4).

God not only comes down and seeks our love and gives us rest in Him, but when He has the heart of man in the embrace of His love, He Himself protects and guards the "sleeping" soul so that it may not be disturbed or awakened by anything from without or from within itself. *VEHEMENTISSIME ZELANS PRO QUIETE DILECTAE SUAE, sollicitus servare inter brachia propria dormientem, ne qua forte molestia vel inquietudine a somno suavissimo deturbetur* (n. {2} [1030]).[342] St. Bernard comments on the exultation he feels at realizing the great love of God for the soul, a love which does not disdain to show itself so openly and without restraint, and which is a pledge of the joys of heaven. "What think you shall she receive there in heaven who here on earth has been graced with such intimate union with Him that she finds herself embraced in the arms of God, cherished in His bosom, guarded by His care and concern, lest she be again awakened by any disturbance whatever" (n. 2 [1030]).[343] {By} implication {he indicates the} great *merit* of contemplation.

3. *Explanation of this sleep* (n. 3ff.): {he explains} what it *is not* {by comparing it to} other kinds of sleep in Scripture—the sleep of death, of sin, or merely bodily sleep—{then shows} what it *is*—a watchful and life-giving sleep which is a beginning of eternal life and puts an end to our "death" here below. *Istiusmodi vitalis vigilque sopor sensum interiorem illuminat, et morte propulsata vitam tribuit sempiternam.*[344] *Sensum . . . illuminat*—what is this sense? {It is} wisdom, love, the knowledge of God by a pure love that has made us like to Him (*caritas illa visio, illa similitudo est*

---

342. Text reads: ". . . *quiete cujusdam dilectae* . . ." ("Most anxiously concerned for the repose of a human Spouse very dear to him, whom with affectionate solicitude He holds in His arms whilst she slumbers lest a sleep so pleasant should be disturbed by any annoyance or agitation" [Luddy, *Sermons on the Canticle*, 2.92]) (copy text omits "2").

343. "*Quid, putas, illic accipiet, quae hic tanta familiaritate donatur, ut Dei brachiis amplecti se sentiat, Dei sinu foveri, Dei cura et studio custodiri, ne dormiens forte a quopiam . . . excitetur?*"

344. Col. 1031A ("[The sleep of the spouse] is wakeful and life-giving; it illuminates the mind, expels the death of sin, and bestows immortality" [Luddy, *Sermons on the Canticle*, 2.94]).

[Sermon 82, n. 8]³⁴⁵). This "sense" of wisdom *awakens* in contemplation when we sleep to the passions and cares of this mortal life. *Dormitio est, quae sensum non sopiat, sed abducat*³⁴⁶ (here the bodily senses). It is a *death* which hides us in Christ (Col. 3:3). In what sense is it a "death" (n. 4)? It delivers us not from life but from the dangers and trials and weaknesses of this mortal flesh. *Sponsae exstasim vocaverim mortem, quae tamen non vita, sed vitae eripiat laqueis . . . Anima nostra sicut passer erepta est de laqueo venantium* (Ps. 123) (n. 4 [1031]).³⁴⁷

1. {As} *mors hominum*,³⁴⁸ the soul is taken out of itself, rises above all earthly things and is hidden in God. It feels no *temptation*, hence does not sin, cannot sin as long as held in this embrace; {it} cannot even be tempted. *Quid enim formidetur luxuria, ubi nec vita sentitur? Excedente anima, etsi non vita, {certe} vitae sensu, necesse est etiam ut nec vitae tentatio {sentiatur}.*³⁴⁹ This is indeed necessary for true rest in this life. "Who will give me the wings of a dove, and I will fly and rest?"³⁵⁰ says St. Bernard. {There is} no feeling of the poison of passion seeping into our prayer, no dullness of

---

345. Col. 1181A ("For that likeness is charity and charity too is that vision" [Luddy, *Sermons on the Canticle*, 2.483]).

346. Col. 1031A, which reads: ". . . *quae tamen sensum* . . ." ("it is a true sleep, which transports rather than stupifies the faculties" [Luddy, *Sermons on the Canticle*, 2.94]).

347. "I describe the ecstasy of the Spouse as a kind of death, not the death which terminates life, but that which delivers her true life from danger. . . . 'Our soul has been delivered as a sparrow out of the snare of the fowlers'" (Luddy, *Sermons on the Canticle*, 2.94) (Ps. 123[124]:7).

348. N. 5 (col. 1031C, which reads: "*Verum haec hominum est*") ("manner of dying . . . peculiar to men" [Luddy, *Sermons on the Canticle*, 2.95]).

349. N. 4 (col. 1031B, which reads: ". . . *Excedente quippe anima* . . .") ("For what has such a soul to fear from sensuality, since she has lost even the faculty of sensation? No longer conscious of material impressions, though remaining still the principle of life to the body, she is necessarily inaccessible to temptations from the senses" [Luddy, *Sermons on the Canticle*, 2.95]) (copy text reads: "certa"; "sensiatur").

350. "*Quis dabit mihi pennas sicut columbae, et volabo, et requiescam?*" (col. 1031B) (Ps. 54[55]:7).

spirit produced by the kinship with the things of the flesh, no heat and unrest of desire {or} avarice, no movements of anger, no anxiety about any cares whatever. *Bona mors, quae vitam non aufert, sed transfert in melius.*[351]

2. {As} *mors angelorum,*[352] it is no longer held by *any image.* To escape from all movement of passion is to die to the things of man's lower nature. But there is another death in contemplation which makes us like to the angels. It is a death to all images and representations and words and reasonings and human concepts and manners of thinking: (a) {it} escapes all consciousness of present things (*praesentium memoria excedens*[353]); (b) {it} escapes not only the *desire,* but also the *similitudes* of bodily things: *rerum se inferiorum corporearumque non modo {cupiditatibus} sed et similitudinibus exuat;*[354] (c) {it} is raised to the society of the angels: *sitque ei pura cum illis conversatio, cum quibus est puritatis similitudo* (1031);[355] (d) ONLY THIS IS TRUE CONTEMPLATION—to be at peace in prayer without any human desires, but still involved in the knowledge and images of material things, is as yet not contemplation. *Talis, ut opinor, excessus aut tantum, aut maxime contemplatio dicitur* (n. 5 [1031]).[356] It is this perfect freedom from images that makes us like angels and gives us perfect virginity of spirit: *corporum vero similitudinibus speculando non involvi, angelicae pu-*

---

351. Col. 1031C ("Happy death which destroys not life, but changes it to better!" [Luddy, *Sermons on the Canticle,* 2.95]).

352. N. 5 (col. 1031C, which reads: "*morte . . . angelorum*") ("the death of the angels" [Luddy, *Sermons on the Canticle,* 2.95]).

353. Col. 1031C ("escaping from the memory of all present things" [Luddy, *Sermons on the Canticle,* 2.95]).

354. Col. 1031C ("she may strip herself, not alone of the desires, but even of the images of inferior and corporeal objects" [Luddy, *Sermons on the Canticle,* 2.95]) (copy text reads: "*cupiditatem*").

355. "and may converse spiritually with them whom she resembles in spirituality!" (Luddy, *Sermons on the Canticle,* 2.95).

356. "The name contemplation, as it seems to me, belongs either solely or principally to such a mental ecstasy" (Luddy, *Sermons on the Canticle,* 2.95).

*ritatis est.*³⁵⁷ *Both these degrees are a gift of God.* Both elevate us above ourselves. Both are at rest in Him. But perfect rest is not found until we are beyond images. *Nondum elongasti, nisi et irruentia undique phantasmata . . . transvolare mentis puritate {praevaleas}.* HUCUSQUE NOLI TIBI PROMITTERE REQUIEM.³⁵⁸ (Read {the} rest of the passage.³⁵⁹) In this rest, obviously, {there are} NO DISTRACTIONS.

357. "to be able to contemplate truth without the help of material or sensible images is the characteristic of angelic purity" (Luddy, *Sermons on the Canticle*, 2.96).

358. "But thou hast not yet flown afar, unless, by purity of thy mind, thou art able to rise above the images of sensible objects. . . . Until thou hast attained to this, do not promise thyself any rest" (Luddy, *Sermons on the Canticle*, 2.96–97).

359. "Thou art in error if thou thinkest that the place of repose, the quiet of solitude, the perfection of light, and the dwelling of peace can be found any nearer. But show me the man who has arrived at this point, and I shall unhesitatingly pronounce him to be at rest and qualified to say, 'Turn, O my soul, into thy rest; for the Lord hath been bountiful to thee.' Here truly is a home in solitude, and a dwelling in the light, and, according to the Prophet Isaias, 'a tabernacle for a shade in the day-time from the heat, and a security and covert from the whirlwind and from the rain.' It is of the same the Psalmist sings, 'For He hath hidden me in His tabernacle; in the day of evils He hath protected me in the secret place of his tabernacle'" (Luddy, *Sermons on the Canticle*, 2.97) (cols. 1031D–1032A) (copy text reads "*praevales*").

# APPENDIX A
## Textual Notes

### Readings Adopted from
### CISTERCIAN FATHERS Multigraph

| | |
|---|---|
| 1 | THE CISTERCIAN . . . 1963] THE LIFE WORKS AND DOCTRINE OF ST BERNARD. *preceded by* HISTORY OF THE ORDER—(to follow Carta Caritatis and Consuetudines) |
| | PART . . . BERNARD] *added* |
| | to begin . . . of *love*.] *added* |
| 2 | Pope Pius XII wishes to] To |
| | He wishes to meditate] To meditate |
| | Bernard's doctrine . . . Scripture.] Based on the Scriptures and Fathers |
| 5 | (read p. 101)] (p. 101) |
| | things" (read p. 102)] things" (102) |
| 6 | etc. (read p. 102)] etc. (p. 102) |
| 8 | to joy] into joy |
| | doctrine of] doctrine on |
| 10 | CAREER] LIFE |
| | BACKGROUND—*The Age*:] 1–*The Age*: |
| 10–11 | the twelfth . . . of the towns.] Important to know some of the characteristics of the Middle Ages, and how different from our own time. *followed by* N.B. Do not have a silly, sentimental idea of the Middle Ages! *added on line* |
| 11 | not felt)] not at all felt) |
| | culture; as] culture. Accepted as |

| | |
|---|---|
| 12 | stands, everybody] stands. Everybody medieval] MA |
| | favorable] the favorable |
| | Orient.] Orient. *Fontaines les Dijon*—where St. B is born in 1090. His saintly Mother, Aleth. *followed by* "raises them for the desert rather than for the court"! *interlined below* |
| 13–31 | AN INTRODUCTION . . . to his works.] *added* |
| 32–33 | to the intervention] to intervention |
| 33 | Bernard . . . again sick] Again—Bernard sick in 1125 *interlined below* |
| | again St. . . . dies] again sick in bed—nearly dies |
| 36 | #95] 95 |
| 44 | health is bad] health bad |
| | the death] death |
| 45 | fall St. Bernard] fall Bernard |
| 46 | for Pope Eugene III] *added* |
| 47 | (Cistercians were exempt)] (Cist. exempt) |
| 48 | 280 and 282] 280) (282) |
| | THE EARLIER . . . BERNARD] THE WRITINGS OF ST BERNARD. |
| 48–68 | The best . . . Eadmer.] *added* |
| 68 | 2. DE DILIGENDO DEO] 1- The *De Diligendo Deo*. (written about 1126) |
| 68–77 | This is perhaps . . . Divine Persons.] Since we are interested in St. Bernard primarily as a doctor of love, and since one of his very first works is in fact about love, it is fitting that we start reading *De Diligendo Deo* before any of his other works. Dom Anselme le Bail says (Dictionnaire de Spiritualité, 1.1474) "It is no paradox to affirm that St. Bernard has only written one single treatise on spirituality, that he has explained but one matter, in dealing with the relations of the soul with God: love. A synthesis of his whole spirituality could very well take the title of one of his works—"On the Love of God"." |

Love the center of St. Bernard's doctrine because
God is Love and Love is the "eternal law" according
to which God has made everything. Man, made in
the image of God, is made for love. Love is the
fulfilment of all his aspirations, love of God for
God's sake alone. Love is man's beatitude.
All St. Bernard's works are concerned in some way
or other with the union of man with God by love.
But here he concentrates on several central
problems namely—how man's natural love is
converted into supernatural love for God, the
degrees by which man ascends to pure love, and
how pure love is the peak of the mystical life and is
itself perfect union with God.

  *De Diligendo Deo*] *preceded by* x'd out before him with the

| | |
|---|---|
| 77 | "*The Problem of Love*":] 2- The Problem of the *De Diligendo*. |

other scholars . . . confusing.] Another reason why it
is good to begin our reading of St. Bernard with
this tract, is that it poses a technical problem for
theologians and there has been a great deal of
discussion about it. Much has been written on
the *De Diligendo* hence, its difficulties are easily
cleared up. One of the best short introductions to
St. Bernard is Gilson's discussion of the *De Diligendo*
in his appendix to chapter xiv of the *Spirit of
Medieval Philosophy*. (p. 289 ff.)
We may summarize it here:

| | |
|---|---|
| 78 | What is . . . love?] It is the *problem of pure love*. |
| | would not] wouldn't |
| 80 | *that in . . . himself*,] that in . . . himself, |
| | Note: this . . . of it.] *added* |
| 81–107 | BERNARD AND GUIGO: . . . in the *De Diligendo*.] *added* |
| 107 | D<small>E</small> D<small>ILIGENDO</small> D<small>EO</small>—Text:] *added* |
| | Part I:] *added* |
| 108 | He has] He has *preceded by* Quis? *in left margin* |
| | 3.] *preceded by* Quos? Quid? *in left margin* |
| | 4.] *preceded by* Quantum *in left margin* |

|       |                                                                 |
|-------|-----------------------------------------------------------------|
|       | 5.] *preceded by* Quomodo—*in left margin*                      |
|       | God's love . . . own Son.] *added*                              |
|       | Chapter 2] *preceded by* food *in left margin*                  |
|       | He gives us breath and air] *preceded by* air *in left margin*  |
|       | He gives . . . eyes] *preceded by* light *in left margin*       |
|       | soul] spirit                                                    |
|       | Here we . . . 977] *added*                                      |
|       | *seek*] seek                                                    |
|       | *clings*] clings                                                |
| 109   | found Him] found Him.) n 2, col. 976.                           |
|       | attributing . . . alone] *added*                                |
|       | *knows our dignity*] knows our dignity                          |
|       | *it comes from God*] it comes from God                          |
|       | *our state . . . beings*] our state . . . beings                |
|       | Without true . . . in God.] *added*                             |
|       | To know . . . to God.] *added*                                  |
|       | This is vainglory. . . . self-sufficient.] *added*              |
| 110   | Here St. Bernard . . . Resurrection of Christ.] *added*         |
| 111–17 | corollary . . . in God by love.] *The Degrees of Love.*        |
|       | (Chapters 8–11)                                                 |
|       | 1- At the end of c. 7 (n 22- col. 987.) Bernard resumes what has gone before and explains again what is contained in the statement CAUSA DILIGENDI DEUM DEUS EST. |
|       | God is not only the *final cause* of our love, but also its *efficient cause*. |
| 117   | stirs] moves                                                    |
|       | true theology of grace!] *added*                                |
| 117–18 | *se in redemptione* . . . finding Him.] *added*                |
| 118   | *Natural Love*] *added*                                         |
|       | (chapter 8: n. 23)] *added*                                     |
|       | are given . . . *of nature.*] are given . . . of nature.        |
|       | subject to God.] subject to God. A disordered love is one in which the will is rebellious to God and emotions are rebellious to the will. |
|       | *Carnal Love*] *added*                                          |
|       | to survive] to survive ourselves                                |
| 119   | It is very . . . in general).] *added*                          |

## Appendix A

|      | |
|------|--|
|      | *Social Love*] added |
|      | love of neighbor] love neighbor |
|      | help our neighbor] help neighbor |
|      | Our "surplus" . . . care of us.] added |
| 120  | "annihilates"] "destroys" |
|      | All this . . . of love."] added |
| 121  | in which *man*] man |
|      | is a natural] a natural |
|      | *Below*] Below |
|      | himself *ordinabiliter* means] himself means |
|      | (St. Augustine)] added |
|      | (*note* . . . to the next)] added |
|      | but he . . . *of necessities*] but he . . . of necessities |
|      | special . . . 988)] |
| 122  | *constantly*] constantly |
|      | With his . . . than ourselves.] added |
|      | We come . . . level.] added |
|      | Love of God . . . bonus.] added |
| 123  | *justus*] just |
|      | will for His sake] will for His sake |
|      | casto . . . mandato] added |
|      | making . . . *freely*] making . . . freely |
|      | (cf. St. Anselm)] added |
| 124  | seeking . . . fourth degree.] added |
|      | OF LOVE] added |
|      | The highest . . . please Him] added |
| 125  | APOLOGIA—1123] APOLOGIA |
| 125–26 | The Controversy . . . very important.] added |
| 126  | Letter 1 of St. Bernard] added |
|      | can see] have seen |
|      | It is . . . letter.] added |
|      | infidelity and tepidity] making virtues out of gluttony, idle talk, and laziness. |
| 126–32 | This must . . . after flight.] added |
| 132–33 | the contrast . . . Cîteaux] the same contrast |
| 133  | ought to say] says |
|      | fantasy.] fantasy and illusion. |
|      | understand the] understand truly the |

| | |
|---|---|
| | About 1123, . . . points mentioned.] *transposed from after their silence.* |
| | mentioned.] mentioned. We do not possess St. Bernard's reply. Note that this action is characteristic of Peter the Venerable, and bears witness to his sanctity. |
| 134–39 | *Two Early . . . about Mohammed.*)] *added* |
| 139 | Many Benedictines] However, the trouble grew, and many Benedictines |
| 140 | you have sent . . . world] you have sent letters all over the wide world: nor are they ordinary letters, but letters full of cutting criticism and malice and mockery . . ." |
| 141 | though the reforms] though they |
| | (v.g. York)] *added* |
| | *Apologia itself*] *Apologia.* |
| | a famine] a great famine |
| 142 | Bernard is for . . . interior.] *added* |
| | fomented] encouraged |
| | He is criticizing . . . attitude.] *added* |
| 143 | some Cistercians] the Cistercians |
| | This conflict . . . wrong.] *added* |
| 144 | This raises . . . others.] *added* |
| 145 | greatness of] greatness and pride and self-love of |
| | is the spirit] is then the spirit |
| | chaps. 2–4] chaps. 2–3–4 |
| | The unity . . . is] the unity of the Church depends on it (iii, 5. col. 901) The various orders in the Church are (see n. 8 [col. 903])] *added* |
| 146 | than the work . . . himself] than the worker himself |
| | virtues] virtue |
| 147 | "With a belly . . . fat."] *added* |
| | here he is . . . follows him] *added* |
| | one who transgresses] he who transgresses |
| 148 | *Laxity is called . . . fellowship*] Laxity is called . . . fellowship |
| 148–49 | true discretion . . . Cluny (#20 [col. 910])] *added* |
| 150 | re-orientating] reorienting |

## Appendix A

|   |   |
|---|---|
|  | *as if it were . . . good*] as if it were . . . good |
|  | with guests] *added* |
|  | (N.B. . . . etc.])] *added* |
| 152 | infractions] they |
| 153 | for such values] for all such values |
| 154 | *as a sign . . . wealth*] as a sign . . . wealth |
| 156 | *Conclusions*] *Conclusion* |
| 157–60 | *Effect of . . . (1044).*] *added* |
| 160 | III.] *added* |
| 160–65 | *Intellectual . . . century).*] *added* |
| 166 | center of new] center of a new |
|  | universals.] universals. *followed by* This problem is of course fundamental, and by no means a waste of time. *added on line followed by* In these schools, though philosophy was hotly debated, theology remained the queen of sciences. The great questions in theology at the time centered on the relation of faith and reason, and the explanation of the Dogma of the Trinity. |
|  | The Victorine . . . elsewhere.] *added* |
|  | but as] but rather as |
|  | had a great popular appeal] was as popular as it was dangerous |
|  | error.] error. In the *Sic et Non* (Yes and No) he listed contradictory statements of the Fathers and underlined the necessity for a critical study of the Patristic authorities in dogmatic theology. This bore fruit in fact in the Scholastic methods like those of St. Thomas Aquinas. |
| 160–96 | Note: Abelard . . . heart" (311).] *added* |
| 196 | *to . . . Life*] *added* |
|  | He did not . . . with them.] *added* |
|  | Bernard strongly] Bernard however strongly |
| 197 | 3. . . . . Abelard.] *added* |
|  | unusual] unexpected |
|  | protest] reaction |
|  | and against . . . stood for.] *added* |

|     |     |
| --- | --- |
|     | of the twelfth century] of Abelard |
|     | who was then] who, then |
|     | and followed] followed |
|     | *The Theme*] Theme |
| 198 | plus a conclusion] *added* |
|     | 3] *added* |
|     | In these . . . union.] *added* |
| 198–99 | opening . . . then treats] In the opening chapter St. Bernard treats |
| 199 | He speaks . . . power!] *added* |
|     | within us (836)] within us (856) |
| 199–200 | He adds that . . . law, etc.] *added* |
| 200 | The man who . . . cor.] *added* |
|     | to feel . . . *killed*] to feel . . . killed |
|     | Only penance . . . (838).] *added* |
| 201 | In fact . . . translation] *added* |
| 202–3 | Whereupon . . . (chap. 6)] (Read Watkin Williams' Translation, p. 15) *followed by* Translation—p. 15, 16, 17 *added in left margin* |
| 203 | Compare . . . *Everyman*] *added* |
|     | *memory*] memory |
|     | *will*] will |
| 203–4 | And now . . . (chap. 6).] (Williams, pp. 16–17) |
| 204 | cause] reason |
|     | "Who is . . . head?"] "Who is . . . head?" |
|     | *Thérèse*] Thérèse n. |
|     | This is . . . to God.] *added* |
| 205 | "It is not . . . to humility."] *added* |
|     | willing . . . commanded] willing . . . commanded |
| 206 | Note at . . . fruit.] *added* |
|     | 1. . . . (chap. 9)] *added* |
|     | 2. *Reason*] 1) *Reason* |
|     | *conversion of the will*] conversion of the will |
|     | READ chaps. 12–13 [Williams, pp. 33–35]] see trans. p. 34 *added in left margin* |
| 208 | These are tasted . . . *conscientia.*] *added* |
| 209 | *Hunger . . . will.*] Hunger . . . will. |
|     | Chapter 13 . . . all this.] *added* |

## Appendix A

|   |   |
|---|---|
| | 3. The soul] 2) The soul |
| | This is . . . p. 41).] *added* |
| | the word of the mercy] by the mercy |
| 210 | "His pardon . . . compunction.] *added* |
| | pour themselves] pours itself |
| 211 | READ translation, p. 43] *added* |
| | Give . . . *pure*] Give . . . pure |
| | Then we . . . heart.] *added* |
| | the *memory*] the *memory* |
| 212 | 4. However] 3) However |
| | see chap. 17] chap. 17 |
| | are actually] they are actually |
| | comparison . . . bitter.] *added* |
| | and wish . . . nobody] *added* |
| | but suffer injury patiently] *added* |
| | win the . . . wrong them] *added* |
| 212–13 | Note . . . to conversion. ] *added* |
| 214 | IV.] *added* |
| | a reply to . . . Chartres.] In 1128 St. Bernard was asked by some Benedictine monks (at St. Pierre de Chartres) whether or not the *Rule* of St. Benedict obliged under pain of sin. This is a hotly debated question, and in order to see St. Bernard's reply in the right light, we must first of all consider the present state of the question today. |
| | 1- *History of the Question.* |
| | Whether or not a given rule obliges under pain of sin depends on the mind of the legislator. There is no doubt whatever that a religious legislator has (or did have) the power to make a rule bind under pain even of mortal sin. |
| | Some rules explicitly bind under pain of mortal sin, in the principal points. Vg., *Rule* of St. Francis. |
| | Others explicitly bind under pain of venial sin on important points, vg the Carmelite *Rule* |
| | Still other rules explicitly state that they do not intend to bind under pain of sin but only *ad poenam*, for instance the *Rule* of St. Dominic. |

Even when the *Rule* does not intend to bind under pain of sin, there will nevertheless be sin (*vi voti*) whenever:

a) The precept transgressed is prescribed by the law of God or of the Church.

b) The precept declares how the vow is to be observed,

c) whenever there is contempt of the *Rule*. (Formal contempt—mortal sin of pride)

d) Whenever there is a sinful motive.

e) Whenever serious harm is caused or scandal is given.

f) Whenever there is a case of real inconstancy.

Today, according to the norms of the Cong. of Bishops and Regulars, 1901 The rules and constitutions of new congregations are not to be observed *vi voti*. Violation of the constitutions is not a sin at least against the vow.

Nevertheless, as theologians and canonists point out, even when the *Rule* itself does not bind under pain of sin—

1) There remains of course a strict moral obligation of obeying the *precepts of the Superior according to the Rule, vi voti*. The obligation is serious when there is a formal command, and remains binding at least sub veniali (*vi virtutis*) even when he does not appeal to his dominative power.

2) As Canon 593 points out it is a duty of state for the religious to tend to perfection according to his rule, and one is bound by the natural law to keep his duty of state. *Hence wilful violations of the rule can easily be violations of the virtue of obedience, if not of the vow*. They are generally imperfections, may be venial sins. Habitual violation of an important point of rule is a venial sin.

In other words *it is false to state* that the *Rule* is simply a body of counsels which one may take or leave at will. The religious cannot act as if he were free to disregard the rule or observances according to his own good pleasure. This would rob religious observance of all its meaning.

Hence, a practical summary: If we break the rule There is sin against the vow 1) Whenever the *Rule* explicitly obliges under the vow.

2) In cases a) to f) above.

There is sin against the virtue—even when the *Rule* does not oblige under sin, in so far as violation of the *Rule* without sufficient reason and in cold blood is a violation of our duty of state.

*The question then arises: Does the Rule of St. Benedict oblige under sin and if so when?*

The *Spiritual Directory* (which is to be taken with a grain of salt) (but is nevertheless quasi official in the Order and represents the mind of the Order between the reunion and the II World War)

1- "When the *Legislator has not defined his intention*, as is the case in our instance, authors commonly admit with Suarez that the obligation does not bind under pain of grave sin" p 206.

2- "In their moral counsels and many disciplinary prescriptions the Rules form matter of the virtue and not of the vow unless they bind under pain of sin," 199.

Then Dom Lehodey cites two opinions:

a) When the rules command under pain of sin, there are always two sins, one against the virtue commanded and the other against religion.

b) One vows to obey *according to* the *Rule*, and the *Rule* simply delimits the field within which the commands of the Superior are to be confined. Hence there is no additional sin (against the vow) when one violates a precept already binding under sin.

Lehodey concludes that we can take either side as "We find nothing in the Holy Rule or in the writings of St. Bernard nor in our traditions that would oblige us to accept either opinion. . . ." 200.

3- In order to see whether the *Rule* of St. Benedict binds under pain of venial sin we must consult the tradition of the Order, and the tradition of St. Bernard, De Rancé etc, (says Lehodey p 206) "and the most learned commentators on the rule" have "created a tradition to this effect."

4- Dom Lehodey then continues:
a) The Moral counsels of the *Rule*—are "nothing else but the Law of God—it obliges us as does the Gospel—allows no dispensation . . ."
b) Disciplinary precepts "which give our Order its religious form"—vg common life, silence, etc—"in all this the Rule binds under pain of sin," 207
c) The Regular penances "oblige in conscience," 209.

All in all this is not entirely clear. The proper distinctions are not clearly made. The decision that the rule binds under sin is based on an appeal to tradition in the order, but the traditional statements of this doctrine are not given.

It is however safe to assume that there is certainly possibility of at least venial sin when we violate those precepts "which give the order its form."

*St. Thomas's opinion.*

One of the clearest and most authoritative treatments of this point remains that of St. Thomas, (Summa, II IIae, Q. 186, a. 9.)

The Angelic Doctor asks: "Does a Religious always sin mortally when he breaks the Rule"?

The answer is No. The only things in the *Rule* that bind under sin are

a) Those which are already commanded by the Law of God, or of nature, or of the Church.

b) Those which come under the vows or formal precepts of the Superior
c) Those which procede from contempt of the *Rule*.
Note he is talking about *mortal sin*.
His explanation:
1) The religious state is supposed to be more secure than the state of those living in the world— it is supposed to be a tranquil harbor, in which one is safe from the raging storms of the sea. But if the rule obliged under pain of sin the religious state would be most perilous because of the multitude of the observances.
2) Some things in the *Rule pertain to the practice of essential virtues* (commanded by the divine law etc)—these oblige under pain of mortal sin—(vg matters of justice, charity, etc)
3) Some points of *Rule* pertain to *exterior observance*,
a) Some of these bear on essentials which have been vowed—vg poverty, obedience, stability. Can bind *sub mortali*
b) Others are simply *means to help us* practice the perfection of the vows. (Various usages—vg silence, mental prayer, lectio) These do not bind under pain of sin unless there is *contempt*—i.e. the *person refuses to submit his will to the rule* (cf. ad 3) and this is *diametrically opposed to the pursuit of perfection* to which the religious is obliged by his very state.
Or if there is some other sinful motive (gluttony, anger, concupiscence) then too there is sin, when a rule is violated. NB *Mortal sin* possible
4) When there is *a formal command of the Superior or Legislator*, according to the *Rule*, then we may sin against our vow of obedience by disobeying.
5) We must be careful of *frequent violations* because they *lead to contempt*. Normally, violations of the rule do not imply contempt because they are committed with a specious *pretext* which though it

may be weak and invalid nevertheless may subjectively save the violator from sin.
Contempt breaks the rule because the violator does not want to keep it.
*Further notes on St. Thomas*:
a) The religious does not vow to keep the whole rule but to obey according to the *Rule*. He sins mortally only when violating those precepts which are explicitly necessary to keep his vow *but he may sin venially* in neglecting those exterior observances which help him keep the vows and direct his whole life to perfection. (ad 1) (Even the Preachers, whose rule does not bind under sin, can sin when they transgress the rule out of negligence or contempt)
b) Those points of rule which are mere statutes or ordinances (for exterior conduct) do not by their nature bind sub mortali (ad 2).
It is clear that St. Thomas takes the *Rule* seriously since there can be mortal sin when it is violated in essential points and there can easily be venial sin even in the neglect of exterior observance, while in these the element of formal contempt makes mortal sin also possible.
DE PRAECEPTO ET DISPENSATIONE.
And now let us turn to St. Bernard himself. Remember that he will serve as a most important witness in our own case, since the answer, for Cistercians, to the question whether the rule binds under pain of sin depends largely on the tradition of the Order, and St. Bernard is the chief spokesman of that tradition.

> Some Rules] *preceded by x'd out* It is of
> Furthermore, any precept, in a Rule, which also falls under the divine law, or even the natural law, binds under pain of sin.
> (*vi voti*)] *added in left margin and marked for insertion preceded by cancelled* (that is an *added sin* against the vow)

of the Church.] *followed by* (In this case too it is an added sin against the vow) *added on line and cancelled*

precept] *altered from* precepts *followed by cancelled* which

declares] *altered from* declare

even when . . . of sin –] *added on line*

*precepts . . . vi voti.*] *altered from* precepts . . . vi voti.

(*vi virtutis*)] *added in left margin and marked for insertion*

even when] *preceded by x'd out* wherever

As] *altered from* as *preceded by cancelled* Since

Hence . . . *of the vow.*] *altered from* Hence . . . of the vow.

*wilful*] *interlined with a caret*

can easily be] *added on line following cancelled* are

are generally] *added on line following cancelled* always

If we break the rule] *added on line*

against the vow] *added in upper margin and marked for insertion*

1) Whenever] *preceded by x'd out vi voti*

duty of state] *followed by* or flows from some sinful motive or [ ] *added on line and cancelled*

*Legislator . . . intention*] *altered from* Legislator . . . intention

dispensation . . ."] *followed by cancelled* This is highly ambiguous.

conscience" 209.] *followed by cancelled* These statements are ambiguous and no one should consider himself obliged to follow them as it is so uncertain what they really mean.

All in all . . . its form."] *added in lower margin following x'd out* He goes on to

a.9] *preceded by x'd out* 9

formal] *typed interlined and marked for insertion*

essentials] *preceded by x'd out* essential points of

|     | subjectively] *followed by x'd out* as |
|     | whether] *preceded by x'd out* the |
| 214 | 1. *Monastic Obedience:*] *added* |
|     | by them. "Are] by them. The form in which they put the question is: "Are |
| 215 | There must . . . change.] The case must be objectively certain. |
|     | 870] 87 |
| 217 | He seeks] seeks |
|     | This is a perfect imitation of] It is a perfect replica of |
|     | follow our . . . things] our own will |
|     | sacrifice.] sacrifice, and a complete sacrifice, somewhere along the line. |
|     | sacrifice of . . . has] sacrifice has |
|     | violated] broken |
|     | pretense. Such is] pretense. And this in a monk who aspires to perfection is a serious compromise. It cannot be tolerated. Such is |
| 218 | unites] *most perfectly unites* |
|     | when he insists . . . already] as it is |
| 219 | accept his] accept their |
|     | criticize his views] criticize them |
|     | it seems] the probability seems |
|     | might be] is |
|     | where the monk] where the soul |
|     | a bad] a totally bad |
|     | monk who] religious who |
|     | can act] will move |
|     | some who] some souls who |
|     | a slavery] slavery |
| 220 | replied] replies |
|     | with legalism] with a kind of legalism |
| 221 | by the *Rule* . . . failings.] by the *Rule*. |
|     | the framework] this framework |
|     | *we admit*] we *admit* |
|     | *who has . . . remedy*] who has . . . remedy |
| 222 | 2. *Some points on stability*] *preceded by four handwritten pages:* St. Bernard on Pure love. |

## Appendix A

1) Nothing should stop us from loving God + from aspiring to union with God.

Not even our sins: if we understand theme aright. Even though our souls are *de*formed it is because there remains in them a form, by which we are aware of the deformity.

This is *image of God*—our freedom.

In sin—freedom is captive to lower passions—all the more reason to seek freedom.

"quo sibi plus displicet in malo quod in se videt, *eo se ardentius ad bonum quod aeque in se videt, trahat.*" Cant 82.7.

a) St. B. not one of those who holds we should never see any good in ourselves

b) Shows us how to use our faults + our limitations.

c) Teaches us that in our faults themselves we can find reasons for hope.

*Importance of knowing how to USE our failings.*

2) *READ*. Beginning of Cant. 83—with Holy Father's comment.

nb. The soul finds *in itself* reason for hope—in the divine image

What to do? Preserve + increase the "caeleste decus" by right conduct

Hence INDUSTRIA.

3) For what—*conformitas Verbo.*—Who lives in us + in Whom we live.

How? By love.

We are life Him by nature. (image)

We must be like Him by love (likeness)

READ. 83:3. "connubium."

Not a contract but an embrace—*intensity* + *purity* of love.

a) Love transforms all other passions into itself

Apply to poverty—

Pauper sum quia amo.

b) quae amat amat, et aliud novit nihil.

c) God accepts no other service if it is not enlivened by love. (even honor—fear—etc.)

For He wants to be loved, not feared.
When He loves, He desires only to be loved in return, because He knows that love will be our beatitude—+ that is what He wills.
d) Magna res amor si tamen ad suum recurrit principium. . . .
A kind of circumincession of love.
e) AMO QUIA AMO—AMO UT AMEM.– love makes us in a sense equal to God.
Grow in purity of love—desiring simply to please God + do His will & be united to Him.
*Summary—if I love, I am CONTENT with fact that what I do pleases God—I seek nothing more.
   *image of*] *interlined above cancelled* likeness of
   Apply to . . . quia amo.] *added in left margin*

   *The First Epistle of St. John.*
Messianic Kingdom of Peace. Recall texts from Isaias.
I. Read Introduction.
* 1 John 1:1-4 The concreteness of the terms
   Jesus is "the Life." Mystery. He in Whom we are, has become "a man" like ourselves.
   Our own life has become a man who is one of us. Abyss of mystery.
   The witness. We declare to you eternal life
   Communion—Incarnation—for the sake of communion with the Father + the Son + with one another
   *That our Joy may be full.*
*The Epistle is a Summary of John's teaching.*
All moral teaching is dependent on the nature of God. ie. all is a matter of conformity to What God is.
   God is light—Therefore we must base our lives on *truth* not on a lie.

## Appendix A

God is holiness—But to love in truth means to love without sin—ie. *in His mercy. + to keep the commandments.*

God is love.

To love God is to separate oneself entirely from the world + from antichrist. The force of the "world" opposed to God, seeks to draw souls into *darkness, sin, hatred.*

+

*God is light. Light + Darkness*

Theme of light + darkness—essential to St. John's Gospel

Lux in tenebris lucet et tenebrae eam non comprehenderunt

*Read.* 1:5-7. God is light. No darkness in Him.

If we are in communion with God—there is light in us + not darkness

The *test*—whether we are in the light + in communion with God, is our union with our brothers (v. 7.)

a *qualification*—we are not sinless—in what sense sin + truth meet in us—confession of sin—dependence on mercy of God—not remaining in sin.

Read 1:8-2:2

*What is meant by light + darkness?*

Light = God = Truth = Holiness.

Truth—*in the sense of exact correspondence between what is SAID + what IS.*

\*READ I.8 (if we say we have not sinned.)

Paradox—if we confess our sin (this is truth) then *by God's mercy* the light is in us

But we must *desire* His light + His mercy

\*READ 3:3-10. The Sons of God *do not sin*—they HAVE sinned in past but once converted they sin no more (cf early doctrine on penance)

\*see especially—(for problem—3:20 + Guardini's interpretation)

*Truth*—in moral sense—exact correspondence of our actions to divinely given norms

(concretely—likeness to actions of Christ).

\*READ 2:3-6.—Keeping His commandments—+ being like Him—"walking as He walked" cf. 3:

\*READ 3:16-18. *Giving* as He did. Sharing all with our brother.

*Truth—as love*—Truth + love are inseparable—*Love is the real source of all moral goodness + of all "truth" in us.*

He who loves—dwells in the light
*will never really sin* (no scandal in him.)
\*READ 2:9-11.
\*READ 3:23-24. Love is God's great commandment, hence real touchstone of truth + holiness.
\*READ also 4:20-5:3

*Truth—in mystical sense*—Is taught by the Holy Spirit, Spirit of love.—
\*READ 2:20-29

Those taught by H. Spirit intuitively know light from darkness.

Those taught by H. Spirit *come to Christ & confess Him*—+ then come to the Father + dwell in the Father + the Son.

And is in communion with all who dwell in God
READ 3:1-2. Sonship in this life—perfect vision in the next. GREAT GROWTH.

*Darkness* = Sin = hatred (disunity) = Antichrist = Nothingness

The Darkness is evanescent, it *passes away*—it is really nothingness. 2:8, 2:17.

(1) *Darkness is hatred* 2:9-11
\*READ 3:12-15 Cain—a son of darkness.

(2) *Darkness is love of the world.*—Hence *false love*. Incompatibility between true love, (charity) + false love (concupiscence)

\*READ 2:15-17
\*READ 5:18-19. The whole world is in the power of the evil one.
>    (3) *Love of the world; source of all ignorance of spiritual realities*
>    Those who love the world cannot know moral truth—2:11
>    (cannot know the *way*)
>    Those who love the world deny the Father + the Son.—2:22-23.
>    Those who love the world cannot "know" (in unity) the children of God. cf. 4:5-6.

\*READ 4:1-6 (4) *Darkness is Antichrist*—working at present in the world—

*Hymn to Charity*

\*READ 4:7-17 First a perfect harmony + summary of *all* we have seen so far.
>    Then, a going beyond—
>    *Charity casts out fear.* The perfection of life in God.

\*READ 4:18-20
>    Confidence—because God has first loved us.
>    Explains what was said about those who love God not sinning.
>    His love will keep them from sin
>    Love the great protective—not fear of punishment.

*The Victory of light over darkness in our lives—by Faith.*
>    The Passion of Christ + the Holy Spirit in our lives—overcome all evil.

\*READ 5:5-12 Mystico-sacramental dogma of redemption.

Afterthoughts—again the problem of sin
>    There is a sin *unto death*—(sin agst Holy Spirit + against Truth) which cannot be forgiven.
>    *If any other sin is committed it will be forgiven due to the intercession of the brethren.*

\*READ 5:14-17.

*The Conclusion*—Summary. *READ 5:20-21.
A.] *added*

223  B.] *added*
the present Code] Canon Law
one was] it was generally
a monk] one
(loosely)] loosely

224  C.] *added*
for instance letters 33, 34, 35] *passim*
*not* transferring] not transferring
prudent] right

224–33  *Some Letters . . . the Spirit").] added*

234  *with God*] with God
believe] say
*Characteristics of self-will*] Characteristics of self-will

235  *Sermon . . . Time*] Sermon . . . Time
tormentors."] tormentors.
clearest] most solid
That we] The fact that we

236  bear] undergo

237  Gospel).] Gospel). Mystical theology is not just a branch
of learning, in the New Testament, it is part and
parcel of the Gospel teaching.

238  term "contemplation"] term contemplation
separated from] separated off from
the "mystics"] "the mystics"

239  some monks] some souls

240  *Garrigou-Lagrange*] Garrigou-Lagrange

241  for instance, . . . "irregularity."] *added*

242  in loving . . . God] passive
passively "infused."] passive

243  Many monks] Souls
that they] that souls
was too weak] is too weak
also . . . now is] *added*
monks *become*] souls *become*
taste for] taste of

## Appendix A

|  |  |
|---|---|
| | Many give up] They give up |
| | "melancholy"] melancholy |
| 244 | Perhaps . . . for many.] *added* |
| | as it is manifested . . . *Ecclesia*).] *added* |
| 246 | the Sermons *in Cantica*] the Sermons *In Cantica* |
| | 4. The Sermons] 4. The *Sermons* |
| | for monks] for the souls of monks |
| 250–53 | St. Bernard, however . . . 111–13)] But St. Bernard In Cantica 83 (see Butler Western Mysticism, p. 111) |
| 253 | *phenomena*] phenomena |
| 253–54 | MEANING. . . . (*Cant*. xxxi. 6).] MEANING cf. passages quoted by Butler, pp. 118, 119. |
| 255 | psycho-physical] physical |
| | conclusion on p.] conclusion, p. |
| 256 | and providential events.] Any other path leads directly into illusion. |
| | Sermons *in Cantica*] Sermons in Cantica |
| | (N.B.: note . . . Clairvaux!)] *added* |
| 257 | is different] is quite different |
| | linguistic, literary and] linguistic and |
| | Conference . . . Science"] Conference |
| | Nesteros] Nesteros on "Spiritual Science" |
| 258 | *acedia*] acedia |
| 260 | this *understanding*] this understanding |
| 261 | towards the Scripture] towards Scripture |
| 262 | you cannot] can't |
| 263 | THE SERMONS . . . themselves.] *added* |
| | final sermons] final *sermons* |
| | *Sermon 1*] Sermon 1 |
| 264 | *Sermon 2*] Sermon 2 |
| | *Sermon 3*] Sermon 3 |
| | *Sermon 4*] Sermon 4 |
| | "spirits"] spirits |
| | "need . . . body."] need . . . body. |
| | *Sermon 5*] Sermon 5 |
| | what this] what brought about this |
| | God is] God |

|     | *Sermon 6*] Sermon 6 |
| --- | --- |
| 265 | *Sermon 7*] Sermon 7 |
| 267 | *Sermon 8*] Sermon 8 |
| 269 | should call] would call |
|     | *Degrees of Humility*] Degrees of Humility |
|     | *grace of compassion*] grace of compassion |
| 270 | spiritual father (or mother!!)] Prelate |
|     | the monks] souls |
|     | of the abbot is] of the Superior is |
| 271 | others. "Do not insist] others. Here, then, St. Bernard paradoxically comes out with a declaration that would be a problem and a scandal to many Cistercians—if they ever read it. "Do not insist |
| 272 | spiritual father's] director's |
| 273 | benevolent paternalism] benevolent bourgeois paternalism |
| 274 | one who] the soul that |
|     | Such a monk] Such a soul |
|     | "a soul lost] it is "lost |
| 276 | praising the Lord] praising God |
|     | of great importance] very important |
| 280 | above themes] above theme |
| 281 | doubtful" (17.4)] doubtful" (14.4) |
| 288 | those who] The souls that |
| 289 | *vehementiam*] *vehementiam* (their indiscrete zeal) |
|     | *obstinatam*] *obstinatam* (attachment to their own will). |
| 290 | He reminds] reminds |
|     | outside obedience] outside of obedience |
| 294 | by His grace] by His Spirit |
| 295 | temptations] temptation |
| 303 | CONTEMPLATION] CONTEMPLATION |
| 304 | an abbot] a Superior |
|     | speaks again] speaking again |
| 305 | the injustice] injustice |
| 306 | [This series . . . here.]] READ in this connection: followed by three handwritten pages St. Bernard Theologien—Jean Mouroux—*Sur les Criteres de l'Experience Spirituelle* |

## Appendix A

1) a true *theology* of Xtian experience "reading in the book of experience."

"un realité donnée à l'interieur de la foi, referée à des normes precises, orientée à des fins definies et vecu tout au long du drame du salut." 253.

2) which is a normal + essential aspect of our return to God

+

3) Framework—Xtian *experience situated within frame of self-knowledge + knowledge of* God.

knowledge in sense of a judgement of faith.

"une prise de conscience de soi; une confrontation à la norme qui est la foi; un jugement concret sur soi même inséré dans l'option d'une liberté." 253.

*Self-knowledge.*—(Serm 35, 55). I am a sinner—I need to return to God.

*Knowledge of God.*—(Serm 36—That He is merciful . . .

(The *idol* of the severe God—38:1-2) (implies a rejection of faith + of the experience of the Church.) 254.

This twofold knowledge is *difficult*

  *necessary*—why? (see effects. p. 254.)

  anticipation of the Last Judgement.

  its effects—compunction—holy fear—*devotio*— (Serm. 10)*

  LOVE—the chief effect.

4) *Christian Love* 3fold Love of Xt. Serm. 20

  Active + affective.—Serm. 50.

  Unitive. Serm. 83–84.

5) *The Church*—all Xtian experience in the Church. Serm 68, 62, 12:11.

  Communio Sanctorum. Serm 62:1. + those united with the Saints. 57:3, 12:11

  Mediation of the holy members. 57:5.

  Each individual Soul is the Church. 57:3, 69:8.

  Brought together by the death of Xt. 68:4.

Our union with Word proportionate to our union with Church 12:11

6) *Faith*—our life in Church is life of faith, enlivened by charity. 24:7-8. –
Possession of the mystery of God. credere invenisse est. 76:6.
But a *hidden* possession. 28:9., 48:6-7.. 31:2.
*Partial* + imperfect knowledge of God. 31:2. 28* cf. p. 259 Mouroux' summary
Yet *source* of experience—*crede ut intelligas*. 38:2.
Faith is the *rule* of religious experience.

7) *Alternations*—"Vicissitudo" rhythm of presences + absences. 31–32.
"Tant qu'on est dans le drame on est dans la vérité, parce que le drame de la vicissitude est l'expression nécessaire de l'existence temporelle et peregrinale et par suite le critère authentique d'une expérience réelle de Dieu."

8) What we see is not the Word but *signs* of His presence What signs

1) Good thoughts + inspirations (32:5-7., 39:1-2)
—a vague + general indication. Insufficient.
2) Forewarnings of the coming of the Word.
a) vigilance + sobriety. 57.*
b) desire (purifies + prepares). 31. (esp. 4) (guardian angel here).
c) Action of the Church through spiritual men—if we respond 57:5-6..
3) Interior signs of His presence.
57, 74.
His presence is entirely invisible etc. 31:6
"Fire" 57:7 f.
"Look"
"Voice".
Light. 69:2-6
Synthesis of all signs. 74* (esp. 5–6)
(Mouroux 265—shows how this transcends experience in faith)

Union of certitude + fear—vigilance—fidelity etc. 57:4-10, 74:2-8.

"Il s'agit d'une crainte fondée sur la certitude même, et portant non pas sur la Présence du Verbe même mais sur les *exigences* de cette présence" 266.
   the chief effect.] *followed by cancelled* 3fold
   57, 74.] *added in left margin*
   "Il s'agit] *followed by cancelled* sur

*Mystical Doctrine of St. Bernard's Sermons in Cantica*
1- Preamble—*Experience* a
Cistercians should ardently desire + seek Myst. Experience.
Serm I 1,3 III,1, I,11
Serm. LXXXIII.1. (+ Doctor Mellifluus).
Magnum bonum quaerere Deum . . . . Serm LXXXIV. 1., - 2 ante quaesitam quam quaerentem
All have *some* experience. Serm 7:9 (of peace with God in His Church)—effect of Incarnation
But the experience of the *osculum oris* is special. III, 1., II, 2.
Given to those who are pacified: II.6 (apatheia) LXXXIII.1. (end).
who have ascended by degrees. III.4., IV, 1. LXXXIII, 5.
2- *The Church + Myst. Experience*
God—angels—when working together in union of charity. LXXV.11.-
Through + beyond the preaching of Church—by love—LXXIX.2.
Xti et Ecclesiae secretas delicias LXXX.1.—also for the soul, id, LXVIII.1,4,
But what soul can take to itself what is said by Sponsa—[ ]?—LXIX. 1,6,7,8
3- Myst Experience in Love
Love the unique theme of C of C's. LXXIX.-1.
Love the only possible bond between man & God that will produce true union. Gilson 127.

In *pure and ardent love* C. LXXXIII Gilson 141*
4- Union of Love with the Word (Image retained + likeness lost.)
    Image + likeness—capax majestatis (image)—appetens (likeness) LXXX.2—Gilson 127*
    Participation by grace (love) in what belongs to Word by Nature. LXXX, LXXXI.
    simplicity—idem esse et vivere—*can become* idem esse et beate esse.
    immortality—lives forever— " " —eternally established in bliss.
    liberty—chooses good or evil " " united to will (+ liberty—Spirit) of God.
By destruction of the *proprium* + restoration of our true nature (Gilson 128* 129* 133*
How? By conversio ad Verbum reformandae per Ipsum. LXXXIII.2
*Love of Jesus*—outline whole Serm. XX in Cantic. Vicissitudo.
(5) *Unitas Spiritus*—last chapter in Gilson
    a) absolutely excludes pantheistic confusion of substances, between man + God. p 121
    "manebit quidem substantia De Dil X.28 cf. Cant 71.9-10* (difference bet. union of soul + God, + union of Father + Son)
    b) Not destruction of the creature but transformation.
    c) Is the *consummation* of restored creation—divinization
    d) *Mutual indwelling of man + God by charity*—Cant LXXI.10.
    e) union of love—precisely *because* God is transcendent Gils 126.
Conformitas maritat animam Verbo. LXXXIII.3.
Si perfecte diligit, nupsit.     " "
Complexus, ubi idem velle, nolle idem, unum facit spiritum de duobus. id.

Amor caeteros in se omnes traducit et captivat affectus. id.

Love above fear + reverence. id. 4. –

Fructus ejus usus ejus. etc. id.

Sponsae res et spes unus est amor- id. 5.

Cunctis renuntians affectionibus aliis, soli et tota incumbit amori. . . . id. 6

Nihil deest ubi totum est—id. 6 (In what sense love of creature comes to equal love of Creator.)

Amor sanctus et castus, amor suavis et dulcis . . . etc. id. 6.

Quam facile magistram de omnibus fecit et magistra unctio et frequens experientia id. 6.

St. *Ailred's Marian Sermons.*

*Our Lady—the Model of Monastic Perfection.*
Serm. 25. Migne P.L. 185:353 ff.

The *Valiant Woman*—cf Proverbs 31.—is first of all the Church, the wife of the New Adam,

"built" out of His side in the Passion, when He slept on the Cross

> Tam fortis ut vincat mundum, tam sapiens ut vincat diabolum, tam bona operaria ut acquirat coelum. 353.

But, he says, this "moral" sense is very often commented.

It is fitting however that the perfections of the Mother (Church) should belong to the children. Hence in the *mulier fortis* we have a form of religious perfection (*forma optimae vitae*)

The strong, valiant soul is the one who has left the world, trampled on the desires of the flesh, + despised the glory of the world.

Who shall find her? Not Moses, not Josue, not Solomon, but He who said "If thou wouldst be perfect, go, sell all that thou hast . . . etc.

*Mary*—the model of all such strong souls.

1) Without any other's example, she despised the world + chose the life of virginity
2) She was "formed" by Xt in the sense that He prepared her for His Mother before the foundation of the world.
3) our monastic vocation—a reproduction of Mary's *strength* and *zeal*.
But—pagan philosophers—left much—yet they were "fools."
robbers—suffered like Paul—but for what motive? Monastic vocation—+ sufferings, tested by the end in view—*pretium—procul et de ultimis finibus pretium ejus*
(1) *Strong in constancy + hope*
*Magna fortitudo philosophorum, magna fortitudo latronum, sed parvum pretium eorum.* 354
Their reward is not "far off" (procul) but close at hand—money—or fame—or honor
But the reward of the monk is "far off"—
it is not seen with the eyes, nor tasted, felt . . . Eye hath not seen . . .
it is as far away as heaven is from earth, as light is from blindness, as happiness is from misery.
He is saying the same as John of the + Ascent I-4.
"All the affections the soul has for creatures are darkness in the sight of God, + the soul that is clothed in them has no capacity for the simple light of God"
"All the being of creatures, compared with God, is nothing." John + - quotes Prov. 31:30.
And it only comes as the "last end." –
The monk is a man who has his hopes fixed on the next life + in eternity
This is his strength—as it was the strength of Mary.
Ailred insists we keep this end in view in our monastic labors, prayers + penances.

The strong soul is "Animam mundum perfecte contemnentem et nihil aliud nisi futura sperantem." 355.
(2) Strong in the vicissitudes of the Spiritual Life.—
*Fidelity*
"*Confidit in ea cor viri sui* . . .
We must be souls on whom Christ, our Spouse, can always depend, whether He sends us trial or consolation.
Such a soul is strong in a truly pure love, that loves Him for Himself + not for His consolations.
*TIMET enim caste, amat perfecte; amat virum suum non propter sua, sed propter se.* 355.
With such a soul, Jesus can come + go as He pleases. He is "secure" in all His dealings with the soul that is *strong, faithful, dependable.*
*Secure abest, secure adest, secure committit ei bona sua* . . . 355.
But He is always everywhere. How does He "leave" the soul? In time of trial.
Happy is the soul who is always strong in her love, no matter what may happen.
Neither downcast + complaining in adversity, nor proud in good times.
Felix mens cum qua secure Deus haec omnia agit.
Vere confidit in ea cor viri sui
Felix mens quae nec adversis frangitur, nec prosperis dissolvitur . . .
Ailred reproves the self complacency of those who, when all goes well, exult and raise themselves over others, but who fall into depression when things go badly.
Describes spiritual trial:
Sordet meditatio, horret oratio, lectio vilescit; insuper impugnat libido . . . mens quasi quibus

 (1) *Strong . . . hope* ] *added in left margin*
 *TIMET*] *interlined above cancelled Timet*

## Additions and Alterations in
## LIFE, WORKS AND DOCTRINE Typescript

| | |
|---|---|
| 2 | This is . . . doctrine.] *interlined* |
| 4 | conformity to God] to God *interlined with a caret* |
| 4–5 | read pp. 100–101–102] *added in left margin* |
| 5 | around them] *followed by x'd out* from time to time and |
| 6 | mightily] *preceded by x'd out* brightly in the |
| 6–7 | read p. 103] *added on line* |
| 7 | it is most . . . are doing.] *added on line* |
| 8 | us into] *followed by x'd out* God |
| 11 | much less standardization] *altered from* much less standardization |
| 12 | wandering clerics] *interlined below and marked for insertion* |
| | realm] *preceded by x'd out* world of si |
| | N.B. . . . everything] *added in left margin and marked for insertion* |
| | One feels . . . problems] *interlined below and marked for insertion* |
| | cultured] *interlined above cancelled* rich |
| | growth] *preceded by x'd out* Fontaines les Dijon— |
| 32 | childhood] *interlined* |
| | First Period] *interlined* |
| | becomes ill] *followed by x'd out* and is confined to cabin |
| | read Letters . . . 5] *interlined and marked for insertion* |
| 33 | entirely] *preceded by x'd out* almost |
| | hardly] *added in left margin preceding cancelled* not yet |
| | he is sick in bed again this year] *added on line* |
| | again St. . . . dies] *interlined* |
| | (approbation . . . Templars)] *interlined and marked for insertion* |
| 34 | Letters . . . 224] *added in left margin* |
| 35 | 1130, Letters] *followed by x'd out* 22 and 40 and |
| | 21] *interlined above cancelled* 20 |
| | 51.3] *interlined above cancelled* 48 |
| 36 | 95] *interlined below and marked for insertion* |
| | (Letter 141)] *interlined* |

|  |  |
|---|---|
|  | Lombardy] *followed by x'd out* Milan (June) |
| 44 | (Letter 239)] *interlined and marked for insertion* |
| 45 | 305] *interlined above cancelled* 228 |
|  | read letter, #2] *added in left margin* |
| 46 | Spires] *followed by x'd out* He fails to get the Emperor and his knights to join the crusade. |
|  | *Fifth Period*] *interlined* |
|  | Letters . . . 408] *added in left margin* |
|  | Malachy;] *followed by* The affair of Nicholas of Clairvaux *added in lower margin and cancelled* |
|  | read Letter 354, p. 431] *added on line* |
| 47 | consultation] *interlined above cancelled* agreement |
|  | (Cistercians were exempt)] (Cist. exempt) *added on line* |
|  | death of Suger] *interlined* |
|  | read Letter 353] *added on line* |
|  | *De Consideratione*] *preceded by x'd out* Writing |
| 48 | death of . . . Champagne] *interlined* |
| 78 | consequent] *preceded by x'd out* of the fall |
|  | tend] *followed by x'd out* in the |
| 79 | then the more] *followed by x'd out* faithful |
| 107 | *The Reasons*] *preceded by x'd out* A more detailed consideration |
|  | What follows . . . Cistercian] *interlined* |
| 108 | How much] *preceded by x'd out* How has He loved us |
|  | 5. He has . . . itself.] *interlined* |
|  | capacity to love] *added on line* |
| 109–10 | yet we . . . crucified] *altered from* yet we . . . crucified |
| 111 | pierced] *preceded by x'd out* nailed to the |
| 119 | necessary for him] *altered from* necessary for Him |
|  | OF LOVE.] *followed by* Clearest case—love of parents for children—St Bernard does not mention this *added in left margin and cancelled* |
| 120 | socialis] *followed by x'd out* For this |
|  | returning to] *preceded by x'd out* our |
|  | one step] *followed by x'd out* and |
| 122 | through danger] *preceded by cancelled* only |
|  | come to love] *preceded by cancelled* can |

| | |
|---|---|
| | tend to] *added in lower margin and marked for insertion to replace cancelled* will only |
| | only] *added in lower margin and marked for insertion* |
| | and the sense of our own {insecurity}] *interlined with a caret* |
| | were] *interlined above cancelled* was |
| | enter] *preceded by x'd out* acknowledge |
| | are spontaneously] *preceded by x'd out* know |
| 123 | as it were] *preceded by x'd out* by our own |
| 125 | Sermons] *preceded by x'd out* Canticle of |
| | pleasure."] *altered from* pleasure. |
| 133 | Whenever . . . fantasy.] *opposite page* |
| | first of all] *added on line* |
| | 1122] *added on line* |
| | short period] *preceded by x'd out* period |
| | "paradise . . . of the air"] *altered from* "paradise . . . of the air" |
| 140 | condemnation] *preceded by x'd out* accusation |
| 141 | and instituted reforms] *interlined and marked for insertion* |
| | certain Cistercians.] *followed by x'd out* Chapters |
| | some] *interlined with a caret* |
| | This is evident . . . of Cluny.] *added on line* |
| 142 | initiated] *preceded by x'd out* tried to |
| | St. Bernard . . . good faith.] *added in lower margin* |
| 143 | He even . . . from within.] *added on line* |
| | became] *preceded by x'd out* lost its power to |
| | to keep] *preceded by x'd out* for each one to |
| | word.] *followed by x'd out* That |
| | these lessons . . . orders.] *interlined* |
| 147 | In short, . . . appear to be.] *opposite page* |
| | precisely] *preceded by x'd out* in order |
| 148 | says that this] *preceded by x'd out* attributes this |
| | monastic values . . . subverted] *altered from* monastic values . . . subverted |
| | "How can . . . the soul?"] *altered from* "How can . . . the soul?" |
| 149 | Carefully . . . qualifies!] *added on line* |
| | attitude] *preceded by x'd out* spirit |

## Appendix A

| | |
|---|---|
| 150 | brings with] *followed by x'd out* a |
| | Bernard accuses Cluny] *interlined with a caret* |
| | life from] *followed by x'd out* flesh to |
| | humility what] *followed by x'd out* is in fact |
| | particular] *preceded by x'd out* cases where |
| 151 | excessive] *followed by x'd out* quantity |
| | 911] *preceded by x'd out* 912. |
| | Other] *preceded by x'd out* Bedding |
| | need] *preceded by x'd out* eat meat |
| | 1) . . . interior spirit] *interlined and marked for insertion* |
| 152 | 2)] *added in left margin* |
| | The second reason] *altered from* The second reason |
| | military] *interlined with a caret* |
| 153 | however] *followed by x'd out* these |
| | other] *interlined with a caret* |
| | decorated] *followed by x'd out* was a |
| 154 | curiousness] *preceded by x'd out* curiosity |
| | these works of art] *typed interlined above x'd out* this |
| | and their cathedrals] *typed interlined and marked for insertion* |
| 155 | continued] *preceded by x'd out* learned |
| | product] *preceded by x'd out* symbol not o |
| | sumptuous] *followed by x'd out* things |
| 156 | fault] *altered from* faults |
| | (918)] *added on line* |
| 196 | felt] *preceded by x'd out* was |
| 197 | occasions] *preceded by x'd out* wickedness |
| | they lived.] *followed by cancelled* A vivid picture of student life to be seen between the lines of this piece. |
| | morals.] *preceded by x'd out* life |
| | a spiritualization] *preceded by x'd out* an entirel |
| | in Christ,] *followed by x'd out* we |
| 198 | This is . . . the Truth.] *interlined* |
| | determined to lead a new life] *interlined above cancelled* converted |
| | likeness] *followed by x'd out* of |
| | and closes . . . 22)] *added on line* |
| 200 | seeks] *preceded by x'd out* lets the |

| | |
|---|---|
| 201 | fasting is useless] is useless *interlined with a caret* |
| | reason] *preceded by x'd out* soul |
| 204 | Note: the . . . order.] *interlined* |
| | by itself] *preceded by x'd out* in i |
| 205 | willing . . . commanded] *added on line* |
| 206 | Here the . . . progressives] *interlined* |
| | Reason. . . pious life] *altered from* Reason. . . pious life |
| | Here the . . . begins.] *added on line* |
| 209 | Hunger . . . will.] *added on line* |
| | The body] *preceded by x'd out* The will is subject to reason, |
| 210 | confident] *preceded by x'd out* assured that |
| | But when . . . trust.] *altered from* But when . . . trust. |
| | Blessed are the merciful] *altered from* Blessed are the merciful |
| | strive to] *followed by x'd out* do |
| 211 | trans. p. 44] *added in left margin* |
| | enlightened] *followed by x'd out* but the |
| | compassion] *followed by x'd out* without |
| 212 | trans. p. 46] *added in left margin* |
| | the period . . . purification] *altered from* the period . . . purification |
| | grateful . . . Father] *altered from* grateful . . . Father |
| 213 | the scandal] *preceded by x'd out* (A Digression |
| | worldly ambition] *altered from* worldly ambition |
| | usurped] *altered from* usurp |
| | had] *altered from* have |
| | many had] *altered from* have |
| | "On] *altered from* On |
| | provoke it."] *altered from* provoke it. |
| | fear] *followed by x'd out* the justice of |
| | it is moderate] it *interlined with a caret* |
| 214 | moderate] *followed by x'd out* frank |
| | the first] *preceded by x'd out* cap 1. |
| 215 | live according to] *interlined above cancelled* keep |
| | every violation] *preceded by x'd out* everything in the *Rule* |
| | does not sin] *preceded by x'd out* and |
| 216 | unintentionally.] *followed by x'd out* He means semi-deliberate faults |

## Appendix A

|     | |
|---|---|
|     | But this . . . not will.] *added on line* |
| 217 | But this gift . . . our part.] *added on line* |
|     | sacrifice, then] *followed by x'd out* in |
| 218 | the most . . . superior] *altered from* the most . . . superior |
|     | evaluating . . . them] *altered from* evaluating . . . them |
| 219 | analyze or] *followed by x'd out* question them. |
|     | The difference . . . difficulty] *altered from* The difference . . . difficulty |
|     | badly] *preceded by x'd out* bad consc |
|     | (d)] *preceded by x'd out* he |
| 220 | The yoke . . . Spirit of Christ] *altered from* The yoke . . . Spirit of Christ |
| 222 | in discussing . . . perseverance.] *opposite page* |
| 223 | remember . . . elsewhere] *added on line* |
| 223–24 | (However St. Thomas . . . generosity.) *opposite page* |
| 234 | *(voluntas propria)*] *interlined with a caret* |
|     | righteous.] *followed by x'd out* (Gilson, p. 57) |
| 235 | on Naaman's . . . Jordan] *added on line* |
|     | But the . . . consilium] *altered from* But the . . . consilium |
|     | everything] *altered from* anything |
| 236 | The distinction . . . intention.] *added on line* |
|     | i.e., we . . . another.] *added on line* |
|     | INFERNUS] *preceded by x'd out* CESSET |
|     | flow] *followed by x'd out* either |
| 237 | mere] *interlined above cancelled* just |
| 238 | "mystical theology" and "contemplation"] *altered from* mystical theology and contemplation |
|     | else. Here] *followed by x'd out* the c |
| 239 | 6] *added in left margin before cancelled* 5 |
|     | discussion] *followed by x'd out* (although there are few |
|     | created] *preceded by x'd out* let |
|     | 7] *added in left margin before cancelled* 6 |
|     | mystics."] *followed by x'd out* but still tends to hold that |
|     | But the contemplative] But *added on line* |
| 240 | these theologians] *interlined* |
|     | gifts of] *preceded by x'd out* seven |
| 241 | (I leave . . . phenomena.)] *interlined* |
|     | 8] *added in left margin before cancelled* 7 |

|  |  |
|---|---|
|  | this or that] *preceded by x'd out* the |
| 242 | building] *preceded by x'd out* adopting a |
|  | to a great] *preceded by x'd out* semi passive |
|  | graces of] *followed by x'd out* mystic |
|  | 9] *added in left margin before cancelled* 8 |
| 243 | Middle Ages,] *followed by x'd out* as the works of Tauler and Ruysbroeck, |
|  | as yet] *followed by x'd out* beyond a vague reproduce |
| 244 | Conclusion: . . . His will] *added in lower margin* |
| 245 | Let us] *followed by x'd out* examine |
|  | If we . . . here] *altered from* If we . . . here |
|  | whole series of] *interlined below cancelled* other |
|  | not only . . . century] *altered from* not only . . . century |
| 246 | remember that the] *followed by x'd out* sermons of |
|  | masterpieces] *preceded by x'd out* literary |
|  | fine] *preceded by x'd out* resume of Patristic doctrine |
| 247 | those who are] *preceded by x'd out* all men |
|  | show the way] *preceded by x'd out* are |
|  | never feels] *preceded by x'd out* is |
|  | quotations] *preceded by x'd out* Scripture |
|  | inspired] *followed by x'd out* and written |
|  | the *mystery*] *preceded by x'd out* God, through the union which the Holy Spirit brings about with |
|  | To study . . . doctrines] *altered from* To study . . . doctrines |
| 248 | enlightened] *preceded by x'd out* speaking |
|  | the *perfection*] *preceded by x'd out* ascend |
|  | But St. Bernard] *preceded by x'd out* Example |
|  | Many mystics . . . hearts.] *added in left margin and marked for insertion* |
| 256–57 | The Sermons: . . . individual soul.] *following* Spirit of God. *and marked for transposition by* Put this after "Bernard's Mysticism." *added in left margin* |
| 256 | humble] *preceded by x'd out* retreat, |
|  | twenty-three] *altered from* twenty-seven |
| 257 | in the light] *preceded by x'd out* their |
|  | Starting from] *followed by x'd out* that, then, they |
| 258 | Pride] *followed by x'd out* is what |

## Appendix A

|     | |
| --- | --- |
|     | divinely] *preceded by x'd out* divine understa |
|     | center] *followed by x'd out* and |
|     | by . . . Spirit] *added on line* |
| 259 | 363] *preceded by x'd out* 362- |
| 260 | story and] *followed by x'd out* the |
|     | quippe] *typed interlined above x'd out* nempe |
|     | banquet of Charity] *altered from* banquet of Charity |
| 261 | monastic] *preceded by x'd out* little |
|     | 74] *altered from* 84 |
| 262 | useful] *interlined above cancelled* helpful |
| 263 | doctrine] *preceded by x'd out* of the |
|     | mentioned in passing] *typed interlined below x'd out* not emphasized |
|     | A General] *preceded by x'd out* The |
|     | peace] *followed by x'd out* and |
| 264 | knowledge of this] *preceded by x'd out* secret |
|     | To explain] *preceded by x'd out* He speaks |
|     | body] *followed by cancelled* Angels, according to him, need to use bodies in their dealings with material creation. Man's spirit dwells in his body. |
|     | beast] *interlined above cancelled* best |
|     | and bodily] *preceded by x'd out* but |
|     | fallen] *followed by x'd out* in the le |
|     | God ] *followed by x'd out* possible |
| 265 | difficulty] *followed by x'd out* raised |
|     | spiritual] *typed in left margin to replace x'd out* mystical |
|     | with God] *followed by x'd out* by love |
|     | love fully] *preceded by x'd out* only |
|     | When the] *followed by x'd out* The mercenary fears—and fear does not produce |
| 266 | Note: love . . . reward etc.] *added on line* |
|     | passage] *typed interlined above x'd out* digression |
| 267 | with the Father] *preceded by x'd out* in the Holy |
|     | manifested] *followed by x'd out* above all |
| 268 | that union] *followed by x'd out* of G |
|     | omnino] *followed by x'd out unde* |
|     | matter of] *followed by x'd out* created |

|   |   |
|---|---|
|   | *paterno*] *preceded by x'd out* se |
| 269 | There are] *preceded by x'd out* Then |
|   | these sermons] *followed by x'd out* the general in |
| 270 | (The patience . . . "breasts.")] *added on line* |
|   | To avoid . . . the monks.] *interlined* |
|   | allusion] *interlined above cancelled* remark |
| 271 | later] *interlined below and marked for insertion* |
|   | (Sermon 18)] *added on line* |
|   | taste] *followed by x'd out* in solut |
|   | discussed] *preceded by x'd out* better |
|   | make two] *preceded by x'd out* touch |
|   | (10.1)] *preceded by x'd out* (9:9-10) |
|   | temporal] *followed by x'd out* and materi |
| 271–72 | However . . . required.] *opposite page* |
| 272 | viewpoint] *followed by x'd out* is i |
|   | (cf. *De Conversione*)] *interlined* |
| 273 | Mercy . . . Gospel!] *added on line* |
| 274 | forgive,] *followed by x'd out* becoming |
|   | so dead . . . for all] *altered from* so dead . . . for all |
|   | This is . . . prisoner.] *added in lower margin and marked for insertion* |
| 275 | the whole] *followed by x'd out* spirit. |
|   | 15] *preceded by x'd out* 16 |
|   | response] *followed by x'd out* must |
| 276 | It is detected . . . virtuous] *added on line* |
|   | trusts] *interlined above cancelled* confides |
| 277 | the good . . . saints] *interlined below cancelled* this example |
|   | upon all the faithful] *interlined and marked for insertion* |
|   | finally] *preceded by x'd out* become kin |
|   | encouraging] *preceded by x'd out* encouragement |
| 278 | when *preached*] *added on line* |
|   | when *meditated*] *added on line* |
|   | counteracts] *preceded by x'd out* heals |
|   | when it is *invoked*] *added on line* |
| 280 | Eliseus'] *interlined below cancelled* the prophet's |
|   | For St. . . . His grace.] *opposite page* |

## Appendix A

| | |
|---|---|
| 281 | Luddy translation, p. 172] *added on line* |
| 282 | Luddy translation, p. 175] *added on line* |
| 284 | importance of . . . waiting] *added on line* |
| | 5–6] *typed interlined above x'd out* 6 |
| | apostolic] *followed by x'd out* mission |
| | (cf. Luddy . . . 181 ff.)] *added on line* |
| 285 | (b) in] *followed by x'd out* addition to |
| | mysterious] *preceded by x'd out* habitual |
| | *Spiritual Canticle*] *added on line following cancelled Living Flame* |
| 286 | "*plenitudo dilectionis*"] *interlined* |
| | *effundit*] *followed by x'd out erumpens* |
| | merely] *preceded by x'd out* a mere "pretty" spiritual |
| | architects] *followed by x'd out* on |
| 287 | *true fullness*] *altered from* true fullness |
| | reality, with] *followed by x'd out* substantial |
| | these words] *preceded by x'd out* these two sermons |
| 288 | beside the point] *preceded by x'd out* outside the |
| 288–89 | You who have but] but *interlined with a caret* |
| 289 | recently] *preceded by cancelled* but |
| | duty of . . . know what they say] *interlined* |
| 290 | *same self-will . . . spiritual life*] *altered from* same self-will . . . spiritual life |
| 293 | (cf. Luddy translation, 198)] *added on line* |
| 294 | It gives us strength . . . (871).] *opposite page* |
| | Luddy 201–202] *interlined* |
| 295 | *effects*] *altered from* effects |
| | This love is . . . (871).] *added on line* |
| | *amor rationabilis Christi*] *added on line* |
| 297 | your power] *preceded by x'd out* our |
| | weaknesses] *typed interlined above x'd out* limitations |
| 298 | subtle] *typed interlined above x'd out* an acute |
| 300 | 23.1] *preceded by x'd out* 33 |
| | the moral sense] *added on line* |
| | arbitrary] arbi- *followed by x'd out* a) *Disciplina* |
| 301 | "The good of nature] *typed interlined above x'd out* "That |
| 303 | 18] *altered from* 19 |

## Readings Adopted from
## LIFE, WORKS AND DOCTRINE Typescript

| | |
|---|---|
| 1 | A most important . . . rewarding.] *interlined* |
| 5 | *can and must*] can and must |
| 7 | *what love is*] what love is |
| | and not just] not just |
| | struggle blindly for] struggle for |
| | "more love"] more love |
| | no idea] no understanding |
| 8 | is a perfect] is perfect |
| | love for the Church of God] *omitted* |
| 11 | *simplicity*] simplicity |
| | *much less*] much less |
| 12 | wandering clerics] *interlined and marked for insertion* |
| | *healthy*] healthy |
| | flourished] purified |
| | their problems] given problems |
| | *Burgundy*] Burgundy |
| 32 | read *Letters . . . 5*] *interlined and marked for insertion* |
| 33 | *Gratia*] Gratis |
| | (approbation . . . Templars)] *interlined and marked for insertion* |
| 35 | Letters, . . . 224] *added in left margin* |
| | 51.3] 51 |
| 36 | (Letter 141)] *interlined* |
| | read letters . . . 165] *added in left margin* |
| 44 | (Letter 239)] *interlined and marked for insertion* |
| 45 | read . . . letter, #2] *added in left margin* |
| 46 | this project] his project |
| | Letters . . . 408] *added in left margin* |
| | read Letter 354, p. 431] *added on line* |
| 47 | consultation] agreement |
| | read Letter 353] *added on line* |
| 78 | ordered to] *ordered* to |
| | vitiated] violated |
| 79 | p. 298] *omitted* |
| 107 | What follows is] This is forever |
| | and yet we] yet we |

## Appendix A

| | |
|---|---|
| 108 | condition . . . itself] condition. |
| | Chapter 2] *omitted* |
| | capacity to love] *added on line* |
| 109 | owe] own |
| 109–10 | yet we . . . *crucified*] yet we . . . crucified |
| 119 | this *amor carnalis*] the *amor carnalis* |
| | necessary for him] necessary for Him |
| 121 | It has to be] It is to be |
| 122 | *experiencing the reality . . . love*] experience the reality . . . love |
| | *love* (c. 9, n. 26)] *love* |
| | gratitude . . . *of God*] gratitude . . . of God |
| | and the sense . . . {insecurity}] *interlined with a caret* |
| | were] was |
| 124 | (c. 10.27-29)] *omitted* |
| | Deum" (990).] Deum." |
| 125 | sake? (n. 28)] sake? |
| 133 | statements made in] statements in |
| 143 | *purity of monasticism*] purity of monasticism |
| | sometimes] sometime |
| | solid] sound |
| | labors] labor |
| 146 | 5.10] 5.18 |
| | corporal observances] corporal observance |
| | *involuta*] *involute* |
| 148 | soul?" (8, n. 16 [908]).] soul?" |
| 151 | *extorquebis*" (911)] *extorquebis*." |
| 153 | consideration] considerations |
| 154 | reason] reasons |
| 196 | v.g.] e.g. |
| | using . . . ambition,] "using . . . ambition," |
| 198 | lived disedifying] led disedifying |
| | in the soul] on the soul |
| 200 | *struggle*] struggle |
| 205 | *poor* and *meek*] poor and meek |
| | *mourn*] mourn |
| 210 | *Blessed are the merciful*] Blessed are the merciful |
| | *DEUM TIBI VIS*] *DEUM VIS* |

| | |
|---|---|
| 212 | trans. p. 46] *added in left margin* |
| 214 | Pierre] Père |
| 215 | live according to] keep |
| 216 | But this does . . . not will.] *added on line* |
| 217 | But this gift . . . our part.] *added on line* |
| 218 | *the most . . . superior*] the most . . . superior |
| | *evaluating . . . them*] evaluating . . . them |
| 219 | views (873)] (873) *omitted* |
| | *The difference . . . difficulty*] The difference . . . difficulty |
| | (e) they] they |
| 220 | *The yoke . . . Spirit of Christ*] The yoke . . . Spirit of Christ |
| | TO BE ACTUALLY] ACTUALLY TO BE |
| | certainly commit . . . not correct] certainly not correct |
| 222 | in discussing . . . perseverance.] *opposite page* |
| | a greater] a *greater* |
| 223 | remember . . . elsewhere] *added on line* |
| 223–24 | (However St. Thomas . . . generosity.) *opposite page* |
| 234 | nothing but] nothing by |
| 236 | *exclusion of*] exclusion of |
| | CESSET VOLUNTAS PROPRIA] CESSIT VOLUNTAS PROPRIUM |
| 237 | us from arriving] us arriving |
| 239 | *the study*] the *study* |
| | has created] have created |
| | *modern . . . theology*] modern . . . theology |
| | *Poulain*] Poulain |
| 240 | *scholastic . . . theory*] scholastic . . . theory |
| | a scholastic] the scholastic |
| 241 | ought to be] should be |
| 242 | *prepared*] prepared |
| | *extraordinary and charismatic*] extraordinary and charismatic |
| 243 | deepening of . . . into] deepening into |
| 245 | whole . . . sermons] sermons—the whole series |
| | *they needed*] they needed |
| 247 | *mystery of . . . God*] mystery of . . . God |
| | *To study . . . doctrines*] To study . . . doctrines |
| 248 | *St. Teresa*] St. Teresa |
| 253 | BUT, as Butler] But, as Butler |

## Appendix A

| | |
|---|---|
| 255 | God!!!] God!!!!! |
| 256 | to the meditation] to meditation |
| | *sermons* are] *sermons* were |
| 258 | Scriptures, by . . . Spirit] Scriptures |
| 259 | tradition of the Fathers] tradition of the Father |
| | *beginning of Sermon 73*] beginning of Sermon 73 |
| 260 | *merely . . . story*] merely . . . story |
| | *gustata*] *gustate* |
| 261 | in *our words*] in *our words* |
| | in *our affections*] in *our affections* |
| | *figure or . . . God*] figure or . . . God |
| | *makes . . . within us*] makes . . . within us |
| | in *sensible realities*] in *sensible realities* |
| | *things of God*] things of God |
| 262 | through bypaths . . . the bypaths *do*] through bypaths which *do* |
| 263 | union, and the . . . and describe] union, and describe |
| 266 | Note: love . . . reward etc.] *interlined* |
| | Laudem] Laudent |
| 267 | *It is . . . Spirit*] It is . . . Spirit |
| 268 | *locum*] *lotum* |
| | beyond all understanding] beyond understanding |
| 269 | correspond] corresponds |
| 271 | *generosity . . . dryness*] generosity . . . dryness |
| 272 | work] works |
| | ourselves] ourself |
| 273 | ointment of *devotio*] ointment of devotion |
| | necessary)] necessary |
| | Him (cf. 11:7)] Him cf. 11) |
| 275 | the chief moral] the moral |
| | *joy*] joy |
| 276 | as contempt] in contempt |
| 280 | a *principal*] the *principal* |
| | all good in . . . grace.] all good . . . |
| | and influencing . . . influence with] and influence with |
| | the *discernment*] *the discernment* |
| 282 | READ 18:2-3—Luddy translation, p. 175] READ 18:2-3 |
| | *EXHIBEBIS*] *EXHIBERIS* |

| | | |
|---|---|---|
| 284 | proceed] provide | |
| | importance of . . . waiting] *interlined* | |
| | (cf. Luddy . . . 181 ff.)] *added on line* | |
| 285 | *coruscamine*] *corpuscamine* | |
| | *Spiritual Canticle*] *Living Flame* | |
| 285–86 | When the soul . . . zeal.] *omitted* | |
| 287 | *true fullness*] true fullness | |
| 288–89 | You who have but] You have but | |
| 290 | *same self-will . . . spiritual life*] same self-will . . . spiritual life | |
| 292 | idea in] idea of | |
| 293 | though *human*] though human | |
| | a *perfect*] a perfect | |
| | (cf. Luddy translation, 198)] *added on line* | |
| 294 | READ n. 6—Luddy 201–2] READ n. 6 | |
| 295 | *effects*] effects | |
| 298 | emerges a subtle] emerges subtle | |
| | *sequi* (21:2)] *sequi* | |
| 298–99 | present in the Incarnate . . . in the world] present in the world | |
| 299 | would say] should say | |
| 302 | *natural,* and good] natural, and good | |

### Readings Adopted from *Monastic Orientations*

| | |
|---|---|
| 17 | on {the} fourteen-year-old] of {the} fourteen-year-old |
| | movement of desire.] movement or desire. |
| 29 | *cum caro*] *cum carne* |
| 311 | of the Psalms] of the psalms |
| | *in voluntate tua deduxisti*] *in voluntate deduxisti* |
| 312 | that he desires] what he desires |
| | with a humble] with humble |
| | consent to do this] consent to this |
| | conform to what *is*] conform to what is |
| 312–13 | joy and gratitude] joy and beatitude |
| 313 | Then, the reason . . . our good:] *omitted* |
| | *Tenet Dominus*] *Tenet Deus* |
| | *Suscipit in coelis*] *Suscepit in coelis* |

## Appendix A

| | |
|---|---|
| 320 | *Psalm 90]* Psalm 90 |
| | *The Lenten fast is a gift]* The Lenten fast is a gift |
| 328 | *vanity]* vanity |
| | *impatience]* impatience |
| 329 | *delectatur]* delectetur |
| | *by other men.]* by others. |
| | *prosperitatibus]* properitatibus |
| | *His* own sake.] his own sake. |
| 330 | His Life unless] His life unless |
| 331 | *revertuntur]* reuertantur |
| 333 | *lacrymarum]* lacrymarus |
| 339 | EXPERIENCED?] EXPERIENCE? |
| 342 | fasts its joys] fasts its joy |
| 348 | *disorder]* disorder |
| 353 | *Effective charity]* Effective charity |
| 362 | finds reason] finds reasons |
| | *why* and *how]* why and how |
| 363 | delivers the *will]* delivers the will |
| 365 | Armed by fortitude] Armed with fortitude |
| | soul's purification] souls' purification |
| 368 | others to {a} *life of virtues]* other to {a} *life of virtues* |
| 370 | *puritas* = {from} *labor]* puritas; labor |
| 372 | *can* be a contemplation] *can* be contemplation |
| 373 | veritatis arcana] *veritatis arcana* |
| | videt invisibilia] invisibilia |
| 374 | CONTEMPLATIONIS II: Another . . . *Love (De]* |
| | CONTEMPLATIONIS II *(De* |
| 375 | which God loves] which God love |
| | VOLUNTAS *ADIMPLETA]* VOLUNTAS ADIMPLETA |
| 380 | *In its most imperfect . . . active life]* In its most imperfect . . . active life |
| | Caritas sponsae] Caritas sponsa |
| 381 | cannot rest—that is, . . . must] cannot rest—must |
| | proderit [distinguish: . . . revealed]. *Vestrum]* distinguish: . . . revealed *marked with asterisk for insertion after* proderit—*not followed in Cistercian Fathers typescript* |
| | profectus] *profectus* |

| | |
|---|---|
| 382 | *Innumeros cernes]* Innumeros cernes |
| | c) (The superiors) *Qui]* c) *Qui* |
| 385 | His judgements. This . . . but so] His judgements, but so |
| 386 | N. 14: distinguishing] N. 14: distinguishes |
| 388 | stat sententia pacis] *stat sententia pacis* |
| 390 | gratitude (*idem*, n. 6). Ingratitudo] gratitude. Ingratitudo |
| | *ventus] ventur* |
| | *rorem misericordiae]* rorem *misericordia* |
| | and the right] and the right hand |
| 391 | *spe.*) {The} point . . . our love. Donec] *spe.*) *Donec* |
| 392 | openly and without] openly without |

## *Monastic Orientations* Variants

| | |
|---|---|
| 13 | AS A PERSON ] II. AS MONK AND MASTER OF THE SPIRITUAL LIFE |
| | we are dealing . . . favorably.] *added* |
| | article on] article read today in refectory on |
| | (he loves . . . goldfinch)] (goldfinch) |
| | Pope is presented] Pope presented |
| | We admire . . . *easily.*] *added* |
| | threat"] threat" (who is really good at nothing!) |
| | in his objectivity] *added* |
| 14 | near Dijon.] near Dijon (Historical background—St. Gregory VII died a few years before—Grande Chartreuse recently founded—Cluny being built—ferment at Molesme will soon lead to foundation of Citeaux—St. Anselm, the great theologian of the time—intellectual ferment—humanism, but strong pull towards primitive monasticism—political background: crusade in Spain.) (Give idea of medieval life here.) |
| | and Alette would] and would |
| 16 | Williams. Bernard more] Williams. More |
| 18–19 | *Nature and Character* . . . and problems.] *added* |
| 25 | 81B] il b. |
| 26 | positive desire] And positively desire |
| | *purely* and *authentically]* purely and authentically |

| | |
|---|---|
| 30 | mortification of desires] mortification of the desires |
| | (this is not] (This not |
| | *zeal for the common life*] zeal for the common life |
| 31 | *zeal for manual labor*] zeal for manual labor |
| | *zeal for prayer and solitude*] zeal for prayer and solitude |
| | *lectio divina*] Lectio Divina |
| | So much . . . works.] *added* |
| 313 | *pie gratias*] *et pie gratias* |
| 321 | N.B. all] all |
| 322 | glory of His resurrection:] glory of His resurrection (2) |
| | *followed by note:* "(2) cf. *Romans* 8: "If any man have not the Spirit of Christ, he is none of His . . . If the Spirit of Him that raised up Jesus from the dead dwell in you, He that raised up Jesus from the dead shall quicken also your mortal bodies because of His Spirit that dwelleth in you. Therefore, brethren, we are debtors not to the flesh, that we should live according to the flesh. For if you live according to the flesh you shall die, but if by the Spirit you mortify the deeds of the flesh you shall live." (*Romans* 8:9-13) (see context) cf. also:" |
| | for {the} Common of Virgins] (Common of Virgins) |
| 324 | a Little One.] a Little One." (Serm. ii, *in Cap. Jejunii*, n.1) |
| 326 | (Serm. 2, n. 2)] (Serm. ii, *Cap. Jejunii*, n.2) *followed by note:* "(3) The *Exordium Magnum* summarizes the Cistercian vocation in three words; "*formula perfectae paenitentiae*". |
| | self-will (cf. Serm. 3 *in Paschal Time*).] self-will. (4) *followed by note:* "(4) cf. Serm. 3 *in Paschal Time*, nn." |
| 326–27 | vice. See St. Thomas, *Summa*, . . . ad. 3).] vice. (5) *followed by note:* "(5) see St. Thomas, *Summa* . . . ad 3) |
| 327 | world, etc. See St. . . . diligimus.] world, etc. (6) *followed by note:* "(6) see St. Thomas, *Summa* . . . *diligimus*." |
| 328 | "root of bitterness,"] "*root of bitterness*" |
| | JOY AND SORROW] *preceded by page headed* Joy and Sorrow *of chart and explanation* |
| | *Rancor*] Rancor |

| | |
|---|---|
| 329 | This means] This means *preceded by* Union with others in joy (charity) *typed in left margin* |
| 335 | I here translate] I translate |
| | *his heart is far from me*] his heart is far from me |
| 337 | no matter what.] no matter what. *followed by* cf. Epistle: First Sunday of Lent *typed in left margin* |
| 338 | "ORDINAVIT IN ME CARITATEM"] ST. BERNARD—SERMONS 49 and 50 "IN CANTICA" "ORDINAVIT IN ME CARITATEM" |
| 339 | DETERMINED OR HELPED] DETERMINED OR HELPED BY A SENSIBLE ATTRACTION] BY A SENSIBLE ATTRACTION |
| | soliloquizes] begins soliloquizing |
| 341 | READ *Dark Night*] READ *Dark Night preceded by* Read John of Cross, vol. I: pp. 351 352 356 364 *typed in left margin* |
| 343 | *Discretio*, a function] "discretion"—a function *preceded by* (1) Balance between mercy and correction—(i.e. how to govern nature without crushing it) *typed in left margin* |
| 344 | Discretion is here] Discretion is here *preceded by* (2) Discretion plus fervent zeal leads to contempt of self and highest contemplation *typed in left margin* |
| 352 | *curae sint universae*] *curae sint universa* |
| 353 | It is regulated] It is regulated *preceded by* "Veritas Caritatis" *typed in left margin* |
| | This is what] This is what *preceded by* "Caritas Veritatis" *typed in left margin* |
| | I am praying] I praying |
| 354 | Degrees of Truth] Degree of Truth—see chapter |
| 355 | One is *completely*] One is *completely preceded by* Affectio Carnalis *typed in left margin* |
| | "Wisdom"] "Wisdom" *preceded by* Affectio sapientalis *typed in left margin* |
| | The "AFFECTUS] The "AFFECTUS *preceded by* Affectio Rationalis *typed in left margin* |
| 356 | infantium] infantium *preceded by* (1) *typed in left margin* |
| | Verbum Patris] Verbum Patris *preceded by* (2) *typed in left margin* |

## Appendix A

|      | |
|------|---|
|      | *eruditio,*] erudition, *preceded by* (1) *typed in left margin* |
|      | AD AETERNUM] AD AETERNUM *preceded by* (2) *typed in left margin* |
| 357  | *intentam {cordis aurem]* intentam cordia surem *preceded by* (3) *typed in left margin* |
| 362  | efforts] effort |
| 364  | This flight] *preceded by* From "Studium" to "Gemitum" *typed in left margin* |
|      | The soul] *preceded by* (From *False Rest* to *True Rest*) *typed in left margin* |
| 365  | *The hunger] preceded by* Fortitude *typed in left margin* |
|      | After this] *preceded by* Mercy *typed in left margin* |
| 367  | *freedom* and *rest] freedom and rest* |
| 368  | *cellars of affection]* "cellars of affection" |
| 370  | *external things]* external things |
| 371  | 4. {The} THIRD] 3. THIRD |
| 379  | (Note: *factus]* "*factus* |
|      | *perditum* and *unus] perditum unus* |
| 380  | *false rest] false rest* |
| 381  | Note n. 6] Note n. 6 *preceded by* "CELLA UNGUENTARIA" *typed in left margin* |
| 382  | belong to the second] belong in the second |
|      | To be both] To be both *preceded by* "CELLA VINARIA" *typed in left margin* |
| 388  | *speaks* His mercy] "speaks" His mercy |
| 390  | "rest." The] "rest" (1028, n. 8) The |
| 391  | Psalm 4] Psalm 90 |
| 392  | what it *is*] what *it is* |
| 394  | man's lower] mans' lower |
|      | to the society] to society |

# APPENDIX B
## Table of Correspondences

*The Cistercian Fathers and Their Monastic Theology—
Lectures and Taped Conferences*

| Date | Page # | Opening Words | TMC CD # | Published Tape Title & # |
|---|---|---|---|---|
| 1/5/63 | 21 | THE EARLIER | 38.2 | Love Casts Out Fear (2134) |
| 1/19/63 | 24 | To understand Bernard | 38.4 | |
| 2/2/63 | 26 | St. Bernard's Mariology | 43.1 | The Virgin Mary (2128) |
| 2/9/63 | 31 | 2. DE DILIGENDO DEO | 43.4 | Love and Purity of Heart (3018) |
| 2/16/63 | 33 | "Theology of Love" | 44.3 | In the Image of God (2135) |
| 2/23/63 | 33 | 3. The condition | 46.2 | In the Image of God (2135) |
| 3/2/63 | 38 | A. GUIGO | 46.4 | Life and truth (I:7a) |
| 3/9/63 | 38 | We should cling | 47.3 | Life and truth (I:7b) |
| 3/23/63 | 41 | CARITAS: | 50.1 | Love is Enough (2907) |
| 3/30/63 | 43 | The Christian is not | 50.3 | Love is Enough (2907) |
| 4/20/63 | 45 | B. Bernard's LETTER | 52.2 | Pure Love (2136) |
| 4/27/63 | 38 | They had been sent | 53.2 | |
| 5/4/63 | — | | 53.4 | Pure Love (2136) |
| 5/11/63 | 48 | 4. UBI PROPRIETAS | 54.3 | Belonging to God (2805) |
| 5/18/63 | 49 | 7. HAEC EST LEX | 56.2 | Love and Purity of Heart (3018?) |
| 5/25/63 | 51 | DE DILIGENDO DEO | 56.4 | Love and Purity of Heart (3018) |
| 6/15/63 | 51 | *dignitas* | 58.2 | Awakening the Heart (2911) |
| 6/22/63 | 52 | God's "re-making" | 58.3 | |
| 7/13/63 | 55 | *Ipse dat occasionem* | 60.2 | Seeking and Finding God (2913) |

|  | | | | |
|---|---|---|---|---|
| 7/20/63 | 55 | Every situation | 60.3 | Seeking and Finding God (2913) |
| 7/27/63 | — | | 61.1 | Life and the Holy Spirit (I:5a) |
| 8/17/63 | 56 | *Natural Love*: | #114A* | |
| 8/26/63 | — | | 65.4 | |
| 8/31/63 | 57 | FIRST DEGREE OF LOVE | 64.3 | Seeking and Finding God (2913) |
| 9/28/63 | 59 | II. ST. BERNARD AND | 73.1 | |
| 10/5/63 | 60 | Bernard admits | 73.2 | |
| 10/12/63 | 62 | *Nn. 10–11* | 73.4 | |
| 10/19/63 | 64 | *manual work* | 80.2 | |
| 10/26/63 | 66 | Letter II, 17 | 80.4 | |
| 11/9/63 | 66 | Many Benedictines | 83.3 | |
| 11/23/63 | 70 | 3. *Criticism of Cluny*: | 86.1 | |
| 1/4/64 | — | | 90.3 | |
| 1/11/64 | 77 | III. *DE CONVERSIONE* | 92.2 | De Conversione (3280) |
| 1/18/64 | 80 | The University of Paris | 92.4 | Love and Hope 1 (III:11b) |
| 2/1/64 | — | | 94.2 | |
| 2/8/64 | 84 | c) *The Problem* | 96.1 | |
| 2/15/64 | — | | 96.2 | |
| 2/22/64 | 83 | b) *Theology*: | 96.4 | |
| 2/29/64 | 84 | *Summary*: | 98.2 | |
| 3/7/64 | 86 | further amplifications | 98.4 | |
| 3/14/64 | 87 | *Quomodo ergo* | 110.2 | |
| 4/4/64 | 90 | *Monastic Doctrine* | 116.2 | |
| 4/11/64 | 90 | *Ut non nostro* | 116.4 | |
| 4/18/64 | 91 | *Numquam consuetudo* | 115.2 | |
| 5/2/64 | 92 | the "wild ass | 115.4 | |
| 5/9/64 | 93 | word *matrona* | 114.2 | |
| 5/16/64 | 95 | *Sermo de Conversione* | 114.4 | |
| 5/23/64 | 97 | Sin is really | 105.2 | De Conversione (3280) |
| 5/30/64 | 100 | Chapter 8 | 105.3 | De Conversione (3280) |
| 6/13/64 | 101 | 3. The soul is now | 118.2 | |
| 6/20/64 | 8 | William of St. Thierry | 118.3 | Thomas Merton and St. Bernard of Clairvaux 1: The First Life of Bernard |

| | | | | |
|---|---|---|---|---|
| 6/27/64 | 10 | What went on in his mind? | 118.4 | Thomas Merton and St. Bernard of Clairvaux 2: Conversion to the Monastic Life |
| 7/18/64 | 13 | 2. *The Voice of Truth*: | 120.3 | Paradox of joy and sorrow (2263); Thomas Merton and St. Bernard of Clairvaux 3: Asceticism in St. Bernard's Time and Ours |
| 8/8/64 | 110 | *Some Letters* | 122.2 | Thomas Merton and St. Bernard of Clairvaux 4: The Letters of St. Bernard |

- Absence of page numbers indicates conference material independent of text

- August 17, 1963, conference inadvertently not reproduced on CD; numbering refers to cassette recording

- Published tapes followed by four-digit number published by Credence Communications; those listed by roman numerals published by Electronic Paperbacks; the final four are available from Now You Know Media

# APPENDIX C
## For Further Reading

### A. Other Writings by Merton on Topics Treated in *The Cistercian Fathers and Their Monastic Theology*

#### General

*In the Valley of Wormwood: Cistercian Blessed and Saints of the Golden Age.* Edited with an Introduction by Patrick Hart, OCSO. Foreword by Brian Patrick McGuire. Cistercian Studies [CS] vol. 233. Collegeville, MN: Cistercian Publications, 2013.
*The Silent Life.* New York: Farrar, Straus & Cudahy, 1957: 95–125.
*The Waters of Siloe.* New York: Harcourt, Brace, 1949.

#### St. Bernard

Foreword to *St. Bernard of Clairvaux Seen through His Selected Letters.* Translated by Bruno Scott James. Chicago: Henry Regnery, 1953: v–viii.
*The Last of the Fathers: Saint Bernard of Clairvaux and the Encyclical Letter,* Doctor Mellifluus. New York: Harcourt, Brace, 1954.
Preface to *Marthe, Marie et Lazare.* In *"Honorable Reader": Reflections on My Work.* Edited by Robert E. Daggy. New York: Crossroad, 1989: 13–22.
"The Sacrament of Advent in the Spirituality of St. Bernard." In *Seasons of Celebration.* New York: Farrar, Straus & Giroux, 1965: 61–87.
"St. Bernard: Monk and Apostle." In *Disputed Questions.* New York: Farrar, Straus & Cudahy, 1960: 208–17.

*The Spirit of Simplicity: Characteristic of the Cistercian Order; An Official Report, Demanded and Approved by the General Chapter; together with Texts from St. Bernard of Clairvaux on Interior Simplicity.* Trappist, KY: Abbey of Gethsemani, 1948.

*Thomas Merton on Saint Bernard.* CS 9. Kalamazoo, MI: Cistercian Publications, 1980.

### Other Cistercian Fathers

"The Feast of Freedom: Monastic Formation according to Adam of Perseigne." Introduction to *Letters of Adam of Perseigne.* Translated by Grace Perigo. Cistercian Fathers [CF], vol. 21. Kalamazoo, MI: Cistercian Publications, 1976: 3–48.

"Guerric of Igny's Easter Sermons," *Cistercian Studies* 7 (1972): 85–95.

Introduction to *The Christmas Sermons of Blessed Guerric of Igny.* Translated by Sr. Rose of Lima. Trappist, KY: Abbey of Gethsemani, 1959: 1–25.

Introduction to Amédée Hallier, ocso, *The Monastic Theology of Aelred of Rievaulx.* Translated by Columban Heaney. CS 8. Spencer, MA: Cistercian Publications, 1969: vii–xiii.

"Isaac of Stella: An Introduction to Selections from his Sermons." *Cistercian Studies* 2 (1967): 243–51.

"Saint Aelred of Rievaulx and the Cistercians." Edited by Patrick Hart, ocso. *Cistercian Studies Quarterly* 20 (1985): 212–23; 21, no. 1 (1986): 30–42; 22, no. 1 (1987): 55–75; 23, no. 1 (1988): 45–62; 24, no. 1 (1989): 50–68.

## B. Significant Writings by Other Authors on Topics Treated in *The Cistercian Fathers and Their Monastic Theology*

### General

Brooke, Odo. *Studies in Monastic Theology.* CS37. Kalamazoo, MI: Cistercian Publications, 1980.

Dutton, Marsha L., Daniel M. La Corte, and Paul Lockey, eds. *Truth as Gift: Studies in Medieval Cistercian History in Honor of John R. Sommerfeldt.* CS 204. Kalamazoo, MI: Cistercian Publications, 2004.

Pennington, M. Basil. *The Cistercians*. Collegeville, MN: Liturgical Press, 1992.

———, ed. *The Last of the Fathers: The Cistercian Fathers of the Twelfth Century*. Still River, MA: St. Bede's Publications, 1983.

## St. Bernard

TRANSLATIONS

*Apologia to Abbot William: Cistercians and Cluniacs*. Translated by Michael Casey, ocso. CF 1. Introduction by Jean Leclercq, osb. Kalamazoo, MI: Cistercian Publications, 1970.

*Five Books on Consideration: Advice to a Pope*. Translated by John Anderson and Elizabeth T. Kennan. CF 37. Kalamazoo, MI: Cistercian Publications, 1976.

*Homilies in Praise of the Blessed Virgin Mary*. Translated by Marie-Bernard Saïd, osb. Introduction by Chrysogonus Waddell, ocso. CF 18A. Kalamazoo, MI: Cistercian Publications, 1993.

*In Praise of the New Knighthood*. Translated by Conrad Greenia, ocso. Introduction by Malcolm Barber. CF 19B. Kalamazoo, MI: Cistercian Publications, 2001.

*The Letters of Saint Bernard of Clairvaux*. Translated by Bruno Scott James. Introduction by Beverly Mayne Kienzle. CF 62. Kalamazoo, MI: Cistercian Publications, 2003.

*The Life and Death of Saint Malachy the Irishman*. Translated by Robert T. Meyer. CF 10. Kalamazoo, MI: Cistercian Publications, 1978.

*On Baptism and the Office of Bishops*. Translated by Pauline Matarasso. Introductions by Martha G. Newman and Emero Stiegman. CF 67. Kalamazoo, MI: Cistercian Publications, 2005.

*On Grace and Free Choice*. Translated by Daniel O'Donovan, ocso. Introduction by Bernard McGinn. CF 19A. Kalamazoo, MI: Cistercian Publications, 1988.

*On Loving God*. Translated by Robert Walton, osb. Introduction by Emero Stiegman. CF 13B. Kalamazoo, MI: Cistercian Publications, 1995.

*The Parables and the Sentences*. Translated by Michael Casey, ocso, and Francis R. Swietek. Introduction by Michael Casey and John R. Sommerfeldt. CF 55. Kalamazoo, MI: Cistercian Publications, 1991.

*Sermons for Advent and the Christmas Season*. Translated by Irene Edmonds, Wendy Beckett and Conrad Greenia, ocso. Edited by E. Rozanne Elder. CF 51. Kalamazoo, MI: Cistercian Publications, 2007.

*Sermons for Autumn*. Translated by Irene Edmonds with Mark Scott, ocso. Introduction by Wim Verbaal. CF 54. Collegeville, MN: Cistercian Publications, 2016.

*Sermons for Lent and the Easter Season*. Edited by John Leinenweber and Mark Scott, ocso. CF 52. Collegeville, MN: Cistercian Publications, 2013.

*Sermons for the Summer Season*. Translated by Beverly Kienzle with James Jarzembowski. CF 53. Kalamazoo, MI: Cistercian Publications, 1991.

*Sermons on Conversion*. Translated with an Introduction by Marie Bernard Saïd, osb. CF 25. Kalamazoo, MI: Cistercian Publications, 1981.

*Sermons on the Song of Songs 1*. Translated by Kilian Walsh, ocso, and Irene Edmonds. CF 4. Kalamazoo, MI: Cistercian Publications, 1971.

*Sermons on the Song of Songs 2*. Translated by Kilian Walsh, ocso, and Irene Edmonds. CF 7. Kalamazoo, MI: Cistercian Publications, 1976.

*Sermons on the Song of Songs 3*. Translated by Kilian Walsh, ocso, and Irene Edmonds. CF 31. Kalamazoo, MI: Cistercian Publications, 1979.

*Sermons on the Song of Songs 4*. Translated by Kilian Walsh, ocso, and Irene Edmonds. CF 40. Kalamazoo, MI: Cistercian Publications, 1980.

*The Steps of Humility and Pride*. Introduction by M. Basil Pennington, ocso. CF 13A. Kalamazoo, MI: Cistercian Publications, 1989.

## Studies

*Bernard of Clairvaux: Studies Presented to Dom Jean Leclercq*. CS 23. Washington, DC: Cistercian Publications, 1973.

Bonowitz, Bernard, ocso. *Saint Bernard's Three-Course Banquet: Humility, Charity, and Contemplation in the* De Gradibus. Monastic Wisdom [MW] 39. Collegeville, MN: Cistercian Publications, 2013.

Appendix C 455

Bredero, Adriaan Hendrik. *Bernard of Clairvaux: Between Cult and History*. Grand Rapids, MI: Eerdmans, 1996.

Casey, Michael, ocso. *Athirst for God: Spiritual Desire in Bernard of Clairvaux's Sermons on the Song of Songs*. CS 77. Kalamazoo, MI: Cistercian Publications, 1986.

Dumont, Charles, ocso. *Pathway of Peace: Cistercian Wisdom According to Saint Bernard*. CS 187. Kalamazoo, MI: Cistercian Publications, 1999.

Evans, Gillian. *Bernard of Clairvaux*. New York: Oxford University Press, 2000.

Gilson, Étienne. *The Mystical Theology of St. Bernard*. Translated by A. H. C. Downes. Preface by Jean Leclercq, osb. CS 120. Kalamazoo, MI: Cistercian Publications, 1990.

Lane, Anthony N. S. *Bernard of Clairvaux: Theologian of the Cross*. CS 248. Collegeville, MN: Cistercian Publications, 2012.

Leclercq, Jean, osb. *Bernard of Clairvaux and the Cistercian Spirit*. Translated by Claire Lavoie. CS 16. Kalamazoo, MI: Cistercian Publications, 1976.

———. *A Second Look at Bernard of Clairvaux*. CS 105. Kalamazoo, MI: Cistercian Publications, 1990.

McGuire, Brian P. *The Difficult Saint: Bernard of Clairvaux and His Tradition*. CS 126. Kalamazoo, MI: Cistercian Publications, 1991.

Rudolph, Conrad. *The "Things of Greater Importance": Bernard of Clairvaux's Apologia and the Medieval Attitude toward Art*. Philadelphia, PA: University of Pennsylvania Press, 1990.

Sommerfeldt, John R. *Bernard of Clairvaux on the Life of the Mind*. New York: Newman Press, 2004.

———. *Bernard of Clairvaux on the Spirituality of Relationship*. New York: Newman Press, 2004.

———. *The Spiritual Teachings of Bernard of Clairvaux: An Intellectual History of the Early Cistercian Order*. CF 125. Kalamazoo, MI: Cistercian Publications, 1991.

Sommerfeldt, John R., ed. *Bernardus Magister: Papers Presented at the Nonacentenary Celebration of the Birth of Saint Bernard of Clairvaux, Kalamazoo, Michigan*. CS 135. Kalamazoo, MI: Cistercian Publications, 1992.

Sommerfeldt, John R., and E. Rozanne Elder, eds. *The Chimaera of His Age: Studies on Bernard of Clairvaux*. CS 63. Kalamazoo, MI: Cistercian Publications, 1980.

## Other Cistercian Fathers

TRANSLATIONS

Adam of Perseigne. *Letters of Adam of Perseigne*. Translated by Grace Perigo. CF 21. Kalamazoo, MI: Cistercian Publications, 1976.

Aelred of Rievaulx. *Dialogue on the Soul*. Translated by C. H. Talbot. CF 22. Kalamazoo, MI: Cistercian Publications, 1981.

———. *For Your Own People: Aelred of Rievaulx's Pastoral Prayer*. Translated by Mark DelCogliano. Edited by Marsha L. Dutton. CF 73. Kalamazoo, MI: Cistercian Publications, 2008.

———. *The Historical Works*. Translated by Jane Patricia Freeland. Edited by Marsha L. Dutton. CF 56. Kalamazoo, MI: Cistercian Publications, 2005.

———. *The Liturgical Sermons: The First Clairvaux Collection. Advent–All Saints*. Translated by Theodore Berkeley. CF 58. Kalamazoo, MI: Cistercian Publications, 2001.

———. *The Liturgical Sermons: The Second Clairvaux Collection. Christmas–All Saints*. Translated by Marie Anne Mayeski. CF 77. Collegeville, MN: Cistercian Publications, 2016.

———. *Lives of the Northern Saints*. Translated by Jane Patricia Freeland. Introduction by Marsha L. Dutton. CF 71. Kalamazoo, MI: Cistercian Publications, 2006.

———. *Mirror of Charity*. Translated by Elizabeth Connor, ocso. Introduction by Charles Dumont, ocso. CF 17. Kalamazoo, MI: Cistercian Publications, 1990.

———. *Spiritual Friendship*. Translated by Lawrence C. Braceland. Edited by Marsha L. Dutton. CF 5. Collegeville, MN: Cistercian Publications, 2010.

———. *Treatises and Pastoral Prayer*. Introduction by David Knowles, osb. CF 2. Kalamazoo, MI: Cistercian Publications, 1995.

Daniel, Walter. *The Life of Aelred of Rievaulx and the Letter to Maurice*. Translated by F. M. Powicke and Jane Patricia Freeland. Introduction by Marsha Dutton. CF 57. Kalamazoo, MI: Cistercian Publications, 1994.

Guerric of Igny. *Liturgical Sermons 1*. Translated by Monks of Mount St. Bernard Abbey. CF 8. Kalamazoo, MI: Cistercian Publications, 1970.

———. *Liturgical Sermons 2*. Translated by Monks of Mount St. Bernard Abbey. CF 32. Kalamazoo, MI: Cistercian Publications, 1999.

Isaac of Stella. *Sermons on the Christian Year 1*. Translated by Hugh McCaffery, ocso. Introduction by Bernard McGinn. CF 11. Kalamazoo, MI: Cistercian Publications, 1979.

*Three Treatises on Man: A Cistercian Anthropology*. Translated by Benjamin Clark, ocso, Bernard McGinn, Erasmo Leiva, and Benedicta Ward, slg. Edited by Bernard McGinn. CF 24. Kalamazoo, MI: Cistercian Publications, 1977.

William of Saint-Thierry. *On Contemplating God, Prayer, Meditations*. Translated by Penelope Lawson, csmv. Introductions by Jacques Hourlier, osb, and J. M. Déchanet, osb. CF 3. Kalamazoo, MI: Cistercian Publications, 1970.

Studies

William of Saint-Thierry, Arnold of Bonneval, and Geoffrey of Auxerre. *The First Life of Bernard of Clairvaux*. Translated by Hilary Costello, ocso. Collegeville, MN: Cistercian Publications, 2015.

William of Saint-Thierry. *The Enigma of Faith*. Translated by John D. Anderson. CF 9. Kalamazoo, MI: Cistercian Publications, 1991.

———. *Exposition on the Epistle to the Romans*. Translated by John Baptist Hasbrouk, ocso. Introduction by John D. Anderson. CF 27. Kalamazoo, MI: Cistercian Publications, 2000.

———. *Exposition on the Song of Songs*. Translated by M. Columba Hart, osb. CF 6. Kalamazoo, MI: Cistercian Publications, 1970.

———. *The Golden Epistle*. Translated Theodore Berkeley, ocso. Introduction by J. M. Déchanet, osb. CF 12. Kalamazoo, MI: Cistercian Publications, 1971.

———. *The Mirror of Faith*. Translated by Thomas X. Davis, ocso. Introduction by E. Rozanne Elder. CF 15. Kalamazoo, MI: Cistercian Publications, 1979.

———. *The Nature and Dignity of Love*. Translated by Thomas X. Davis, ocso. Introduction by David N. Bell. CF 30. Kalamazoo, MI: Cistercian Publications, 1981.

Bell, David N. *The Image and Likeness: The Augustinian Spirit of William of St. Thierry*. CS 78. Kalamazoo, MI: Cistercian Publications, 1984.

Déchanet, Jean, osb. *William of St. Thierry: The Man and His Work*. Translated by Richard Strachan. CS 10. Spencer, MA: Cistercian Publications, 1972.

Hallier, Amédée, ocso, *The Monastic Theology of Aelred of Rievaulx*. Translated by Columban Heaney. CS 8. Spencer, MA: Cistercian Publications, 1969.

McGinn, Bernard. *The Golden Chain: A Study in the Theological Anthropology of Isaac of Stella*. CS 15. Washington, DC: Cistercian Publications, 1972.

Morson, John. *Christ the Way: The Christology of Guerric of Igny*. CS 25. Kalamazoo, MI: Cistercian Publications, 1972.

Sergent, F. Tyler, Aage Rydstrøm-Poulsen, and Marsha L. Dutton, eds. *Unity of Spirit: Studies on William of Saint-Thierry in Honor of E. Rozanne Elder*. Foreword by Bernard McGinn. Afterword by John R. Sommerfeldt. CS 268. Collegeville, MN: Cistercian Publications, 2015.

Sommerfeldt, John R. *Aelred of Rievaulx: On Love and Order in the World and the Church*. New York: Newman Press, 2006.

———. *Aelred of Rievaulx: Pursuing Perfect Happiness*. Mahwah, NJ: Newman Press, 2005.

Squire, Aelred. *Aelred of Rievaulx: A Study*. CS 50. Kalamazoo, MI: Cistercian Publications, 1981.

# INDEX

abandonment: 145, 277, 324; of self: 220, 242, 275

abbess: 193

abbey(s), Benedictine: 148; Cistercian: xix

abbot(s): lxxiv, xciv, 33, 140, 152, 224, 230–31; angry: 226; as contemplative: 269; as father of souls: 269, 271; as spouse: 382; Benedictine: 140, 225; Cistercian: 37, 46; Cluniac: 134–35; discipline of: 270; interior life of: 271; life of: 304; obedience to: 290; permission of: 224; teaching role of: 52

Abelard, Peter: lxii, xci–xciv, cvii, 11, 35, 44, 166–97; absolved of heresy: 186; adversaries of: 177; all-night vigil of: 169; and Heloise: xci–xcii, 166–72; and women: 168; as adversary of St. Bernard: 167; as aggressive: 167; as agitated: 178; as ambitious: 167; as apostle of free thought: xci, 167; as cleric: 168; as combative: 178; as dialectician: 177; as director of Heloise: 169; as embodiment of new era: cvii; as faithless rebel: xci, 167; as figure of controversy: cvii; as first modern intellectual: 167; as first professor: 167; as first rationalist: xci, 167; as founder of Paraclete: 169; as founder of St. Genevieve: 166; as free-thinker: 173; as heathen: 179; as heretic: 183, 186; as innovator: xci, cvii; as knight of dialectic: 167; as legislator: xciv; as master: 177; as monastic founder: cvii, xciv; as monk: xci–xciii, 167–69; as philosopher of Christ: 185; as proud: 167, 178; as rambunctious intellectual: 167; as rationalist: 173; as rebel: xciv, 192; as rebellious: 167; as restless: 167; as servant of Christ: 185; as student: 167; as systematic theologian: 172–73; as teacher: 176–77, 185; as thinker: 176; as theologian: 177; as treasure: 185; as turbulent: 178; as unredeemed: 181; as vain: 167; attitude of: 178; books of: 183–84; burial of: 186; career of: 168, 176; case of: xci, 167–97; censorship of: 183; character of: xci, 178; condemnations of: xcii, 44, 172, 177, 180–81, 183; conduct of: 185; conventional Catholic view of: 167; death of: xci–xcii, 167, 171–72, 184–86; disciples of: 177; doctrine of: 181, 183; errors of: xxi, 167, 170, 172, 178; *Fidei Confessio* of: 170, 183; flaws of: xci; genius of: 168; humility of: 185; hymns of: 168; illness of: 185–86; influence of: xcii, 176, 197; ingratitude of: 178; intellectual brilliance of: 167; intellectual problems

459

considered by: 172–78; language of: 176; last days of: 184–86; life of: 167–72; love affair of: 168; love for prayer of: 185; love for reading of: 185; love songs of: 168; marriage of: 167–70; Merton's fascination for: xci; method of: 177, 183; mind of: 178, 185; monastic doctrine of: xcii–xciii, 167, 186–96; monastic letters of: 169; mutilation of: 169; myth of: 167; obligations of: 168; passions of: 167–68; Platonism of: 178–79; poverty of: 185; prayer of: 170–71; pupil of: 197; rationalism of: xcii; real: 167; reductive myths about: xci; restlessness of: 176; retirement to Cluny of: xcii, 183–86; rule of: 169; sanctity of: 185; *Scito Teipsum* of: 175; sermons of: 170; *Sic et Non* of: 172; silencing of: 183, 186; simplicity of: 185; spirit of: 178; teaching of: 185; theology of: 172–78; thought of: xcii, 178; tomb of: 186; tongue of: 185; vanity of: xci, 176; weaknesses of: xci; work of: 185; writings of: 176
ability: 24; of others: 329; to give: 217
abnegation: 332
Abraham: lxxii
absolution: 128; apostolic: 129
absorption, of soul: 28
abstinence: xc, 157, 159, 196, 322; continual: 140; increase in: 140
abundance, place of: 368
abuse(s): lxi, lxiv, 148, 151, 153, 194, 213–14, 241
abyss, terrible: 205
Academicians: 181
academy: 184
acceptance, joyful: 275; loving: 310
accidentals: 137, 253; variety in: cvi
accommodations: 191
accusations: 133, 142, 146
*acedia*: 258

achievements, ascetic: xxxviii; mystical: xxxviii
acknowledgement: 234
act(s): 176, 199, 362; arbitrary: 115; as end in itself: 116; destructive: 85; evil: 199; lascivious: 186; of will: 115; sinful: lxiv
action(s): xxx–xxxi, lxxv, cvii, 152, 257, 263, 271, 277, 346, 349–51, 355, 376–77, 381; centered on Christ: 280; directed to Christ: 280; divine: civ, 205; exterior: 345; fatigues of: 284; fruitful: xxxvi; good: 372; intemperate: 37; liberating: 122; line of: 230; liturgical: 49; natural: 345; of evil one: 280; of Father: xcvii, 371; of God's love: 324; of one's spirit: 280; of soul: 372; of Spirit: 258, 280, 371; of Word: 370–71; rule of: 298; social: 86; spiritual: 286, 341; unified: 253
actives: 350
activism, dangers of: xxiv; restless: 284
activity: 163, 340, 350, 353, 355, 359, 362–63, 371, 384–85; fruitful: 274; good: 363, 370; painful: 385; spiritual: 154; transcendent: 372; useless: 362; vital: 274
Adam: xxxix, 121, 135, 362–63, 366; children of: 105; fall of: 128; sin of: 67, 173
Adam of Perseigne xliv–xlv, li–lii, c, 356–59; letters of: li–lii, c, 356–59; Marian writings of: li, c; on silence: c, 356–59
adaptation(s), legitimate: 150; valid: 157; wrong: 362
administrators: xxx
admiration: 93, 163, 251; spontaneous: xxii
admission, monastic: 230
*adolescentulae*: lxxv, 277, 287–91, 299–300; as escort of Bride: 287; as infants in Christ: 288

## Index

advance, interior: 270
advantage: 381
Advent(s): cvi, 38, 256, 333; as paschal season: xxvii; as sacrament: xxvii–xxviii, xxxi, xli, 321; present: xxviii; three: xxviii
adversary: 325
adversity: 34, 95, 163, 328, 337
advice, letters of: 225
affairs, of state: 35; public: 35; secular: 33
affection(s): 4, 74, 98, 116–17, 207, 251–52, 261, 294–95, 303, 343–44, 354, 361, 354, 364, 370; attractive: 355; capacity for: 301; carnal: 355; cellars of: 368; chaste: 69; comforting: 69; effusive: xciii, 227; evil: 355; exercise of: 4; fraternal: 302; good: 355; holy: 9, 69, 278; human: lxxvi, 261, 293, 378–79; lack of: 355; natural: 118, 301; of wisdom: 355; ordering of: 355; pure: lxxviii, 303; rational: 355; sensible: 293; subjection of: 355; sweet: 69; tender: 293; three: 355
*affectus*: 72, 77, 99–101, 116, 370; *caritatis*: 343; *rationalis*: 354–55; *sapientalis*: 355
affinity, spiritual: 228
affirmations, dogmatic: 166
affliction: 38, 304, 328
*agape*: civ
age, commercial: 11
agitation: 306, 392; of senses: lxxix
Agnes, Mother, OCD (Pauline Martin): 376
agreement, rational: 72; spiritual: 72
*ahimsa*: lxxxviii, 86
aid(s): 190, 274
Ailred (Aelred) of Rievaulx, St.: xxi, xliv–xlviii, lxxxi, 187, 262; character of: xlvi; death of: xlvi; life of: xlvi; meditations of: xlvii; sermons of: xlvi; works of: xlvi; WORKS: *De Anima*: xlvi; Marian sermons of: lvi; *Rule for Recluses*: xlvii, 187; *Spiritual Friendship*: 262
air: 108
alarm: 391
Albert, Br.: liii
Albigenses: 45
Alcuin: 68
Aleth (Alette), Bl.: 14; as Christian wife: 14; as model: 14; as mother: 14; death of: 17, 32; example of: 17; influence of: 17–18; sanctity of: 18
Alexander of Lincoln, Bp., letter to: 34, 227–28
alienation: xxxix, 85
aliens: 227
Allchin, A. M.: xlix
allegorization: 50
allegory: 280; anti-Jewish: xlviii–xlix
alliance: 4
alms: lxii, 93
almsgiving, corporal: 364
aloes, bitter: 341
alternation: 298
Amadeus of Lausanne: xliv
ambiguity: 173
ambition(s): 22, 24, 26, 63, 294
Ambrose of Milan, St.: 246
ambition(s): lxxxv, 17, 25, 189, 196; gratification of: 167; worldly: xx, lxiii, 213
ambivalence: 353
amends: 332
amnesia, spiritual: cvii
*amor*: civ, 72–73; *affectualis*: 355; *carnalis*: lxxvi, 78, 96, 113, 118–19, 210, 293–95, 374; *castus*: 123; *fortis*: lxxvi, 297; *gratus*: 123; *justus*: 123, 374; *rationalis*: lxxvi, 295–97; *sanctus*: 374; *socialis*: 119–20, 122
*amplexus*: 72–73, 77
Anacletus II (Peter de Leone), Antipope: 44, 256, 299
Ananias: 40

Anchin, Abbey of: 228–29
Anchin, Abbot of: 228–29
anchoresses: 193
Andrew, St.: xliii
angel(s): 55–57, 66, 124, 132, 145, 163, 175, 231, 264, 266, 272, 394; as brothers: 56; as companions: xliii; as messengers: 52, 55–56; as power of God: 56; as servants: 56; bread of: 206; death of: 394; glory of: 351; guardian: xliii; hierarchy of: 56, 288; intelligible bodies of: 55; orders of: 55; society of: 394; spirit of: 282, 308; spiritual bodies of: 55–56, 282
anger: 9, 63, 69, 176, 201, 226, 232, 274, 281, 337; movements of: 394
anguish, peaceful: 333
*anima*: 206
*anima mundi*: 103
animal(s): 109, 156; lower: 264
*animus*: 206
Anjou, Count of: 47
annihilation: xvii
annoyance: 392
Annunciation: lxxxv–lxxxvi, 51
anointing: 283, 329, 331; interior: 329; of head: 324, 335; of soul: lxxiv, 269–74, 329; triple: lxxiv, 272–73
Anselm of Canterbury, St.: lxxxiv, 61, 68, 112, 123, 150–51, 173–77
Anthony of Egypt, St.: 23, 148–49, 189
anthropology, theocentric: 74
Antichrist: 182
anti-clericalism: 11
anti-Semitism, medieval: xlviii–xlix
ants: 82
anxiety: xxxix, lxxxiv, xcvii, 23, 32, 43, 127, 132, 298, 306, 325, 342, 346, 362–63, 365, 369, 389, 394; restless: xcix
*apatheia*: 84
apathy, quietistic: 8
apostasy: 223
apostates: 134–35

apostles: 135, 176, 189, 347; love for Christ of: 294; spirit of: 308
apostolate: xxx, 283, 285
appearance: 83, 334
appetite(s): 101, 130; blind: 342; inordinate: 120
applause: 196
apples: 361, 372
application: 258
approach, aesthetic: lxxxvi; ascetic: 244; biblical: 55; dialectical: 172; existential: 55; psychological: 244; rational: 172; reasoned: 177; sacramental: 244; sapiential: lvii; scholastic: lvii; scientific: lxxxvi; speculative: lvii; theological: 244; to mystery: 172
appropriation, of mysteries of faith: lxxi
approval, ecclesiastical: 184
Apulia: 39, 44
Arabia: 227
Arabs: 162
Arca de Sardinia, Evora: ciii
archangel: 172
Archibald, Sub-dean of Orleans: 41
architects, Cistercian: 286
architecture, Cistercian: xix, 153–54; Romanesque: 11
Archpoet: 165
argument(s): 134, 137; irrefutable: 231; scriptural: 135–36
Aristotle: civ, 160, 162, 170; legacy of: 177; *Organon* of: 160
arithmetic: 16
*armarium*: 194
army, German: 43; of Lord: 184
Arnold of Bonneval: 256
Arnold of Brescia: 45, 183
Arnold of Morimond, Abbot: 32–33
arrogance: 364
Arsenius, St.: 191
art(s): 154–56, 162; as display: 154; as sign of wealth: 154; as sign of worldliness: 154; in cloister: 156; literary:

## Index

246; love of: 141–42, 155; plastic: 155; religious: 153–54; Romanesque: 153, 156; true: 154; work of: lxx, 246
ascent: 370; ascetic: 198; degrees of: lxiii, 198, 264–65; into heaven: 373; mystical: 198; to God: lxiii, 198; to pure love: 284
ascesis, monastic: 120
asceticism: 120, 206, 284, 300; exterior: 334; false: 334; of Origen: 80; resources of: lxxviii
ascetics, hardy: 155
Ash Wednesday: liv; epistle of: 334; gospel of: 324; liturgy of: 323
Asia: xlvii
aspirations: 352, 377
Assumption, Feast of: 314
assurance: 306
astonishment: 251
Astrolabe: 168, 186; prebend for: 186
astronomy: 13, 16
atonement: 173
attachment(s): 333, 346; shackles of: 333; to judgment: lxvii, 234–35, 237; to self: 121; to will: 235
attacks, Cistercian: 139
attendants, of Bride: lxxviii
attention: 376
attentiveness: 189; spiritual: 28; to Word: c
attitude: 142; fleshly: 149; humane: 177; legalistic: lxvi; practical: 177
attraction: 251, 352, 354; deification of: 348; good: 349; individual: 348; kinds of: 349; natural: 349; sensible: 339; supernatural: 349; to spiritual things: 217
attribute: divine: 389
audacity: 41
Augustine of Hippo, St.: xlv, 88, 94, 99, 121, 135–36, 173–74, 177, 188–89, 238, 246
austerity: l, 27, 127, 139, 143, 145, 158, 320; Cistercian: 131, 133; lack of: cvi

authenticity: lxiv, 320, 328; lack of: 328
authorities, ecclesiastical: 184; monastic: lxi
authority: 55, 161–62, 176, 288, 311; Church: 197; guidance of: 348; medieval concepts of: 167; of word: 337; papal: 8
automatism: 355; psychic: 119
autonomy, desire for: xxxix; illusory: xxxix
Autpert, Ambrose: 67–68, 313
Autun: 154
Auxerre, episcopal election at: 48
avarice: lxxviii, 22, 63, 148, 155, 201, 304, 394; thirst of: 279
aversion: 323, 332
*avidya*: lxxxviii, 82–83, 109
awakening: 373; time of: 160
awareness, of divine will: 306; prudent: 345
awe, sacred: lxxxvi, 54

backbiting: 147, 312
balance: 120; discreet: 348; of nature: 120; perfect: 353; psychological: 12; right: 343; true: 362
Baldwin, Br.: 39
Baldwin of Ford (and Canterbury): xcix–c, 313–14, 317–20, 366
balsam, divine: 285
Bamberg: 36
banquet, heavenly: 146; secret: 277
baptism: xxxix, 240, 328, 347
Bari: 43
Barré, Henri, CSSP: 58–60, 63
basilica(s): 159; size of: 154
Basse-Font, Abbey of: 232
baths: 195
battle(s): 131–32; matter for: 176; physical: 97; spiritual: 97
Bay of Pigs: ciii
beans: 131, 147, 157
bear: 157–58
beast(s): 158, 264

beatitude, foretaste of: 377
beatitudes: lxiii, 205–12, 365
beatniks: 165
beauty: 82, 154, 214, 345; austere: xix; of monastic life: 307; of vocation: lxiv
Becket, St. Thomas: xlvi, 162–63
bed: 132, 201–2, 211; bridal: 164; feather: 131; hard: 131; of contemplation: 187, 190
bedchamber: lxxviii–lxxix, xcviii, 303, 380, 389; of King: 383, 385; security of: 386
bedclothes: 151
bedding: 152
bee: 2
beggar: 309
beginners: 341; faults of: 289; fervor of: 341; inordinate zeal of: 288; spiritual: lxxvi, 287
behavior: 342
Being: xii, civ; infinite: 389; itself: 112; transcendent: 112
being(s): civ, 112, 376; contingent: 112; created: lxxvii, 264, 297; fallen: 109; intuition of: 112; mortal: 290; rational: 88; spiritual: 264; true: 109; whole: 110, 118, 197, 305, 323, 333–34, 338
Belgium: 32
belief(s), common: 11; problems of: 177
believers, unbelief of: 112
Bellarmine University: xxvii–xxviii, cxi
belly: 22, 84, 147
Benedict, St.: 129, 136, 361; as lawgiver: 129; as servant of God: 129; mind of: 19
Benedictines: 134–36, 139, 141–43, 156, 220, 225; and transfers: lxvi–lxvii, xciii–xciv, 224–33; Black: lxiv, 126; Cluniac: lxi; holy: 143; less strict: 156; life of: 126
Benedictinism: 142
benediction: 252–53

benefices: 213
benefit: 381; common: 90; undivided: 91
benignity: 330
Berchmans, Mother M., ocso: 204, 376–77
Bernard of Clairvaux, St.: vii, xvi; acquaintance with: 262; activities of: xxiii–xxiv, xxvi, xxxiv, lviii; admiration for: xxiv; admiration for Cluny of: lxi; advice of: 133; aggressivity of: lxxxiv, 18; and Scriptures: liv, 257–61; anger of: xxiv, xxxiv; anniversary commemorations of: xxiii–xxxvii, lxxxii, 1–2; anthropology of: 108–9; aphoristic remarks of: xxiv; apostolate of: xxvi; application of: 28, 30; approach to scriptures of: lxviii; ardor of: xxxvi, 65; artistry of: lxx, lxxiii; asceticism of: lxxxv, 70; as abbot: xxiii, lxxiii, 271; as anti-intellectual: lxii; as artist: 246; as charismatic: 13; as *citharista Mariae*: 59; as clever: xciv; as conservative: 61; as cynical: xciv, 229; as Doctor of Church: xli, 1, 246, 259; as extraordinary: 13; as father: xli, 27; as father of souls: 271, 351; as genius: lxxxvi, 48, 246; as gracious: xciii; as guide: lviii, 10; as inspiration: lxxxv; as instrument of God: lxxxv; as last of fathers: xx, xl, 1, 246; as literary stylist: lx, 16, 61; as long-suffering: xxiv; as man: lxxix; as man of God: lxxxiv, 14; as Marian theologian: lxxxvi, 59–62; as master of souls: 27; as model: lviii, 10; as monastic leader: cviii; as monk: xxiii, xli, lxxix, 30; as mystic: 27, 61, 70; as mystical doctor: 247; as novice: lxxxv, 25, 30–31; as opponent of theological innovation: xxv; as person: lxxxii, cviii, 13–31, 339–40; as poet: 16; as polemicist: lx; as politician:

## Index

xciii, 226; as preacher: 61; as preacher of crusade: xxv, xxxiv; as proponent of devotion: xxv–xxvi; as public figure: xxiii; as pugnacious: xciv; as reformer of Church: xxv, 304; as reformer of society: 304; as rival of Abelard: 177–78; as saint: lxiv, lxxxiv–lxxxvi, 14, 48, 214, 246; as satirist: lx; as sign of God: xxvi, lxxxiv, 14; as speculative mystic: 247–48; as spiritual master: xli; as superhuman: 13; as theologian: xxxv, 17, 247; as theologian of desire: 76; as theologian of love: 73; as traditionalist: 61; as witness to Christ: xxv; as writer: lxxix, lxxxv–lxxxvi, cv, 35, 48; ascetic theology of: 120; ascetical teaching of: 1; asceticism of: xxv; attitude toward intellectual life of: 196–97; attitude toward philosophy of: 2; austerity of: 27; authority of: lxxiii; background of: lxxxii, cii, 10–12; biographer of: xlv, 256; biography of: xxxii, liii, lviii, lxxxii–lxxxv, xciv, cvii–cviii; birth of: 12, 14; body of: 39; brethren of: 39; brothers of: xlv, 40, 42–44, 247; canonization of: 48; career of: xxiii, lviii, lxxxiii, 10–14, 33; character of: xxxiii, xliii, lxxxii, xci, 18–19, 247; childhood of: 14; chronology of: lvii–lviii; comments of: xxiv; community of: 287; companions of: 27, 32; compassion of: xxiv; complexity of: lxxxiv; consolations of: 39; contemplation of: xxiv, 3, 384; contradictions of: 19; conversion of: xlii, lviii, lxxxiii, lxxxiv, cvii, 19–27, 32; critique of Abelard by: 179–82; critique of Cluny by: lxi–lxii, 126–33, 141–60; death of: xxiii, lviii, 48, 245; depth of: xxi; devotion to: 9–10; devotion to Mary of: 9; doctrinal unity in: 71; doctrine of: xxi, xxxiv–xxxvi, xliii, lvii, lxx, 2–4, 88–89, 98, 237, 245, 263, 293; doctrine of love of: lix, lxxxix, 1, 7–8, 78, 234; dream-vision of: 15, 18; earlier works of: 48–125; early formation of: 14–19; early life of: lxxxiii; early maturity of: lxxvii; early monastic life of: lviii, cvii–cviii; education of: lxxxiii–lxxxiv, 14–17; eloquence of: 17; entrance to Cîteaux of: 27, 32; example of: 2; exile of: 38; experience(s) of: xxxvi, lxxvii, lxxxv, cii, 26, 48–49, 51, 74, 244–45, 247, 258, 299, 304, 384–85; fame for sanctity of: 27; family of: 24; faults of: xxiv; Feast of: xliii, lxxxiv; fervor of: 9–10, 59, 61; frailty of: xxiv; friendships of: lxii; generosity of: lxxxv, cviii, 28, 30; gentleness of: xxiv, cvi; gifts of: 1, 27–30; good looks of: 17; graces of: lxxxv, cviii, 1, 14–15, 27–29; graciousness of: 15; grief of: 39, 43; health of: lxxxv, cvi, 29–30, 39, 44; heart of: 258, 271; historical background of: cii; holiness of: 81; humanity of: xxiv; humanness of: 227; humility of: 8; illness of: lviii, 48; imagination of: 142; imitation of: xxiv; impatience of: xxiv, xxvi; imprudence of: cvi; indignation of: xxiv, 154; influence of: xxi; initiatives of: 18; inner unity of: xxxv; insight of: 59; instruction of: lxxiii; insufficiency of: 43; intelligence of: 15; interactions of: lviii; interior life of: 271, 339; journey of: 43; judgments of: 140; kindness of: 15; labors of: 39, 43, 256; lack of discretion of: cvi; legends of: civ, 59–60; life of: xx–xxi, xxxiii, xliii, liii, lvii–lviii, xcvi, 32–48, 245, 247; love for: xxiv; love for Christ of: xix, 9; love for Cluny of: lxi; love of: 51, 61; lyricism of: xxi; manners of: 17; Mariology of: xxxiii, xxxvi, xlii, lxxxv–lxxxvi, 58–68; meditations of: 2, 256; memory of: 28; merits of: 2; message of: lxviii; mind of: lxxxvi, 17, 19, 48, 56; miracles of: 32, 43; misfortune of: 39; modesty in: xli, 43; monastic career of: 18; monastic formation of: 27–31; monks of: xcvi, 245, 247, 300, 308, 339–40; mortification of: lxxxv; mystical doctrine of: lvi, 244–306; mystical teaching of: xix, lxviii, 1; mystical theology of: 4–7, 66, 70, 120; mysticism of: 70, 78; natural gifts of: lxxxiv–lxxxv, cviii, 1, 15, 17, 28–29; nature of: lxxxii, 18–19, 29; nobility of: 27; novitiate of: xlii, lxxxiii, lxxxv, 27–31; obedience of: 15; ordinary routines of: xciv; originality of: xcvi; parents of: xlv, 14, 17–18, 32; passion of: xxiv, 65; patience of: xxiv; pen of: 142; personal problem of: 339–40, 351–56; personality of: xxi, xxiv, lxxxiv; power of: 19; power-drives of: lxxxiv, 18; practice of: xciv; prayer of: 43; prayer-life of: 245; preaching of: xxxv, 245; private obligations of: lxxi; profession of: 32; psychology of: 276; public life of: xxiii; public obligations of: lxxi; reading of: 48; religious experience of: 96; responsibilities of: xcvi, 43; rhetorical strategy of: lxiv; sanctity of: 2, 8; sapiential approach of: lvii, 2; seal of: 46–47; self-defense of: 141, 145–46; self-discipline of: lxxxv; sermons of: viii–ix, xxxv, xli, lxxi–lxxiii, 43, 59, 67, 257, 262; severity of: cvi, 127; shyness of: lxxxiv, 15, 18; sickness of: 32–33, 44, 71; sins of: 43; sister of: xlv, 14, 44; soliloquy of: 351; sons of: 38–39, 243, 246; sorrow(s) of: 39, 43; soul of: 8, 26, 39, 43; spirit of: xxix, 1, 7; spirit of charity of: 7; spiritual experiences of: lxx, 246; spirituality of: xxvii, xcv, 9, 18, 56, 70, 110, 275–76; standards of: lxii, 143; stereotyped image of: cviii; strength of: 8, 38; strength of character of: 28; struggles of: 33; studies of: 3, 15; style of: xix, xxxiv, lvii, ci, 4, 155; submissiveness of: 15; taste for: 262; teaching(s) of: ix, xv, xviii–xx, xxviii, xxxvi–xxxvii, lxviii, lxx, lxxiii, 1, 5, 74, 244–45; teaching on love of: cv, 68; temptation of: 17; theology of: xv, xxiv, lix, 16, 48; thought(s) of: xxxix, 247, 339; thoughtfulness of: 15; times of: 247; travels of: lviii, lxxii; treatises of: xxxv, lxxxiv; trials of: 17, 33; troubles of: 39; understanding of: 237, 262; union with God of: 8; upbringing of: lxxxiv; vanity of: xci; violence of: xxi; virtue of: 15; vocation of: xxv, lxxxiii, 18–31, 300, 304; vocation letters of: cviii, 126, 224–33; voice of: lxxiii; will of: 39; wisdom of: lxxiii, 2, 15; works of: xxxiii, 10, 31; worship of: lxxxv, cii, 48; wound of: 43; writings of: xxxv–xxxvi, lviii, lxxxiv, 1, 6; zeal of: lxxxv, 8, 30; WORKS: Advent sermons: xxvii–xxviii, xcv; Assumption sermon: xlii, 349; *Apologia*: xviii, liii, lx–lxii, lxxxix–xc, cvi, cviii, 33, 125, 132–33, 139–57; *De Aquaeductu*: xliii, 67; *De Consideratione*: xxxiii, lix, lxxix, 46–47, 55; *De Conversione*: lxii–lxiv, xc, xcii–xciii, cvi–cviii, 16, 19–22, 160, 197–214, 262, 272; *De Diligendo Deo*: xi–xii, xiv–xvi, xxiv, xli, liii, lv, lix–lxi, lxxxv, lxxxvii, xcvii–xcviii, civ–cv, 7, 18, 33, 68, 70, 72–73, 77–79, 88–89, 94–95, 107–25, 262, 265, 269, 273, 292, 307, 374–81; *De Diversis*: xcv, 66, 77, 88, 163, 179, 200, 307–11, 329, 338; *De Gradibus Humilitatis*: xix, xxxix, xli, lxxix,

# Index

xcvii, 17, 33, 71–72, 82, 89, 109, 211, 262, 269, 354, 359–74; *De Gratia et Libero Arbitrio*: lxxix, 33, 71, 88, 94, 117; *De Laude Novae Militiae*: 33; *De Moribus Episcoporum*: 9, 35; *De Praecepto et Dispensatione*: xli, liv–lv, lxiv–lxvii, lxxix, xciii–xciv, cviii–cix, 44, 75, 214–24, 262; *Epistola* 1 to Robert of Châtillon: 126–33; *Epistola* 11 to Guigo: xxiv, lxxxvii–lxxxviii, civ, 72, 81, 89, 96–107; *Homilies on Missus Est*: xliii, lxxxv–lxxxvii, cii–civ, 50–68, 86; Lenten sermons: xli, xcv–xcvi, 320–38; letters of: xxi, xxiii–xxv, lxxix, xciii–xciv, 9, 24–26, 32–48, 60–61, 73, 76, 88, 96–107, 126–33, 163–64, 180, 224–33, 329; *Life of St. Malachy*: 46; *Sermones in Cantica*: xiii–xiv, xvi, xviii, xxxv–xxxvi, xxxix–xli, liv, lviii, lxviii–lxxx, xcvi–xcviii, cviii, 3–5, 9, 37–40, 54–55, 66–67, 70, 72–73, 75–76, 78, 86, 89, 96, 125, 210, 237, 243–306, 338–56, 368–74, 378, 380–95; sermons for All Saints: 366; sermons for Dedication of Church: xli, xliii–xlix, 76; sermons for Epiphany: cvi; sermons for Feast of St. Andrew: xliii; sermons for Feast of Sts. Peter and Paul: xliii; sermons for Nativity of John the Baptist: 3, 329; sermons for Pentecost: xli; sermon in octave of Assumption: 67; sermons on Psalm 90: xliii, 8, 44, 70, 75; sermons on Resurrection: liv–lv, lxvii–lxviii, lxxix, cviii, 90, 234–37, 343, 364; *Tractatus adversus Abaelardum*: 179–82
Bernard the Carthusian: 39–40; letters to: 40, 42–43
betrothal, spiritual: xvii–xviii
Bible: lxxii, 16, 31, 64, 178; Septuagint: 16; Vulgate: 257, 347
Biddle, Arthur: xiii
birds: 158, 320

birth, virgin: 66
bishop(s): 34, 137, 152, 154, 176, 183, 213, 348; accommodations for: 191; splendor of: 141; teaching role of: 52
bitings, grievous: 320
bitterness: 199, 250, 328
blame: 149, 244, 366; shared: 127
blankets: 151
bleeding: 195
Blessed Sacrament: 332
blessedness: 205
blessing(s): 97–98, 228, 342; Lord's: 27; of obedience: 196
blindness, spiritual: 278
block, stumbling: 371
blood: 29, 41
bloodshed: 41
boar: 157
Bochen, Christine M.: xv, xxxvii
body: 4, 29, 38, 62, 84, 130, 148, 156, 200, 203–4, 207, 209, 250, 264, 347–49, 365, 378, 380; as impediment: 349; bowing of: 93; care of: 152; corruptible: 310; eyes of: 254; feculence of: 38; food for: 149; glorified: 380; love of: 107; members of: 347; mortal: 377, 380; mystical: 121; of angels: 55–56, 264; of Christ: xxx, xcvi, 244, 302, 347–48; properly clothed: 136; protection of: 138; resumption of: 380; sense of: 28; spiritual: 264; tabernacle of: 316; whole: 328
boldness: 2
Bonaventure, St.: 23, 177
bond, charity as: 248; nuptial: 171, 251
bondage: 203, 227
bone: 259
book(s): 164; censorship of: 183–84; condemnation of: 183; copying of: 194; denunciation of: 183; distribution of: 194; sacred: 163; sapiential: 381; text: 373
boorishness: 148

bosom, of Father: xcix, 316, 383
Bourges, Archbishop of: 44
Bouyer, Louis: lxxxii, lxxxiv, xci, 18
bowing: 137
box, common: 194
Braine, Abbey of: 233
Braine, Abbot of: 233
bread: 25, 94, 131, 154; daily: 108; heavenly: 149; of angels: 206; of souls: 149; white: 130
breast(s), naked: 202; of Bride: xxi, 270; of Spouse: xiii, xxi, 270, 288; sweet: 341
breath, gift of: 108; poisonous: 202
brethren: 137, 160, 225–26, 236, 256, 259, 302, 324, 329; compassion toward: xxxviii; false: 46; hearts of: 368; labor for: 366; love for: 366–67; monastic: 130, 261; need of: 50; peace with: 149, 367; preoccupation with: 366; single-hearted: 132
briars: 208
bricks: 362
Bride: lxxviii–lxxix, 251, 287; breasts of: xxi, 270; escort of: 287; example of: lxxv; following: lxxvi, 287; footsteps of: lxxv; mystical: xxxviii; pope as guardian of: 41; soul as: 4; voice of: 247
Bridegroom: 251, 298, 389; arm of: 390; decrees of: 384; divine: 389; friend of: 286; hand of: 390; home of: 384; judgments of: 254; law of: 254; love of: 252, 287; ointments of: 298; place of: 387; pope as friend of: 41; presence of: 254; testimonies of: 254; visits of: xviii, 256; voice of: 247; words of: 254
Brittany: 36, 47, 169
brother(s): ci, 119, 231, 234, 328, 371; advantage to: 91; benefit of: 236; compassion for: 270; concern for: ci; family: 137; fugitive: 225; gift to: 121; imperfection of: 364; risk for: 121; selfless love for: 122; serfs as: 136; service to: 91; simple professed: ci; solemn professed: ci; truth in: 369; weakness of: 364; whipping of: 160
bruises: 132
Bruno, Br.: 40
Buddhism: lxxxviii, 82–83
buildings, monastic: xv, 148
burden(s): lxxiv, 104, 274, 286; insupportable: 105; light: 105, 276; of brothers: 269; of charity: 105; of work: 316
Burgundy: lviii, 12; Duke of: 14
burial: 195
Busch, Jan: 193
business: 5, 13; Father's: 288
Butler, Cuthbert, OSB: 240, 253–54
buzzard: 158

calf, fatted: 294
Calixtus II, Pope: 33
calumny: 147
Calvary: 67; continual: 355
camp, of Lord: 192; of world: 192
canals: lxxv, 282–83
candelabra: 158–59
candlestick: 152
canes: 151
Canon Law, Code of 223
canon(s): 11; Augustinian: 193; Premonstratensian: 232; scandalous: 232
canons, legal: 230
Canterbury: xcix
Canticle of Canticles: 43, 71, 256, 261, 263, 269; as human love story: 260; as love song of Christ and Church: lxxiii, 247
capacity, human: 109
captivity: 311
care(s): 43, 70, 306, 389, 393–94; apostolic: lxxviii, 303; bitter: 320; conscientious: 95; for others: xxx; of souls: 303, 352; worldly: 115

Index

career, ecclesiastical: 17, 24
caritas: civ, 72–73, 88–89, 104, 107; actualis: 354; affectualis: 354; gift of God as: 89, 102; God as: 89, 102
Carmelites: lxiv
Carta Caritatis: liii, lxxix
Carthusian(s): xlv, civ, 81, 225; as mediators of charity: 96; as saints: 96
Casey, Michael, ocso: lxvii
Cassian, John: liv, 80, 115, 257, 289, 344
Cassiodorus: 16
castles: 11
cathedrals: 154
caution: 87, 261, 282, 289
cautiousness, illusory: 219
Cavallera, F.: 71
cellar(s): xcviii, 368–74, 380–83; of grace: lxxviii, 303; of Spouse: lxxvii–lxxviii, 299–306; three: 300
cellaress: 193, 195
censorship: xxxvii, 183–84; ecclesiastical: 183; repressive: 183
centaurs: 156
ceremony: 342; clothing: 158
certitude: 23, 54, 173, 208, 281, 387–88; light of: 279
cesspit: 201, 212
chaff: 259
chalices: 261
Châlons: 32, 186, 225
chamber, bridal: 113, 381; council: 384; of King: 361, 372
change(s): 298; accidental: 138; inner: lxx, 242
chantress: 193–95
chapter, monastic: 232
chapter room: vii
character: 255
charisms: lxxv, 282
charity: xii, xv, xxxi, xxxvii, lxii–lxiii, lxviii, lxxviii, lxxxix–xc, xcv, cvi, 3–4, 25, 73, 77, 83, 89–90, 94, 98, 134–39, 143, 146, 150, 159, 172, 197– 98, 208, 211, 215, 232, 234, 236, 244, 248, 250, 271, 274, 283, 287, 291, 303, 316, 318–19, 322, 327–30, 332, 334, 337, 343, 348, 359, 361, 363, 366–67, 383, 391, 393; act of: 326; active: 353, 381; affective: xcvi, 352–56; apostolic: xxxvi; ardent: 382; as gift of God: 89, 102; as God: 89, 102; as great rule: 139; as obstacle: 377; banquet of: 260; breadth of: 216; burden of: 105; Christlike: 135; commitment to: lxvii; conformity of: 4; degree of: 295; delights of: 208; divine: 7, 69, 172; doctrine of: 1, 7; effect of: 326; effective: xcvi, 352–56; ends of: 345; excessus of: 374; exercise of: 377; experience of: 96; exterior order of: 347–48; false sense of: lxi, 148; fervor of: 344; fire of: 3, 96, 273, 369; fraternal: 8, 269, 286, 318, 343, 380; genuine: 135; God as: 102, 107, 287; guidance of: 3; Holy Spirit as: 103; immaculate: 102; infinite: xxxvii; joy of: 327, 330; lack of: cvi, 144, 146, 156; Lady: 70; law of: xxxvii, lix, cv, 79, 96, 102, 106; meaning of: 234; of Christ: xxxviii, xlviii; of spouse: 300, 380–81; of superior: lxxviii; order(s) of: 107, 354; ordering of: xli, xcvi–xcvii, 338–56; passionate: 345; perfect: 4, 338; perfection of: 123–24, 215, 248, 339; principle of: xc, cvi, 139; promotion of: lxvi; quality of: 89, 103; roots of: 319; rule of: 137–38; school of: xli, 68–69, 77, 338; sincere: 98, 214; spirit of: 7, 348; springs of: 334; storehouse of: 361; substance of: 89, 103; supernatural: 104; theology of: 96; true: 98, 208, 256; truth of: 353; two: 353–55; unity in: 139, 145; virtue of: 102, 345; wine of: 382; without wrinkle: 364; yoke of: 105
Charlemagne: 11; monastic idea of: 134

Chartres: 214, 220; Council of: 46; humanists of: 11; School of: 103–4; theologians of: 103
Chase, Neil: cxii
chastity: xc, 159; interior: 186; of body: 186; of soul: 186; paradisal: xxvi; spirit of: 186; toward God: 91; vow of: lxv
Châtillon: 14, 16
Chautard, Jean-Baptiste, ocso: xiv
check, etymology of: 160–61
checkers: 161
cheerfulness: 207; human: 325
cheese: 157
Chenu, Marie-Dominique, op: 49–50, 103–4
chess: 161
chickens: 157
child, offering of: 233; tender: 341
childhood, spiritual: c, 359
children: 199, 324, 342; feeble: 341
choice, clear-sighted: 175; free: 175; spontaneous: 175
choir(s): 135, 194, 196, 261, 266; angelic: 288
Christ, Jesus: xxi, xxxv, 38, 57, 132, 163, 184, 187, 197, 199, 273, 335; abiding of: 180; action of: 329; allegiance to: 191; army of: 25; as Almighty God: 279; as Anointed: 328; as ascending: 294; as Author of Life: 111; as being: 291; as Beloved: 266, 277, 285, 383–84; as boy: 288; as Bridegroom: lxxvii, xcviii, 113, 164, 247, 251; as center: lxxv; as center of everything: 314; as center of revelation: lxxi, 258; as chaste: 279; as child: 290; as consolation: 171; as crucified Savior: xix; as divine Person: lxxv; as divine Spouse: lxxvi–lxxviii, xcvii, 72, 170; as dying: 294; as expectation: 171; as gift of God: 108, 278; as God–man: 253, 294; as graciousness: 171; as guest: 111; as Head of Body: 322, 330; as Head of Church: 328; as hope: 171; as humble of heart: 324; as Image of Father: xl; as Incarnate Word: xxxviii, xlviii, lxxi, lxxv, 275, 279, 298, 314, 357; as Justice: lxxvii, 299; as kind: 279; as King of Angels: 4; as Lamb: 322; as life: 291; as light: 291; as Lord of Majesty: 111; as man: 294; as Master: 164, 357; as Master of gentleness and humility: 330; as meek: 324; as merciful: 279; as merciful Father: 171; as model: 291–92; as *mons coagulatus*: 53, 281; as *mons pinguis*: 53, 281; as new Eliseus: lxxv; as only-begotten Son: 111, 275; as pastor: 97; as perfect: 279; as perfect peace: 317; as portion: 171; as Power of God: 56; as purifier: 171; as Redeemer: 181; as Redemption: lxxvii, 299; as rest: 317; as risen Lord: xxvii; as rising: 294; as Sanctification: lxxvii, 299; as sanctuary of God: xxvi; as Savior: 9, 162, 250, 275; as Second Adam: xxxix; as sober: 279; as Son of God: 21, 108, 113, 174–75, 267, 348, 360–61; as Son of Man: 180; as Son of Mary: li; as source of consolation: 275; as source of good: lxxiv, 275; as strength of God: 56; as Sun of Justice: 65; as Tabernacle: xcix, 318; as teacher: 330; as teaching: 294; as Truth: xxi, lxiii, 26, 82, 188, 296; as Way: 291; as wellspring of knowledge: 275; as wellspring of virtue: 275; as Wisdom: lxviii, lxxvii, xcix, 237, 299, 360; as Word: xxviii, xxxi, xl, xlviii, xcvii, xcix, 72; as Word made flesh: 65, 67; as Word of Father: 21, 289, 357, 360; Ascension of: 114, 265, 294–95; beauty of: 38, 113; believer in: 259; birth of: xlviii, 15, 253, 256; blood of: 6, 25, 175, 179; Body of:

xxx, xcvi, 244, 302, 347–48; bosom of: 390; breast of: 383; bride of: lxxiv, 196, 247; brothers in: 6; call of: lxxvii; charity of: xxxviii, xlviii; coming of: xxvii–xxviii; compassion of: lxxvi; conformation to: xxxv, lxxi, lxxx, 4; consolation of: 369; contact with: 314; conversation of: 351; countenance of: 351; cross of: xlviii, 111, 114–15, 144, 173, 186, 250, 254, 293, 296, 374; crucified: xix, lxviii, lxxx, 110, 237, 254, 278; crucified in His people: lxxii; crucifixion of: 110; death of: xxvii, 40, 111, 114, 128, 149, 173–75, 181, 217, 253, 293, 295, 374; desire for: lxxv, 314; desires of: 237; devotion to: xxvi; disciples of: xlix; divinity of: xix, lxxiii, 174, 287, 295; dying with: xxvi, xxxix; effect of: 180; enemies of: 292, 323; example of: 114, 294; experience of: 179; face of: 351; fast of: 322; Father of: 237; feet of: 350–51; finding: 314, 317; flesh of: xxvi, lxxvi, 113, 164, 253–54, 294–96; focusing on: lxx; followers of: lxii, 143; following: xxvi, 135, 144, 163, 187, 214, 298; friends of: 111, 292, 323; gift of: 321–22, 347; gift of self to: lxxxv, 26; glorification of: xxvii, lxxi, lxxv, 258; glory of: 110, 115, 321; grace of: 280; growth of: 348; handmaid(s) of: 171, 185; heart of: xxvi, 296; help of: 279; hidden in: 393; hidden life of: 250; human: xix, lxxvi, 174; human nature of: 92; humanity of: xxvi, lxxiii, xcix, 113, 175, 248, 250, 287, 318; humility of: 58, 144, 235, 237, 250, 279; image of: 253, 294; imitation of: lxvi, 279, 299, 368; in world: 321; incarnate: lxxvi, 254, 295; Incarnation of: xxvi–xxvii, lix, lxxiii, 15, 57, 235, 250, 265, 267, 277, 318, 321, 324; infancy of: li–lii, 145, 253, 324; Infant: xlviii, 145; inheritance of: 318; inner life of: 116; interest of: 352; interests of: 286; kenosis of: 358; Kingdom of: 180; knowledge of: xix, 108, 254; liberty of: 175; life in: xxxix, xliii, 237, 244, 274, 291–92; life of: 111, 250, 280, 299; life with: xxxix; light of: lxxvi, 261, 296; likeness to: 69; lips of: 351; looking at: 244; love for: xix, lxxvi, xcvii, 10, 15, 111, 170, 273, 277, 291–97, 299, 364, 383; love for Father of: lxxiv, 268, 317; love in: 42; love of: lxxvi–lxxvii, 110, 113, 115, 163, 170, 291–93, 296; love of Father for: 317, 330; lowly life of: 250; majesty of: 171; manger of: 144, 189; manner of life of: 324; maturity in: xxxi; meekness of: 279; member(s) of: 151, 261, 328; memory of: 111, 115; merciful love of: 110; mercy of: 114, 171; merits of: 321; mind of: 179; ministers of: 338; miracles of: 171; mortal life of: 279; mortification of: 320; mouth of: 351; mystery of: xxvii, xxx–xxxi, xxxv, lxviii–lxix, xcv, 57, 180, 235, 237, 295, 297, 321; mystical: 247; Mystical Body of: xxvi, xcv, 321–22, 330, 340; nakedness of: 187; name of: lxxiv–lxxv, 9, 274–75, 277–80; need for: 277; new life in: 142; obedience of: lxviii, 58, 217, 237, 288–90; omnipotence of: 279; parents of: 288; passage through world of: xxvii; Passion of: xix, lxviii, 111–13, 182, 235, 237, 250, 254, 295, 299, 320, 368; patience of: xxiv; person of: xxxvii, lxiii, lxxi, lxxv, 264, 314; physical body of: xxvi; place of: 187; poverty of: 235, 320; power of: 114, 199, 279, 293; precepts of: 294; presence of: xxv, xxvii–xxviii, l, xcv, 58, 111, 115, 253, 265, 278, 295; radiation of: xxvi; reading of: 163; rebirth in:

xl; receiving of: 309; redemption by: lix, c, 6, 112–13, 173–74, 181, 267, 318; renunciation of: 237; rest in: 316–17; rest of: 366; restoration in: 301; resurrection of: xxvii, xlix, lxviii, 110–14, 235, 253, 320–22; revelation of: 142; risen: xl, lxxx, 132; risen humanity of: 280; rising with: xxvi, xxxix; Sacred Heart of: 250; sacrifice of: 175; school of: xxxvii, 163, 338; seamless garment of: 145; seeking of: 316; self-emptying of: xxvii–xxviii; self-gift of: 175; self-surrender of: lxviii; sensible presence of: 295; service of: 225, 346; sheep of: 139; side of: xxvi, 383; silence of: 235; soldier(s) of: 131, 225; soul of: 111; speech of: 351; Spirit of: xlviii, 220, 246, 268; spiritualization in: 55; standards of: 303; strength of: lxxvi; subjective act of love of: 174; suffering(s) of: 154, 250, 296, 321–22, 328; swaddling clothes of: 144; sweetness of: 351; teaching of: lxxi, 253; thoughts of: 112; tormentors of: 235; triumph of: 110; true self as: xl; true self in: xxxviii, xl; truth of: lxxvi, 296–97; understanding of: 291; union with: lxvi, lxxi, xxiv, 111, 235, 247, 258, 264, 292, 314, 318, 320–22, 326, 328, 332, 334; unity in: 144, 321; voice of: 351; virtues of: 299; whole: xxvii; will of: 244, 294; wings of: 314; wisdom of: lxxvi; withdrawal of: 190; word(s) of: 142, 199, 351; wound(s) of: xxvi, 254; yoke of: 23, 26, 207, 220

Christendom, feudal: 11

Christian(s): 237, 260, 321; faithful: 110, 276; first: 151; heart of: 333; true: 320–21

Christianity, Biblical: 82; contemplative: viii–x

Christina of Markyate: 185

Christmas: xxviii, 18, 324; dawn Mass of: 51; midnight Mass of: 51

Christoffersen, Hans: cxi

Chrysogonus, Lord: 40

Church: xxv–xxvi, xxx, xxxv, xlviii, lxi, lxx–lxxi, 18, 41, 61, 68, 110–11, 135, 142–43, 181, 183, 208, 234, 244, 258, 283, 347; as Bride of Christ: xxxviii, 247; as mother: xlviii, 145; as Queen: 145; as resting place of Lord: 318; as spouse: 145; as tabernacle: 318; authority of: 173; child of: 145; Christ's presence in: xxv; contemplation in: 241–44; development of: 348; discord in: 147; diversity in: 145; Eastern: l, 246; evils in: 41; faith in: 98; fruitfulness of: lxiv; functions in: 348; glory of: 163; guidance of 248; holy: 214, 247; joy of: 98; lands of: 228; Lords of: 141; life in: 244; life of: xxxv, lxxi; liturgy of: 259; living: xliv; love for: 8, 98; majesty of: 163; member of: lxxiii; mind of: 297; monastic: 261; monastic conception of: 228; moral teaching of: 165; mystical life of: 242; order of: xxxv, xcvi, 348; power of: 11; present-day: lxviii; princes of: 304; reform of: 134; revolt against: 11; strength of: 41; tabernacle of: xcix, 318; thinking with: 244; unity of: 8, 145, 348; vitality of: 247; voice of: 316; welfare of: 214; Western: 246; wound of: 41

church(es): 353; adornment of: lxii, 142, 153; Benedictine: 142, 155; Cluniac: 141, 158; monastic: lxii, 154–55; Negro: ciii; parish: 134; splendor of: 153

Cicero: 16

circuit: 315

circumspection: 296

circumvention: 315

Cistercian(s): xxxvii–xxxviii, lxi–lxii, lxvi, lxxxix–xc, xciii, cvi, 1–2, 10–11, 103, 107, 133, 136–39, 143, 153, 155, 167, 186, 224, 226, 246, 379; American: xxix; charges against: 143–45; combative severity of: 141; Common Observance: xxxii; contemporary: lxxxv; early: 69, 246; exemption from tithes of: 47; expansion of: 27; function in Church: 68; Serlo of Wilton as: 165; severity of: 141; strict: 156; twelfth-century: xliv

Cistercianism, aggressiveness of: 126; early: xxxv, xliv, 125; English: xlvi; essence of: 126; militancy of: 126; theological notions of: xxxvii

Cîteaux, Abbey of: xxxvii, xlii, lviii, lxxxiii–lxxxiv, cvi, 10, 18, 23, 26–27, 32, 45, 60, 127, 130, 133, 224; austerity of: 26; calling to: 145; controversy with Cluny of: 125–60; criticism of: 26; founders of: 224, 320; hard life at: 26; instability of: 26; manuscripts of: 155; poverty of: 26; reputation of: 26

city, holy: 227

civil rights movement: ciii

Clairvaux, Abbey of: xlviii, lviii, lxi, lxvii, lxxii, 18, 33–34, 38, 41, 44, 46, 48, 81–82, 126, 227–30, 232, 256; as Jerusalem: xciv, 227–28; *conventus* of: 52; difficulties of: 33; economic crisis at: 32; foundation of: 32; foundations of: 32–33, 35–36, 44; hermitage at: 256; letter to: 38–40; monks of: 38, 245; new church of: 44; papal visit to: 35

classes, scripture: ciii

*claustrales*: 193–94; compared to knights: 194

clay: 95

cleanliness: 148

clemency, divine: 98

clergy: lxiii, 7, 41–42, 69, 213; laxity of: 198; pastoral duties of: 191; regular: 145; secular: 17, 145; sins of: 213

cleric(s): lxiv, xciii, cvii, 162–63, 214, 385; as men of God: 214; authentic: 214; Cluniac monks as: 134; wandering: 12

Clermont, Bishop of: 47

climate: 135–36

cloister: 7, 158, 184, 231, 333; art in: 156; Cistercian: xxxviii; regularity of: 192

cloth, coarse: 152; color of: 152; precious: 130

clothing: xv, 131, 134–35, 148, 151–52, 159, 185, 288; moderate: 130; regulations on: xc; stealing of: 160; unnecessary: 130; warm: 139

Cluniacs: lxi–lxii, lxxxix, 81, 136, 154; silence of: 134

Cluny, Abbey of: lxi–lxii, lxxxix–xcii, cvi, 12, 32, 45, 47, 125–30, 133–60, 167, 183–85, 224, 226, 233; abuses of: 147; accusations of: 133–35; as center of Christianizing influence: 134; as center of economic prosperity and power: 134; as center of liturgical worship: 134; as center of reform: 134; as centralized and conservative: 134; as nursery of bishops: 134; as nursery of saints: 145; calling to: 145; chapter at: 158; chapter of: 159; Cistercian criticism of: 141, 148–56; complacency of: 157; customs of: 158; defense of: 135–39, 147; economic life of: 158; fervor of: 133, 137; formation at: 134; founders of: 148; gifts to Church of: lxi; grand prior of: 128; hospitality of: 145; lavishness of: 133; lax spirit of: 133; monks of: 149–50; observance(s) of: 133, 137, 149, 158, 224; pomp of: 140, 145; prayers of: 145; priors of: 158; purity of: 143;

reform of: xc, 139, 141–42, 157–60; St. Bernard's critique of: lxi–lxii, lxxxix–xc, 126–33, 140–60; St. Bernard's praise of: 140, 145; splendor of: 133; statutes of: 158–60; tradition of: 159; worldly greatness of: 145; worldly spirit of: 133
coats, fur: 135
coldness: 268
color, charm of: 254
combat, spiritual: 320
comfort(s): 39, 229, 310; cult of: 150; lack of: 11; superfluous: 119; temporal: 271; useless: 142
command(s): 193, 201, 219; of Father: 175; onerous: lxvi; reasonable: 188; unclear: lxvi
commandment(s): 19, 123, 162–64; first: 118, 377
commentary, scriptural: 172
commitment: 77; free: 116; mature: lxxvi, lxxxvi; personal: lxxxvi; religious: lxxxvi; responsible: lxxvi; to charity: lxvii; to common will: lxvii; to truth: lxiii
communication(s): 366; difficulty of: 11
communion, spiritual: lxxv, 75, 279; with God: 77; with truth: lxiii
communists, hypocrisy of: 305; injustice of: 305
community: 366; deficiencies in: 222; disorder in: 350; judgment of: 237; life in: lxxviii; monastic: xxxviii, xliv, xlviii, lxxvi, xcii, xcv, 77, 228, 234, 307; officers of: 193–96; religious: 194–95, 307; rest in: 318; structure of: 193; theology of: xlvii
companion: 302
comparisons, disinclination for: 256
compassion: viii, xix, xxiv, 89–90, 123, 205, 211, 213, 293, 331, 363–64, 366–67, 371; false: 365–66; feeling of: 370; fraternal: lxxiv, 122, 273; grace of: 269; merciful: xcvii; self-

less: xxxviii; toward brethren: xxxviii, 270; wrinkle in: 366
Compèigne: 46
compensation: 47
competition: 326; spirit of: 334
complacency: xc, 280, 331–32, 334
complaint(s): 129, 227, 232–33
*complexus*: 251, 253
complication, reduction of: 158
compline: 391
composition, Latin: 16
comprehension: 54
compromise(s): 23, 325, 333
compulsion, exterior: 270
compunction: xxviii, xxxvii, xlii, lxxiv, xcv, 210, 213, 272, 280, 284, 292, 310, 325, 329–30, 369–70, 374, 387; as source of strength: 333–34; Lenten: 332–34; school of: 332; spirit of: 310; tears of: 210
conceit(s): 276, 289
concept(s): 172, 214; abstract: lxiv; death to: 394; human: xcviii, 394; Pelagian: 176; philosophical: 389; theological: 389
conceptualism: 166, 172
concern(s), human: 378; personal: 125; tender: 195
concupiscence: xcv, 24, 119; carnal: 24; fire of: 279
condemnation: 210, 311; complete: 214; frank: 214; moderate: 214; nonviolent: 214
conduct, canons of: 289; devout: 185; guidance of: 3; holy: 185; humble: 185
conduits: 283
conferences, novitiate: xi, xl, xlii, lviii, lxvii; appendices to: xciv–ci; contents of: lxxix; current events in: ciii; dating of: liii–lv, lxxx; recordings of: lxxx, lxxxiii, ci–cviii, cx; revised version of: lxxx, lxxxii; schedule for:

lii–lv, c–ci; texts of: lv–lvii, lxviii, lxxx–lxxxii, cviii–cix
confessions: 280
confessors: 342
confidence: lxxiv–lxxv, 4, 45, 132, 250, 270, 277, 279, 306, 311, 388; perfect: 390
conflict(s): xx, xcviii, 104, 143, 249, 312; intellectual: 160; of love and fear: 127; of spirit and letter: 127; personal: 126; within monasticism: 127
conformity: 250, 312; external: xxxvii; mystical: 253; of life: 228; to outward objects: 109; to will of God: 80; to Word 253
confusion: 21, 34, 193, 204, 210, 239, 243–44, 349
Conon: 176
conscience: 19, 24, 63, 129–30, 199, 208, 272, 288, 325, 329, 362, 391; bad: xlix, 200; badly formed: 219; book of: 21, 200; false: 222; good: 208, 352; nature of: 200; perverted: 200; problems of: 177; sting of: 200; testimony of: 268; voice of: 362
consciousness: 394
*consensus*: 77
consent: 175, 312; of spiritual father: 288; wicked: 176
consolation(s): xlv, lxiii, lxxvii, 19, 36, 38–39, 43, 111, 114, 203, 205, 242, 250, 295, 298, 307, 309, 331, 341–42, 368–69; divine: 270; of God: 272; of Scriptures: 309; sacrifice of: 355; sensible: xcv, 309; spiritual: 270, 340
consoler: 207
constancy: lxxvi, 230, 297, 346
*Consuetudines*: liii–liv, lxxix
consumerism, religious: lxii
contemplation: xix, xxii, xxx–xxxii, lv, lxviii–lxix, lxxvii, xcvi, 1, 3, 5, 8–9, 27, 65, 70, 89, 110–11, 217, 237–44, 257, 263, 269, 271, 283–84, 299–300, 304–5, 340, 344, 349, 351–55, 367–68,

371–74, 377, 381, 386–87, 389, 393–94; approach to: 244; arm-chair: 242; as apostolic: 381; authentic: lxx; bed of: 187, 190; bridal chamber of: 381; call to: 303; capacity for: 377; dark: 372; death in: 394; degrees of: 243, 385; desire for: 263–68; devout: 63; ecstasy of: 344, 370, 389, 394; forms of: 239; freedom of: 367; fruits of: lxxv; gifts of: lxxv; graces of: lxx, 29, 242; highest: xxvii, 238; holy: 263; infused: 313; intellectual: lxxviii, 304–5, 384, 386; joy(s) of: 271, 367; knowledge of: 241; land of: 269; levels of: 383; lifelong: 244; light of: 383; loving: 383–84; mansions of: 383; merit of: 392; mystical: 386–87; objectivity of: 384; of good: 104; of Mary: 66; place of: 240; primacy of: 353; privacy of: 383; profession of: 238; pure: xvii, xxx–xxxi; quiet of: 389; repose of: xcvii–xcviii, 359–95; rest of: xcvii, 365, 367; sacrifice of: xcvii, 354; sharing of: 283; sleep of: 285; spirit of: 10, 239; study of: 239; symbol of: 303; taste for: 243; terrible: 387; true: lxxix, 304–6, 372, 374, 388, 391, 394; unmixed: xxx–xxxi; vocation to: 308–9
contemplative(s): xxx, 238, 241–42, 300, 340, 350, 359; abbot as: 269; Cistercian: 242–44, 246; lack of: 241; soul of: 272
contempt: lxiv, 216, 222, 249–50; for God: 24; for others: lxxv, 276; of Creator: 176
contention(s): 6, 201, 312
contentment: 116, 151
continence: 186, 207
contingency, human: lx
contract: 77, 116, 251
*contractus*: 77, 116
contradiction: 249
contrition: 269; ointments of: lxxiv

control, episcopal: 134
controversy: 312; monastic: 126
convalescence: 284; period of: lii, 212; salutary: 211
*conversae*: 193–94; compared to infantry: 194
conversion: xxviii, xli, lxiii, lxvii, lxxi, 14, 19–27, 100, 198–214, 250, 323–24, 332, 336, 341; agony of: 201; appearance of: 334; call to: cviii; full: 204; helps to: 198; integral: 333; interior: xcv, 323; meaning of: lxiii; need for: cvii; of apostles: 199; of memory: 204, 209–12; of mind: 204; of saints: 23; of soul(s): 199, 204; of will: 204, 206; outward form of: 334; pattern of: 326; problems of: 198; process of: xli, lxiii; pseudo-: lxiii; radical: lxxx; reality of: 334; stages of: lxiii; struggle for: 200; struggles of: 198; total: xcvi, 330, 334, 338; true: 99; work of: 203
conversion of manners, vow of: li, 150, 232
conviction: 388
cooperation, generous: 222
Coran (Qu'ran): 139
corn: 164, 282
correction: 22, 343; rod of: 171
correctives: 272
corruption(s): 143, 344; land of: 88; weakness of: 380
cosmos: 104; as object of scientific thought: 11; as religious epiphany: 11; beauty of: 175
Coulton, G. C.: 153
council(s), Church: 35; monastic: 188
counsel(s): xlv, 214–15, 283, 346, 364; gift of: 369; spirit of: 365
country, far: 200
courage: 114, 130, 132, 205; renewal of: 9, 279
course, better: 209
covenant, breaker of: 228

coverlets, dainty: 130
covert: 395
cow: 282
cowardice: 325
cowl: 151–52
craftsmen: 11–12
created: 49
creation: xxvii, xxxix, l, lxix, lxxxviii, xcvii, 103, 110, 317, 375; human: 171; new: 111, 113; order of: lxxxviii
creature(s): 5, 84, 88, 106, 238, 251–52, 357; rational: 357, 385
Cremona: 36; opposition of: 36; prosperity of: 36
crime: 279
*crimen*: lxvi, 215–16
criminal: 249
crises, ecclesiastical: xciv; political: xciv
criticism, aggressive: 144; of others: 144, 210; rationalistic: 257; scientific: 257
Croiset, Jean, SJ: 249
cross: 82, 195; carrying of: 186–88; disgrace of: 115; folly of: xxiii; love of: xliii; mystery of: xxiii, xxvii; of Christ: xlviii, 111, 114–15, 144, 173, 186, 250, 254, 293, 296, 374; simple: 195; tree of: 111
crow: 158
crowd: 11
crucifix: 332
cruelty: 22
Crusade (s): 165; First: 12; new: 46; Second: xxv, xxxiv, lviii, lxxii, 45–46
crusaders: 12
crystal: 250
*cubiculum*: lxxviii, 300, 303–4, 306, 372, 380, 383–84; true: 388
culpability, moral: cvii
culprits: 171
cultivation, of mind: 16
culture, unity of: 11; vitality of: 12
cummin: 130

Cunningham, Lawrence S.: xxii, 100
cupidity: 94, 234, 319; poison of: 282
cure, period of: lii
curiosity: xxxix, xli, lxxix, 17, 28–29, 67, 70, 109, 202, 268, 305–6; false: xxxvi; restlessness of: 206; unquiet: 389
curiousness: 154
custom(s): 188; appeal to: 189; Cistercian: lxii; Cluniac: lxi–lxii; good: 224; monastic: 139, 224; power of: 138
Cyprian, St.: 188

Daggy, Robert E.: xiii, xxv, xxxvi, cxi, 185
Dalai Lama: ci
danger(s): 9, 19, 63, 65, 122, 132, 205, 279, 281, 290, 296, 385, 387, 393
Daniel of Morley: 161–62
Daniel, Walter: xlvii
Daniélou, Jean, sj: 240
Daniel-Rops, Henri: xxiii
daring, holy: 266
darkness: xxii, 132, 205, 238, 278, 284, 298, 351, 373; angel of: 289; bitter: 212; interior: 212; outer: 131; salutary: 212; soothing: 212; things of: 21; works of 278
Darwin, Francis: 193
daughter, of Father: 268
David, King: 274; dwelling place of: 163; family of: 52; House of: 51
day: 278, 361; of Lord: 308
day-dreaming: 285
deaconess: 193–95; example of: 194; obedience to: 188; of mature years: 194; virtue of: 194
dead: 20; living: 355; supernaturally: 291
dealings: 353; business: 150
death(s): xii, xcviii, 34, 38–39, 83, 113, 127, 132, 195, 203–4, 228, 259–60, 293, 297, 342, 392–93; choice of: xxxix; degrees of: 395; false desire for: 376; for love of Christ: 297; happy: 394; love of: xii; mystical: lx; of angels: 394; of men: 393; of sin: 392; overcoming of: lxxvi, 173; rest in: 380; snare of: 9, 279; spiritual: 80, 280, 299; taste for: xxxix; threat of: 297; to self: xl, lx
debate, world of: 166
Deborah: 184
debt(s): 211; of humanity: 174; to devil: 173–74
deceit: 6, 22
deception(s): 84, 335
decrees, divine: 384
deeds, evil: 182; good: 203, 361, 372; great: 20
defaulter: 228
defeat, fear of: 132
defendant: 128
deficiencies: 210, 244; in community: 222
degrees, of contemplation: 300, 384; of interior life: 284; of spiritual life: 238, 241
deification: 79, 379
Dekar, Paul R.: xv
de la Roche, Geoffrey, Bp.: 33, 44
Delfgaauw, Pacificus, ocso: xxii, lxxxvii, 70–77, 103
delicacies, exotic: 157; royal: 157
delight(s): 69, 72, 206, 253, 256, 299, 341–42, 384; spiritual: 346
deliverance: 127, 231
Dell'Isola, Frank: xxv
demon(s): 24, 182; ways of: 315
*demonstratio*: 49
denial, of nature: lxviii; of orientation: lxviii
Denis (Dionysius), St., legend of: 169
deordination: 350
departure, contentious: 223
dependence, human: lx; necessary: 110
deposition: 34
deprivation, pride in: cvi

depth(s), spiritual: 176, 257
Derby Day: ciii
descent, necessary: 377; negligent: 223
desert: 14, 21, 150, 152, 155, 184, 190–91, 206, 366; Chosen People in: 190; Christ in: 190; journey in: 57
desertion: 132
desire(s): xxxii, cv, 4, 10, 19, 43, 73, 76, 86, 117, 125, 235, 242, 251–52, 281, 285, 306, 317, 332–33, 335–36, 342, 345, 351, 394; allurement of: 105; ardent: xxxi, 72, 250, 264, 380; attraction of: 105; bitter: 329; bodily: 148; centered on God: 338; evil: 294, 320; for action: 350; for autonomy: xxxix; for easier life: 192; for experience: 245; for God: 76, 308; for knowledge: xli; for mystical union: 263; for perfection: 156; for self-assertion: xxxix; for self-gift: 26; for true rest: 319; force of: 345; human: 5, 394; law(s) of: lxxxviii, 107; mortification of: 30; of soul: 76, 100, 336, 372; ordinate: lxxxviii, 107; passionate: civ; restless: xcviii; satisfaction of: lxvii; sweet: 72; transformation of: 107; true end of: 88; unlawful: 279; unrest of: 394; worldly: xx, 115
desolation(s): lxxvii, 205, 298
despair: 4, 63, 85, 101, 205
desperation: 9, 279
destiny: 343, 375
destroyers: 312
detachment: 85, 244, 337, 383; interior: xcv; perfect: 277
determination: 130
detraction(s): 63, 146, 156
detractors: 146
development(s), individual: 11; normal: 239; of love: 169; organic: 284; spiritual: lxxi, lxxv, 239; theological: xxi
devil, 24, 40, 57, 84, 87, 128, 170, 174, 182, 280–81, 325, 342; angels of: 281;

as jailer: 182; debt to: 173–74; noonday: 351; payment to: 173; power of: xcii, 174, 181–82; rights of: 173–74, 181–82; will of: 182
devotion(s): 51, 154, 186, 256, 261, 269, 271–72, 321–22, 324–25; fervent: 273, 321; Marian: 68; official: 134; ointments of: lxxiv, 272–73; originality in: 66; sentiments of: 296; sweetness of: 268; to flesh of Christ: 253; true: 309; whole-hearted: 228
dew, heavenly: 164
dialectic(s): 11, 177; sterile: 198
dialecticians: 2–3, 11
dictating: 194
differences, accidental: 11
difficulties: 63, 297; absence of: 219; innumerable: 219; presence of: 219
diffidence: 225
*dignitas*: 108, 110
dignity: xxx, lix, 45, 108–9, 127; ecclesiastical: 41; human: 78; knowledge of: 109; natural: xvii, 67; personal: 86; source of: 109; supreme: 108
Dijon: 12, 14
*dilectio*: civ, 72–73
Dionysius, Pseudo-: 56
Dionysius the Areopagite: 169
direction, aimless: 243; spiritual: viii, lxxxix, 95
director, spiritual: 239, 271, 289–90, 349, 373
disadvantage: 331
disappointment: 42
disaster: 243
discernment: lxxv, c, 280, 373
disciple(s): xlix, c, 92, 265, 289, 301–3, 357, 358, 381; love of: lxxvii
discipline: 301–2, 381; ascetic: 302; intellectual: 177; life of: 302; monastic: 31, 270; observance of: 288; of gospel: lxxiii; of mind: 16; of submission: lxxviii; of superior: 270; spiritual: 29, 201; system of: 195; way of: 209

discomfort: ci
discord: 6
discouragement: 204, 208, 298, 371, 377
discretion: xxxvii, lxvi, lxxvi, xcvi, cvi, 146–50, 216, 268, 280, 282, 289, 296, 340, 343–46, 348–50, 353–55, 383; as mother of virtues: 344, 382; as theory: 344; dead: 344; function(s) of: 339, 345; inert: 344; influence of: 340; norms for: 345–46, 352; sterile: 344
disease: 202; spiritual: lxvii
disgust: 22; weariness of: 279
disobedience: xcviii, 216, 218, 311–13; cure for: 222; formal: lxvi, 216; sloth of: 301
disorder: 348
dispensation(s): lxi, lxvi, 147–48, 215, 223–24; Jewish: 57; legitimate: 150; old: 112; rightful: 148; valid: 222
display: xviii, 142; cult of: 150
disposition(s), evil: 329; free: 311; good: 51, 278; honorable: 9, 278; interior: 325; perfect: 321; right: 242
disputations: 338
dispute(s): 127, 164; scholastic: 196
dissention: 6, 69
dissimilitude: 80
dissipation: 148
distraction(s): xcviii–xcix, 29, 154, 306, 319, 395; worldly: 257
distress: 21
distrust: 252
disturbance(s): 27, 343, 359, 392
diversity: lxi
divinity, fullness of: 316
divinization: 300–301, 379; of human nature: lxxviii, 301
division(s): 193; healing of: 134; social: xcviii, 312
docility: xix, 244, 349
doctor(s): 87, 92, 95, 238, 347; arguments of: 196; monk as: 230–31; of Church: lxxi, 259; quack: 32

doctrine(s): 3, 245, 267; Cistercian: 2, 245; living: 246; Marian: lxxxvi, 60–61, 66; monastic: 289; mystical: 245, 247; of gospel: 6; of love: 6, 246; patristic: xl, 2; sacred: 172; sapiential: 2; scholastic: 2; spiritual: lxx, 245; wind(s) of: 316, 348
dog: 208
dogma(s): lxix, 162, 166, 238, 240; experience of: 238; reality of: 238
domination, appetite for: 188
Dominicans: lxiv
donations: lxii
dormitory: 160
double-mindedness: 308
doubt(s): 4, 63, 279, 281
dove(s): 157; wings of: 393
dread: lxxviii, 251; of judgment: 63
dress: lxii
drink: lxii, 141, 147–48, 151; of good works: 54; of prayer: 54
drives, compulsive: xxxix
Drogo: 225–27
drunkenness: 201
dryness: 271
Dumont, Charles, ocso: xxix, li, 187
duplicity: xvi, 308
Dutton, Marsha: 262
duty: 92, 97, 152, 213, 246, 256, 271, 292, 339, 352–55; formal: 51; of superior: lxxviii
dying: 195; manner of: 393

Eadmer: 68, 150–51
Earll, Mary Beth: cxii
ear(s): 163–64, 201–2, 207, 254, 323, 347, 351; Holy Name as melody in: 9, 278; of heart: 358
earth: 27, 114, 144, 171, 207–9, 282, 299, 308, 313, 316, 332, 351, 353, 355, 357, 373, 377, 380, 392
earthiness: 12
ease, bourgeois: 242
Easter: xlix, liv

eating: 149; excessive: 151
Ecclesiasticus (Sirach): xliii
Eckhart, Meister: 100
economy, divine: 55, 238; twelfth-century: 11
ecstasy: 11, 77, 253, 374, 389, 393; mental: 394; public: 342; secret: 342
edification: 156
education, monastic: xlviii; of heart: 196; of tongue: 196
effect(s), bodily: 253; interior: 387; psychophysical: 248, 255; subjective: 387
efficacy: 8, 341
effort(s): 304, 311, 373; ascetic: 375; fruitless: 206; human: 379; intellectual: 305; vain: 362
eggs: 149, 157
ego: 83; worship of: xx
egotism: 76
Egypt: 157, 162; treasure of: 184; world as: 319
Egyptians: 162
elect: 22, 319; community of: 319; souls of: 247
election(s): 388–89; episcopal: 141; papal: 35
element(s), bodily: 147; exterior: 147; progressive: 160; spiritual: 147; traditional: 160
elevation, illusory spiritual: lxx
eleventh century, as conservative: 10–11; as static: 10–11
Elias (Elijah): 136, 283
Eliseus (Elisha): lxxv, 280; action of: 280
eloquence: 53, 59, 162, 282; divine: 357; eternal: 357
emaciation, public: 324
embrace(s): 74, 251, 253, 392–93; desired: 361, 372; mystical: 4; of spouse: xcviii, 390; spiritual: 4–5
emergencies: 353
emotion(s): lxxvi, cv, 118, 236, 294
empathy: 92

Emperor(s), Holy Roman: 39, 43, 46, 134
Empire, Holy Roman: 134
emptiness: xvii, 100
emulation: 349
enclosure, service of: 193
encounter, heavenly: 379
end(s): 381; eternal: 353; natural: 367; supernatural: 367
endurance: 325; feats of: 30
enemies: 34–36, 87, 132, 281, 291, 361, 364; gentleness toward: 87; hand of: 181; of God: 108
energy: 83, 344
engagement, existential: lxxxv
England: 161–62
enjoyment: 110; earthly: 187
enmity: 6
environment, power of: 139
envy: 22, 147, 156, 350; wound of: 9, 279
epistemology, theory of: 177
equity: 6, 69
*eros*: civ
error(s): 127, 166, 176–77, 268, 281, 395; danger of: 295; dangerous: xxi; dogmatic: 197; invincible: 83; spirit of: 3, 289
espousals, mystical: 72, 243
essence: 55
essentials: 253; agreement on: 11
esteem: 352
Étampes, Council of: 35, 46
eternity: 171, 200, 388; joys of: 314; wedding of: 186
etymologies, fanciful: lxxxvi
Eugene III, Pope: lviii–lix, lxxii, 45–46, 48; letters to: 46–48
Europe: 243
Evagrius Ponticus: 84
evaluation: 218
evanescence: 85
evangelicals, protomendicant: lxxxii
evangelism: 11
evangelists, Cistercian: xliv

# Index

evasion, motives for: 219
Eve: 135, 362–63, 366; will as: 206
events, providential: 256
*Everyman*: 203
evidence: 281, 388
evil(s): lxiii, lxxviii, lxxxviii, 6, 10, 58, 67, 83, 86–87, 95, 99–101, 117, 147, 176, 200–201, 203–4, 209, 212, 218, 226, 304, 310, 328, 337, 355, 388; avoiding: 96; day of: 395; detachment from: 213; discernment of: 373; done: 310; forces of: 173; inability to will: 94; joy in: 332; knowledge of: xxxix; mystery of: lxxviii, 305; objective: 175; open: 305; resistance to: lxxvi–lxxvii, 297; roots of: 305; spirit of: 87; suffered: 310; traps of: 164
evisceration: 200
exaggeration, rhetorical: 142
exaltation, way of: 326
example, teaching by: 194
excesses: 171
*excessus*: 370, 378, 381, 389; *amoris*: 374
exchequer, English: 161
excommunicate(s): 230
exegesis, allegorical: lxxiii
exegete: 257
exemption:137; history of: 137
exercise(s): 158, 285, 346; community: 50–51; hard: 131; spiritual: 136, 341
exhaustion, physical: 362
exile: 1, 4, 88, 227, 327; desert of: 184; happy: 163; land of: 250
existence: 121; natural: 85; new mode of: 379; processes of: 85
exodus: 57
*Exordium Parvum*: 320
expectation, eschatological: xxvi
expense, futile: 344
experience(s): lxiv, lxix, lxxi, 167, 179, 208–9, 214, 263, 305, 310, 354, 386, 387–88; Christian: 214; common: 177; contemplative: lxx; direct: 338;

246; obedience of: 52; principles of: 297; pure: 337; question of: 173; sense of: 179; understanding of: 180; unfeigned: 98; word of: 52
faithful: lxix, lxxv, 155, 162, 171, 241, 277, 314, 347
faithfulness: 252
fall(s): xxxviii–xxxix, 67, 78, 88, 132, 318; as collapse into ambivalence: xxxix–xl; as descent from supernatural to natural: xxxix
falsehood(s): 20, 83
falseness: 82
falsity, recognition of: 82; truth of: civ: 82
familiars, non-monastic: 158
famine: 141
fancy: 348
fast(s): xxxviii, 131, 157, 201; austere: 150; breaking: 150; exterior: 325; joy of: 341–42; Lenten: 320–23, 326; merit of: 325; monastic: 159; regular: 288
fasters: 323
fasting: lxvi, xc, 120, 134, 140–41, 144, 149, 159, 196, 201, 216, 320, 322–25; exterior: 334; joy in: 328–29; rule of: 335; triumph in: 329
Fathers, Apostolic: lxix, 237; Cistercian: xxi, xliv–xlv, lxxxi, xciv, cxi, 70, 144, 307, 313–14; Desert: 190, 194, 293; Greek: lxix, 16, 238, 300, 379; Latin: lxix, 16, 238; monastic: viii, 134; of Church: lxxi, 2, 51, 55, 61, 74, 80, 162, 172, 178, 240–41, 246–47, 257, 259, 262, 277; spiritual: lxxiv, lxxvi, 270, 272, 288
fatigue: 304, 385
fault(s): 22, 43, 127, 141, 169, 171, 215, 220–21, 229, 276, 310, 319, 341, 371, 376; apparent: 371; involuntary: 309; of frailty: lxvi, 216, 221; of negligence: 215; of others: 364, 371; of weakness: lxvi, 215

faultlessness: 286
favor, human: 335
fear(s): xii, xlii, lxvi, cv, 9, 40, 42, 63, 80, 93, 99, 132, 204, 207, 210, 213, 220, 226, 249–51, 266, 279, 282, 302, 305, 325, 332, 335–36, 338, 357, 365, 381, 386–88, 391; as natural affection: 118; chaste: lxxxviii, 107; coercion of: 105; compulsion of: 93; gift of: 369; law of: lxxxviii, 101, 107, 127; of defeat: 132; of judgment: xcviii, 206, 265, 390; of Lord: lxxviii, lxxxiv, 19, 23, 305, 381; painful: 251; place of: 305; servile: 390
feast, Marian: xcix
feast days: 151, 158
feeling(s): lxxvi, 179, 251, 255, 295, 310; angelistic: 286; exile from: 88; human: 177, 297; natural: 177
fellowship, good: 148
ferment, intellectual: xci, cvii
fervor: 59, 61, 269, 290, 294–97, 308, 324, 332, 341–45, 349, 352, 383; blind: 268; exemplary: 137; impetuousity of: 344; movements of: xcvi, 339; of divine love: 7, 69, 344–45; regulation of: 345; sensible: 308, 340–41, 345; spiritual: lxxvi, 290; superficial: lxxvi
fidelity: lxxvi, 162, 186, 286; conjugal: 202; to vow: 138
field(s): 31, 113, 190, 233; fruitful: 208
figure(s), outward: 58; vs. realization: 55
filth: 102, 201, 203
Finley, James: vii–x, cxi; as novice: vii
fire: xlix, 96, 212, 353, 379; brush: ciii; of zeal: 286
fire-fighting: 353
fish: 20, 130, 149, 151, 156–57, 199
fishermen: 164
Flahiff, G. B.: 183–84
flame(s): 376; of love: 285; throne of: 250; tongues of: c, 357

Index 483

Flanders: 35, 45
flatterers: 130
flattery: 34
flavor: 130–31
flax: 195
Flay, Abbey of: 229–31
Flay, abbot of: 229–31
Flay, monks of: 229–31
fleas: 143
flesh: 22, 24, 29–30, 57, 63, 84, 107, 150, 170–71, 201, 203, 205, 211, 253, 259–60, 265, 289, 293–95, 360, 362–63, 370, 378; appetites of: 354; desires of: 295; liberation from: 169; likeness of: 254; mortal: 393; mortification of: 345; need of: 377, 380; of Christ: xxvi, lxxvi, 113, 164, 253–54, 294–96; passions of: 279; poison of: 361; sinful: 22; sufferings of: 380; things of: 394; visible: 294; weak: 254; weakness of: 359, 393; works of: 265
flexibility: cvi
flight: 131–32
flour: 151
flower(s): 57, 67, 111, 113, 206–7, 361, 372
foe: 132
Foliot, Gilbert: xlvi
Fontaines: 14
food(s): lxii, 29–30, 67, 130–31, 136, 140–41, 147–50, 185, 260, 288, 325; bloody: 158; coarse: 14; for body: 149; frugal: 130; Holy Name as: 9, 275, 278–79; necessary: 118; of good works: 54, 284; of prayer: 54; pleasant: 341; self-satisfaction as: 236; simple: 14; soft: 341; solid: 288; spiritual: 9, 260, 278; substantial: 346; tasty: 151; Tibetan: ci
fools: 291, 311
foot: 347, 368
footprint, of Beloved: 285
force, brute: 41
foresight: 362

forest(s): 31, 53, 157
forgery: 46–47
forgetfulness: 209
forgiveness: 203, 210, 274; of others: cvii; of self: cvii
form(s): 334; fruition of: 93; love of: 93; of bodies: 94; outward: 58; spiritual: 333
formalism: lxxxix, xcv, 135, 335; monastic: 334–35; pure: 334; rigid: 221; scrupulous: 221
formalist: 335
formalities, external: xc, 160
formation: 381; Cistercian: 1, 245; Cluniac: 134; directors of: lxxxi; monastic: li–lii, lxxx, civ, 196; regulations on: xc
fornication(s): 22, 85; spiritual: 344
fortitude: 279; gift of: c, 358, 369; spirit of: 359, 365
fortune, good: 329
foundation, firm: 286; lack of: 243; monastic: 19
fountain(s): 252, 275; of Savior: 164; sealed: 207
fowl: 157
fowler, snare of: 393
Fox, James, ocso: xxviii, xlvii
Fox, Peggy: cxi
fragrance: 335
frailty: 171, 222; faults of: lxvi, 221; human: 221–22, 310
France: l, 35–36, 41, 44; medieval: lxxix
Francis of Assisi, St.: 23, 70
Franciscans: lxiv
freedom: xii, xxxvii, xlviii, xcv, 13, 74, 79–80, 85–86, 101, 105, 109, 115, 274, 337–38, 367; authentic: xiii, xlviii, cv; feast of: lii; from passions: 84; law of: 106; loss of: 94; man of: 42; of counsel: 94; Pelagian concept of: 176; perfect: xli, 79, 394; problem of: 175–76; spirit of: 106; spiritual: 71
Fremund of Prémontré, Br.: 232

frequency, habitual: 367
friends: 232
friendship(s): 96, 232, 302; dangerous: 17; importance of: lxxxvii; love of: civ; sacramental concept of: 97; stormy: 17; theology of: xlvii
frivolity: 45; spirit of: 32–33
Fromer, Anne: 13
fruit(s): 57, 67, 111–13, 206, 208, 299; communicating: 381; insipid: 346; of labor: 314
fruitfulness: 286; for Church: 214; for souls: 214; of Church: lxiv; of preaching: 271
fruition: 72
frustration(s): 74, 317; constant: 104; life of: xl; of wishes: lxviii
fugitives: 134, 225
Fulbert, Canon: 167–69
Fulbert of Chartres: 61, 63–64, 68
fulfillment: 73, 80, 114; genuine: lxxvi; human: lxviii; lack of: xl; of commandment: 377; perfect: 332, 377; true: lxviii
Fulk, letter to: 24–26; uncle of: 25–26
fullness: 73
function, ascetic: 193; assigned: 348; educational: 193; individual: 348
fur(s): 130, 146, 151, 159

Gabriel, Archangel: 50–51, 55, 66, 231; mission of: 57; name of: 52, 56–57
gaity: 45
Galilee: 51
gambling: 165
games, Persian: 161
Gandhi: 86
garden(s): lxxviii, 206–7, 300, 381; enclosed: 207; of agony: 237; spiritual: 206
garments: 22, 323, 334; fur: 138–39; of skins: 135
Garrigou-Lagrange, Reginald, OP: 240–41

Gasparri, Cardinal Peter: 223
gate, of monastery: 137
*gemüt*: 100
General Chapter, Benedictine: 141
General Chapter, Cistercian: xiv, xliv, xlvi, li, 37, 45; letter to: 37–38
generation, divine: 79
generosity: xxxvii, xcix, 7–8, 123, 138, 175, 217, 271, 317; lack of: 224
Genesis: xlix
Geneviève of the Holy Face, OCD (Céline Martin): 204
Genoa: 36
gentiles: 155, 278, 347
gentleness: xix, lxxviii, 303, 330, 367; need for: 127
Geoffrey of Auxerre: 197
geometry: 16
Gerard, Bl.: 40, 247; death of: lviii, 44, 247; illness of: 42–43; sanctity of: 247
Germanus of Auxerre, St.: 185
Germany: 46
Gethsemani, Abbey of: vii, xii–xiii, xxii, xxvii, xl, xlviii, lii, lix, cii; daughter house of: ciii
gift(s): 75, 300; active: 339; better: 347; charismatic: lxx, 242, 282; contemplative: 339; diversity of: lxxvii, 299; divine: xxxii, 102, 268, 300; extraordinary: lxx, 242; generous: 220; natural: 146; of God: xlviii, c, 27, 89, 102, 108–10, 222, 303, 319, 368, 373, 395; of heart: 334; of life: xxxix; of nature: 1, 110; of others: 329; of self: c, 23, 26–27, 80, 89, 102, 108–10, 222, 303, 319, 368, 373, 395; of will: 217; preoccupation with: 258; pure: 373; qualitative: 217; to God: 335
Gigny, Abbey of: 47, 141
Gilbert of Hoyland: xlvii, 298
Gilson, Étienne: xi, xiii, xxii, lv, lix, lxvii, lxxxvii, xci, civ, 69–71, 73–81, 88–90, 107, 109, 111, 153–55, 166–69,

*Index* 485

173, 234, 240, 292, 298, 338, 364, 374, 379
ginger: 130
Giroux, Robert: xx, xxxi–xxxiii, xlvi
giver, cheerful: 325
gladness: 54, 207, 307
glory: 3, 109–10, 145–46, 175, 285, 309, 311, 351, 376, 380; companions in: xliii; divine: 110; eternal: 39; experience of: 371; fleeting: 8; house of: 204; human: 331; light of: 115; of Ascension: 295; of heaven: 145; of Lord: 115; of Resurrection: 112, 322; personal: 196; reflected: 145; rest in: 380; to God: 321; worldly: 8, 34
gluttony: 150, 201; spiritual: 289–90
*gnosis*: 84
God: xxii, lxvii, 200, 215, 218, 234, 236–37, 248, 255; abiding in: xxx; absorption in: 28; acting for: 236; aid of: 121; arms of: 372, 392; as absolute Being: 54, 107; as Author: 312; as Author of goods: 234; as Author of nature: 118–20; as *caritas*: 89, 102; as charity: 102, 107, 287; as charity by essence: 79; as concept: 112; as created by: 117; as Creator: xxxix, lxxxviii, 5–6, 22, 88, 103–4, 251–52, 316, 375; as Defender of orphans: 281; as Divine King: 154; as eternal: 95; as faithful: 171; as Father: xxvii, xxxviii, lxviii, 113, 175, 251, 267, 316, 331, 347, 357–58, 361, 370, 383; as Father of fatherless: 281; as Giver of goods: 234; as Giver of Himself: 110; as Giver of life: xxxix; as good: 99, 330; as Heavenly Father: 330; as Heavenly King: 36; as hidden: 278; as immaterial spirit: lxxiii, 55–56; as immeasurable: 95; as Judge: 312, 385; as just: 277; as just Judge: 101; as kind: 277; as lovable: lx; as Love: xii, 7, 69, 73–74, 79, 88, 107, 116, 265–66, 330; as loving Father: 6; as loving Mother: 341; as merciful: 277; as merciful Father: 171; as merciful Judge: 39; as Most High: 391; as omnipotent: 249; as powerful: 99; as pure love: 107; as reason for loving God: 7, 69, 95, 107; as Redeemer: 375; as refuge: 117; as Ruler: 312; as Source of intelligibility: 112; as Source of life: 7; as supreme end: 7; as Supreme Giver: 5; as supreme Goodness: 107; as terrible: 277; as Trinity: lx, lxxx, 72, 77, 79, 102, 172–73, 183, 238, 267, 357–58; as Truth: xxi, 109, 231, 372; as Wisdom: 3, 289; as Word: 54; ascent to: lxiii, 198; attaining: 87; attention to: 242; attraction to: 122; attribute of: 55; becoming: xvi, 80; Being of: 389; benefits of: 390; blessing of: 243; bosom of: 392; bounty of: 368; call of: 50, 222; care of: 392; centered on: 338; charity of: 34; clinging to: 108; commandments of: 137, 164; communion with: 77; concern of: 392; condemnation of: 304; consecration to: 338; consolations of: 272; contacts with: 285; contemplation of: lxix, 238, 372; creative action of: 317; decrees of: 387–88; dedication to: 186; definition of: 107; dependence on: xxxix; designs of: 249; desire for: 76, 308; desire of: 248–49; devotion to: 190; divine majesty of: 315; dream of: 284; embrace of: lxxix; enemy of: 211, 236; enjoyment of: 365; epiphany of: 112; essence of: 180; existence of: xi, 112; experience of: lxix, lxxix, 28, 248, 264, 305, 384, 386–87; eyes of: 375; face of: 27, 362; fatherhood of: 6; fear of: 35, 41, 180, 305–6, 318, 381, 387–88; feet of: 265; figure of: 261; filled with: lxxv, 287; finding of: xcv, 118, 366; forgiveness of: 388; free for: 190; friends of: xcvi,

338; gift(s) of: xlviii, c, 27, 89, 102, 108–10, 222, 303, 319, 368, 373, 395; glory of: 9, 20–21, 41, 154, 214, 231, 336, 341, 386, 388; glory to: cv; good things of: 234; goodness of: 28, 122–24, 175, 249, 267, 272, 327, 330, 332, 355, 375, 391; grace of: 242, 249, 303, 341; gratitude to: 269, 273; greatness of: 386; guidance of: ix; hand(s) of: 80, 226, 242, 302; happiness of: 124; heart of: 249, 391; hiding from 363; holiness of: lxxviii, 305; honor of: 154, 175, 213, 236, 336; honor to: cv, 119; hope in: 226; house of: 305, 386; household of: 227; image of: xii, xv–xvi, xxxviii, xl, lix, 71, 74, 100; ingratitude toward: 188; intimacy with: 245; invisible: 294; journey to: lxxvii; judgments of: 180, 385–86; justice of: 105, 180, 182, 304, 306; kindness of: 391; Kingdom of: xxvii, lxxi, 11, 129, 146, 151, 198, 258, 319, 323; knowing: lxix; knowing about: lxix, 238; knowledge of: lx, lxix, 2, 84, 125, 166, 238, 264, 267, 305, 372, 381, 392; lavishness for: 154; law(s) of: lxxxviii, cv, 72, 79, 99, 101, 105, 164, 287, 355, 371; liberality of: 249; life in: 58, 77, 330; light of: 278, 284; likeness to: xv–xvi, xviii, xxxviii, lix, lxiii, xcix, 4, 8, 74, 80, 90, 198, 317, 338, 375, 3; living: 366; lost in: lix, 79; love for: xxx, xxxvi, xxxviii, xliv, lx, lxxvi–lxxvii, lxxix, xcvii, 2, 5–6, 8, 10, 77–80, 84, 94, 101, 105, 107–25, 135, 166, 211, 215, 218, 222, 269, 273, 276–77, 289, 291, 297, 300, 302, 309, 319, 327, 331, 333, 335–36, 338, 346, 352, 354, 367, 374–80, 390–92; love of: ix, xiii, xxxvi, lx, lxxvii, civ–cv, 6, 70, 72, 76, 79, 108, 122, 125, 178, 220, 253, 267–68, 273, 276, 292, 298, 300, 307–8, 324, 327, 331, 371, 375, 391–92; loving concern of: 175; majesty of: 108, 249, 266; memory of: xlvii; mercy of: xxxviii, lxxiv, 37, 111, 114, 122, 146, 204, 209, 222, 231, 249, 270, 272, 277, 281, 299, 306–7, 364, 375–76, 387–89, 391; mystery of: 268; name of: 218, 281, 386; nature of: xi; obedience to: xcix, 105, 123, 312, 374; occupied with: 190; of love: 272, 285; of power: 277; offenses against: 288; one spirit with: 124; openness to: 29; opposition to: lxviii, 236; order of: 237; ordinances of: 311; patience of: 270; peace of: 228; people of: 50; picture of: 261; place of: 305, 386; plans of: 248; pleasing: 58, 219, 236, 317; possession of: 372, 386–87; power of: lxxv, lxxvii, 56–57, 114, 199, 297, 306, 379; praise of: lxxiv, 124, 357; presence of: ix, lxx, cv, 114, 121, 206, 231, 255, 284–85, 363; providence of: 122, 312; purpose(s) of: xxxv, 302, 388; quest for: 74, 308; reality of: xcvii, 373; reasons for loving: lix, 7, 69, 107–25; relationship to: xcviii; relishing: 381; rest in: xxx, lxxix, xcix, 306, 317, 355, 359, 365, 384, 395; rest of: xcix, 306, 317–18, 389; return to: 72; revelation of: xxvi; reverence for: 375; revolt against: 234; righteousness of: 20, 388; road to: 346; sacrifices to: 345; salvation of: 359; sanctity of: 386; sanctuary of: xxvi; search for: viii, 308; secrets of: 2, 268; seeking of: xcv, 74, 108, 118, 307–9; seeking by: 307; self in: 377; separation from: 105; serenity of: 389; servant of servants of: 9; servants of: 157; service of: 29–30, 54, 119, 139, 230, 341; severity of: 385; sight of: 375; sign of: xxvi; son(s) of: 106, 109, 212, 309, 315, 330; soul of: 318; Spirit of: 67, 75, 237, 247, 268; spiritual identification with: lxxiii; strength of: 56–57; strong: 366; submission of will to: lxvi; substance of: xiii, 358; sweetness of: 28–29, 122, 365; things of: 256, 391; thirst for: xxvi, civ, 76, 366; tranquillity of: 306, 389; truce of: 134; trumpet of: 172; trust in: 269; truth of: 197, 237; turn to: 121, 204; union with: xv–xvi, xxvi, xxxviii, xl, lvii, lxviii, lxx, lxxiii, xcvi, 3, 5, 7, 22–23, 69, 71, 78, 82, 90, 100, 115, 117, 166, 197–98, 247–48, 255, 264–68, 270–72, 301, 330, 332–33, 338, 352, 354–55, 363–64, 371–72, 381, 390; voice of: 19, 199, 362; way to: x, 86, 139, 326; ways of: 243, 304; will of: lxviii, lxxvi, xcix, cv, 7, 20, 22, 52, 80, 100, 120, 123, 125, 145, 175–76, 218–20, 233–34, 256, 271, 306, 311–13, 317, 324, 328, 337, 352–53, 366, 375–78, 382, 387; wisdom of: 316–17; word of: lxxi, 19–21, 23, 51–52, 54, 74, 199, 209, 257, 265, 337, 357; work(s) of: lxxxv, 43, 57, 265, 317, 384; worship of: xx; wrath of: 213

Godfrey of Chartres, Bp.: 183
godless, sins of: 304
Godwin of Anchin: 228–29
gold: 54, 95, 154, 185
Goldwater, Barry: ciii
goliards: 168; as non-conformists: 165; as rebels: 165; as wanderers: 165
good: lxii–lxiii, 86–87, 94, 98, 101, 109, 124, 198, 201, 204, 209, 212, 222, 226, 265, 270, 275, 280, 300, 310, 388; common: lxvii, 90, 236; desire for: cvii; discernment of: 373; divine: xxxix, 327, 329; false: 329; great: 300; greater: lxvi, 222; highest: 74, 88; knowledge of: xxxix; lasting: 88; lesser: lxvi, 222; love of: cvii, 96, 236; of all: 237; of another: 124, 236; of charity: 222; of neighbors: 98; of others: 329; one's own: 98–99; opposition of: 86; perseverance in: 155; pleasure in: 236; real: lxvii, 236, 329; source of: 313; spiritual: lxxiv, 150, 275; supreme: 88; taste for: 381; temporal: 294; true: 92; ultimate: 88; universal: lxvii, 236; zeal for: 340
goodness: 97, 99, 276, 279; natural: 367; of God: 28, 122–24, 175, 249, 267, 272, 327, 330, 332, 355, 375, 391
goods: 93; material: 88; of spirit: 209; temporal: 34; worldly: 34, 209, 235
goose: 157
gospel(s): 6, 20, 51, 164, 178, 184, 237, 273, 275, 288, 320, 324; as fable: 181; begotten in: 38; call of: lxxx; message of: xxiii, xl; preaching of: 116, 145; words of: 54
gossip: 149–50
governments: 347
grace(s): lxxxiii–lxxxv, 9–10, 19, 31, 39, 54, 65, 78, 80, 110, 113, 120–21, 169, 172, 199–200, 202, 242, 249, 255, 260, 264, 270–71, 282, 284, 294–95, 301, 303, 308, 314, 321, 329, 331–32, 338, 341, 343, 343, 351, 354–55, 368, 373–74, 376, 381, 383, 385; action of: 204; actual: 23; cellars of: lxxviii, 303; charismatic: lxxvi, 238, 287; divine: 247, 270; effect(s) of: 280; exterior: 282; extraordinary: 238; fullness of: 303; gift(s) of: 109, 111, 276; guidance of: 238; instrument of: 343; interior: 282, 330; justifying: 179; life of: lxix, 239–40, 330; mediation of: 61; mystical: lxx, 2, 242, 359, 375, 385, 388; necessity of: 110, 120; objective: 298; of God: 242, 249, 303, 341; of healing: 347; of Holy Spirit: xxvi, 290; of Passion: 112; of prayer: xlii, 27, 29, 240, 242–43, 255, 271–72, 287, 341; prevenient: 29; real: 341; repercussions of: 345; response to: 76; sanctifying: lxxvi, 287; savor of:

2; special: 246, 347–48; spiritual: 28; springs of: 390; stream of: 331, 337; theology of: 117; treasure of 282; work of: 367
Graham, Aelred, OSB: ciii
grain: 259
grammar: 16
Grande Chartreuse, Abbey of: 12, 81, 98
grandeur, infinite: 249
gratification(s): 85, 235; private: 237
gratitude: lx, lxxiv, xcix, 35, 73, 122, 170, 222, 234, 270, 272–73, 275–76, 281, 313, 331, 374, 390; hymn of: 263; spirit of: 267
grave: 203
greatness, human: 75
greed: 101, 119, 130
Greek: 160, 162
Gregory of Nyssa, St.: 80, 246
Gregory the Great, St.: xcvi, 64, 68, 77, 136, 138, 179, 191, 238
Gregory VII, Pope: 10, 12
grief: 22, 43, 127, 202, 205, 336
Grinberg, Miguel: ciii
groaning: 211, 364
growth, laws of: 284; living: 284; silent: 284; spiritual: lxiii, lxv, lxix, 270
Grube, K.: 193
*grund*: 100
Guerric of Igny, Bl.: xliv–xlv, xlviii–xlix, lxxi, xcix, 298, 313–17; Advent sermons of: xlix; Assumption sermons of: xcix, 313–17; Christmas sermons of: xlviii, lxxi, 276; Easter sermons of: xlix
guests: 135, 137, 150, 316
guidance, divine: ix; human: 250; of charity: 6; trustworthy: x
guides: 312
Guigo the Carthusian: lxxxvii–xc, xciv, civ, 81–101, 104–6; as genius: lxxxix; as greatest Carthusian: lxxxix; as prior: 43, 81; *Customs* of: 81–82; doctrine of: lxxxviii, 86; existential approach of: 82; fervor of: lxxxix; letter of St. Bernard to: xxiv, lxxxvii–lxxxviii, civ, 72, 81, 89, 96–107; letters of: 97–98; letter on solitude of: lxxxix; maxims of: lxxxix; *Meditations* of: lxxxviii–lxxxix, 81–97, 99–101, 104–6; on attachments: lxxxviii; on power of good: lxxxviii; on self-love: lxxxviii; on true and false charity: lxxxviii; on truth: lxxxviii; on worldly peace: lxxxviii; parables of: 95; reflections of: lxxxviii; seriousness of: lxxxix; style of: lxxxix
guile: 315, 351
guilt: 282; neurotic: cvii; rational: cvii
guilty, sins of: 369
gullet: 84, 202–3
Guy, brother of St. Bernard, death of: 44

habit(s), bad: 309; color of: cvi, 135, 139; former: 132; monastic: 194; religious: 129, 194
hardship: 317–18
Haimeric, Cardinal, papal chancellor: 18, 35, 39, 72, 97
Haiti: ciii
Hallier, Amédée, OCSO: xlvii
hand(s): 201, 347
happiness: civ, 69, 88, 106, 250, 271, 287, 375; human: 175; infinite: 3; perfection of: 124; promise of: 207–8
hares: 157
harmony: 72, 367
harshness: 15, 364
Hart, Patrick, OCSO: xii, xiv, xxiii, xlv–xlvii, lii, cxi, 68
harvest: 307
hate(s): 87; land of: 88
hatred: 6
hawks: 157
head: 347, 390

## Index

healing: 43, 278, 347
health: 87, 139, 147, 279, 282, 363; good: 157; lack of: 12; of kingdom: 36
hearing: 142
heart(s): ix, xx, xxvi, lxxiv, xcix, 3, 5–7, 9, 20–21, 30, 37–38, 53–54, 63, 66–67, 69, 93–94, 96, 111, 114, 117, 127, 130, 132, 147, 151, 164, 180, 199, 204, 244, 254, 260, 270, 277, 279, 281, 285, 287, 289, 291–92, 295, 306, 310, 316–18, 320, 323, 325, 331, 333, 335, 337, 348, 361, 368–69, 378; affection of: 294; awakened: 373; change of: lxiii, 99, 198; cleansing of: 22, 211; contrite: 228; custody of: 30; dry: 355; ear(s) of: 20, 358–59; exchange of: 248; eyes of: 21, 207; fulfilling of: 287; fullness of: 73; gift of: 334; hardening of: 328; hardness of: 279, 329, 332; heavy: 207; Holy Name as jubilation in: 278; humble: 279; kingly: 233; knowledge of: 305; leprosy of: 235; listening of: 357; love of: 253, 294; malice of: 320; meek: 279; of child: 145; of doctrine: 246; of fallen man: 318; of imperfect: 277; of man: 124, 295, 392; perversity of: 199; pure: 98, 212; purification of: 76, 217, 257, 365, 374; purity of: lxiii, 30, 264, 267; rending of: 323, 325, 333–34, 337; restless: 316; sabbath of: 358; softening of: 329; solitude of: 31; treasure of: 152; upright: 180; vain: 152; veil of: 259; vessel of: 164; watchful: 384; whole: 118, 124, 294, 296, 336
heat: 255, 394–95
heaven(s): 5, 62, 69, 111, 163, 171–72, 206, 227–28, 265, 272, 281–82, 308–9, 313–14, 353, 355, 366, 375, 377, 390, 392; ascent into: 373; desire for: 325; discipline of: 316; distant: 208; foretaste of: 314; freedom of: 185; gate(s) of: 38, 305, 386; glory of: 145; hope of: xcviii, 390; joys of: 34, 392; kingdom of: 20, 25, 259, 324; life of: 125, 319; rest in: xcix, 314, 316; ruling of: 226; secrets of: 231; silence in: 361, 372; third: 383; voice from: 201

Hebrews: 162
Heliodorus: 131, 191
hell: xcv, 25, 236; arrows of: 164; fear of: 218; flame(s) of: 131, 236; way to: cvi, 144
Heloise: xci–xcii, 166–72, 184–86; all-night vigil of: 169; as abbess of Paraclete: xci, 169, 184–86; as disciple of truth: 184; as fighting woman: 184; as nun: 184; as partner of Abelard: 170; as philosophical woman: 184; as sister of Abelard: 170; as teacher of humility: 184; as wife of Abelard: 170; child of: 168; heart of: 184; learning of: 184; letter of: 186; love affair of: 167–68; marriage of: xci, 168–70; Merton's admiration for: xci; passion of: 168; seduction of: 168; self-sacrifiing nobility of: 169; studies of: 184
help(s): 347, 395
helplessness: 122
Henry I of England, King: 35–36; letters to: 35–36
Henry IV, Emperor: 12
Henry of Sens, Abp.: 34–35
herbs, medicinal: 279
heresy: 2, 11, 184, 247, 348
heritage: 227
hermit(s): 12, 166, 230; ancient: 148; talkative: 189
hesitation: 281
hesychasts: 1
hierarchies, angelic: 56, 288
Hinduism: 109
*historia*: 49, 51–53
history: 143; Cistercian: lx, lxxix, 247; reality of: 49

holiness: lxx, 288, 304, 310
holocaust: 325
Holy Land: 32, 35, 46
Holy Spirit: xxxv, xlv, lx, lxxiv, xcvii, 37, 54–55, 58, 67, 76, 93, 98, 102, 106, 114, 125, 133, 145, 170, 181, 189, 208, 220, 233, 237, 245, 247–48, 253, 258–60, 269, 288–89, 293, 309, 315, 321, 328, 330, 347–48, 358, 361, 363–64, 368–71, 391; absence of: 281; action of: lxxv, civ, 69, 246, 258, 280, 282, 340, 370; anointing by: 269, 276; as bond of Father and Son: 79, 267; as charity: 103; as indivisible unity: 267; as kiss: 267–68; as undivided love: 267; bond of: 332; desire for: 281; direction of: 344; gift(s) of: xxvi, xlix, lii, lxxiv, c, 145, 163, 258, 281, 295, 297, 359; glorification of: 281; grace of: xxvi, 290; guidance of: 361; infusion of: 55, 267, 282; inspiration of: 23, 240; joy of: 330; movements of: 281; obedience to: 244; of Lord: 337; of truth: 391; operations of: 269; power of: xxv, lix, 29, 297; presence of: lxxv, 103–4, 280–81; receptivity to: c; sword of: 337; testimony of: 106; unity in: 347; work of: lxxvi, 260, 272, 287
homeland: 310
homily: 50–51
honesty: l
honey: 2, 9, 53–54, 151, 164, 261; name of Jesus as: 278; of love: 251; sweetness of: 252
honeycomb: 54, 261
honor(s): 8, 24, 33, 143, 233, 251, 347; divine: 174–75; ecclesiastical: 41; exhibition of: 4
hoods, ample: 130
hope(s): lxiii, 9, 24, 28, 47, 85, 114, 127, 203, 205, 208, 228, 252, 265, 279, 300, 309, 314, 318, 335–36, 377, 388–89, 391; certitude of: 388; Christian: 208; confident: 332; experience of: 388; motives for: 208; of heaven: xcviii, 390; perfect: 391; positive: 207; true: 391

Horace: 16
horror: 388; of sin: 304; of soul: 304
hospitality: 316
hostility: 188, 319
household, of Lord: 286
houses, guest: 191
housework: 160
Hugh, Br.: 226
Hugh, Grand Master of Templars: 97
Hugh of Amiens: 140
Hugh of Cluny, St.: 133
Hugh of Pontigny, Abbot: 226–27
Hugh of Prémontré, Abbot: xciv, 232–33
Hugh of St. Victor: 50, 166, 196
humanism: xlvii, lxxxii, 11, 149–50; twelfth-century: 168
humanist: 155
*humanitas*: lxxviii, 303
humanities, city of: 163
humanity: 182, 358; anguished: 6, 69; sinful: 305; worn: 6, 69
Humbeline, sister of St. Bernard: xlv, 14; death of: 44
humiliation(s): 249–50, 272, 315, 337, 376
humility: ix, xxxvii, xli, xlviii, lii, lvii, lxvi, lxxiv, xc, xcv, xcvii, 10, 31, 58, 82, 89, 120, 135, 145–46, 150, 159, 205, 211, 213, 215, 221, 243–44, 255, 264, 272, 298, 301, 308, 316, 318–19, 329–30, 332, 343, 357–59, 361–63, 367, 370, 374, 381–82, 387; Christian: 8–9; conversion as: 199; degrees of: 135, 224, 301, 360–61; false: 362; fullness of: 316; hyssop of: 361; indiscreet: 282; life of: li; school of: 361; true: 280; work of: 370
hunger: 130–31, 149; spiritual: lxiii, 208–9, 260

hunters: 156–57
husband, of shameless woman: 91–92
Huygens, R. B. C.: 368
hymns, sweet: 322
hypocrisy: 305, 328–29
hypocrite(s): 334–35

idea, and name: 55
ideal: 353; attainment of: 353; Cistercian: 126; contemplative: 313, 352; monastic: 143; renunciation of: 352; spiritual: lxi
identification, spiritual: 265
identity, human: xiii, xl; illusory: xl; inner: 109; spiritual: 109; true: xl, civ
idleness: 131, 149; bed of: 365
idol(s), graven: 155
idolatry: cviii, 85, 234
Ignatius of Loyola, St.: 244
ignominy: 110
ignorance: xcvii, 65, 82–83, 92, 109, 176, 201, 360, 362–63, 369–70; feigned: 231; land of: 88
Igny, Abbey of: xlviii, 33, 233; lay-brother of: 233
illness: 223; psychosomatic: 200
ills, spiritual: 280
illumination: 279, 284, 296; of soul: 238; passive: 238
illusion(s): xcvii, cvii, 23–24, 120, 235, 292, 334, 354–55, 362; choice of: xxxix; conversion from: lxxxiv, 23; flight from: lxxxiv, 26–27; pursuit of: lxxxiv, 23
ill-will: 342
image(s): lxxiii, xcviii, 365, 394–95; Biblical: lxxi; bodily: lxxiii, 254, 389; death to: 394; defacing of: xlvii–xlviii; divine: xii, xvi, xxxviii, xl, xlv, xlvii, lix, xcix, civ, 4, 71, 74–75, 77–80, 100, 109, 198, 317, 375; eternal: xl; material: lxxiii, 394–95; of Father: xl; of mercy: 376; of Savior: 195;

sensible: 395; theology of: xv, civ; uncreated: xl
imagination: cv
immorality: 213
immortality: 392
impatience: 156, 235, 328, 376
imperfection(s): xcvii, 309, 333, 341–43, 362, 375–76
impiety: 312
importunity: 43
impressions, material: 393
imprudence: 288–89
impulse: 348; holy: 348
impunity: 42
impurity: 102, 186
inability: 362
inadvertence, transgressions of: lxvi, 216
incapacity, of created being: 297
Incarnation: xxvi–xxvii, lix, lxxiii, 15, 57, 235, 250, 267, 318, 321, 324; as manifestation of divine power: 57–58; as work of divine power: 57; desire for: 264; drama of: lxxvi; motives for: 173, 178; mystery of: lxxxvi, 9, 53, 57, 66, 178, 247, 298–99; of Word: xxxviii, xlviii, lxxi, lxxv, 265, 275, 279, 298, 314, 357; prolongation of: lxxi, 248
incense: 54
inclination: 346
inconstancy: 223; habitual: lxiv
incontinence, remedy for: 171
independence: 197; fatal: 301; of externals: 362
indifference, callous: lxxviii, 304
indignation: 207
individual: 11–12, 340; rest in: 318
individualism, false: 301
individuality: 11
inequality: 251
inertia: 8
infallibility: 8; illusions of: 280

infancy, divine: li–lii, 145, 324; spiritual: 357
infants, hearts of: 281; lips of: 281; mouth of: 281; speechless: 359
infidelity, Cluniac: 126
infidels: 162
infirmarian: 193, 195
infirmary: 151, 160
infirmity: 249, 298, 332
influences, diabolic: lxxv; natural: lxxv
infractions: 152; of observances: 216; of *Rule*: lxvi
ingratitude: lxxv, 110, 276, 390
inheritance: 266; of Lord: 318
iniquity: 100
injury: 127–28, 130, 228; grave: 211; personal: 126; suffering: 212; to self: 211
injustice: 201, 305; alliance of: 366; economic: 136; victims of: 33
innocence: 357
innocent: 164
Innocent II, Pope: lviii, 35–37, 39, 42–44, 169, 180, 183; anger of: 36; letters to: 36–37, 40–42; wrath of: 37
insecurity: 122
insight: 291, 391; contemplative: 258; into Scripture: 258; mystical: 66; originality of: 66; psychological: xlvii; spiritual: lxxi, 177
inspiration: 371
instability: 222, 319
instinct, good: 373; natural: 78
instruction: 386
instrument, natural: 343
insufficiency: 363
insult(s): 111; personal: 126
integration, of dioceses: xxxv; of individuals: xxxv; of monasteries: xxxv; of nations: xxxv
integrity, of Cistercian life: xx
intellect: 365, 385; exercise of: 109
intellectualism, of scholastics: xxi; sterile: lxiii, 197

intelligence: 42
intemperance: 141–42, 150
intention(s): 130, 310; analysis of: 175; impure: 328; order of: 353; purity of: 139, 267, 282, 328; real: 236; subjective: 175
interest(s), detachment from: 383; lasting: 353; of one's own: 125, 231, 346; private: 102; spiritual: 294
intimacy: 308; degrees of: 264; spiritual: lxxiii
introspection: 280; morbid: lxx
intuition, mystical: 1
invocation, of Holy Name: 279–80
Ireland: 165; monastic foundation in: 44
iron: 379
irregularity: 241
irreverence: 373
Isaac of Stella: xliv–xlv, xlix–l, xcviii–xcix, 311–13; sermons of: xlix–l, xcviii–xcix, 311–13; teaching of prayer of: 1
Isaias (Isaiah): lxxii, 53, 56, 318, 385, 395
Isidore of Seville, St.: 55
isolation, inner: xx, outer: xx
Israel, as God's beloved: 209; as Lord's inheritance: 318; as People of God: lxxii; as Servant of Yahweh: lxxii; children of: 278; history of: 57; judgments on: 385; monastery as: 319; persecution of: lxxii
Israelites: 362
Italy: 36, 42, 256
Ivo, Master: 40

Jacob the Patriarch: xlix, 62, 97, 209; ladder of: 163
James, Bruno Scott: xxiii, 25, 41, 96, 98, 128, 163, 225, 227
jealousies: 63, 84, 329
Jeremias (Jeremiah): 385
Jerome, Pseudo-: 63, 187

Jerome, St.: xciii, 131, 168, 187, 190–91, 193, 196
Jerusalem: xciii, 33, 163–64, 288; citizen of: 227; daughters of: 389; earthly: 227; free: 227; heavenly: lxxi, 227–28, 258; pilgrimage to: 227
Jews: xlviii–xlix, lxxi–lxxii, 40, 259–60, 280, 347; as type: 277; portion of: 259; salvation from: lxxii; spirit of: 276
Job: 274
Joel: 53, 334
John of Salisbury: 162–64, 196
John of the Cross, Saint: xiii, xvi–xviii, xx, xxii–xxiii, xxx, xcv, 212, 238, 255, 285, 289–90, 328, 335–39, 341–43, 346, 385
John the Baptist, St.: 136
John the Evangelist, St.: xxx, 89, 94, 107, 383; First Epistle of: lv; Gospel of: xxx, 237
Johnson, Lyndon B.: lxxxiii
jokes: 150
jongleurs: 12
Jorannus of St. Nicasius, Abbot: 225–27
Jordan River: lxviii, 190, 235
Joseph, St.: lxviii, 51, 57, 237; as poor artisan: 289; as spouse of Virgin: 52; name of: 52
Joseph the Patriarch: xlix, 40, 145, 274
Jouarre, Council of: 97
journey: lxxxvi, 227, 333, 384–85; human: lxxvii; to God: lxxvii
joy(s): xviii, xlv, xcv, xcix, 7–9, 36, 69, 72, 85, 98, 124, 127, 206–8, 250, 268, 273, 275, 307, 318, 320, 324–25, 328, 335–37, 342, 368, 372, 375, 388; anointing of: 328, 330; as natural affection: 118; capacity for: 377; deep: 329; degree of: 367; earthly: 187; eternal: 34; evil: xcv; false: 333, 337; human: 333; hymn of: 263; interior: 325; in Lent: 326–32; in penance: 328; in sorrow: 328; life of: 312; natural: 367; of charity: 327, 330; of contemplation: 271, 367; of eternity: 314; of heaven: 34, 392; of Holy Spirit: 330; of spirit: 314; pledge of: 392; renouncement of: 187; shallow: 333; sincere: 329; spirit of: xlviii; spiritual: 325, 327, 330; spontaneous: 367; true: xcv, 337
Judaism, affirmation of: lxxii; denial of: lxxii
Judaizer: 188
Judas Iscariot: 213
judge: 22, 360
judgment: xvi, xcix, 40–41, 104, 128, 183, 218, 237, 312, 363–64; attachment to: lxvii, 234–35, 237; clear: 296; detached: 296; disease of: 234; extreme: 216; fear of: xcviii, 206, 265, 390; last: 132; mere: 237; rejection of: lxviii; terrible: 385; terror of: 386; true: 128
Jung, C. G.: 206
junior: 137
justice: xcvii, 6, 14, 35–36, 40–42, 53, 69, 86, 174, 179, 233, 265, 276–77, 297, 306, 312, 346, 363–64, 366, 369; divine: 74, 105, 174, 305, 381, 387; false: 366; hunger for: 209, 363, 365, 369; indifference to: lxxviii, 304; inexorable: 304; laws of: 127; natural: 110; of God: 105, 180, 182, 304, 306; outraged: 126; standard of: 146; strict: lxxix; thirst for: 209, 363, 365, 369; toward brother: 91; transcendent: 175; zeal for: 297
justification: 114

Kennedy, John F., assassination of: ciii
Kentucky: cxi; rural: lxxix
kernel, inner: 260
kindness: lxxviii, 303, 331
Kingdom, heavenly: 25; of Christ: 180; of God: xxvii, lxxi, 11, 129, 146, 151,

198, 258, 319, 323; of heaven: 20, 25, 259, 324
kings: 278; Norman: 161
kinship, with things of flesh: 394
kiss(es): 74; Holy Spirit as: 267–68; mystical: 2; of feet: lxxiii, 264–65; of hands: lxxiii, 264–65; of mouth: lxxiii–lxxiv, 211, 264–67
kitchen: 157
Kleiner, Sighard, ocist: xxxii
knight: 225
Knights Templar: 33, 97
knowledge: xvi, xxxvi, lvii, lix, 3, 109, 197, 208, 231, 266, 268, 281, 283, 340, 358, 361, 373, 394; about God: 238; as possession: xxxix; cold: 267–68; complete: 95; contemplative: 2; desire for: xli; existential: xxxix; experiential: 66, 238; gift of: 257, 343; hidden: lxix, 238; highest: xvi; illusory: 109; infusion of: 264; key of: 213; lack of: 84, 234; light of: 2, 267–68, 345; lower: 373; of creature: 84; of divine Good: xxxix; of evil: xxxix; of God: lx, lxix, 2, 84, 125, 166, 238, 264, 267, 305, 372, 381, 392; of good: xxxix; of self: 70; of things of God: 2; order of: 2; passive: 305; popular: lxix; practical: 70; proud: 267–68; quasi-experiential: 305; speculative: xliii, 2; spiritual: 258; theological: 163; through love: 166; true: 109; vain: 109
Knowles, David, osb: lxxxiv, xcii, 173, 176–78
Knox, Ronald: 29
Kramer, Victor A.: xlix

labor(s): xxxviii, lxxxiv, 8–9, 11, 21, 23, 37–38, 69, 86, 132, 143, 164, 192, 201, 206, 254, 273, 298, 304, 307, 314, 316–18, 320, 358, 362–66, 371, 385; avoiding: 314; futile: 362; grievous: 362; harvest: 314; manual: xc, 29, 31, 120, 131, 134, 136, 158–60, 308; multiple: 362; of fear: 362; relief for: 43; terrible: 362
laity: 163
lamb, gentleness of 252
lament: 22, 151
lance: 111
Landgraf, Arthur: 77–78
Langres, Archdeacon of: 25; Diocese of: 14, 44
Languedoc: 45
lantern: 152
Lateran Council: 140
Laughlin, James: lii
laughter: 149
lavishness, of decoration: 153–54
law(s): 104, 106, 196, 276, 282; authority of: 200; bad: 104; canon: 16, 129–30, 230; changeable: 158–59; Christian: 41; common: 104; divine: 79, 215; eternal: 103, 105; exterior: 107; fulfilling of: 287; fullness of: 73; good: 104; inner: 101; interior: 107; just: 105; knowledge of: 16; letter of: lxvi, 216; love of: 371; meditation on: 254; moral: lxiv–lxv; natural: 230; of being: 86; of charity: xxxvii, lix, cv, 79, 96, 102, 106; of desire: lxxxviii, 107; of divine liberty: xxxvii; of fear: lxxxviii, 101, 107, 127; of freedom: 106; of God: lxxxviii, cv, 72, 79, 99, 101, 105, 164, 287, 355, 371; of Lord: 102; of self: 104–5; of sons: 101, 106; old: 276–77, 344; penal: 215; Roman: 16; sense of: xxxvii
Lawson, Penelope, slg: xlix–l
lawsuits: 312; advocates in: 137
Lax, Robert: xiii
laxists: 147
laxity: 143, 146, 148
lay-brothers: 32
Lazarus: xxx, 349–51; vocation of: xxxii, 349–50
laziness: 8; justification of: 135

## Index

learning: 3, 24, 194; secular: 184
leaves, fig: 362
Le Bail, Anselme, OCR: 71–72:
Leclercq, Jean, OSB: xiv, xxii, xxv, liv, lxxxii, lxxxiv, lxxxviii, 18, 140, 158, 262
*lectio*: 51
*lectio divina*: 31, 261, 262
legalism: 220
legate, papal: 141
legends, Marian: 59
Le Goff, Jacques: 161–63, 165, 167, 169
Lehodey, Vital, OCSO: lxv, 241–42
leisure: 132, 192, 256, 262; man of: 42
leniency: 225
Lent: liv, 44, 320–38; as conversion: 322–24; as gift: 322; as humility: 324–26; as mystery: xcvi, 321–22, 328; as sacrament: xcv, 321–22, 332; as transformation: 322–24; compunction of: 332–34; fast of: 320–22, 324–25, 329; fruit of: xcvi, 338; grace of: xcvi, 338; joy of: 325–31; mystery of: 334, 338; sacrifice of: 325, 332–33; sorrow of: 328–30, 332; spirituality of: xcv, 320–30; theology of: 330–31
Lentfoehr, Thérèse, SDS: xxxii
Leonius of St. Bertin, Abbot: 233
leprosy, bodily: 22; inward: 22; of Naaman: lxvii–lxviii, 235
lessons, ascetic: 58; moral: 58
letter: 154; as secondary: 147; of Benedictine life: lxii; of Cistercian life: xx; of law: lxvi; unpalatable: 259; unprofitable: 259; vs. spirit: 55, 141, 260; violation of: lxii
letters, monastic: 140; of exhortation: 224
levels, of spiritual life: xlv
levity: 156; danger of: 224
liberal arts: 15–16, 55; *quadrivium*: 16, 162; *trivium*: 16
liberality: 148
liberation: lii, 71, 376

libertinism: 197; spirit of: 197
liberty: xcix, 93, 217, 250, 265, 311–13, 330, 337; divine: xxxvii; joyous: 175; of spirit: xcix; precious: 219; spirit of: 106; tranquil: 191; true: 93
license: 301; moral: 197
lie(s): 83, 326; living: 334
life: xxxix, 38, 282, 362, 367, 378, 393; active: xvii, xxx, 257, 282–87, 351, 364, 367, 380; angelic: 27, 142, 313; apostolic: 257; ascetic: 58, 300, 303; bad: cvii; Benedictine: lxii; busy: 191, 247; cenobitic: xxxvii, 51; Christ-centered: lxxvi; Christian: lviii, lxii, lxxi, 214, 240, 291; Cistercian: xix–xx, xxxvii, lxxix, 126; clerical: lxiv, 214; Cluniac: 145; common: xcix, 30, 49, 77, 189, 288, 290, 301, 318; community: xx, lxxxv, 302, 307, 359; concrete circumstances of: 352; contemplative: xxvi, xxx–xxxi, lxx, lxxiii, 238–39, 242, 244, 257, 271, 282–87, 313, 367; convent: 170; daily: 5; dangerous: 11; decent: 230; devoted: 247; disedifying: 198; divine: lxxv, 247, 328, 330–31; earthly: xxviii; easier: 130, 223; ecclesiastical: xxi, 304; entrance into: 20; eternal: xcviii, 19, 164, 208, 222, 353, 392; everyday: 5, 256; faithful: lxii; family: 7; finding: 85; for spirit: 260; fullness of: 247, 372; gift of: xxxix; good: cvii; harder: 130; hidden: 27, 30; higher: 130, 223; holy: 41; human: lviii, 75, 150; illuminative: lxxiv, 269; in God: 58, 77, 330; in mind: lxiii, 197; individual: 6; infinite: 173; inner: xxxiv, 281, 334; intellectual: xci, 160–66; interior: xxviii, xxxi, lxxvii, xcvi, 155, 270–71, 284, 299, 303–4, 333, 339, 348; liturgical: xc; meaning of: lix; mixed: xxx; modern: 244; monastic: xxx, xxxviii, xli, xlviii, lii, lviii, lxi–lxii,

lxviii, lxx, lxxix, xc, xcii, cvi, 23, 26, 68, 72, 141–42, 149–50, 186, 192, 220, 234, 243–44, 291, 307, 316, 319, 333, 355; moral: 58; more perfect: 130; mortal: 3, 5, 124, 377, 393; mystical: lxix, lxxiv, 3, 5, 153, 240–42, 247, 263, 274; necessities of: 120, 152; new: 113; newness of: li, 198; of Church: xxxv, lxxi; of faith: lxix, 313; of frustration: xl; of grace: lxxv; of humility: li; of meditation: 170; of penance: xxx; of prayer: lxix, 170, 237–38; of silence: li; of soul: xxxi, xxxiv–xxxv, 83; of virtue: lxiii, xcvi, 208, 257, 296, 368; ordinary: 256; outer: xxxiv; pious: 206; political: xxi, 12; prayer: lxx; present: 327, 353; purpose of: 78; quiet: 382; regular: 224; religious: lxv–lxvii, xci, 170, 186, 190, 222–23, 288, 308; resurrected: xcviii; sanctity of: 297; science of: xliii; secular: 191; social: 6, 319; solitary: 191; source of: 260; spiritual: xlv, lxiv, lxxvi, lxxviii, 168, 209, 212, 214, 238, 241, 246, 264, 271, 273, 277, 290–91, 293–94, 296–300; spiritualization of: 197; stricter: 156, 223; student: 160–66, 197; supernatural: 120, 280; treasures of: 259; tree of: 207; true: 20, 292, 393; unitive; xvii; way of: 131; whole: 197; wretched: 333

light(s): 3, 21, 65, 132, 199, 255, 271, 278, 285, 304, 351, 385; angel of: 289; armor of: 278; divine: 238; dwelling in: 395; gift of: 108; Holy Name as: 9, 275, 278–79; mysticism of: 275; of faith: 278, 340; of God: 278, 284; of truth: civ; perfection of: 395; place of: lxxviii, 304; ray of: 21; serenest: 205; true: 198, 206; virtuous: 299; way of: 230

likeness, divine: xv–xvi, xviii, xxxviii, lix, lxiii, xcix, 4, 8, 74, 80, 90, 198, 317, 338, 375, 393; lost: 88, 338; restoration of: 78, 198; theology of: xv, civ; to Word: xl

lilies: 207

limitation(s): 210–11, 273–74, 376; human: lx, 125; serious: 294

lions: 156

lips: 66, 358

Lipsey, Roger: xlvii

listening, importance of: 284

literalism, extreme: 143; sterile: lxxi

literature: lxxxix, 155; Cistercian: 71; classical: 192–93; medieval: 246

littleness: 145

liturgy: 16, 51, 322, 332; Ash Wednesday: 323; Christmas: 51; of Easter Vigil: xxxix; reform of: cvi; simplicity in: xv; vernacular: ciii

living, high: 130

loathing: 209

loaves, warm: 164

Lochman, Jan: ciii

*locus terribilis*: lxxviii

locutions, successive: 255

logic: 16, 177, 184

Lombardy: 36

Longpont, abbot of: 233

Louis VII of France, King: 44–48

love(s): xii, xvi, xix, xxxvi, lvii, lix, lxvii, lxxxvi, xcvi, 2–5, 10, 38, 54, 69, 71, 73, 75, 80, 84, 91, 93–94, 105, 117, 127, 138, 145, 149, 170, 175, 180, 217, 222, 234, 236, 250, 252–53, 255, 268, 284–85, 302, 306, 331, 338–39, 374, 377, 379, 388–89, 392; ability to: 78; act of: 50; act of supreme: xxxi; affect of: 180; affective: 354–55; appeal to: 135; ardent: 9, 266, 287, 371; as all-sufficient: 4–5; as cause: 251; as commitment: 77; as *consensus*: 72; as fruit: 251; as great reality: 251; as knowledge: 77, 88, 179; as merit: 251; as natural affection: 118; as recompense: 251; as understanding:

179; beginning of: 107; blissful: 390; bond of: 4; brotherly: 6; capacity for: xix, 234, 301, 377; carnal: lxxvi, 76, 78, 118–19, 253, 293–95, 374; chaste: 5, 253, 266; communion of: 319; compassionate: 273; concepts of: 77; condescending: 371; consummate: 73; consummation of: 107, 118; deep: 367; degrees of: xli, lx, lxxxvii, xcvii–xcviii, cv, 71–72, 107, 120–25, 265, 269, 374–80; delightful: 253; dignity of: xlv; disordered: cv, 119, 121; divine: xxvi, 5–7, 69, 76, 98, 285; doctrine of: lix, 5–8, 234; dynamic of: 116; earthly: 169; ecstasy of: 374; ecstatic: 77; effect of: 327; effective: 354–55; embrace of: xxxv; eternal: 75; evil: 88; exile from: 88; experience of: 54, 75, 122, 340; fatherly: 228; feelings of: 123; fervent: 7, 69, 340, 374; filial: 309; fire of: 268, 285, 361; flame(s) of: 267, 285; fleshly: lx, 266; for all: lx; for brethren: 366–67; for Christ: xix, lxxvi, xcvii, 10, 15, 111, 170, 273, 277, 291–97, 299, 364, 383; for Church: 8, 98; for God: xxx, xxxvi, xxxviii, xliv, lx, lxxvi–lxxvii, lxxix, xcvii, 2, 5–6, 8, 10, 77–80, 84, 94, 101, 105, 107–25, 135, 166, 211, 215, 218, 222, 269, 273, 276–77, 289, 291, 297, 300, 302, 309, 319, 327, 331, 333, 335–36, 338, 346, 352, 354, 367, 374–80, 390–92; for King: 361; for Master: 297; for monastic ideal: lxi; for others: 374, 383; for sake of loving: 5, 125; for souls: 286; for spiritually underprivileged: 364; for Spouse: 288; force of: 100; fraternal: 72, 368, 377; free: 167; freely given: lx, 123; fullness of: 286; generosity of: 175; God as: xii, 7, 69, 73–74, 79, 88, 107, 116, 265–66, 330; grateful: 124; gratuitous: 124; higher: 295; highest: 124; holy: 5, 253, 266; human: 118, 169, 292–94, 296, 391; ill-directed: 288; immensity of: 307; imperfect: xii, 219; in word: 123; in truth: 123; inebriated with: 266; infinite: 292; inflamed with: 288; influence of: 3; inordinate: 288, 301, 328; inscrutable: 75; intense: lxi, 143, 374; interested: 99; intimate: 5, 253; intuitions of: 285; just: lx, 119, 123; lack of: 110; law of: 104, 106; made for: cv; measure of: 69; merciful: 49, 75, 110, 273, 376; mercenary: 91–96, 105, 115, 252; misdirected: cv; motivations for: lxxxvii, 288; mutual: xxxvi, 5, 79, 253; mystical: 11, 72, 286; natural: 118, 120–21, 302, 374; natural power to: lxxviii; nature of: xlv; nonviolent: lxxxviii, 86; obedience as: 216; object of: xi, 78, 116; objectivity of: 119; obstacles to: 327; of abstraction: lxxvi, 291; of another: 124; of Bride: 252; of Bridegroom: 252, 287; of brother: 122; of Christ: lxxvi–lxxvii, 110, 113, 115, 163, 170, 291–93, 296; of cross: xliii; of death: xii; of enemies: 353; of Father: 175, 268; of fellow man: 374; of God: ix, xiii, xxxvi, lx, lxxvii, civ–cv, 6, 70, 72, 76, 79, 108, 122, 125, 178, 220, 253, 267–68, 273, 276, 292, 298, 300, 307–8, 324, 327, 331, 371, 375, 391–92; of heart: 253, 294; of Holy Name: lxxv, 279; of Jesus: 9, 15; of knowledge: 163; of law: 371; of Mary: 9–10, 15; of nature: 103; of neighbor: lx, 119, 121, 273, 319, 327, 367; of others: 274; of person: lxxvi, 291; of poor: 14; of relatives: 187; of self: lx, xcvii–xcviii, 34, 76–78, 80, 99, 124, 327, 346, 374–80; of soul: 4, 72, 107, 253, 293, 392; of truth: lxxxviii, 2, 82, 86–87, 99, 197, 354; of virtue: 70, 253, 294; of whole heart: lxxvi; of whole mind: lxxvi; of world: 87, 99, 155; openness to: xlvii; ordered: 118; ordinate: 119–20; passionate: lxi, 143; path of: 3; perfect: lxxvii, 4, 69, 79, 124, 266, 297, 302, 327, 377, 380, 391; perfection of: lxiv, 214, 367; personal: 296, 367; physical: 77; pleasant: 5; power of: lx, 266; power to: 76, 302, 344; powerful: 253; presence of: 54; principle of: 265; problem of: xi, 76–81, 107; prudent: 293; pure: xviii, xxiv, xxxviii, lv, lix–lx, lxxiii–lxxiv, xcviii, 5, 75, 78, 89, 99, 115, 122–23, 232, 246, 248, 252, 265–66, 269, 277, 284, 286, 300, 335, 375, 377–79, 390–92; purification of: 77, 255, 296; purity of: 7, 77, 99, 115, 375; quality of: 374; rational: 295–96; real: lxvii, 236; reciprocal: 252; return of: 331; savor of: 285; school of: 338; self-centered: lxxviii, 302; self-forgetful: xcviii; selfish: lxxviii, 76, 302; selfless: xxxvii, lii, lxxx, lxxxvii, 103, 330, 368; sensible: 295; sentiments of: 296; serene: 5, 253; servile: 105; sincere: 253; social: lx, 119; Spirit of: 106; spiritual: lxxvii, 266, 293, 295–96; spontaneous: xii, 123; state of: 367; stream of: 252; strength of: 172; strong: 5, 286, 292, 296–97; superabundant: 125; supernatural: 120, 302, 345, 378; supreme: 69; sweet: 5, 253; sweetness of: 90; teaching on: lxxxvii; temperate: 119; tender: 292–96, 341, 367; tepid: 7; theology of: lxxxvii, 70–81; transcendent: 175; treatises on: 71–72; Trinitarian: lxxiv, 267; true: 72, 99, 115–16, 149, 266, 291, 354; types of: cv; understanding of: civ; understanding through: 180; union of: xviii, lxxiv, 72; unitive: lxxi; vehement: 288; vitality of: 330; well-ordered: 120–21; wise: 292, 296–97; without limit: 8, 94–95; work of: 128; wound of: 67; zealous: 286

lowliness: 256

loyalty: 37

Luddy, Ailbe, OCSO: 50, 259, 261, 263–68, 270, 274–75, 278–87, 289–306, 340, 343–45, 352–54, 368–69, 372, 378, 380–95

Luke, Lord: 39

Luke of Cuissy, Abbot: 232

Luke the Evangelist, St.: 51, 53

lust(s): xx, 17, 119, 130, 176; gratification of: 167

luxury: 119, 141–42, 148, 151; cult of: 150

Lyons, canons of: 60

Mabillon, Jean, OSB: 25, 133

machinations: lxxix

magisterium, infallible: 8

maidens, young: lxxv, 277, 287–91, 299–300

Malachy, St.: 44

maladies: 279

malice: lxvi, 25, 66–67, 83, 233, 319, 380; of heart: 320

man, active: 19; as creature of God: 175; carnal: 295; common: 11; creation of: 292; essence of: 80; fallen: 110, 174, 318; gifted: 19; glorification of: 317; good: 229; heart of: 392; hired: 101; holy: 229; humble: 316; hungry: 116; impious: 316; iniquitous: 318; just: 318; nature of: 264; new: lii, 320; outer: 316; perfect: 328; quiet: 316; sick: 284; sinful: 109; spiritual: 346; stubborn: 312; ungrateful: 331; universal: 121; wicked: 205; wretched: 334

manger: 294

manhood, perfect: 348

Manichaeans: 136

manna, hidden: 73, 208

manners, wantonness of: 301

Manrique, Angel: 16–17
mansion(s): 304, 384
manuscripts, Arabic: 160
Marcigny, Convent of: 184–85; recluses at: 185
Margaret Mary Alacoque, St.: 238, 248–50
Marie d'Oignies: 368
Marie-Eugène de l'Enfant-Jésus, OCD: 241
marks, vain: 335
Marne, valley of: xlviii
marriage, as sacrament: 171; experience of: 194; full: 252; mystical: xvi–xviii, 4–5, 243, 248–49, 263, 277, 377; of Church and Word: 257; of Word and soul: 257; perfect: 252; sacred: 251; spiritual: xvii–xviii, 4, 251, 257; with Word: 4, 250, 252
marrow: 259
Martha, St.: xxx, 349–51; house of: 349; vocation of: xxxii, 349–50
Martin of Tours, St.: 135, 185–87, 191
martyrdom: 296
martyrs: 137, 299, 380
Mary, Blessed Virgin: li, lxxxv–lxxxvi, 9–10, 50–68, 204, 237, 311, 313; actions of: 316; annunciation to: 57; apparitions of: 242; as consort of Joseph: 289; as ideal of monks: 67–68; as model: xxxi, 313; as mother of contemplation: 67; as Mother of God: xix, xxvi, 65, 314; as Mother of Jesus: lvii, 67; as pattern: xcix, 316; as pure creature: 66; as Queen of angels and saints: 313; as Queen of Cistercian Order: 313; as Queen of Heaven: 59; as royal way: xxviii; as rule of monks: 67–68, 313; as Star of the Sea: xxxvi, xliii, lxxxvi, 62–65; as universal mediatrix: xxxvi, xliii; as way: li; Assumption of: 313–14; body of: xxxi; breast of: 294; compassion of: 67; contemplation of: 66; devotion to: xxvi, xxxviii, lxxxvi, 10, 66; example of: 63; flesh of: xcix, 316; freedom of: 66; grace of: 65; Holy Name of: xliii; humility of: 58, 66; Immaculate Conception of: lxxxvi, civ, 60–61; Immaculate Heart of: xliii; invocation of: 63; love of: 9–10, 15; mediation of: xxvi, lii, 9, 61, 67; merit of: 65; motherhood of: xxxvi; mystery of: lxxxvi, 59, 66; mystical love of: 67; mystical martyrdom of: 67; name of: lxxxvi, 51, 62–65; obedience of: 58; obedience of Jesus to: lxviii, 58; power of: 66; praise(s) of: 50–51, 60; prayer of: 63; prayer to: 10; prerogatives of: 60; rest of: 314; service of: 67; Son of: 62; soul of: xxxi; trust in: 10; virginal motherhood of: 50–51, 59, 62, 66; virginity of: 58, 65; virginity of body of: 66; virginity of soul of: 66; virginity of spirit of: 66; virtues of: 59, 67; voice of: 316
Mary of Bethany, St.: xxx, 349–51; spirit of: 349; vocation of: xxxii, 349–50
Mary (Mariam), sister of Moses: 22
Mass, conventual: 159, 307
master(s): 303; of others: 382; spiritual: 342; supervision of: 382
mat, rush: 131
materialization, of symbol: 50
mathematics: 160
matron: 192–94; as married woman: 193; as superior: 192–94; commands of: 193
Mattathias: 40
matter, as source of impurity: 102; grave: 216
matters, ecclesial: lviii; political: lviii; spiritual: lxxvi, 342; temporal: 228; worldly: 15
Matthew of Albano: 141
maturity, spiritual: xxxi, 348
Maurus, St.: 136

Maximus the Confessor, St.: 374, 379
McCann, Justin, OSB: 74, 135, 142, 189, 192, 216, 218, 301–2, 361
McCormick, Anne: cxi
McDonnell, Thomas P.: xxiii
McGowan, Patrick: cxi
McGuire, Brian P.: xlv
mead: 159
Meade, Mark C.: cxi
meal(s): 151; at Cluny: 149–51; multicourse: 149; readings at: xiii
meaning, inner: 260; of life: lix; of universals: 172; question of: 172; problem of: 172; spiritual: 261; thirst for: civ
means, natural: 121
measure: 345
meat: 140, 146, 150–51, 157, 159, 195–96, 250, 259; strong: 372
medicine(s): 95; art of: 231; care in: 195; Greek: 160; healing: 278; Holy Name as: 9, 275, 278–79
mediocrity, spiritual: 153
meditation: 3, 28, 31, 95, 107, 111, 113–14, 273, 317, 388; diligent: 112; of Holy Name: lxxv, 278–79; personal: 51
meekness: lxiii, lxxviii, 205–6, 244, 303, 330, 367
melancholy: 243; uncharitable: 148
Mellifont, Abbey of, foundation of: 44
melody, Holy Name as: 9, 278
members, bodily: 201–3, 264, 347; feeble: 347; less honorable: 347; of Body of Christ: 322, 347–48
*memoria*: 111–12, 199, 314, 365; *Christi*: 114–15, 210
memory: lxiii, 21–22, 30, 38, 74, 199, 203–4, 209–12, 394; of Christ: 114, 210; of Passion: 114, 368; purification of: cvii, 211, 365; sweet: 114
men: 264; fighting: 130; hearts of: 233; poor: 232; sons of: 316, 351; worldly: 192

*mens*: 100
mentality, symbolic: lxxxvi, 54
mercenary: xii, 89, 99, 101, 265; *affectus* of: 100; hope of reward of: lxxxvii, 89; love of: 101
merchants: 11, 151
merciful: 273
mercy: 45, 53, 89, 104, 111, 114, 129, 170, 210–11, 228, 269–70, 273, 276, 293, 306, 316, 330, 343, 361, 363–66, 369, 371, 376–77, 388; action of: 371; all-powerful: 97; compassionate: 371; decree of: 306, 388; dews of: 390; divine: xxvi, lxiii, lxxiv–lxxv, lxxix, xcvii, 210–11, 270, 389; eternal: 387; experience of: 270; hope of: 4, 265; infinite: 387; of God: xxxviii, lxxiv, 37, 111, 114, 122, 146, 204, 209, 222, 231, 249, 270, 272, 277, 281, 299, 306–7, 364, 375–76, 387–89, 391; oil of: 273; toward others: lxiii; understanding of: 388; vastness of: 171; works of: 364
merit(s): 117–18, 144, 276, 304, 310, 346, 377; principle of: 353
Merton, Thomas, anthropology of: xxxviii; as good student: ix; as good teacher: ix; as master of novices: xl, xlii, li–lii, ci, cviii–cix; as master of students: xxii, xxix, xl–xlii, lxxxii; as spiritual director: viii; as spiritual teacher: viii; attitude of toward St. Bernard: xiii, xxi–xxii, lxxxiv; back problems of: cvi; baptism of: xii, lix; conversion of: xi; death of: xiv; entrance into monastery of: lix; guidance of: vii–viii; hermitage of: l, cviii; Holy Week retreat of: xii; hospitalization of: cvi; humor of: vii, civ; insight of: vii; interests of: xciv; monastic formation of: xliv; novitiate conferences of: vii–xi, xxi, xxxvi, xlii–xliv, lii–lviii, lxxx–lxxxii, ci–cii, cviii; novitiate of: xiii, xlv;

Index                                                                                                    501

prayer of: l; projected works of: xliv; scholasticate conferences of: li, xciv–xcv; solitude of: l; soteriology of: xxxviii; spiritual teaching of: xliv; sympathies of: xciv; taped conferences of: xlix–l, ci–cviii; vocation crises of: xlv; WORKS: *Ascent to Truth*: xx–xxi, xciv; *Asian Journal*: lii; *Cassian and the Fathers*: xlii, xlv, 23, 80, 115, 131, 257, 289; *Charter, Customs, Constitutions of the Cistercians*: xlii, liii; *Christmas Sermons of Bl. Guerric of Igny*: xlviii, 276; *Conjectures of a Guilty Bystander*: xlviii–xlix, lxxii, xci, 165; *Contemplation in a World of Action*: lii; *Dancing in the Water of Life*: xxxvi, l, lxxxiv, xciii, cvi, 185; *Disputed Questions*: xxv–xxvi; *Early Essays*: 242; *Entering the Silence*, xiii, xvi–xvii, xxi–xxii, xlv, li, lxxxviii, 376; *Exile Ends in Glory*: 204, 377; *Faith and Violence*: 85; "Feast of Freedom": li, 356; *Gandhi on Non-Violence*: 86; "Guerric of Igny's Easter Sermons": xlix; *Hidden Ground of Love*: xlix–l, lxxx; "Honorable Reader": xxv, xxxi–xxxii, lvii; *In the Valley of Wormwood*: xliv–xlv; *Introduction to Christian Mysticism*: xlii, xlv, 79, 84, 100, 239, 379; "Introduction to Cistercian Theology": xl–xli; "Introduction" to *Monastic Theology of Aelred of Rievaulx*: xlvii–xlviii; "Isaac of Stella: Introduction": l; *Last of the Fathers*: xxxii–xxxvii, lvii, 1–10, 68–70, 246; "Lectio Divina": 261; *Life of the Vows*: xlii, xlv, 150, 215; "Life, Works and Doctrine of St. Bernard": lii–lxxxiii, lxxxvii, xciii, cix; "Liturgical Feasts and Seasons": xliii–xliv, xlvii; *Marthe, Marie et Lazare*: xxv, xxxi, lvii; *Merton-Giroux Letters*: xx, xxxi–xxxiii, xlvi; *Monastic Journey*: 68; *Monastic Observances*: xlii, 261; "Monastic Orientation 3": xxvii, xli, li, lxiv, xcv–xcvi, c; "Monastic Orientation 4": xli–xlii, lxxxii, xcvii; "Monastic Orientation 5": xlii; "Monastic Orientation 6": xlii, xcviii; *New Man*: xxxviii–xl; *No Man Is an Island*: 331; *Other Side of the Mountain*: xlvii; *Pre-Benedictine Monasticism*: xlii, xlv, lxxx, 80, 115, 131, 257; "Reflections on Some Recent Studies of St. Anselm": 173–75; *Road to Joy*, xiii, xxxii; *Rule of Saint Benedict*: xlii, 142; *Run to the Mountain*: xii–xiii; "St. Aelred of Rievaulx and the Cistercians": xlvi–xlvii; "St. Anselm and His Argument": 112, 173; "Saint Bernard et l'Amérique": xxviii–xxix; *School of Charity*: xxiii, xxix, xxxvii–xxxviii, xlviii, li, lxx, lxxxix; *Search for Solitude*: xxii, xxxviii, liii, lv, lxxii, 100, 165; *Seasons of Celebration*: xxvii–xxviii, 66–67, 321; *Seven Storey Mountain*: xi–xiii, xliv, cv; *Silent Life*: xxxvii–xxxviii, l; *Solitary Life: A Letter of Guigo*: lxxxix; *Spirit of Simplicity*: xiv–xvi, xxxix, lxvii, 109, 153; *Survival or Prophecy?*: xiv, liv, lxxxix; *Thomas Merton on St. Bernard*: xiv–xviii, xxx–xxxi, 349; *Thomas Merton Reader*: xxiii–xxv; *Turning toward the World*: xlix, lxxx, lxxxix, ci; *Waters of Siloe*: xviii–xx, xxix, xlv; *When Prophecy Still Had a Voice*: xiii; *Wisdom of the Desert*: 191; *Zen and the Birds of Appetite*: 82–83

message, divine: 55
messengers, of Lord: 36
*metanoia*: lxiii, lxx, 20, 198, 242
method, scholastic: xxi; speculative: 240
metrics: 16
Metz: 48
Michael, Archangel: 231

Middle Ages: xx, 11–12; early: 165; High: lviii; late: lxix, 59, 238; symbolic mentality of: 54
might, way of: 326
Migne, J.-P.: xiv, xlv, 3, 133–34, 307, 356
Milan: 36–37; See of: 37
mildness: 376
milk: 164, 270, 288; spiritual: 341; sweet: 341
mill: 150
mind(s): ix, lxiii, cv, 3–4, 22, 70, 84, 88, 95, 125, 149, 151–52, 179, 189, 203, 208, 279, 294, 305, 386, 389; cheerful: 217; death of: 8; dedication of: 82; detached: 262; devoted: 351; donkey as: 189; eager: 254; feeding: 150; free: 262; generous: 217; great: 146; illumination of: 392; life in: lxiii, 197; life of: 8; light for: 3; peaceful: 262; purity of: 395; satisfaction of: 268; state of: 262; striving of: lxxix, 306; weary: 278; whole: 124, 296
miracle(s): 57, 136, 287, 347; workers of: 347
Miroir, Abbey of: 47, 141
mirror: 212
miserable, miseries of: 369
misery: 22, 192, 204–5, 273, 277, 319, 353, 369; recognition of: 82
misfortune(s): 85, 279
mission(s): 6; apostolic: lxxv, 284; charismatic: lxxv, 284; invisible: 277; of Holy Spirit: 274–87; of Son: 274–87; of Word 277; revelation of: 277; visible: 277
mistakes, useless: 362
mitigation(s): lxi, 149–50; wholesale: 148
moderation, in eating: 149
modes, human: 125
modesty: 367
Mohammed (Muhammad): 139
Molesme, Abbey of: 12

monastery: lxvi–lxvii, lxxiv, civ, 15, 19, 26, 30, 52, 77, 137, 142, 151–52, 155, 165, 192, 216, 225, 231–32, 289, 333, 368; as Israel: 319; as school of charity: 338; as school of Christ: xxxvii, 163, 329; Benedictine: lxxxix, 126, 149, 156; Cistercian: xxi–xxii, lxx, 48, 126, 241, 243, 245, 348–49; Cluniac: 141; contemplatives in: 242; customs of: 224; decoration of: 153; irregular: lxvi; known: 224, 230; lavishness of: 133; lax: 224; leaving: 130, 139, 223; less strict: lxvi, 223; location of: xix; love for: 307; of men: 194; of nuns: 194; order in: xcvi, 348–49; regular: 223; relaxed: 223; splendor of: 133; stability in: 222–24; stricter: lxvi, 223–24; unknown: 231; well-ordered: 223
monasticism, Benedictine: lxi; clerical: 134; decadent: xviii; eremitic: xxxvii; purity of: 143; twelfth-century: 167
money: 155, 161, 231; love of: 155; waste of: 156
monk(s): xv, xxvi, xxix, xliii, xlviii, lxii, lxiv, cii, 2, 7, 10, 12, 18, 32, 56, 68, 135–39, 142–43, 149, 151, 155, 157, 190–91, 214, 223–24, 230–31, 243, 246–47, 269–71, 274, 284, 292, 301, 307–9, 321, 323, 365; as clerics: 134; as contemplatives: 243; as wild ass: 191; ascetic: 147; average: 142; beat: 165; Benedictine: lxxxix, 126, 142, 155, 214; Cistercian: lxxxix, 126, 133; Cluniac: 126, 135, 149; criticism of: 191; decision of: 233; early: 150; Egyptian: 130; first: 190; heart of: 333; holy: 157; imperfect: 219; individual: lxii, 143; life of: 332; lost: 165; meat-eating: 157; newly professed: xl, lxxx, ci; obedient: 151; pessimistic: xlix; poor: 230; prayer life of: lxx; present-day: cii, civ,

cviii; privacy of: 158; relations of: 269; sated: 157; self-examination by: 239; severe: xlix; sincere: 219; true: 143, 320–21, 334; vain: 151; vocation of: 191; wandering: 165, 192
monkeys: 156
Montaldo, Jonathan: xiii, 376
Monte Cassino, Abbey of: 43
moons, new: 318
morality, Christian: 6, 69
morals: lxiii, 8, 197; discipline of: 297
mortals: 7, 69, 289
mortification(s): lxii, 27, 140, 142–43, 244, 272, 346; desire for: 320; lack of: 141; of desires: 30; of members: 114; of passions: 114; of senses: 30; technique of: 28
Moruela, Abbey of, foundation of: 36
Moses: 40
mother, bosom of: 341; spiritual: 270
moths: 143
motion, spiritual: 358
motives: 51, 199; for gratitude: 273; natural: 346; selfish: 303; sinful: lxv; wrong: 328, 362
Mott, Michael: liii
mountain, curdled: 53, 281; fat: 53, 281
mourners: lxiii, 205
mourning: 205, 323
Mouroux, Jean: lv–lvi
mouth(s): 279, 359; Holy Name as honey in: 278; of babes and sucklings: 357; parched: 202
movement(s): 342; Cistercian: 73; freedom of: 202; mendicant: 11
Murdac, Henry: 163–64
murmuring: 138–39, 193, 235, 311–12
Murphy, Lauren: cxi
music: 16
mysteries: 51, 57, 145, 172, 179, 247, 261, 358; Christian: 177, 181; divine: xcii, 49, 261; inner: 58; Lent as: xcvi, 321; of Christ: xxvii, lxviii, 235; of cross: xxvii; of divine union: 332; of faith: lxix, lxxi, 16, 238, 246; of God's love: 273, 300; of Incarnate Word: 275, 359; of Incarnation: 246–47, 264; of Kingdom of God: 319, 323–24; of redemption: 246–48; of revelation: 53; of Trinity: 172–73; paschal: xxxix, liv; reality of: lxxxv–lxxxvi, civ; sense of: 179; substance of: 53; supernal: 53; veil of: 259
mystic(s): viii, x, 238–39, 248, 340; extraordinary: 238; Rhenish: 100
mysticism: lxix, 238–41, 247, 275; Christian: xxi; Cistercian: xi, 67, 78–80, 81, 245; contemporary: lxx; divorce from theology: 74; false: 348; historical approach to: lxix; medieval: 78–80; monumental: 11; nature: xix; of light: 275; patristic approach to: lxix; phenomenological approach to: lxix; post-Tridentine: 300; speculative approach to: lxix, 166; study of: 239
myth: 388

Naaman: lxvii–lxviii, 235
nails: 111
nakedness: 187, 362
name(s), and idea: 55; holy: 386; meaning of: 52, 55; new: 208; power of: 55; relation to essence of: 55; terrible: 386
Nantes: 167
*narratio*: 52
narrowness: 364
nature: xix, 11, 82, 104, 108, 110, 120, 288, 300, 338, 341, 343–44, 367; aid of: 29; as ordered to grace: 78; as ordered to supernatural: 104; bodily: 264; denial of: lxviii; divine: 102; enemy of: 119; fallen: 104, 120, 338; gift(s) of: 1, 110; good of: 301; goods of: 119; historical: xl; human: xvi–xvii, lxxviii, cv, 74–75, 78, 86, 119, 250, 255, 290, 292–94, 300–302,

319; individual: 75; life according to: lxxviii, cv; lower: 394; meaning of: 78; need of: 105; of soul: xix, 302–3; perfection of: 343; ruin of: 343; sensible: 293; sensual: 346; spiritual: 264; true: 80; unstable: 223; weary: 196
Nazareth: 51, 278, 288; name of: 57
Nazis: 305
necessity: 116, 121, 123, 217, 375; law of: 353; limits of: 119; natural: lx, 119; of life: 120; of men: 354; of poor: 369; order of: 353; servile: 312
nectar: 90
need(s): lx, 65, 90, 122, 136, 273–74, 353, 369; bodily: 353; deepest: 349; immediate: 353; just: 119; of others: 90; time of: 121
neighbor(s): 211, 361, 369, 372; as other self: 119; benefit of: 282; care for: 367; compassion for: xix; concerns of: 367; hearts of: 361; love of: lx, 119, 121, 273, 319, 327, 367; needs of: 367; service of: xcvii, 119, 282, 354
Nesmy, Claude Jean, OSB: xxviii–xxix
Nesteros, Abbot: 257–58
New Testament: xxx, xlviii, lxviii–lxix, lxxii
Newman, John Henry: xxiii
news, trivial: 150
Nicholas of Clairvaux: 46, 60
Nicholas of St. Albans: 60
night: 278, 361, 373; dark: xvii, lxxviii, 212, 304–5, 342, 385
nobility, contact with: 194
nocturns: xliii
nominalism: 55, 166
non-being: xii
non-violence: lxxviii, 86, 303
Normandy: li, 47
nothingness: 291, 329, 363; human: xxvi, lx, 122
Notier, John: 41–42
Notier, Theobald: 41–42

Notre Dame, School of: 166
nourishment, spiritual: 196
novice(s): vii, xl, lviii, lxii, lxx, lxxix, lxxxi, ci–cii, 74, 195, 225, 243, 287, 289; brother: ci; Cluniac: 135, 138, 160; former: ciii
novitiate(s): lii, lviii; brothers': lxxx; choir: lxxx; Cluniac: 134, 160; merging of: lxxx
nuns: 186–96; service of: 194

oath: 231
Obazine, Abbey of: 48
obedience: xvi, xxii, xliii, lxv–lxvi, lxxvi, xciii, 23, 120, 146, 175, 186–88, 192–93, 216–22, 232, 244, 249, 255, 270–71, 288–90, 301, 311–12, 318, 349, 358–59, 367, 381, 387; concept of: xcii, 192; degrees of: 218–19; doctrine on: 234; false view of: 219; function of: 193; good of: 216; imperfect: lxvi, 216, 219–20; inert: 216; labor of: 301; limits of: 221; monastic: 135, 193, 214–22; perfect: lxvi, 216–18, 220; pretended: 217; qualities of: 193; real: 217; servile: 216, 218; sin against: 220; spirituality of: 193; to God: xcix, 105, 123, 312, 374; to members: 201; true: 217; virtue of: lxiv; vow of: lxv, 157, 221
objects, corporeal: 394; inferior: 394; sensible: 395
oblation, formal: 129
obligation(s), common: 322; degree of: lxiv; monastic: lxv, 150, 220; moral: 215; religious: lxiv–lxv; to love Christ: 291
obols: 162
Obrecht, Edmond, OCSO: xiii
observance(s): xciii, 149; austere: 144; Cistercian: 156; Cluniac: 137, 141, 158; corporal: 146; details of: 139; documents on: lxxix; exterior: 146, 322–23; fidelity to: lxii; infractions

of: 216; interior: 334; lax: 146; legitimate: 147; Lentan: 334; less strict: 147; level of: 142; monastic: xxxvii–xxxviii, lxii, lxv–lxvii, 215; points of: 126; purpose of: 215; religious: lxv, 190, 222, 230; spirit of: lxii, 142
obstacles: 332–33, 377; ordinary: 377
obstinacy: 237, 315
occasion: 117
occupations, multiplicity of: 351; useless: 362; vile: 136
ocean: 275
O'Connell, Patrick F.: xv, xvii, xxx, xxxvi, xlii, lvii, 23, 79–80, 142, 150, 242, 379
Odilo of Cluny, St.: 64–65
Odo of Cluny, St.: 68
odor: 207; fragrant: 113; sweet: 272, 298–99
offense(s): 171, 382
offerings: 155
office(s), burden of: 33; discontent with: 348; good: 302; holy: 41; monastic: 348, 350, 352
office, divine: 135, 159, 194, 196, 260, 266; night: 151; Sunday: 159
officers, monastic: xcii, 194; weekly: 194
oil(s): lxxiv–lxxv, 9, 53, 164, 202, 270, 274–75, 277–78, 281, 283–84, 288, 299, 361; healing: lxxv; heavenly: 361; of mercy: 273
ointment(s): 207, 270, 272–73, 276, 302; gradations of: 273; mystical: lxxvii, 299; precious: 368
Old Testament: xlviii, lxxii
omniscience, illusions of: 280
operation, mental: 115
opinion: 55
opposition, to God: lxviii, 236
oppressed, anxieties of: 369
oppressor: 127
optimism: 208
oratories: 136, 195

order: 86, 345; affective: 354; Christian: 41; exterior: 348; of creation: 175; of execution: 353; of intention: 353; of nature: 28; restoration of: 6, 69, 175; violated: 175
order(s), active: xxxi; Benedictine: 32; Cistercian: xx–xxi, lxv, lxxxiv, 7, 33, 46, 69, 125, 129, 142, 225, 242, 313; contemplative: xxxi; less rigorous: 223; major: 168; monastic: 139, 142–43, 148; penitential: 242; religious: xxxi, xxxvii, lxiv–lxv, lxxxii, 223–24, 232; unity of: 145
ordinance: 128
ordinariness: 255; exterior: 243
ordination: 350; priestly: lxxx, 158, 213
Origen: 16, 80, 246
outlook: 142
Ovid: 16
Oxford, schools at: 44

pagans: 109
page, sacred: 172
pain: 249, 368, 391; outward: 311; remedy for: 200
painting, curious: 154
palace, of King: 383
palate: 22, 130, 149
pallet, painful: 207
Paraclete, Convent of: xcii, 35, 169, 186, 192
paradise: 362–63; name of: 231; return to: 113; spiritual: 209; trees of: 362
pardon: 169, 210, 252; hope of: 4, 299, 332, 368
parents, offering by: 233
Paris: lxii, xci, 44, 47, 160–66, 186; archbishop of: 35, 197; as center of student life: 177; bishop of: 169; intellectual life in: 160–66; Latin Quarter of: 166; twelfth-century: 160–66; University of: lxii, 166
Paris, Julian: 320
parousia: xxviii

participation, in divine love: lxxiv, 330; in mysteries of faith: lxxi
partridges: 157
Pascal, Blaise: lxxxix
Paschasius Radbertus: 63–64
passion(s): cvii, 24, 26, 337, 343, 345–46, 389, 393; allurement of: 4; carnal: 294; four: 336; freedom from: 84; holy: 346; inordinate: 371; land of: 88; mortification of: 114; movement of: 394; poison of: 393; supernaturalized: 345; worldly: 115
paternalism, benevolent: 273
patience: ix, xcv, 129, 212, 244, 262, 309–10
patient: 95
patriarchs: lxxiii, 57, 264
Paul, St.: xxvii, xxx, xl, xlviii–xlix, 5, 14, 73, 116, 130, 149, 169–71, 179–80, 184, 188, 194, 208, 231, 233, 253, 259, 274, 278, 289, 310, 321, 347, 372, 383
Paul VI, Pope: ciii
Paulinus of Nola, St.: 190
Pavia: 36
payment: 101
peace: xvi, xxx, lxxix, xcviii–c, 7, 11, 27, 34, 45, 47–48, 53, 69, 72, 80, 82, 86, 97–98, 127, 129, 134, 151, 166, 211–12, 231, 235–36, 263, 267–68, 287, 301, 306, 310, 312, 314, 319, 325, 333, 358, 363, 370–71, 377, 382, 388–91, 394; among orders: 145; bonds of: 38, 102; degrees of: 382; destroyer of: 234; dwelling of: 395; false: 83; feelings of: 388; God of: 97, 334; highest: 377; illusory: lxxxviii; inner: 236; interior: xxxv, xxxviii, 93, 210; invisible: xxxv; mediators of: 213; monastic: xxxviii, xlii; of Church: 10, 39; of kingdom: 36; perfect: 8, 82, 309; perpetual: 97; profound: 250; promise of: 207–8; realms of: 383; serene: 6, 69; true: 82–83, 228, 306, 333, 371; with brethren: 149, 367; with others: xxxviii; worldly: lxxxviii, 82
peacemaker(s): lxiii, 213; as blessed: 212; kinds of: 212; office of: 213; true: 212
Pearson, Paul M.: cxi
*peccatum*: lxvi, 215–16
Peers, E. Allison: 243, 255, 285, 290, 328, 342, 346
penalties: 132, 215; ecclesiastical: 41; unjust: 176
penance: lxvi, xcv, 17, 19, 37, 40, 56, 114, 135, 147, 200, 213, 215, 221, 232, 269, 272, 284, 290, 310, 328, 332–34, 341–42, 363, 365–66, 368–69; counsel of: 221; desire for: 320; excessive: 29; joy in: 328; life of: xxx; men of: lxii, 143; spirit of: 310, 333; symbols of: 135; work of: 365
penitents: 299, 323, 350
Pennington, M. Basil, ocso: xv, xxxiii–xxxiv, xliv
Pentecost: 294, 297
people, holy: 89; hostility to: 188; ignorant: 92; sick: 92; spiritual: 179
pepper: 130
perfect, example of: 277; influence of: 277
perfection: lxv, 198, 212, 222, 231, 277, 291, 317, 353, 355; call to: 339; desire for: 156; experience of: 339; habit of: 341; higher: 156; mount of: 124; natural: 301; nature of: 198; of charity: lxxviii; of love: lxiv, 214; of rest: 359; progress in: 346; spiritual: 291, 293; way to: lxxvi, 291; willed: 339
perfectionists: 222
perfume: 288
peril, gravest: 280
period, feudal: 10
permanence: 345
perpetuity: 345
perplexity: ix
persecution: 127, 213; anti-Jewish: lxxii

persecutor: 127
perseverance: 30, 222, 226, 309; prayer for: 222
persistence: 341
Persius: 16
person(s), excommunicated: 230; human: xxxviii, 195, 203; inequality of: 4; of superior: lxvi; respect for: 195; spiritual: 281, 341; whole: 197
personalities, diverse: lxxvii; individuated: 206
perversion: 150; of true love: 72
Peter Damian, St.: 63, 133-34
Peter Lombard: 102-3, 196-97
Peter of Celle: 60, 163-64
Peter, St.: 20, 40, 63, 188, 199, 278, 297, 383-84
Peter the Venerable, Abbot of Cluny: lxi, lxxxix-xc, xcii, xciv, cvi, 47, 97, 133-42, 147, 157-61, 184-86; and Abelard: xcii, 171-72, 184-86; apparent sophistries of: 139; as friend of St. Bernard: xc; defense of Cluny of: 134-39; humility of: 147; leadership of: xc; letters of: xc-xcii, 133-41, 157-58, 171-72, 184-86; letters to: 45-46, 97-98, 186; observance of: 147; practice of: xc, 139; principles of: xc, 137-39, 147; reform by: 139, 141-42, 157-60
pettiness: lxxix
pharaoh: 362
pharisaism: 153, 335
Pharisee(s): lxxv, 83, 146, 209, 213, 276, 323; Cistercians as: 135, 143; Jorannus as: 227; long faces of: 324
pheasants: 157
phenomena, mystical: 241, 247; psychophysical: 253; supernatural: lxix
phenomenology: 239
philanthropy, condescending: 273; self-satisfied: 273
*philia*: civ
Philip of Harveng: 163

Philip of Lincoln, Canon: 34, 227-28
Philippe, Paul, OP: lxxx
philosopher(s): 2, 162, 170; activities of: 163; pagan: 162, 173
philosophy: 16, 168, 196; cosmic: 103; Greek: 238; true: 184; vain: 2
Phinees (Phineas): 40-41
physician: 276; human: 279; spiritual: 205
physicists: 104
physics: 184
*pietas*: 276, 296; ointments of: lxxiv, 273-74, 276
piety: 14, 296, 299, 365-66; appearance of: 334; fake: 335; false: xcv, 335; fountains of: 390; gift of: 369; life of: 368; Marian: 68; school of: 164; unguent of: 368
pig: 84
pilgrimage: xciv, 163, 227; earthly: 111
pilgrims: 12
Pisa: 36; Council of: 36
pittances: 130
pity: 38, 43, 201, 205, 208, 283, 370; multitude of: 211; spirit of: 37
Pius XI, Pope: 348
Pius XII, Pope: xxxvi, xlii, lxxxii, 1-10, 68, 246; article on: lxxxii, 13; as vicar of Christ: xxxvi; ascetic appearance of: 13; death of: lxxxii; *Doctor Mellifluus* of: xxxii-xxxvi, lvii-lviii, lxxxii, 1-10, 68-70, 246; pet goldfinch of: 13
place(s), lofty: 384; of Bridegroom: 387; quiet: 387; regular: 137; secret: 384, 395; solitary: 190; terrible: 386
plaintiffs: 128
plan(s), detachment from: 383; divine: xxvii; providential: 169
plasticity, complete: 337
Plato: 162, 184; attitude of Abelard toward: 178-79; *Timaeus* of: 103
Platonism: 16, 102
plays, morality: 203

pleasure(s): 17, 24, 82–83, 85, 88, 93, 125, 200–202, 204, 341–42, 346, 375; angelic: 84; bestial: 84; carnal: 284; deceitful: 34; desire for: 332; diabolical: 84; exile from: 88; false: 34; instinct for: 346; inward: 207; legitimate: 325; manifold: 91; of belly: 84; of gullet: 84; of taste: 151; paradise of: 206–7; philosophical: 84; sensible: 294; sensual: 206, 235; worldly: 17, 34, 322; wretched: 22
plenty, storerooms of: 368
pliancy: 205
poets: 12
poison: 95, 196, 200
Poitiers: 41
Poitou: 36
polemics, atmosphere of: 125–26
pomp(s): xviii, 142
Pontifical Academy of Sciences: 13
Pontigny, Abbey of: 226–27
Pontius of Cluny, Abbot: lxi, 133–34
poor: lxii–lxiii, xcix, 95, 141, 154, 164, 195, 309, 316; in spirit: 204; love of: 14; necessities of: 369; proud: 144
pope(s): 8, 128, 134, 137, 183–84, 232
popularizations, of mysticism: 240–41
Porion, Jean-Baptiste, OCart: xxii, lxxxix
pork: 157
porter: 135
portress: xciii, 193, 195
positions: 24
possessions: 24; earthly: 187; loss of: 34; love of: 34; useless: 362
Poulain, Augustin-François, SJ: 239, 241
Pourrat, Pierre: 59, 70
poverty: xxxviii, xlii, xcv, 11, 120, 141, 146, 148, 186–87, 195, 210, 250, 309, 320; evangelical: 11; interior: 187; lack of: 151; Lady: 70; monastic: 153; of spirit: 31; spirit of: 187; vow of: lxv

power(s): lxxxv, 11, 26, 34, 93, 174, 207, 249–50, 297, 309, 319, 338, 380; diabolical: 174; divine: 58, 279, 305, 381, 387; dynamic: 100; ecclesiastical: 192; frail: xcv; from God: 87; healing: 273; human: lxxvii, c; infinite: 175; intellectual: xcii; just: 181–82; love of: 176; man of: 85; merciful: 97; name of: 9, 279; natural: 344; of binding and loosing: 176; of devil: 181–82; of divine presence: 295; of God: lxxv, lxxvii, 56–57, 114, 199, 297, 306, 379; of Holy Spirit: xxv, lix, 29, 297; of Passion: 182; of Resurrection: 111; of sons of God: 309; of soul: xlv, cvii, 198, 339, 344, 360; papal: 10; quest for: lxxix; secular: 41, 192; transforming: 286; voice of: 20–21; world of: 11
powerlessness: 94
practice(s): 143, 218, 344; ascetical: xix, xc; exterior: xc, 334; inefficacious: 120; of virtue: xc, 159; outward: lxiii; penitential: xcv, 242; pious: 201; singular: 335; unusual: 335
*praesentia*: 111–12, 115
praise(s): 73, 165, 202, 266, 277–78, 285, 322, 331; divine: 273; of Lord: 276; of men: 84; perfected: 281; spirit of: 267; to God: 11
prayer(s), ix, xxxi, l, lxxxv, 5, 8, 10, 17, 31, 37, 39, 45, 56, 66, 93, 122, 129, 136, 138, 142, 155, 164, 171, 228, 246, 253, 285, 308, 334, 341–42, 351, 363, 376, 383, 393–94; active: 339; affective: 242, 340; confident: 119, 121; consolation(s) in: 242, 271; contemplative: viii, lxix, 19, 142, 241–43; degrees of: 239, 241, 243, 374, 384–85; devotion in: 271; devout: 340; distraction from: lxii; fervent: 9, 340; grace(s) of: xlii, 27, 29, 240, 242–43, 255, 271–72, 287, 341; holo-

## Index

causts of: 294; imageless: 142; inefficacious: 120; life of: lxix, 170, 237–38; men of: lxii, 143; mystical: xix, 240, 242, 340; of Church: 39; of princes: 39; of quiet: 243; of simplicity: 242; of union: 243; passive: 339; peace of: 285; period of: 242; potion of: 284; rest in: 191; sensual: 344; soul of: 255; state(s) of: 239, 367; to Father: 87; true: 154; zeal for: 31
preachers: xxx
preaching: 11, 213, 278; fruitfulness of: 271
prebend: 228
precepts, bodily: 147; Christian: 6; interior: 146; obligatory: lxv; spiritual: 146–47, 205
precipitation: 344
predestination: 222
preferences, personal: 217
prelacy: 303
prelate(s): lxxviii, 168, 188, 304–5
Premonstratensians: 233
Prémontré, brothers of: 232–33
preparation, lack of: 243
presence, apophatic: 112; delightful: 304; divine: xvii, xcviii, 115, 249, 254, 371; of Beloved: 383; of Christ: 112; of God: ix, lxx, cv, 114, 121, 206, 231, 255, 284–85, 363; of Holy Spirit: lxxv, 103–4, 280–81; of spouse: 304; secret: 304, 383
prestige, human: lxiii, 213; political: lxiii, 213; social: 194
presumption: 220, 315, 342
pretension, arrogant: 144
prevarication: 218
pride: xii, xxxix, lxi, lxxviii, lxxxiv, cvi, 9, 22, 26, 31, 63, 67, 83–84, 109, 142, 144, 146–47, 169, 176, 186, 210, 237, 258, 276, 282–83, 301, 304, 315, 323, 342, 363–64; degrees of: 17, 72, 109, 361; intellectual: 167; of life: 24; pharisaic: lxi, 144; psychology of: 276; self-righteous: xxxviii; spiritual: 290; swellings of: 279
priest(s): 168, 241, 348; good: 213; Jewish: 136; life of: 191; pastoral duties of: 191; sinful: 213; vocation of: 191
priesthood: 213; Catholic: 348; Jewish: 57
princes: 8; of evil: 315
principle(s), abstract: 177, 214; application of: 138
priors, Cistercian: 225; Cluniac: 141, 157
probity: 382
problem(s): 19, 164; ethical: 177; juridical: 233; linguistic: 257; literary: 257; philosophical: xcii; textual: 257; theological: xcii, 177
Prodigal Son: 128
profession, Cistercian: 197, 313; holy: 191; infidelity to: 192; monastic: 128–29, 134, 220–21, 230, 319; religious: 170
professor: 164
profit, for soul: 34
progress: 160, 209, 282, 343, 367; in virtue: lxiii; material: 12; of others: 352; secret of: 274; spiritual: lxxvi, 12, 205, 270
progressives: lxxviii, 206, 300
promise, divine: 388
property: 186; monastic: 136
prophecies, fulfillment of: 58
prophet(s): lxxiii, 20, 136, 163–64, 231, 264, 283, 308, 347, 358; experiences of: 385; message of: 280; predictions of: 57; sons of: 190; spirit of: 308; visions of: 57
proportion, due: 348
proprietorship, exterior: 189; interior: 189
prosperity: 34, 163, 337; economic: 134; material: 271
prostration: 135

protection: 114; against devil: 182
protest, implicit: 349
Proverbs, Book of: 282
providence: 170; action of: 238
prudence: lxxvii, 224, 226, 286, 299, 343, 370
psalm(s): 159, 260–61, 266, 311, 332, 335, 371
psalmist: 259, 395
psalmody: 131
Psalter: 15
psychology, deep: 339; mercenary: 96; modern: 92; of fraternal compassion: 273; spiritual: 105
publican: 83, 146
Pullen, Cardinal Robert: 44, 196
punishment(s): cv, 41, 43, 100, 105, 175, 182, 272, 310, 388; bodily: 311; fear of: 96, 301; in time: 171; sin as: 96
purgation, consoling: 371; pleasant: 371; sweet: 371
Purgatory, Mount: cv
purification(s): 56, 212, 284, 365; of body: 365; of intention: 116; of love: 77, 255, 296; of memory: cvii, 211, 365; of soul: 342, 354, 365; of spirit: 365; of will: 209, 365; passive: 212; severe: 212; three: 365; total: 214
puritanism: 153
*puritas amoris*: 374
purity: 58, 190, 213, 286, 359, 370, 372–73; angelic: 378, 395; ecstasy of: 378; of heart: lxiii, 30, 264, 267; of intention: xc, 144; of love: 7, 77, 99, 115, 375; of mind: 395
putrifaction: 345

*quadrivium*: 16, 162
quiet: 191, 304, 306, 357–58, 388; contemplative: xli; exterior: 383; place of: 368, 387; realm of: 383; state of: 242; true: 387
quietism: 277, 381
quietness: 45

quietude: 206, 316
Qumran: 190

rabbits: 157
raiment, soft: 130
rain: 275, 395
rancor: 328
Raphael, Archangel: 231
rapine: 22
rapture: 124, 253, 374, 375, 377, 381, 386; transient: 380
*raptus*: xcvii, 374, 381
raving: 87
Ré, Isle of: 1
reading(s): 10, 52, 194; aimless: 243; art of: viii; background: 262; contemplative: ix, lxxi, 258; labor of: 258; monastic: xiii; spiritual: ix
realism: 55, 166
reality: lxxv, 55, 214, 221, 278, 287, 296, 312; absolute: 112; adaptation to: xcix, 312, 362; concrete: 354; conflict with: 104–5; conformity to: 312; contact with: 243; conversion to: lxxxiv, 23; everyday: xcvii, 373; experience of: 237–38; facing: cvii, 298; fullness of: lxxv, 287; God as personal: 112; invisible: lxxxvi, 54, 370; nature of: 83; objective: 244; of acts: 199; of divine providence: 122; of motives: 199; of mystery: 48; ordinary: 373; psychological: 214; pure: 112; revealed: 112; sacred: lxxxvi, 48, 54; sensible: 261; submission to: xcix, 312; supernatural: 291; supreme: lxxxvi, 58; transcendent: 112; truth of: 338; unseen: 373
realization, experiential: 238; vs. figure: 55
reason(s): xcvii, 21, 55, 110, 166, 188–89, 201, 203, 206, 209, 211, 288–90, 293, 313, 335–36, 340, 342, 345–46, 354, 360–63, 365, 370–72; activity of: 296; arguments from: 178; as accuser:

361; as critical instrument: 166; as deputy: 360; as judge: 360–61, 363; as prosecutor: 363; as vicar: 363, 370; as witness: 361, 363; autonomy of: 11; conversion of: cvii; for injunctions: 219; judgment of: 296, 348; quiet of: 363; resourceless: 203; rule of: 354; subjection to: 206, 355
reasoning(s): xcviii, 173; abstract: 338; chain of: cv; circuits of: 3; death to: 394; human: 3; logical: 112
rebellion, of emotions: 236; of senses: 236; of will: 363
receiving, importance of: 284
reception: 355
recluse(s): 186–87, 191, 193; English: 185
reclusion, rite of: 193
recollection: 115, 361; of sin: 210
recommendations, letters of: 225
reconciliation: 212
recovery, facility of: 203
recreation(s): 314; monastic: 148, 160
redemption: lxix, xcvii, 66, 118, 173, 179–82, 292, 375; dogma of: 174; mystery of: 246–48; price of: 173–74
refectory: xlii, lxxxii; community: 137
reflection(s), impromptu: 339; objective: 339; sacred: 189
reform(s), Benedictine: 141–42; Cluniac: lxi, xc, 139, 141–42; letter of: 158; monastic: 12; religious: 10; spirit of: 158
reformation, image of: 338
refreshment, abode of: 207
regalia, pontifical: 140
regret(s): 127, 381, 389
regularity: 141, 221
regulations, canonical: lxiv; Cluniac: xc, 158; on office: xc
rejection, of judgment: lxviii
relation(s), human: 378
relationality: civ

relationship, false: xxxix
relatives, carnal: 187
relaxation(s): 150, 241
relief: 10, 205, 216
religion: 12, 276; as empty form: 335; Catholic: 6, 69; conversion to: 184; Christian: 97; habit of: 335; holy: 230; life in: 14
religious: 158, 223, 241–42, 367; bad: 219; dedicated: lxvi; good: 219, 229, 371; ordinary: lxix, 241; perfect: 217; young: 243
relish: 354
remedies: 6, 38, 110, 130, 215, 235, 237, 280; for sin: 205; normal: 221; penitential: lxvi; sovereign: 279
remembrance: 314
remorse, spirit of: 333
Renaissance: lxix, 238
renewal: cvi
renunciation: lxii, 143, 153, 244, 303; monastic: 131, 191; perfect: 142
reparation: 67
repentance: 203, 210–11, 310
repose: 305, 374, 382, 389–90; eternal: 64; of soul: xxxv; perfect: 70, 372, 385, 389; place of: 395; quiet of: 305, 386
representations, death to: 394
reprobate, condemnation of: 304
repugnance: 196
resemblance, way of: 77
resentment: 210, 229, 319
reservoirs: lxxv, 282–83
resistance, interior: 325
responsibility: 288; personal: 219; to community: xcvi
rest: lxxix, 23, 26, 70, 228, 249, 268, 284, 300, 304, 306, 314–15, 317–18, 365, 367–68, 370–72, 374, 380, 385, 389–92, 395; ascent to: 359; bed of: 191; contemplation of: 306; contemplative: xcvii, 8, 97; degrees of: 390; eternal: 317; everlasting: lxxix;

experience of: 387; false: 380; for God: xcix, 306, 317–18, 389; from sin: xcix; in certitude: lxxxiv; in Christ: xcix; in community: 318; in God: xxx, lxxix, xcix, 306, 317, 355, 359, 365, 384, 395; in heaven: xcix, 314, 316; perfect: 371, 391, 395; place of: lxxviii, 304, 306, 318, 384, 389; richer: 207; spiritual: xcix–c, 313–20; to soul: 70, 306, 318, 366, 380, 389; true: xcix–c, 69, 306, 319, 366, 389, 393
restitution: 47
restlessness: 206, 224, 235, 304
restorative: 279
restraint: 392
restoration: 175; of human nature: lxxviii, 301
resurrection, general: xcii, 172
retreat: 249, 256
retribution: 101
revelation: 74; Christ as center of: lxxi; scriptural: lxix, 71
revelation(s): lxxi, 56, 108, 173, 238, 248, 253, 258, 267; mystery of: 53; of angel: 56; phenomenology of: 55
revenge: 105
reverence: 4, 222, 249–51, 285, 357; for priesthood: 41
revival, monastic: 10; religious: 10
revolution, intellectual: 197; spirit of: 197
reward: 89, 91, 115–18, 266, 288, 300, 314, 355; eternal: 39, 208; final: 115; full: 151; highest: 124; love as: 115
Rheims, Archbishop of: 98, 226; Archbishopric of: 44; province of: 141
rhetoric: cv, 4, 16
Rhine River: 46
Rhineland: 36, 46
Rice, Edward; xxiii
Richard I, King: li
riches: 145, 155, 299
riddle: 212

Rievaulx, Abbey of, foundation of: 35
right: 42
righteous: 20
righteousness: lxxviii, 45, 234; of God: 388; of man: 388; sense of: 234
rights: lx
rigidity: xc, 135, 143; false: 133
ring: 248
risk, of failure: lxvii
rites: 49
ritual, Old Testament: xlviii
rivalry: 340
rivals: 326
river(s): 275, 331
Rivière, J.: 182
robbers: 230
robbery: 201
Robert of Arbrissel: 11
Robert of Châtillon: lxi, lxxxix, cvi, 126–33, 226, 233; apostasy of: 130; as cousin of Bernard: 126; conscience of: 130; fall of: 128; given as child to Cluny: 126; letter to: lxi, lxxxix, cvi, 32, 126–33; parents of: 128–30; transfer without permission: 126; vows of: 130; weakness of: 130–31
Robert of Prémontré, Br.: 232
Roberts, Abp. Thomas, SJ: ciii
Rochais, H. M.: xiv
Rochester, Bishop of: 44
rock(s): 53, 164
Roger: 185
Roger of Sicily: 44
Roloff, Ronald, OSB: lxxx
Romans: 162
Rome: xxii, 36, 44, 128, 134, 256; Bishop of: 137; court of: 183
roots: 131; of charity: 319
Roscelinus: 166
roughness: 364
Roulland, Adolphe: 146
Rousselot, Pierre: 70–71, 76, 78, 107
routines, absurd: 158

## Index

rule(s): 127, 215, 223; ecclesiastical: 137; hard: 19; inabililty to keep: 224; kinds of: 221; relaxation of: 225; religious: lxiv, xciii, 156, 192, 220; spirit of: 249; strict: 223; violation of: lxv
Rule of St. Benedict: xxxvii, lxiv–lxvii, 74, 131, 135–40, 142, 146–47, 150, 189, 192, 215–16, 220–22, 224, 288, 290, 301, 308; dispensation from: lxi; essence of: 147; infidelity to: 134; infractions of: lxvi; letter of: xxxvii, lxi, 138, 141; literal observance of: 126; obedience to: 157; observance of: 221; ordering principle of: 138; points of: 157; precepts of: lxv, 129, 214–15, 220–21; prescriptions of: lxv, 214; remedies of: 221–22; spirit of: lxi, 141, 150; submission to: lxxviii; violation of: 215, 230; prologue: 301; c. 1: 192; c. 4: 142; c. 5: 218; c. 7: 301, 361; c. 41: 135; c. 42: 189; c. 58: 74; c. 61: 230; c. 68: 217; c. 71: 216
rumors: 150, 195
Rupert of Deutz: 59, 61
rust: 102
Rusticus: 131

sabbath, contemplative: lii; true: 93
sacrament(s): 54, 171–72, 341; last: 186; of name of Jesus: lxxv, 279; saint as: xxv
sacred, sense of: lxxxv, civ, 48–49
sacrifice(s): 39, 122, 138, 174–75, 217, 233, 272, 288, 325, 345, 352, 354; daily: 228; interior: 325; spirit of: 332; vain: 318
sacrilege: lxxviii, 220, 304
sacristan: 193
sad, sorrows of: 369
sadness: 63, 326–27
safety: 130
sage: 130
saint(s): xxiv, xxvi, lxxv, 120, 130, 145, 226, 239, 270, 277, 310, 343, 352, 366,
378; as sacrament: xxv; assembly of: 318; communion of: 98; feasts of: 159; fellow citizen of: 227; land of: 385; lives of: 193; mark of: 87
St. Denis, Abbey of: 45, 169
St. Follian, Abbey of: 233; interdict of: 233
St. Genevieve, School of: 166
St. Marcel, Priory of: 186
St. Medard, abbot of: 229
St. John's University: liii; conference on psychiatry at: liii
St. Nicasius, Abbey of: 225–26
St. Pierre, Abbey of: 214
St. Victor, School of: 166
St. Vincent, Abbey of: 68
St. Vorles, canons of: 14, 32
salt: 9, 130, 278, 344–45
salutation, of brethren: 137
salvation: xvi, xxi, lxvi, 8, 56, 64, 98, 130, 175, 203–4, 282–83, 294, 311, 326, 359; economy of: 113; gift of: lxxv; gratuity of: lxxv, 276–77; human: 138, 238; of others: 282; of soul(s): 36, 149, 135, 171, 231; pledge of: 308
Samway, Patrick, SJ: xx
sanctification: xxx, 169, 222, 282, 355
sanction, of spiritual father: 288
sanctity: xxi, 10, 12, 19, 24, 81, 115, 279, 302, 310; call to: xxxvi; high: 376; nature of: xxv; pledge of: 377; signs of: 58; vocation to: 214
sanctuary, holy: 38; interior: 151; of church: 154; service of: 136
sanity: 120
Sarepta (Zarephath): 283
Sartre, Jean-Paul: xlviii
satiety: 147, 209
satire: 144
satisfaction: 127–28, 203, 209, 216, 231, 233, 235, 250, 332, 354; adequate: 228; material: xcvii; of desires: lxvii, 372; permanent: xxxix; theory of: 174–75

savages: 161
Savigny, Abbey of: 48
savor: 305, 381, 387
scandal: xxiii, lxiv, lxvi, 143, 156, 213, 222, 224, 229, 304, 323; danger of: lxvii; grave: 216; great: 335; public: 232
Schachter, Zalman: ciii
schism(s): 247, 348; confusion caused by: 41; in body: 347; local: 36; papal: lviii, lxxix, 35–36, 44, 299
Schmitz, Philibert, osb: 123
scholarship, world of: 166
scholasticism: lxii, 11, 177, 238
school(s), Carmelite: 241; cathedral: 12; Cistercian: xix; cloister: 12; conflict in: 55; intellectual level of: 176–77; of charity: xli, 68–69, 77, 338; of Christ: xxxvii, 163–64; Parisian: lxii, xci; twelfth-century: 56
Schroen, Mother M. L.: lxxx
science(s): 16, 160, 196, 387
*scientia*: 108–10, 208, 258, 296
Scripture(s): xxviii, l, lxxi, lxxxvi, 2, 23, 49, 52, 58, 149, 162, 192, 229, 238, 247, 315, 348, 377, 379, 391–92; allegorical approach to: xxix; and liturgy: 259; consolation of: 309; imagery in: lxxiii; insight into: 258; linguistic problems of 257; literal sense of: lxxi, 257; literary problems of 257; reading of: 196, 258; St. Bernard and: liv, lxxi, 15, 257–61; sense(s) of: 258, 300, 381; study of: 257–58; text of: lxxii, cx; textual problems of: 257
sculpture, lavish: 154
sea: 275
season, harvest: liv
secrecy: lxxix, 306, 373
secret(s): 324, 373; divine: 384; intimate: 384; of Beloved: 384; of God's love: 268; of place: 384; of truth: 373
secularism: 11
seculars: lxxxviii, 158, 160, 194

security: 41, 121, 128, 306, 316, 391, 395
Sedulius: 165
Sedulius Scotus: 165
See , Apostolic: 39; Holy: 41, 128, 223
seeing: 142
seeking: 304
Seius: 162
Séjalon, Hugo: 320
Séjourné, Paul, osb: 364
self: 207, 236, 364, 378; autonomous: 125; becoming: 80; contempt of: 344; death to: lx; emptying of: 75, 378; exterior: 85; false: xvi, xx; forgetfulness of: 8; gift of: xlviii, c, 23, 26–27, 80, 89, 102, 108–10, 222, 303, 319, 368, 373, 395; higher: 75; in Christ: xxxviii; inner: 22; interior: 324; loss of: 34, 378–79; love of: lx, xcvii–xcviii, 34, 76–78, 80, 99, 124, 327, 346, 374–80; real: xvi, xx; reflection on: 378; renunciation of: 217, 234, 303; transient: 85; true: xvi, xxxviii, lxxxiv, civ, 79–80
self-absorption: lxx
self-affirmation: 85
self-assertion, desire for: xxxix
self-complacency: 258, 274, 286, 335
self-confidence: 36, 298
self-consecration: 67
self-contempt: 369
self-contradiction: lxviii
self-deception: 280
self-defense: 229
self-denial: 23, 257, 332, 359
self-discipline: lxxxv
self-discovery: xiii
self-display: lxxxv, 26
self-distrust: 369
self-emptying: lii, 324
self-esteem: 102
self-forgetfulness: lxxiv, xcix, 274, 317, 378, 382; moral: 378; mystical: 378
self-gift: lix
self-hatred: 200, 210

## Index

selfhood: xxviii; authentic: xxxix
self-indulgence; 325
self-interest: lx, 80, 323
selfishness: 276, 302, 319, 329, 363, 375–76
self-knowledge: xvi, xix, xli, lix, lxxv, xcvii, 109, 235, 363
self-love: xii, lxxvi, 67, 76, 78, 80, 102, 118, 120–21, 219, 235, 291, 326; law of: 321
self-preservation: lix–lx, 78
self-regard: lxxv
self-renunciaton: 324
self-sacrifice: 274, 325, 367
self-satisfaction: lxxvi, 83, 109, 280, 332
self-seeking: 101–2
self-surrender: lx
self-transcendence: 75
self-will: xvi, xli, lxvii, lxxvi, xcviii, cviii, 71–72, 79, 104–5, 120–21, 234–36, 268, 288, 290–91, 301, 311–13, 326
seminarians: cvii
Seneca: 16, 168
seniors, counsel of: 288, 290; example of: 288, 290
Sens, Council of: xcii, 183–84, 197
sensation: 378; faculty of: 393
sense(s): lxxv, 21, 26, 84, 236, 280, 351, 373, 393; alienation of: 253; allegorical: 258; anagogical: 258; attractions of: 293; bodily: 201, 393; common: 243; exterior: lxxix, 306; good: 382; historical: 258; interior: lxxix, 306; literal: lxxviii, 258–60, 287, 300, 381; moral: lxxvii, 300, 381; mortification of: lxxxv; mystical: xlviii, lxxviii; physical: 255; spiritual: lxxviii, 181, 209, 258, 260, 266, 288–89, 300, 303–4, 381; tropological: 258
sensibility, religious: lxxxv
sensuality: 29, 294, 393
sentiment(s): 296; Christian: 154
sentimentality: 274
Sept-Fons, Abbey of: xiv

seraph: 56
serenity, spiritual: xix
serfs: 136
seriousness: xxi, 316
Serlo of Wilton: 165
serpent: 24
servant(s), faithful: 286; of God: 79; of Yahweh: lxxii; poor: 164; wise: 286
service: lxiv; divine: xliv; instrument of: 29; military: 320; of neighbor: xcvii, 119, 282, 354; painstaking: 202; reasonable: 289; to curiosity: 202; to pleasure: 202; to vanity: 202
servitude: 192; spirit of: 391
severity: 127
shadows, land of: 88
shame: 34, 362
Shannon, William H.: xv, xxxiii–xxxiv, xxxviii, xlix
shaving: 158
sheep: 143, 196, 282; led to slaughter: 235; lost: 234
sheep-shearing: 195
shell: 259; outer: 260
shelter: 119, 204
shepherd, pope as: 41
ships, ballast in: 316
shirts, woolen: 130
Sicily, monastic foundation in: 44
sick: 195–96; in body: 195; in soul: 195; love of: 14
sickbed: 365
sickness(es): 87, 92, 362, 376; bed of: 207
sighs: 342
sign(s): 57, 189; external: 49, 58
Signy, Abbey of: lxi
silence: viii, xxii, xlviii, lxvi, xcii, 45, 63, 131, 137, 148, 160, 162, 186, 189, 195, 216, 281, 284, 351, 356–59, 366; criminal: 282; discipline of: 358; exterior: c; friend of: 357; fruitful: c; great: 189; interior: c; life of: li; regulations on: xc; violation of: 216; zeal for: 308

silver: 154
similitudes: 394
simony: lxxviii, 304
simplicity: xv, xviii, l, xcii, 23, 148, 195, 225, 261, 320; Cistercian: 195; essential: 11; externals of: xv; intellectual: xvi; interior: xiv–xv, 243; monastic: 142; natural: xv; original: xvi; perfect: xvi; spirit of: 142, 153; true 308
simplification: 158
simulation: 351
sin(s): xvii, lix, lxvi, 4, 12, 21, 24, 29, 38, 78, 84, 88, 94, 96, 100, 114, 128, 169, 175–76, 200–201, 208–10, 212, 214, 216, 218, 232, 234, 250, 272, 284, 293, 310, 318, 327, 332, 343, 354, 360, 362–65, 369–70, 388, 393; act of: 176; after-effects of: cvii; bad effects of: 278; burden of: 310–11; capital: 341; correction of: 220; defilement of: 209; depth of: 205; freedom from: 388; healing of: 278; horror of: 304; inability to: 93; inclination to: 176; increase of: 220; life of: 206; matter of: lxv; mortal: 121; occasions of: 195, 197, 230; of godless: 304; of tongue: 195; original: xxxix, 83, 174, 264, 301; pain of: lxiv–lxv, xciii, 215; past: 210–11, 311; real: lxvi, 201, 216; remission of: 210; rest from: xcix; serious: lxv–lxvi, 216; slave of: 94; sorrow for: 325; unwillingness to: 93; venial: lxv; web of: 200
Sinai, Mount: 227; God of: 281
sincerity: ci, 144, 243
sinfulness: 200
singing: 194, 196, 260
sinner(s): xxiv, 9, 20, 63, 108, 123, 128–29, 176, 200, 270, 277; anger of: 281; forgiven: cvii, 388; great: 211; grievous: 211; guilt of: 359; inner motives of: 175; oil of: 202
sister(s), lay: 194; of Son: 268
situation, present: 354

skin(s): 136; anointed: 364; pliable: 361; stretched: 364
slave(s): xii, 99, 101, 265, 358; *affectus* of: 100; fear of: lxxxvii, 89; of devil: 174; of sin: 94
slavery: 80; bitter: 364; to self-love: 219; to self-will: 71; yoke of: 79
sleep: 29, 195–96, 205, 372, 389–90; as awakening: xcvii; bodily: 392; explanation of: 392–95; life-giving: xcviii, 372, 392; of death: 392; of sin: 392; of spouse: 392; pleasant: 392; true: 393; vigilant: 372; wakeful: 372, 392; watchful: xcviii, 392
sleeves, long: 130
sloth: 8, 45, 282, 365; tepidity of: 279
smells, sweet: 207
smoke, sweet: 54
snake: 156
snare, of fowler: 393
sobriety: 148
society: 120; Christian influence on: 134; contact with: 301; feudal: 10, 18; human: 6–7, 69; medieval: 12; on high: 319; urban: 165
*socius*: 302–3
softness: 148
Soissons, Council of: 172, 183
soldiers: 32, 156
solemnities: 318
solicitude: 149; affectionate: 392
solidarity: 388
solitary: 192
solitude(s): viii, xx, xxxviii, l, lxxxix, xcii, 11, 31, 189–92, 284, 308, 320, 395; as protection: 192; in community: xx; interior: 359, 366; quiet of: 190, 359, 395; secret of: 190; tropes of: 190–91; true: 376; wild: 131; zeal for: 31
Solomon, King: 163, 283
Somerville, Mary: cxi
son(s): 99, 252, 265; elder: 260; liberty of: 79; of God: 79; prodigal: 260;

selfless love of: lxxxvii, 89; spiritual: lxxiv, 269; true: 309; wise: 229
song: 151
*Song of Roland*: 12
sonship, spirit of: 268
sophisms: 164
sophistry: 2
sorrow(s): lxxiv, xcv, 85, 127, 230, 250, 272, 274, 295, 327–29, 332, 335, 337, 362, 366, 368–69; as natural affection: 118; evil: xcv, 329; false: 337; for sin: 325; good: 329; interior: 333; joy in: 328–29; object of: 337; real: 325; true: xcv, 337
Sortais, Gabriel, ocso: xxxvii–xxxviii
soul(s): xvi, xviii–xix, xxvi, xxxi, xxxv, lxiii, lxxiii, lxxv–lxxvi, lxxviii, cv, 3–5, 7, 9, 19–23, 34, 38, 40, 56, 62–63, 65–66, 69–70, 76, 78, 92, 97, 99, 102, 116–17, 127–28, 130, 138, 143, 148–49, 165, 195, 198, 200, 203–5, 207–8, 210–12, 217, 235, 247–48, 250, 252–54, 257, 260–61, 264–66, 268–72, 274, 278, 280, 282–87, 294–95, 305–6, 328–30, 334, 336–37, 341–43, 355, 359, 364–65, 367, 371–72, 378, 381, 383, 385, 388, 390–91, 393, 395; ability of: 336; actions of: 372; activity of: 255; acts of: 102; affections of: 91, 251; anointing of: lxxiv, 269–74, 329; apostolic: 213; as spirit: 254; as spouse: xcviii, 76, 113, 265–66, 277, 361, 380; blessed: 361, 372; blindness of: 334; capacity of: 286; captive: 118; care of: 303, 352; Christian: 328; cleansing of: 342; concern for: 213; contemplative: 359, 380, 384; conversion of: 199; danger to: 141, 144, 148, 151, 230; deception of: 164; depths of: lxxxiv, 23, 80; desire(s) of: 76, 100, 336, 372; destiny of: 71; detached: xcv, 337; disposition of; 234; emotions of: 5; essence of: 100; faculties of: lxiii, 71, 336; faithful: 115, 249; father of: 271; feelings of: 5, 251; fervent: 340, 380; fervor of: 254; generous: 19; gifts to: 108; great: 146; ground of: 100; harshness of: 364; hatred of: 187; holy: 118, 389; human: 79, 84; imperfect: 328; impure: 102; individual: 258; infected: 22; inner movements of: 236; languors of: 279; learned: 258; leprosy of: lxviii, 22; less advanced: 287; life of: xxxi, xxxiv–xxxv, 83; love of: 4, 72, 107, 253, 293, 392; meek: 205; mourning: 205; movements of: 251, 350, 354; mystical: 113; natural movement of: 74; nature of: xix, 71, 302–3; night of: 243; passion(s) of: 335, 345; passivity of: 385; penitential: 19; perfect: 277; perfected: 361; poor: 205; power(s) of: xlv, cvii, 198, 339, 344, 360; priestly: 213; purification of: 342, 354, 365; purity of: 98; quiet: 387; religious: 221; rest to: 70, 306, 318, 366, 380, 389; safety of: 230; salvation of: 36, 149, 135, 171, 231; sanctuary of: 199; sentiments of: 5; sleeping: xcviii, 392; strength of: 100, 336; substance of: xviii, 21; summit of: 100, 329; tongue of: 254; torpor of: 21; transformation of: 379; treatises on: 71; unmerciful: 211; virtues of: 372; visitations of: 111; whole: 21, 124; wise: 316; wound of: 311
South Carolina: ciii
Southern, R. W.: 150
sow: 208
Spain: 33, 36, 139, 162
spark: 285
sparrow: 393
speaking, useless: 160
speculation: 70, 354, 388; empty: 3; profound: 339; theological: 177
speech(es): 63; interpretations of: 347
spices: 130, 299

spider: 200
Spires, Diet of: 46
spirit(s): 9, 28–29, 106–7, 129, 150, 179, 204, 218, 253, 259–60, 264, 279, 281, 308, 325, 342, 348, 363; affliction of: 205; angelic: 282, 308; animal: 264; authentic: 333; blessed: 231; Carthusian: lxxxix; Cistercian: 125, 145, 324; competitive: 15; created: 264; discernment of: 280; divine: 55; dullness of: 393–94; fleshly: 147; food of: 259; good: 289, 291; goods of: 209; heavenly: 20; human: xxxix, 22, 75; interior: 151; joy of: 314; lax: 133; Lenten: 325; liberty of: 266, 317; monastic: 143, 178; obedience to: 29; of apostles: 308; of Benedictine life: lxii; of charity: 7, 348; of Christ: xlviii, 220, 246, 268; of Cistercian life: xx; of counsel: 365; of faith: 169; of fortitude: 365; of God: 67, 75, 237, 247, 268; of joy: xlviii; of Lord: 233, 337; of poverty: 187; of understanding: 2, 365; of wisdom: 2, 365; pharisaical: lxxiv–lxxv, 275–76; poverty of: 31; purification of: 365; rancor of: 279; refined: 262; religious: 133; single: 347; subjection to: 206; things of: 339; tranquil: 351; treasures of: 259; true: 133; undivided: 5; unity of: xvi, 4–5, 251, 379; vs. letter: 55, 141; violation of: lxi–lxii; virginity of: 394; walking in: 308; wise: 158; worldly: 133, 142, 147, 152
spirituality: xlviii, lxxxix, 141, 394; Bernardine: 18; Christian: 59; Cistercian: xx, xxxvii–xxxviii, lxxix, 1, 10, 18, 245, 324; conventional: 105; illusory: 291; medieval: 12; modern: 296; monastic: lxxx, 262; negative: 208
spiritualization, excessive: 50; of love: 169
splendor, spiritual: 154

spontaneity: 116, 234
spouse: lxxv, 113, 207, 251, 267–68, 277, 297, 299, 304, 371, 391; abbot as: 382; arms of: 97–98; Beloved of: 288, 297; breasts of: xiii, xxi, 270, 288; cellars of: lxxvii–lxxviii, 299–306; charity of: 300, 380–81; Christ as: 287–91; Church as: xxxviii, 145; companions of: 381; embrace of: xcviii, 390; glorious: 361, 371; heart of: 113, 115; human: 392; love of maidens for: 287–91; monk as: xxxviii; of God: 271; of Son: 268; request of: lxxvii; rest for: 115; sleep of: 392; soul as: xcviii, 76, 113, 265–66, 277, 361, 380; visits of: 253, 374
stability: lxvi–lxvii, 128, 232; change of: 222–33; love of: 222; points on: xciii, 222–24
stag: 157
stain: 209
Stanbrook Abbey: lxxxix
standardization: 11
star: 62–65; morning: 65
starvation: 157
state, duties of: 167; fallen: 109; married: 145; peaceful: 316; religious: 367; secure: 316; supernatural: 367
statistics: 13
statues: 195
status: lxiv
*status quo*, feudal: 136
*Statuta*, Cluniac: xc, 140, 158–60
Stella, Abbey of: 1
stench: 201
Stephen of Clairvaux, Cardinal: 44
sterility: 348
Stiller, Colleen: cxi
stillness: lii, xcix
Stolz, Anselm, OSB: 240
stomach: 149, 200
stone(s): xlix, 164, 351; hardest: 53; precious: 54, 185; rolling: 231
Stone, Naomi Burton: lii

storerooms: 368, 381; of Spouse: lxxvii, 299
stories: 351; Biblical: lxxi
strain: lxxix, 306
stranger: 229
straw, bricks without: 362
strength: xxi, lxxvii, 31, 57, 136, 156, 200, 278, 286, 294, 297, 299, 314, 319, 333; habits of: 341; of Christ's love: lxxvii; physical: 225; spiritual: 325; whole: lxxvii, 108
strife: 201
striving(s), earnest: 341; human: 268; term of: 377
structure, organizational: lxxix
struggle(s): lxiii, lxxiv, 92, 311, 332, 363; companions in: xliii; of flesh against spirit: 29
students: 92; in Paris: lxii–lxiii, 167, 197; theological: lxiv
study: ix, xxii, lxxviii, 3, 189, 245, 304, 338; of Fathers: 31; of Scripture: 31, 258; passion for: 161; theological: 74
studying: 10, 52
subjection: 381; yoke of: 382
subjectivity: civ; inordinate: 244
submission: 311; blind: 175; discipline of: lxxviii; of will: lxvi; to God: lxvi; to others: 301; to superior: lxvi; to truth: 83
substance: 144, 379–80; divine: xvi, 89
success: 24
suffering(s): lxviii, 83–84, 114, 128, 200, 236, 249–50, 273–74, 328, 332, 369; for love of Christ: 297; love of: 8; psychology of: 326; source of: 326
Suger of St. Denis, Abbot: 44, 46; death of: 47
Sulpicius Severus: 187
summer: 113, 131, 195; long hot: ciii
sun: 250; brilliance of: 252
superfluities: 121
superior(s): 92, 135, 137, 150, 152, 188, 215, 232, 249, 256, 288, 303, 342, 349, 351, 382; argument with: 223; cellar of: lxxviii; charity of: lxxviii; command of: 187, 216; discipline of: 270; duty of: 232; eyes of: 382; fault of: 14; good: 382; humble: 382; judgment of: 218–19; life under: 221; obedience to: 220; office of: 219; permission of: lxvi, 223; rank of: 382; role of: xcvi; single: 193; submission to: lxvi; views of: 219; virtue in: 194; virtues of: 383; will of: 217–18
superioress: 192–93; as married woman: 193
superiority: 329; moral: lxi
superiorship: 303, 383
supper, Lord's: 149
suppliant: 171
supplication: 332
survey, theological: 177
suspense: 38
sweat: 318
sweetness: lxxvii, 90, 164, 208, 253, 294, 346, 368, 376, 385; blessings of: 28; divine: 74; heavenly: 53; odor of: 54; of God: 28–29, 122, 365; of God's love: civ; sorry: 22
swine: 208
Switzerland: 46
sword, double-edged: 209; of Holy Spirit: 337; spiritual: 41
syllogisms: 3; true: 261
symbolism: lxxxv–lxxxvi; Old Testament: xlviii
symbol(s): 48–50, 54, 332; mediation of: civ; of penance: 135; scriptural: 54
sympathy: 274; paternal: 272
synagogue: xlviii, 276
synthesis, theological: 177

tabernacle: 319, 395; of body: 316; precious: 184
table, abbot's: 137
tableware: 152

Talbot, C. H.: xiv, 60, 185
talents: 19, 24
tanning, of leather: 195
taste(s): 151, 341, 351
Tauler, John: 100
teacher: 92; office of: 92; true: 92
teaching: 194; evangelical: xxx; false: 184; heretical: 183; informal: 151; method of: 177; monastic: xxx; mystical: 4; patristic: xxxviii, 379; theological: 172; twofold: 338
tears: 38, 129, 205, 210–11, 249, 325, 333, 376; bread of: 333; devotional: 279
techniques, of prayer: 238
teeth, gnashing of: 131, 202
temperament: 176, 255; modern: 244
temperance, virtue of: 176
temple: 40, 164; Jewish: 57
temptation(s): xcviii–xcix, 17, 24, 56, 117, 138, 171, 190–91, 205, 223, 282, 294–95, 298, 314, 319, 393
tendencies, lax: 143
tepidity, Cluniac: 126; league of: 366
Terence: 16
Teresa of Avila, St.: cv, 238, 241, 243, 248
terminology, heretical: 173
terror: 9, 279, 391
Tertullian: 188
Tescelin: 14; retirement to Clairvaux: 32
testament, everlasting: 97
testimonies: 111, 268
testing: 381
thanks: 276, 285; devout: 210
thanksgiving: 169, 277–78; act of: 169
theft: 100
Theobald of Champagne, Count: 33, 45; death of: 48
*theologia*: lxix, 238
theologian(s): 104, 240; mystical: xx, 238; perfect: 238
theology: xxxv–xxxvi, 16, 172, 196, 237–38; as highest contemplation: 238; as *summa*:172; ascetical: 246; Benedictine: 74; Cistercian: lxxxvii,

1, 70–81, 96, 338; concepts of: 167; divorce from mysticism: 74; dogmatic: lxix, 246; infused: 16–17; liberal: 173; modern: 173; monastic: xlvii, lxxx, xciv; moral: 246; mystical: lv, lxviii–lxix, 7, 77, 237–44, 246; of Abelard: 172–78; of charity: 96; of community: xlvii; of friendship: xlvii; of love: lxxxvii, 1, 70–81; of spiritual life: 246; of Trinity: 79; parts of: 172; patristic: xx, 74, 240, 246; post-Tridentine: 300; scholastic: xx; synthetic: lxxxvii, 71; systematic: lxxxvii, 71; traditional: 166, 178
Theophrastus: 168
*theoria*: lxix, 238
theory, mystical: 70; scholastic: 240; Thomistic: 240
therapy, monastic: lii
Thérèse of Lisieux, St.: 145–46, 204, 376–77
thing(s), bodily: 389, 394; changeable: 86; dead: 373; divine: 28, 245, 248, 341; earthly: 5, 328, 389, 393; evanescent: 85; external: 151, 200, 325, 362, 370; good: 6, 69, 300, 318, 330, 368, 380; heavenly: 5, 9; internal: 363; invisible: 261; material: 349, 394; nature of: lxxxvii; of God: 29, 261, 380; outward: 360; perishable: 84; present: 394; sensible: 155; spiritual: 28, 150, 217, 361; temporal: 5, 85, 93; unknown: 261; wicked: 385
thinking: 52; manners of: xcviii, 394
thirst, for doctrine: 245; for God: xxvi, civ, 76, 366; spiritual: lxiii, 208
thistles: 111
Thomas Aquinas, St.: xxi, lxv, xcvi, civ, 54, 177, 182, 223, 326–27, 330, 344–45, 366–67
Thomas, Br.: 233
Thomas Merton Center: xxvii–xxix, xxxvii, cxi

Thomas of Marla: 225
Thomas of St. Victor, Prior: 40–41
Thomas the Apostle, St.: 383
thorns: 111, 208; crown of: 250
thought(s), Cistercian: lxxxvii, 73; ethical: 175; free: 167; good: 209; medieval: 176; Moslem (Muslim): 160; orthodox: 177; philosophical: 166; pious: 114; scientific: 162
thoughtlessness: 15
throne, royal: 359
tigers: 156
Tilburg, Abbey of: xxii
time, free: 351; fullness of: 321; passage of: 319
tithes: 134, 141; reception of: 136
Titus: 162
toil: 211
Toledo: 160, 162
tomb: 350
tone, dramatic: 126; emotional: 126; passionate: 126; personal: 126
tongue(s): 202, 357; distribution of: 358; kinds of: 347; of flame: c, 358
Tonkin Gulf: ciii
tonsure: 335
tools: 135
torments: 200
tortures: 297
Tours: 36
towns: 11; around monasteries: 191–92; walled: 11
tradition(s): cvi, 11; Benedictine: 289; Christian: viii; Cistercian: xv, lxv, lxxxi; Cluniac: 134; desert: xcii; mystical: viii; patristic: xxxix, lxx–lxxi, 240, 259; Platonic: 88; resources of: lxxiii; valid: 157
tragedy: 334
training, bad: 219; lack of monastic: 134
tranquillity: 7, 9, 69, 279, 358; of God: 8, 70; of mind: 8
transaction, juridical: 174
transcendence, divine: xxi

transcendent: 49
transfers, monastic: lxvi–lxvii, xciii–xciv, 126, 224–33
Transfiguration, Feast of: 159
transformation: lxxi, 20, 324, 332–33; inner: li, lxiii, 323; spiritual: ix
transgression(s): 128, 218; of inadvertence; lxvi; of weakness: lxvi
transiency: 85
*transitus*: 126
*translatio*: 49–50
translations, Arabic: 161
trappers: 157
travel: 158; curious: 130; equipage for: 148; vain: 130
trial(s): 1, 66, 69, 122, 170, 242, 297–98, 319, 328, 390, 393
tribulation: 22, 69, 122
trifles: 149
Trinity Holy: lx, 72, 102, 183, 238, 267, 357–58; life of: lxxx; life in: 77; mystery of: 172–73; reasoning about: 173; theology of: 79; union with: 72
Trois Fontaines, Abbey of: 32
trope(s), conventional: 13; Platonic: 88; rhetorical: 65
tropology: 50
troubadour: 59
trouble(s): 10, 156, 192, 269, 319; day of: 279; worldly: xx
Troyes: 169; Council of: 33
trust: lxxiv, xcv, 117, 272, 292, 310, 377; greater: 210; humble: 210; in Word: l
truth(s): xxxix, civ, cvii, 22, 24, 53, 57, 82, 84, 86, 91, 94, 109, 137, 164, 166, 175, 188–89, 198, 207, 212, 235, 281, 320, 325, 336, 354, 363, 369, 371, 386, 391; abstract concept of: cvii; action of: 26; approaches to: 55; as adversary: 83; as Incarnate Word: 197; as life: 83; as person: 197; assurance of: 281; battle against: 362; bitterness of: 82–83; call of: lxxxiv, 23; caring:

370; Christ as: xxi, lxiii, 26, 82, 188, 296; commitment to: lxiii; communion with: lxiii, 197; consequences of: 337; contemplation of: 197, 395; conversion to: lxxxiv, 23–26; defended by: 93; defender of: 93; degrees of: xcvii, 71, 82, 89, 211, 269, 354, 359–74, 378, 382; destruction of: 334; divine: 27; evidence of: 43; experience of: 54; flight from: 362; God as: xxi, 109, 231, 372; incommunicable: 373; indifference to: lxxviii, 304; infinite: 173; knowledge of: 289; lack of: 328; light of: civ, 384; love of: lxxxviii, 2, 82, 86–87, 99, 197, 354; minister of: 83, 92; mysteries of: 373; naked: 364; needy: 364; of Redemption: 114; office of: 360; pen of: 200; pure: 207, 370; rays of: 3; recognition of: 82; resting in: 363; return to: 82; secrets of: 361, 373; seeking: 83; severe: 370; Spirit of: 361, 391; stamp of: 334; submission to: 83; substantial: 82–83; summit of: 3; supreme: 3; unbelievable: 391; understanding of: 2; union with: 197; voice of: 26, 199; weak: 364; Word of: 361; zeal for: 214, 297
tumult: 190, 359
tunics: 146
turmoil: 371
turtle-dove: 207
twelfth century, as age of awakening: 10; as Age of Bernard: 1; as age of transition: 10; fasting in: 321; intellectual climate of: 55; religious sensibility of: 48
typology, biblical: 49
tyrants: 230

ugliness, cult of: 153
Ulpien: 161
unbeliever(s): 108, 110, 112
uncharitableness: 146
unction: 164, 208
undergarments: 136
understanding: xxxv–xxxvi, lxxi, 4, 55, 173, 259–60, 268, 358, 365–66; circumspection of: 296; gift of: 240; light of: 112; mystical: xlviii; natural: 255; spirit of: 2, 365; Spirit of: 268; spiritual: 258, 260, 266; teeth of: 261; vigilance of: 296
ungodliness: 205
unguent: 302, 368
unholiness: 304
union: 383; contemplative: xix, xxxvi, xcvii, 3, 344, 359; covenant of: 4; degrees of: 390; desire for: 81; destiny to: 71; divine: xxvi, xxxvi, xl, civ, 10, 74, 272, 383; eternal: 115; experience of: 387; in Christ: xcv, 328, 332; in Holy Spirit: lxxiv, xcv, 332; intimate: xxxi, 392; joy of: 372; life of: 238; manner of: 321; means of: 321; moral: 253; motives for: 321; mystical: xxxviii, lxiii, lxxvii, 72, 248, 253, 263, 265, 387; nature of: 198, 263; nuptial: 263; of Bride with Spouse: lxxviii; of Christ and Church: lxxiii, 258, 263; of faculties: xviii; of Father and Son: 267; of fervor and discretion: 383; of God and soul: 71, 254; of knowledge; lxxiv, 267; of love: xviii, xxxix, lxxiv, 77, 267, 372; of Spirit and will: 361; of spirits: lxiii, 265; of wills: xvi, xviii, lxviii, lxxiii, 234, 253, 265; of Word and reason: 361; perfect: xviii, 4, 264, 352, 354, 371; personal: lxxiii, xcvi; seeking of: 381; supernatural: xl, 302; transforming: xvii; with Christ: lxvi, lxxi, lxxiv, 111, 235, 247, 258, 264, 292, 314, 318, 320–22, 326, 328, 332, 334; with Creator: xxxix; with divine Spouse: xcvii; with Father: lxxiv, xcv, 321, 332; with

Index 523

God: xv–xvi, xxvi, xxxviii, xl, lvii, lxviii, lxx, lxxiii, xcvi, 3, 5, 7, 22–23, 69, 71, 78, 82, 90, 100, 115, 117, 166, 197–98, 247–48, 255, 264–68, 270–72, 301, 330, 332–33, 338, 352, 354–55, 363–64, 371–72, 381, 390; with Incarnate Word: 246, 313; with Infant Christ: 145; with Trinity: 72; with truth: 197; with will of God: 80; with Word: 300

unity: 38, 302, 328, 347–49; common: 348; destroyer of: 234; in Christ: 144, 321; in contemplation: 3; in diversity: lxi; moral: 248; of Body of Christ: 348; of Church: 8, 145, 348; of common life: 318; of divine life: 79; of monk: 365; of social life: 319; of spirit: xvi, 4–5, 251, 379; psychological: 248; sign of: 322; vocation to: 5

universals: 166, 172

universe: 66, 175; fictitious: 104; interpretation of: 104; sinful: 67

universities: 12

unknowing: ix

unlikeness: 77; land of: xl–xli, 88, 200

unreality: 104

unrest: 311, 371, 385

unselfishness: 286

untruth: 104

unworthiness: 256, 369

upheaval, social: cvii

Ur: 37

Urban, Fr., ocso: 376

Urban II, Pope: 12, 137

usages, altering: lxvi; Cluniac: xc; enforcing: lxvi

usefulness: 159

utterance, mystical: 261; sacred: 261

vainglory: 109, 151, 282, 288; as arrogant: 109; as self-sufficient: 109

valleys: 164

value(s): 5; aesthetic: 153; artistic: 153; higher: 153; highest: 354; human: 150; in God: xcvi, 353; in themselves: xcvi; inordinate: 323; inviolable: 85; monastic: 141, 148; natural: 323; objective: 339; practical: 345; religious: 136; spiritual: 153, 200, 332, 345; symbolic: 50; true: 354; worldly: 150, 323

vanity: lxxv, 24, 38, 151, 155, 201–2, 205, 274, 287, 290, 328; action of: 26; conversion from: lxxxiv, 23–26; escape from: 27; exterior: 152

vassal, of Lord: 36

Vatican Council, Second: ciii

vegetables: 131, 136

vengeance: 40; just: 385; secret: 385; severe: 385

venison: 157

verbiage, empty: 2

*verecundia*: 18

vernacular, in literature: 11; in preaching: 11

versatility: 13

verses, Latin: 16

vespers: vii, xliii, 321

vessel, broken: 379

vestiarian: xciii, 193, 195

vexation: 231

Vézelay: 154

*viaticum*: xxviii

vice(s): c, 4, 62, 65–66, 88, 147–48, 151, 164, 176, 206, 325–28, 333, 342–43, 366; atmosphere of: 197; totality of: 359; tumult of: 359;

vicissitudes: lxxvii, 263, 298

victim: 249; innocent: 249

Victorines: 11, 166, 197

victory: 131–32; corporal: 97; spiritual: 97

Vietnam, coup in: ciii

view, common: 237; false: 83; speculative: 218

vigilance: 296

vigils: 131, 159, 195, 288

vigor: 217

villages, monastic ownership of: 136
violations, deliberate: lxvi; of rules: 215; sinful: lxvi
violence: 9, 12, 203, 206, 259; of anger: 279
Virgil: 16
virgin(s): 322; common of: 322; foolish: 186; wise: 186
virginity: 58; monastic: 322; of spirit: 394; spiritual: 93
virtue(s): lix, lxxv, lxxvii, 7–10, 37, 62, 65–66, 69, 98, 109, 147–48, 150, 152, 176, 198, 206, 222, 244, 277–78, 282, 298–99, 326, 334, 341–43, 391; appearance of: 289; cardinal: 120; concern for: 213; essence of: 159; fourfold: 207; governess of: 344; governing of: 345; guardian of: 344; holy: 361, 372; hunger for: 208; interior: 146; joy of: 209; life of: lxiii, xcvi, 208, 257, 296, 368; love of: 70, 253, 294; mere: 277; mother of: 344, 382; of obedience: lxiv; ordinary: lxx; perfecting of: 345; practice of: xc, 159; progress in: lxiii; rewards of: 208; spiritual: 207; theological: 345; thirst for: 208; true: 159, 365; weakness of: 328
*virtus*: 108, 110
vision(s): lxxi, 70, 248, 253–54, 386, 393; beatific: 111; fullness of: 228; imaginary: 248; nobler: 254; sweet: 254; sublime: 254; terrible: 387–88
visit(s), of Beloved: 285; of Bridegroom: xviii, 256; of spouse:253, 374
Visitation: 97
vitality, supernatural: 330
Vitry, Cardinal Jacques de: 368
vocation(s): xxx, xxxii 5, 233, 243, 249, 255, 307, 349, 385; active: 349–50; advice on: xciii–xciv; angelic: xxvi; apostolic: xxvi, xxxi; as gift of God: 222; as pledge of eternal life: 222; as sign of predestination: 222; beauty of: lxiv; Christian: xxvi, lxiv, 214; Cistercian: 308, 359; Cluniac: 160; contemplative: 349–50; diversity of: lxxvii, 145, 299, 304; divine: 353; frustration of: 222; highest: 19; individual: 383; infidelity to: 167; letters on: xciii–xciv, 225; monastic: xxvi, xlii, 7, 26, 365; of penitent: 349–50; personal: 233; prophetic: xxvi; recommendations on: xciii–xciv; ruin of: 222; special: 368; to sanctity: lxiv, 214
voice, divine: 20–21, 199, 207; human: 20, 199; interior: 20; of Beloved: 255; of Bridegroom: 247; of Church: 316; of God: 19, 199, 362; of power: 20–21; of wisdom: 315–17; sweet: 207
Volturno River: 68
vow(s): 126, 128–29, 134, 138, 145, 215–17, 220; Abelard on: xcii; dispensation of: 222; infidelity to: 157; monastic: 220; of chastity: lxv; of conversion of manners: li, 150, 232; of obedience: lxv, 157, 221; of poverty: lxv; simple: lxxx; sin against: 221; suppliant: 207; understanding of: 221; violation of: lxv, 221
vultures: 157

Waddell, Chrysogonus, ocso: xiv–xv, xxv, xxviii–xxix, xxxii, xxxiv–xxxv, xli, xliv–xlv, cix–cx
Waddell, Helen: 165
waiting, importance of: 284
wanderers: 12
wandering, inquisitive: 223; unsettled: 223
war: 134
warfare, bodily: 208
washing: 158
wasteland: 206
water(s): 131, 147, 152, 196, 205, 212, 275, 283, 379; clear: 164; dark: 164; living: xliii

Index 525

waterboys: liv
Watkin, E. I.: lxxx
wax: 2, 95, 261
way: 310; bad: 310; human: 295; illuminative: lxxiv, lxxviii, 198, 270; purgative: 198; of life: 230; sensible: 295; to God: x, 86, 139, 326; unholy: 230; unitive: 198; wise: 377
weak: 130, 150
weakness(es): xix, xcvii, 38, 202, 222–23, 249, 278, 293, 297–98, 319, 328, 333, 346, 366, 369, 376, 393; faults of: lxvi; fundamental: 219; human: xcix; justification of: 135; transgressions of: lxvi, 216
wealth: lxiii, 213
weariness: 318, 385
wedding, spiritual: 256
weeping: 131, 323
wheel: 314
whims: 316
whips: 160
whirlwind: 395
whisper, divine: 351
wicked: 289, 314–15; paths of: 315; prince of: 315
wickedness: 87, 208
widows: 194
wife: 194, 202
will(s): lxiii, xcix, cv, 22, 88, 93, 109, 118, 125, 187–88, 201, 203, 206–7, 209, 211, 217–18, 220, 234, 250, 255, 285, 305, 311–12, 314–15, 336, 361, 365, 372, 378, 386; abandoned: 236; act of: 115; action of: 345; arbitrary: 175; as tyrant: 105; assertion of: 102; attachment to: 235; bad: 95, 215; common: xix–xx, xli, liv, lxvii–lxviii, cviii, 90, 234, 236–37, 366; concurrence of: 251; conformity of: 387; control of: 119; conversion of: 206, 209; correspondence of 251; corruption of: 235–36; deep: 100; deliverance of: 363; denial of: 346; desire of: 207, 346; divine: 19, 65, 205, 306, 311, 321; effort of: 337; exercise of: 285; faculty of: 361; free: 108, 363; force of: 355; generous: 216; gift of: 217; good: 45, 95, 211, 221, 225, 228, 297; hardness of: 100; harmony of: 4; human: 361; humble: 312; incomprehensible: 175; inert: 203; intention of: 378; irritated: 207; known: 218; languid: 203; of Christ: 244, 294; of Father: lxviii, 52; of God: lxviii, lxxvi, xcix, cv, 7, 20, 22, 52, 80, 100, 120, 123, 125, 145, 175–76, 218–20, 233–34, 256, 271, 306, 311–13, 317, 324, 328, 337, 352–53, 366, 375–78, 382, 387; of superior: 218; omnipotent: 357; poisoned: 370; poor: 207; primacy of: 71; proper: liv, 234–35; purification of: 209, 365; reasonable: 209; renunciation of one's: xcviii, 244; sacrifice of: 217; simplification of: xvi; strong: 205; submission of: lxvi; supple: 363; sweet: 34; to obey: 217; union of: xvi, xviii, lxviii, lxxiii, 234, 253, 265; weak: 204, 219; wretched: 202
willfulness: 364
William of Angoulême: 36
William of Champeaux, Bp.: 32, 166, 196
William of St. Thierry: xliv–xlv, lii, lxi, lxxxi, 13–17, 19, 23, 26–28, 32, 68–69, 71–74, 77, 139, 338; and Abelard: xcii, 173–74, 178–81, 183; as biographer: xlv, lii, lxxii–lxxv, cvii–cviii, 13–17, 19, 26–31, 35; as friend of St. Bernard: 13, 19; as hagiographer: lxxxii–lxxxiii, 13; as mystic: xlv; as panegyrist: lxxxiii, 14; as theologian: xlv, 178; WORKS: *Commentary on Song of Songs*: 77, 179; *De Contemplando Deo*: 72–74; *Disputatio adversus Abaelardum*: 77, 178–81; *Golden Epistle*: xlv, 77, 179, 262; *Nature and*

*Dignity of Love*: xlv, 68–69, 72, 338;
*Vita Prima*: xlv, lii, lxxxii–lxxxv, cvii–cviii, 9, 13–15, 17, 19, 26–31, 35, 71
Williams, Watkin: 16, 22, 166, 198–213
willingness: 189
will-power: 84
Wilmart, André, OSB: lxxxviii, 81–96, 99–101, 104, 106
Winandy, Jacques: 68
wind, burning: 390; north: 207; south: 207
wine: lxxviii, 91, 130, 147, 151–52, 165, 196, 270, 299, 379, 382; honey: 130; of spirit: 284; of vainglory: 282; spiced: 285
wine-cellar: lxxviii, 266, 303, 340, 344, 382
winter: 112, 131
wisdom: viii, xxxv, xxxix, lvii, lxix, lxxvii: 21, 67, 72, 86, 162, 180, 207–8, 261, 282, 299, 316, 354–55, 358, 361, 366, 381, 392–93; affection of: 355; ancient: x; beginning of: lxxviii, 305, 318; Christ as: lxviii, lxxvii, xcix, 237, 299, 360; Christian: 2; contemplative: vii, ix; discernment of: 345; divine: xcix, 67; eternal: 164; God as: 3, 289; gift of: 240; guidance of: 15; human: 177; mystical: xxxvi, 386–87; non-Christian: lxxxviii; wisdom of: lxxvi; of Father: 289, 316; of God: 316–17; overcomes malice: 66, 86; profundity of: 384; pursuit of: 368; spirit of: 2, 365; Spirit of: 268; spiritual: x; theological: 240; theology as: 238; true: 3; voice of: 315–17; zeal for: 299
wishes, frustration of: lxviii
witness(es): 129; active: xxx; faithful: 180
woe, endless: 34
wolf: 129, 143, 158
woman: 170; strong: 195

women: 17, 24
wonder: 94
wood(s): 31, 157, 164
wool: 139, 195
word(s): xcviii, civ, 189, 259, 278, 351, 361, 392; bodily: 254; doer of: 52; from silence: c; good: 282; human: 20, 261; idle: 130–31; lascivious: 186; necessary: 189; of Fathers: 74; spoken: 54; true: c; unspeakable: 231; written: 54, 164
Word: civ, 100, 163, 199, 250, 252, 254, 358, 362–63, 369, 391; abridged: 358; absence of: 390; action of: 370; arm(s) of: 390; as flesh: 253; as holiness: 254; as image: 75; as justice: 254, 296; as piety: 296; as power: 296; as sanctity: 296; as spirit: 254; as truth: 254, 296; as will: 198; as Wisdom: 253, 296; Christ as: xxviii, xxxi, xl, xlviii, xcvii, xcix, 72; coeternal: 358; conception of: 58; condescension of: 254; conformity to: 250; creation in: 292; devotion to: xxxviii; divine: lxiii; embrace of: 390; face of: 254; generation of: c, 357–58; guidance of: 253; immersion in: lxxi; Incarnate: xxxviii, 246, 248, 292, 313, 357, 359; ineffable: 357; listening to: c; Living: 209; love for: 287–88; love of: 391; marriage to: 4, 250; made flesh: 65, 67; obscure: 358; of Father: 21, 289, 357, 360; of God: lxxi, 19–21, 23, 51–52, 54, 74, 199, 209, 257, 265, 337, 357; of Lord: 19, 199; of Truth: 361; omnipotent: 357; possession of: 307–8; power of: 199, 254; powerful: 209; presence of: 390; reformation by: 250; reverence for: 360, 363; saving: c; Spirit of: 357–58; tongue of 254; trust in: l; turning to: 250; union with: 254, 266; vicar of: 370; visits of: 56, 111; wedded to: 250

Wordsworth, William: xix
work(s): lxxvi, lxxxv, 31, 136, 138, 146, 194, 196, 202, 218, 277, 307, 309, 316, 324, 341–42, 351, 355, 363, 385; active: 350; avaricious: 344; for God: 316; good: 284, 296–97, 346; hard: 131; harvesting: xcix; manual: 131, 136; of effective charity: 356; of God: lxxxv, 43, 57, 265, 317, 384; of Holy Spirit: lxxvi, 260, 272, 287; outward: 285
world: xxvii, xxxv, 10, 19, 26, 58, 62, 83, 104, 129–30, 150, 170, 190, 198, 208, 214, 236, 238, 257, 277–78, 299, 321, 323, 328, 333, 353; adversities of: 328; as Egypt: 319; attire of: 129; attraction of: 17; beauty of: 104; children of: xx; Christian: 133; creation of: 162; eyes of: 274; fallen: lxxix; flight from: 11; goodness of: 104; goods of: 209; higher: 54; love of: 87, 99, 155; men of: 225; new: 373; of limitations: xcviii; of responsibilities: xcviii; of space and time: xcviii; offering to: xxxi; order of: 104; physical: 104; princes of: 230; redeemed: 113; renewal of: 110; renunciation of: 194; return to: 138, 192; secular: 158; service of: 225, 230; separation from: 142; sins of: 175, 327; spirit of: 178; things of: 155; truth of: 104; ways of: 142; whole: 64; wicked: 205, 380; withdrawal from: xx–xxi, 17
worldliness: lxxxiv, 15, 26, 150
worldlings: 335
world-soul: 103–4
worldview, medieval: l; of modernity: l

worm: 200; hidden: 335
worries: 5, 38, 231
worship: 49, 93; divine: 278; liturgical: 134; of ego: xx
wound(s): 127, 132, 202, 210–11; adorable: 250
wrath, sons of: 213; sword of: 171
writers, spiritual: 120, 234
writing(s): 194; good: 155; postscriptural Christian: lxix

year, liturgical: xliii, 333
yogi, arrival of: ciii
yoke, easy: 276; of charity: 105; of Christ: 23, 26, 207, 220; sweet: 105
York, Archbishopric of: 44–45, 141

zeal: 3, 19, 42, 108, 163, 268, 286, 296, 340–41, 343, 345–46, 382; active: 8; apostolic: 8; ardent: 295, 300, 340–41; assiduous: 8; blind: 296; efficient: 8; false: 369; fervent: lxxviii, 303; for charity: 256; for Church: 10; for common life: 30; for glory of God: 41, 214; for justice: 297; for manual labor: 31; for prayer: 31; for service of God: 30; for solitude: 31; for souls: 10; for truth: 214, 297; for welfare of Church: 214; fruitless: 343; harmful: 343; illuminated: 296; indiscreet: 288–89, 291; inordinate: 288; lack of: 234, 297; misdirected: 289; moderation of: 345; of Lord: 281; spiritual: 286; to seek God: 108; true: 287; uneasy: 343
zero, discovery of: 160
Zilboorg, Gregory: liii

www.ingramcontent.com/pod-product-compliance
Lightning Source LLC
Chambersburg PA
CBHW020630300426
44112CB00007B/72